CW01306482

Prison Or The Paralympics?

Autobiography. A book documenting the story of a near death experience that gave her the strength and spiritual guidance to fight the unjust justice system and to rehabilitate herself back to competitive sports

Penny Walker

Text copyright © Penny Walker 2021

Penny Walker has asserted her right to be identified as the author of this work in accordance with the copyright, Designs and Patents Act 1988

The moral right of the author has been asserted.

All rights reserved. No part of this publication may be reproduced, stored in a retrieval system, or transmitted in any form or by any means electronic, mechanical, photocopying, recording or otherwise, without the prior permission of the copyright owner.

ISBN 9798751394790 Paperback

Dedicated to Trevor and Valerie Walker, the parents who gave everything!

Contents

Acknowledgements

A Note From The Author

Introduction

Prologue

Chapter 1: The Accident

Chapter 2: In The Beginning.

Chapter 3: Saying Goodbye, Thanks For All You Did For Me

Chapter 4: The Life That Once Was

Chapter 5: My Guardian Angels And The Show Must Go On

Chapter 6: Special People, Dewsbury Rugby League Club And The UK Finals

Chapter 7: The Waiting Game And The Game Of Poo!

Chapter 8: More Rugby, More Study And Football

Chapter 9: Stubby Is Born, The Mental Battle And A New Home

Chapter 10: Bramley Rugby League Club, Wembley, Formula 1 And A Master's Degree

Chapter 11: Some Of My Recordings At Nantes Hospital

Chapter 12: A Funeral, More Formula 1, And Superbikes

Chapter 13: Recordings At Nantes Hospital, Food At Last And My Reality

Chapter 14: Around The World Trip

Chapter 15: Recordings At Nantes Hospital, Birthing Stubby And I Move To Plastics

Chapter 16: Subaru, Bathurst, Barmy Army And Perth Glory FC

Chapter 17: Recordings At Nantes Hospital, Stubby Is Being Naughty, Moaning And More Delays

Chapter 18: Recordings At Nantes Hospital And Phone Conversations At Last

Chapter 19: My Last Recordings At Nantes And My First Recording At The Grand Feu

Chapter 20: Dubai 7s And New Year In Perth

Chapter 21: The Grand Feu, No One Understands Me And Neither Do I

Chapter 22: Study Must Come First And A Trip To China

Chapter 23: A Friend For Stubby, Life At The Grand Feu And Visits Home

Chapter 24: The Disability Is Seen But Not The Person And Further Recordings At The Grand Feu

Chapter 25: The Beginning Of The Next Generation

Chapter 26: My Small World Just Got Bigger And The Strength Of The Young

Chapter 27: Police Interrogation And My January 2017 Recordings

Chapter 28: Re-living The Nightmare, Boxes, Another Operation And Court

Chapter 29: Dahlias, The Return To The Grand Feu, Driving Lessons And The Spitting

Chapter 30: Peace Pad, My Daily Walk, A Driving Test, A Trip To The UK And The Announcement

Chapter 31: Confirmation, Boys Get A Holiday, The Runner, A New Hospital And Back To Nantes

Chapter 32: The Gifts From APF And Thrown To The Lions

Chapter 33: A Massive Pile Of Nothing And My Last Recording In July 2019

Chapter 34: The Gentle Goodbye, An Appeal, The Gym Gods And My First Competition

Chapter 35: Appeal Papers, The Volunteer, Fear Of The Truth And My Pen Is Mightier Than The Courts

Chapter 36: The Sentence

Chapter 37: Closure, Handing It Over To The People's Justice And The Universe

'The Tank'

Appendix

Acknowledgements

To my sons Harvey and Elliott, throughout everything you never left my side, I love you from every inch of my heart and soul. To mum and dad thank you! To Kay and Denbo, you know what you have done thank you! Cede Nullis you are simply the best. To Pat and Robin, Sharon and Richard, Mel and Robert, Susan and Peter, Andy, Lisa and Rob Tyers, Debbie and Lee, Chris and Marie, Deirdre, Davina and Warren, Kelly and Alex, you never gave up on me thank you!! To those who never judged, gossiped or turned their backs on me, you are few in number, but your loyalty and kindness was and still is amazing thank you! For those who walked away thank you, in doing so you strengthened me.

To all those who came to my rescue on that day thank you. To the wonderful teams at Nantes hospital France and at the Grand Feu Niort France thank you! You were my team of angels working endlessly to get me back on track. Every step I managed to take since is because of you. To APF (Association des Paralysés de France) the fantastic team in Niort France, you supported, guided, and believed in me thank you! To Pasquay you were willing to listen to my needs and your expertise allowed me to follow my dreams, amazing thank you. For all at CHP Haltérophile gym Poitiers (now called Stade Poitevin) your acceptance, guidance and good humour gave me hope and self-belief thank you! To Danny Taylor at Taylor's Gym Liverpool England, I asked if you were up for some challenges, you didn't hesitate to say yes. You are some smart dude thanks for being who you are and the knowledge you give so willingly. You are a hidden treasure!

I also need to thank Elvis Presley, I loved you when I was a teenager and in my darkest times your voice cleansed and healed my soul, thank you!

To all the disabled people in the world, you are the real champions. Be strong, love who you are, believe in yourself, never let doubt or fear own you! Go for your dreams never give up hope, it's the best medicine we have. Love to you all! The song I give to us is 'We Are The Champions' Queen. You have inspired me and continue to do so everyday thank you!

A Note From The Author

"To hell with circumstances. I create opportunities."

- Bruce Lee

We often see our circumstances as what is meant to be but by going within you are given all the guidance and tools needed to create your own dreams, desires, and destiny. Accept self-love and those opportunities are limitless. Do not turn to ego or self-fulfilment, but make your actions based on passion and the desire to help others. Love is all the ingredients you need. With that comes strength, determination, the truth, patience, hope and divine intervention. Everything is possible and possibilities are endless. When you search within, all the gifts of the universe are bestowed on you with guidance that is hard to explain. It just is.

By telling my story I hope to enlighten, encourage, and give support to others, allowing them to see how powerful they really are. To assist them on their journey of healing and enlightenment. Being different from what the world perceives is 'normal' and 'correct' is a gift given to you so you can teach others in their 'normal' life or world the real purpose of life on planet earth.

I am guided and compelled to put these words on paper and create a book. I do so with love not anger or judgement. Some may be hurt by the brutal truth but if you hide from the truth and do not acknowledge its existence it will slowly consume you. Love brings truth and the truth will if accepted always bring love and spiritual growth. Many of us do not tap into our inner strengths but seek comfort and acceptance from an external world or energy that leads us down many a fictitious reality. This false guidance results in self-doubt, unhappiness, judgement of others and deep sadness! Turn your energies to going within, love yourself first and you will automatically be free to love and accept what you feel is important in your unique and beautiful world. You will empower yourself to achieve great things and you will set yourself free to be who you really are. An amazing loving soul.

Throughout my journey I was given divine guidance which presented itself in many ways. One of these ways was through song. I will therefore acknowledge these songs throughout this book. The impact that they had was guidance, healing, hope and exposing the reality of many difficult situations. I hope you enjoy reading my story.

Introduction

"We are here to learn to love each other. I don't know what the others are here for"

- W.H. Auden

On the 2nd of April 2016 my whole world was turned upside down in a negative way or so I thought! The journey I was then given was painful, scary, lonely, challenging, depressing, exhausting, both physically and mentally, confusing, torturous, numbing, embarrassing, self-doubting and there was a huge feeling of being a burden with no self-worth or purpose. A deep, deep feeling that your soul was dead or dying with no desire to live. But the universe had other plans for me. As I eventually came to realise that the universe did this for me, not to me, my life slowly started to change.

In a brief summary, my life had been blessed by a good fulfilling career which allowed me to connect with amazing, courageous and strong people who taught me many things and gave me so much insight to the true meaning of why we exist on this planet. Many of these wonderful people have passed on but their energies remain.

The universe also guided me back to my passion of being in the gym which I had been ignoring for several years. I also found the guidance and strength to find my inner soul so many of us ignore so we can do what others want us to do or fit into the boxes that we think we should be in.

My car accident changed all that now being classed as 80% disabled, meant both I and society no longer had a box for me to fit into. The result being you are left out in the cold, blinded and disorientated, confused and lost. It doesn't take people long before they turn and look the other way. You are then left alone with your pain, disabilities, thoughts, anger, disappointment and fear. Life becomes very dark, lonely and cruel. One disaster after another keeps knocking you down, but I came to realise that the important thing was not how hard or how many times you get knocked down, but how many times you get up again and face the challenge that knocked you down. It's that which gives you strength to carry on!

Prologue

I was looking down I wasn't sitting, I seemed to be out of my body I was looking down. I kept watching myself from above and I was sort of lifted into fresh air. I can only feel the top half, I am struggling I am squashed. I can smell earth, like an earthy smell like, I suppose an engine smell when you lift the bonnet up after you have been driving. I can also hear people, very, very noisy, the lights are flashing. I am trying to stop bleeding I have got my arm pressed against something. I am not sure if I can move, I think I can move my arm to try and stop it bleeding. Oh no I can see blood! What's happened please tell me. No, it's too difficult. Now I can hear voices again and see flashing lights, people are talking to me, really nice voices. I am talking back, I'm talking back I am talking to them, I think I can hear my own voice and I can't seem to get any oxygen. I feel as if I am floating away. I am floating out of my body I am looking down, I am looking down. So much noise, noise. I can't see my hand; I don't know what's happened to my hand. I am worried about the eggs, I am worried about the eggs, ohhh, what's happening? I can't find my hand I am looking for my hand, a voice, is it my own voice? He's talking on a phone very panicky. Oh God I hope I remember more.

Chapter 1: The Accident

"All truths go through three stages. First, it is ridiculed. Then, it is violently opposed. Finally, it is accepted as self-evident."

-Arthur Schopenhauer

I write about this part of my life to help others. When I finally came out of intensive care, I was able to start reading, there was very little else I could do. It was as if these books had been gifted to me. A guidance, reassurance, messages to give hope that things would improve. A dear friend I class as one of my divine guides is Melody (Mel). She always seemed to bring books that gave support and an understanding of what was going through my mind. One author was Norman Vincent Peale the one by my bed was 'The Power of Positive Thinking'.

The books that guided and inspired me through this difficult time were many. Once I was out of intensive care, I also had a dicta-phone. I recorded my experiences, though difficult for me to re-listen to, it captures what I was going through in a real and raw way. These recordings I will use, and it will be seen how low a person can get, how much a person can endure and how often a person can get back up. When 'your soul whispers love but your ego shouts fear!' I will not sugar coat anything if I do there would be no point in writing it. I did find it difficult to write and to re-live it. It is purely from my point of view and experience others involved may see it differently, I have no problem with that. I have my integrity, honesty and personality trait of needing justice, truth, and fairness. After all I am a Libran, the sign of balance and the scales of justice how very ironic. Names will be included for I have no fear to what people may say or do it's all already been said and done. Living in one's truth is how we should seek to live.

My aim is not to hurt others but also not to give others the permission to control and hurt me either. This is my insight, my experience, and my reality. I am vibrating from an energy of love, truth, and peace. The establishments or others will never take that away from me again! Fear cannot exist if there is honesty and love cannot exist if there is fear. I had a long, difficult, and lonely journey which I had to travel to get to my inner peace and self-love. I have no anger to what was done to me I know it was done for me, so I could become a better person, a stronger person and a person who accepts that sometimes people act out of fear which means there is no honesty. My journey has brought me to the simple conclusion which the Beatles already concluded many years before, 'All You Need Is Love'!

We had bought our old French farm in 2004 and spent Easter and the summers there until moving to live there in 2008. The house needed a lot of work but slowly with my partner Robert Mitchell we were fixing it up. I had always loved gardening and growing veg, my dad is a good gardener and always had allotments. I remember when I was 9 or 10 having a few chickens in an old wardrobe and a little run in my mum and dad's small back garden at Thornhill Dewsbury.

The animals we had in 2016 on the farm in France included chickens, guinea fowl, geese, turkeys, rabbits, goats, and pigs, all for our own consumption. I took care of the small holding and had four pigs. Buster the very beautiful Berkshire male, his girlfriend or distraction whichever way you want to look at it, Myrtle-May another pure breed but this time a Gloucestershire Old Spot, her sister Dolly and one of Dolly's daughters a cross breed between Buster the Berkshire and Dolly the Gloucestershire Old Spot. Myrtle-May couldn't get pregnant, so it allowed Buster to have a companion while they were out in the field. Like most animals it's better if they have company.

On the 2nd of April we were busy preparing the house for guests. Robin and Pat were visiting us for three weeks, I was busy all-day cleaning as we do when we are about to have friends stay. I had left the guest bedroom for my last job. First, I needed to go and get the boys Harvey and Elliott who had been out for the day with friends at the beach. Yes, the weather was nice it was like summer had arrived early. I got a text saying they were just going to have a pizza and then they would be ready for me to pick them up. I got some eggs ready for them and finished my cup of tea and set off. It was around 8:15 pm.

The next memory I have is being in this strange place, Rob was talking to me. I said, "Where am I?" "You're in hospital you have been in a car accident". My response "They were all over the road they were pissed! Where's the boys?" Rob's reply "They are okay it was just you in the car".

I was in the intensive care unit (ICU). I found out that I had been flown in by helicopter to Nantes hospital, was operated on and was in a coma for at least a day. I couldn't move and I had a collar on with loads of wires and machines connected to me. My legs and left arm in pot, my right hand bandaged up. I didn't feel well at all!

Robin and Pat came to visit the next day, a lovely couple. Robin, I meet around 1995 through treating him. If Pat and Robin were there it must have been a few days after the 2nd of April for they weren't due until the 3rd of April. I got to know Pat through

Robin, Robin had left the fire service and was looking for another career. He was very interested in the massage, so I said why don't you train at the Northern College of Massage in Blackpool in the UK. So, he did and was good at last I could get some good hands-on treatment. It was around this time that I was doing my master's degree in acupuncture. Robin was fascinated by it, and I suggested he considered doing the course which he eventually did and he graduated in 2004. Now I could get acupuncture as well as massage from an excellent therapist.

Pat's recollection of that visit was that I was unrecognisable as my face was so swollen my hand was totally bandaged, the size of a balloon. They came again and the ends of my fingers were black, I was still in ICU and in a lot of pain. The memory of my 10/11 days in ICU were sometimes very clear and sometimes not so clear, I can only write about what I remembered. I did remember Rob coming and telling me I had been in a car accident that's when my first sentence was, they were all over the road they appeared pissed and then my concern was for the boys. Rob told me they were okay, but I didn't believe him for why weren't they here. I remember thinking they don't want to tell me anything because I am so weak and fragile.

Marc a neighbour in the village came to visit, a volunteer fire fighter for many years, but he had to leave my ICU room because he was so upset with how I looked. It was probably at this time that all the gossip started about the accident. I won't go into it here because it wasn't till much later that I found out what was going on.

I was in so much pain, I couldn't move, and they kept taking me off for operations. There were so many people in my room all surrounding me but wouldn't let me see their faces. Some would argue that it was the drugs, but I was never in my ICU bed. I would go off with these people to all kinds of places. I remember we went to my barn back on the farm and then into this beautiful wood. I always complained when they brought me back. I could see the white sterile ICU room as I looked down and begged them not to take me back. They said I had to go back but I was so happy being with these faceless beings, I could go where I wanted easily without pain or restrictions.

There are a few things I remember while being in ICU but not sure in which order they occurred. There was a small window in my door, and I could see things going on. The couple of rooms whose doors I could see were busy with people coming and going. One room I saw trolleys being pushed out with body bags on. I remember thinking that's not a very lucky room to be in. I wondered if that would be how I would leave my room. I could also hear noises which seemed to come from beneath my room. I couldn't sleep due to the pain and discomfort, that was normal, but the noise was new, I thought there was a fight going on there was so much shouting and it sounded like so many people. I was concerned for the staff the people sounded agitated. I asked the next day if there had been any problems, they said no. I never did find out what it was I suppose you can blame the drugs or say it was my mind just replaying the horror it had just witnessed.

I was slowly learning about my injuries, due to my work I wanted to know. The oxygen mask and neck brace came off first. But I still had so many wires and machines stuck to me and I later found out that one of my lungs had collapsed. I had a lot of pain in my back, hips, legs, arms and an unbearable pain coming from my right hand that was all bandaged up. Once when the staff were moving me, a thing I came to dread, one was a little bit careless and grabbed me to turn me the pain was out of this world. I found out much later why. I had broken my left hip the innominate bone in two places and had four broken lumbar vertebrae, plus all the breaks in my legs and left arm.

When I had the energy, I talked with the staff firstly because I naturally talk a lot and secondly because I wanted to gain information about me. The language barrier made it difficult, but we could communicate, pain being a universal language. One doctor on the ICU spoke good English and we chatted whenever he visited me. He had been on duty in the early hours that they took me to casualty. He was possibly the first doctor at Nantes hospital to see me. I remember his first name being Louie or sounded like that. He said they had a lot to sort out and they got a specialist in to reattach my right hand. I won't go into details of the accident, that's a whole other chapter but my right hand had been ripped or sliced off during the accident, everybody was looking for it, even me! I never was unconscious and was trapped in my car for about three hours. I found out later that they only found my hand when a pompier (fireman) went across the road from where my car was to have a pee (peeing outside is a very French thing to do) and he found my hand. I wondered what sign it was giving. Maybe thumbing a lift? Well, a lift my hand got, straight into a plastic bag!

In my ICU bed I tried to remain cheerful and happy, not so easy to do when the pain is so bad. This doctor was chatty, I remember he always came to say hello even when he was on nights. I would joke saying where are we going tonight, not the disco again. When he was telling me about the night I got taken in by helicopter, he said to calm and rest the body which had lost a lot of blood and to let everything rest and start to recover they put me in a coma. I don't know what that entails I am guessing some sort of anaesthetical state. This doctor who was speaking in English to me said "We put you to sleep for ten years" "Wow" I said, "That's a long time." (For all I know I could have been there 20 years). "No, I mean ten days, no I mean hours". At the time it was funny.

The staff were excellent, I was assessed constantly. The oxygen went, then the drips of antibiotics but that wasn't good they said I could take powder. The moment I took it I was violently sick. In fact, when Robin and Pat came to visit, I had just had some and threw up before I got the chance to say hello. I told the staff I couldn't take the powder. After three bad reactions I point blank refused I couldn't cope with the added pain of feeling more ill and then the physical pain of having to vomit so I went back on the drip.

My pain was getting worse and worse I was beside myself with an indescribable pain. My patience for people who moan about any sort of pain is not very high these days. Cutting your finger or twisting your ankle, that's not pain.

I could see my fingers on my right hand were black and I could smell them. Some doctors came to look at my right hand and then went into the corner to chat about it. I told them I wanted it to go to the decheterie, French for tip. I said I cannot stand the pain or the smell. Take it off please! As you may have guessed my right hand had gangrene, parts of it dead. I came to the realisation that pain is bad but it's a message from your body that there is something wrong, a sort of protection and a signal to stop using the part that's in pain. Through my profession I knew that there are different sorts of pain and indeed some you must work through to actually promote recovery and healing. But this pain in my hand was different if I had been given a gun, I would have shot myself or given the means at least chopped it off. I believe healing pain is good pain, but pain from something rotting and dying is not. This pain is not bearable no matter how many drugs you take it's a whole different level of crucifying and suicidal pain that is impossible to cope with. You read stories of people chopping off limbs in the trenches during the wars. I would have done the same if the opportunity was made available. The decision was made my right hand had to be removed!

Chapter 2: In The Beginning.

"I maintain my edge by always being a student, you will always have something to learn"

- Jackie Joyner-Kersee

I was born in Dewsbury West Yorkshire England in 1964. I am a twin and have an elder brother. My father was a professional rugby league player nicknamed 'Tank' because of his ability and strength to get over the try line while knocking or carrying any other player trying to stop him scoring out of his path. Maybe I inherited some sort of inner strength in my genes! I know my grandfather (my dad's dad) Sam Walker was to me such a powerful kind and funny Yorkshire gem. In the days when my father played rugby you had to hold down a job as well. He was a taxi driver. My mum was extremely strong too working hard at night as an auxiliary nurse bringing up three children and keeping the home fires burning. She was so strong but deeply sad which I did not realise until my thirties. She seemed to carry everyone's problems on her shoulders, and it weighed her down. Her childhood had been difficult. Her father was taken into Stores Hall mental institute because he had epilepsy and never came out. That left my grandma Doris Broadbent on her own with two children and no income, it was the era of no handouts. My mum therefore left schooling to get a job and never stopped working throughout her life.

I was a very quiet, shy, and withdrawn child and liked my own company. I had many imaginary friends who were very real to me. My twin Caroline was much bigger than me and craved all my mum's attention. So, from an early age I just accepted the situation and didn't push myself forwards. I don't remember what was wrong with me, it never got spoken about. But I struggled to walk in my early years and was pushed around in a pram while my sister ran around and helped push me. I have a feeling it was some sort of hip problem. Apparently when I did start walking, I would not speak very much and walked around carrying and looking at the pictures of a children's bible book. When asked what I wanted to be when I grew up, I answered a nun.

My life continued going to school and getting on with things. Thornhill High

School was the secondary school I went to. It has had a documentary made about it which I have yet to see. I liked school though I found the work was not easy, I had to work hard to understand it. I made the decision that I had no choice but to be there and so I may as well get something out of it.

I respected the teachers though in my first week there I ended up having a fight with the PE (Physical Education) teacher Mrs Sanderson. She was a typical 70's PE teacher not very kind, hard faced and wore very short gym skirts what seemed to be 24 hours a day.

The fight was physical, and she ripped my Aertex PE shirt while she dragged me around. The fight was because she wanted me to go into the hall with just my knickers and short gym skirt on. I didn't have any gym knickers for the first week of high school because being a twin my parents had to buy double of everything in relation to school uniform. They just couldn't afford the gym knickers for the first week of school.

I had already given Mrs Sanderson a note to say I couldn't have a shower because I was on my period much to great embarrassment to me. At home we never got the talk about life, when I had my first period, I thought I was bleeding to death and got given a sanitary belt and sanitary towels. For those of you who don't know what these things are (thankfully the choices have improved today compared to the 70's), they were a belt you put around your waist and then you fixed this nappy like pad to it. Discreet did not come into it.

So, this P.E. teacher wanted me to run around, climb up wall bars and jump about in a short skirt without any gym knickers. I plucked up the courage to explain this to the teacher in front of the class who I didn't really know. She shouted at me (you may have seen the brilliant film Kes, the realistic scenes with Kes' P.E. teacher, that is exactly how we were treated in that era). I am now distraught, terrified, and very upset. I said the boys may see me, she replied that they won't be in the hall (in fact they were and did do their lesson in there I later found out).

I started to get my school uniform and said I can't go into the hall and left to go to the door. That's when she dragged me back and started pulling me and shouting at me. I was scared and being attacked so I fought back to try and release the strong hold she had on me. It wasn't pleasant it was an actual fight, but I managed to break free and ran all the way home, tears rolling down my face.

Not a good start to my first week at high school. This teacher already had a reputation of being a cow and I had just made myself public enemy number one. There must have been other complaints because much to my relief she left a couple of years later. This incident never left me, and I promised myself that no-one would ever push me around again. I would always stand up for myself and fight for what I believed in, speak the truth, never giving in to bullies whatever shape or form they presented themselves. Little did I know then that I would one day have to take on the whole French 'Justice' system single handedly, literally!

My time at high school came to an end, I worked really hard and got good grades, in those days' 'O' levels and CSE's. I did drama for one of my subjects and in our individual presentation, in front of the examiner you had 'to perform' an improvisation. I had so much work for my other subjects that I hadn't really thought about my drama. I had to think on my feet. I sat on the floor knees up against my chest arms wrapped around my knees and started rocking and talking to myself, imagining I was hearing voices and a bit crazy (seeing I had spent most of my childhood hearing and talking to voices, it wasn't so difficult to do). The dramatic examiner was so impressed with my performance he said I had to continue and take this further; I was so 'talented'!

So, my path was chosen I would go to DABTAC Dewsbury do 'A' levels and go to university to do a drama degree, sorted or so I thought. I started at DABTAC in September I was still 16 but would be 17 in the October. A dear friend Betty was an ex-driving instructor, so I began lessons. She was excellent, no dual peddles, and, in the car, I shared with my twin Caroline an old blue Ford Escort Mark II, I passed my driving test the first time at the age of 17. I had some independence now, I loved driving and I had been taught by an expert advance driving instructor who gave to me her knowledge and excellence. This gave me a deep love of driving and respect for the powerful machine that I had in my control. I could drive anything and would drive anywhere. I had been given the gifts of making me a very good driver hence why I didn't have a car accident until 36 years later even though I drove all over the world.

I spent many hours in the DABTAC library doing my 3 'A' levels, sociology, history, and general studies. It was at this time that a teacher asked me to do a test for dyslexia, I agreed to do it and was diagnosed with dyslexia, but I never wanted the label and just carried on without help but now at least I knew why everything, to me seemed such hard work compared to how the other students saw it. It was also at this time that I discovered a Martial Arts gym five minutes' walk from DABTAC on Bradford Road. At the age of 17 I discovered weights. We were now in the early 80's and so it was all about women in lycra with leggings around their ankles (remember Flash Dance and the song What A Feeling!) jumping around doing aerobics. That was not for me, I wanted to be in the gym lifting weights with the men. So that's what I did. There were very few women hitting the weights it was seen as wrong and not very feminine. But I loved it I wanted more and didn't care what others thought. I hadn't fitted into stereotypes all my life, so I didn't need to now.

Two years later I had successfully passed my three 'A' levels on the 19th of September 1983. I also had been accepted at Liverpool University to do a drama degree.

Although the degree was from the University of Liverpool, I attended and lived at a teaching college at Aigburth just a fifteen-minute walk from Penny Lane. There were two colleges, Christ, and Notre Dame (the catholic one) and Saint Katherine's across the road (the protestant one). All students mixed and took their lessons as one. I remember at the interview day realising that the very small rooms were bigger at Christ and Notre Dame, so I said it would be nice to lodge there even though I was not catholic to have an opportunity to experience a different religion. It worked and I got a place in Angela Hall where I lived for the first two years of my three-year degree course.

My main subject was drama, with psychology and American Studies. In year two you had to let one subject go to concentrate on just two subjects, I dropped American Studies. However, a big change was made in the first week. I realised I didn't want to do drama, the students seemed too dramatic. The college was a teaching college and had a good reputation for their Physical Education department. I expressed my unsettlement in my choice of subject and was allowed to change to P.E. which I was so pleased about because I was still training hard with the weights and was preparing to compete in an EFBB (European Federation of Bodybuilding) under 21 competition near my hometown at the Frontier. It was formally Batley Variety Club where many famous singers such as Shirley Bassey and Roy Orbison appeared in the 1960's. My dad's stories confirming this as being a professional rugby player for Dewsbury, Batley and Huyton and later a coach, the tradition was to go out as a team after the game for a few beers. I am sure in the 60's the games were played on a Saturday afternoon in the winter months. They were later moved to Sundays and then later still to the summer months.

The Physical Education course was just what I was interested in. We covered physiology, biomechanics, history and politics of sport and sports psychology. With my other subject being psychology, I enjoyed my subjects. The work was hard, and I was training on my own for a competition which included dieting to get to be my best and into my weight class which was under 52kg.

It may be hard to believe this, but a P.E. college did not have any facilities for weight training, but it was the mid 1980's. The head of P.E. did get me a room, well a shed set up with a bench and some weights. Very basic but it's one's ability to use what is available and be inventive, that's what counts. Where there is a will there is always a way. The only time I ever put myself in danger while lifting was in that shed when I nearly throttled myself doing benching. Somehow, I managed to roll the weighted barbell down my chest to my hips and get myself free. Any of you guys out there who have experienced this will know that it's scary.

When my fellow students got to know me and realised, I was a bit mad, some would come into the hut (its basic facilities were for all the students, very few used them), and help me train. A native Liverpudlian Harry was the main person who was interested in weight training, but he didn't live at the college, so we trained together only when time allowed. I had a mission, so I was always in there while the typical student's life of drink, sex and rock and roll carried on around me. Don't misunderstand me, I did enjoy the student life but if I was preparing for a competition it had to come second, of course the studying always came first, well some of the time! The rest of the girls on my floor must have had fond memories of me for I often filled the hall with the sweet smell of cooking. Fish and cabbage in my pressure cooker, it became a big joke, "Oh Penny's cooking again!"

My first bodybuilding show was on the 21st of October 1984. I got fourth and was probably too fat. I needed the experience and knowledge to prepare for my next competition which was on the 7th of April 1985 for the British under 21's. Now less than a year to prepare. This date the 7th of April would turn out to be a very special and significant date for me.

My world continued back at Liverpool University. I still have all my training and food diaries and I took a lot of supplements in the 1980's. The supplements were desiccated liver tablets or liquid, brewer's yeast, boldo and lecithin, B complex, vitamin C. In 1984 I added four Alfalfa and 6 kelp tablets three times a day, amino acids and cut up capsules. At the time of writing (2020) I take only cider vinegar, but I am looking into which supplements I need. It must be noted that in the 80's supplements were not the scientific industry that it is today. My view with supplementation is to keep it simple but recognise that the quality of food available and the realistic amount of food I can consume means I need to add supplements.

I was very lucky at my time at Liverpool University to have a friend on my P.E. course whose sister's boyfriend was a NABBA Mr. Universe, Owen Neil, a big guy with an even bigger loving soul. I went with my friend Peter to Nottingham to train with Owen, get advice and go through my posing. Owen was so encouraging and supportive and gave me the spirit and determination to continue with my passion. Bodybuilding is a very lonely and isolating sport, or it was in the 1980's for few women got seriously involved. It was seen as somewhat weird and strange and not accepted especially for women bodybuilders. Looking at today's (2020) acceptance, muscle is accepted, and the industry is huge. With the likes of CrossFit and powerlifting, muscle is in fashion.

America was way more advanced in the 1980's in the world of bodybuilding with the likes of Jo Weider and magazines such as Muscle and Fitness which I bought every month. My heroes included Arnold Schwarzenegger, ("I'll be back" being very apt for me now!) Franco Columbo, Bob Paris, Lee Haney, Frank Zane, Tom Platz, Albert Beckles, Gary Strydom, Bertil Fox. The women included Cory Everson, Elles Von Moais, Bev Francis, Carla Dunlap and Gladys Portuguese. I did go to a few seminars in the 80's, one of them being Lee Haney (8x Mr Olympia), Cory Everson, Bev Francis, Gary Strydom and Tom Platz.

In 1984 I went on two trips abroad. In the Easter break from university on April the 15th to the 26th I went to Florida USA with my family, and I took the opportunity to go to the famous Gold's Gym in Tampa. I still have the original training vest which I brought back, it's now back in use. Also, in 1984 from the 1st - 15th of July I went hitch-hiking with my friend from university Emma Pitman. All the guys at university laughed at us and said we would never go but we did and got to Corfu Greece. It was a friend of my father's who later became a great friend of mine Bobby Stocks who got us from Dewsbury to Germany on our first lift. He was an international truck driver with Edwards a great start for us.

In January 1985 back at university my work was increasing but I still wanted to compete in the EFBB British under 21's class the venue being near my hometown at the Frontier nightclub Batley. In the October I would be 22 years old, so it was my only chance. I knew it would be difficult being away from home plus the academic demands and just having the very basic facilities in the little hut at college, but it wasn't impossible. I think this is when the cabbage and fish smell in Angela Hall was at its best!

What I didn't plan in my preparation for my British under 21's qualifying competition was a back injury. On the 5th of February 1985 I pulled my back doing hyper extensions, I continued training but there are notes in my training diaries stating my back was giving me a problem. It took me until the 7th of March to try and put the intensity back into my training. On the 14th of March it took a turn for the worse and I could hardly walk. So not training I eventually got to see an osteopath who said I had a twisted hip. Slowly I got back to training with some back discomfort. Not so good so close to a competition.

Sunday April 7th, 1985, Frontier Batley EFFB Yorkshire Championships. The place was packed and a group of my friends from university came to give me support. Emma, Tosh (Mark Parcell), David and Kathy stayed at my family house where they experienced their first Yorkshire puddings with gravy. They didn't stop talking about them for weeks. My mum's Yorkshire puddings were always great not that I could have any on this occasion. I did my competition and was placed 3rd but not good enough to get to the British Championships only 1st place got you there.

So, 1985 continued and on the 28th of April I went to a show at Winsford and entered a bench press competition at Latham's gym and got 2nd. I was unaware then that nearly 35 years later, with shall I say a more mature body, I would be raising the bar again 'single handedly'. In May 1985 I also went to the British Finals in Blackpool, to learn and be inspired. My goal now was to one day compete at a UK final.

On July the 7th I was also inspired in a different way when I went to see the Boss in concert. My friend at Liverpool University Tosh loved Bruce Springsteen and I went along with the gang too. It was amazing! My other live concerts would include Madness at Liverpool University, it cost 50p a ticket, yes 50p! Also, at the University I saw Gary Glitter. In the 80's his real identity wasn't known and his music danceable in an 80's sort of way. Now his songs such as 'Do You Want To Be In My Gang' make me nauseous. Oh, the innocence of the 1980's (but writing in 2020 how the 'mighty' are falling and not quick enough in my opinion). I also saw Oasis, Bon Jovi, Tina Turner, Jimmy Barnes, Spice Girls and others over the next decade or so.

Getting back to my study work in May of 1985 I stopped training to revise for my exams. On the 11th of June I had my American Studies paper. My psychology exam was on the 13th, on the 14th of June my Physical Education paper 1 and then on the 18th paper 2.

We had to move back home for the summer and on the 29th of July I started working nights at Fox's Biscuits Batley which made training interesting, but I still trained. I finished working at the end of August and then I was back at Liverpool by the 2nd of September to start year two of my degree.

During the summer I had managed to train with a local amateur rugby league team Dewsbury Celtic. My dad had been player coach there having finished playing professionally for Dewsbury, Batley and then later Huyton. I wanted to get fitter for my bodybuilding however in 1985 I was not aware of how important rugby league would become in my life, must be in my genes.

Celtic was a very good team, the guys were all encouraging and supportive, a lot of them remembering me in my pram when I was taken to see my dad play. Then my interests were more on the sweets and cakes on offer than watching 'Tank' (my dad) bulldoze his way over the try line with 2 or 3 men going with him. My dad's position was prop and for a lot of years he was in the Guinness Book of Records for scoring the most tries as a prop. It's got to be remembered that the game was so different then, one of the rules being you kept the ball until you lost it to your opponents no change over after 6 tackles.

On the 7th of October 1985 I was 21 and on the 12th of October 1985 with my twin sister Caroline we had our 21st birthday party in West Yorkshire at a working man's club on Huddersfield Road Ravensthorpe. A coach load from Liverpool University came and a good time was had by all. One of the biggest things that my university friends wouldn't get over was the fact that we served mushy peas and pork pies and jacket potatoes, not your usual birthday food. On Dewsbury market there was (maybe it's still there) a stall that was famous for its pork pies and its belly pork, Cross's, how delicious they are/were? My friends from Liverpool clubbed together and got me a ghetto blaster which I still have today, a radio cassette player. I remember my friends every time I see it. Thanks guys!

Over the next 12 months I continued to train, entered some competitions but now being 21 years old I had to go into weight classes. I was in the under 52kg ladies and the over 52kg ladies and came 3rd in both. Being in my final year of university, after a competition on the 20th of April 1986, my revision had to come first as my final exams would begin in June.

In my final year at Liverpool University, I made the decision to move out of the halls of residence and rented a one room flat on Smithdown Road just off Penny Lane (The place the Beatles famously made a song about). I was actually there when the famous riots happened. I wasn't far from them but was oblivious for I had my head down revising. Finding academia not easy meant that work, work, and more work was the only way I was going to get through my exams. Determination and focus being part of my being and character.

It was interesting that my dissertation special study paper for my third year P.E. Physiology course was titled 'An Investigation of the Physiological Adaptations of Muscle After Sport Injuries, with a Brief Account of Examples of Injuries, Treatment, Prevention and Services Available' March 1986 tutor Mark Seddon. This title describes what would later be the essence of my whole professional career, maybe a force was guiding me even then. I must re-read that paper; I may re-learn something.

By the middle of June 1986, I was back living in Yorkshire, my life in Liverpool coming to an end. Liverpool and its wonderful characters and unique personalities was now in my blood, there is something amazingly unique and special about that city and it's not just because of the Beatles. It has a deep, loving, passionate soul which vibrates regardless of difficulties. It was possibly this or some universal energy that would guide me back to that city 33 years later and to an amazing person, Danny who would not hesitate to help me, on what I believe to be my destined path. The ultimate reason for me treading this path being to help others believe and love themselves, no matter what life has delivered and challenged them with.

I returned to Liverpool on the 8th of July 1986 to graduate, yes, I managed it! It was a special day; my family came including my granddad Sam who never went anywhere. Now what had life got in store for me?

Chapter 3: Saying Goodbye, Thanks For All You Did For Me

"You are only limited to what you push yourself to."

- Lindsey Vonn

The decision was made I think the doctors were worried about making it. For me there was no choice the level of pain was sending me mental. It's hard to put into words only someone who's experienced it would understand. Asking for my limb to be chopped off was not a debate but a plea to end the pain. If I was to make a comparison to giving birth I would without exaggeration say my rotting right hand was a hundred times more painful without any let up.

Once the decision had been made that I needed an operation I was glad. My other injuries needed attention too and I remember a really nice lady came to my bedside with a mobile x-ray machine to x-ray my left leg. I told her I didn't have pain in my left leg but really bad pain in my right leg. She telephoned the doctor, and it was my left leg that she needed to x-ray. That was about the only part of me that wasn't in pain.

Both my legs had broken bones, the toes on my left foot were all broken. The doctor, Dr. Pietu who fixed all my sticking out bones when I was taken by helicopter to Nantes hospital also needed to put what I can only describe as barbecue skewers into all of my four toes on my left foot. Dr. Pietu had already put a metal pole through my right femur (I named it my dancing pole) with screws and bolts at the top and bottom of it. He also had to put some screws and bolts through my right ankle, which was all smashed up, and a metal plate in my left wrist. My hip was broken in two places and the four lumbar vertebrae that were broken had to be left to heal. Because I was not allowed to move for about 6 weeks, never once getting out of bed, my bones got healing time. It wasn't until the last few days at Nantes hospital that I tried to sit in a chair. I would eventually have to be transported, still in a bed to a rehabilitation place in Niort, the Grand Feu. I later realised that I had been taken to Hotel Dieu in Nantes, translated to God's hotel and then I was going to the Grand Feu in Niort, translated to The Big Fire. My first day at the Grand Feu did feel like hell but at least God decided I was going to be allowed to leave his hotel. Some don't!

There were so many different doctors involved in my operations but the two that I saw at my bedside the most were Dr. Pietu and Dr. Lescour the plastic surgeon. Both doctors came to describe their intended procedures. Dr. Pietu saying that if he didn't straighten my toes, I wouldn't be able to walk. Dr. Lescour described how the hand would be taken off and then how the rest of my arm would have to be sewn into my right groin so it could live there for three weeks. After the three weeks another operation would be performed to take my arm out of my groin and then the groin would be sewn up again. That sounded like a walk in the park! All I knew was that I could not continue with the pain. I wasn't happy, scared in fact to be having an operation because they had to put you to sleep. My fear was from the dentist when a child who put you to sleep to pull teeth out, coming round after was always so painful and scary. My mum always gave us either Heinz tomato or chicken soup after the ordeal.

The only time I was really sick in my life was around the early 70's. I had a bad fever that took me out of it for days. I remember Dr. Twist our family doctor visiting and a vague memory of the vicar Webb coming. I can't remember how I got sick it was only me not my sister or brother. But I do remember that my mum stopped us going to Sunday school because of a trip we had been on with the Sunday school. The coach's windscreen got smashed so the coach had to be driven back without a windscreen. The vicar, Webb who had been sat on the front seat for the whole of the journey suddenly decided he wanted to move further down the bus once there was no windscreen. My sister and I were put on the front seat while vicar Webb went on our seat, very Christian of him. I may well have been ill from that. My mum was furious, and we never went to the church again. So, either the vicar visited because I was ill after that coach trip or because it was touch and go whether I lived.

One of the few childhood memories I have is of being ill on the sofa. I knew I must have been really ill because I had a bottle of Lucozade wrapped in that orange-coloured noisy wrapping, you only got that if you were really sick and then Heinz cream of chicken soup. I can remember coming back to planet earth and watching a programme on the TV. In those days there was no remote control, only three channels and it shut down at 11pm to the National Anthem 'God Save The Queen' then made a loud buzz that would wake up anyone who had fallen asleep on the sofa. The programme I woke up to was Sam. Years after I would ask people if they had watched Sam as a kid, I could describe the storyline to them, but no one had seen or heard of it. But I remembered it so vividly, eventually I concluded I must have dreamt it all up, until one day I saw the full box set for sale on Amazon. Yes, I bought it and had a few weeks of nostalgia. The crazy thing was a lot of it was filmed in the area I grew up in.

Back to the intensive care April 2016. The doctors had seen me, and I remember suggesting that it could be a good idea if all the stuff that had to be done was done at the same time. The barbecue skewers in my left foot and I think my plate in my left wrist was put in then but not sure. The scaffolding in my right leg and ankle had been done already. They were all compound fractures sticking out of my body if I understood correctly. I do think that all the ends of the fingers that I had left were broken and my toes because they are all misshaped now. Also, the chopping off of my right hand and placing my arm in the pocket that they had created in my groin, all being done under one big operation, it made sense to me.

The less you have of a dangerous anaesthetic the better, I had more fear of that than anything it stays in your system and makes you a bit mental. I knew that I had to have these drugs that my body wasn't used to. Living a healthy, sporty life from the age of 17 not even really drinking meant my body would react to these strong chemicals but they would also save my life. I suppose I just wanted it all over with, the doctors agreed. They probably already had decided to do it all at the same time, but I was saying let's get on with it, it's okay.

What happened next was torturous. When you are due to have an operation, you can't eat or drink anything from around early evening. That wasn't such a problem for me except I got really thirsty as the evening went on. I think the bigger problem is knowing they mean business if you have been told you can't eat or drink and then your mind starts to work overtime.

I was scared but this feeling was not as prevalent as the dying pain in my hand. It was sending me insane there are no words to describe it but now I had hope that the pain would be taken away. Unfortunately, this situation went on for three days and I was getting more and more down. The ICU doctor came in one evening to see me and chat, he was concerned because I wasn't the same person, I had no spirit left in me and when your spirit is broken your will to carry on is too. I explained the pain was unbearable and getting worse. My hopes and fears were raised everyday only to be shattered when I got told I wasn't having the operation that day. I knew that I wasn't the only patient and indeed someone else may have just been brought in by helicopter and need their attention to save their lives just as they had done for me. But with the amount of pain, I was in I just got disappointed when the operation didn't happen.

My ICU doctor came to see me on the Saturday night that's when he realised, I was losing my will to live. He was going on holiday for a couple of weeks, and I never got to see him again. I believe 99.9% of the people who took care of me were earth angels and he most definitely was! As he left my room, I thought no way would I get my operation tomorrow it was a Sunday. I prayed anyway that I would.

Prison Or The Paralympics

My prayers must have been heard because after the painful wait I was going to the block to have my hand chopped off, my left toes wired up and anything else my smashed-up body needed.

It was now time to say goodbye. Some may think it odd to say goodbye to a part of your body that was about to be taken away from you, but my right hand had been my right-hand man for as long as I could remember. I used it every day of my life, I held my milk bottle in it when I was a baby, held my teddy bear with it to bring me comfort as I slept, did my first drawings and words with it and probably picked my nose with it and yes spent over 50 years wiping my bottom with it!

It never once let me down, I never fell out of a tree or fell off a swing. I learnt how to roll pastry out with my grandma and how to put my granddad's dahlias in with guidance and help. I wiped my tears away with it when I was sad or hurt and rubbed my bruised knees with it. I caressed my pets with it and held the lead of my first dog Skippy with it. I was able to go on adventures with Enid Blyton and the Famous Five while sat at the top of the stairs with it and held the new born chick I had hatched with it. I did all my schoolwork with it and balled the rounders ball in the school's rounders team with it. I held the hand of my first boyfriend with it and put my Elvis records on the record player with it.

With it I brushed my hair and put my make up on. It spent two years writing my 'A' levels. It spent nearly 20 years lifting weights for me and the best part of 25 years passing exams for me. It gave healing and massage to thousands of people, and it learnt how to give acupuncture. It cooked, cleaned, gardened, and decorated. It waved, it shook hands and on rare occasion gave a signal or two to someone it disapproved of. It drove all over the world in all sorts of vehicles. It held my babies with security and love and rocked them to sleep and held them tight if they were ill or had awoken with a bad dream. It had never let me down and never left my side until through no fault of its own it was ripped off and discarded, thrown to one side, into a hedge and left to die.

On that Saturday night suicidal with pain, I thought of all the things my right hand had allowed me to do. It was because of it that I had accomplished so much and lived the life I had. What would I do without it? How would I cope without it? But I knew it was dying and it sacrificed itself so I could live on. I took gratitude that I had been reunited with it and I got that chance. If my right hand had not been found and it was destiny it was because despite everyone's efforts to find it, even me, it was found by someone needing to have a wee far from where I was. If not found I believe for the rest of my life I would have wondered about its fate. If it hadn't had been found, did it stay there rotting? Did a rat or fox get it? Did the birds pick at it? My acceptance of it leaving me may have never fully happened. Although the pain was indescribable and one may ask why it was re-attached, surely dead after being on its own for over three hours. But I am so grateful to Dr. Fournier, Dr. Waast, Dr. Lescour, Dr. Mahe and Dr. Pietu and all the staff involved in my treatment and care at Nantes hospital and who took the time to reunite us. Physically it may have caused extreme pain and discomfort but psychologically it was healing and comforting to be reunited. I thank them all from the bottom of my heart for giving me that.

Chapter 4: The Life That Once Was

"Keep working even when no one is watching"

- Alex Morgan

I said earlier that this date, the 7th of April, would be significant to me. The first person I met who had the 7th of April as their birthday was Dennis (Denbo). I met Denbo via Kay his wife who I met while working at Shapers Gym Wakefield Yorkshire in 1986 when I had come back to live in Yorkshire after finishing my degree in Liverpool. I believe that throughout your life people cross your path to guide you and give you lessons. Some of these lessons we really don't like, and they can be extremely painful. But some of these lessons and guides get us back onto our life's purpose. Kay definitely did this when she gave me some information on a sports massage college, the Northern College of Massage, Blackpool UK. Though I had done my degree in physical education and psychology from Liverpool, the massage course would be the basis of my future career for 25 years of my life.

The summer of 1986 consisted of me working as much as possible at any job I could get to enable me to pay off my debt from being at university. I worked behind a bar in a night club at the weekend, a couple of days at an old folk's home, a sports summer camp at the local sports centre and a few days at Shapers gym Wakefield. I was crazy busy and also training but most of these jobs were just for the summer, so I just did it.

As previously said, Shapers was where I met Kay and then later her husband Dennis. These fated relationships are still as strong as ever and still as important to me over 30 years later. They are incredible people who I am blessed to have in my life. Remember it was Kay who gave me a prospectus for the Northern College of Massage in Blackpool. It was at this college in 1986 – 1987 I completed my diploma in remedial massage. I continued until 1993 getting my diploma in sports therapy and advanced remedial massage. I would continue to study for the next ten years (I have included the list of my qualification in the appendix).

In March 1987 Kay and Dennis took over Muscle World Gym in Horbury,

Wakefield. I continued to train mainly at Muscle World, it was near to home, well equipped and a great atmosphere of being relaxed, caring and very passionate. When Denbo entered the equation a few months after Kay had taken over, an element of craziness infected the atmosphere in Muscle World gym, created by Denbo. Life was sweet, I trained hard surrounded by good people, studied hard and was slowly building a client base for my massage treatments.

There were many amazing people who helped and inspired me during this time, far too many to mention all of them here, but they know who they are! However, there are a few I would like to mention. Michael Thomas, he was Kay's brother Malcom's son. Kay's brother had spent his life working in Botswana setting up a co-operative and helping the local people. Micky was half Welsh and half Botswanan. He came to live with Kay and Dennis when he was very young, Malcom understanding the benefits of educating his son in England. There were some cultural differences for example he didn't know what the purpose of a knife and fork was and at the beginning Rem, Kay and Denbo's beautiful Red Setter, got it in the neck because dogs were not seen as pets where Micky came from. He soon got the idea, and I am sure having Tracy, Kay and Denbo's young daughter, to guide him, made his transition quicker.

Micky was a natural long distance runner amazing talent which seemed to come so easily. He did have so much support from his new family and having Denbo, an ocean of knowledge, positiveness and understanding on his team was a big bonus! If Denbo didn't know something he would seek out the most knowledgeable person and further his own knowledge in order to give his best in the situation. I know I benefited from Denbo's drive and passion when we trained and so did many of the Wakefield Trinity rugby league team. David Topliss and Andy Kelly's brother to Neil Kelly, who I worked with at Dewsbury Rugby club, would send players to Muscle World gym and Denbo and Kay would guide them and drastically improve the player.

I even did hill runs when Denbo took Micky for some extra training. Micky's main training was at the athletic club at Wakefield, the Wakefield Harriers. Denbo got a respectful reputation for sorting athletes out and many benefited from his input. One particular person who benefited was an overseas player from Australia, Matt Fuller. I believe Denbo saved his rugby career at Wakefield, taking down the chip on his shoulder a little and not only building up his body but his confidence too. I treated Matty many times and his whole drive and outlook changed. I think some of the foundations laid by Denbo for Matty can be seen today with his very successful gym and coaching abilities in Perth Australia. Good on ya mate! Love to you and your family.

Micky inspired me, he was a natural and achieved a lot in his junior years. He always made it look so easy. Mick was a relaxed, chilled kind of runner. He would often stay at the back and then in the next lap he would have passed all the others and be in front, the rest of the pack metres behind. He ran for the England schools National at Gateshead which he won and Frank Bruno the famous boxer presented him with the trophy. He has over 200 trophies and one of my favourite photos, which I had on my clinic wall for years, was Micky at around the age of 16 running for Wakefield Harriers at Huddersfield. The race being a typical race tactic of Micky's staying at the back and then totally eliminating the rest of the runners with speed and grace.

Micky went back to live in Botswana in his early 20's. He didn't continue his competitive running but did start to play rugby union for Botswana. When he was 24, he played at the Rugby Union International rugby 7's tournament in Dubai. The same tournament I helped at but not the same year. When I was there, the Fijians won the tournament, and they also did when Micky played in the tournament. The Fijians were always amazing in the 7's, they are so strong and fast.

I haven't seen Micky for a few years, but I am sure our paths will cross again. You are a star Micky remember to keep shining, you are special!

Another talented runner slightly older than Micky but also running for the Wakefield Harriers was Darren Spawforth. He was also a distance and cross-country runner. It was probably through Micky and Denbo that I started to treat Darren. Darren had a fierce determined fire in his belly and unlike Micky he seemed to have to work extra to achieve his goals. Micky worked hard but the fire in his belly wasn't as fierce as Darren's. The inspiration I got from Darren was his sheer determination to overcome the things that knocked him down, mainly injuries.

At the level that they were competing it was tough, if you didn't have a support system around you it was even tougher or virtually impossible. Darren's support was his family especially his father a keen cyclist and mentor for him. Darren remembers in some of his dark times his father would tell him "You may have lost your fitness, but you can't lose your natural talent". Darren recently lost his father suddenly and it hit him hard. But I have a feeling that the foundations given to him by his father will continue to guide Darren throughout his life and he will continue to achieve great things. Despite his run of bad luck with injuries Darren achieved so much. He ran for Yorkshire, the North of England, England, Great Britain. He won the Durham International Cross Country twice in 1991 and 1993. This was a big race and was televised. His races were around the 3,000 meters mark but he did also do some track races as well as the cross country. Like Micky he won at Gateshead and then was selected to run in Hong Kong, a race opened to the world and called the Hong Kong Golden Mile. I remember he was injured before this race, and I treated him a lot for shin splints. He was only given 5 weeks to prepare for this race, but he still got third, that's how talented and hardworking he was and still is. Darren finally got his constant problem with his shins sorted out by going to get some orthotics for his shoes.

It's ironic, or is it? That Darren and his wife, Sheryl, now own what used to be Kay and Denbo's gym Muscle World Horbury West Yorkshire. It is now named Fitness Muscle World Gym. Darren and Chez kindly let me train there whenever I am in England, thanks guys! Darren you are still an inspiration to me today!

Like I said, there were many great people around me another being Martin. A guy who trained at Muscle World in Horbury and lived in Ossett not far from Horbury. A little further on from Ossett was a small village called Gawthorpe. At Gawthorpe there was and still is a years old tradition on May Day. On this day there is a day of celebrations, a May Queen and Maypole dancing. Not sure how much of the original events occur now but I do know that the World Coal Carrying Competition still goes on and now people come from all over the world to enter in the race. The small village was an old coal mining village so I can imagine years ago a challenge was set more than likely in one of the pubs there, for a coal carrying challenge.

I remember as a kid we all had coal fires, there were working pits all over in the past. We even played on the local slag heaps and got told off for getting so dirty when we got home but we still played on them. They were huge and it was great fun to run up them and try and run down without falling! They were left for years so there was always loads of wildlife, newts, tadpoles, and sticklebacks (little fish). We took an old jam jar and tried to get a pet. They never lived long but there were so many and their habitat then in the 1970's was natural and rarely disturbed or destroyed. For us kids it was a magical place full of enchantment, adventure, imagination, and happiness. I also remember George Brown our coalman delivering sacks of coal to us and putting it in the 'coil ole' (coal hole). The sacks were big, difficult to get hold of and appeared very heavy.

Martin loved his training; he was a no bullshit sort of guy and kept himself to himself. He came across as being a bit angry with the world on a number of occasions. I liked his no bullshit attitude and got on well with him. He was training for the coal race and challenged me to enter the women's race. Of course, I took up the challenge. Five years earlier in 1986 I had entered and got third. But when Martin challenged me in 1991, I was not dieting for a bodybuilding competition and was actually at Keighley Rugby League Club, not only treating them but helping them to get fitter. So, I felt fitter and more up to the challenge. The challenge was on! Martin and I started to do running and then practice the course at Gawthorpe.

In the 1980's and 1990's the women had to run a different course from the men, now I think both women and men do the same course. The year I did it the race distance was much shorter, but you had to sprint it the best you could with a sack of 'coil' (coal) on your back.

Belinda Archer came second. She was not happy and complained about the crowds being in her way. It was the same for all of us. She was complaining that much that I offered to give her the trophy I had just won, she said no! If the crowd had got in her path that wasn't my fault. I remember her trying to push past me, in those days the race path narrowed to get to the finish line at the Maypole, there wasn't the space, and I was in front anyway!

I never got around to doing the race again, so I stayed undefeated. Martin was over the moon, as the photo shows as I cross the finish line first. He did compete in the longer men's race up a difficult incline and I think he finished mid field, a very good achievement in such a difficult challenge. Thanks Martin I couldn't have done it without you!

Around 1987-88 I started to do voluntary work for the under 19's rugby league team at Dewsbury Rugby League club. The club was at Crown Flatt's ground, the original pitch with its famous nine-hole slope or hill depending on which direction you were playing. To give you a little history of Dewsbury Rugby club. It was founded in 1875 or 1876. In 1877-1878 the club issued their first ever fixture card. In the 1880-1881 season the team was successful in the Yorkshire Challenge Cup. Victory over Wakefield Trinity in the final was achieved by a drop goal from Alfred Newsome. Changes were seen at the club in 1898 but Crown Flatt has been the centre of Dewsbury rugby club since 1876.

It wasn't until 80 plus years later that my dad Trevor 'The Tank' Walker would be running around the rugby pitch at Crown Flatt and it would be over 100 years later that I would be running on and off the very same pitch. Although I don't know the path my dad took in his junior years as a rugby player, he did play his first professional games for Dewsbury and continued to play there in the mid 1950's and 60's. I was born in 1964 and my dad was playing there then. It was thought that my elder brother Philip would follow the tradition, but Philip didn't have any interest in the sport. It was I who was into sport with my bodybuilding and my twin Caroline wasn't interested in sport but rather in horses.

It's quite unique that I would become known for my involvement with Dewsbury Rugby Club, and I was given an amazing honour when Dewsbury RLFC supporters club awarded me club person of the year 1989-1990. I was even more proud to see all the great names that were on this trophy, one of them being my dad's in the 1965-66 season. Now as my dad is in his 80's and not as active, it warms my heart to have the common achievement. It encourages one to embrace one's life no matter how difficult it may be, because we have only a certain amount of allotted time in which to be the person our soul wants us to be and to try to make the world a better place. Thank you to all the supporters club for giving this to me.

I must also mention that there is a much more famous rugby family from the Dewsbury area who I was blessed to know but more of that later, let's get back to 'The Tank'.

My dad was playing for Dewsbury and from the wonderful book published by Bob Fox, Tony Scargill and Ken Crabtree in 1989 (I was physio at Dewsbury at this time), ' The Official History of Dewsbury Rugby League Football Club', there are first team photos with 'Tank' on them for the 1957-58 season and the 1965-66 season. I have also found newspaper cuttings that stated that a local lad from the Shaw cross team at 18 and weighing 15 stone was signed by Dewsbury. His first team debut being against Huddersfield when he was 19 years old. I know my dad only played professional rugby for Dewsbury and later Batley, with a short spell at Huyton. He stayed with Dewsbury for many seasons. I remember going to the games when I was very young. When I became involved with the club many years later it was the smell of the wintergreen that brought my memories back as a very young child. They came flooding back giving a wonderful calming feeling of contentment.

In the Dewsbury Rugby book on page 56 (my age as I am writing this!), there are some photos that hit the headlines on the 16th of April 1966 at Station Road Swinton. Dewsbury V St Helens, attendance 13,046 a big crowd. According to my dad, and I believe it is this match, a lady (Minnie Cotton) came on the pitch with her umbrella about to hit one of the Dewsbury players. 'Tank' took it from her saving the Dewsbury player's head from attack and proceeded to break the umbrella across his thigh! In 1966 I am sure it would have been made of wood. The match result was Dewsbury 5 St Helens 12. Obviously, a game with much drama and excitement for both the crowd and the players!

My dad also played at Batley and coached there; I think he was player coach for a number of seasons. He went to Batley with a fellow Dewsbury player Mike Sullivane. When I asked dad why he left Dewsbury the short answer was someone on the committee. How strange my reason for leaving too! Dad also has a fond memory of a certain referee Eric Clay: "That robbing bastard robbed us of two semi-finals". Now surely dad you can't be suggesting back handers were being taken, allegedly. We will never know!

I remember as a young child people visiting us connected with rugby, usually my dad's rugby mates. I can't remember them all but there was Rodney, Colin Cook and Mick Doyle. Colin and Mick were mine and my twin's godfathers. I distinctively remember Mick being a builder and building our extension at Overthorpe road Thornhill. That was exciting because my sister and I would then get our own bedrooms. In the decades to come I would continue to meet my dad's fellow teammates, it seemed that everyone I met in the rugby arena, if of a certain generation knew 'The Tank'. It was always great to hear their stories and made me even more proud and connected with the 'Tank's' rugby achievements.

Before 'The Tank' left his professional rugby career he went to help his friend Dave Cox at Huyton, Liverpool (I am not sure exactly when 'Tank' left Dewsbury to go to Batley, I am guessing it was around 1966-67). I know he was at Huyton in the early 1970's because I have his player's season ticket little red book for 1972-73. Dad says he went there to play and help his friend but trained at Celtic amateur club in Yorkshire because of the long distance. There wasn't any M62 then. The M62 opened up in stages between 1971 and 1976. After Huyton, 'Tank' continued with Celtic and became involved with the amateurs.

When dad finished his professional career, he continued to play amateur at the famous Dewsbury Celtic Rugby Club at the Irish National Club West Town Dewsbury. As I have already mentioned I joined the men to train with them to develop my bodybuilding. A wonderful atmosphere and great characters many of them having played professional. Like so many of the local amateur clubs they were a force to be reckoned with. In my profession I spent a number of seasons working with amateur clubs, Dewsbury Moor and Thornhill rugby club being two of them. I worked with an amazing coach and man, Johnny Harpin, who used to play alongside my dad. How one's world intertwines in amazing connections, or is it all already predetermined by the forces that be?

Dad never played for Great Britain or International. I believe he got a shoulder injury at selection time. I vividly remember dad coming home one Saturday evening. I was excited to see dad back and went to jump up at him but was stopped and then I saw his arm fastened up in a sling. He looked in pain and was very sad for a good while after. At such a young age I didn't understand what was going on, but I think he lost out on playing for Great Britain. He did however get into the Guinness Book of Records for the most tries for a prop and that record was held for a number of years. He got 17 tries in that season but dislocated his shoulder and there were still 7 games to play, so 'The Tank' could have got even more. I am not sure who has the record now.

An interesting story dad tells is that a chief's son from Fiji wanted to take 'Tank' to play for them, but my mum wouldn't go. Now that would have been an amazing experience and place to grow up. I had the honour of helping out the Fijian Rugby Union team at the Dubai 7's in 1998 when I took myself around the world (more on that later). But for now, the story was this giant of a man had a dead leg, and anyone who has seen them play knows how powerful they are, it's in the genes. They came into the changing room when I had just finished treating the young team from New Zealand, the Warblers, that I was working with. I saw this giant limping and offered to help. My goodness I have never tried to treat someone with such solid muscles, and I have treated some big muscle guys before, one being Geoff Capes. For those who do not know the name he was the world's strongest man, just like Eddy Hall from Leeds. Geoff Capes was at an event demonstrating his strengths and somehow, I ended up trying to treat his shoulders. But this Fijian's leg was the toughest challenge of my career. He did get back on the pitch and the Fiji team won the tournament, so I must have helped him a little bit.

My life that once was involved lots of study, enjoyable hard work, bodybuilding and being surrounded by like-minded people who taught me so much in so many areas of my life. I am eternally grateful to them all! I do believe these lessons have helped me to develop commitment, strength, both mental and physical and the will to keep going, no matter the odds. Or is this just the Yorkshire grit that is buried deep inside of me? Or possibly sheer bloody mindedness? Who knows whatever the elements may be, together they allowed me the strength to carry on when life just kept knocking me down. My message to anyone experiencing life's lessons is to believe in yourself, to give love to yourself and to be kind to yourself. Forgiveness and love will strengthen you and slowly a way out of darkness will be illuminated allowing you to take one step at a time into a bright, peaceful and happy existence. This will bring you inner peace and a love for your life. A gift that you can pass on to others. Never give up hope!

Chapter 5: My Guardian Angels And The Show Must Go On

"On the occasion of every accident that befalls you, remember to turn to yourself to inquire what power you have for turning it to use."

- Epictetus

I had very little sleep that Saturday night and had many visitors, I begged them all to take me with them so I could be free from the pain and confusion. They refused but their presence was calming and healing. They were my team of guardians, my angels who never left my side and are still by my side today. Throughout they have given me signs and messages of hope and later they exposed lies and cover ups that were being carried out by a very low vibing and corrupt world. They also demonstrated to me that others don't have the integrity or honesty that I value so highly and live by. Naively I thought others especially in positions of authority did too!

I still wasn't certain that my operation would go ahead especially on a Sunday and the fact that it hadn't gone ahead a number of times before. But they came for me and pushed me out of my ICU room and on a journey that was terrifying. All you can see are the lights in the ceiling as you are pushed on your bed. Everything is slow motion and very, very scary. Having to have so many operations I got used to this journey and tried to chat with the person pushing me about anything, the weather, their job, just to break the haunting silence. On my first trip on this journey, I was scared but also relieved that at last the pain would be taken away. If I died so, be it but I couldn't continue to live with this rotten smelling, torturous pain, that I did know!

The reader must understand that I was further confused and powerless because my understanding of the French language was limited. Over the years I concluded that some of the French had an arrogance and were impatient with anyone they didn't choose to understand. This choice was often dictated by their personalities, they managed to understand if it was work or gaining money. Some even if fluent in English choose to act dumb if you had a complaint or didn't agree with them.

In the hospital I didn't see this very often, but outside of that environment I sure did. This went to a whole new level after my accident. The big multimillion international insurance company Allianz never once translated any important legal papers concerning my accident and gave me a non-English speaking solicitor Hugo Riposseau from Niort and Bressuire Cabinet AOV. In the end I was starting to believe he was working more for the other party's solicitor a big famous one from Bordeaux, Coubris, Courtois and Associates (allegedly).

Some may have the opinion that if I choose to live in France, I should speak the language and I totally agree with you. I do try but my Yorkshire accent and the complex French language gives me challenges. I have some very dear French friends and we communicated very well, both parties must want to be understood. I never spoke in English with them, I tried to communicate in French. That's easier if you know the subject but when it gets beyond your vocabulary like the law system even French people don't understand. It's just one of the ways these people gain power over others. Confusion and big, long words whatever language it is in. It's keeping you in the dark making things exclusively just for their members. Think of politicians, the justice system, your small print on your insurance policy. It's all done with intent, consciously to feed their egos, their importance and to create a distance from mainstream society. It empowers them or they think it does. This is a global practice and even when dealing with your own native language, the intentional confusion and 'elitist' protection is so obvious. As Albert Einstein put it "Unthinking respect for authority is the greatest enemy of the truth." I'll second that!!

When I got to the block (operating theatre) there were three surgeons waiting I told them I was so grateful but if it hadn't happened today, I was going to the boucherie to ask them to chop it off (that's butchers in English). They then said they were very professional at their work which I had no doubt they were, but they didn't get my sense of humour.

Another scary thing is the actual theatre room it's full of machines and monitors, bright white and freezing, it's scary! The doctor who was in charge of my general anaesthetic spoke English and she looked familiar. She had these beautiful blue eyes which stood out even with her gown and hat on in preparation for surgery. She said, "It's nice to see you looking like this and chatty." (Chatty was my camouflage for scared shitless). I said, "Have you seen me before?" her reply "Yes when you were brought in by helicopter, you didn't look too good then" "Oh my God" I said, "You were one of the team that saved my life! Thank you so much for all you did for me." With her beautiful smile shining down on me she said, "That's okay it's my job."

This earth angel became my sign that everything was going to be okay, she had a calming reassuring presence and gave me hope and confidence that things were going to be alright. My earth angel was my anaesthetist, the part I feared the most. If your anaesthetist isn't good, then it's goodnight and lights out. I was blessed to be surrounded by excellent teams of medical people.

Another who sent me this message was Bob Marley, remember I said songs and books became signs and information from the universe, I think I had a direct line with Bob. His songs 'Three Little Birds' with the lyric "Everything Gonna Be Alright" and 'No Woman No Cry' again telling me "Everything Gonna Be Alright" were just two of them and I couldn't believe the songs he sent me when I left the court.

It's a Queen song that I associate with my time in ICU 'The Show Must Go On', though at times you question what the hell's the point! The universe will always show you and direct you to the point. In my case writing this book is a very important healing and hopefully encouraging to others sort of point.

Another scary part is coming round it's terrifying. It amazes me they can put you half dead with drugs to cut into you and in my case chop things off and you won't feel it. What happens to your aura or Qi in Chinese medicine and the spirit? Surely these are already out of balance with the accident or disease that the patient has got. How do you correct those? Is that part of the horrendous fear, confusion and disorientation you feel as you come round after a general anaesthetic?

When I came round after this particular operation, I felt petrified. At first you wake up, but you are paralysed and very scared. Your mind tells you to move but you can't then you start to panic. I thought they had left me in a garage, I was cold and felt abandoned crying heavily shouting for help (maybe again my mind took me back to my accident). I was so scared I was all alone left in what I thought was a garage. It turned out that I was back in my ICU room but that's not what I thought. The experience was so horrifying that I expressed my fears of coming round after my operation. They said I could be given something to help that. I can't remember if I took them up on their offer for my next operation, but I definitely did for the rest. Throughout this journey I have probably had about 15 procedures, that's a lot of anaesthetic for one's body to deal with.

I stayed in my ICU room for a few more days until I was moved to another part of the hospital, the trauma unit. I was guided to ask someone to get me a dicta-phone so I could record my experiences. I don't know why I wanted one, but I asked for one. Maybe part of me wasn't convinced that I was going to make it and the dicta-phone would at least allow me to say goodbye to the ones I loved.

Chapter 6: Special People, Dewsbury Rugby League Club And The UK Finals

"Your vision will become clear only when you can look into your own heart. Who looks outside dreams, who looks inside awakes"

- Carl Jung

In the early 1990's I bought my first house and set up my clinic. It was a Victorian house with high ceilings and two big reception rooms. I decided to turn one of the three bedrooms into my living room and use the downstairs as my clinic area. The house was called West Grove so that's the name I gave my clinic. I loved the Victorian era, 'Upstairs, Downstairs' being one of my favourite TV series, a love I shared with Mrs Hirst. Mrs Hirst was my English teacher and the senior mistress at Thornhill High School, who later became a patient of mine. A fun, amazing woman who I was blessed to get to know. She died of cancer, and I felt her loss. I really connected with her. Hilary was kind enough to leave me all her 'Upstairs Downstairs' videos which I cherish to this day. Thank you, Hilary.

A few years before getting my own place to work from, I was concentrating on home visits to treat friends and their families. But it was my voluntary work with the under 19's Dewsbury Rugby League Club team that led me down my destined work path. My theory was I could help the team and also get hands on experience that no textbook or teacher could ever give me. Boy what a shock I got when I did my first match. The problem is that people believe you know everything. I believe the day anyone thinks they have no more to learn from any person no matter what it is or the background that person comes from, is a day when you may as well stop breathing.

On this first match I had to run on the pitch to a damaged shoulder, A-C joint injury, a dislocated finger, damaged thumb, head injury and many other knocks and bruises, it was crazy. But I was hooked and my love and passion for the game remains to this day.

In the late 80's and 90's the game was very different than it is today. Moving to summer rugby I believed was a bad move. I voiced my concerns, but I think the move was more to do with Sky Television and profit than the spirit of the game. When matches were played on a wet muddy field there were fewer general injuries. On cold frosty days the officials decided whether the pitch was too hard for the game to commence. But when summer rugby arrived nobody seemed to acknowledge that a dry spell and even the English sun could bake the ground and make my injury count increase not to mention the problem of dehydration.

There was something magical about rugby in winter. The fans went for a drink, got their rugby fix and then went home, usually via the pub to a traditional Sunday dinner, with Yorkshire puddings of course and then would watch Scrum Down on TV, usually falling asleep at the same time!!

Rugby has advanced so much today and they don't even wear shoulder pads! Maybe I am just nostalgic for the time that I was professionally involved with this wonderful sport of rugby league.

I was asked to help with the other teams not just the under 19's, which I did willingly (I was hungry for knowledge and to gain first-hand experience of injuries and treating them). This is when I started working with the first and second teams. Because my work was hands on massage, not just machines, the guys preferred my treatment. My first sole responsibility for Dewsbury came about in a somewhat dramatic way. We were all on the bus an early start because we were playing away at one of the Cumbrian teams. We were just about to set off when these cars appeared at speed. The men came on the bus and proceeded to escort the Dewsbury physio off, Keith Shaw. To this day I don't know what happened, but he never came back. I was asked if I would take over and help them out for the match. Of course, I would but I was very nervous. Being thrown in at the deep end you either sink or swim. With the help of the lads doing their own strapping and helping me out I didn't sink, it was more like treading water than actually swimming, but together we got through it.

I was blessed with a kind, funny and at times crazy but respectful and loving group of guys. Passionate about their sport and dedicated (well 90% of the time) to doing the work to recover from any injuries that they may have had. I mentioned earlier a famous rugby family from the Dewsbury West Yorkshire area, Liversedge to be exact. The father of this family, Mark Burgess was a strong, powerful player, a gentle soul with a wicked sense of humour. I remember his family coming to watch him play and anyone who is a fan of rugby league will know about his four boys Luke, Sam, George, and Tom. The famous Burgess boys, making history by eventually all four of them playing for the same professional rugby team in Oz, the Rabbirtos at the same time, on the same day, in the same team. What an achievement, the genes and passion given to them and the encouragement at a young age obviously paying off.

When I have seen them play, I see their father's grit and strength and intelligence of the game within them.

I worked with Mark for several years, because of his fearlessness and the position he played (number 8), he was often on the treatment table. I remember on one occasion while playing at Crown Flatt, Mark got a head high tackle, which was allowed in those days. Though I often searched out the other team's head high tackler after the match and gave them a piece of my mind. It's such a dangerous, cowardly, and unnecessary movement often carried out by those who lacked the skill or courage to do a proper tackle. I understand that it can happen by accident but in some teams, they seemed to have a designated hit man who got my opinion after the match, no matter who they were and that would include my own players.

Going back to Mark he was down in the 9-hole area (the slope on the pitch of Crown Flatt). As I got to him, he was sort of having a fit his eyes rolling back, and he was speaking in a foreign language which I think was French. I tried desperately to open up his airways, but the slope and Mark's weight made it impossible to move him. I then saw he couldn't breathe because his tongue had fallen back and was blocking his airway. I made the quick decision, an instinctive one, to get hold of his tongue, a dangerous thing to do as he could have bitten my fingers for, he was fitting, but I wasn't going to let him die. The game continued, the referee not stopping (he got a piece of my mind after the game and tried to patronise me by saying "Now let me explain the rules of the game to you" idiot!). It must be noted that there were very few female physiotherapists working with professional rugby teams at this time and we got a lot of flak in this male dominated environment.

Back on the pitch I was trying to hold Mark's tongue and support his body while he was fitting, the game going on around us. The scene must have looked serious because some of the crowds nearby were climbing over the small fence to get to me and Mark. Eventually, the match was stopped. I think the crowd's shouts had some effect. With help we managed to get Mark in the recovery position, and he was coming round. By now there were St. John's Ambulance on the pitch with a stretcher as well as Dewsbury's coach Maurice Bamford, ex-Great Britain coach and a person my dad knew well, plus the officials. I was trying to get Mark off the pitch and to hospital while the referee and Maurice Bamford were having a full-blown argument about the match. I was livid. Mark was seriously unwell, and these guys were shouting and arguing over the top of him. I gave them a bollocking and they stopped but then the ref wouldn't let the St. John's Ambulance stretcher Mark straight off the pitch but made them carry him the longest way to the dressing rooms. What!!

Throughout my years I got several 'speaking's to' by referees who stopped the game to do so. It was usually because I had run the shortest distance to get to my player that was down. My job was to get the players off that pitch with minimum injury and not in a body bag. All of these refs got my opinion and a piece of my mind after the match. They were feeding their power and ego and not their common sense. Eventually my protective and no bullshit reputation went before me.

Mark recovered and got back playing the game he loved and was so passionate for. He did do some coaching and no doubt was busy with his four boys who were starting to be noticed in the rugby arena.

As is so typical of life, you come in contact with people on your path of life and then you venture down a different path and your paths may never cross again. But sometimes your paths are destined to cross again for one reason or another. When Mark Burgess and my paths crossed again it was a painful and difficult one nearly 15 years later.

I got to hear that Mark wasn't very well and amateur clubs such as Thornhill and Dewsbury Moor were holding fundraising events to raise money for Mark. I had bumped into Mark a few times over the years, but I was no longer involved in rugby. Mark had gone on to do some coaching, one of those teams being at Nottingham. He asked me to physio for them, but I just didn't have the time. He also coached his four sons who all played rugby. When I heard that he wasn't well I went to see him. Since that day on the nine hole at Crown Flatt I had a certain bond with him, a need to make sure he was okay, a need to help and take care of him. I had this feeling with all those who were in my life but the sheer fear and shock of seeing Mark struggling that day on the rugby pitch gave us an unspoken connection.

I remember being in a Dewsbury pub one weekend, a thing I rarely did, it may have been someone's birthday or something, but Mark was there. It was great to see him, and we chatted. Someone else came to chat too, another rugby player and Mark explained that I had saved his life, I never saw it like that. All I saw was one of my players having a problem and I did all I could to stop that problem I was never going to give up on him. All these years later, I knew his diagnosis was serious but maybe I could help him now.

I visited his home at Liversedge many times to help with massage and acupuncture. Mark struggled to talk but his personality was still the same being funny and being the person, I remembered. His physical appearance however was so different the big powerful body that used to knock players out of his way and tackle like a man possessed was no longer there, but Mark was. I don't know if what I was doing even helped his physical body, but we had a laugh, had some sadness and took the piss out of each other. From a psychological point I think my visits uplifted him. But

Motor Neurone is a cruel, devastating, soul destroying imprisonment in your own body. It's torturous for those whose body is fighting it but equally as torturous for the people around who have to watch this slow, painful process taking away every bodily function from the person they love, the person that had been their rock, their source of strength, their mentor, their guiding light, their coach, and their father.

Sam was the one I saw the most who was Mark's main carer and lived with his dad, his two younger brothers George and Tom and their beautiful, intelligent, empathic black Labrador. I saw Luke on my visits also but not George or Tom too often, they may have been at school. Both Sam and Luke were playing professional rugby Sam at Bradford Northern and Luke at Leeds Rhinos. It was probably around 2006 when I went to see and treat Mark.

The disease affects muscle movements, slowly destroying the cells that are supposed to send messages to allow movement. Eventually the muscles are weakened and waste away. Seeing this shadow of the former big, strong, muscular, professional rugby player sat with his loyal dog by his side broke my heart.

Mark still had his sense of humour, and he joked a lot, I wanted to treat Mark as I had always done, not seeing the diseased body but his spirit which was courageous and strong. As time passed it was more and more difficult to understand his words so he would write things down. I knew that this cruel disease would eventually get the better of this amazing human being and my treatments wouldn't stop that, but I would continue while ever he wanted me to visit him.

I got to know Sam and Luke and even took a look at an injury or two. Their respect and love for their dad was so obvious. They had this wonderful banter and positivity with each other no self-pity or selfishness, just unconditional love. Sam was at Bradford Northern, and he was getting into the first team, he must have only just turned 17. We talked a lot about rugby and his dream of visiting Australia. I had connections with Australia and encouraged him to visit, the world being his oyster.

The last time I saw Mark was when I turned up at his house to treat him, but he must have forgot our arrangement because Sam was carrying Mark down the drive to put him in the car. Sam then went back into the house, and I stayed talking to Mark who was sat in the front passenger's seat, tears rolling down his cheeks he looked so very sad. I chatted to him gave him a big hug and a kiss on his cheek. Sam came back they seemed to be in a rush to be somewhere, I said my goodbyes and went to my car. Now I had tears rolling down my cheeks I knew I would never see him again. In my mind I was questioning the cruelty of our world, why did it have to pick on the good ones. I was angry with the universe and angry with myself for not being able to help Mark as I had been able to do all those years before.

Mark died in 2007 and there were that many people at his funeral that the police had to be there to control the traffic. The small church at Liversedge was packed inside and outside. It was so sad but at the same time so beautiful to see all the people that Mark and his family had connected with. Players from Bradford Northern and Leeds Rhinos were there and some of the overseas players wore their traditional clothing as a sign of respect for Mark and his family. There were many people from the rugby environment, and it was amazing to see them all toast Mark in the pub after. My friend Andy Tyers was there from Sheffield who got to know Mark while he was at Nottingham, which gave us a chance to catch up.

On that day the strength of character of his four boys shone through with pride, honour, respect and a deep love for the man that had been their foundation built out of granite, love and a passion for a sport that they would continue to build on and to reach amazing levels of success in. Mark's legacy living on through them and I believe he has never left their side, watching over them with pride and of course that wicked sense of humour that he had. One of life's unsung heroes Mark Burgess!

I didn't send them a card but wrote them a poem instead. I believe it was sent to them from their loving father:

Another interesting situation which occurred involved Neil Kelly known as Ned. It was a home game at Crown Flatt, Neil took a knock on his arm, I ran on with my 'magic sponge' and he continued playing. I wasn't happy with the way he was holding and protecting his arm, it was not Ned's style. I kept a close eye on him and was on and off the pitch going to Ned. I told him to come off, but he wouldn't. We got to half time and the doctor took a look at Ned.

Half time in the dressing room was a bit crazy, I was re-strapping and looking at any concerns that any of the players had, encouraging them and assessing their injury. Often the coach would be shouting, the volume dictated by how the game was going. On this occasion it was Maurice Bamford whose coaching methods involved a lot of shouting and swearing. He had demanded that the doctor look at Ned because he had gone down so much but always got back up. The doctor said he had badly bruised his arm. On the way out for the second half I managed to say to Ned that he needed to go down at the first tackle and stay down for his arm was not right.

It must be noted that Maurice Bamford did not agree with females being involved with rugby and was always questioning my reason for treating the players. In fact, on one occasion, he came into the treatment area and one of the players (I think it may have been David Watkinson who had a knee injury, a ligament pull or tear, he was waiting for the specialist appointment) was under the heat lamp. Maurice said, "Now let me ask you something, you can keep that heat lamp on for one minute, one hour or a week and it won't repair a tear, so why are you treating him?" My reply was "Yes you are correct, but I am using the lamp to warm the area up, encourage blood flow (I had already massaged the thigh and knee area including the back of the knee and hamstrings to encourage healing), but what you haven't taken into consideration is the psychological aspect of an athlete with an injury. He will be more confident and feel less anxiety about his problem which will help him through his training, and it gives me an opportunity to feel, see and assess his injury before and after training". Maurice left the room he had nothing more to say. It must be noted that I was in my early 20's Maurice Bamford was a formidable character an ex-Great Britain coach and if you knew what was good for you, you didn't get on the wrong side of him, especially if you were a player.

I was speaking the truth; I wasn't there to feel a rugby players leg but to do my job. I think he (Maurice) gave me a tiny bit of respect after that, though he kept it well hidden. Remember I was supposed to be at home making Yorkshire puddings, that's what he once announced on the team bus one Sunday night on our long trip back from Cumbria. I think he didn't like the fact that I got on well with the players and had their respect while Maurice could feel any respect, he had from them was slowly being eroded by the way he treated some of them. All that said, I did like Maurice it's a case of better the devil you know. That's why I went to work with him a few years later at Bramley.

Back to the second half of the game. Ned did not stay down on his first tackle, his second or third, I was on and off the pitch. He was holding his arm so badly. Each time I went on Maurice would give me a mouthful of abuse "Stop f.... fussing over him bla bla bla f... bla." On my third return from running onto Neil who I had just told I think he had a broken arm, and he must not get up after his next tackle, Maurice was out of the dugout and shouting at me. I then picked my wet sponge up and threw it at him saying "Treat him your fucking self, he has a broken arm and should have been off in the first half!" The next tackle Neil did stay down and came off and went to the hospital. Maurice was not happy with me and reminded me that the doctor had seen the arm and it was only bruised and I was pissing about and fussing too much. Later in the club house Neil returned from hospital with a pot on his broken arm! Maurice was a little kinder to me from that day, but I still think he believed I should be at home on Sundays making the Sunday dinner.

There were so many great personalities and friendships formed at Dewsbury rugby club it was a caring family atmosphere. The partners and wives of the players were supportive and involved which I believe is essential. The only thing that they didn't get involved with was the end of session piss up, usually a weekend away. I remember going on a couple, one being with Dewsbury and spent most of my time laughing at their drunken activities and making sure they were safe. I was never a drinker; I was training for my bodybuilding and felt a bit of a duty of care to get them home safe.

I never really drank after games for I always had to drive home, even after away matches. Drink driving being one of my lifetime disapprovals. I was knowledgeable of the effects it would have on a person's body and their physical and mental reactions through my profession and my bodybuilding. It was my number one pet hate. I was known to take beer off the players if they had for example a dead leg after the match. Explaining recovery needs to be allowed to start straight away and I would not be treating them on Monday if they drunk and as was the tradition, staying out and even going to a nightclub. I remember one of the Lancashire signings, a good player who came from St Helens or Widnes if I remember correctly, who had an injury, and he went on a bit of a night out. I refused to treat him for the whole week. He was not happy, but he was not being responsible and thought I had a pair of magic wands not a pair of hands. I knew I could work miracles with my dedication and massage but if you will not do your bit I will dedicate my energy to those that will!

Going back to drink driving, I believe that the law should be zero alcohol in your system, then no chances could be taken. I remember one drinking person said that would not be fair because you may still have alcohol in your system from the day or night before and therefore should be allowed to have some in your system. If there is any alcohol or drugs in your system it will affect a person's ability to drive, end of story! How ironic that my car accident would involve an aged driver who liked a drink and who no doubt was on prescribed drugs, none of which was investigated. But more on that later.

Back to the personalities of Dewsbury rugby team. Part of the fixtures and fittings there was a guy nicknamed Chilly, Chris Hill. He was the kit man along with a man named Keith Fortis. Keith often took down statistics during the matches. Chilly was a quiet man but he saw and heard everything. If you wanted anything, more strapping, another pair of socks, Chilly was the man. He had a bunch of keys, was always there and worked really hard. The club played a big part in his life often being undervalued. I had a good connection with Chilly and he taught me a lot. I was in my 20's spent my life in education surrounded by the 'educated ones'. But Chilly taught me how much you could learn from people of all walks of life. Society tends to make judgements of a person by what they have, what they have achieved and their academic background. The biggest thing Chilly demonstrated to me was contentment with one's life, to be kind and caring and to be just who you are no matter how others see you or judge you. It's a difficult act to follow Chilly but at least I got shown it existed.

Thank you Chilly. Your father who was on the committee at Dewsbury, he was also a tireless worker for the club. He was also a kind, gentle soul. Rare in this day and age but I believe the new decade, 2021 is the time of change and a movement towards Chilly and his father's attributes. Here's hoping.

Others involved in rugby league that I was lucky to meet included Ray Abbey, Shaun Dunford and Jack Addy to name but a few. These men also had connections with Crown Flatt and when I knew them their involvement was on the coaching side. I was around Jack Addy for a longer spell than Ray Abbey, I liked their personalities and passion for the game. Jack was a bit of a ladies' man with a mischievous cheek to him. He once told me that he could have been my dad because he tried to date my mum, but I think her heart had already been taken by 'The Tank'.

It's sad to see these passionate characters of the past slowly leaving us for the rugby pitches far, far away, but I have no doubt that they keep an eye on things. In fact, Jack was a bit put out that I had forgotten to mention him (remember I hear voices). I hadn't really Jack, how can you and your fellow rugby generation ever be forgotten. Dad as I write is still kicking, maybe not a rugby ball but the inevitable time machine is catching up to him and since we lost my mum a couple of years ago, I think he misses her company and care. But they have all lived their lives with courage and passion and being involved with the best northern sport there is! Giving hours of drama, entertainment and dedication for others to watch and be a part of. In these strange times (2020/21) we must do all we can to keep this sport alive and kicking for the next generations to benefit from. It's part of the northern people's DNA!!

So why did I leave Dewsbury rugby league team? Another important lesson I learnt was not to believe or trust a person, especially a chairman that won't look you in the eye. Alias Rodney Hardcastle. This is how it went. I used to block out Monday evenings at my clinic from 6pm for any of the players to come for treatment they used to train Tuesdays and Thursdays, I went to the club on these days. It was essential to treat them as soon as possible after a match and it also allowed players with ongoing injuries to still train yet be able to have some treatment on Monday. The number that showed up didn't matter, if I worked till midnight so be it, I wanted them to be back fit and available for team selection.

There is a big element of psychology in sport in fact everything we do in life. Getting into the players' heads and them trusting you being vital for progress. I was blessed to have that from my training partner for my bodybuilding, Denbo. He was in my head, and I trusted him, I still do! I never questioned anything but gave him 100% a 100% of the time that's how we got to the EFBB UK Bodybuilding Championships Grand Finals in Harrogate Yorkshire Sunday the 15th of October 1989.

I mentioned earlier in the note from the author that certain songs guided me and were significant in my life. The song that Denbo and I had for our training was Tina Turner's 'Simply the Best' it's still powerful today and only last year I sent Kay and Denbo two roses for their garden. A beautiful perfumed one for Kay as she talked about her fond memories of a perfumed rose around her childhood home's front door. The rose I sent for Kay was called Nostalgia, with a strong perfume, cream and red in colour. Denbo's was a yellow peachy coloured one called, yes you guessed it 'Simply The Best'! In the 90's I also surprised them by taking them to a Tina Turner concert at Woburn Abbey Bedfordshire England. That song even today allows me to work harder and realise how blessed I am to have such amazing people in my world.

Back to the story of leaving Dewsbury rugby club. Mr Hardcastle questioned why I billed the club for two hours (£30) when maybe only one player or no players turned up (that never happened!). My answer was I close my clinic to anyone else, so I am free to concentrate on the Dewsbury players. He said we can't keep paying it. I think I may have asked for a small increase in my rate for match days and training nights a few weeks before. I got no travel expenses and was the only medical person responsible for the first, second and under 19's teams, as well as for anyone else. The only other medical person involved was Dr. J. H. Lee a really nice person but was only really there at first team home matches, and to help arrange any appointments needed with specialists.

My chat with Mr. Hardcastle happened in the treatment area, and we were the only ones there. He suggested I sit in my clinic on Monday nights and just bill them if anyone showed up. I explained I had a busy clinic, evenings being the most sought-after appointments. I already gave them Tuesday and Thursday, sometimes Fridays (at the drop of a hat) and that my request for a retainer for Mondays was fair, I would often treat at least six players. The mistake I made was not going in front of the committee who understood my dedication, passion and hard work to do all I could to help the team be successful. He basically went back to the committee, told them that I wanted more money and that I would not negotiate. I obviously didn't find this out until much later and that was the end of that.

The paper article on this matter went like this:

The club are looking for a new physiotherapist after Penny Walker has decided to step down because of her expanding business commitments. Chairman Rodney Hardcastle said: "We are very sorry to see her go. She has done a great job for the club."

Interesting, what a lying toad, if I had that many business commitments why would I go and physio at Keighley, which was miles out of my way.

Now regarding my bodybuilding training and competitions at this time, I was still training and had all the facilities of a fully equipped gym not just the extremely limited equipment (a bench, barbell, and dumbbells) in my shed at Liverpool University. In the summer of 1986, I was back living in Yorkshire having finished my degree in Liverpool. The last competition I did was the Northeast Championship on the 20th of April 1986 just before starting my revision for my final exams at Liverpool University. From the summer of 1986 onwards, my world involved a lot of jobs to earn money to pay off my student debt, training in a properly equipped gym and studying at the Northern College of Massage.

By 1987 my regular gym was at Muscle World Horbury. Towards the end of 1987 into 1988 I started to train with Denbo. In the August of 1988 I entered an EFBB show in Oldham, and I think I got placed fourth. I weighed in at 9.7 so was probably carrying too much fat. Photos taken at Muscle World Gym a couple of days later showed I had the muscle, and I had the shape, I just needed the condition. We continued to train hard, and I dieted more. The next competition being in December 1988. I weighed in at 8.4, my condition was better, and I got first and qualified for the UK Finals. Remember me mentioning going to Blackpool to watch the UK Finals in May 1985 and making the decision that this was going to be my next goal. Well three years later I had the ticket! It was now when Denbo and I had to really pull out all the stops and get the work done back in the gym. Challenge set, game on, Cede Nullis!!

At the same time, I was also studying, slowly building up a client base for my massage and juggling life but enjoying every minute. I then added a further juggle which you already know about when I volunteered to help the under 19's rugby league team at Dewsbury. With all the genuine support and care around me I was able to train really hard, get my exams and develop some wonderful connections and friendships at Dewsbury rugby club. The year 1989 was the year I was physio for the professional Dewsbury Rugby League team. I have already written about my time at Dewsbury Rugby club so I will finish this decade off by detailing what would turn out to be my last bodybuilding competition, the UK Finals Harrogate 1989.

From the end of 1988 Denbo and I knew I had a place in the UK Finals, the weight class would have to be decided nearer the competition date. The idea in the off season was to eat enough food to have good strength to grow muscle, eating the right food to allow repair and thus growth of your muscle fibres. The two nutrition books I had in the 80's were 'Muscle Growth' and the 'Ultimate Nutrition' both by Bernard Beverley and Arthur Fairhurst, very informative. I also got the Muscle and Fitness magazine every month which often covered nutrition. But just as with your training it takes years to figure your own body out, what works for one person will not necessarily work for another person. Bodybuilding is all about patience and a long-term investment. So many today, now that muscle is accepted and fashionable, expect overnight results but you are talking years of hard basic training just to get a foundation. After that you can start to adapt and concentrate on bringing up weak areas and developing the look you want. Listening and watching others is important but the thing is to connect to yourself. The mind, body and muscle connection, you either have it or you don't! Bodybuilding being a very mind driven sport.

For some reason at this time, probably my workload, studying, setting up my clinic, rugby and training, I stopped writing training and diet journals so all I can say is that I trained whatever we decided and let Denbo do the programming. I do remember him having me run up and down the fire escape stairs at the side of the gym after a leg session to get more definition. I just did whatever he said. I trusted him he knew his stuff and was in my head, a place any good coach should be if the coach/athlete relationship is to reach heights in training never before achieved. If you have someone in your corner that can do that you are very, very lucky indeed. I was very, very, very lucky!

Denbo recalls during this preparation time how after finishing a training session during the strict dieting phase, I was shredded, veins popping out everywhere. Usually you are quite flat, tired and very hungry at this stage. He asked me what I had had to eat, I said a tin of tuna, but I really shouldn't have. He said, "Well whatever you ate it's gone straight into your muscles."

I was interviewed and photographed by a magazine called Muscle and Co. It was probably after qualifying in December 1988. In the interview I speak about how complicated the pre-competition diet can be.

"People think bodybuilding is very complex" explains Penny, "They make it complicated themselves. It is really very simple, but they get too bogged down with all fancy exercises and diets that they lose track of what they are doing. They would be much better off getting a basic physiology book and just read what muscles are comprised of. A big problem with a lot of bodybuilders is rest and recuperation. They just don't rest enough. They over-train all the time. The muscle grows during the rest period. Also, people make competition preparation very complicated when it doesn't need to be. All this sodium loading and carbohydrate loading, your body wants to be balanced, if it's not balanced it tries desperately to balance itself. If you don't have water, your body will retain the water that you have got. It automatically thinks there is a drought on, so it holds water even more. People make the sport so complicated." (The rest of the article is in the appendix).

      The competition day arrived, EFBB UK Bodybuilding Championship Finals Sunday the 15th of October Harrogate Yorkshire 1989. We had both worked really hard, my condition was good my body fat low and now it was time to show what we had managed to achieve. There is a mysterious story connected to my UK final preparation. I have photos of my qualifying win, Kay, and Dennis on the stage with me December 1988. There are photos taken at Muscle World Gym at the end of January 1989 of me in out of competition condition, taken so comparisons could be made throughout our UK preparations. But that's it and where the mystery begins. To this day Denbo doesn't know what happened to the film (remember there were no smartphones (I call them spy phones) and God knows what else) back then we just had plain old cameras with films that you had to take to be developed. I have got about four photos taken by someone else of me on stage but that's it no real record of what we had managed to achieve. Denbo was gutted and I still tease him to this day. "Denbo was I really that bad that you had to destroy the photos?" or "Did you put a film in the camera Denbo?". It isn't and wasn't a big drama, I know from the few photos I have that I was in the best shape I had ever been in and that was all down to Denbo.

      It was a real big show and being quite local to us some of the rugby lads came to support me. I hope I get this right please forgive me if I don't. I remember from the under 19's Nathan Graham, Mick Tong and Mark Hirst came to support me. It's difficult when you are so dieted down it affects your concentration and brain function so many details of that day I can't remember. Denbo remembers that I had a very good posing routine and described it as stunning. I am not a hundred percent sure, but I think the music I used was Patti Smith's 'Because the Night' I had to make up a routine which would show all the compulsory poses, highlighting my best features and provide enchantment, grace and a certain amount of seduction. You are showcasing your hard work, all the times you did those extra reps all those times you pushed yourself beyond your limits because your coach had your back and was in your head. I never wanted to fail or let down the person I trusted the most in the world my coach Denbo.

      In front of my bedroom mirror, I put together my moves, practised and changed them until I was happy. You didn't get long to pose but a good, well put together interesting presentation could get you the points to place you higher. Although I always found it very nerve racking, I enjoyed the posing routine part of competing. This is what Denbo said about my routine at the UK Finals "It was stunning and I can remember after your posing, Ken Latham (the organiser compère for the show, who had vast experience, knowledge and years of running shows and judging them) looked at me and Kay where we sat and put one finger up and moved it as if to say she's got it number one, if he had put his thumb up I would have thought he meant you looked okay but putting his index finger up and moving it mouthing first I thought yes she's done it all that work never missing a training session and she's done it".

Looking at the few photos I have of that day I definitely was ripped especially my abdominals and the detail on my back double biceps pose was crazy. It's difficult to see on the four photos I have, maybe my glutes could have been better more ripped possibly?

While backstage I overheard one of the girls say that she hadn't been training that long and you could tell. The muscle has a different look when the foundation of years of hard work is missing. She was a bit puffy and her skin condition on her back was not good.

The result, I got fourth the one who was saying she hadn't been training long beating me. It was a shock and I hurt more for Denbo than myself. He was so upset when he came backstage, but I said never mind Denbo you got 1st place for coaching, here's your trophy. I had got him a small trophy with World's No.1 Coach and Cede Nullis (yield to no-one) engraved on it. He had to walk away for a little while to compose himself he was so gutted for me.

I wasn't angry just disappointed with the politics. The girl that really shouldn't have beaten me waving to one of the judges, apparently, she trained at that judge's gym. This was a big show, this was the EFBB UK Finals! The reader can draw their own conclusions. It was while we were still backstage after presenting Denbo with his trophy and giving him the biggest hug for all he had sacrificed, that I announced my retirement from bodybuilding competitions. I said "Denbo it's taken us two hard years to get here, and I don't want to compete with people that have just been training for a short while and taken short cuts that I am not prepared to take for the sake of a trophy. It's not what bodybuilding is about. It should be about making your body healthier, stronger, more functional not taking health risks. I love my training but the shows, I'm done with them."

When I got out into the main hall people, I didn't know stopped me and said that they couldn't believe what had happened and that I was robbed. This gave me some confidence back that I hadn't totally let everyone down because I was doing the show as much for my supporters as I was for myself. The rugby lads that were there were really gutted, and I was sad that they were sad. I was so grateful to all the support and love that people showed me that day but now this chapter of my life was closed, and new chapters would begin, but first let me eat some food I was starving!

Chapter 7: The Waiting Game And The Game Of Poo!

"Perseverance is critical. I achieve whatever success I achieve because I was unwilling to stop."

- Nadia Comaneci

I was taken from ICU to trauma and orthopaedics it was a long corridor with doors on either side. I am not sure if half was trauma and half was orthopaedics, I just knew I was placed in a room. My bed was against a wall as I lie there. There was a big window to my right and a small room with a toilet and sink to my left (not that I could ever use it). As I lie, I would stare at the wall in front which had a TV which I never used. I didn't watch telly at home, just DVDs so I wasn't the slightest bit interested in French TV. I really did not have the energy to be bothered with it. The state I was in when I arrived was that my right hand was sewn into my right groin, I was not allowed to move that arm at all. I had my pots on my legs and I am sure I had a pot on my left arm. No break-dancing for me then!

I felt anxious about leaving ICU, you were watched like a hawk, you felt safe. The feeling I had when I moved to trauma was different, I saw it as progress but also feared if I was ready to be exposed to the world again. The bubble wrapping which I saw the ICU giving a person was removed and now my overall protection was not as protective. It is of course all fear-based emotion. Fear of the unknown, fear of change from an environment you trusted to one you knew nothing about. Fear of the fear itself.

Trusting the process helps but you constantly must install that trust into yourself while battling with your over-active, doubting and questioning mind. I had many conversations with myself, realising that I was physically paralysed to change my situation but not mentally paralysed.

Some after the sort of trauma I had aren't so lucky. For those around me, I think me having brain damage was their biggest fear.

One of the reasons for my drive and desire to help others today is because I was protected from such a fate. To this day I wonder how my head was saved from permanent brain trauma. Oh yes you have mental trauma, but I had seemed to have escaped actual physical brain trauma. That's when I realised this was done for me not to me. The universe had a mission for me, all I had to do was have patience, listen, be guided and accept the challenges placed before me. Easy right?! As my dicta-phone recordings revealed at times these challenges were unbearable and I struggled badly with them. But I always had a tiny voice in my head saying, "Believe it is going to be okay."

Through my mental persuasion I accepted this new environment and trusted the process. The staff were caring and very helpful. I only had an issue with one who didn't seem to have the same level of compassion as the others. I got the feeling she didn't want to be there. Neither did I!

My memory of this time as I write is a little vague, maybe the dicta-phone recordings will be more informative, but I want to write this before listening and writing that information down. The reason for doing it this way is because I want to write my story in a reflective way after knowing all the events that happened on this journey.

I remember having had my right hand chopped off and sewn into my right groin by the time I was in trauma and still wearing my Chanel tuber grip dress, which my plastic surgeon had kindly put me into. This tuber grip dress was around my shoulder and to the top of my thighs. Its purpose was to keep my sewn in arm from moving, no movement allowed, no turning, no change of position, nothing for over three weeks. I was trying to accept my fate of not being able to move and tried to think of an animal or a creature that had no arms or legs that could move and how did they cope.

I came up with an earth worm, being a gardener, they were my special friends who were working hard to improve my soil. It's always a bad sign if your soil is wormless, it means to me that the soil is of poor quality and lacks nourishment. Having chickens, I was always sad and shooed them away if they came to collect a quick snack on my worms. But the chickens aren't stupid for they knew the value of earthworms as I found out when I did my diploma in Chinese herbal medicine. In Chinese herbal medicine the 'di long' was used for a tonic for the blood. The use of di long is banned now but nobody has told my chickens. Maybe I need to have a word with them!

So, I am a worm that's all the movement I am allowed and can do just pretend you are a worm and then you will feel less frustrated, that's what I kept telling myself. Being a worm was okay until the worm became very, very sick with diarrhoea, dysentery or whatever the hell it was. The worm was not happy and in a lot of pain. Every time a bout of excruciating pain came, I imagined it must have felt the same for the earthworms every time I accidentally spiked them with my garden fork, a thing I tried to avoid doing and always felt bad when it happened and instantly apologised to the worm.

Hospitals are obsessed with poo; bowel movements and God help you if they think your poo isn't enough or if it's stuck. My world in that room was just about to change in a painful and smelly sort of way. I am not sure if I had had the operation to put barbecue skewers (pins) in my left toes before this problem started but I think I had. I can't imagine it being physically possible to operate on anyone in the state I was in. But I did have many procedures, I was always on the block, the operating table. I counted around fifteen procedures at Nantes hospital, the block was my second home. I didn't like going there but what choice did I have. I knew that all the staff were helping me to recover but it still was a scary journey every time. By now I had taken them up on the offer of giving me something to make my coming round after an operation less traumatic to me. I don't know what they gave me but just before the porter came to push me down that terrifying route, someone would bring me a tablet that they had to put under my tongue.

This tablet worked because in comparison to the times I didn't take it my anxiety and coming around was so much calmer and far less frightening.

For some reason I remember vividly a time that I had an operation, I don't think I was in ICU, I must have just moved. Maybe it was the operation to put the plate in my left wrist. If it was, it was before I took them up on the offer of the tablet. I was wheeled down corridors and into lifts (Nantes hospital is huge). It was a different route to the one I went on from my ICU room. I was so scared. When you are lying in your bed the only thing you see are the lights in the ceiling, flashing past. The porter walked and pushed quick, but everything is in slow motion.

The fact that you were being taken to the block didn't help. The meaning of this from the English history books being that you are being taken for your inevitable death and your head cut off. My picture of this being reinforced when someone brought me an historic based novel where they had all been sent to the block. However, when I started taking that little pill under the tongue, I didn't really care about going to the block. But even with the tablet the whole experience was still very psychologically distressing.

On the above occasion I remember I was very anxious about going to the block again. I had concerns for my sewn in right arm and maybe when they were moving me and operating, they would damage or rip it out. I knew they were all extremely professional and amazing medical people, I was so lucky to have them. But what if, like the nurse in ICU they forgot about my other injuries and turn me too quick and pull on my right arm, my mind was working overtime. I tried to talk to the porter to distract my overactive brain, but I was scared stiff.

Prison Or The Paralympics

As I got to the block, I was wheeled to a waiting bay just outside the big glass automatic doors which led to the operation area, the block! I remember thinking that it was like a bus station. Trolleys arriving parked up in their little bays, stationary until they moved off to their next destination. The purpose of this bus station like environment was for someone to come and check your name tag, your date of birth and the operation that you were about to have. They took your blood pressure and put your line in. Then you had to wait and wait until they were ready for you. From each bay you could see a TV and I remember some French programme going on about politics. Instead of being distracted by the TV I spoke to my team who had visited me in my ICU room. I asked if they would come with me into my operation because I was really scared. Would they mind just watching over me and all the medical staff as they had done before and as they did while I was stuck in the car. I gave my fate up to the universe but put in a request to be around for longer, I still had things to do. I was very emotional and wanted to burst into tears and run away but I was still a worm and couldn't run anywhere.

A person arrived dressed differently than the person who had taken my details, she had a hair net on like the previous person had put on me. It reminded me of the time I worked at Fox's Biscuits in Batley West Yorkshire as a student over thirty years earlier. Then my only stress was the chocolate bourbons that I struggled to pick up off the conveyor belt to place in boxes. They often went flying up in the air, I preferred doing custard creams they seemed to behave themselves better. She had a nice friendly face and smiled, checked my name, and then pushed me through the large glass automatic doors. I passed another area that had bays in it and some beds with people wrapped in sheets and blankets, surrounded by machine. She pushed me through some more doors and then into the block.

In this sterile clinical place people gowned up were busy doing things. Every time I got pushed into the block area I always went cold; I don't know if that's because the room was actually cold, or I felt cold from its atmosphere. It's then time for the countdown. You are put into position, I remember when they were taking my right hand off, when I was in ICU, they placed my arm on some sort of platform attached to the side of the operating table.

Then the next thing is to be transferred from the bed to the operating table. The transfer from the bed to the operating table was always a manoeuvre I dreaded but usually there were four people to transfer you. It was always painful and the block never comfortable to lie on. On this occasion I think I am correct in thinking it was my left hand getting all the attention for the metal plate to be put in. I also think Dr. Lescour came to keep an eye on my right arm, check it out and redress it while I was knocked out. My recording of this is maybe more accurate because I can't remember if my pins in my left toes were already in or if they were done on this occasion. What I do know is my earth angel was here again and that always brought me some inner peace.

The anaesthetist talks to you while tightly holding the mask over your face and someone else is connecting you up via the line that was placed in your vein when you were in the bus station. It's all very weird and trying to let go of your natural desire to fight what they are doing to your body is so scary and difficult to do. The counting distracts you and you are taken somewhere which allows you to stay alive but not feel the brutal procedure you are about to have. All my fears of being at the dentist as a young child rushing back to the forefront of my memory.

I never asked how long my operation took and how long I was in this semi-dead state, but we are talking hours. I remember coming round after this particular operation being really scared as I opened my eyes, I could see people in other beds at various stages of recovery. Tears were rolling down my face as I was paralysed, I tried to shout but there was no noise. I was so scared it was like awaking from a really bad nightmare, confusion, panic, pain and desperation all stuck together in one large lump of emotion. This feeling which seemed to last forever but it could have only been about 15-20 minutes. But what is time? Does time differ when you are put in this semi-dead state, does time even exist at all? What is time?

The scariest thing is the disconnection of your mind and body or is it a disconnection from your soul? Your body is there but you can't feel or move it, your voice is there loud and clear in your head but there is no sound. Has your spiritual connection with self been put on pause and it's the Universe's decision if you are reunited? Whatever it is it's damn scary and I don't think after this disconnection you are ever quite the same again. It's as if you now vibrate differently, you see life clearer in a new way. It's as if you have been given a new set of eyes, ears and a new understanding of life. It's as if you have had a cleansing of your soul. It's not just the medical staff working on you while you were in this ego free state but some other universal energy that empowers you with emotions and feelings that you failed to feel before. I didn't know then, but this change would create many internal battles, they were like tests to see in which direction I would go. Back to my programmed way that society had shown me or take a different isolated less travelled overgrown path that only a few choose to go down.

The reconnection of either my soul, spirit or mind to my physical body started to happen. First, I could move my head and then sound, though weak and very quiet came out of my mouth. I was so very cold, and the rest of my body took a while before I felt it again. In fact, I think I didn't get the full reconnection of my legs until I was back in my trauma room. This process of disconnection and reconnection was so traumatic to me that I requested assistance for my next block visit, this would come in the form of a little tablet placed under your tongue that I mentioned earlier.

Now getting back to the poor sick worm with diarrhoea. From the moment I was taken by the helicopter to hospital to moving to my room on the trauma ward I had not had a bowel movement, about two weeks. This did not concern me I wasn't eating, I wasn't moving at all, was on medication known to cause constipation, nature would take its time, all in due course. No not in hospital the fact that I had been living off medication my body full of drugs and still having the residual of them, didn't seem to matter. I honestly believed if they had given my body another week with fruit and veg and the permanent removal of the heavier drugs, my poo would have arrived in its own sweet time. But no, no, no! I was sent for an x-ray which gave them the ammunition to start the brutal attack on my intestines, I was told I had a blockage. Maybe the poo was having a rest, taking its time to get to its destination, how did they know it wasn't moving they only x-rayed me once for the bowels.

I am well aware that they were worried about bowel movement, but my bowels were having to adapt to different circumstances, so their usual pattern of behaviour was bound to be different. They had all the evidence they needed to begin my nightmare of pain, embarrassment, stench and sheer soul-destroying torture. They became obsessed with my bowel movement, or lack of it. I was given this disgusting powder in my water glass, the only glass I had so if I wanted to drink any water which I was trying to do to keep hydrated, I had no choice but to drink it. Remember at this stage I could do nothing for myself I was bed ridden. My only hand wasn't so good because of the operation it had had to put the metal plate in. Holding my glass of water and a spoon at this stage being the only two things I could do with some pain and difficulty. I forced myself to switch on the portable little radio I had and to start recording on my dicta-phone both difficult tasks but ones I persevered with. I was not only given the powder but petroleum jelly, raspberry flavour and no doubt some sort of tablet. Their mission was accomplished, very soon the flood gates opened and never stopped for about ten days.

Let me set the scene for you I am virtually paralysed in my bed, pots on both legs my Chanel dress protecting my right arm sewn into my right groin then suddenly a severe wave of pain hits your stomach area. You can't even double yourself up to try to make it go away. You know Niagara Falls is due any minute, you buzz for help which naturally takes 10-15 minutes (they were always so busy and had a lot of people to care for). By the time your SOS is answered you are covered in the stuff. Not pleasant, soul destroying and very embarrassing. It happened many times a day, it never stopped. If I had a visitor, they often had to leave the room due to them having to change me and the smell! None of my visitors complained but it can't have been pleasant for them. I was getting weaker and weaker even taking a sip of water would set it off, but they still insisted on the powder and jelly and then they added soup. Not just any old nutritional soup like you got as a kid when you were sick but special soup. It was special alright, it looked and tasted like dirty washing up water. I came to the conclusion that they were trying to kill me. The thing that puzzled and concerned me was where was all this stuff coming from? I hadn't eaten for weeks, not properly. In the end I refused to take any more powder, soup or raspberry flavoured petroleum jelly or the prune compote that they tried to make me have.

    I really couldn't give a shit (no that's wrong that's all I could do!) if I lived or died, I was losing a lot of weight, probably looked green and was in so much pain. The nurse with a bit of an attitude and didn't want to be there, who started this whole thing off then came up with a 'brilliant' idea to give me a drug to bung me up. What! I said "Oh no you are not!! You started this, if I die, I die but you are not giving me any more of your crazy drugs. Where is the shit going to go if you do that?"

    During this time my plastic surgeon visited me and the don't want to be there nurse transformed into a caring, concerned, loving nurse in front of my very eyes. I think it was more for the doctor's benefit than mine. Then a funny thing happened he said his goodbyes and left the room with the nurse. Within five minutes he was back again and said that he had been told I wasn't eating (wonder who told him that?) I said I would start eating if they stopped making me shit all the time with their soup and potions and offered me some real food instead! Why couldn't this topic have been discussed in front of me instead of behind closed doors? I wasn't stupid I had spent most of my life studying the function of the body and how to treat it. I had never come across any research that said making someone have dysentery for over a week and then blocking it up with drugs was a good medical procedure!

    I did however find something out in the early hours of one morning when I had to buzz the night staff. By the time they got to me I was covered from top to bottom in the stuff. When they came in, they said "Not you as well, why didn't you buzz?" I said, "I did!" Apparently, the whole trauma ward had the same problem. They must have all been given the same soup, jelly and powder that I had been given. The girls cleaned me up and then put a nappy on me. Great now I can sit in it until morning.

    I did come up with a solution for the problem. I called it 'Dyno-Poo', you may have heard of Dyno-Rod who you phone when your pipes are blocked. Why couldn't they come round and give everyone colonial irrigation, problem solved. No pain, no soup, powder or jelly and no shitty bed sheets! I patent this idea here and now. I probably talk more about this on my recordings, but I think we need to swiftly move on from this topic.

The turning point in my situation came when one of the nurse angels came back on duty, a lovely girl who just seemed to get it. She asked if I was okay, and I said no I really need to start eating proper food to heal this bowel problem and give the intestines the chance to work properly. Can I have some kiwi for breakfast and some pineapple juice, I need to feed my body something other than that medication stuff that they force me to have. (I think by now I refused to have any more of their pooing medicine). She said yes I will see what I can do. That day I had kiwi fruit, green beans for lunch and some more vegetables for my evening meal. It all stayed good, and I felt like a different person. Slowly though, I had to be careful just small amounts of plain food, but the dysentery stopped, and I could at last try to feed my body so I could aid my repair and recovery.

I can't remember the exact days and time scale that I continued with a sensitive bowel it used to come and go but I was now carefully trying to use food rather than medication to improve the situation.

There was one time when the porter came to take me for my legs x-raying but he couldn't because my bowels had just decided to play up. I suppose I should have been grateful it didn't happen in the x-ray room, how embarrassing would that have been! The people taking care of you don't judge you, but it is still soul destroying and embarrassing each time it happened. An adult shouldn't poo their pants even if they are paper pants.

I got told a few times I was moving to plastics but then it got delayed. I was probably in the trauma room over two weeks, with most of that time being allocated to very painful dysentery. But some good things happened while I was there, I got my dicta-phone a strange comfort to me to talk about my emotions and things that were happening to me. I also got my radio from Robin and Pat which I listened to when sleep just wouldn't happen and my mind started working overtime and you begin to think too much. What's that quote 'Make sure your worst enemy doesn't lie between your own two ears.' Laird Hamilton, boy can your mind have power over you. The key is to keep it all balanced, not so easy with some of the challenges life tends to throw at you.

Two other productive and pleasant things that happened was getting some massage and physio on my legs, she was very nice and good to talk to. From the very moment I got out of ICU, I tried to do some massage on my legs (when my left hand allowed remember that it had a metal plate in). I knew the value of massage from my years of administering it to others and I could feel a haematoma in my right thigh. I was careful not to disturb the stitching, my broken bones in my legs were all compound fractured and had come through the tissue and my skin. The other positive and relaxing thing that happened was a lady coming to give me a facial. That was so appreciated and relaxing.

My day-to-day activities continued in trauma, and I just had to wait for the decision to operate on my right arm and groin. Another mountain to climb but I didn't think the Universe would have given me Mount Everest but that's what I got or that's what it felt like to me!

Chapter 8: More Rugby, More Study And Football

"Don't wait until you've reached your goal to be proud of yourself. Be proud of every step you take towards reaching that goal."

- Author unknown

I can't remember the exact way I ended up at Keighley rugby league club. I think they needed someone, heard I had left Dewsbury and contacted me. When I got to Keighley the coach was a big bearded Welsh guy called Tony Fisher and his assistant was Peter Astbury nicknamed Razza a crazy Neil Diamond fan, (I remember he went to see him in concert). They both knew my dad for they began their careers probably around the same time. Tony Fisher was full of passion and the half time coaching was on the same decibels as those of Maurice Bamford's half time coaching. There is no doubt that these men achieved so much and gave so much of their lives to rugby. I am not judging their methods often it worked. However, sometimes I had to pick up and heal the psychological scars some of the players had from these coaching methods and often the respect for the coach soon being lost. I didn't have many problems with Maurice and Tony but after Fisher left the next coach was a Mr Peter Roe, now things became interesting, he could never look you in the eye.

The general feeling at Keighley was different than the one at Dewsbury, it was a little bit frosty maybe there were struggles going on behind the scenes. I knew the smaller clubs always struggled financially. I suppose I was spoilt at Dewsbury from the family like atmosphere that was given off as soon as I got there. Keighley seemed to need time to accept any newcomer.

The team appeared to have a lot of injuries, little problems that needed a week off playing to get them back on track. When you first start with a team and especially the coaching staff, it takes a while for your suggestions to be heard. You have a coach under pressure to keep his team's position, and you have the players under pressure to keep their place in the team, be it in the first or second team. Tensions can be high and it's the physio's job to try and keep the players calm, confident and fit. I didn't have too many problems with Tony Fisher or Peter Astbury if you proved your worth, worked hard and were dedicated, you would earn their respect. But when Peter Roe arrived within a very short space of time, I realised that there was no respect and eventually my respect for him slowly eroded. I knew a new broom sweeps clean, but there is a right and a wrong way, an agitating way, or a calm way. Agitation was growing fast amongst the players, we were all treading on eggshells.

Roe's favourite saying to me when I was treating someone was that it was all in their minds and that they should run it off. He had played with some fantastic injury and according to him, he kept going, what a hero! While sat in the dugout one Saturday for a home game for the second team with Peter Roe and his assistant Ian Fairhurst, Peter said to me "I have a bad back can you take a look?" I turned to him and said, "Peter that's just all in your mind" and then I had to run on to one of my players. I had no respect for the man, and I think the feeling was mutual. I showed him minimum attention, only when I had to. Every week the players and I would guess who was going to get the boot next. One player, Andy Tyers, who had an ongoing knee injury, said he thought it wouldn't be long before he was gone. I stated that it might be me before you, and it was!

There were a number of things I rebelled against while 'working' with Peter Roe, one was being on the players bus for away games. I lived in Dewsbury, Keighley was about an hour away if the traffic was good going either around Bradford or over the tops. It was always busy, roadworks and often bad weather, remember rugby was still played in the winter. On one particular day we had an A team match away, but the team's ground was nearer for me to drive straight there rather than driving to Keighley to sit on the team bus, to be on the bus which goes back to where I had just come from. Logic, right? I told them it made more sense to meet them at the ground. I think it was at this game that I had an argument with the coach, I was sticking up for one of the players. When the coaching staff wanted someone gone, they would start to pick on them and try to trigger them. I saw this so many times. I had already made my mind up that I would leave at the end of the season, staying because I was contracted to do so and for the players. I didn't want to let them down.

I turned up at the club the next day, a Sunday for a first team home match. Peter Roe told me I was sacked. Boy, must I have had a power over him for him to be that scared that he had to get rid of me. His actions amounted to a cowardly, weak, frightened individual, probably going back to some childhood or life wounding. We all have such woundings, it's whether we acknowledge them and deal and heal them that determines how much of that shit we choose to carry around with us and ultimately blame others or situations for that shit!

His actions were not only childish and immature but illegal, I had a contract with the club, he had no authority to sack me. It was obviously calculated because he already had a person there to be physio. His weakness and childishness continued the following week when I returned to the club for a meeting with the committee. Having realised what had happened at Dewsbury with the chairman Rodney Hardcastle I took a friend with me Glynn Robinson. I knew him from the gym, he was involved with the unions, a spokesperson for the nursing union. Glynn was used to dealing with disputes and bullshit!

Roe kept us waiting out in the cold before he would come to the 'meeting', he was sat in the stand like a king on his throne. The players were running around the pitch, and I was stood at the corner. Most of the lads acknowledged me and said hi, but a couple didn't, one of them being Ayres a 'star' player who I had to work on a lot he was injured on a regular basis. I thought to myself you yellow bellied toad. One of life's lessons, some people are takers, and some people are givers, some weak, some strong, some cowards, some brave. You meet them all in life the key is trying to recognise them and keep your own integrity and standards.

When the meeting finally got going Roe told a load of lies and I told some home truths. He was very agitated, aggressive in his manner and eventually stood up and shouted in the meeting "Either she goes, or I go!" and then stormed off. He had a paddy like a young child. Like I said I must have scared him with my power of honesty. I call his syndrome the 'small balls syndrome' and what usually goes with small balls, yes you guessed it, a big arrogant ego!

So that was that, again there is a bit of a pattern emerging here but seeing how some of the players had been treated I realised it was a gift. I needed to be away from this environment, the deeper problems at the club coming to light a little later when they went bankrupt!

Keighley then refused to pay me what they owed me! Within a week of that meeting Maurice Bamford was on the phone asking me to go to Bramley, as he was the coach there. I was at Keighley from the middle of 1990 to 1993, going to Bramley in 1993. One ex-Keighley player described Peter Roe as a "Petty, vindictive, bullying coach with his favourites and that is why he faded away." I would say that was a fair summary. There were some very good players at Keighley, but I think being close to the Bradford Northern club sort of overshadowed them and the club.

The people involved in the Bramley club were businessmen, an accountant, solicitors and a pharmacist who had a number of chemist shops. One of these Leeds solicitors put a letter together for me to send to Keighley. They said they had not got the money to pay me this meant I could make them insolvent don't remember all the legal laws of it but it only took one letter before I got the money, they owed me.

Before moving on to Bramley I must mention a person who I met through working at the Keighley club, Andy Tyers. A big guy who unfortunately had ongoing knee problems throughout his rugby career. He was one of those intelligent, thinking, and knowledgeable rugby players and it could be seen when he played. I think his bad luck with injuries never allowed Andy to reach his full potential. His passion and love for the game was infectious. He was a good man manager, knew how to talk to people told you things straight while having compassion, understanding and concern. He got shipped off to play for Nottingham not long after I had left Keighley.

Throughout this period, I was still training though as you all know I decided in 1989 to stop competing and concentrated on my business, do more study and the rugby. I continued to study at the Northern college of Massage and in 1990 completing the sports therapy course and in 1993 completing the advanced remedial massage course. Also, between 1992-1994 I went to the Football Association centre of Excellence at Lilleshall to complete their Treatment of Injuries course, a very intense, difficult but informative course. It was a residential course and the group of people on the course supported each other coming from different backgrounds usually involving football.

Lilleshall is the place where all the famous footballers were sent to have intense treatment and rehabilitation when they were injured. The likes of Gaza (Paul Gascoigne) and David Beckham all going there. Because we were residential, we ate in the same place as the footballers, but I didn't know who the hell they were, my fellow students did and they used to say look who's here, I didn't have a clue. While in the line for food one day I heard a Yorkshire accent so started chatting to this young lad who was at Leeds United, I think. He looked young but later I found out that big clubs would sign up any young lad who stood out, keep them at the club bringing them up the ranks and releasing them at 17 or 18 if they didn't come up to expectations. How cruel and psychologically disturbing was that for a young teenager? This young lad was Alan Smith whose career did take off. Another player there who I talked to for quite a while was Michael Thomas from Liverpool. I felt connected to the name because of Micky my runner who had the same name, he was a Michael Thomas also.

In fact, Denbo and I brought Micky to Lilleshall to get a fitness test for information that could enhance his running. I think when we got there the man doing the tests thought it was the Liverpool player Michael Thomas not our Michael Thomas, because there were newspapers and photos in the room there, about Michael Thomas the football player. Maybe he wanted an autograph, he didn't mention anything, and we started the fitness testing.

The test was long, it tested lungs, blood oxygen, flexibility, strength, etc, etc. Our little Micky who was still at school was on the treadmill about 40 minutes they kept increasing the resistance and Micky just kept going. Denbo and I left Micky with his testing, and we went to the canteen to get some food. Also, there were the Widnes Rugby League team, who were there at training camp before a big final. I think the year was 1993. If it had been 1993 the final at Wembley would have been the Challenge Cup with Widnes v Wigan, arch-rivals. Wigan won the match, the score 20 – 14. The Widnes team were eating, and the Widnes players were taking the mickey out of Jonathan Davis (making fun of) because he was getting salad while the others were having pies and chips, just anything but salad.

We went back to get Micky and discuss his fitness test. Micky had short hamstring muscles which would need stretching and flexibility, the full results coming later three pages. The person who tested Mick said he was the third best he had ever tested the other two being world class runners. What a fit young lad, that was a very impressive result Micky!

Also, in the 1990's another dedicated young man, passionate to his dreams, would visit my clinic. I helped him, with tight hamstrings and any other injuries that affected him. He lived in Mirfield the next village on from my clinic on Huddersfield Road. I sort of knew him and his father through my work with the amateur rugby club at Dewsbury Moor. Richard Silverwood was just beginning his journey, I would conclude a fated journey. At first it was amateur rugby league which Richard was refereeing, that soon changed. I remember he came for his leg massage before his first pro game, between York and Batley Bulldogs. He was nervous but also excited. I was pleased for him, I had watched his progress and dedication over the years and had a feeling he would do well, he was so dedicated. He did do well he became an international referee.

Richard's achievements are impressive, his first Super League game was Halifax v Salford in 2001 at the young age of 24. He refereed 415 Super League games including the finals in 2010, 2012 and 2013. He also was awarded rugby league ref of the year in 2006 and in 2010 plus awarded international ref of the year. His achievements don't stop there. Richard also was the ref four times for Australia v New Zealand in 2009, 2010, 2011 and 2012. The Four Nations also in 2010 again Australia v New Zealand. He was also the ref at the Rugby League World Cup Final in 2013 and the Challenge Cup final in 2006, 2010 and 2012. Amazing Richard your dedication and hard work paid off. I am so pleased for you and proud of all your achievements!

Another rugby league official who was a regular at my clinic was a linesman / touch judge called John Glover. He was very interesting to listen to and he kindly gave me a photo of himself and the other linesmen when he went to the Wembley final. An achievement he was so proud of, and rightly so. The photo hung on my clinic wall amongst all the other amazing photos.

Just like all the other people I was blessed to help and have a connection with, I was able to see them grow and achieve the challenge that they had set themselves. It was so encouraging and pleasing to me. I embraced their strengths, they all gave lessons to me on how to continue even when the odds may have been stacked against them. These lessons did not just come from the athletes I treated but many others. Three that are no longer with us included Mrs Colbeck from Ossett. When she had to go into care, I promised to have her dog, Suzie. I did and she lived to a grand old age just like Mrs Colbeck. Mrs Colbeck once told me that her mum said to her that her tongue was so sharp that she would cut herself. Mrs Colbeck's response "No it won't because I always speak the truth". And she did, I told her she would make a good Prime Minister she was so wise.

Another amazing lady was called Lily Armstrong she lived in Crigglestone before moving to her daughter's house in Horbury. Her legs had given up but not her mind. Her life story was unbelievable. Living in a mining area her husband was a miner and you can hear Lily's story at the Yorkshire Mining Museum. There was also Brian Holroyd another star who came to me after his stroke. I got him to the gym, and he got strong and started walking. He walked everywhere, miles and miles he even took ramblers out on the famous walks in the Yorkshire area. A very intelligent man who achieved a lot in his career. All three of these people were my mentors, they had so much life experience and had been dealt some harsh battles that life has a tendency to throw at people. But they never gave in.

Another great lady also from Ossett is Bessie Sykes who has just turned a hundred years old, and still living in her own house. These amazing people were my university of knowledge about the real way of living, very rare, beautiful gems, that I will be eternally grateful to.

An experience I was grateful to have that occurred in my career was working with the Yorkshire Ladies rugby league team again in the 90's. I have a medal given to me from the Lancashire v Yorkshire women's Rugby League match Warrington 1991. I also remembered going to Old Trafford with the Yorkshire team where they played before the men's premiership final. I remember because Alex Murphy was in the dugout taking the mickey out of women's rugby. He was known as 'Murphy The Mouth' and he knew I was 'Tank's' daughter. I had some banter with him and then he left the dug out to coach his team. Of course, the ladies Yorkshire rugby team won!

At Lilleshall besides Alan Smith the footballer there was another Alan on the course and again I noticed the Yorkshire accent. Alan Jackson was helping at Bradford

City football club, the youth side. Because of location we kept in touch. I went to some football games to help out and he came to help at some rugby games so we could further our experience and knowledge. It's a very sad day when a person thinks they know everything, you must keep learning, expanding and growing, it's the essence of life no matter who you are. Every day presents an opportunity to learn, and I always try and embrace that opportunity.

Alan was involved with the youth side of Braford City FC and he asked if I would be interested in helping them in a tournament in Hamm Germany. Of course, was my reply, I hadn't had so much experience with treating football players, so I was pleased to further my knowledge and experience. This occurred in 1995 (I still have and wear the tee-shirt!) Not only was the tournament for the young lads from Bradford City but the veterans which included Alan. This veterans game was quite light-hearted not as serious as the main tournament, so much so that our team of veterans had trays of beer brought out at half time instead of pieces of orange.

The event was full on, we were staying in a beautiful old château and were given pickled cabbage with every meal, but the village and area was stunning. I think Hamm was and probably still is a twin town of Bradford formerly the twin town to Shipley a district of Bradford.

Only ten years earlier in 1985 the Bradford club had a devastating fatal fire where 56 people lost their lives and over 265 people got injured. I was at Liverpool university at the time, and it was shocking to hear the news, I was deeply saddened by it, it was my county. I wasn't to know then that nearly ten years later I would be involved with the young up and coming players of the future at the same club.

The team that Bradford took was full of talented young men. Some were on loan from teams like Everton and I think Liverpool, but they were being released from Bradford and more than likely that would be the end of their professional football career. I felt for these young lads, they all had their dreams, desires and wishes squashed. I hoped for them, that they would find their calling in life without too much psychological scarring. These young men gave it their all, I suppose in their position you never know who is watching, maybe a scout for another club. Our team got to the final but drew with the other team which took us into extra time, then penalties, then the golden shoot out. It was so exciting and also very nerve racking. I so badly wanted them to win, they deserved to, I had got to know them and they were good lads. They did win, fantastic! It was worth eating all that cold meat and pickled cabbage, hey lads?

I can' leave this chapter without mentioning another football disaster a few years after the Bradford City fire. In 1989, by now I was back living in Yorkshire, which made the impact of the disaster so much closer to home. With the love of Liverpool and its people, this horrific 'mistake' really got to me as it did to most of the UK. It was the Hillsborough disaster.

I already had connections with Liverpool and a few years later a connection to the Sheffield area. I was also going to end up having a connection with the year that the truth and justice finally was acknowledged for the Hillsborough victims. That was the year 2016, 27 years later for the victims and their families. Believe me when you are accused of something you didn't do and there are lies, cover ups and only half of the information presented you fight to get the truth out there no matter how long it takes. It's the only closure you have to the devastation and sorrow that is thrown at you. The year 2016 was also the year of my accident.

Looking into the Hillsborough disaster, the investigation throws up the same shit and legal games that I was put through. The games are performed to blame the weak, innocent victims to save the face of the establishments. My conclusion from my own personal experience is that the police, lawyers, insurance, courts, judges, media and the government all piss in the same pot! Making the weak and vulnerable their scapegoat. This is in order to cover up their mistakes, protect their positions, polish their egos, save their careers and their big fat pensions. All because they made a mistake and didn't do their job. Although I experienced this in a different country, not the UK, it's the same game, same shit!

It can clearly be seen in the case of the Hillsborough investigation how the blame game began before any investigation was begun. Hillsborough disaster was a fatal crush of humans at a football match at Hillsborough Stadium in Sheffield South Yorkshire England on the 15th of April 1989. It was the Football Association Cup semi-final between Liverpool and Nottingham Forest. The police match commander David Duckenfield ordered exit gate C to be opened leading to an influx in the two standing only central pens in the Leppings lane stand allocated to the Liverpool supporters. This led to overcrowding and the crush. A total of 96 people were killed, 94 of them dying at the scene and 766 were injured. The match was replayed in May at Old Trafford with Liverpool winning and going on to the final to win the FA Cup.

Days and weeks after the disaster the police fed the press false stories implying that hooliganism and drunkenness by Liverpool supporters had caused the disaster. This blame continued to be directed at the Liverpool fans even after the Taylor report of 1990 found the main cause was the South Yorkshire Police's failure to control the situation. The director of Public Prosecutions ruled there was no evidence to justify prosecution of any individuals or institutions. I bet they did!

The first coroner's inquest regarding this disaster completed in the year 1991 concluded that all the deaths were accidental. This finding was rejected by the families, and they fought to have the case re-opened. It was Lord Justice Stuart Smith who concluded that there was no justification (he was right about that no justice!) for a new inquiry in the year 1997. It can be seen how the game plays out, slam any door supposedly there to obtain the truth, in the faces of the innocent victims who they then try to silence and paralyse by should I say an allegedly corrupt system, it stinks!!

There are good honest people in this corrupt world that will not be bullied, lied to or used by anyone or any establishment. These families had to set up a support group bringing private prosecutions against Duckenfield and his deputy Bernard Murray. It's no surprise that these private prosecutions failed in 2000. As I write this in 2020, we are already seeing the beginning of change. How the 'mighty' will fall we already have Jeffrey Epstein, Ghislaine Maxwell, Andrew (I don't count him as a prince!) and many more will be exposed, brought down by the people's justice. There are much bigger fish in these poisonous oceans, but I believe they will be caught, gutted and salted eventually.

The Hillsborough Independent Panel was formed in 2009 to review the evidence. In 2012 this report confirmed Taylor's 1990 criticisms revealing details about the extent of police reports to shift blame onto fans, the error of the first coroner's inquests and the role of the other emergency services. Thus, accidental death ruled previously being quashed and the creation of new coroner's inquests.

Also, in 2012 Operation Resolve was produced, two criminal investigations led by the police, to look into the causes of the disaster and by the Independent Police Complaints Commission (IPCC) to examine actions by police in the aftermath. In April 2016 the second coroner's inquests ruled the supporters were unlawfully killed due to grossly negligent failures by police and ambulance services to fulfil their duty of care.

This is an horrendous disaster and equally horrendous is the way the victims and their families and friends were treated for 27 years! It just is not acceptable, how many other cover ups are there? How many that did get swept under this huge carpet of lies, cover ups and injustice? It just shows where we are as a human race. People with power, position, and usually money believe that they can do what they like and get away with it. This is slowly being eroded by people speaking up and sharing their story. The more people that do this, the more other people will find courage to tell their story and the more people will stop turning and looking the other way. The truth is powerful, and the universe will assist someone in their truth.

My story is extremely mild compared to others, but it still devastated my world and I still had to tread that lonely dark path looking for a glimmer of light. But it can be done and slowly and surely the glimmer of light will appear. One of the main reasons for this book is for me to bring closure on an extremely difficult and life changing event that occurred in my life. Another important reason is to help give hope to anyone who reads my story and help them believe that all is not lost. For it isn't, you just have to find another way there is always another option and sometimes you must be the one to create that option. Be bold, be brave and be truthful. You will need a lot of patience, justice can take a long, long time to arrive, but fighting for it makes the way ahead clearer for the person behind you. Sadly, the same injustice that was done to you, will be done to others. Remember 'divided we fall, but united we stand!'

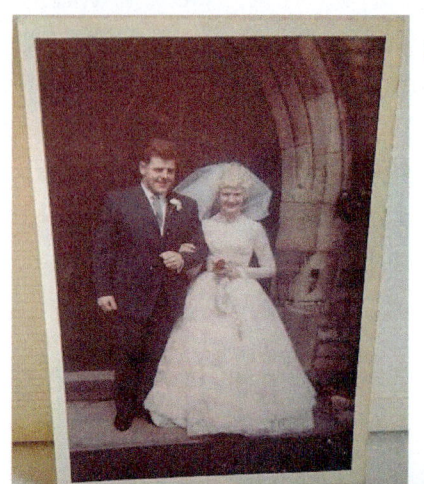

Prison Or The Paralympics

Mum & Dad's Wedding

Mum & Dad With The Three Kids

Chicks

Snow 1979 & Skippy

Class Photo

Bowling In The Rounders Team
Mum Helping

Sheriffe

Skippy

Blaze

Grandad Sam And His Sister Phyllis At Our 18th Birthday Party

Angela Hall Liverpool University (I'm Wearing Gloves)

Florida Holiday 1984 With Grandma Dixon & Grandma Walker

Disneyland, Florida & At Frank's House

Mum With My Second Car

My Under 21s Bodybuilding Competition 1985

Owen Neil, NABBA Mr. Universe

Graduation Ball Which Took Place At The Adelphi Liverpool

Graduation Day Liverpool 1986

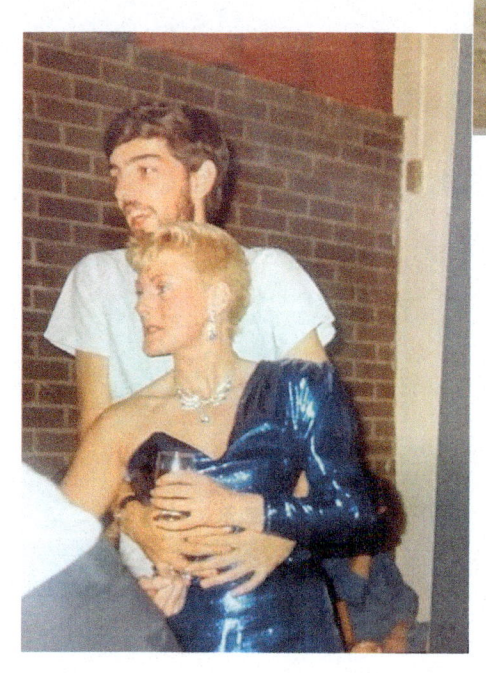

21st Birthday Party With Stewart One Of The Gang From Liverpool University

Training At Muscle World

Kay & Me

The Shapers Rowing Team

Prison Or The Paralympics

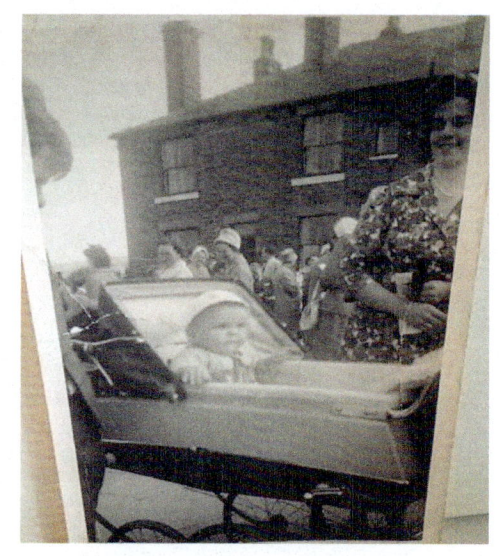

Tank In His Pram

Dad Playing For Dewsbury Celtic Against Hull K.R. (Feb 1975)

70

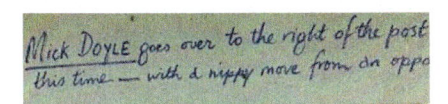

Mick Doyle *goes over to the right of the post this time — with a nippy move from an oppo*

Mick Doyle

Johnny Harpin

Me, Gary Cocks & Chris Haigh When I Was Physio

Chilly, Keith & Me On The Bench

Hamm Football Tournament

Dewsbury Team 1989-1990

Prison Or The Paralympics

Qualifying For The UK Finals December 1988

My Posing Routine At The December 1988 Competition

Photos Taken After The Competition

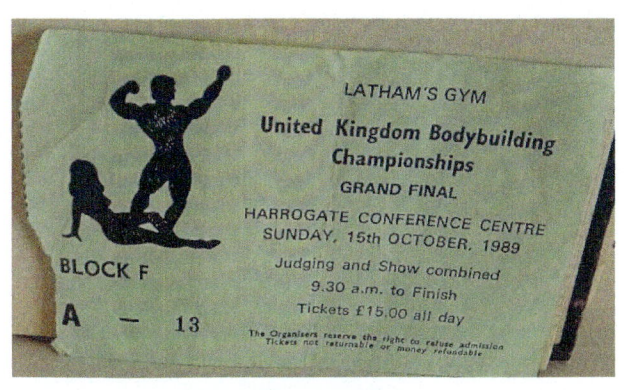

I Had The Ticket

My Mentor Denbo

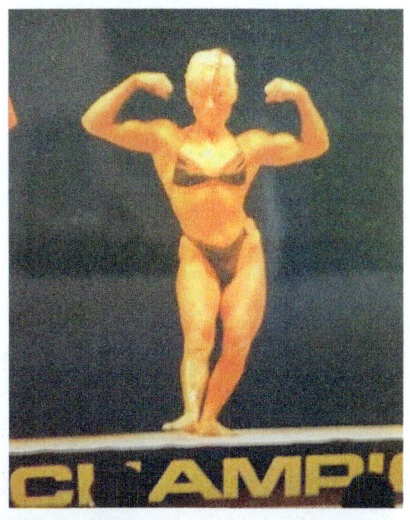

Photos Of The Uk Finals

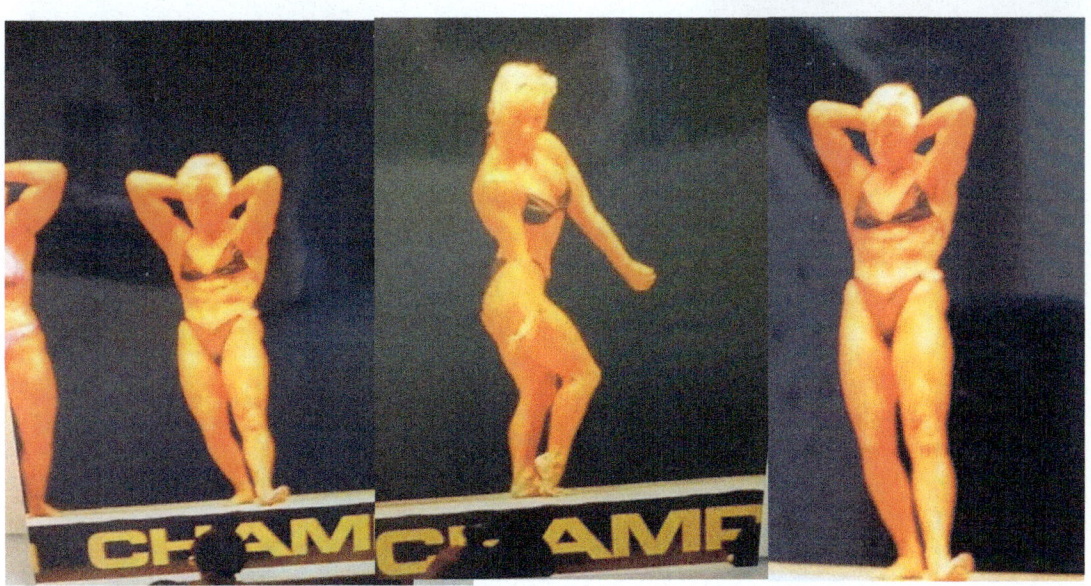

Prison Or The Paralympics

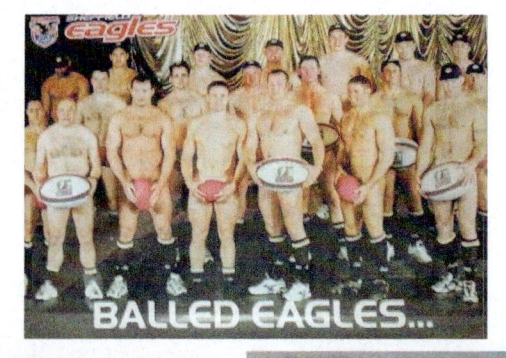

Rob & Andy Tyers With The Trophy Sheffield Eagles Had Just Won At Wembley & Sheffield Eagles (Top Right)

Mark Burgess Playing The Fairy Godmother At The Christmas Play At Dewsbury Rugby League Club

Wining The Coal Race

Mick Doing His Thing At Huddersfield

Drama as RL team sets off

DRAMA surrounded Dewsbury Rugby League players as they were about to set off for the Second Division clash with Workington yesterday.

For as the team coach was leaving the Crown Flatt ground for the long haul to Cumbria, two unmarked police cars arrived and officers escorted the team's physiotherapist Keith Adrian Shaw off the bus.

A police spokesman said today that Mr Shaw had been taken to Leeds to help with inquiries involving a car.

Dewsbury manager Maurice Bamford said that although he had been surprised by the incident it had not materially affected the team's performance.

"We lost 10-2 but I think Workington were fired up to beat me, their former coach, rather than the Dewsbury team," he said.

The physio duties meanwhile were carried out by Penny Walker, daughter of former Batley and Dewsbury prop Trevor Walker. "And she did a good job too," said Maurice.

The Paper Article About When I Was Physio For The First Team

74

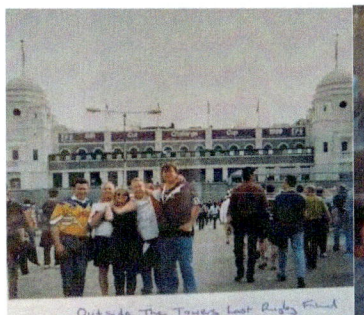

The Last Rugby Match At Wembley & Andy Falls Asleep

Dean Hall Playing For Bramley With Ray Ashton Player Coach

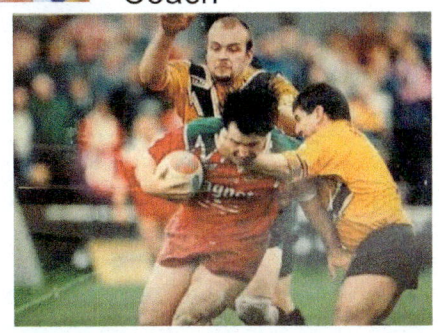

Perth Reds At Muscle World Gym

At Keighley Rugby Club

Matt Fuller Playing For Wakefield Trinity

Matt And Me Going To See The Spice Girls

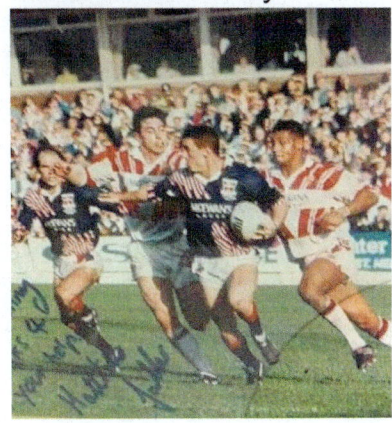

75

Chapter 9: Stubby Is Born, The Mental Battle And A New Home

"I don't want to not live because of my fear of what could happen."

- Laird Hamilton

I remember waking up in a different room. My bed in a different position though the lay out was the same. I was coming round from the operation to remove my right arm from my groin. I was now in plastics.

I can't remember the specifics of the actual operation my memory of all my block adventures sort of lumped together in one big memory. This is probably due to the basic routine of the block procedure being the same just different faces administering the same procedures.

I remember in my days in my physio clinic and with my athletes being careful not to install fear into the person, explaining that operations are not a walk in the park. You have to be mentally prepared for your loss of mobility and pain be it different from the pain that got you the operation in the first place, but still there is post operative pain. The doctors and specialists tend not to highlight this probably on purpose for the patient's sake. The result is there is a lack of mental and physical preparation for the challenges ahead. I remember my work with Dean Hall, a professional rugby player his situation being a good example of the need to guide and protect a person while on their path of recovery and healing (You will get to know Dean's story in chapter 10).

My surgeon Dr. Pietu (who I saw as my little Buddha of hope, inspiration and expertise), was an amazing surgeon as were all the other doctors who operated on me. I was extremely lucky to have all of them on my team. Dr. Pietu spoke English well and I saw a lot of him. From the moment I was taken by helicopter to his hospital, he put me back together with my dancing pole, plates, nuts and bolts and his great expertise. As we got to know each other there was a mutual respect which I saw was given to him from his staff also, always a good sign. He was at the top of his game but yet he had an earthly grounded nonegocentric vibe about him. From day one I had respect for him.

I don't feel the need to give respect if it's not there, it's got to be earned (remember my time with a certain coach at Keighley rugby club!). With Dr. Pietu if you asked an intelligent question, you would get an informative intelligent answer back. He did shock me once however when I was asking about the plate in my right ankle and when that would be removed. He had already said the dancing pole and nuts and bolts in my right leg would be in about two years. The plate in my ankle he wasn't sure because he had concerns about the nerve dying that had been damaged. He said, "The nerve could die", I said "It won't, I won't let it." Then he said, "At one point we thought we would have to chop your right foot off." "Oh" was my reply. From that day on I moved my toes at least three times a day and any other movement I could on that foot. I sent blood to it and healing from my mind and prayed. I already had an image of my movement being like Quasimodo or a zombie with my broken hips, back, legs not to mention my handless silhouette. Losing the right foot would have definitely got me a part in a zombie movie!

Though I had all this experience and knowledge of post operative pain and the need for recovery, I somehow thought the removal of my handless arm out of my groin would not be such a big thing, it won't be that painful. How wrong can one be!

I think this operation happened on the 1st or 2nd of May 2016. If the 2nd that would make it exactly a month after my accident and I was still having operations to 'fix' the trauma my body had been given by the accident and was still being put through. I realised more than I had ever done before how amazing this body of ours is and more so how powerful our minds are within this body. The mind controlling the level of success or failure the body can achieve. As a human most of us do not tap into this mind body connection and I would add to that the soul or spiritual connection that we have with our bodies, a thing I was now trying to do.

The only way I can describe the pain in my newly birthed right arm was a pressure feeling like you have been run over by a combine-harvester. It was unbelievably painful even with the high amount of pain relief I was on. In comparison to the pain, I had in ICU when my hand was dying, it was totally different. This was a very tight pressure like feeling, as if it was trapped under some extreme weight. I could feel all my fingers, thumb and hand even though they were not physically there (it was heavily bandaged so I couldn't see it) it was throbbing and torturous, especially when the tablet, again under my tongue started wearing off. The pain in ICU was one that filled my whole body and internal organs with a sick feeling, a sheer desperate pain. Don't get me wrong the pain in plastics was desperate but it seemed to just stay in my right arm not my whole body. I knew my body had had a month of healing and repair so that will have helped me to have more strength generally then when I was in ICU. But the psychological pain was very similar in both cases.

Pain is fascinating its messages from your body to your brain and vice versa. Not so much in ICU, I was in such a physical and mental state it wasn't possible. But in plastics I tried all sorts to get me through the pain. I mentally pictured white healing light surrounding me, I imagined massaging the arm, the fingers, thumb and hand, giving them permission to relax and come out of painful spasm. (I still have to do that today) I talked to it, and I accepted it. My soul loved it so my body could connect and heal it. As soon as I got to physically see it, he was named Stubby. All the nurses and doctors referred to him as Stubby. He was accepted not rejected even though he had a lot of work and lots of healing to do. I always, even today introduce him to people as Stubby and I talk to him all the time. Why is he a he? I don't know he just is.

When I eventually would leave Nantes hospital to go to my next place of residence, I would realise how significantly important my act of connecting to my amputation was. How I had saved myself from so much time and anguish allowing myself the permission to be different, disabled and special. Though the road was a rocky one and I stumbled many times often not knowing how to get up again because assistance never seemed to be there when you fell. But the saddest thing I learnt on this treacherous rocky path was that often you would be pushed down by others that couldn't or wouldn't accept your amputation. Being an amputee made you a danger to a lot of society. They think you may be contagious, they may catch the amputation and then they will become mad and mentally unstable just like the amputee. Best distance oneself from them, make out they are mad and better still turn our backs and walk away. I am jumping the gun a bit here I still haven't got out of plastics and still oblivious to the way disabled people are looked upon and treated. But that would come soon enough!

My world had become very small it consisted of a bed and a small table which at times frustrated the hell out of me because the cleaner or a couple of times the nursing staff would have moved it to my right side, how the hell was I supposed to get anything off it then? I never left this bed world, no toilet world, no other world at all. If I went, which I often did for an operation or x-ray, I still stayed in my bed world. I was even transferred into a bed world like trolley so I could be hosed down when they finally gave me a shower and washed my hair. This first took place in plastics, probably after Stubby had settled down a bit. Although it was cold lying on this slab on wheels, it felt great to have a 'proper' shower and your hair washed. The girls in trauma were great they would brush my hair, clean my teeth and give me a bed bath every day. But to actually have water showered over you after over a month was something I was so grateful for.

My parents managed to visit me while I was in Nantes. They flew from the UK to France and stayed about ten days. My parents may have visited twice but the journey to the hospital was a four hour round trip. By this time Robin and Pat would have returned to the UK. There were still the animals to take care of and the boys to sort out with everyday life. Elliott being thirteen was still at school and Harvey who had just turned sixteen a few days after my accident was in his final year of college doing his exams in June. Their lives had to continue as normal as it was possible. I was told very little about what was really going on back at the ranch.

It was so wonderful to see my parents. They put on a brave face but were shocked at seeing me as I was. They also happened to visit just after the birth of Stubby and at the time of some of my worst pain, I know they wanted to change places with me, but they couldn't. Even seeing me in pain was better than not seeing me and I think they got some comfort that I appeared to still be able to make conversation, smile and be present in their company. I think it was a case of one seeing was better than a thousand tellings, they could assess their daughter with their own eyes which gave them some level of peace but also sadness and worry too.

It was around this time that my dear friends Kay and Denbo got told about my accident. Pat and Robin lived close by, so they visited them on their return to the UK to break the news of my accident. Seeing as they got to France less than 24 hours after my accident, they were well informed and could explain the situation with correct information.

Pat and Robin went to Kay and Denbo's house and told them there had been an accident. Denbo recalls thinking "I've fucking lost her she's dead, I've fucking lost her!" He recalls it being a shock, a big, big, big shock. Kay was in shock too they were all upset and sat chatting about me, about the past and what we had done. Denbo said he couldn't remember much because he sat numb and in shock.

When I eventually got to visit them the first thing Denbo did when he saw me was roll up my right sleeve and kissed Stubby and said hello. He was the first person to do that, and it meant so much to me. It told me he loved my disability as much as he loved me, and it was going to be alright. Every time I visit, which isn't very often, Stubby is always the first to get attention. Denbo explaining he only kisses Stubby because he knows I can't wipe my bottom with him. Oh, so that's the only reason hey Denbo?

I will leave plastics now because my dicta-phone recordings will have more information of my time there and be more accurate.

I would like to thank every single person who took care of me. Just like the staff in trauma and ICU they were kind, cheerful and hardworking, having to deal with difficult people in difficult circumstances. I thank each and every one of you.

The day arrived that I was going to leave plastics and Nantes hospital, to go to my new place of residence. The leaving date had been changed a few times mainly due to availability of a room for me. Building up to this departure certain things had to be accomplished, and my doctors happy with the state of my condition. I still had my barbecue skewers in my four left toes, so they needed to be removed before I left. This happened on the day before leaving I think or maybe even the day I was leaving. I was really stressed and terrified how it would happen.

Two young men came into my room said bonjour and then started unwrapping my left foot from the bedding covering it and it's bandaging. I asked what they were doing I had never seen them before and I didn't know who they were. "We are going to remove your pins" was the answer "But Dr. Pietu is doing that" was my response, they ignored me. In fact, I no longer existed. I was very scared, they can't have had much experience they looked too young, one was almost certainly a student. The one who looked in charge had a phone which rang, he answered it and then just left not even bothering to cover up my foot indicating they would be back. I was now panicking and very worried. Firstly, my gut was shouting don't let them do it and my mind was angry with their bedside manner or none existence of it. They had this dismissive, cocky, arrogant attitude and I didn't even exist. I pushed my red button and buzzed I wanted to know what was going on, where was my 'Buddha' the one I trusted and had total respect for.

The nurse came in and I told her my concerns and asked if she could cover up my foot again. I also told her I was a person not a piece of meat. I had feelings and there was no reason to be treated like I just had been, no matter how important they thought they were. She left and I went into panic mode waiting for these two to return. In my desperation to calm myself down I turned to one of my books on my small side table and opened it at a random page. "I can do all things through Christ which strengthens me" stared back at me, page 203, first paragraph. The book 'The Power Of Positive Thinking' by Norman Vincent Peale. At the bottom of this page, it offered eight principles of a constructive nature that you could do if a loved one or you are ill. "In sickness send for your minister even as you send for your doctor." That is believe that spiritual forces as well as medical procedures and techniques are important in recovery and healing. I couldn't believe the page I had randomly opened. I calmed myself closed my eyes, prayed that the correct person to do this for me would be sent. It was then dinner time, and my food was brought to me. Minutes later Dr. Pietu came into the room to do my toes, was I pleased to see him!

He saw I had my food and said he would come back, I said no stay the food doesn't matter. He said no I will come back, "Bon apetit" I said, "What with this food?" he laughed and left. So now I prayed again that he would return before the other two.

About 20 minutes later there was a knock at my door and Dr. Pietu walked in, my prayers had been answered and I gave thanks. "Right" announced Dr. Pietu "I am going to pull these out." "Will I get any pain relief before you do?" I asked. "No, it won't hurt" the doctor replied. "How do you know have you had barbecue skewers pulled out of your feet before?" He laughed and put all his weight behind pulling the first skewer out, then the next and the next until all four were out. They were long but his steady hand, expertise and the spiritual forces involved meant I didn't feel a thing! The other two doctors (I assumed they were doctors) arrived just as Dr. Pietu had finished. My faith in the divine intervention again being tested and again not letting me down!

The other thing I had to do before my adventure to my new home could begin was to actually be put into a chair to get my body used to sitting again. It sounds simple but it wasn't. The first time I was propped up by pillows and the nurses held me, I lasted about 5 minutes before my head felt really funny and dizzy. Over the next few days, they managed with a hoist to swing me out of bed and into a chair where I stayed about thirty to forty minutes.

Even though the physio had been treating my legs with some sort of machine that they wrapped around them, my body movements were so few and limited (lifting a piece of coal would have been a challenge never mind a 25kg sack). The other thing that the staff had managed to achieve was getting the stitches out which were many. Now I just had to wait for the ambulance to come and collect me.

Two ambulance men arrived and I was transferred out of my bed world and into another and pushed out of my room with the few belongings I had resting on my chest. I said my goodbyes, thanked the staff who were on duty and entered a world I hadn't seen for over six weeks. It was very surreal, I saw the sky and clouds that were grey and they had movement, I saw a tree and lots of cars which actually scared me. It was so very strange, it's as if I had never seen these things before, they were alien to me not part of my world. The noise, the smells and the busyness making me uneasy and nervous. Part of me wanted the safety of my hospital bed and the staff around me and part of me wanted that tablet under my tongue and then part of me wanted to scream out loud that I had made it I was alive!

Despite all that had happened to me I was given, for some unknown reason to me, the strength to carry on. I didn't know in this moment of exhilaration, of a feeling of a certain degree of freedom that this feeling over the course of time, would be cruelly and unlawfully taken away from me.

Chapter 10: Bramley Rugby League Club, Wembley, Formula 1 And A Master's Degree

"When anyone tells me I can't do something I'm just not listening anymore"

- Florence Griffith Joyner

So here I am at Bramley, the coach who thought I should be at home on Sundays making Yorkshire puddings, obviously didn't want me in the kitchen until after I had looked after his team. Like I said I liked Maurice Bamford, he shouted a lot but he had an undying love for the game. I got to see another side of Maurice when he asked if I could help his wife who was suffering from MS, if I remember correctly. He hoped that some massage would ease her pain. I gladly went to his house near Morley, she was lovely and he was so caring and loving. I visited a number of times to try and help Maurice and his wife.

They say you can't judge a book by its cover, I believe if you look at a person's soul you will find their truth. The problem is that the soul is often buried under fear, conditionings, other's judgements and conformity. All the soul needs and wants is a real and truthful love. When the soul is cared for there is a beam of light that radiates out from the person who has such a soul. It can be seen in the eyes no matter what that person's age may be.

I have come to realise while writing this book that every professional rugby team I was involved with seemed to have a problem. At Dewsbury it occurred before I became involved and that was the fire at the old stand at Crown Flatt in September 1988. Sixty firemen fought the blaze, but nothing could be saved. The stand and over 1000 seats were destroyed, the changing rooms, kit room, secretary's office plus all the history of the rugby league club, photos, records and official documents were all gone.

I was around after the fall out, the treatment and changing area were then put together and I sadly never got to see the historic facilities that I had visited as a young child, but the smells were the same, strong wintergreen.

I don't want to get into the politics of it all, but I felt what I felt and observed what I saw. There was something not right with the relationship, with the miraculous appearance of Dunken Development, I smelt a rat. I don't think their motives were coming from the love of the club or the game of rugby especially the father who referred to me as the veterinary and he seemed to spend a lot of his time in the committee room, with the free booze. This is just my opinion, and I am so pleased that the players and the fans found a new home where new memories and history have been made and continue to be made. Dewsbury rugby club has a special place in my heart. Both the players and the fans gave me support and encouragement with a warmth of love I never found at any other professional rugby club. Thank you!

Keighley's problems were financial. There was a history of financial problems which haunted the club. But after dissolving in liquidation, the club did reform in 2001 and thankfully continues today. Bramley's problems appeared to also be financial, so much so that their ground was sold for housing by the businessmen directors of the club. I always wondered why professional Leeds businessmen were interested in a small rugby club. I suppose the prime location and area of land involved was a big attraction. I thought these businessmen didn't seem to have the passion and genuine love for the club that I saw at Dewsbury.

I remember one Bramley director, an accountant by profession who always dressed expensively (all the committee did), asked if I could just come and treat the players and not bother with match days. I couldn't believe my ears. He said they had to cut back. I said that he was insulting my profession, the most important time to assess and prevent long term injuries was the moment they happened, not two or three days later. Also, there would be no one to stand up to the coach and bring a player off the field to avoid aggravating the injury further. I told him the essence of keeping a fit team was to assess, treat and rehab as soon as any problems occurred. The fact that he thought my presence on match days was not needed totally shocked me. Did he think I sat there knitting? I told him if he wanted to take the responsibility of the lives of the players than he was welcome to do so but I wasn't prepared to take responsibility of keeping the team fit if I wasn't there on match days.

It is sad but fatalities do happen in sport. My dad was playing for Batley when such a tragedy occurred. It occurred at Crown Flatt on the 15th of April 1969. Dewsbury had beaten Batley 8 points to 7. The Dewsbury player loose forward John Davis, a signing from Leeds in January was injured in the 60th minute. He was doubled up in pain and the game was stopped so he could have treatment. The coach for Dewsbury, Alvin Newall appealed for a doctor from the crowd. Two were available in the dressing room when John Davis was carried off. One gave the kiss of life the other heart massage. A police escort was given to the ambulance which took Davis to Dewsbury Infirmary. There five doctors attempted to revive the injured player who had been unconscious since being carried off.

John Davis was a teacher and left a wife and two children. A former Welsh rugby union international, he joined Leeds in December 1962. He had a reputation of being one of the fastest forwards in the game.

Dewsbury abandoned a Yorkshire Cup senior competition and gave the tie to Wakefield Trinity. A few weeks later a combined Dewsbury and Batley team (I believe my dad played), played Leeds at Headingly in a match which helped to raise funds for John's widow and family. The responsibility and duty of care in such a physical sport is huge and should never be taken lightly.

I was back with the devil I knew at Bramley and a mutual degree of respect existed between us. Maurice shouted and sweared, I mopped up the injuries and we had an understanding. The Bramley lads were a passionate, hard working group of players with some great characters and personalities amongst them. All uniquely different and all very passionate about the game they played and loved.

When Bamford left an existing player took over the coaching, Ray Ashton. Ashton and Bamford had had a number of misunderstandings. Ray had achieved a lot in his career, he was a fiery player who had flare and skill, but he was coming to the back end of his prime. I remember Ashton being knocked out for a very short time at an away game at either Whitehaven or Workington. I am inclined to think it may have been Workington and Ashton had previously been player coach there. I think some scores had to be settled and hence he was knocked out.

Bamford and Ashton had a real go at each other after the game, I was pig in the middle. I didn't know how bad he had been hit on the field so had to watch him, no alcohol or sleep on the long journey back to Bramley. Bamford was agitated, coaches tend to get that way when they sense their days of coaching at that particular club are numbered. I stuck up for Ashton as I would have done for any of my players who had an injury, especially an invisible head injury. I was therefore disappointed to see the change in Ashton's attitude towards an injured player when he became player coach at Bramley.

Throughout my career I have seen a lot of bad injuries. One such injury occurred at Keighley. A player had an unusual injury that thankfully, I only saw once. This poor guy had totally ripped open his scrotum sack. He was not only in immense pain but embarrassed to show me. I told him that I needed to see his injury, it was bad. I suggested he had to go to the hospital, the Keighley doctor came to take a look, but I managed to persuade the player to go to casualty and not to let the club doctor stitch him up. I had concerns about letting the doctor loose on this situation. Stitching a cut above the eye is one thing, but this situation was a whole lot different.

The doctors that I worked with in my time with professional rugby teams included Dr. Lee at Dewsbury who was lovely, genuinely interested in sports injury and we worked well together. The doctor at Keighley was a gynaecologist, I suppose essential at a rugby club! I tried to keep the players at a distance, he was always pissed, courtesy of the club's free bar. The doctor at Bramley I didn't have a lot of dealings with, however on one particular day he hindered more than helped the situation.

The situation occurred at the Bramley home game. One of my players, Dean Hall (remember I mentioned him in chapter 9), who was from Mirfield, took a bad knock just under the post, in fact I think he may have even hit the post. I understood and got Dean, he was different, quiet and mysterious. A bit of a lad, I think some of his social crowds were a bit wild. I knew Dean and his mum from Dewsbury rugby league club. The support his mum gave him, especially during matches was wonderful. However, the people close by did often leave with tingling in their ears. In those days I would give anyone three chances to prove to me it was worth giving them my time and energy. Today people only get one chance, that's the beauty of knowledge, of experience and age. Dean was the sort of guy who needed his rugby career to keep him on the straight and narrow. He came across as not giving a shit, but he did. Dean didn't need any second chances from me, he didn't let me down once!

Dean took this knock while playing for Bramley. As I ran on, I could hear his screams. He was a tough player and a hard player, I knew instantly that he was in serious trouble! I tried to calm him down and told him that he had injured his knee and I needed to strap his ankles and possibly his thighs together before we could stretcher him off. I needed to try and stabilise his legs before we moved him. His body language and screams telling me all I needed to know. At that point the club doctor ran on and wanted to do a knee test. I shouted, "No stop, don't touch his knee, he has probably ruptured all the ligaments, let's just get him to the hospital!" To me the evidence of the damage was in Dean's face!!

One of the biggest problems today, I think, is that a lot of medical people don't look for the obvious signs, the simple, little signs (some don't even look at the patient at all) but rely only on the textbook for symptoms and diagnosis. Yes, you need to know these but there are so many clues that a person will present to give you information, rolling around holding your knee screaming being just one of these clues!

Dean got stretchered into the dressing room and the ambulance called. I had to get back on the bench for the game continued and I had to take care of the rest of my players. There was no one else to do it. My fears of leaving the doctor with Dean came true he did test the knee. This not being such a good thing to do risking and possibly causing further damage, but that we will never know.

Dean was strapped up, given painkillers, anti-inflammatories, and sent home to wait for a specialist's appointment. I think I pushed to get Dean seen privately and we went to a place in Bradford which dealt with Bradford city football club and had a good reputation. Surgery was needed he had ruptured his ligaments and a total knee reconstruction was the only way to go. He had a Gazza injury, (Paul Gascoigne the footballer) Dean had the same injury, his cruciates in his knee were badly damaged, reconstruction was needed.

I liked treating knee injuries compared to the shoulder joint, the knee joint is less complex. With the sports I was involved with knee injuries were common in my work. I remembered an amateur footballer came to my clinic, he had been everywhere, including the Leeds United physio who told him it was arthritis and put him on a machine. I don't think he had much hope that I could help him. During his history taking I realised that he hadn't really been treated. I asked him to lay face down on the treatment couch and he said, "But the pain is at the front of my knee." I told him I needed to check his hamstrings and the popliteal muscle. My treatments always involved a lot of massage and later traditional Chinese acupuncture. When I began to assess and massage him, he nearly hit the roof, there was so much tightness in the area. I always said that my hands were a gift from the universe. They were big, looked old and didn't match the rest of me. But they knew how to feel problems like they were radars. I once said to a lovely old gentleman, Mr Heppingstall, who I did home visits for, (he had painful and arthritic knees) "I think my hands will end up arthritic with all the massaging I do." His reply "Nay lass, if God's given you a gift, he won't take it away." Interesting!

I treated the footballer two or three times with deep massage getting the whole area of his knee front and back relaxed. He was delighted to be back playing Sunday football for another season.

Another interesting knee case I had involved a neighbour of mine. He had had problems for a while probably due to his rugby days, I took a look and could feel what I thought was a small piece of bone at the back of his knee just a little away from his ligaments. He was in Bupa the health insurance company (don't get me started on them) so he had a knee procedure to resolve the pain and gain back the mobility of his knee. The procedure involved cutting the patella tendon, pulling the patella back to get to the knee joint. Clean the knee area, sort out any cartilage damage and sew the patella back to its position. A big procedure, right? The weeks passed but the exact problem still haunted him. I took another look/feel and sure enough the piece of bone was still lodged there. I suggested that he should go back to his expensive health company and tell them, I even drew a mark around the area where his appointment was due indicating the bit of floating bone. He returned home after another less invasive procedure with the fairly large piece of bone in a jar. He didn't have the same pain again and could get on with his life.

Dean Hall had his reconstructive surgery and I took him to see the specialist in Leeds. The specialist told him he would never ever be able to play rugby again. What a shock!! On the journey back from Leeds to Mirfield Dean did not speak once. Yet again I saw this man in deep pain but this time it was emotional pain.

"Right Dean", I said, "We either work really hard to get you back playing rugby and you must do everything I say, no excuses. Or you wallow in self-pity with the would've, should've, could've and drown your sorrows in beer while pretending that it doesn't bother you. I will be with you every step of the way but the key to this is keeping you away from pre-season training at Bramley." Dean chose to believe in me and we spent weeks rehabilitating him.

The first thing I told him to do was to stop limping, not an easy thing to do. I took him to the gym, trained in the local park and gave him treatment. I told him I wouldn't let him back on the rugby pitch until he could jump off one of my chairs in a pain-free, stable movement.

The season was about to begin, and Bramley had organised a 'friendly match' at Bramley with Leeds Rhinos. Why they are called 'friendlies' is beyond my comprehension, it's a physio's worst nightmare! It was on a Sunday Dean had been training with the lads once he could jump off my chair and he was ready. I had got into his psyche, we were ready mentally and physically. As I strapped his knee, I told him I wouldn't say he was ready if he wasn't. Our trust and connection had been built over the weeks that we had worked together. I could see it in his eyes, he was ready! I was extremely proud of him. Against all odds he was about to run onto the rugby pitch and that was down to him, his hard work, courage and belief in himself! Later in my life I would have to find those strengths in myself, but Dean was one of the many people that I was blessed to know who showed me how it was done.

I explained to Ray Ashton that he needed to put Dean on the wing and not in the pack just to allow Dean's confidence to grow. It had been a long, hard road to get him back on the pitch, especially when the specialist said he would never play again. It would also make sense for him not to play the full game, after all it was only a 'friendly'. Ashton listened to about 70% of my suggestions and towards the end Dean was driving the ball in, in midfield against Leeds Rhinos' big, powerful forwards. After the game Dean was so happy, he had even scored a try while on the wing.

Prison Or The Paralympics

I told Dean that he should not go and get pissed up that night, we still had a lot of work to do on keeping him fit. I also expected to see him at my clinic on Monday evening with any of the rest of the team if they needed any treatment.

Bramley for some reason had an away game on the Tuesday or Wednesday night. It could have been Doncaster I think it was at a dog track. This meant none of the players had time for recovery and I made it clear to Ashton that no way should Dean be involved. There hadn't been enough time to see how his reconstructed knee had held up. The coach, Ray Ashton phoned me while I was treating the lads that Monday evening and asked about the injuries and Dean. Again, I said Dean should not be considered for the mid-week game.

The day of the game arrived the team including Dean were on the coach. We had to meet some of the Lancashire players, but one hadn't turned up, I think it was Paul Garrett (he did however get there in time for the game). In the changing room Ashton announced the team, he included Dean Hall. I was mad but couldn't show it, I didn't want to put any doubt or negative thoughts into Dean's head, I just had to pray. My opinion, hard work (I didn't bill the club for rehabilitating Dean) and my professional input all being wiped aside. Dean was on the bench to start with but was soon on the field in the pack!! After the game I sought out the Bramley committee man who was there and told him I was giving my notice and would be leaving in the next few weeks. What was the point of me being there?

The time now would be about the mid 1990's. My studies continued in the 90's at the Northern College of Acupuncture. A four-year master's degree in Traditional Chinese acupuncture which began in 1995 and finished in 1999.

Once I left the professional rugby league arena, I still helped some amateur sides. Two of these teams were coached by Andy Tyers, remember him from Keighley. Andy coached at Clown and later Rotherham. I helped Andy out whenever I could. Andy asked if I would mind looking at his brother Robert's knee (it must run in the family these knee problems). Robert lived in Oxfordshire but the next time he was up to visit Andy in Sheffield he would try and sort out a treatment. The brothers came to my clinic and as always, I began by taking some case history and general information. Robert said his job was a pump attendant, ok they had them in those days, I am thinking a Shell or Q8 petrol station. He said he wouldn't be in Yorkshire the following weekend because he had to work at a place called Silverstone. Ok no problem whenever you are up north, we will see if we can treat you again.

On the Monday I was training with Denbo and Glynn (the guy who came to the Keighley meeting with me), we were chatting about this and that and I think I asked if they knew the name Silverstone. Glynn knew straight away I still didn't get it. He asked if I could get tickets, I said I can phone and ask Robert. That week two tickets arrived with a note from Rob saying his mum will be there and if I find her, he will see me after he had finished working. The date on the tickets being the 16th of July 1995 that weekend. At the last-minute Glynn had to pull out because of work. I did not know what to do. This guy had taken the time to send me tickets, I had to go, or I would feel bad. Remember at this point I had never heard of car racing or anything to do with it. I decided to go on my own so as not to embarrass myself in front of Andy's brother and let him think I didn't appreciate him taking the time to post the tickets to me.

As I got nearer to my destination the traffic got heavier and we had to queue. I am thinking what's going on here, why so much traffic? Once I got into the place the fun began, I had to go to a certain entrance, it took me ages to find it. I ended up with a strain to my leg for walking around so much. At last, I found my entrance, the guy who was looking at my ticket said to me "Who are you Schumacher's girlfriend?" My reply "Who's Schumacher?" I didn't know the name, never heard it before. So here I am sat in this special area with all the families and friends of the people who worked at this place called Silverstone. I was close to this track, and I could see a lot of people, I thought this place must be popular. Music was playing and even today if I hear this song, it reminds me of this day. The song is Edwyn Collins' "A Girl Like You".

At last, there was something happening. These funny looking 'cars' making a hell of a racket started to go around the track. I found out a long while after that was the warmup laps to warm the tyres up. What struck me the most was these cars looked like toy cars. They didn't even look like a car. We were surrounded by big TV screens and there was a drama with someone called Damon Hill and Michael Schumacher. They had crashed and were out of the race. I thought they can't be good drivers then, can they? The race continued with all that racket that they make lap after lap, after lap. Eventually it ended and someone called Johnny Herbert won.

Right, what do I do now? People were leaving our seating area. Okay find Rob's mum. I asked a couple of ladies if they were Rob's mum, but they weren't. So, I followed the crowd, we were in a place close to another place called the paddock. Did they have horse races here too? I thought. I got to this big gate and there was someone stood there with this colourful shirt on which had the name Williams on it. I asked if he could help me, I was looking for Rob Tyer's mum. He opened the gate and said follow me. I followed him into what he called the garage, it didn't look like a garage to me, the floor was so clean! There was one of those toy cars there, blue and white with a wheel missing. There were also a group of guys drinking out of this massive bottle. Rob saw me and came over and offered me a drink, it felt heavy even with my bodybuilding training. I said, "What sort of shit is that?" it tasted awful. Now, having tasted it, I know why they try to get rid of it by showering each other with it. I went to look at the car I was told it was Damon Hill's "Who?" I asked. I went on to say "I make no wonder that they crash, look at the state of the car, it's touching the floor! Why is it so low and small?" Rob just laughed and then we left to walk around the paddock. I was still expecting to see a line of stables full of horses. No horses, but there was someone singing and playing a guitar. He was singing 'Go Johnny, Go', singing and playing the song 'Johnny B Goode' a Chuck Berry song from 1959. I thought good, things are starting to liven up! Rob told me it was Damon Hill playing. "Who?" Again. "It's because Johnny Herbert won." "Okay" I am thinking I have never heard of either of them. An interesting fact in the same year 1995 at a concert in Cleveland Ohio, Chuck Berry with Bruce Springsteen, played the same song, awesome.

We partied the night away and I never saw one horse. Rob kept pointing people out, but I was oblivious to who they were. There was an international rugby union player there I chatted to him I told him he should try playing the real rugby game that is rugby league, the one we play up north, not like that pussy game they call rugby union. I said the ball spends more time in the crowd than on the pitch with all the kicking you do. But I suppose you southern softies need to keep stopping and starting to get a rest in the game. I think he thought I was mad, but I thought it was an honest and valid observation.

I was back training in the gym the next week and telling Denbo and Glynn what happened, where I went and what I saw. Glynn who followed F1 a little wouldn't believe me. He said you don't get into the paddock. I said I did! Even my grandma said you can't get into these places. I did and I didn't know what all the fuss was about.

The next Silverstone I went to was with Lisa, Andy's wife, Andy and a few others. Andy had never been before even though his brother was the pump attendant. Rob was the guy who filled up the racing cars with fuel in the pit stops. He was with the Williams team, the top team in those days. I did go to other F1 races I had caught the bug and understood it a little more but more about that later.

I was still helping Andy out with the team he was coaching when I could but the work for my master's degree in Traditional Chinese Acupuncture was increasing. The College was in York North Yorkshire, so it wasn't too far away for me.

However, in 1998 I was part of the group who went on another crazy weekend. I think I was the only lass amongst the group of rugby players from Clown and the Rotherham teams. This was a very special outing for the Sheffield lads because we were on our way to watch Sheffield Eagles play Wigan at Wembley in the Challenge Cup final. The celebrations began as soon as they sat on the train on that early morning. Rob, Andy's brother came along too. He may spend his life in the fast lane, surrounded by 'Brolly Dollies' and famous people but no way was Rob going to miss out on this weekend. Fortunately for him there was no F1 racing that weekend. Spirits were high although I sensed amongst the group that they didn't expect Sheffield to beat Wigan. I said, "I am not so sure, I feel Sheffield may win!"

I admit to this day I have yet to see this match. Yes, I was there. My first Wembley Final and I soaked up the amazing atmosphere, but I did fall asleep. I had a beer or two, something I didn't really do so often, and I was tired with all the excitement and travelling. I think there were quite a few of us who grabbed 40 winks, not just me. I will watch the game one day, I have it on VHS (does anyone remember them?). The final score Sheffield Eagles 17, Wigan 8 what!! So that was it back to Sheffield to party the night away. We did lose one of our gang but he got back safe and sound a day later.

If you knew Andy, you could guess what happened next. Though he lived in Sheffield he wasn't going to spoil this celebration so the lads who could get away with it, booked into a hotel in the city. Then we continued to celebrate this fantastic result in the city of Sheffield. It was one of those moments that you can't plan for, a rare moment that needs to be embraced before you have to come back down to reality.

The next day tired and in need for the 'hair of the dog', we made our way to the place Andy knew he could find the victorious team. The team was there with the trophy. I remember the smile on Robs face when he held the trophy (beats that shitty champagne doesn't it Rob?). A weekend to savour and remember.

It's probably around 10 years since I have actually seen Andy and longer for Rob, but we keep in touch. In 2000 Andy became involved with Sheffield Eagles when Mark Ashton asked him to join the coaching team as Academy coach. Then Andy became the assist coach with the first team and eventually onto the board culminating as CEO from 2019 (I write this in 2020 Andy is still CEO for Sheffield Eagles and Rob now works with McLaren on their super cars). I am proud to be your friend guys our friendship journey has been a long, loyal and a supportive one. We have all had mountains to climb, obstacles to jump over, crawl under or bulldoze down. I am grateful for our friendships and know you are only a phone call away.

The only other time I went to Wembley was in 1999 Leeds V London Broncos. It was the last ever rugby final there because the historic Wembley was being knocked down. Of course, Andy was there, the final score Leeds 52 London 16. This time it was Andy who fell asleep during the game, and I have the photo to prove it.

Before I move on to the end of the 90's and the new millennium, I will go back a little. There were a few things that occurred which involved rugby teams, two happened with the Keighley team. We were on the team bus heading to Cumbria,

Barrow in fact. These journeys are always long and I was chatting with some of the players. From a young age I have always known things, I think everybody does it's whether you listen to the information or not. I was giving some information to a player and the Aussie that was about to get a trial with Keighley was laughing and said, "Hey Penny there's a black cat over there (he was looking out of the bus window) is it yours?" I connected to him straight away and said "No but are you planning on going skiing? Because if you are be careful. I can see a pot on your leg." He laughed along with the rest of the players sat nearby. We said no more and continued our journey to Barrow.

The usual routine occurred in the dressing room. Players getting their kit on any strapping needed being done and officials checking the player's hands and studs on their boots. It must have been 10 minutes into the first half when the Aussie took a hit went down and was carried off with a broken leg. I felt awful, I didn't want any injuries for any players even the Barrow players and here was one of my players with an injury I had seen him have on the bus. The lads remembered what I said and couldn't believe it. I saw the player the following week at Keighley. He was good had his pot on his leg, I told him I never wished for him to break his leg, I just saw him with a pot on. He was cool about it and he didn't think it was my fault, but I noticed he spoke a little less harsh to me from that point on. In fact, most of the team seemed to have a bit more respect.

It was normal for me to give messages to people as I treated them, I was guided to the ones that were ready to receive a message. A couple of regular patients would ask me if I had any predictions or messages. One such person was Steven Wolfenden. I knew and treated most of the family. I remember going to his mum's funeral and the songs played even today remind me of his mum and the family. They were mad on cricket and his mum would sit in the sun watching it for hours. So, the song by Elton John, 'Don't Let The Sun Go Down On Me' was so appropriate and also was 'Empty Chairs And Empty Tables' from Les Misérables, what an atmospheric song, both were played at her funeral.

The theatre production of Les Misérables was also special to me because I took one of my very first patients who I did home visits for, Mrs Haigh to Manchester to see Les Misérables. An amazing lady with a very kind and talented daughter Christine. Christine was a fashion designer and she made any dress that I needed for special events which included my 18th and 21st birthday parties plus my graduation ball at Adelphi Hotel in Liverpool. Her abilities and flare never getting the recognition they deserved.

After his mum's funeral Steven continued to visit my clinic and we often chatted. I commented how significant the music was at his mum's funeral and I learnt that they were his choices. He then asked me if I had any predictions, I said all I can see is an event that is going to stop the world. Writing this in December 2020, in the middle of a second lockdown I could say I predicted it 30 years ago. But I think I predicted what happened on the 31st of August 1997 because that night I had a dream which made me sit bolt straight up in bed. More on that later.

My messages about the lockdown are many but I feel it is a sorting out and a wakeup call to the human race to look within themselves. To connect with their heart and soul and take guidance from them not the false, cruel, soulless misdirection that blocks that love. The divine gift, a gift that every person is given at birth the gift of love, a soulful love that now needs to be allowed to blossom. Many of us turning this soul love into a man-made one, the divine's gift no longer accessible. This man-made soulless love begins searching in all the wrong places, believing that love can be found in greed, possessions, power, control, ego and money. The soul slowly suffocates, and its person is left sad, depressed, lonely, unfulfilled, and empty. But self-love can bring a person's soul love back to life, ridding the fears from the person and allowing inner contentment and peace by connecting back to oneself with love.

Back to the past and the second event that happened while I was at Keighley was them drawing Wigan away in the Challenge Cup. A big, big game for the players who were both anxious and excited. Around this time the value of nutrition was being introduced to rugby. Being involved with the sport of bodybuilding I already got and understood its important value. On this big match day, it was therefore decided that the team would have a breakfast all together on the way to Wigan. I was sat on the bus and eventually I started thinking we seem to be travelling a long time and it's not the way I would have gone to Wigan. But when the landscape started turning into sheep after sheep, I thought hold on a minute I was up here a few weeks ago. My god we are going to Cumbria or are already in Cumbria. Some person had booked this breakfast on the way to Cumbria. It didn't go down well! We were running that late that the players started getting their kit on while still on the bus and I started strapping them on the bus!

While at Dewsbury there were a couple of occasions (well more than a couple!) where the fans from the team we were playing got to me. I don't know why these fans always seem to plant themselves near the dugouts. On one occasion Dewsbury were playing Hull K.R. Yes, I know they are a very passionate group of fans but just a few make their comments too personal. This woman was shouting abuse throughout the game and then I think Gary Cocks got sin binned so she had a real go at him, and he took the bait. If anyone knows Gary, he is a hard man on the field but a true, kind gentleman off the field. So, I had to intervene "Just sit-down Gary, ignore her she's only a gypsy." The reason I said that was because she had loads of earring dangling from her ears and I was trying to diffuse and make light of the situation. Gary had just been sin binned not a good time for a total stranger to start verbally attacking him. She continued throughout the game and we all just ignored her.

I never gave it another minute's thought. The weeks passed and it was eventually time to play Hull K.R. at their ground. In those days Hull K.R. was always a tough and physical team to play. I knew there would be more than average knocks to deal with later. The thing I didn't know was that, shall we call her the earring lady, had obviously been boiling away over the incident at Dewsbury weeks ago. She wanted my blood! I had once had the pleasure of going round the pubs in Hull and you don't stare at people or look at them too long or you are inviting trouble, and that's just the women. This was just my observations at the time, I am sure it's totally different now, hope so.

She was at it again all through the match, I ignored her, but she wasn't satisfied. After the game, she accosted me giving me a mouthful. I just threw what water I had left in my sponge bucket at her and went into the changing rooms. About 15-20 minutes later someone came to tell me someone was at the door to see me. Yes, it was my biggest fan, the woman with the earrings. She had another go at me. I told her to go home and read her tea leaves, then shut the door.

The only other time I threw water at the fans was at Wigan (not sure if it was while at Dewsbury or Keighley). Again, the person was near the dugout all the match. They were making racial comments about some of my players. After the match I said "It's amazing, do you make comments like that when Ellery Hanley plays for you?" More racial abuse so I threw the water left in my bucket at them. Fortunately, I always kept hold of my bucket and never threw that as well.

After finishing working with the professional rugby teams, I did continue to work with some of the local amateur teams, the main local two being Dewsbury Moor and Thornhill. I worked a lot with Johnny Harpin, a very fair and knowledgeable coach. He had played professional rugby and was part of the Dewsbury Celtic ARLFC team that gave the professional sides a run for their money.

Dewsbury Celtic was part of the Dewsbury Irish National league club which has a long history and is still very much alive and kicking today. Celtic became one of the most famous names in amateur rugby league. Many professional clubs feared their name if drawn against them in the rugby league challenge cup.

My dad as well as Johnny was involved with the club in the 1970's. Newspaper comments in the 70's saying it all.

"Humberside ARL were shattered by the heavy defeat of an Ace-of-clubs at the hands of Dewsbury Celtic" (Hull Sports Mail 7/12/74)

"Salute Dewsbury Celtic who against all odds at Hull won the B.A.R.L.A Yorkshire Cup, proving once again to be the leading light of the Amateur R.L. World" (Dewsbury Reporter 27/12/74)

Celtic V Leigh 1973
"Celtic played it open with a magnificent spirit and they tackled and defended with outstanding courage" (Leigh star Feb 1973)

Celtic V Featherstone 1972
"Celtic put up a magnificent defensive display and showed ideas in attack" (Sunday People 30/1/72)

"Amateurs fight a hard battle" (Green Post 29/1/72)

Johnny Harpin was the captain for the games against Featherstone and Leigh.

Dad was given a scrap book by Jerry Swift "All For The Good Of The Game". It includes the official souvenir programme costing 5p of the R.L. Challenge Cup 1st round at Mount Pleasant Batley, on Saturday the 8th of February 1975 kick off 3pm. The teams Dewsbury Celtic V Hull Kingston Rovers (oh no not Hull K.R., wonder if the woman with the earrings went?) The scrap book is full of black and white photos of the game. Mick Doyle being captain for Celtic and Roger Millward being captain for Hull K.R. There was a big crowd on these action-packed photos taken at the game, dad and Johnny being on some of the photos. (I didn't recognise you Johnny, you had long hair and sideburns!) He also had a wicked sidestep and attack.

"With a great break by Johnny Harpin (6) who covers at least 30 yards" Swift

"From the play of the ball Trevor Walker gives the defence a pile of trouble as he ploughs to within a yard of the line" Swift

The half time score Celtic 2 HKR 13. The second half

"Celtic was getting more and more on top with increasing fervour" Swift

"Trevor Walker rolled over on the line in the corner after taking on four defenders five yards out" Swift

"Harpin comes across field in a storming run" Swift

"An important factor in the game the dismissal. A difference of opinion between Trevor Walker and Millington Hull K.R. leads to an 'early bath' for both – David Foster coach (Celtic) approaches Trevor" Swift

"Bob Walker is inches away from glory as the balls skids over the line and the referee on the spot gives a lost ball" Swift

Try no.1
"Mick Doyle drives over left of the posts in spite of Wallace's attention" Swift

Try no.2
"Mick Doyle goes over to the right of the post this time with a nippy move from an opportunist chip" Swift

The crowd rise to their tip toes

"From a Doyle kick to the right-wing Brian Pepper thrills the crowd as he beats Sullivan and Smithies with the try line in view." Try No.3 "This try is the result, Sullivan is astounded but the referee had already awarded the try in spite of Hull K.R.'s clearance of the ball after grounding" Swift

Final score Celtic 15 Hull K.R. 31.

The pen pictures Dewsbury Celtic 1974-75.

J. Harpin (standoff) Age 27, 11 ½ stone miner, Ex-Hunslet. Very experienced player who has the ability to win matches for his team – great tactician and superb cover tackler. One half of a grand half back pair.

M.Doyle (scrumhalf) Captain. Age 25. 12 stone. Bricklayer. Ex-Batley, Bradford, Huyton and Wakefield. Mick combines a great insight into the game with the guile and cunning of all good scrum halves. A superb leader who inspires his team at all times.

T. Walker (prop) vice-captain. Age 35, 20 stone. Transport executive (taxi driver to you and me). Ex-Dewsbury and Batley. Pack leader whose great experience rubs off on the rest of the Celtic pack. Strong in the scrum and devastating in the loose. Holder of the world record for tries in a season by a prop (17) whilst playing for Batley. Has been in charge of the interleague side this season.

Fate put me in Johnny's path while he was coaching the amateurs. Johnny was a good man manager and very well respected. This event I am about to describe indirectly involves rugby. After a home game in 1996 (think it was at Thornhill or Dewsbury Moor club) Johnny invited the whole club house to his 50th birthday party at his home the following weekend. Eileen, his wife had not expected this and was left with the task of organising a party for who knows how many. Johnny was away at Barrow Island Cumbria with the players. I think I may have been at college doing my acupuncture degree in York. I got to the party and there were loads of people especially those connected to rugby. Eileen had done an amazing job getting a marquee and everything organised, she worked so hard. The party was at full swing, and I was talking with some of the players asking what they had got Johnny. I also asked if they had organised a stripper gram (very popular in the 90's), no they hadn't. I couldn't believe it. I said right get the yellow pages (it's now replaced by Google) let's have a whip round and get him a stripper.

We were fortunate enough to get one at such short notice which entertained all the fellas not just Johnny. Eileen said the only thing she can remember is a load of lads standing outside, at the window where they could see the stripper better and licking the window! That's one way to wash windows. Johnny had a good 50th birthday party. He always took care of everyone, he was a pleasure to work with. Thanks Johnny I gained much knowledge from being around you.

My final rugby story involved a New Zealander who came to my clinic for treatment. He was working as a youth worker and also played rugby. He also became one of the characters in a TV series with Sarah Lancashire that was being filmed in the Huddersfield area. It was the series 'Where The Heart Is'. A few years ago, I re-watched it, I love Sarah Lancashire, especially in 'Happy Valley'. I must admit Arnie Homa played his character wonderfully, he was a rugby player!

Chapter 11: Some Of My Recordings At Nantes Hospital

"We are all faced with a series of great opportunities brilliantly disguised as impossible situations."

- Charles Swindall

I had this strong drive or message to record my experiences I didn't have the choice to be able to write it and maybe in the beginning it was a way of talking to my family and friends if I didn't make it. Between April 2016 and July 2019, I recorded when I felt the need to and never re-listened to my recordings until the end of January 2021 after writing from memory about being in Nantes hospital.

The recordings are raw nothing has been changed so sentences are sometimes not finished or not grammatically correct. When I was talking to the dictaphone I was unaware of a lot of the things that were going on or some of the information that I would later find out. Also, in some of the recordings I was very ill, in a lot of pain and on medication for my injuries. On occasions what I say on my recordings is different from what I have written in 2020-2021. There are a number of reasons for this, firstly my memory was in and out for a long time after the accident and I could only record what I remembered. Also, the mental and psychological battle was only just beginning I was on a journey of darkness, despair, disappointment and sheer frustration with a lot of physical and mental pain.

Some of this recorded information may be repeating and differ from my memory writings but all is important to the journey which I had to travel.

My First Recording: April 2016

Hello, my name in Penelope Walker I am going to record my experiences over the next few weeks and maybe use it to help other people. I will jump about a bit because it's going to be confusing for me enough but first of all I would like to go to the first week when I was in intensive care. Today's date is the actual 20th, it's about 3:05 in the morning on the Tuesday I am not in intensive care now but lying-in trauma.

Here's my story from intensive.

I remember waking up to lights surrounding me and wondering why I couldn't move and where I was. I was very dazed and didn't really understand my situation. Then after, how long I don't know Rob appeared in the room, beloved Rob with a smile but an awkward look on his face. I thought to myself at least Rob's okay but where are the boys? He then informed me that I had been in a car accident which was really quite shocking to me as I take pride in being fair and very none risking and also being courteous and respecting the road. My response "They were pissed they were all over the road". I thought well and never thought no more of it. I asked him "Where's the boys?" he said they were okay I accepted his answer but deep down I didn't believe him because I didn't know I hadn't seen them. Then I believe, this may be right, or this may be wrong, but I do believe he said Robin's here, and I started to remember that our dear friends Robin and Pat were arriving that weekend. I can remember them due to arrive and staying with us and we were looking forward to seeing them. Such a dear couple but they are now not only such a special couple, I even put them in that they are both saints. I think they are angels put on this earth to help people, and they have certainly helped us. (I got very emotional at this point on the recording).

Robin came in with a smiling face and his long hair and it was good to see him. Then if I remember correctly Rob said that Pat Robin's wife and Claire our dear friend also was here so they changed over positions after bits of talk about this that but not much really. I got to see Pat and Claire. It was so good to see them I now think that I must have looked quite a picture because I don't know if my face was black or blue, nobody told me, so I just assumed it was normal. The relief on people's faces when I seemed to be myself. I was myself, the only problem was that I was in so much pain and that I could not remember what had happened. I tried frustratedly to remember for I wanted to know and then I just thought do I really need to know. In this condition do I need to know any details like that, to haunt me, or to just not be pleasant memories. So, I accepted the fact that I would not know and maybe one day I would get to know. I bombarded Rob with questions, and he explained to me that I had been coming to pick up Harvey and Elliott from Claire and Steven who had spent a day at the beach. So, I then realised on what route I was on. I could not remember any of the day I could not remember getting in the car or anything.

Then he did inform me there was another car involved in which an elderly couple were in. I spent a few days pondering and thinking and then I made myself realise it was not good to think. I would never remember it, it's no good I knew in my heart I would never have put anybody's life in danger. I would never have taken risks for the simple reason that years ago I decided that it's better to arrive five minutes late than not to arrive at all. So, I calmed myself and my mind about the situation and accepted it was just one of those things that had happened.

Intensive care I class as intensive, a place that is bubble wrapped. Everything is bubble wrapped, you are bubble wrapped and it's a safe place. I was in an individual room which I think is normal. I found out there were 30 rooms in this particular place and that I was transferred by helicopter to the hospital in the early hours of the 3rd of April. A few days later while talking to my doctor who was so sweet, he was called Louis, I would find out that when I arrived, he said that he had to put me on morphine for ten years I did say did you mean ten days? No ten hours. If I had been there ten years that's a long time. I had a collapsed lung and I had various injuries, open wounds and broken legs and a very bad hand, that they operated on. So, he said I did not know what to do with you, you were in quite a state.

I tried to cheer up and just be normal with people. I remember saying to the doctor whose first name was Louis, every time in came in because he was a night doctor, you have come for me to go to the discothèque, we can dance, and he laughed. I remember him, probably the 3rd of 4th night he came in and said madame Walker you are so sad tonight. I said I am sorry, there is no disco tonight, I am just tired with the pain, mainly of my hand, just tired of the pain.

By this stage I had had some doctors come to me to look at the hand I had no problem looking at my hand I could only describe it as something out of Dr. Who! It had gone all gangrenous, it was black and solid and wouldn't move and the smell was quite horrendous. I had no hesitation in telling the medical staff that it had to go. There was no problem it had to go, I did not think twice about it because my logic was if I am trying to deal with that it's taking too much energy away from my body to deal with the rest of my injuries. Although it's my right hand and it has done so much for me over the years, I had to be logical. So, I accepted it, I am not saying that there weren't going to be dramas later on and I realised the frustrations I was going to have but I could not keep that gangrenous hand and unfortunately it had to go.

All the doctors were in agreement probably relieved that I was not adamant but confident that it needs to go and they said they would organise to remove it. That was fine but it seemed to take ages. I understand I am not the only person in the hospital, but it was like four or five days and the pain was out of this world. It was just so different from the rest of the pain. I classed the pain from the legs and the other places to be sort of repairing and in pain, good pain but this hand was so draining it was sending me really, really, really crazy, the pain was so bad. We had a few moments of yes you are going down at 10 am, yes, you are going down at 8 am and I never went. Yes you are having your operation then didn't.

On the last day I think it was a Friday, so I had been in just under a week arriving in the early hours the Saturday before. I just said I can't take the pain I need this hand to go, I really, really need this doing to allow progress with the rest of my injuries. To give me a chance to recover to give me a chance just to look forward really. Eventually on Sunday they would come to take me down it was a relief.

I wasn't eating I was on drip, after drip connected to wire after wire but the problem was you couldn't drink after late evening when you were due to go on the block as they say in France which is an operation. Many times, I didn't drink and then late afternoon they would tell me it wasn't happening, but at least I could drink. When the time eventually came and they took me down I actually came out of my room, room number 19 and thought oh it's a different world. We had to go downstairs in a lift and we then had to start the process of three doctors explained to me what was going off. I did say to them that I am so glad they are doing it today because if they hadn't have done it today, I was going to go to the butcher's and ask them to chop it off. I think they did get the joke, but one did say we are very professional. I said I know, I don't think you are going to butcher me it means it's time for it to go!

So, they prepared me I had no problems I had no fear they just made me feel so calm. The lady who was the anaesthetist said, "Bonjour I met you last Saturday" I said, "Oh my God, thank you so much for saving my life and giving me my life." She said, "I prefer to see you like this then before." I said, "You know I cannot believe it was a car accident, I have tried and tried to think." She said, "No we gave you something to stop you thinking, to forget that time." I said, "Oh thank you." That's handy I thought and an image of KGB flashed through my mind. I don't know if they can, but I am grateful if they did because I really could not have coped with the flashbacks. She was a lovely, lovely girl and we got to work. The next thing I knew I was in my room but didn't realise I was in my room. I thought they had put me in a garage and I was so distressed that they had put me in a garage. I suppose it's the drugs playing games with your mind and I just cried out not to leave me here, don't leave me here I don't want to be left alone and then suddenly I realised the number 19 on my door. It was a glass sliding door and you could see through it and I thought no I am in my room I am where I should be and that made everything okay.

So that was the block, the first block I had that I was conscious of. I then slowly could feel pain, it wasn't as bad and the smell had gone. Progress had been made I felt at least I could cope and look forward. What the surgeons did do is they took the hand away and grafted my arm into my lower tummy and groin, so it appears as if I have an arm growing out of my groin and what the surgeon wanted to do is for me to keep perfectly still for three weeks. Then it would grow the skin, cut the skin off and cover the end of my arm which was bone. I think he wanted, I don't know how much he wanted to keep but I think he wanted to keep the two bones the ulna and radius so my arm would turn. I have the full length of my arm I think, I don't know how much had to come off the end but obviously they had to get rid of the gangrene, that needed to go!

At the time of this recording, I am in trauma and still weak, they are happy with it, it gives me quite a lot of pain! The phantom hand flying around everywhere or that's how it feels. I think the doctors were happy at this stage.

My experience in intensive care I find intensive. You are given everything intravenously, they slowly start giving you drugs instead but generally you really didn't move. The problem was for me at one stage, I wasn't sure where I was. I wasn't sure if I was in a torture chamber or I don't know, some sort of? It didn't feel at stages that I was being helped because when they kept moving you when you had just got the pain to a comfortable level when they decided they needed to change you or wash you or turn you. I was only allowed to turn onto my left because of my arm. My new hand/arm growing in my groin. But my right leg was so painful, and they always seemed to grab that, in fact I said I needed that to be re x-rayed. My left leg was fine in my opinion, and I am thinking good I have my left leg and then the doctor came around and said you have to go to the block. You need an operation for dislocated metatarsals on your left foot and we need to pin them. Oh what, I thought but at least it's not my big toe where all the pivot comes from.

So, I just waited for them to take me down again and by bon chance (good luck) the lovely lady was there again. She said I am your personal anaesthetist. I said I think you are. She explained things and said I could have half I didn't need to have a full anaesthetic I opted for half the quicker I can get out of my body's disconnect after an operation the better. Before we went down for the block the plastic surgeon came to sort out and dress the hand. He gave me a new dress, he gave me this beautiful tuber grip dress. A little short but beautiful which I said to him thank you have you given me a new dress, is it Chanel? So, the joke continued for many days that I had my Chanel dress and the doctor had got me a Chanel dress.

My concern was people not being aware of my arm while I was on the block, but he said no he would take care of it, and it was better to have the operation now while we are resting this and growing the hand or the skin than to operate after. He said don't worry I will be there and true to his word he was. I saw another guy come into the operation and I thought I recognised him, and it was the specialist. So, as I was under having my pins put into my foot he sorted the arm out, re-dressed it had a good look at it which was amazing really. A good idea to do it all at the same time. So that was okay that went well, my recovery was quicker because I only had half and I didn't feel that dazed. Just lost that's how you feel with all the anaesthetic and gas and everything else that they do to you.

I have ten survival tips for people in intensive care. I will start them, but I have sort of forgotten a bit of the intensive care because of the new experiences I have had in trauma. My main tip was to make sure you kept getting water, bear in mind you cannot move, you have to make sure they have got your table in a position where you can reach it. The nurses and the people who take care of you don't do this on purpose, but some come in to do something, move your table out of the way and you can't get to it.

Although you have a buzzer you can press to call them, I really tried not to use it too often because I thought they were so busy and unless it's really, really essential I didn't buzz. I tried when anybody did come in to ask them if they would fill my glass up and got them to just make sure I could get to my water. Water probably being my 10-commandment number five. I think the first commandment is politeness you have to respect the people, you have got to be polite, you have got to realise what such a hard job they were doing. I am not just saying that I mean it. I have taught my two sons, Harvey and Elliott that they must be polite I think it goes without saying to be polite. So, politeness and respect are the first two commandments. The third is cheerfulness, well as much as you can be when in so much pain. There have been many times, and no one ever knew, in the first week I absolutely cried myself to death well nearly, especially in the dead of the night. Not because of pity, I won't do pity, but because of the pain. I suppose mainly, just the pain but maybe also a reaction to the drugs and sheer frustration to it all. But it was mainly the pain especially when the gangrene was there. I was absolutely frustrated of not having the hand taken off that really got me down, but I tried not to show it a lot of the times but when I had no choice, and the pain was so bad you got really down. It wasn't the staff's fault.

The problem is if you show yourself to be too down you end up with another tablet. A tablet to calm you, a tablet to do this a tablet to do that. I tried to just do it quietly until it got too much then I had no choice they had to see my situation and my depression.

Probably the next commandment would be being aware of your surroundings. I am so fortunate, I still don't know how but I bless the powers that be that they must have put cotton wool around me in the car accident, to not damage my head or my internal organs.

Now in trauma I know the extent of my injuries especially on the right. I smashed all my femur and I have got what I call my dancing pole in, my right ankle has a plate in. My left arm's wrist has been plated the right arm sewn into my groin. I think staying in this position for so long may cause problems in the shoulder and arm later but it's just a matter of spending quite a bit of time working on it. I feel as if I have quite a big haematoma on my right thigh. I massage it daily. The physio has just started to come, I can move it but because it was open wounds, I have many stitches which limits movement. Because of the pressure on the stitching the last thing I wanted to do is open the wound and cause more healing and more options for infection. I am careful I do not push the right leg. I will probably have to add to the commandments as I remember now but at least you have five.

In intensive I was fortunate to have marvellous people. They're all different and they do work in different ways, and I was lucky not to get anybody that was not caring. People have different levels of care. I feel that they must have to have some immunity of other people's pain, it is part of their job. At times when you are really down you think oh no, they don't care about me, they just leave me, it's not that at all it's just they are so busy. So intensive care summary would be it's probably the safest place I have felt. You are cocooned you are bubble wrapped everything is so clean, I did not feel exposed in there.

There was one thing that did really stress me in there when they started giving me antibiotic powder. I had it by drip like all the other medication and then they decided to give me it in powder, the moment I took it it made me so ill, violently ill wanting to vomit. I did vomit just as Pat and Robin entered the room on a visit.

I told the staff I couldn't take it. I said maybe I am allergic. I took it two more times and on the third time I managed to hide some of the powder in my food it may have been liquid, I don't remember but I managed to get rid of some. I then said I can't take any more and they put me back on a drip. It was causing me to be upset which would affect the hand that had just been put into my groin. They didn't want me to have stress.

Another time I remember when I was due to leave ICU, they said I would be moved in the next few hours. This guy who I only saw once was good because he gave me all my drugs at 6am and said we don't want to see you stressed so I will give you your drugs. I thought great bring it on. He also decided to take out my catheter, oh I thought that means progress maybe I can't move out of intensive care unless I have got that out. But I didn't quite work it out how I was going to pee seeing as I couldn't move but I accepted it. Then at the last minute it was decided I wasn't getting moved to plastics but stay where I was. Which wasn't a problem for me I knew the routine I knew what happened, I knew how they treated me, so it wasn't a drama for me to stay a bit longer.

The problem was I couldn't pee. I tried and I got so stressed the pain was so intense in my bladder, I had to buzz them and say it is really difficult. We tried the bedpan, but it was really difficult because of my hand, and I wasn't supposed to be turned very much. I tried but I just couldn't pee! I don't know if it was psychological because I was in a bed. I remember my mum saying to me that I would never wee in the bed as a child I always got outside of my bed and peed on the carpet which meant I ruined the carpet, but I never wet my bed.

The doctor came and ultra-sounded my bladder and said yes, it's really full it needs emptying. Then they assisted me and emptied it and left me with a nappy on which irritated me because it was so hot in those rooms and then by early morning I think, well very soon after they decided to put the catheter back in much to my relief because it was just one thing to not have to think about.

Now the other thing is their obsession with poo. They want you to poo, the fact that you are not moving, you are not eating, you are on lots of drugs especially the pain killing drugs I'll remember it in a minute, the pain killing drug morphine which makes you constipated. I remember at one point a lovely woman she was so thorough, I don't know how she did it because I couldn't see but she said I had a bit of dry poo that was stuck. She persevered and got it, but constipation was obviously a problem (more on that later). But other than that, the toilet seemed to have been taken care of.

The bed bath was fine, and people were respectful, you just got used to being naked. Bed baths were painful at the time but afterwards you felt better for it. Having been freshened up, new bedsheets and whatever else.

Okay I am now going to stop and if I think of anything else I will add it to my intensive care summary. There is one thing I think I probably would remember is that I thought to myself I cannot move, I cannot move so what creature or animal am I like. What can I copy? The one that I came up with was a worm. So, every time I wanted to move or do something I pretended I was just a worm but not just any old worm I was a worm that had been pecked many times by a bird or a chicken. So, I was an injured worm. I was a little pecked earthworm that's how I pictured myself and how I still do now to a certain extent except the dress has been changed. Now I am in a Dior dress (tuber grip) which is a bit transparent, you can see through it but it's still a dress. And some new shoes, casts on my broken legs so ready for anything really. So that's how I visualised myself I had forgotten I was human. I used my eyes and just wriggled my way around which wasn't very far because I am obviously bedridden and accepted that was my limit for now. Right thank you so much I will be back.

38 minutes

Prison Or The Paralympics

Hi, it's me again first of all I need to change the date of my last (first) recording, I said it was about the 20th of April 2016, but I was a few days in front. I think today is the 20th it's about 4:00 in the morning, I am actually feeling for the first time in about six days better. Before I had six days of bad poo!!

35 seconds

I managed to have two sweets just now and a full glass of water without feeling sick or without going to the toilet. It's has been quite a big drama it's not only been going to the toilet it's been Niagara Falls! It is apparently due to my body getting rid of all the drugs which I can understand but they have been giving me so much stuff to move the bowels. I had an x-ray a couple of days ago that showed there was a blockage so it's really dangerous and you do need to keep it moving. If the stomach and the bowels continue as they feel now then I think I am over the worse, but it's been so tiring and so, so depressing, I suppose because you can't eat what they give you to eat.

What they give you to eat is all about bowel movement. This lovely soup that you think you are getting is like dish water, which is basically weak water, it's warm but I am hoping I am past the worse. It's a shame that yesterday I had Jenny and Jude who came to visit and three times they had to leave. Once it was just horrendous it even came up to my dressing on the groin which is where the arm skin is growing. I can really do without that it even went down to the bandages on my legs, but we are hoping, I am hoping that today is going to bring a change it can't continue.

Also, I feel quite positive I may be changing and going to plastics. I feel I need to go there just so they can deal with this hand and maybe towards the end of this week they will cut the skin off the hand, and I can maybe sit up and move more.

It's difficult, it's difficult (big sigh) just having people clean you all the time. It's difficult not being able to just eat really when you know that you have to, but it seems to be normal to them and just a lot of hard work for the girls. So, the obsession of poo is definitely well and truly alive in hospitals. I was trying to think of a way of getting round it, why couldn't they just have an irrigation man come round and clean everybody out and have it done with. But maybe that's my new invention, setting up the irrigation of poo in hospitals!

It was so nice to see Jenny and Jude their smiling faces and, I was lucky that Pat and Robin called in just before. I had no disturbances, no poo arrivals and we could have a good chat for about an hour and a half. They are going up to the ferry at St Malo to go back home. I feel disappointed that I haven't really seen them, but I am sure they need to go back just for a rest. I can't really start to thank them for what they have done, they have just been so unbelievable.

I suppose my next thoughts are, oh my tummy is starting now maybe it's the water or the two sweets? If I cut this short you know why. But I am trying to think of anything else I have missed out about intensive care. I think in intensive it just probably hard to remember because of the condition you are in when you are in there. If I remember things, I will add things. But I am now in trauma. Sorry I spoke too soon I think my stomach is turning over, but I will continue all the same. I am in trauma (yawn) I am so tired I remember leaving intensive and noticing I was out of my safe world (ICU) and into the real world with the bugs, viruses and anything else that lives out there? It wasn't a long journey, and I came into room number 56. Totally different, clean but not clinically clean and I have been here ever since. That was on the Tuesday and on the Wednesday, I went down on the block for my left four metatarsals being pinned fortunately the big toe seems to be good. I am sure I am going to have dramas putting my foot down when they take the pins out. The right leg is still struggling, for two reasons, one, because my groin is growing skin and is above that leg, I don't want to force that and two there is a lot of stitches around the kneecap where they put my dancing pole into the femur. Also, I have got a broken ankle which is pinned and has got a metal plate so that leg will cause no ends of challenges. I am not worried too much but I can't work it too much because I can't push it until all the stitches are out and it heals and see what happens with my groin.

I have a physio now she is lovely she just moves the legs it's a start. I am just hoping I feel better today than I have done for days in the hope that I will be moving and that things are progressing. They are such lovely staff here they do so much hard work. But I need to move on I need to feel I am moving forwards and also so they can really concentrate on my arm. No one seems too worried about my legs or the arm with the plate which was x-rayed a few days ago. I don't know the results of that, but poor thing is having to be used anyway. All in all, things are not bad. If I had recorded this a few days ago, a few hours ago I would have felt differently. When the poo arrives, it makes you feel so bad, so very bad. As long as the colon has no problems, progresses and gets back working then I will be happy. I have to just put up with the horrendous time that I have had and I am still having.

I also will talk about the rest of the week's visitors. Yesterday which was Tuesday, I got Pat and Robin, Jenny and Jude and Monday I got Marc, Harvey, Elliott and Rob. They came mainly to sort out some paperwork and to have a bit of a meeting with the doctor. It was a simple meeting, I think he just wanted me to understand what was going to happen. I did anyway but he runs through the French with an interpreter, alias Harvey to make sure. It was great to see them, Marc and Rob were out a little of the time doing paperwork. The boys seemed good Harvey may have got an apprenticeship at Lion d'Or. He is going for a trial period next week. I think it's good for him that he's got it, if he doesn't like it, he has just got to say. I know it's a good opportunity, but he's got to not feel obliged. He is such a pleasing child and mustn't just take it to please others for it's for two years and two years really hard labour.

Elliott is still his smiling self, obviously doing well glad that mum's not as black and blue as she was. But I did get to know yesterday about his chick, his combatant we managed to hatch. I did tell them on Monday that the chicks were far too young to be outside they needed to be in a box covered up on a night and so I think it's died, there are a couple died now. I think they are struggling working back at the ranch although I don't know how Rob will get on now Pat and Robin are going. He just needs to get a little bit more organised because he is thinking of going back to work if they offer him a contract while I am still in hospital. But that will mean he really needs to be organised with the animals. There is nothing I can do I have to accept whatever happens. But I know I am very upset about the chicks dying because I know I would have never let them die. I am not saying they have let them die I am saying they just don't get how delicate they are at this time of year. It's all good I think I am trying not to stress myself about it.

Pat did tell me that I had to give Rob some slack, but she says it every time she sees me, so I don't know what she means. I am saying that I am not putting him under any pressure at all. I am just a very big doer, homes are very hard work, but I just do it there and then and get it done. Rob tends to just have to think about things just a little bit which is the difference I suppose. It must have been good for him when Robin and Pat arrived. They both look well despite having to be dropped into this big dramatic situation.

They went last night to Pierre Eric's for a galette, and pancakes and I can't believe it, but Robin managed to eat two. It's unheard of, Robin is such a fit guy he does his climbing, and he just has no fat on him, I think they had a nice evening. So that's all real good and I have just told Harvey to ask for help because Rob won't. I have also told Jenny that he won't ask so just be there. Who knows let's see but the main thing is that I have another week here and then in the next few days, hopefully in plastics? Then get the hand sorted out and look forwards and maybe go to Niort for rehabilitation.

Is there anything else I want to add? I am feeling quite uplifted even though it's four in the morning, I think it's just because the tummy is not bad. But I do need to eat some food, let's hope I am praying and asking every angel in the universe to help me get through this! Right, that will be it for now and I will speak of my experiences in intensive no not intensive this place which is orthopaedics / trauma, soon thank you bye!

16 Minutes

These were my first ever recordings in April 2016. I had nobody to talk to, so it felt like I had someone who was listening and understanding how I felt. I didn't know then how long and challenging this journey would be and how cruel my environment would become. Nearly five years later these recordings would offer me an insight to the enormity of the struggles that I just had to endure and get through. Somehow.

Chapter 12: A Funeral, More Formula 1 And Superbikes

"The mysteries of life speak to those who are willing to listen"

- Long Walker

Did I see the event that unfolded on the 31st of August 1997? I was actually in Portugal on holiday with my dear friend Bobby Stocks. Bobby was a long-time friend of my dad's, a mad rugby fan and a mad wonderful personality. We got on so well, Bobby was quite unique, not your average bloke. He drove lorries for a living for Edwards International based on Huddersfield Road Ravensthorpe. Bobby was part of the gang of fellas including my dad who would arrange guys only trips in the 1970s to New York, Florida, Las Vegas and other places. In fact, it's because of one of these trips that dad persuaded my mum that he needed to buy a Dodge people carrier, a big American car. This would allow him to take more passengers at the same time in his taxi business. We ended up with dad getting such a vehicle shipped back to the UK and it lived on our drive. He kept it for quite a number of years and replaced it with the first black London cab in Dewsbury. 'Tank' was a kind of adventurous, risk-taking soul but my mum much less so, she just saw the need to keep a roof over the family's head. The result being that many of dad's pipe dreams never materialised, but we always had a roof over our heads, thanks to mum. Dad would often go with Bobby on his long-distance trips to Europe which allowed him to express some of the adventurous side that bubbled up deep down inside of him.

Bobby often went on holiday on his own and I did go a couple of times with him, once to Rhodes Greece and then the Algarve Portugal. Bobby was loved by everyone an easy-going sort of guy who was happy in his life. But boy could he talk. I have been accused of having the same problem. Only this year 2020 two amazing and caring friends Warren and Davina gave me a Christmas present. A three-metre roll of duct tape re-named mouth tape! Thanks guys I appreciate your wonderful gift, but you are mistaken to think that will stop me!

On the 31st of August 1997, our weeks holiday was coming to an end. I was fast asleep when suddenly I heard this loud bang that woke me up. I thought "Oh no someone has had a really bad crash on these narrow streets." We were staying right in the centre. The next morning at breakfast I asked Bobby if he had heard that car crash last night, "No" he said my reaction "You must have it was so loud." "No, I didn't hear a thing." We went to look up the narrow streets I was convinced it must have been really close because it had been so loud. Nothing not any sign of any crash which confused me. The weather was good, and we went for a walk knowing tomorrow we would be flying back to England. As we walked total strangers were stopping us to tell us that Princess Diana was killed in a car accident. I am sure all who read this and are old enough to remember this day, will do, it did indeed stop the world.

Bobby and I went to sit on the rocks on the beach we were in shock. I said to Bobby "She was killed you know, months ago I saw something was about to happen that would stop the world, but I thought it was going to be an assassination of the American President. What I see now Bobby are crowds of people and flowers, but the most significant flowers are small white roses placed somewhere different." We were both sad and just wanted to go home.

I wasn't a strong royalist, but I didn't mind them, I believed the history books and like so many people accepted them and didn't question the reason why they existed. Diana's death, which from day one I thought suspicious, hit me hard, it wasn't tears but a deep feeling of loss inside me.

I was guided to go to London the need to go being so powerful. I re-arranged my appointments and set off around the 3rd of September. I was very sad on the drive down and a song I associate with the journey is REM's 'Everybody Hurts' which came on the radio. This is now my song from Diana, it's helped me many times especially when my world becomes dark, challenging, scary, painful, lonely and empty. I believe Diana was about to pull the plug on some serious shit that was going on, hence she had to go.

I have to smile at some of the words in this song 'don't throw your hand oh, no don't throw your hand.' I did but it wasn't a boomerang, it didn't come back straight away! This song is so powerful I love it. I believe you are never alone you have always got you never forget that!

I spent three nights sleeping on the Mall. When I arrived, I could choose my spot there weren't many people there, boy did that change. Charities were there on the second day giving out blankets and hot drinks. Even Harrods came and were handing things out, but they weren't as friendly as some of the other people giving out things. Portable toilets were being placed all over and the traffic was stopped. I got myself quite organised with cardboard and a plastic bread tray which I slept on because of course it rained. I went to watch her coffin arrive on the Friday night. People were queuing to sign the book of remembrance, but I didn't sign it. The number of flowers and the perfume they gave off was indescribable. The whole atmosphere was something I will never experience again. There was this powerful, uplifting energy, sadness but peace all at the same time. It felt to be this amazing healthy energy that was also delivering a message to the soul of humanity. Very, very powerful and it also made every single person the same, people in pin-striped suits carrying flowers, no class division. It was a oneness, a wholeness, a kindness and an acceptance that every single person had a right to be there no first class or second class. Just one united class for a moment in time in a divided world.

Also, in the 1990's I would find myself in another paddock. This time it involved two tyres and the likes of Jamie Whitham, a fellow Yorkshireman walking around, with that beautiful Yorkshire accent. Jamie did come to my clinic for a treatment for his lower back. Having felt the weight of a superbike, I just don't know how they moved it so gracefully and took it so low on the track. Anyone who follows the superbikes will know that Jamie missed the 1995 season because he had cancer but was back racing in 1997. Now that's inspiration for anyone, this scary word 'cancer' wasn't going to stop or define him. Jamie had his dreams to fulfil, amazing what a guy!

I didn't go to a lot of the biking racing even though I found the races very exciting. The Paddock (I still didn't see any horses) was like a big family coming together every few weeks. I knew Jeanette and Kevin, Jeanette helped the riders if they needed massage or had an injury, Kevin worked on the bikes, both jobs essential. On one occasion at a race Jeanette asked if I could take a look at one of the riders who had a groin injury. It was a standard joke while I was working with the rugby players that their groin needed a rub, little did they know how extremely painful it was to have a groin injury treated.

In my early days working with Dewsbury rugby team one player was trying to tease, embarrass or test me. He told me he had a bad groin strain (I knew he hadn't) and asked if I could treat his groin, I truthfully and naively answered "You will only come once after a groin treatment" his reply "I'll be happy with that." I quickly learnt that you had to be quick witted and not easily offended, then you became one of the lads. So much so that they often let the door shut in my face, not holding it open for a woman, it's just Penny. That was a sign that I had been allowed into their male world.

I said I had to learn fast and think on my feet and so I did. Another attempt to embarrass me in my early days at Dewsbury was after a training night. I was treating someone, and the other lads were going into the sheep dip, they all got into a long bath that to me looked like a sheep dip. One player decided to have some fun and came waltzing into the area where I was treating players, he had a towel around his waist and a protrusion at the front under his towel. He asked if I had any treatment for this? My reply being I did but the problem was I didn't have my magnifying glass with me so I wouldn't be able to see his problem. All the lads then laughed at him and not me. By the way it was a coat hanger he had under his towel. After that I was part of the gang, respected, we had banter and a genuine band of friendships were made. I thank all the rugby lads whole heartedly for their kindness and acceptance.

Back at the superbikes, this rider was not part of the superbikes, but he had to start the last race to win the overall Artisans category and I think it was the last race of that season. I took a look at him it was bad, the minimum I thought he had done was torn some of his adductors and or abductors muscles at worst he had totally ripped them off the bone. He was in a lot of pain but he was desperate to start the race so he could take the title. I told him and Jeanette that it wasn't looking good and if he could even get on the bike, he risked making his injury far worse. I said the decision laid with the rider, Jeanette and the team but whatever the decision I would help in any way I could.

I did work on his leg to try and relax the whole of his leg reducing as much of the muscle spasm, increasing blood flow and helping him from a psychological aspect because I knew by the rider's face, he was going to start the race whatever it took.

It took a lot! Jeanette and I decided we had to strap the thigh up to give it some support and then somehow get him on his bike. We made it quite clear that he just starts the race, he didn't even have to finish it to win the season, but then he had to promise to go straight to casualty. "Okay I will." Nobody could know about his injury, or he wouldn't have been allowed to race. The garage shutters came down just before the race so he could be literally lifted onto his bike. Once on the bike with his adrenalin and the fact he was not actually weight bearing he was comfortable in a painful sort of a way and stable. We all watched from the track with tension, willingness and prayers. I think everyone of us was on that bike with him.

Once I saw him sat on his bike, I knew he would be okay and after all he promised to stop after completing the first lap. I should have known better from experience, just like Neil Kelly not staying down on the rugby pitch after each tackle with a broken arm, this guy was not going to just do one lap. He finished his race and got his victory once he had been secretly lifted back off his bike. I learnt later that he did end up having an operation, I think it was for a Gilmore groin but not a hundred percent sure.

Gilmore's groin was discovered in the 1980's by the surgeon Gerry Gilmore. I was fortunate to go to a lecture by this surgeon in the 80's organised by the Society of Sports Therapy with a colleague and a dear friend, James Briggs who I knew from the

Northern Institute of Massage in Blackpool who was involved with this society (The founder of this society being Graham Smith). James was a teacher before changing his career to sports therapist and later osteopath, a very knowledgeable man and very academic. James eventually lectured at both the Northern College and the Society of sports therapy. He wrote several books his first one Sports Therapy Theoretical and Practical Thoughts and Considerations, which he kindly gave me a signed copy of. We were both lucky enough to attend this lecture of Gilmore's.

In the early days before James lecturing and book writing took up all his time along with his busy clinic, we would see each other on the courses that we attended. He was sportive, a runner and loved his football. He got an opportunity to go on a tour down-under with a local amateur side from Lancashire a rugby league team. He asked if he could come and watch some of the rugby games that I was working at to gain hands on experience and soak up the general atmosphere. At the time I was at Bramley, and I was happy for him to be there. The rugby tour was successful, and Jim had a great and wonderful experience. The nearest I got to such a trip was being reserve physio for a Barla tour of Fiji. I got to hear later that the tour was difficult because a lot of the team and staff went down with food poisoning. That wouldn't have been a pleasant tour.

I remember Paul Shuttleworth while playing at Dewsbury got a groin injury and I am almost certain he had a Gilmore's groin and he had to have the Gilmore's groin operation. It may well have been Gilmore who operated on him for it was not widely understood or recognised in the late 1980's.

Another attempt to assist one of my patient's injury involved a piece of gym equipment and a journey to Oxford. Remember Rob Tyers, the pump attendant from Formula 1, well it was difficult for him to get consistent treatment on his knee due to his crazy working hours and consistent world travelling. I came up with an idea when Kay and Denbo were investing in a new leg extension machine made by a local lad Martyn Stables. The old machine was up for grabs, and I thought Rob could at least be able to build up his quads and legs to make them stronger and therefore taking some of the pressure off his injured knee. I contacted Rob and he was up for it and I thought and hoped that maybe Martyn would deliver it and set it up for him. Martyn said he would help. He was a F1 fan, but he was the sort of bloke who would have helped anyway. Martyn is a very talented and clever workman, his equipment amazing. (Check out his machines, link is in the appendix).

The date was set and off we went in Martyn's van to Oxfordshire. Rob was grateful and so pleased. He showed us around the Williams workplace and Martyn got to sit in the racing car. He was very happy so much so that 20 odd years later when I went to visit Martyn and his wife Julie at their workplace in Barnsley, the first thing he showed me was the picture on his wall of him sat in the F1 car. Awesome so glad you got that experience Martyn.

In 1997 another adventure occurred. I had caught the Formula 1 bug and wanted to see other racetracks in different locations, which usually meant different countries. The last race of the season was planned to be in Portugal not too far away so I booked a place to stay in Lisbon early on knowing the availability may soon be booked. It was announced later that the track in Portugal was not up to safety regs and so the race was moved to Spain Jerez. I understood the need for safety only a few years before there had been tragedies. It was the year before my first very naive visit to Formula 1, remember I was expecting to see horses in the paddock area! That was at Silverstone 1995. The year before in 1994 at San Marino Grand Prix in Imola Italy an extremely bad weekend unfolded.

The first tragedy was on the 30$^{th of}$ April, not even during the race but during the previous day's qualifying sessions for the race when Roland Ratzenderger was killed. However, the crash Rubens Barrichello had the day before Ratzenderger fatal crash when Dr. Sid Watkins told Barrichello that he lost him and he died for 6 minutes, he was, the next day, thankfully walking around at the Imola track. Probably the most documented death on this weekend was on the 1st of May the day after the tragic loss of Ratzenderger. It was Ayrton Senna crashing into a concrete barrier while he was leading the 1994 San Marino Grand Prix Imola (Schumacher won this race, his first victory in Formula 1). Senna was with the Williams team, Rob's team, he was the pump attendant that would have given Senna's car it's fuel. I didn't meet Rob until the following year, knew nothing about F1 so had no clue that these tragedies had happened. As I got to understand the sport more, I would ask questions, one being about the personalities of some of the drivers. That's the only time I heard Rob mention Ayrton Senna the pain was still raw, but it was obvious that this man was given a lot of respect from Rob and his loss was deeply felt at Williams.

We spend so much time in our lives wasting it, yet it can go within minutes. It seems we put so much of our precious time into negative thinking, fear filled behaviour and ego driven actions at the expense of feeling love of oneself and others, contentment, internal harmony, and peace. We need to break free from these negative time-wasting energies. Talking of these crashes makes me think it's down to some extraordinary force of fate that decides the outcome. Think of John Davies, the Dewsbury rugby player who died in 1969, Ratzenderger, Senna dying but Barrichello was spared at Imola in 1994, Princess Diana, Dodie, Henry Paul but Trevor Rees-Jones spared 1997. Me spared in 2016, what or who makes that decision? If spared, then what task are you then given what missions must you perform and for what purpose. I know if I hadn't had my accident, I probably wouldn't be writing this book!

It would seem the purpose of Ratzenderger and Senna's death was to prevent other deaths on the racing track. The whole safety issues being reviewed and improved. I don't think there are any concrete walls left exposed on the racing tracks any more. It's the same after the Hillsborough disaster, changes were made to prevent the same tragedy happening again. Do tragedies and accidents have to happen in order to highlight, expose and change environments and situations. Do some survive these tragic events to expose, improve and prevent the same mistakes been made to others. Becoming the voice, the word that is the spotlight that must be shone brightly if there is any hope of changes being made.

As I said I booked my accommodation in Portugal early and a refund wasn't possible. I am therefore in Lisbon with my friend Janette and the F1 race is in Spain. Not one to be defeated, it was decided that a few days in Lisbon a nice city, the rooms were already paid for. We could then fly down to the Algarve Faro airport and hire a car, Faro not that far from Seville Spain and drive to get to the racing. I am not sure if it was because of ticket availability or the time it would take us to drive there but getting to the actual race was going to be difficult. So, plan B, okay we can't get to the race so we will just go to the party after the race. I asked Rob to let me know where the party would be and I will try and get some accommodation nearby. The party was at this yacht club and our hotel within walking distance to the place of the party. Great sorted, Rob said he would put us on the guest list wonderful!

There were several famous people staying at the same hotel, I didn't recognise most of them. One person was the actor who played James Bond, Pierce Brosnan. I think most of them must have been to the race. I suppose James Bond, action and fast cars fits in with F1.

We approach the door to the entrance for the F1 party. I gave my name, I was on the list so no problem. The guy said, "You are not on the list", I said "I am Robert Tyers put us on it." "No, you aren't on the list." "Look I have come all this way why would I do that if I didn't think I was on the list and how did I know to come here if I didn't have a contact within the F1." The guy behind said "You can come in as my guest." I said, "No Rob promised to put me on the list I want to see him, he is with the Williams team." The guy then let us in. I found Rob sat down he had damaged his knee again and was in some pain but was happy because their driver Vielleuve had won the race and the championship. After the famous hit by Schumacher and then Schumacher no longer in the race, Vielleuve only had to finish in the top six to win the 1997 title with 22 laps still to go.

Though the Williams car had taken a whack in the left it turned out the battery housing had been smashed and the only thing keeping it in place was the wiring loop that was keeping the car running. Vielleuve said the car felt very strange after that hit which was harder than it appeared on camera. Schumacher was possibly hoping that Vielleuve's car was damaged enough so that it would not finish the race. If it didn't finish the race Schumacher would win the title by one point, the same scenario that happened in the 1994 season at Adelaide Australia.

Vielleuve managed to finish the race and won the 1997 championship. At first there was no investigation, but later Williams were accused of match fixing and went to court. Schumacher accusing Vielleuve as using him as a break and denying any wrongdoing. Instead of Schumacher being dragged before the courts Williams and McLaren were done instead charged with match fixing. It was thrown out of court and the courts felt it essential to investigate lap 48 and the collision. Sixteen days after the race Schumacher was found guilty of trying to intentionally take out another driver of a race and secure a world championship.

It would appear in our world if you have some sort of power or advantage over another and are prepared to bare face lie then you can potentially get away with anything. Until one day the powerless accused person fights back and never gives up until the truth is acknowledged and then the accused person is set free by the lies being exposed.

At the party at Jerez despite his painful knee Rob and his team were in good spirits and were grateful for the result. It was on this occasion I got to hear Damon Hill playing his guitar again. He was playing in front of a group of people as Janette and I walked back to our hotel room.

In between all this travelling I was very busy working and doing my master's degree. I began the course in 1995. At this time, I was halfway through the course and eligible to do the master's degree because I already had a degree (Liverpool) and I also worked in the field (my clinic). Out of 30 odd students only 12 qualified to do the master's which was from Bangor University Wales, the first degree in Acupuncture to be recognised in the UK. An important academic milestone for Traditional Chinese Acupuncture. Around this time 1998 I began a course at Shezen College Manchester with Shulan Tang. Shulan who trained in China was an amazing acupuncturist and herbalist. Her depth of knowledge and wisdom was mind blowing. She was famous for her work with gynaecological problems and since I had decided to do my research paper for my master's on the menopause and HRT, I was grateful to be one of her students. I studied with her from 1998 – 2001.

It's funny but I was advised by Hugh the principal of Northern College of

Acupuncture that maybe I would struggle with the workload of a master's degree. He really meant that I was a bit thick. I had never found academia particularly easy, but I could sense the needs of my patients. I observed a lot, felt a lot and asked questions. The key to getting the right answers is to ask the right questions. For example, if someone was going through separation, just lost a loved one or changing their job, it was all relevant to that person's health and therefore the necessary treatment one decided should be given.

The solution for Hugh's concerns about me was to give me an extra piece of work to show my capabilities. Cheers Hugh! I was already running a busy clinic and a home, still involved with rugby to a certain degree and training although it was not as serious as when I was competing. I decided if I had to do this extra work then I had to make it profitable for me. I decided he can have his extra piece of work, but it would be my introduction to my research paper, therefore starting my master's. Over the course for the master's out of the 12 people able to do it some deferred it for another year the main excuse being they didn't have time! In the end it was down to 8 who finally did the master's degree, I was one of these 8.

It may sound like sheer madness that in the middle of all this that I would take off for a few weeks. I had all the research information collected I just needed to put it all together and present it to my tutor at the start of 1999. In 1998 I set off on my trip. It was October the 27th when I set off to Tokyo Japan.

Chapter 13: Recordings At Nantes Hospital, Food At Last And My Reality

"You don't need someone to complete you, you only need someone to accept you completely."

- Buddha

It's the 21st of April (2016) it's about 8 o'clock at night the girls have been in to do their last arranging of the bed and moving me, shut the shutter and now hopefully, bladder permitting that should be it until morning. Last night was quite difficult for me after I had finished recording. I listened to the radio which Pat and Robin got me yesterday and it was good to have the company. A song came on from R.E.M not sure of its title, 'everyone cries' I can't sing but it goes like this: 'everyone hurts sometimes, everyone cries sometimes' Anyway you don't want any more of that, but I remember listening to it on the radio randomly a few times. The first time I really listened to the words was when I was on my way down the M1 to Princess Diana's funeral. When you listen to the words it's so unbelievable really and it came on my radio last night. It made me quite sad but then in a way it was bizarre all those years ago driving my car after the shock of Diana's car crash and here I am lying in a bed after a car accident as well. The difference I have hopefully got through!! Diana didn't manage it she had too much trauma internally, I think. So, it made me really think.

I must tell you of my experience at that funeral, it's quite entertaining really but I must tell you that a few days before I was on holiday in Portugal. I remember the night of the accident of Diana's been suddenly woke up with a noise of a bad crash. I told my friend Bobby and I asked if he had heard a noise, but he hadn't. I was shocked because it was so loud, so real, I said whoever has been in that accident is not good. We did look around the next day to see if there had been an accident but there was no accident.

People then started telling us even in Portugal of the news of Diana. It was such a shock. What was even more weird is that many months before this funeral people I used to treat asked if I had any messages to pass on to them. One or two used to ask what predictions I had. The only prediction I had was that there would be a death that would stop the world. That would stop everything still. I assumed it was some sort of American president, an assassination but then I realised it was Diana's death because it did really stop the world.

Everyone was in shock, and I remember going down to the funeral. People thought I was crazy, but I just had to go, there was something telling me to go.

I was very ill prepared for sleeping on the streets, but I was one of the first there and I looked for my position. I went to the cathedral and that was probably not a good place and then went back to the bottom of the Mall and settled myself there thinking as they turned, they will need to slow down to go under the archway. I was there for three days. I managed to get a plastic bread container and some cardboard, courtesy of Harrods although Harrods wasn't as courteous when I asked for more cardboard. They said they couldn't possibly give me any more for whatever reason but at least I was off the ground and could keep off the damp.

I got a good position people just kept coming. I remembered on the first day, I must have gone down on a Thursday because I remember the night, they moved the coffin to the house where it would be taken from for the funeral. We all went down to watch. People were talking to each other, and someone said how are you doing, did you sleep last night? I answered I didn't sleep very well at all I have got these two nut cases next to me, she has got a bit of a bad eye and a club foot, but they do nothing but argue all day and night, I got very little sleep they are doing my head in. This guy said I know who they are, it's my mum and dad. Talk about putting your foot in it, but he knew that they were a bit mental. Then I got next to a lady who was telling me all about how her husband died of gonorrhoea, so you got to know all sorts of people.

There were newspaper people from Australia, people getting interviewed and slowly things got settled. Toilets arrived, I remember borrowing a blanket from the Red Cross. A newspaper man, a reporter borrowed it and I said you've got to bring it back because I promised I would take it back, but he never did.

Being there was an absolutely out of this world experience, just the amount of people, just the sombre atmosphere, just the number of flowers and just the smell of those flowers. It must have been a world record of people buying flowers that week. People sort of started arriving and trying to take your spot, you had to be fairly tough. I remember being stood on my plastic bread container and people who had only just arrived and had not slept outside in the cold and wet were complaining to me. I just turned around to them and said "If I was 6 foot 2 would you ask me to chop my legs off? Right no, well pretend I am 6 foot 2 because I am not moving. I have been here three nights in the cold and wet and I am not not going to see anything. So there!" I was right at the front and then the boys came, Diana's sons.

What was also weird as we left Portugal, was that I said to Bobby there is going to be some roses that are going to be really significant. And there they were, a beautiful ring of white roses sent from the two boys to their mother.

Last night I was fairly upset because when you think about it the boys, though they were younger than my boys, when they lost their mum, at least I have got my boys who I will have time with and still be with. My boys may find me difficult at times, but Diana didn't have that, and her poor boys were motherless. That gave me courage (I get upset now) to be blessed that I wasn't dead that I could have some time with Harvey and Elliott and Rob. I was grateful because I think I was so close to not being here. It gave me strength even though it was upsetting. It made me realise that life can go on. Poor Diana didn't have that choice. I still think it was organised, but no one will ever prove that!

It's nice to see her boys have grown up but when I saw them marching down the Mall, there was a tear in everyone's eyes even the police officers. It was such a sombre time and when her brother made a speech, we all clapped and would not stop clapping. All I can say is that experience is one I will never experience again, it was so out of this world.

Anyway, I'm going to talk about today, I have had a bit of a sombre night and feeling sad but grateful at the same time. Most of the nurses are nice one of the friendly nurses came and said was I alright. I wasn't really alright because I think I was hungry, and it was near breakfast time, and I thought they are going to give me all that stuff that they had been giving me and I just know I need food. I don't need constipation powder and pills, soup like dishwater. So, I said to her please, please can I just have some kiwi fruit, just some fruit. She gave me two kiwi fruits and two cracker like biscuits it was a feast, it was so nice. I just knew I needed to eat. It cheered me up a bit because I think I was just getting further and further down from lack of food, proper food. Then at dinner time I had a big plateful of green beans we call them runner beans French call them haricot vert, I let the butter melt over them, wonderful! Also, some kiwi fruit and tonight I had another dish-full of vegetables and a pear. So far, I have had one problem, but it is not liquid, it's getting there I feel. They did offer me (or try to) some more of that powder stuff, but I said please just let me use fruit.

Today the doctor has been I think he is the doctor who I have seen quite a bit who seems to organise people's stay in hospital. He informs me I will be moving tomorrow, thanks goodness it means progress. So, I don't know when the operation will be but at least I am moving tomorrow. I hope I can get the same breakfast without any more stuff for the bowels. I am sure that's what killed me off, I am not used to medication, and they gave me so much. I don't know where it comes from. I think I could have filled an irrigation tanker myself. So, if my idea ever comes off, irrigation of the bowels, they will have to have plenty of room in the tank if mine is anything to go by!

What else am I saying? Right, I still think there are things I have missed from intensive but all I can say about intensive is that it is so hard, it's so intense you are at your worst. You are either going to live or die in intensive. I did see a couple of electronic funeral trolleys go out at the end of my stay. I think I probably can't really remember it while I was going through it, I asked for a lot of help, and I got a lot of people around me. They wouldn't show their faces, but I felt surrounded by people. They would just sit at the side of me or just be around. Amazing really, more often or not I wasn't even in the room. People says it's the drugs, but I honestly think it could be something beyond our comprehension. If you believe in the spirits, angels, God, or anything else. I did ask them to come and take care of me and I think they, on various occasions came and took me for a trip. For I was often in a barn or in a wood or just travelling around with them, not in any sort of crazy way travelling around going places, seeing people. I didn't feel spaced out, I didn't fell drugged up I just felt as if I was being taken places. Out of body experiences I don't know what you call it, but we were off doing things all the time that week and a few days I was in intensive care.

So, this is probably my last night in this room, number 56 in trauma. The girls have been brilliant here, even though there has been just a couple of girls that stressed me a little bit, I think it's amazing what they do. They do long hours and have a lot of mess to clean up which they do so well. I am sort of relieved to be going because it means I am going to the next stage. I am also glad that I have got to this stage because it's a long time to be in this position. A physio comes to me I think we will be alright depending on how my foot and ankle are. Everything is going to be x-rayed again.

The way I feel now unless it changes during the night, is that the food I have eaten today has stayed in my intestines so the vegetables with the fibre will hopefully be helping the intestines to heal. That is such a positive thing. I will probably have not much more to say here except they have been really good. I have been here a week I have been blessed with visitors I will go through them.

First it was Rob, and I am sure he brought Pat, Robin and Claire. Although I threw up the moment Pat and Robin walked in, I think that was the second time they came to ICU. For the distance they have to travel it's so good to have visitors. Then Rob and the boys came which was good. I didn't really know what my face looked like I think it was quite badly bruised, the boys especially Elliott kept saying that I had black eyes. I remember Elliott saying "Wow!!" when he arrived so maybe that meant I was quite black and blue. I suppose I would have to be really. The visit by the boys was good, I think it put their mind at rest because Rob had probably mentioned to them that sometimes people aren't the same after accidents, but it was good to see them, and Marc came too.

Dear, poor Marc he kept having to leave the room I think he got a bit upset but I think he was happy that I was alright. He has seen a lot for he has been a pompier (fireman). Funnily enough so has Robin, he has been in the fire service for many years too.

Then I think the next visitors were Claire, Steven and Lewis and he drew me the most wonderful picture. He kept leaving, it's a bit much in intensive care, it's a lot for a five-year-old or is he six now? I can't remember. I think he is six, he has just gone six in April, it was his birthday. It's quite a big thing for a child to take in as it is for adults. I asked Rob to take all the cards and his picture back home mainly, so they don't get damaged or lost. We had a good chat they are just brilliant people. One day I will chat to them and see what happened at their end because I don't know if it was a matter of life or death. I know Claire and Steven came to the hospital while Rob stayed at home with all the boys. I think he probably wanted it that way because if it was the end, he wanted to tell the boys.

I had a visit from Mel and Sheila, but I can't remember the day. They are good company we had a good chat and they cheered me up. I don't think I had started with the bowel problem then, it may have just started, but we didn't get interrupted. I did tell them that the nurse had just informed me I was growing mushrooms, champignon in the nether regions. I said well they do grow in dark, damp places. It's just probably due to having the catheter and just being in the hot room and in intensive care. The staff don't seem worried, I think it's gone now. The staff did entertain me when they said I was growing mushrooms I thought the image was funny.

It was good to see Mel and Sheila, Mel cancelled her birthday party due to my accident because she was so upset her birthday was on the Saturday after my accident. Mel said she just couldn't have a party which was so sweet of her. I then got a visit from Michelle and Eric they were on their way to pick Audrey up from the airport in London. I was quite ill with poo, and they did have to experience it. They stayed a good while but had to leave to get the ferry. It was nice to see them, I think they told Rob to use their second car whenever he wanted to. Now Rob's got Annie's car so he should be okay.

Who else has visited? The boys, Rob and Marc revisited, and we had a meeting with the doctor and the paperwork sorted out. The boys seemed good because they were on school holidays. Then I had Pat and Robin visit me again they were on the way to the ferry Saint Malo. Then Jenny and Jude, they dropped their daughter (Jude's sister) back off at Nantes airport, such good people, I am blessed, really blessed. I have just got to have the courage to ask for help and not be too independent. Rob needs to ask for help but he won't.

Is there anything else I need to cover here? It's been a week of being fine until the poo arrived. That's been a challenge with so much pain. I am on strong pain killers so the pain must be bad, so hopefully touch wood. I had three lots of food today and it's all calm. I wish they had listened to me first of all. I just wanted food, fruit and vegetables, what I am used to not processed stuff.

Now I am going to try and sleep it's about nine o'clock. I am tired but at the present time I feel quite balanced and okay it's probably because I have had food. We will see what the next stage brings. I will try not to get too emotional about all the people who are helping and have helped. I can't wait to see the boys and Rob again and maybe I will be in a position to give them a hug. The first time I was all wired up, the second time I said don't touch me because of my bowels I wasn't sure if I had something contagious. One day I will be able to give them all a hug. Right, I think that will be it for now if there is anything I remember during the night I'll just add to it. But it is looking like sometime tomorrow I will be on manoeuvres to plastics, progress one hopes! Bye for now.

30 Minutes

Hello, it's me, it's the 22nd of April early morning not a bad night, no problems with the bowel but yesterday morning was quite different. First thing yesterday I had a problem with the bowels, but it's improved in texture, if you like for want of a better description. Very painful and I can't imagine how painful it actually is because I am on so many pain killers. Then it settled down, the girls arrived and gave me my usual fruit and crackers and that was good. The guy who co-ordinates things I don't know if he is a doctor, I see him quite a bit, came to tell me that I was going to get my legs x-rayed that morning, but he didn't know about plastics. I am still in trauma not in plastics, don't know why, probably just availability of beds. So, the morning was quite sad for me.

I got chatting to the young nurse while she was washing me. She had been to Australia and had visited Adelaide the place where we used to live. It was nice to have a chat with her about Australia. As I was waiting for the guy to take me to radio (x-ray) the bowels movement started again with a vengeance. At the same time poor Harvey phoned but she never gave me the phone, so I didn't get to speak to him. The porter had to leave and then I had to wait for another guy to come. But that was it for yesterday which I think was very good compared to previous days of my bowel's activity. For the last two days I have eaten mainly fruit and haricots verts. I have had haricots verts for dinner and tea for two days running which isn't a problem for it's better to eat rather than be given medication.

My medication seems extensive, I get nine tablets on a morning at some point I am going to try and find out what they are for and see if they are all essential. I think having never taken medication before it's a bit rough on my body and it is fighting it. I will see when the time comes if I am able to reduce them.

After going to my x-ray, maybe it was just the trip out of my room, I felt a bit better. Also, as I was on my trip I passed and saw this middle-aged guy sat in his wheelchair and I thought yes, he's probably had an accident too. I am so lucky, I am hoping, (I haven't tried standing up yet) but I can feel my legs except the right, which is a bit numb, but I can feel my legs! I am hoping there is no spine damage. They say there isn't and if so, I am very, very fortunate and grateful.

When I come back to my room I spend the whole of the afternoon, after dinner (my haricots verts), just looking through a magazine that Jenny had brought me, a home magazine. The afternoon went quick, and I am looking forward to seeing the boys, tomorrow. I have asked them to bring me some kiwis and some pineapple. I think if I can eat proper fruit, it may keep things moving. Today I hope to be in higher spirits and hope the bowels behave themselves. This chat is becoming more of a story about bowels but that's what's happening at the moment. It is very, very obsessive in hospitals. I still think they should employ a dyno poo man or woman. It could be called dyno poo or poo's r us? I am sure that there is a place to try and improve the horrendous time people have with diarrhoea. I suppose I really ought to say a little bit about myself.

I have not mentioned it but I am a 52 year old female, a Yorkshire lass born in Dewsbury. At the moment I am a little concerned about Rob, he is doing so much. When the time is right, and we get to catch up I need to check that he is doing fine. Then there's Harvey, just gone 16, he is a lovely boy, turned out to be very tall and very, very kind and gentle. Very polite but that's how I expect them to be. Since the age of 8 he has wanted to do chocolate, in order to do chocolate, you must do boulangerie and patisserie. He has had a few work experiences but one he went to really put him off. So, he said he is thinking he doesn't want to do it and would rather do cooking. I said that's fine and to go and get an apprenticeship.

Then there is Elliott absolute live wire such a card, such a character he is now 13 he has a love for the outdoors loves all the animals and we are showing bantam chickens. He has a great personality he is a good kid. He finds school a bit of a challenge and he would rather be at home and then so would Harvey, but he doesn't complain so much, but it is difficult being in French school.

I hope today is straightforward, I haven't a clue if I am moving. Looking forward to seeing my visitors and hope the bowels behave themselves. I will try and think of something more interesting to say next time. Maybe what I have done in my life and what my poor right hand has given me all its life. Thank you.

17 Minutes

Hello, it's Saturday morning about 3am, date 23rd of 24th, I am not sure? I am still in trauma just had to get the girls in to bring me a bassin (bedpan) for the bowels but at least there seems a pattern now because for three days it's been early morning. I have managed to get enough notice to get the bedpan which makes life so much easier. Yesterday I did quite well I ate what they gave me I even had black pudding. Knowing what it's made from having pigs I was a bit sad to think what I was eating, black pudding that has come from intensive farming. I always find it difficult when the pig trucks or any of the animal trucks come past.

Our pigs are traditional rare breeds. We have Buster the Berkshire pig, a beautiful boy a gentle giant really, except when food is around. Then we have two Old Spot pigs, Myrtle May and Dolly. Myrtle May can't get pregnant. Dolly has had one litter, just three, but they were beauties. I think with my condition now Rob made a decision that the pigs have got to go. Buster has been put up for sale because he is such a good breed and it's a shame for him not to carry on breeding. Myrtle-May because she is infertile will go. Some friends, Lorraine and David, came over to help Rob decide and to help sell Buster. I am hoping by the time Dolly is due in three months, three weeks and three days that she gives birth when I am back at home. I am hopeful, depending on mobility to be there for her when she is giving birth. She is a lovely pig and I think she understands and likes me to be around.

Yesterday I was fairly good (wincing in pain) sorry my hands just hurting "oh, oh, oh pain" (then a few seconds of silence) I got told by the plastic surgeon who came to look at my hand and he informed me it would be a week on Monday when he does the operation. I will be in here (trauma) another week. It's not a problem, I just don't think about it.

I got good news when Rob came to see me yesterday for more paperwork to be handed in. He told me that tomorrow, which is today now, that Mel and Sheila are coming to visit. (Pause pain) Wow! God this hand. Also, another Rob, electrician Rob was going to visit. Which means this weekend I have something to look forward to and then it will be Monday another week and then it will be operation time. The only problem is on that day of the operation, probably the 2nd of May 2016 my parents come for a visit on the 1st of May.

Although Rob has told them I have had a car accident, he hasn't told them the extent of my injuries and he hasn't told them I have lost my right hand. Mainly because it's no good worrying them, they are elderly and it's a difficult thing to say over the phone. So, I don't know when they are going to visit. Tuesday is maybe a good day, but Rob's back at work next week, so maybe he can ask for half a day off on Wednesday possibly? It's going to be difficult, but my parents will want to visit me. I am sure everything will be sorted.

Yesterday was not too bad I am just really waiting for instructions. Rob brought me some more kiwi, I just need to keep eating fruit and veg, and get some fibre and not having any more medicine for my stomach. I honestly think it will never be the same again. I am in so much pain when I have to go to the toilet and that's with all these pain killers. I think all the drugs I had to have to save me has stripped the lining of my intestines or made it really raw. So hopefully with time and good food it will right itself. It seems a bit crazy that all I seem to talk about is poo but there are certain stages to this world I find myself in.

You have intensive (ICU) which is all about pain and recovery and just getting through whatever. The next chapter seems to be the poo stage/chapter, just trying to get yourself back on track. The body rejecting all the poisons needed to be given to you to keep you alive. Probably with being laid for so long, not moving, not really eating, the whole system has to kick start again. I am hopefully out of the poo phase and going forwards to the possible rehabilitation phase. The only thing is that I know of two more operations coming, one for the hand which will be a full anaesthetic which always sends me a bit crazy. The other one for the pins in my left metatarsals which I hope will just be half of an anaesthetic which is much easier. So, there we have it.

I was going to discuss a tribute to my right hand, what it has done for me, I will start and see how far I will get.

I suppose you can say you are born with it, it helps you walk, helps you eat, it helps you do all sorts. It helps you write at school being right-handed. So, it did all these things, gave me so much pleasure as a child playing with toys and loving my pets. (Groan now it's my legs that are hurting) But my right hand has done far more than that. After school I did all my 'A' levels with my right hand in the 1980's, when you wrote everything, when there were no computers, everything had to be written. So, the hand got plenty of work. I went on to do my 'A' levels in history, sociology and did a general study paper passed them all and that was a lot of writing. At the same time, I went to a gym and that became a lifelong love of working out.

My hands have done plenty of weightlifting I even went into competing. I got as far as the British finals in Harrogate. So, my right hand has done much work and much lifting besides all my writing. I am trying to work out a plan later where I can somehow strap a dumbbell to this right arm so I can carry on training with weights. Though I have got weights at home, with all the animals and work with them plus everything else in the house, my training was very scatty and not regular. I am really going to be starting from the beginning again, having seen the condition of my body, everything has gone, muscle, mobility and strength. The skin is hanging off me, the muscle gone but I do try and do some work while I am in here. I use my water bottle as my dumbbell, and I at least try and keep my left arm, shoulder, triceps and bicep going. Hopefully when this other arm, my right arm has calmed down and been cut out of my groin, I will be able to at least move and lift it and get that going. But I need time, patience, patience and more patience.

I then went on to do a degree at Liverpool University it was a Physical Education and Psychology degree, again much writing especially in lectures. I then went on to start a physio course and I also did a course at the Northern Institute of massage and really enjoyed it, again lots of writing. I spent many years working with professional rugby league players. I worked at Dewsbury, Keighley and Bramley. I set up my clinic and was very busy. So, this right hand which I favoured in the treatments has given much pain out but has also saved a lot of discomfort and saved a lot of people's sporting careers for want of a better description. I didn't finish my work until 2008 when we moved to France.

My right hand also helped me with my love of gardening. I had an allotment and I fondly remember Mr and Mrs Heppinstall who had the allotment before me. They lived in a one up and one down with this allotment just at the back ironically their street was called Walker Street. It was a wonderful allotment, he even had an air raid shelter still there from the war. Also, a greenhouse with an ancient grape vine running through it, the roots outside the old greenhouse. I got to know Mr. Heppinstall and treated him because he had really bad knees, he was a blacksmith all his working life. He was involved in inventing the shutter on the submarines during the Second World War a very clever man. His television was always turned away. One day I said, "You don't watch TV?" In his good strong Yorkshire accent, he said "Nay lass I don't watch that because there will come a day when I am forced to watch it. Why would I want to watch other people do stuff when I can do it? One day I won't be able to do it and then I will then be forced to sit in front of that thing." He went on to say, "I only watch animal programmes the rest is no good." I remember saying to him how correct he was. We have become a nation of TV and computers while at the same time we miss out on life. We miss out on doing things it's bad because I think we have created a generation of people that just sit and don't do things, don't create things. I think I am lucky because my two, Harvey and Elliott seem to be busy doing things with interests inside and outside the house. I think it's a good healthy balance to be in.

I took Mr. Heppinstall's advice and have always tried to be active and to do things. There is a pleasure of being in a garden, I am already wondering how I can fasten a garden fork onto my right arm.

My right hand has done quite a bit, I thank my right hand for all it did, and gave to me. It has healed many people, it has helped many people, and it's been a close friend of mine, which I will sadly miss. So, thank you, right hand, God bless you. That's the story of the hand and I am sure I have missed loads out. I will leave it for now I don't want everybody to be bored. I hope today it's straight forward with no dramas thank you.

27 Minutes

Hi, it's Sunday evening I think it's the 23rd of April or maybe the 24th. The weekend has gone I wasn't really looking forward to the weekend, but it's passed fairly well, and I had lots of visitors. I am sort of fairly cosy, I am sat in the bed I have been sat in for over a week. When I was in intensive care they lifted me into a different bed, much to my horror, when they were going to move me. But they did it so professionally I didn't feel anything. So, this is my second bed I have had while I have been here. It's been decided now the following Monday, not tomorrow I will be having the operation for the hand I hope it is! That means another week of being still, which is difficult but what can one do? I am actually growing the skin from my groin, to cover the end of my right arm. The only problem is my right leg is quite sore, although they have taken the stitches out of my knee, it's a bit raw and has a funny feeling. Every day, twice a day I massage my legs. I feel I have quite a big haematoma, but I have reduced that quite a bit. I am gentle with my leg for two reasons. I don't want to disturb my groin which has the arm skin growing in it and also, I want to just protect it and be cautious. Massage and slight movement is all I am doing at the moment.

The left leg is fairly mobile I massage that it feels good to try and tense the muscles up. I still have pins in the four left metatarsals not sure what's happening or how long they will stay in, but it will probably be another operation to take them out. I have just done my exercises with my water bottle for my left arm, shoulder, triceps and bicep, trying to keep them strong. It's amazing that the body and muscle has just withered away in a relatively short time. Though I didn't train very regularly I did have some muscle but that has just gone. But then I haven't been moving or lifting or doing anything. I am slowly trying to get everything going, it's important to do a little bit so things don't get too stiff even if it's just tensing the muscle.

Talking about medical issues, the poo is still arriving early mornings which I am pleased about. It is quite painful, but it seems to be once or twice in the mornings and then it stays away (except for some gas), until the next morning. That's fine I can deal with that though it's difficult being on the bedpan with the state of my legs and the sewn in arm. I think at least I can deal with it and they are not on my case about going to the toilet with this obsession they have of pooing. I am eating as much as I can of what they give me especially if it's vegetables.

I had my first bit of meat today, I felt my stomach was ready for that. I have also been blessed with gifts from people who have been. The people that have been included Rob on Friday on his own because the boys had gone to the beach with Jenny and Jude. They have gone to an island just off from here it's supposed to be beautiful. It's got a beach and little pools to look for fish. Harvey's gone too so I am hoping they had a good time. Rob is going to go back to theirs for a curry so that's really nice for them. When he is here, because of the distance he has always got to get back for the animals. But he brought some more paperwork. The hospital needed my wage slips from when I worked at the Bonne Vie.

The Bonne Vie were not very helpful but Carol and Carl are not the most cooperative of people. I lasted at the restaurant for two months. So many people I know have had issues with them. It's sad really because I don't know why they are like this, but they are! We eventually got the wage slips because Sheila just decided she would chase them up. Good Sheila, even though she worked there and had issues with them too.

My visitors on Saturday, first Mel and Sheila came to visit again so we had a good laugh they brought me bits and bobs some biscuits. We had a good time and we chatted. I try not to, but its inevitable people ask how you are. I try not to talk about what's going off but fortunately now the poo saga is coming to a slow end (I hope it doesn't stop totally because then I will be in trouble again) we didn't get disturbed. Then to my surprise Chris and Marie came which was brilliant. I know they work such long hours and they have given up their Saturday to come over and visit me.

It was nice to see them, Marie being a nurse I think she understood the situation. They brought me lots of tins of pineapple, yum, yum! I have a tin of pineapple on a morning they also brought me some individual chocolate cakes which are in my drawer. I didn't fancy them but each day I am getting more and more to fancy them. Whoever comes to visit can have one, the boys can have one and I might even get to the point of wanting them. It was good to see them we had a long chat and then they left.

Then on Sunday, today Robert the electrician came a lovely, lovely person. His wife had gone to the airport, so Kim didn't come. Being an ex-policeman in the UK he explained things and that I will have to be interviewed about the accident. They have already interviewed Rob. I thought it was a little bit unfair what they did to him. It was good to get Robert the electrician's explanation and experience and just to chat. We chatted about so many different things. It was good he was here to give me his informed opinion, but it was also good that he had so much time to chat. He stayed quite a while and I always feel a little bad when they stay quite a while because the journey is long, and people have things to do. He brought me some grapes and some wonderful porridge fruit bars which I am sure will be great for my digestion. Not a bad weekend for me.

Monday, tomorrow I am just going to do the week and do it as calmly and carefully as I can and not stress about it. Before I know it it will then be the operation, then the next stage, maybe it's sitting up, maybe moving my arm, who knows. Is there anything else to add? No not really. I think I mentioned feeling like a pecked worm in a Chanel dress. I have actually got a new dress now, they cut the Dior one up and it's gone in the bin. Hopefully this tape works because it got dropped and all the pictures at the front are not working. So, I will say bye for now.

11 Minutes

Hi, I think it's now the 25th of April it's a Monday evening about nine o'clock I have finished reading and now need to go to sleep. The evenings are always really difficult it's just you want to be home with the family, but I am trying to be strong. Today has been pleasant, usual breakfast my tin of pineapple with some crackers and then not long after that you get someone coming to wash and clean you and then there is the re-dressing of your injuries. The arm needed to be looked at and dressed. Some stitches in my leg needed to come out which was a bit painful, then the legs re-dressed.

I was lucky today for a lady came to give me a facial and a manicure, be it only on my one hand, it was good it passed an hour. I was very lucky and grateful.

The orthopaedic doctor is back off his holiday, he had a very quick visit to see me which was good. The physio has been and said the right leg the femur is quite shattered. So, for two reasons I am not pushing it too much. She did work it a little bit but told me not to do too much with it. One because of the arm and the groin and two because it needs three months to repair. That was that, then it's usually dinner time, then the cleaner came, then the lady with books, then a lady from the hospital, so it was busy. Then they say 'bonne nuit' (good night) pull the shutters down and that's when it gets difficult. But Monday is done now I have just got to get to sleep, I have just got this week to go before the operation. I don't really want to go and have another operation, but I know it will mean progress.

I was thinking and maybe I have already said this about blood as I had to have a blood transfusion. Am I now French? Because I had a lot of blood and apparently here but not sure, if you are English, you cannot give blood because of the foot and mouth disease but I may have that wrong, so I assume I just got blood from French blood donors. So, I got myself thinking of whose blood have I got. At first, I thought it would be just one person's blood but Rob the electrician said they mix it all together and then bag it up. So, I have probably got a mixture of blood. I amused myself by thinking what if I have an insomniac's blood what if blood has the characteristics of that person. What if I have some from someone who was an alcoholic what if I got some from, I don't know there could be multiple possibilities. I found it amusing, if blood has personalities, then I could have a different personality now, because I have got different blood. But that's just me with my vivid imagination. I am disappointed that I can't give blood because others gave theirs to me.

While in ICU, the nice doctor on nights, when he came to visit me said that he didn't know what to do with me, he just put me on morphine for ten years, when he really meant ten hours. He said to me which I found quite interesting. He said, "You had a star looking over you that night." I found that quite amazing because that's how I felt, something must have happened to protect me. I never felt I went down a white tunnel or saw it. I never could remember any of the accident, but I feel really, really sure that somehow, something be it my injuries quite severe, somehow protected me. My head, my vital organs, my back, it's as if they could cradle me. I feel as if something watched over me. I still don't ask the question why I suppose my natural curiosity says why, but I am not really bothered about why I was in an accident, I just was!

I just want the strength from the powers that be, God, angels, anybody to just get through it. To not break down in front of the kids or Rob and to just be as strong as I can be. There are emotions but is that self-pity? I don't know. I just need to get through this week as cheerfully and as strong as I can then that will bring me to the next phase.

So, there is not much more I want to say except it's difficult, but I am sure it's all going to be okay. Tomorrow is another day I must force myself to wake up happy and well. I send all my love to everyone, and I also wish and pray that everything is taken care of, and the boys are happy, and Rob is not too over stressed. He goes back to work tomorrow so I think in a weird way it will do his mind good. I am just sad that I am here for a while, but they are back at school, maybe I will see them at the weekend. Going to try and get some sleep and continue to be positive and by the way I dropped this again today (dicta-phone) so I am hoping it is still working. Bye.

8 Minutes

Hi, it's Wednesday teatime I thought I would speak now because it is fairly quiet, and I don't think anyone will visit. I have just had the nurse with the bedpan, and I have managed to have the poo. I was terrified I wasn't going to have one because I do not want them to think I have got constipation and give me all those medicines again, which drove my stomach insane. I am pleased, no matter what it is at some point each day, that I have at least some sort of movement just to keep them off my case.

It's been a fairly good few days I am glad we are now on Wednesday evening. The evenings are quite difficult, I do sometimes get a little upset, but I try not to. It's just not being at home really. It's the little things, sitting in front of the fire. Brewing the pot of tea for Elliott, me, and Rob to have, Harvey doesn't drink tea. Dipping your biscuits in your tea watching the television, although we don't have television, we just have DVDs which I think is amazing no advertisements. Rob moans about the sport but for nearly two and a half years now we have not had TV and we just watched DVDs. The kids have never complained once.

It is amazing how draining the television is, you automatically put it on then if someone's got the controls they flick and flick through all the channels, which is most irritating. If you actually watch something it stops and starts with advertisements and then inevitably you get the news which is sad to say but I really don't want to know anymore. It doesn't depress me, but I take it on board. If there has been a disaster, I feel sorry for all the people involved and I question why there are all these attacks and wars and everything else. To be honest I think a lot of people would be much happier if they didn't have a telly. What we do is that we pick the series we want to watch. The only danger with that is you end up watching another one and another and it becomes late, but it does mean you can't be bombarded with all the things that are going on in the world. I just need to concentrate on my own little world and my own surrounding people and family and just try and make that a pleasant place to be. I think it's healthier, I am convinced it is healthier.

I had all the doctors except the plastic surgeon visit me. I think it's still on for Monday which is good because it's four days away. The orthopaedic surgeon said that it is possible that my right leg in the ankle area, where the nerve was crushed, is possibly not good but he is not sure. But he also told me on Monday they will take a pin or metal out of my left hand and take the four metatarsals out of my left foot. I am glad about this because it means there is less anaesthetic. So, although it will be sore, I'm glad of the operation, but like any operation I have some reservations, but I am under the hands of good doctors. It's just when I am coming out, I always feel a bit lost and upset when I have a full anaesthetic. I am not sure, and I know everyone will take care of me and hopefully that will be the last operation, although the doctor did say the plate in my left hand would have to come out after a year. Anyway, I will try and stay positive.

This week has been difficult just because of being here but I am more than halfway through, progress hopefully as soon as they can get this hand, I mean arm from my groin. I am sure I will be able to start moving more or maybe even sit in a chair. I know I can't weight bare for another two or more months but at least I may be able to sit up. The other thing I was going to mention is how difficult it is being in one spot not moving. But I am reading and at the moment I am reading two books that Jenny gave me. I also have Bob Flowerdew's organic gardening book that Rob, and Kim brought for me. Plus, Mel's book, a book on positive thinking.

Chris and Marie got me some tins of pineapple so each morning I have a tin. Don't know why I am craving pineapple there must be something in it I am wanting. The surgeon says I need to put more fat on I try and eat especially vegetables I know I need to eat. They don't understand I don't really ever eat big amounts even when I am active.

The night shift doesn't come in anymore because my bowels have settled so I hardly see them. Though they do disturb me twice, now I have taken to pretending that I am asleep. They read my urine or whatever they do and then they leave me. Then they always come and check me and say goodbye in the morning which is usually about 6am. It's turned quite cold so at the moment I have got two blankets on, I can't get my upper body warm. That's because I have not got my thermal vest on anymore.

Then not long after that someone comes and washes you and more often than not a nurse comes at the same time to do the dressings. By the time all that's happened, and they have changed your sheets and move you up the bed which feels wonderful, it's round about 11:00, so I either read or sleep. Then it's dinner time. Now it's about 5 o'clock so before too long it will be food again. As daft as it sounds you actually look forward to the food because it just passes some time on and gives you something to do. I am hoping and praying for another night of sleep and peace no upsets even though it is upsetting not to be with the family. I am trying to be strong that's all you can be and just knock another day off so it will soon be Monday. Bye for now.

9 Minutes

Well, it is now Friday evening, this recording may (hopefully it won't be) full of self-pity I have had a difficult week just trying to get to the end of a week. It's been (and on Monday it will be a month now), and I have not moved. I have not been able to sit up or anything. So, I am finding it quite difficult. I suppose the most difficult thing is on an evening not being with the family and I haven't seen them all week due to school and work. I just hope they can find time to come Saturday. I know they can't come Sunday because they have to go to the airport to pick my mum and dad up. So, I don't know what to say really except I have got to keep strong I haven't got to weaken. I daren't show the nurse or the staff any sort of emotional breakdown, because no doubt they will end up giving me some antidepressants which I don't want.

This morning to my horror the nurse brought me some more laxatives, the petroleum jelly stuff and the powder, four lots!! I went "Whooo what's that for?" I said, "No I have had a poo, I've had a poo for the last four days regularly." The nurse said, "Oh the nurse didn't put it down." I thought "Oh no don't start me on that one again. I am three days away from having my operation if I start with all that pooing stuff again it will be a nightmare!"

So even though I am not really hungry I am eating every veg they give me and fruit. Unfortunately, my water, my bottled water ran out, so I am on their tap water which I do believe irritates my stomach, I am drinking it but not too much. I hope they bring me some when they visit.

It's just been such a difficult time and I am trying to stay positive. I thought I would just talk about something and cheer myself up. I suppose I am just tired and need to get the operation over and done with and see where I am after that. I am not under any illusion but if I can just sit up and move and stop any bed sores developing on my bottom that will be a plus.

I know the leg is going to take a long time but if I can just move forwards with the arm. It makes you really appreciate freedom. You also appreciate that so many people must be lonely, be it in their own homes, be it in a care home, be it an illness. It's very frustrating to have no control of what you do and it's just something that we will probably all experience at some time.

My observation is to spend the next 20 years being as active and as lively as possible. There comes a point when you can't be active and that's going to be difficult. On a cheery note, I have got this dam leg to get right, which is going to be a challenge because it doesn't look so good, but we will see. Stay positive stay calm and try not to get upset about things that you are missing. I think that's all really. So over and out.

5 Minutes

This recording is a song that Elliott composed for me and sang it to me. Beautiful thank you Elliott.

"I'm sailing the seas to find my lassie

sailing the seas to find my lass

I am looking for her everywhere until I see her there.

I'm sailing the seas to find me bairn

I'm sailing the seas to find me bairn

I'm looking for him everywhere until I see his teddy bear."

Elliott after the song said to me "That's the end".

27 Seconds (Elliott)

Chapter 14: Around The World Trip

"Start by doing what is necessary, then do what's possible, and suddenly you are doing the impossible."

-Francis of Assisi

I had booked my first night in a hotel in Tokyo heading off to another part of Japan the next day. I began to try and ask for directions it was very complicated, so I decided to not sleep at the hotel but continue my journey. The kind lady gave me some instructions in Japanese on a piece of paper and that's what I used to get my train tickets. I had 3 trains to try and catch. The trains were so organised, and you had to be quick to get on it before the doors shut and you were left standing on the platform. I really didn't have a clue if I was getting the correct train. In fact, on the second train, I had the whole carriage discussing my trip in Japanese. Some said I was going in the wrong direction and others said I was going in the right direction. With jet lag setting in and hanging on to my only source of food, a tuna sandwich, I resorted to praying. Someone must have listened because I did get to my final train the Bullet train which would take me to Suzuka.

This train I believe is the fastest in the world or it was in 1998, what an experience! I was so tired but didn't want to fall asleep for fear of missing my stop. The train was very comfortable and so clean. It wasn't packed but being a people watcher, I watched the ones that were on the train and noticed they were wearing feet gloves which I had never seen before. The men wore shoes a bit like flip flops or thongs and their socks had a place for every toe. It intrigued me I thought it was a good idea.

I was so jet lagged so my first day at Suzuka was sleeping but then on the Friday morning it was down to the racing track. If you haven't guessed, it by now I was at the final race of the F1 1998 season a very interesting race.

There is so much hard work that goes on behind the scenes by the team and in the 3 days I spent in the Williams garage I saw the good, the bad and the ugly. The guys were so down to earth in a very plastic sort of world, but this plastic sort of world was only evident on race day. There was a comradeship, a respect for each other and the guys had a common goal. Every single team member working so hard knowing the importance and obsessive need for perfection, double and even triple checking some things. The intensity and stress were extremely high, but it was all sprinkled with good humour and taking the piss out of each other.

Although Friday was a long hard day for these guys I got to know and observe their characters in a true atmosphere because the glitz and glamour that is part of F1 would not arrive until tomorrow when the qualification times were done. I saw a lot of the same things in this hard-working team as I had done in the rugby and football teams I worked with. They were good at their job, at the top of their game and no room for egos. The Williams team were a good bunch of lads.

The Friday involved a lot of testing and weighing. Yes, the cars have to be weighed. Every time a car went out of the garage, they would cover it. I jokingly asked if it was to keep it warm. No, it's so that photos can't be taken and other teams copying their cars. Right, it really is a very cutthroat industry, spies are in the mist and security is essential. Security was high, they even have someone watching over the tyres. Their driver was still Villeneuve, he was around on the Friday but more so on the Saturday.

Another important job and essential is feeding everyone. For this team the responsibility was down to a guy named Paul. Paul the chef was probably the nicest guy that Rob introduced me to, again he worked so hard with his team. Throughout the weekend I try and stay in the background but on the Saturday, I found myself eating breakfast with Villeneuve, there was only us two eating the lads having eaten earlier and back to work. Believe it or not I felt uncomfortable. God knows why he is only another human being and probably a really nice guy, but the media builds these people up to be some sort of superstar when in reality they have to be grounded and down to earth to get on with their lives. It's the law of Karma. I think because his physio came in fussing over him, I left, I would have loved a chat with him about how he mentally prepares himself. Throughout the day his physio was like a mother hen fussing and I am thinking if I was looking after him, he would have to get his own bloody water bottle. I may be being unfair to the physio maybe he was expected to act like that but F1 job or no F1 job I wouldn't be wiping their arse. The physio just appeared too in awe of the whole situation not my style. I would have been more likely to have done my job but taken the piss out of him as well.

The big day, Sunday the 1st of November 1998 Suzuka. Schumacher was in pole position but even the start of the race was filled with drama. First Jarno Trulli stalled on the grid forcing an aborted start I don't think he went to the back of the grid. Then Schumacher did the same on the grid leaving himself with the task of fighting his way from the back to the front if he had any hope of taking the world championship. Call me a bit paranoid but when I have been involved with a race, I have never seen Schumacher finish a race! This one Suzuka 1998, Jerez 1997 and Silverstone 1995, how bizarre! In this race at Suzuka Schumacher's tyres fell off and Hakkinen won the world championship for the first time.

Now it must be noted that Williams was the top team at this time and so they had the first garage which was next door to the winner's enclosure. I was very close to it watching the top three drivers come into the enclosure. Michael Schumacher had to ask me to move so he could get into the winner's enclosure to shake Hakkinen's hand. Then the lucky guy had to squeeze past me again when he left the enclosure. Bet he never forgot meeting me!

The work starts all over again, packing everything up but before that the Williams team had planned a little surprise. Now this is the bits you won't get to see on the TV with Murry Walker's (no relation) commentary, but another commentator named Walker, me! Murry had come into the garage over the weekend and just stared at me and he probably wondered who the hell I was and why I was in the garage. The commentary by Penny Walker:

"Okay and they're off, the Williams team have captured the four deserters they have them in position ready to 'lap' the tape around them. In first position the technical guy who is going to work for Ferrari next season, second position is Gary could this help to stop him moaning. Coming up at the rear in third and fourth two other Williams team members taking it all in their stride. Now the action begins, first they swiftly and expertly cover the four in leftover food, nice, then it's a quick shift of gear as the four are sprayed with foam and finally in the last circuit the water hose. What a fantastic event its a photo finish to see who got the most crap thrown over them. I feel it may be Gary who just manages to get the title. Well, done you have worked hard for this victory, congratulations Gaz, your moaning paid off!"

I better explain this event. This race was the last of the season and four people were leaving the Williams team to join different teams. It is a tradition, I think to capture those leaving and give them a leaving present which involves covering them in food and spraying them with foam and water. It's a token of love from the team mates they are leaving behind. What a beautiful and extremely funny, for those not tied up, race to watch.

After all the jobs were done and the cars covered up and put to bed the hard-working team could let their hair down and go for a beer or two. As we were in Japan the country of karaoke that had to be done too. Where the after-race party was they had small karaoke rooms where groups of people could go to sing. I found myself in a booth with the two Schumacher's singing 'My Way'. But to be honest nobody can sing that song better than Elvis did in June 1977 his final concert, dying shortly afterwards. When I learnt of his death, I stayed in my bedroom for days playing my Elvis records I was devastated. He died at the age of 42 on the 16th of August 1977 just two months after singing this song. Did he already know that the end was near and facing his final curtain? His music got me through some of my darkest times after my accident. He never fails to heal, I believe he was sent to guide this troubled world. Princess Diana was sent for the same reason.

I was lucky enough to be sent a negative of a photo taken of Elvis by a freelance photographer in America. I had a Saturday job at the Mermaid Fish shop restaurant in Dewsbury which was owned by Norman Lodge. The freelance photographer was his brother who lived in Florida. We went to visit him when we went to America in the 1980's on our family holiday. He must have remembered I was an Elvis fan and sent me the negative, thanks Frank.

Chapter 15: Recordings At Nantes Hospital, Birthing Stubby And I Move To Plastics

"We are not humans on a spiritual journey. We are spiritual beings on a human journey."

-Stephen Covey

It's now the Sunday night before my operation for my hand. So, it's probably the 1st of May. It's come fairly quickly though I did struggle mid-week for a time, feeling a bit sorry for myself and a bit lonely. Now I have just got to get a good night's sleep then tomorrow morning, I am hoping, it's morning when I go for the operation.

This weekend has been good Mel and Sheila came yesterday they are always good fun. I think we spent the first thirty minutes talking about farting. Don't know why probably I started that conversation. It's good that they are jolly, and I can't believe they have come every week. It's good they really do cheer me up.

Then today I have been lucky because Rob and the boys came, they always make me feel better even though sometimes I get information about the animals I don't need. Like the mama rabbit is out and about, running wild. But yesterday or the day before the goat Marcus and the young pig Christopher went. So, bye to Marcus and Christopher. We have got Marcus' son Mars who is lovely. It will make Rob and the boy's life a bit easier because he did cause quite a few problems. He battered the metal gate down and just generally was mischievous. But I will sadly miss Marcus, but I couldn't have tackled him with one hand, it would have been impossible and dangerous.

There are various other things today that happened my mum and dad arrived, and kindly Phil and Carol have picked them up from Poitiers's airport, allowing Rob to visit me. I am hoping my mum won't be too stressed because they won't get to see me until Thursday if Rob's working which will annoy her. But it's no good them coming tomorrow because I will have just had my operation. They can come Thursday and Saturday, but we will see. Also, Marc and Martine were visiting their friends in Nantes, so they called for a while which was good, it made the day pass.

I got a little stressed later on when she brought my medication because she changed it. She said I had to have two at 8 o'clock and all the time I have had one. So I asked her why and she said something, remembering it's all in French, but I didn't quite understand. I didn't want more medication just before my operation I wanted the routine the same. She got a little bit annoyed which upset me so I said I would take the tablets, "I will just take them I am not bothered." But she did come back later and sort of apologised and took the other tablet away and said just stick to that tablet. I haven't got a clue what the other tablet was for.

If they would only explain to me. If they knew my horror of taking medication, I am just taking it because I have to, I know I must. But I don't want to take things I don't need to take. It really threw me, and I got quite upset. I have taken the medication and she has taken the extra one back that I don't normally have, and I don't even know what it was for. Now all is good I hope everything goes to plan tomorrow. That the surgery is good. I have just got to come out of the anaesthetic quietly and calmly without too much stress and then we will see what the next stage is. For now, I am going to try and get a good night's sleep bye.

6 Minutes

It is the 4th of May Wednesday morning the operation has been done that was done on the 2nd of May on the Monday. They got me ready, and I went down about 10-10:30. Just before I went down they gave me a pink tablet to go under my tongue and another tablet but I don't know what that was for but I can't remember having any problems after the operation. Normally I get confused and upset and everything else with the anaesthetic.

I will talk you through the day. I was quite relaxed and relieved that the week had gone, and it was time for the operation. The only concerns I really have after the operation is whether I would be confused, upset and whatever else I went through, but that didn't happen.

I actually have had a permanent line to the angels and God while I have been in here and although people are sometimes embarrassed to say they are religious I have sort of got over that. I have always talked to the angels, I just have. I can't believe that there isn't something if you look at all the history. The paintings many years ago, if you look at the churches there is always some sort of angel around. Whether it's just got weakened over time, but I believe there is something. It wasn't a problem, but God always seemed a bit of an embarrassment to me in some sort of way. I worked it out over the last few days, it's not God I am quite happy to talk to God and believe in God, but I am confused with what has happened in the name of religion. So, the way I have dealt with it is I talk to God while not being any part of a religious establishment, not part of any service or method of religion. I have just decided I will talk to him in my own way which makes things so much easier. I am not feeling I have to be loyal to a certain type of religion. I just talk and ask, and you would not believe, if you truly ask the simple questions, ask for simple assistance, it comes. I asked if he/she (who knows? But for me he is a he), if he would make sure that I was fine after the operation and I cannot even remember any stress coming around, I just woke up.

Continuing the day, they took me down and it was like being in a, I don't know a bus station. You are all queued up in cubicles created by these temporary dividing walls that were bright orange. I loved the colour it really cheered me up, everything had orange on it. You were in stalls waiting for your turn. There was a little problem because for some reason they had got me down as the 17th of October for my date of birth, but it's on the 7th. That caused me a little bit of delay because the lady had to phone up, but she managed to get some stickers and re-stuck all the information with the correct date. Then you just have to wait. There were televisions which I watched a little bit, I was trying not to watch the people because I just didn't want to see their fear or their pain, I just wanted to focus on being positive, happy and confident.

Then it was eventually my turn to go and when I went in, I went into a different area to where most people were going and there were two nice girls and they started doing all the preparations, sticking things on you and things like that and asking you questions. Then she put a table at the side of me and she said that's for your, I don't know if she said hand or arm, remembering this is all in French. I said "Oh, it's not for my tasse de thé (cup of tea)." "Oh no, no, you like tea?" I said "Yes" She said, "Green or black tea?" I said, "It's got to be Yorkshire black tea with milk." She asked, "You have milk with it?" Then the other girl said, "Yes I have milk with mine." I said, "Oh yes and do you have biscuits and dunk the biscuits in?" She said "Yes, yes, obligatoire." By doing things like that it just makes things more relaxed. Having said that she was about to put the mask over my face for the gas which for some people, including me, it can be quite suffocating. But I just took myself to a place that Elliott and I go just before we go to sleep, on to his special beach a place of peace and harmony.

I was taking deep breaths in because the gas obviously helps. But then this guy on my left hand was doing something, they had already put a line in, but I could feel what he was doing and it was painful. I am trying to tell him through my mask but then within minutes I was asleep, I think he had just started working on me a wee bit too early for the gas to have taken effect. That was that I don't know how long I was there, but I didn't get back to my room until 5 o'clock or 5:30. I am not sure, but I think I am now in plastics. Nice room, with yellow walls, bright room I have a nice view, I can't see much but I can see the helicopters coming and going.

I was here at last; I didn't feel too bad at all. I managed to eat a little bit. But just before I came to my room, they sent me for an x-ray and the guy from the x-ray put my newly birthed hand down on the x-ray table and asked me to turn it but I couldn't turn it. So, he tried turning it, oh my God he pushed his thumb on to my arm and that set it off and I screamed. Then he just put a piece of wood there or some sort of wedge why he didn't do that in the first place I don't know!

I then came back, not sure if that set it off but as soon as I got back (I suppose I hadn't had any painkillers for a while or my normal medication for the day the general medication that my body had got used to had all been changed or not given because of the operation). I may have just run out of pain relief and possibly the fact it's just been cut off and taken out of my groin. Sorry I didn't explain, my hand/arm is now free from the groin. I haven't looked at the groin yet because of the dressing but I think they are going to change it today. I have looked at the arm because the doctor came to look at that.

As I was eating tea the wave of pain in this arm was so unbearable, it was just a nightmare. It just suddenly appeared, I pressed my buzzer, I know they are really busy. Somebody came and then she said she would go and see somebody, but she never came back. I don't press my buzzer unless I really, really, really, really have to! I then had to press my buzzer again. At last, they gave me some morphine which is a tablet you put under your tongue, and it acts fairly rapidly within 15 minutes. The pain was so bad but then it calmed down and everything was good, and I actually got some sleep. It was not a lot because I had obviously been asleep most of the day in the operation.

So that was Monday done and the operation done too, which I was grateful for. Tuesday, I woke up and the girls were really good they washed my hair!! That was brilliant because after a month of not washing your hair it is about time, you need to wash it! They had this really wonderful plastic thing that had a place for your head to go, and then it had like a pipe to let the water out, you just having your head over the bed. I suppose it was easier because my arm isn't attached to my groin anymore.

Then Rob and my mum and dad appeared they had arrived on the Sunday. They are both looking old, but my mum was looking more aged than my dad. I found out that Harvey, bless him, had let slip or Grandma managed to get it out of him that I had lost my hand, so they knew before they visited. I had wanted to tell them when they were here, so she didn't have a bit of a drama and get upset while she and dad were in the UK. Mum said she had got time to prepare, and it was better for her to find out there than here.

They were fine, no problems and brought a card from Georgina, Darby, Caroline, and Peter (my sister and her family). My parents were happy enough although they read too many newspapers and watch the news too much and all the world dramas lay heavy on their hearts especially my mum's. They are here till Sunday; I think they are coming back on Friday. Carol and Philip have offered to bring them, they actually picked them up from the airport, this allowed Rob and the boys to come and visit me. When Rob and the boys visited, I found out that mama rabbit plus others are still running around free, but they don't know where my mama rabbit is, my guess is a fox. On Tuesday, yesterday I found out that the geese have hatched some babies, 3 so far, which is wonderful let's hope that they stay good. Papa goose Gandy is being very protective, and no one can get near, so they have to keep away, he's just doing his job of looking after his girl and his babies and sometimes he sits on the eggs as well. I have read that they partner for life. One of the babies will be for Christmas and hopefully they will hatch more. I would like to show some if it's possible.

I do want to reduce the animals; I want to concentrate on maybe a couple of things that we show and show well. It just gives an interest which I think will be good for me and Elliott.

What else? Nothing much, probably tonight I will maybe talk about a few things which I may have already said because I am trying not to forget anything and sometimes, I say it twice. Oh, that was it the doctor came and said on Tuesday I am going to Niort, I am now in Nantes which is an hour and a half away from home. Niort is about 40 minutes away, it's the place where the rehabilitation is, I don't know how that will go.

Yesterday the girls, as always have been really good she had me sitting up to eat which I found quite hard, I was very dizzy. They then wanted me to go in a chair and I said it's not possible my right knee is really being quite naughty. I don't want to push it because the surgeon said it needs at least another 2 months for the bone to lay down. I don't want to risk it and push it, but at least I sat up which felt so weird.

I suppose I did a bit too much yesterday my mum, dad and Rob were here which I didn't have a problem with it was great to see them but after just having the operation and the sitting up, the visitors it seemed quite a lot to be doing.

Now this morning the hand was again throbbing. The only thing I can describe it as is a pressure. You see those big tractors, if you imagine (no don't try to imagine it), God blimey, I can't imagine it how awful! But if you imagine your arm under one of its tyres that's how it feels, just like a pressure, really restricting pressure. But the girls gave me some morphine and my medicine and it's now starting to calm down. I have had a bit of breakfast I will give it 10 more minutes and then I will need to buzz for a bedpan. Yesterday they took out my catheter so that's progress. I have got to make sure I ask them for a bedpan which I will. I have already done a wee and they are happy as long as I do some sort of poo once a day, I think that will make them and me happy as well. So that's my aims today regular wees and a poo.

Also, Rob brought me some books, so I have got a Hugh Fearnley-Whittingstall book, it's about various things and then I have got 'Lacy Street' by Lynn Andrews, it's about Liverpool so at least I have something to concentrate on. Right, I am going to stop waffling and try and remember tonight to tie everything up because I am sure before long, I will be whisked off to another place and then that will be a new adventure, so bye for now.

17 Minutes

It's now Thursday evening 7:30 ish I am still in plastics, I have been here since Monday after my operation. It's gone fairly quick, yesterday nobody came which wasn't a problem, I just read my book and rested quite a bit. I did have a couple of bad bouts of pain with the hand (phantom) and the arm. This morning unfortunately because I am now not using my left hand because it gave way yesterday, I thought I can't risk losing this function, I need one hand please! I have stopped lifting myself up and helping, I can't because it's a broken wrist and I am pushing my luck with it.

This morning the girls come in I am busy trying to protect both hands. Then I can't believe I didn't stop them, but they put their hands up under my legs and moved me up the bed which was absolutely crippling. I screamed the place down. They were obviously very sorry, but it put me into a lot of pain for quite a while.

Today I had a visit from Kelly and Alex and their new three-week-old son although he wasn't allowed in the room, the nurse told them, but we managed to have a good chat. Ethan, their elder son and a good friend of Elliott's was there as well, though he looked a bit bored, bless him. They looked well, the baby is well though he has got a bit of colic. We had a good chat, the only problem was my hand/arm set off again.

They don't seem to give me enough morphine. Now I am waiting, and I am going to ask when I finish recording this for some morphine because they seem to give me it too late, when the pain has well and truly set in. It means that my pain is too intense then. I don't know why the morphine is not given earlier, but there you go. I am also on antibiotics now because I have a bladder infection. They took my catheter out a couple of days ago and I am still managing to use the bedpan.

It was unfortunate that I had a very painful time when Alex and Kelly were here. Tomorrow I think mum and dad, Carol and Philip are here and then it's the weekend. Then somehow, they are moving me. I will just have to make sure I get painkillers. I am fine, just a bit exhausted today with the pain. Over and out.

3 Minutes

Very stressed in this recording:

Hi, I am back now because I am in a real load of pain (crying), I have been all day. Three times I have tried to explain that I need my medication before the pain arrives (very upset, in a lot of pain). It's only the morphine that takes the pain away from my hand which is really, really painful. One of the girls came and I asked her, and she gave me some doliprane (paracetamol) but it didn't help. I asked her if it was morphine, she said yes, but it can't have been. The pain just got worse and worse, and I had to buzz them again. She came in and said what's your problem as if she couldn't fucking see! (Big sigh) Then she eventually came with the morphine you put under your tongue which is really quick acting. But I am still in a lot of agony now. (I am getting really upset) It's three times now, they shouldn't let you get into so much pain (crying) they don't give me my medicine, it's stupid. I don't ask for it if I don't have to, I put up with a lot of pain, but I can't put up with this. I'll see what the doctor says tomorrow.

I don't know, I keep asking them to shut this bloody window four times. Four people I have asked to shut this window and they just keep ignoring me. Oh God give me strength! Let me get out of here please!!

1 minute

See now I am back again, and the drugs have kicked in. I am going to have one of my Werther's toffees that Kelly and Alex brought me. Why should I have to go through all that pain? Just for the sake of giving me a tablet (big sigh). I am back to normal now and the pain has subsided.

But I have had my suspicions this is going on to another subject now. I don't know why I just sense it because there is so much gossip going on about my accident. There is someone talking, and I don't do Facebook, I think it's the devil's hand. I think it's people who have nothing better to do in their lives. Most are nosey, interfering busybodies that's what I think some of the people on Facebook are. I have friends who use Facebook but it's what I think of it at the moment. (I am actually on Facebook now be it not very often, so I am a nosey busybody too. At the time of the recording, I was not happy with the gossip on Facebook, it felt so unkind).

Apparently, someone has been on Facebook asking loads of questions about the accident not very pleasant. Fortunately, Kelly responded and said it was inappropriate they shouldn't be asking questions, you should think about the family and it's nothing to do with her. It was Nicola's whatever it is website, face site. I am debating whether to have a stern word with her. Why don't people just leave you alone? I am not on Facebook, I don't need or want to be on Facebook, and I don't want my family on Facebook.

Why are people so interfering in your lives? It's one of my other annoyances today. Maybe I will just let it all be because sometimes the more you talk about these things the more you feed them. Hopefully I am yesterday's news! It is annoying that you can't even have a private life anymore!

But hey, so I am going to enjoy my Werther's now and read a book. Thank you drug for giving me my life back for a little while. Over and out.

2 Minutes

I am very stressed and upset on this recording:

Hi, it's Friday morning, pretty early I have woken up and my hand is starting again. I have buzzed for the nurse, a really nice lady came but she said I can only have doliprane (paracetamol). I have taken what they gave me, why can't they give me anything stronger? (Crying and in extreme pain) I don't really know why I am just waiting, because all the signs are here that it's going to kick in. It's really, really painful, God it's so stupid. I feel like Marie Antoinette waiting to go to the bloody block, you know the pain's coming, and you can't do anything about it but wait. I am in such absolute agony, but they won't give me morphine I just don't understand why! It's at least 8 o'clock and the last time I had some was last night! I understand they don't want to give you hard drugs, but God I can't carry on with this pain, they need to help me out.

I am just going to try and relax and try and ride the wave. But as soon as this gets worse, I am buzzing them, they have got to give me some medication, they have got to, it's cruelty. (A very stressed recording I was obviously in extreme pain).

1 Minute

Another upset and stressful recording:

I can't believe it, a lovely woman who was talking to me, who gave me the paracetamol (I don't think she is a nurse) she has been back she has just finished her night shift. She has been back with a tablet and the morphine! God, she doesn't know how much that means to me (crying). I think it's the first time I have seen her because you do get different staff all the time. I think she is an angel, been sent to help me. (A big pain wave) It's still getting worse, but I know the morphine will just take it away. Now at least I don't have to wait for the next set of staff.

So, thank you God, thank you, thank you, thank you! I don't know what she did, but she managed to get me some. Maybe she just understands the stupidity of it all, of me having so much pain. (It's not as if I am going to be like Michael Jackson or Liz Taylor. I am not surprised they got addicted to prescribed drugs, they had so much plastic surgery and operations). But once this pain goes, I will find some other way of helping any pain. This pain at the moment, it's phantom, it can't last forever but it's bad! Without medication it's bad (big sigh).

Oh God I am so relieved, so relieved it's hard, it's like when you are just going back into labour. You think what the hell I know what's coming. Although I would say this pain is far greater than any labour pain. Labour pain is productive, it progresses, you get somewhere and there is an end result. I suppose there is an end result with this (big wave of pain came) but I can't quite see it at the moment. Hopefully the next recording will be more cheerful.

I don't know what's happening today, they will probably review the medication. I have just got to try and be patient. I do want to be moved nearer home but I am not looking forward to them transporting me. Especially when I don't know how bad my legs are so that's why I want this pain to be better by Monday. Bye.

3 Minutes

It's still Friday morning the pain has passed and now I have got breakfast consisting of four biscuits with butter, a pear which I asked her to peel but she didn't quite understand me, so she has cut it into four, but the skin is still on. I didn't want to eat the skin it looked a bit worse for wear, but I ate the flesh. I also got this juice thing which everybody says I have to drink it's good for me. But for many years, I have woken up to the fact that anything messed with, manufactured, or created, is basically full of artificial chemicals.

I have said it to so many people a lot of years ago, why do you buy that low fat spread stuff? All it is chemicals, it's not good for your digestion. I think it could even be the cause of some cancers and irritable bowel. I have always said you are better off buying organic. I know it's expensive. But having had it confirmed, last year that they spray things to death and pretend they have not sprayed them, it's dangerous to even rely on organic. Every time they sprayed when we were picking apples, I was ill, so ill, tired, ached and had a headache, it's just ridiculous what they are allowed to do. But it's in the name of profit isn't it!

I am finding it hard to eat this stuff, but I will try. When I have meat, I apologise to the animal because I know that it has probably suffered an horrendous life just to feed me.

The nurse came with my tablets, she is talking to me and asking me if I need to see a psychologist. I said the only reason I am crying is because of the amount of pain I am in. I am not crying because of the accident, I am not crying because of my situation (well I do but I do it in the dead of night when no one can see me, I don't want antidepressants). But I am crying because it's emotional. I have not really gone into shock I'm crying because I miss my family and miss my situation that I had in my life. I am missing simple things, the baby geese and everything I have worked hard to create in the last two years, I am missing my life that was.

I told the nurse no, no it's not in my head, I am not crying because it's in there I am crying because of this bloody hand and my medication needs sorting out to reduce the pain. I don't know, I think I have dodged that one, but we will see. I have a degree in psychology, I could psychologise myself.

My dream before my accident was to get a nice little Jersey cow. So, I could have the cream, make the butter and my biggest dream was to make an ice-cream, like the one I remembered as a kid. A simple beautiful, tasty ice-cream without all that greasy after taste that so many ice-creams leave in your mouth. Every time I have an ice-cream, even a good quality ice-cream, there is this grease left on your tongue. I can't remember it being like that when I was a kid.

As children we went to Caddy's and Crossley's. Crossley's was in Ravensthorpe where my Granddad and Grandma Walker lived. Caddy's was in Dewsbury a bit posher. In the yard of Crossley's, you could see his ice-cream making machines in the wooden hut he had, it having been there for many years I used to go to his little open hatch, and he would lean against the work surface look down on you, I would excitedly look up and ask for a 99. The 99 had a chocolate flake in it and you could get some 100's and 1000's bits thrown over it, it was just delicious. You could also get a sandwich ice-cream. It was ice-cream between two wafers, plain of chocolate ones. Then there were the oysters shell, they were shaped like a shell, half of the shell was filled with this wonderful ice-cream. Caddy's and Crossley's ice-cream was delicious!! (This is not on my recordings but an interesting fact to me is that my dad used to keep fit in the off season, which was summer in the 1950's, by pulling a small Crossley's ice-cream cart. He would pull it around Ravensthorpe so people could buy an ice-cream. He saw it as part of his fitness regime for his rugby and he also got some pocket money too.)

I don't know if that's going to happen now because I was going to struggle with two hands milking a cow, so I don't know if I could even think of milking one with one hand. But I had got all the paperwork and had all that ready to buy a cow. A pedigree cow with a calf is about one thousand five hundred euros, you need a good pedigree for the quality milk. So, I don't know if that's going to happen. Maybe I am better off investing in a small ice-cream making machine and get milk. I think there is a place not far away in Bressuire that's got Jersey cows, so I could try and buy the milk from them. Or there is a butter making place in Pamplie, quite famous I even found it in a supermarket in South Australia, Pamplie butter. I could buy cream from them. I had an image of having a little van going around selling ice-cream.

When Crossley died nobody wanted to carry on his work so his secret recipe may have gone. I might have to have a word with him and ask if he could send me his recipe from wherever he is, you never know, he might do! Less of my waffling you might have noticed I am a lot happier now that's because I have not got pain. Bye.

11 Minutes

It's still Friday, Friday evening about 9:30. I thought I ought to really check in again because my recordings this morning were somewhat desperate. So, the day has been good, I think I managed to persuade the nurse that I need morphine at least three times a day.

My parents came with Philip and Carol, they stayed for a good while which was great. The pain was just starting I asked for some pain relief, and she actually gave me some. I don't know if it's because there was a crowd there (my visitors) or she had had a discussion with the doctor or she just realised I needed it because she also gave me one at 8 o'clock this evening before the real dramatic pain could get a hold. Stubby is a bit pulsey tonight but I have just been exercising him (he should not really be him he should be a her, but he's not).

Also, this afternoon a nice girl came, she wasn't a physio she was a masseur plus something else, she was really good. We did some exercises and she got me an ice pack for the right knee. She exercised my right arm which was a bit painful, and she gave me some homework. I think she is really good, but unfortunately, I am only here until Thursday, I think? But who knows because things, dates and decisions change in this place all the time? So, all is good the only thing is the nurse now just said goodbye and she if off for the weekend which means another nurse. But the medication is hopefully down on the record sheet now so I will get my morphine. I will just ask for it if I have to. By that angel giving me my drug this morning it meant I didn't have to sit around waiting and waiting and the pain getting worse and worse. I hope I get it again tomorrow morning because it's all about timing and stopping the pain before it can get a hold of me.

It was good to have mum and dad here it meant the day passed fairly quick. Tomorrow is Saturday I doubt anyone will come knowing I am going to Niort, but we will see.

Is there any other information to give you? Not really, I am just a bit tired I am going to just eat one of my Werther's toffees and maybe read but I am really quite tired. There is something else, I must still be growing mushrooms because they gave me something for it, so I must have still got an infection, but I am feeling much better and I thought I would let you all know. Hopefully things will be moving forwards and Stubby won't be playing up so much. Bye for now.

4 Minutes

The pain was not good when I did these recordings, but I tried to endure it and get through the pain the best I could.

Chapter 16: Subaru, Bathurst, Barmy Army And Perth Glory FC

"Freedom comes when you stop caring about what others think of you."

-Buddha

The F1 season had finished so that meant Robert was on holiday and seeing as Japan is halfway to Oz (sort of) that was the next place to head for. A group of us headed for the Bullet train the next day and tried to find our way to Tokyo airport. They thought I had a clue how to achieve this, but I didn't, even though I had done the exact journey to get to the racing. The fact that I got to Suzuka at all was a miracle.

I was heading to Perth to see the Fullers, Matt and Laura (Matt's first wife) and Rob was going to help at the Subaru rally team and also visit some friends. Paul was travelling there too, he was also the chef for the Subaru team not just the F1 Williams team.

Matty and Laura took me to see some of Perth. Fremantle and a special hill where you could see the whole of Perth. We went to this special sight-seeing place when it was dark to see Perth lit up it was amazing. Someone had the same idea and turned up in a white limo. A guy got out and I asked him if he wanted my autograph, for some reason he said no. I noticed the British accent and he kindly allowed me to have a photo with him. I hadn't got a clue who he was, I thought I heard Kevin McRae. I found out later it was Collin McRae who was there for the rally driving race and he was driving for Subaru. I still didn't have a clue who he was.

I planned to go and watch some of the rally driving, why not! I told Matt and Laura if they did what I said I could get them into the paddock (by now I knew there wouldn't be any horses in the paddock, maybe a kangaroo though). Matty was not so convinced and was unsure if it was worth his time going. But I got them exactly in the place I said I would get them the Subaru garage looking at McRae's car. It's not what you know but who you know. Paul even fed us, I told you he was a nice guy.

My next adventure was flying to Sydney on the 6th of November to stay at Laura's mum's house. Matty's brother was having his 30th birthday party so we all went. Of course, it was a barbecue, my first Australian barbie and it was thundering and lightning. At the party I got talking to Laurie about the F1 race. He was on his way to Bathurst because he worked for Kodak in the days when you needed films to take a photo. I asked if I could have a lift and he said I could.

Rob arrived at Laura's mum's house in Sydney after finishing with the rally racing in Perth. Rob was a huge rugby fan and Matty having played professional rugby at Wakefield Trinity in the UK and in Perth, resulted in them being a little in awe of each other. Matty was sat with a F1 mechanic and Rob with a professional rugby player. Shirts were exchanged and a friendship developed. Rob soon left Sydney heading for the Bathurst V8's race where he was helping out the Denistron team. You get about a bit Robert but why not when you have the connections and the talent!

I spent a wonderful time sightseeing with Matt and Laura and then I also set off to Bathurst with Laurie. This world trip although planned to a certain degree was turning out to be some amazing opportunities that you needed to grasp with both hands and take these once in a lifetime chance. Again, I had never heard of Bathurst, didn't know what a V8 was but learnt that it was a massive event in Australia and seeing that I was in Oz why not experience it. I didn't have a ticket so as we approached, I hid in the back of Laurie's van. He was working there selling his camera films, so he had his pass. Once inside I thanked him for his kindness which he had no problems with the Aussies tending to be helpful to others, an attitude "No drama mate". A good laid-back sort of attitude.

I went off to find the paddock. Here I am again in a team's garage watching them work on what looked like a normal sort of car. The drivers (there were 2 drivers because the race was so long) were Mezera and Menu. Alain Menu's wife was also at the race. They were French, I got on well with her it can become quite boring all the waiting around, so I think she was glad of some company.

At Bathurst there is a long-standing tradition that you camp on the mountain to get the best view of the race. This place is filled with characters, eskies to keep your beer cold, of course essential in the hot Australian sun. These folks were prepared and organised, one group even had a small train of eskies that even moved like a small train, brilliant! The mountain was supposed to have a reputation of being a little rough. Beer, burn outs, dope and crazy fun. Not the same décor of your corporate boxes or sponsors seating area, the mountain was much more raw and realistic. So where do you think I headed? Yes, and I took Alain Menu's wife with me.

We were positioned to watch the race. The pre-race lap occurred, all the drivers waving to the crowds while been driven in vintage cars. Then the 100 odd lap race would begin. First the warmup lap, Tomas Menzera was driving first, great at last the race started. Caroline (Alain's wife) and I watching from the mountain. The cars came flying past but no Densitron. Then the safety car came out to slow down the race it was out for a long time so long that even Rob had got bored and had fallen asleep on the grass. It turned out the car Densitron had broken down after the warmup lap and that was the end of the race for them. I was upset for the guys who had worked on the car they were really nice guys but that's motor racing for you. Mr Menu was not impressed that I had taken his wife up to the mountain, but it was a fantastic place to watch the race. The race, the atmosphere and characters were 'far out' as they say in Oz.

After the race there is always celebrations or the drowning of one's sorrows in the case of the Densitron team. This time it wasn't Damon Hill who provided the entertainment, but this guy called Jimmy Barnes. Yes, the Aussie icon (the other being AC/DC). I of course had never heard of him, what a sheltered life I must have lived.

Jimmy Barnes was originally in the band Cold Chisel, then they broke up and then got back together. Jimmy Barnes being a true Aussie legend even though he is Scottish. In 1998 I think the band Cold Chisel did tour but all I can remember at Bathurst was the strong gravelly, deep, rocky amazing voice of Jimmy Barnes. The performance was mesmerising, a true entertainer. I have been lucky to experience some fantastic artists live including Jimmy, Tina Turner, in fact remember the 'Simply The Best' song, Denbo's song, well Tina and Jimmy recorded that song together. How life weaves it's magic synchronistics. I think Tina also did some singing with the Boss Bruce Springsteen.

While still in Oz I bought a Barnes CD some of my favourite work of his are the 'Workingman', 'Driving Wheel's', 'Stone Cold' and 'Cry To Me', ('Cry To Me', originally sung by Solomon Burke).

After Bathurst it was back to Perth. A visit to Rottnest Island to see the Quakkas that live there, they look like a very small kangaroo. Then trying to water ski with Matt and Laura's friend Greg. After that a long drive which allowed me to see my first kangaroo and many of his mates also dead on the road. In the UK it's usually hedgehogs or rabbits, in Oz it's big kangaroos usually hit by the large double trailered monster trucks they have.

When you live in the UK it's hard to get to grips with the size of Australia. I remember having the flight from Perth to Sydney about seven hours and I offered my passport at check in, the lady kindly pointed out that it was not necessary for I was not leaving the country, of course!

Next destination was Monkey Mia where after a wait luck allowed the amazing experience of seeing a dolphin and its baby up close. The baby was such a show-off. The baby will stay with it's mum for 5 to 6 years. After that wonderful experience it was to the Pinnacles which is at Namburg National Park Western Australia, it's a conservation area. What are the Pinnacle's? The Yued people believe they are the remains of young men lost to the shifting sands. They were warned not to enter but some did stand in the sand and the Pinnacles are the fingertips of the young men that didn't listen to their elders. Scientists have a different theory which concludes that it was due to conspiring natural forces over 500,000 years ago. They are massive sand dunes rich in calcium carbonate which is broken down marine life. There was heavy rainfall that dissolved the calcium carbonate in the sand dunes and allowed it to deposit on the bottom on the sand dunes as a layer of limestone. I prefer the Yued people's theory.

Now back at Matt and Laura's it's the 18th of November 1998. A Saturday morning preparing breakfast on the barbie before going to my first ever cricket game which was at the Wacca Perth. It was the second test match Australia v England. We were in a box at the Wacca a privileged place to be to watch the important game. I didn't understand the rules and while England was batting all I kept seeing on the huge TV screens was this animated duck walking on the screen. I didn't get it but later learnt that if you are out without a run, it's called out for a duck. Right got it, so logical, why couldn't I figure that one out?!

It was a good view from the box, and I could see and hear a group of people having way too much fun. I was told it's a group of English supporters that follows the cricket and are called the Barmy Army (I have just realised put b in front of army and you get barmy, clever). The story behind the Barmy Army goes back to 1994 when a group of fans were supporting the tour down-under. They were named by the local media as the Barmy Army because they were supporting such a hopeless team, the captain for the 94-95 tour was Michael Atherton. A founding member Paul Burham tells the story that a gang of supporters at the Adelaide test got 100 tee-shirts printed with Atherton's Army printed on it with a union flag and the new nickname Barmy Army. Other fans wanted to have one, so they had to have another 3000 printed.

Being intrigued by the singing the action and the sunshine I was beckoned. So, I told Matty that I was going to sit with the Barmy Army. I will admit I was a little bored, nothing seemed to be happening in this sport and it goes on for hours and hours. Matty looked a bit concerned warning me that it may not be a safe thing to do. I said they are only some English fans having a good time, what's unsafe about that! So, I left and joined the area where the Barmy Army where they were lovely. In 1998 it was only the second tour down-under for the Army, so a relatively small number compared to today's Army. They sang, drank and were happy. Every time England got a 6, they would do the conga and I would join in. Fortunately, or unfortunately at the Wacca in November 1998 there weren't that many congas needed.

Later, I would be joined by Matty and co from the sponsors box and they joined in the atmosphere too. To say Matty was a professional rugby league player he was sometimes reserved. I also remember the time when he was in the UK playing for Wakefield Trinity and I took them on a surprise adventure. There was Matt and Laura, Jeanette and me. I took them all to Sheffield to see the Spice Girls in concert. They loved it, but I bet they never would have dreamt of going.

In life you must think out of the box. Seize opportunities don't fear what others say or think. If you are not harming anyone or yourself then do it. People will always judge and gossip about you. To have memories you must first live a life worth remembering. Don't be fearful about who you are. Be authentic and you will be happy. Fear the judgement and thoughts of others and you will be stuck. Go and experience things for yourself and then decide how you feel, don't fear being different, being different is being free!

After the cricket match, I got the signatures of the English cricketers not that I can read anyone's name. Matt also got my Barmy Army hat signed by the Aussie team. After the day's result the hat is probably of more value than the signatures of the English players. However, a very wonderful day even though England got stuffed.

The next day I found myself in another VIP box watching the newly formed, just two years before, Perth Glory Soccer team. Perth has problems due to its location with expenses of travel having to fly everywhere and other teams having the expense of flying to Perth to play which is an added challenge for establishing new professional teams. Today the Perth Glory Soccer team are still very much alive and kicking, I was lucky to have experienced their beginnings and happy that they went from strength to strength. Unfortunately, the same cannot be said for the Western Perth Reds professional rugby league team formed in 1995.

Matt Fuller was one of their players (I think it was a Reds rugby shirt that he gave to Rob in exchange for a F1 shirt). When Matty had been playing for Wakefield, he had faith in me fixing any injuries he had. It's always difficult to get a good hands-on treatment at the rugby club. There is usually only one physio and loads of players to take care of and they are usually training too. I told Matty I would come and help the new club out when I got my degree finished. But alas it wasn't meant to be, the club becoming extinct in just three years. I am sure one day there will be another Western Reds rugby league team, let's hope so.

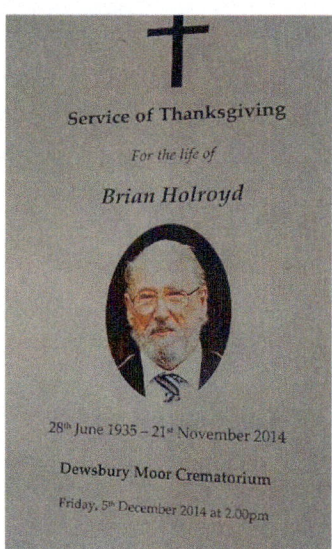

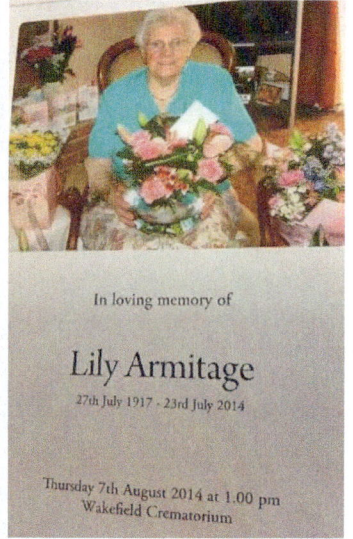

Prison Or The Paralympics

Brian Holroyd & Lily Armitage

Mel Wilson & Castel

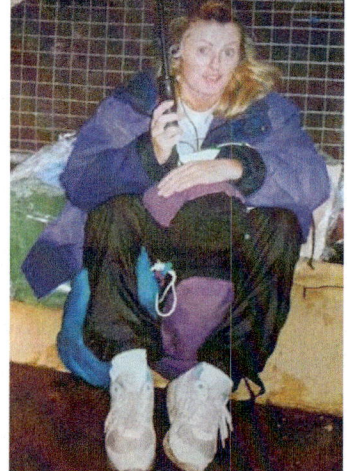

Jerez F1 1997 (Damon Hill On Guitar)

Sleeping On The Mall For Princess Diana's Funeral

Martyn In The F1 Car

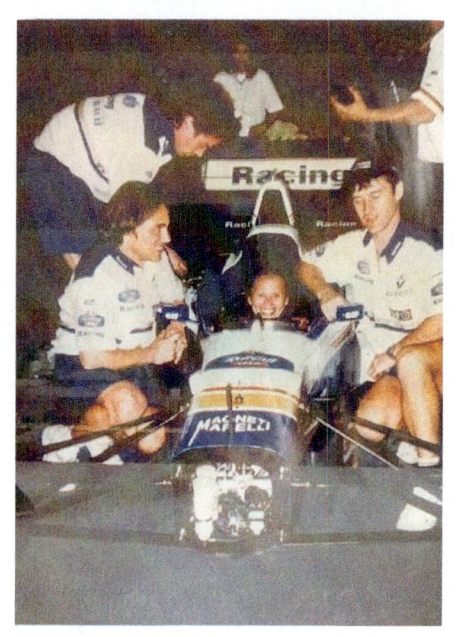

Silverstone

Penny Walker

The Bullet Train

F1 Pass

Villeneuve

Formula 1 At Suzuka

The Lads Backstage Before The Final

Dripping Wet.

Michael back on his way to Squeeze Past me again (lucky man).

OK Gary Can't Leave You Got Testing On Monday.

Rob & Matty

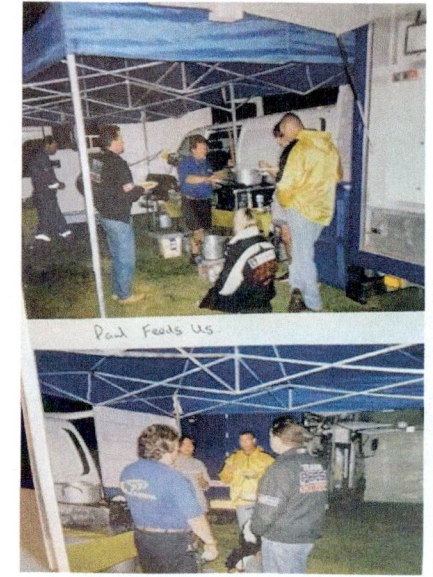

Paul Feeding Us

Bathurst Pass

Colin McRae Perth, Australia

Subaru, Perth Rally

Densitron Team Bathurst

160

Penny Walker

Quokka On Rottnest Island, Perth

Dolphins, Monkey Mia

Pinnacles, Western Australia

Me & Matt At The Wacca

My Passes, For Perth Glory & Dubai 7s

Conga With The Barmy Army

161

Prison Or The Paralympics

Salt & Pepper

Snowy's Offspring

Pekin Pullets & Fancypants The Cockerel

Guinea Fowl With Colonel The Combatant Cockerel In The Background

Guinea Fowl In Winter

Guinea Fowl In A Group

162

Colonel The Combatant

The Turkeys Ken & Deirdre

Ken The Turkey (Named After A Good Friend)

Geese (Gandy Is The White One)

Rabbits

Marcus The Male Goat

Star My Beautiful Female Goat

Robin Feeding Mars

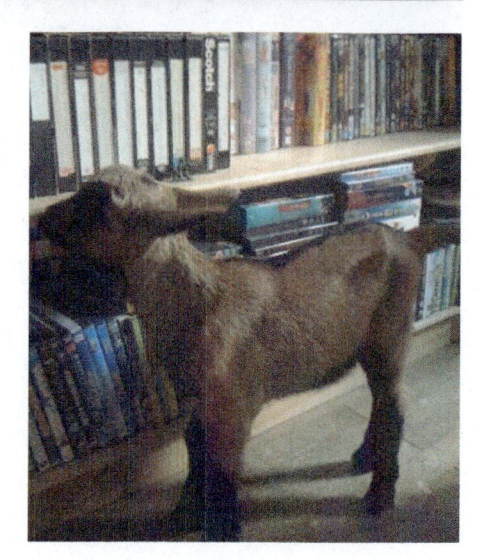

Mars The Baby Goat Sleeping In The House

Dolly & Myrtle May (Dolly Is The One With Black On Her Right Ear)

'Tank' Helping Dolly With Her First Litter

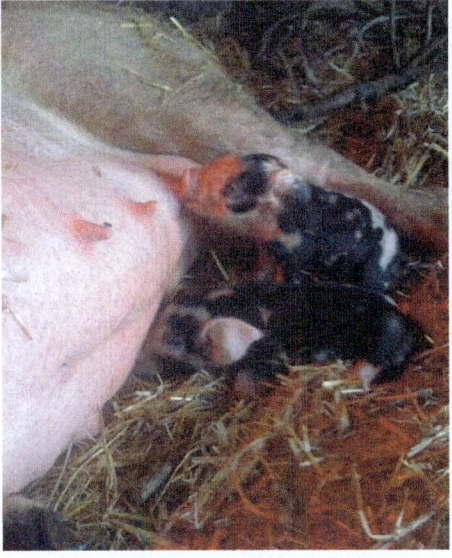

Buster And Myrtle May

Dolly Giving Birth To 13

Chapter 17: Recordings At Nantes Hospital, Stubby Is Being Naughty, Moaning And More Delays

"You have to do something in your life that is honourable and not cowardly if you are to live in peace with yourself."

- Larry Brown

It's about 9:30 Saturday evening I have just asked for my morphine (a big wave of pain comes) my hand is playing up a bit, but it's definitely going longer between the needs to have morphine. It will be fine in the next 5 minutes now that I have had the morphine (another wave of pain) oh it's still quite bad.

I have had a really good day because the Golden Girls (Mel and Sheila) arrived "Oh sod off Stubby!" (Another pain attack). It's the name I have given to my arm Stubby, but at the moment he is not playing very nicely. "Oh Stubby!" (Another pain influx). What happens is that it just tightens, tightens, tightens, and then tightens some more and won't relax. Now all my arm is in spasm and tightening, it's painful. I know the drug, if she had given me the right one, she told me to swallow it but if it's the right one you put it under your tongue. I am sure it will be the right one, I will know if this pain doesn't go in the next five minutes and they have given me the crap one, not the correct one. "Oh Stubby!!" (Pain again)

It was good I can't believe they have been every week (Golden Girls). They just come and they are good fun and they chat about poo and farts for some reason, it's good, real good company but I didn't really expect them to come today because I told Rob to tell them that I might be going on Tuesday and also to tell them where I was going, Niort. They did actually go to my old room in trauma. Mel went in and she saw this person with a cover over them with black hair so she slipped out and said "Oops, wrong place!" They then took ages trying to find me "Oh! Stubby behave!" I think he is calming down I am not sure. Oh God!! (pain)

That was nice it passed on Saturday. Sunday will be boring I suppose but I can finish my book. Then Monday they will be messing about with me, going for x-rays and whatever else is needed, then just waiting to see if I am going on Tuesday. I don't even know if I am allowed to go in their clothing (hospital gown) or whether I put my own on, but I think they were all cut off including my shoes and thrown away. I won't be able to get my underwear on I have no chance, it will be impossible!! (Another wave of pain) " Tu, tu, tu, tu Stubby calm down!" (Big sigh) I think he is calming down now. Today the girl who is quite a bit pushy in a nice way had me sitting up. It was difficult but I did sit up for about twenty minutes I don't know if she is on tomorrow, but no doubt if she is, she will have me sitting up again. She did suggest the chair, but I said I am not ready for the chair. I don't want to do anything because I am moving, and I want to be in the place that knows about rehabilitation. So, I am going to avoid that chair, she's not getting me in a chair. If they want me in a chair when I move, that's different. I will sit up for her because I know I can handle that. But I am not going in the chair because I have got to get from the bed into a chair, and from the chair back into the bed. Which to me that means weight bearing or someone getting hold of me and making me scream. So, I will just say no to that one.

I don't think there is anything else (in a whisper) "Stubby is finally calming down." I am alright but at the beginning of the week, as you will probably have read, I had some horrendous times with the pain. At last, at last they don't seem to argue when I ask for pain relief. I don't know what's happened there, if someone has had a word with them or if I have got through to them, I don't know. I only hope the one she has given me is the right one, but we will see. If it isn't I will have to buzz them again. I am now going to turn the light off and try to go to sleep that often calms him down. There you have it another day gone.

5 Minutes

It's now Sunday dinner time I haven't got a clue what date it is, it must be the 8th, 9th or 10th of May. I had a good sleep. They have been to wash me, clean me, change me and all the other stuff. The nurse has been to change my dressings. Stubby has been quite naughty today he has just been redressed he played up a bit so the nurse after changing the dressings on my legs and groin came back with my morphine. Hopefully Stubby will behave himself for a while. If you turn a certain position, he just starts playing up a bit. The doctor has been and had a quick look. The nurse said he was worried because my leg and groin area was warm. I think they are worried about an infection but to be honest the leg has been warm since day one. I think it's the metal in my femur and the many bolts, it's just a foreign body my body doesn't like. Tomorrow I get everything x-rayed they may be able to find something out.

So there you go, the sun is sort of out it's fairly quiet because it's a Sunday. I am just slowly reading through my book eating a few chocolates hiding the wrappers, so the nurses don't tell me off and waiting for the go ahead for movement. I suppose either tonight or tomorrow I will summarise this place before I leave hopefully remember all the things that happened here. I may repeat myself, I can't really think of much to say except it's been a challenge, it's been hard, painful, depressing and I think there is more of that to come.

I want Stubby to calm himself down now, it's nearly a week, it's a week tomorrow when he arrived and was born. I have got to calm him down a bit, he needs to calm down. But as Mel said once he's calmed down, I will probably feel all the pain in my leg. It's all just things I have to get through, isn't it?

If I have missed anything I am sorry it may come back to me I need to record it as I remember. "Stubby, Stubby!" He is just kicking off again. All in all, I have survived a month, I am sure I can survive a couple more. Bye.

4 Minutes

Hi, it must be the 9th of May today because it's Monday and I had my operation on my hand last Monday which was the 2nd. So, 7 add 2 is 9 so it's the 9th of May. Been sort of a good weekend I didn't expect anyone to come. I know my mum, dad, Philip and Carol came on Friday, but I didn't realise the Golden Girls would come on Saturday. So that was good, they did get lost and went to my old room!

Sunday no one was here and today which is Monday a few hours ago Eric, Michelle and Audrey visited which was nice they had just been to Ikea, so they called here as well. She did ask the nurse about where I was going and when and said that I wasn't likely to go tomorrow or the day after. But I had just had a woman in who does the files or checks you out. I couldn't talk to her because I was on my bedpan, but I managed to ask her if I was going tomorrow. She said we are just waiting for a place. So I don't know what's happening. But Michelle's given her number as well so at least she will understand the French because when they ring Rob he only understands to a certain point. There I was hoping tonight to summarise this place, but maybe I will be here a bit longer.

Today the physio came and worked on my arm and leg and put me on this machine that slowly bends your leg. If I have to stay here a few more days at least that's a bonus because she is really good, though she hurts me.

I don't think I have forgotten anything. Yes, I have forgotten something, today although it's just starting now, but not too bad. Today I have gone all day without needing morphine for Stubby. I am going to get some at 8 o'clock. I think it will be too much for me to go all night as well, but I have gone all day. I had some this morning but none midday so that's progress. He is starting to get a bit naughty now so I will buzz them at 8 if the nurse hasn't been.

I had all my x-rays done today. I am trying to explain to the nurse that my cast irritates the sore on my left leg, but she doesn't understand me. I don't think it will ever heal while it's getting irritated. No doubt the doctor will be here tomorrow with the results, and I will find out more.

I am a bit fed up that I am not moving on but, in this place, nothing is when they say it's going to be. For a week they have been saying I am going on Tuesday, and they don't really know. It's just a matter of waiting, the only problem is I am struggling with the food. I just want plain veg and fruit but it's always messed up, but at least I got a banana tonight and had a poo so they can't hassle me about that!! But getting on those bedpans is absolutely challenging and wrecks me and I have got a really bad bedsore on my bottom which doesn't help. I am sure it's the bedpan that's caused it but they say it's not, but I am bloody sure it is because they have to drag me on to them.

Oh, what a way to go. But anyway, I am going to try and stay positive, read my book and just get through another night which will then take me to Tuesday. Okay over and out.

6 Minutes

This will be quite quick because I am not sure when they are coming to wash me. It's now Tuesday morning I am not going to Niort. I have had both doctors in Dr. Pietu, he is the orthopaedic surgeon I like him he is quite funny; he looks a bit like the guy out of the two Ronnies, Ronnie Barker the bigger one with the white hair but my doctor hasn't got white hair. He does have glasses; he's got round black glasses not the big ones that Ronnie wore. I find him good he has a bit of a joke about him. At first, he comes across as really serious and then I think he realised he could talk to me. He speaks very posh English. He has seen the x-rays everything is good I need a bit longer with the barbecue skewers in my left four toes. Everything is fine but I still need, or he prefers me to have another two months without weight bearing on my right leg.

The plastic surgeon Dr Lecons he is more like George Clooney though he did look a bit rough this morning. I like him too. He sometimes looks a bit unkempt probably because they have to stay here some nights, I don't know. But he is the chef (boss) of the clinic. I see him quite a lot I don't even know if he does the operations or oversees them, I have never asked. He is very much in contact with me a lot and speaks with

Prison Or The Paralympics

me a lot about the whole thing. He was examining me, and everything is good he is happy but if I only went and let gas out (farted) in front of George Clooney!! I just said "Pardon" and he said "Pas grave" no problem, how embarrassing but then again what hasn't he witnessed of mine. I think it's the medication or maybe the processed food I have to eat. He was alright about it he is a doctor after all.

The nurse has just been, I get new nurses all the time. I honestly think the nurses' aim each day is to see how many people they can get to scream! She has got me again; they don't seem to acknowledge people's discomfort or inability to move. A couple of nurses have been trying to pick this scab off on the lower right ankle. It's a big scab, I was always told to leave scabs on, but nurses are obsessed with taking them off. This is the last scab remaining it's big and thick, so she tried her best until I screamed my head off, she then stopped. I thought bloody hell as if I haven't got enough to cope with. Leave my scab alone (big sigh) so now the scab is half off and half on and giving me discomfort.

The plastic surgeon doctor has recommended I see a psychologist, everyone is trying to get me to see a psychologist, he says it's a big thing (sigh) I said to him I have already got a degree in psychology. If they want me to see one, I will see one, but I don't know what depths they will reveal. They might section me if they get talking to me!!

Anyway, Stubby at the moment is tight and playing up but I think that's because he has been examined. I need to relax him and my elbow and shoulder. I did ask for some morphine because he did get a bit rough. Now I ask for it before he gets too rough, I have learnt the hard way, but I don't let the staff know that. I know I need the morphine under the tongue, no matter how much they tell me the other one works, it doesn't. Last night the girl came, and she gave me two of those little white tablets and said they were morphine. I said they don't work and then five minutes later she came back with the one for under your tongue. This was at 8 o'clock at night and the only other one I have is at 7:30 – 8 o'clock in a morning, I try and go all day until 8pm. I don't want to be on morphine, but I don't want to be in pain either.

Now they have just taken my blood pressure and there will be someone in to wash me. I think I am getting a bald patch at the back of my head. What else is there to say, that's it really. I probably won't have any visitors, people are busy. I think Michelle said yesterday that Rob was working this week and the boys were at school, so that's it we will see what happens this week I can't see me moving before Thursday there has to be a place for me or there is no point sending me. Okay from a fairly content if that's the right word, person who is trying to get through all the hoops and the dramas, over and out!

6 Minutes

It's still Tuesday about 9:00 Tuesday evening I am back recording because I think I need a good old moan. The day wasn't a bad day I think I had got up to them washing me and I am struggling with the food. I am trying to eat some of the food (sigh) I suppose there are a number of reasons why I can't eat it. One because if it's meat I really struggle to eat it knowing what the animals have gone through in intensive farming. The whole point of us having our own animals for eating is to not support that system. I got some pork the other day and I couldn't tell what it was, it was black. I asked what it was, thinking what's she giving me here! She said it was pork I must of pulled a face and she took it away and brought back boiled ham. They also keep giving me these drinks and saying it's good for me.

For example, tonight it was rice pudding. Well, I make good rice pudding it's not like what they gave me. The rice wasn't cooked, and it tasted as if it had loads of sweeteners in it. I could only take a few mouthfuls and then I am over it and I can't eat any more.

Then I get things in tubes which are supposed to be high calorie, it's from Nestles scientific health department whatever that is? It's high in calories but on the container, it never gives you what's in there. There are no ingredients on it whatsoever. So, I haven't got a clue what's in them probably laboratory fortified chemicals which happens to be high in calories. (Big sigh) I also get this drink, no fibre, no fat, high calorie drink. Well, what's in that? Again, no ingredients on it, all I want is normal food. I know it's difficult because they are supplying the whole of this massive hospital. It's probably manufactured outside and that's why the soup is made out of powder. I have had this theory for years that a lot of the food they are trying to get us to eat is really not healthy. I believe that the food we eat causes half of the problems that we get.

Why is it so weird to be organic? Organic is really being normal, it's even got a word now why isn't everything organic or should I say normal and natural? Not that long ago we didn't need to define things as being organic because that was all there was before the big farmer and supermarkets balls it up for our 'convenience'! So that's my moan about food.

Also, the physio came back, she is good she left me on the machine for 30 minutes which was fine but I did later have to massage my leg because it was quite painful. She tried to move my shoulder, but I think she has actually strained some of the muscles the last time she moved it. The problem is they want to move joints but when I was working, I always spent a couple of sessions massaging giving them a full hour before trying to move things. What is the point of moving something that's in spasm, it won't happen, all you do is force it to break the fibres down then you have got two problems to look after. I don't know if I will be able to get that across to her tomorrow, but I will try and massage it when I have finished this. But I still haven't had any more morphine, so I don't know whether to try and not have any tonight, I don't know. I think I will definitely try and go a couple more hours because the night staff will be on now.

I told you before that I wasn't going which is frustrating because I need to move now really. After the physio and dinner, they put me in a chair, put me in a harness and put me in a chair. I sat there for an hour absolutely hated it but knew I had to do it. I felt really dizzy, didn't feel happy all I wanted to do was fall asleep and be left alone. They eventually put me back and then it was teatime. We had like a shepherd's pie I knew the potatoes wasn't mashed potatoes (packet) but I can't complain, some people are starving and I am sat here complaining. I did get a banana which was good, and I also got a banana yesterday, which was good too.

This woman came I have to have an injection every day to stop blood clots. That woman I swear to God she is trying to torture me. I had just got my first mouthful of food. It could be my own fault because they used to come in the middle of the night, but I did used to be half asleep and the night staff would come with this big needle and inject me. I asked can't you do it before now I am just asleep when you do it. But this woman I swear I have got a bloody scar from what that woman did. Some put it in, and you don't feel a thing but the couple that have given me real pain have actually made me terrified of it now. Tonight, I screamed and shouted "Shit!" because of pain she couldn't put a needle in. I will now cringe every time she comes. Now I am going to be more stressed. I hope to God she's off tomorrow, but she did say "À demain" (see you tomorrow) I hope she's off. I need someone else to give me it, some give it without any problems. If it's her I will have to give her my dead leg, my dead side because she hurts me so much.

They must all be trained the same, but some just don't have the knack. I am going to have to pray a lot tonight that I have a better day tomorrow. I am getting really down at the moment not because of my situation, just because I want to move forwards. I need to keep thinking positive. Told you it would be a moaning one didn't I. I just want to get proper food, at least in Niort I can get some provisions. I would like things such as almonds, figs from the bio shop. I know it costs more but at least I'll know I won't be trying to fight the chemicals. I have enough chemicals in my system as it is without the food containing them.

I will have to buzz later and get them to shut my shutters and pull me up this bed and probably have another pee. A good thing is that I had a poo today believe me that's a big thing in hospital. Oh my God I will have to tell you this (I hope you don't tell above a dozen) this is quite embarrassing. I am full of gas and farty I have never been as farty in my life, I am putting it down to my medicine and the food. I couldn't believe it this afternoon a bit of poo came out. I thought oh no sugar! So fortunately, I had my toilet paper next to me. I managed to get it there was only a tiny bit, I was worried that my bowel problems was coming back and it could delay my leaving the hospital. I thought what do I do? What do I do? So, I buzzed and asked for a bedpan I had my wrapped up small piece and so I put it into the bedpan because it was too embarrassing to tell her. There was no problem, I just got her to pass me some of the stuff you wash your hands with, well hand! It was a bit dramatic for me I do hope the poo isn't coming back. Right I will leave you all in peace now. Sorry about the moaning but it's got to be said because I will forget it when I leave if I can ever get out of 544 that's my room number. Bye.

15 Minutes

Right I am going to have my last moan of the day. It is still Tuesday it's probably about 11 o'clock at night. I buzzed the night staff because I wanted the shutters shutting and a cover putting on and I also had a problem with how the nurse had bandaged my right leg it's too tight and irritating me. Eventually this nurse comes I also had a problem with my bed it was way too hard. They have to unplug this airbed when you go to the block (theatre) or x-rays and when they put it back in it never feels quite the same it goes really hard, it was hard and is getting me uncomfortable. So, this girl came, I am sure she was a nurse, her badge said she was a nurse. I said my bed's a bit hard can you please turn it down she said "No it isn't" I am thinking why, are you lying in it? How do you know! I replied alright then leave it she did mess about with it, but it was still rock solid, hard and uncomfortable. I will ask the nice one tomorrow to do it. Then I said could you look at my bandage. I don't know if she was just nasty with me because I can't speak French properly or what, but she was huffing and puffing. I said it's too tight and she said, "It isn't it isn't" and gave a big sigh. I said, "Oh forget it!" Then she said I'll go and get my colleague or whatever they call them "Tout de suite" (right away). An hour later nothing and by that time I was wanting a pee desperately and I am waiting to get the shutters shut and wanting to go to bed (sleep I'm already in bed!) I knew she wasn't coming back.

So, I had to buzz again and this other nurse came, different again, the first one had got me quite upset. I don't want to be in this situation, who wants people running after them I can't even have a pee on my own (getting upset, crying) then they can't be arsed even to listen to you. I hardly ever ask for help, only if I have to! The one that came before why does she do this job if she doesn't want to help people? I thought to myself "Shite to all the lot of you I'll sleep and if I piss in the bed that will be okay, if my foot falls off from tight bandages it falls off! But I can't pee my bed I just couldn't, so I had to buzz again. But the other woman came who was nice and she said, "Just buzz anytime it's not a problem" (big sigh) maybe not for her but the young nurse had a huge problem with it.

But it is a problem the whole thing is a big problem. I am trying so hard to get through it, but I don't know how much more of this I can take! I think if they move me, it will be a different environment and a different challenge. I think I am isolated I know I get visitors I am really lucky with visitors, but I have no phone. Rob was supposed to give me bloody Eric's phone because when I said that I have no phone to them yesterday they looked at each other and said, "Well we have given Rob a phone." So obviously that phone was supposed to be given to me so I could keep in contact with Rob, but he hasn't given me it for some reason?!!! So, I am just frigging abandoned here in frigging Nantes (big, big sigh). Anyway, such is life over and out moaning over.

4 Minutes

It's Wednesday morning I have just had breakfast, fruit and two biscuits. A woman came I don't know who she is, but she is always walking around with files in her hands. She looked at my hip or whatever she looked at and then said you are just waiting for a place, so it might be a week, talk about how to upset somebody.

I was already a bit fed up, I don't know I just think it's going to be one of those times where I might be up and down then up and down again (big sigh). Sheer frustration sheer boredom, if I could get hold of a good book, it might distract me from what's going on. I am a bit emotional today, but the two nice girls have come the one that lives next to Madagascar she goes back in July, she is a student here. The other one is quite active, she gets things done she is really nice, she is big into the use of arnica which I am, and she knows about alternative things.

I am proud to say I didn't have any more morphine last night so went all night without morphine. I went all day as well I think I only had morphine in the morning. My hope today is to just have the morphine I have just had now, I felt I needed it. I am not sure if it was mental, I don't know. For whatever reason I felt that I needed some. I know it's got loads of side effects, but I need to slowly reduce it, if I am down to one a day I will be happy. I don't want to totally get rid of it because I don't know what the journey is going to be like whenever I set off to the Grand Feu Niort. By the way things are going I will probably be all 'healed' and ready for dancing!

I am frustrated because I am not seeing the family. Rob's not here I want to shout why? I don't know, I just don't know, it's too difficult. We will see what today brings.

No doubt they are determined to get me into that chair again which isn't a problem it needs to happen it's just that I suppose I am sad that I am stuck in the same place. I should be grateful that I am in a bed, and I am but it's not easy. So, I will read the rest of this magazine I have got. They are full of kack really and advertisements, that's why I don't buy these expensive mags that tell and show you how your life should be. But I have got Bob Flowerdew's to finish, I am saving the radio, I am not using it too much in case my batteries run out. I will just have to wait for the nod at least I have got the psychiatrist to look forward to, now that will be interesting! After speaking to me he might section me and keep me in a different department, who knows?

I suppose they have got to be looking to be doing everything (which they are I am so blessed) they can in case there is any problems later on. About four times they have tried to get me to see a psychiatrist it was only because George Clooney asked me that I have said yes.

Alright then I will try and stay positive, but I think I have to try and accept that I am going to be upset. I think it's just a process of healing. Not to get too focused on it, if I am upset, I am upset and it's part of my emotions, part of everything that's going on.

I have asked and asked and prayed for a positive good forward moving day no dramas, here's hoping, okay.

4 Minutes

Well, it's now Wednesday evening 10:30ish today has been fine after breakfast, which I didn't have or did I? Yes, I did have morphine with my breakfast and tablets but not anything since. Things have been fine, not excruciating pain but painish. After breakfast I had my toilet and they washed me and then they actually did my hair. They asked me if they could wash my hair which is quite hard because you have to lie backwards. How anyone coped in a normal bed when they were ill I don't know at least these beds you can change their positions to try and get some sort of comfort and it's an advantage because they can turn the bed right up. I also had my dressings looked at by one of the nice nurses. She took the stitches out of Stubby and then she checked the left leg which I asked the night staff to do yesterday but she said there was nothing wrong with it, so I gave up but today she took it off. Then this other nurse came an older woman and they put, which I wanted them to do, put like this sticky stuff but it's padded on the sore which was rubbing. They also put it on the other side which was all red in between my little toe and my next toe because the nail on my little toe is causing a problem with the next toe.

She took the stitches out really well and everything was fine, but they have done it tight I will ask them if they don't mind loosening it off a bit tomorrow. They also found quite a few stitches left in which I thought when I was massaging it, what's that I can feel something but don't know what it is. I know it's not good to have stitches left in they go septic. There were a couple on my knee and a couple down at the bottom of my ankle. I am pleased that they checked and found them. That's two positive things, they washed me and got my stitches out.

Also, another girl gave me my injection remember yesterday it was really painful and awful but with this nurse I didn't even know she had been. I said, "Right you are booked for tomorrow, are you working tomorrow?" She answered "Yes" I said, "Can you please do it tomorrow the other one was a nightmare."

Then I had to sit in my chair, I don't mind sitting in the chair, but it does show how ill I am because it makes me feel tired a bit wobbly and insecure, I suppose. But when she put me back in the chair, she did it on her own with the harness she is really good, but she was going to let go of my legs and I said "No, no, no my leg" so that's hurting a bit I have given it a good massage. It could have been from the physio yesterday also leaning backwards today for quite a while that seems to hurt it. The physio didn't come today and, in a way, I was glad because I think I maybe needed a rest or the body needed a rest. She will be back tomorrow.

What else is there to say, nothing really. I keep thinking I should go on about other things because if this book ever gets put together is it just going to be about poo, and me complaining about food. This dinner time it was a chicken salad, I had to apologise to the chicken because I knew of the life it had had. Then we had eggs and what was it? Broccoli so I ate all the broccoli. The eggs were boiled eggs, but they just don't taste like eggs. I have been spoilt with our eggs which are wonderful.

Another day tomorrow I have the meeting with the psychologist, so a shrink is coming to see if they can sort me out, I might end up interviewing him or her! So, we will see what's going to be said, I just hope I am in a good place tomorrow, so I don't come across as depressed. Who wouldn't be depressed in this situation?

I had my last antibiotics for the bladder infection thank goodness, they are like horse tablets, and I don't like taking antibiotics I think they just strip away your own immune system. I just hope I can get my body back to its normal self without too much trouble. I needed the medicine when I arrived it saved my life and I probably still need it now, but I hope there is a way of me not having anything in the future. I have just got to be patient. I know this knee; I need it to move I hope this knee will move. The ankle I think will be a pain, but I can get it moving. This knee is still very swollen so I don't know what's happened there we will have to just see. Right over and out.

9 Minutes

Although things were slowly improving the pain still brought me challenges, and Stubby's character was starting to emerge.

Chapter 18: Recordings At Nantes Hospital And Phone Conversations At Last

"It's not death that a man should fear but he should fear never beginning to live."

-Marcus Aurelius

I am going to talk about the day of the accident and what has been told to me because I had forgotten, and Rob told me what I was doing. I was going to meet my friends Claire and Steven who had the boys at the beach for the day. I was meeting them halfway to bring them home we only had one phone (Rob had lost his at Adelaide airport) I had taken the phone; I obviously didn't get to where I was supposed to be meeting them. Claire was phoning me, but nobody was answering, in the end they came to the house. Rob didn't have an idea what was going on he knew that if I had gone to their house I would have sat and had a cuppa, so he wasn't worried about the time.

We only had one car, the boys were a bit panicky, but they were told that mum had broken down and Steven and Rob were going to go and sort it out. They had come a different way fortunately, so the boys didn't come across the accident and see the drama of all the ambulances, the police and the cars.

Rob said I know which way she has gone and so they found me. I don't know what their reaction was, I haven't really had chance to talk to Rob properly and being a Yorkshire male, he is all tough and everything else. Apparently, they were just cutting me out and they were explaining to Rob that they were taking me by ambulance to get into a helicopter to go to Nantes hospital. It wasn't looking very good at all!

Rob and Steven went back to our house I wasn't actually that far away about 15 minutes. Rob decided as it was getting late by now, he wanted to stay with the boys. The boys were told that someone had to go back and help mum sort it out and they had just come to get some stuff to help the car. So, the boys didn't worry or wonder where I was. They gave them a story about just needing to repair it so then the boys were satisfied and went to bed.

Rob stayed at home, Claire and Steven left Lewis sleeping with Peggy, Skitty and Mars on the sofa. The dog, cat and the baby goat, Lewis loved it. Unfortunately, the week before my accident my beautiful female goat Star died. She had given birth and I had lost one of her babies and I lost her which was really sad because she was such a beautiful character. For a while we had Mars, the baby goat in the room sleeping much to Peggy and Skitty's annoyance, but he was motherless, and we had to feed him constantly by a bottle.

Rob stayed at home I think he feared the worst and thought it was only right to be with the boys when the phone call came. Claire and Steven went all the way to Nantes hospital, I haven't had chance to speak to them. I think they waited quite a while to see if they could get any information. The information was not good it was 50-50 and they feared the worst on a lot of things. I don't know when they got back to their house probably in the early hours I would think.

Rob and Steven then came on Sunday, apparently they came to see me but I can't remember anyone coming. I was probably well and truly out of it. The doctor in ICU told me he didn't know what to do with me, so he put me on morphine and I was then in a coma for ten years he said and I said I have been here ten years? But he meant ten hours. The doctors had to start patching me up. My legs they were both broken my bones were sticking out. They have had to put, (I call it my dancing pole) into the femur on my right leg. I also broke my tibia and fibula. The surgeon had to go in from below my knee and there were various other things. The hand, there was so much gossip about the hand, they had to search for my hand, and I lost a lot of blood.

People say that I am being strong, they don't see my tears running down my cheeks on a night. I am not strong I am just trying to be practical, trying to be logical. I can't get my hand back; I actually think having my own hand that was just going to be stuck out rigid would probably be far worse than having it removed. I am already thinking of ways in which I can add things to it once it has healed, so I can dig in the garden, bake, and do other things.

My prayer and I tell you something I have had a permanent line to that energy and all the angels, is that the leg is good, if I can walk and bend and move it fairly normally. I just hope I can bring humour, hope and maybe able to give guidance to others. Thanks bye.

28 Minutes

It's Thursday evening it's got to be the 12th of May. Today has been okay the usual wash and then I got sat in my chair. I think the nice woman who does seem to want to do a lot for me, put me in the harness herself. This really scared me because I can't really let my right leg go down it needs someone to hold it. So, I hung on to it but I couldn't reach it at all, but we managed and we get me into the chair. Getting back on the bed was a little bit of a drama but there was someone else there who could hold my leg. I am so relieved when I get back on my bed. It is so tiring being in that chair, I think it's because usually my head is in a different position, and I am using different muscles. Once I got back in my bed I had quite a long sleep.

The doctor said that I was going to get a trickologist, a psychologist here today but nobody turned up. Like everything else it never happens on the day they say it's going to happen here.

A bit before tea and definitely after tea I felt quite sad, really sad. I think I was frustrated, I felt abandoned because I hadn't seen Rob and the boys. I haven't got any phone, I am not communicating with anybody, I just felt really, really bad. Rob doesn't communicate well if at all, it's got to improve because it's not good enough! I want him to phone me, I want to be able to speak to him there has got to be a massive improvement. It's not right because I get upset and feel angry with his lack of care and concern. I have no books to read which helps to distract me and passes time on. I asked the nurse the one who is so nice and has been looking after me (she is going back to her island that is next to Madagascar in July) about being away from home. But her answer didn't help but upset me more. She said she Skypes or phones her boyfriend every day that she has been here, everyday!!! I said do you mind telling that to Rob when he comes.

Anyway, she passed me out a book that I hadn't had out for a while Mel, my friend's book 'The Power Of Positive Thinking'. I just randomly open a page and it made me feel so much better. It basically said you have to think how you think about some things, before you ever start to do something. It will dictate the end result of what you do. For example, if you have faith in something and believe in something you are going to be more likely to achieve that. But if you start out thinking that you are not going to be achieving it or you are not going to be good, then you won't be. Norman Vincent Peale, the author gave an example of some baseball team that were losing and then there was a preacher who everyone believed in, and he took all their bats down in a wheelbarrow and had them blessed. The next day and forever more they just believed in themselves, and they were hitting runs. So, I am going to spend some time just thinking and try and get positive, though it's really difficult but I am going to try and be positive, okay bye.

4 Minutes

Penny Walker

It's Friday dinnertime I have just had dinner and it's usually quiet for a little while when they have taken your plates back there is usually half an hour of peace. This morning went fairly quick I got my bandages changed. Stubby now doesn't have any cover on him. All stitches are out, the only thing left to do is to take the barbecue skewers out of my left toes.

Both doctors visited they are happy with things. The doctor said I don't know if it's Wednesday or Thursday (others seem to think it's Wednesday) when I leave. Doctor Pietu will come back either the day before or that morning to pull out my barbecue skewers. He said he can do it here in my room and there is only four seconds of pain (big sigh). I am not thinking about that I will just have to bite the covers (bed covers). All stitches are out, and he said I probably don't need the cast but to use it on a night to keep the foot in the right place. That's all good, I think? I am trying to think of anything that I have forgotten to mention to add onto this.

Only thing I have forgotten to mention which is a bit strange, was when I was in intensive care there was one who was a very efficient nurse. Once when they cleaned and washed me while giving me my bed bath she said, "You have a very good bottom" so let's hope my 'Very good bottom' returns, it's just probably because I used to train quite a lot. Also, I have been climbing over loads of things and fences and God knows what else to feed and clean all the animals. It's probably toned up while doing that. All that now needs working on in the future.

I am quite positive today although yesterday I was quite sad about feeling abandoned, today I don't feel so abandoned. I am hoping I get visitors at the weekend. Rob has got to come because I haven't seen him for so long and he needs to bring me some stuff. Also, a woman has been, and he needs to sort out my tax returns. I suggested he gets Marie to help him. Well, if it's been done or not I don't know so he needs to come to sort that out. They have got to be in by the 30th of May which isn't far off.

I also had a meeting with the trickologist the psychologist. I don't know I just talked him to death for half an hour. He said I had got a very strong good attitude and he may come back before I leave, just to have a chat, I don't know. They have just got to do things it's better for the hospital especially when they are passing me onto another place, that they have everything tied up. Me talking to a psychologist means at least they can say that they looked at my mind in case I go cuckoo when I get somewhere else.

It's just been a very boring time although I am reading. I do hope Rob comes tomorrow with the boys. Bye.

5 Minutes

It's Friday night 10 o'clock I have just finished reading and need to go to sleep now. I just got the night staff in; my covers were all over the place. I have got like a metal frame thing over my legs to stop the bedding landing on my legs. I have a blanket but it's just too heavy it's not worth having it so I have taken that off and got the staff in and at the same time had a pee and hopefully I can get to sleep. I thought I would just tune in because I have been going to do this for ages.

It's the bassin (bedpan) talking about the bedpan it's been an absolute nightmare. I am actually grateful that I am peeing myself although I have finished the antibiotics, I don't know if I am still growing mushrooms or not? But one has just got to go with what they say and tell you. The bedpan I suppose is a good invention and people are really nice they have a little bottle of spray that they spray on it which means it gets a bit slippy. I have hardly seen it used here in plastics, but I did see it in trauma, not many used it but one or two insisted on using it.

Another week on from having had my arm removed from my groin and Stubby is calming down and he has had his stitches out I am more flexible, and my legs have improved. By getting more physio I can actually move a little better. But when I first started to use a bedpan oh my God it was so difficult and painful. First of all, I needed two people, I just couldn't do it. Now I sort of lift myself up and they put it underneath me, so you only need one person. I dreaded having to use it because it was so hard to actually get on it and get on it right. I was always worried about missing it and peeing or pooing in the bed, so I often had to move it around which is difficult. It's probably easier now because every week you are getting stronger and are moving forwards a tiny bit.

Like tonight it was in the totally wrong place, so I had to hoist myself up with my left broken hand, which I am keeping an eye on, but I had no choice but to use it. I had to move myself into a totally different place, then sit myself on it. I try and move my knees up as much as they will move, so I actually feel in a position to pee. I don't know if anyone had tried to pee uphill but it's really hard to do, well virtually impossible! I therefore have to try and fidget about with the right position. Then they have to take it away, so more moving positions and trying to hold yourself off the bedpan with a broken hand.

I just feel it's one of these things that is taken for granted. It's been so hard just getting on a bedpan without pain. But then I look at the positive, at least I am peeing, and I haven't got a catheter in which although it's good because you don't have to think about it, it can cause bacteria and over a long period of time I think it would be harmful to your bladder function. I had it for four weeks which is long enough.

So never take peeing or pooing for granted! I can't wait until I can sit on my toilet and have a poo and a pee in peace, although I never could have a poo in peace because invariably someone shouted me, wants me or suddenly they need the toilet or to clean their teeth. But to actually be able to pee on my own, on a toilet would be a major achievement. Right, that's the basin dealt with. Believe you and me I have found that quite a hard thing to do but one gets over these things! Bye.

5 Minutes

It's about 2-2:30 Saturday morning the nurses have just done the exact same thing they do every night. They come in open the door wide open so all the light floods in and I wake up, startled, just to ask me if I'm alright! Now I am agitated and can't get back to sleep, where's the logic? (sigh) What's the point of coming in at 2 o'clock to see if I am alright? I could have been dead on the floor by now. Why don't they come at 9 o'clock or 10 o'clock? (sigh) Anyway I am going to ask the boss it's wrong, every night now I am having disturbed sleep and then I can't get back to sleep. It's stupid, that's my moan over with.

1 Minute

It's now about 8:30-9:00 o'clock Saturday evening, it's been a good day. The boys arrived in good time although I was a bit angry, well not angry, just out of sorts and disappointed that Rob didn't get me a phone and I was looking forward to getting a phone. I wasn't feeling well either because I had a bit of sickness and diarrhoea. I believe it's the antibiotics they gave me for five days, I think it is just coming out of my system, because I have been to the toilet three times today and it's painful. I was agitated and then obviously poor Rob got it all. He shouldn't really because he has got so much to do at home.

The boys have been so good as well it is so frustrating that I am stuck here. Rob says he has been ringing the hospital, but no one has passed on any messages. You just start thinking well I have been abandoned, I have not got a phone and I can't speak to anybody. It's not been good for five days, so Rob got it in the neck. Elliott said (me laughing) "I am going to sit over here so I don't get shouted at." I wasn't really shouting I just (big sigh) needed to express my sheer frustration (I am feeling a bit sick so if I stop this it's because I feel sick, long sigh).

But they brought me some figs and some almonds. Also, some royal jelly which actually tastes awful, so I will have to find a way of eating that. None of that has given me this feeling I have been feeling sick for a few days really. Two assistants came in when the family were here and I wasn't that happy, so I don't know what they made of it all. Why am I left here for weeks without a phone? (Big sigh) It makes me beside myself with mental torture because I can't communicate with anybody!

There's Kay and Denbo I haven't spoken to them or some of my other dear friends that are all worrying about me, Susan in Yorkshire and Sharon in Australia, my parents, why can't I have my phone and why haven't I been given Eric's phone? It's ridiculous it's as if Rob is controlling who I can talk to it's not normal! I need to talk to someone it should be Rob, but he obviously doesn't want to. Christ, I have just been on my deathbed doesn't he think I need emotional support and reassurance it doesn't feel right.

I am not signing up for a hospital phone because they have kept moving me and saying I am leaving and I also think they are really expensive to use for both parties, bit of a con (big sigh).

All is good now I will have to just make sure I am in a nice mood the next time I see Rob. I will be sending him all my love through the airwaves and hope he gets it.

I did get to speak to my mum and dad because they phoned Rob while they were visiting me which was lucky though they got me on a bit of a downer which then upset my mum but what can I do? You can't hide it all the time. Mum had a chat, and everyone is saying how strong you are, how brave (big sigh getting upset). Then I spoke to my dad who said you are doing really well. Sometimes my dad seems his age and his brain is not like it used to be, but when (crying now) he spoke to me today it was as if he had gone back forty years he was just knowing and so present and wise. He just said how I had done so well and how proud he is of how I am coping and that just made me feel worse and grateful to have them by my side (break down crying). I hope they are not upset too much it's difficult to hear your child in pain whatever that child's age. It was so good to hear them.

I put the phone down and it rang again, it was Claire, Steven and Lewis. Nobody expected me to answer so they were all over the moon when they heard my voice because I hadn't had the means to talk to them. She was just so happy, and Lewis was so happy. He is only a young kid, but he understands what's going on. She just said she couldn't believe because she had to have a fairly big operation and she said she couldn't stick it for five days in hospital. Yet here I am six weeks later and without any phone (big sigh again).

Now I have spoken to a few people I don't feel as desperate for a phone I am over worrying about the bloody phone!! Claire said she had spoken to Sharon in Australia because Sharon phoned me, but she could only phone the nurses' phone and I only could say a few words, this was when I was in trauma. The nurse stood there and was not happy, Sharon sounded upset but I couldn't talk with her. Claire said Sharon was very upset and wanted to come over but couldn't. I don't expect her to come over from Australia. That's the next person I need to make contact with, I need to speak to my dear friend.

It was good to hear Claire and Steven they are coming over in two weeks so I will get to see them again. I put the phone down again and it rang again, and it was Kay who didn't expect to hear me. She was so pleased to hear me. I forget what people are going through out there it's been such a serious accident. You forget people actually do care about you and it's been a shock to a lot of people. Pat and Robin went to tell Kay and Denbo about my accident. Kay said on the phone that they were both in such a big shock (getting upset) sorry I am sorry, I am causing so many people so much sadness. I had a really good chat to Kay, and she then felt so much better and then Denbo came on Denbo absolutely bless him (big sigh). He is having some troubles of his own. When I was in England and we trained together many years ago, I think I kept him a bit sane, and we helped each other. He is having quite a difficult time because of my accident. I spoke to him and said my situation is no different to his and I am going to send him so much love and healing he is a very good man one in a million. Kay has also had her own health challenges, so my aim is to send them love and prayers it was so nice to actually talk to them.

Then I get to talk to Kelly, briefly, she is good, and the baby is good no more colic so that was good news. Then because they were visiting, I got to chat to the boys and Rob, and they stayed quite a while. I won't probably get to see them now for another week. I just hope that I still go on Wednesday, I hope I can be strong!

I have got two more reading books so they should keep me out of mischief, and I have got Mel's book, that is saving me to some extent. I am trying to remember I think it says in it, I still can't remember it "I can do everything through Christ." Oh, I will have to look it up I can't remember there it is "I can do all things through Christ which strengthens me." So, the book is all about having faith in things and it is extremely good but it's not religions in a religious sort of way it's just common sense. Hey why can't that work? Because the way the world's going there's nothing else that's going to work. In the world everybody just seems to hate each other. Right, I am going to have to go now because I still feel sick. Bye for now, bye!

11 Minutes

A week on from the big operation and the arrival of Stubby, brought many frustrations and questions, the biggest one being why I couldn't have a phone?

Chapter 19: My Last Recordings At Nantes And My First Recording At The Grand Feu

"Thinking is difficult, that's why most people judge."

- Carl Jung

I think it's the 15th not sure, Sunday night I am just giving you a bit of an update because I know there may only be a few days left here so I am trying to get all the information in before I go. Today has been good I slept really well last night, I didn't even notice them coming in to see me at 2:00 am, but I think now they just open the door slightly, so the light doesn't wake me up.

Today no visitors but I have had a shower the first in six weeks! Though they are really good at giving you bed baths, every day they give you a bed bath and they make you feel like a new person. The shower is very clever, they lift you onto another trolley which is all plastic, quite hard on your back, it makes my air mattress on this bed seem quite soft. They can put the sides up and then they take you down the hall to this wet room, you lie there, and they shower you. The only disadvantage which I would change is she washed my hair first and put water over my body, so I was quite cold and shivering because the room wasn't really warm. If she had done my body first, she then could have covered my body up while she washed my hair. It was good it was another experience. Then you are brought back, and they put you back in your bed, it's all good!

Because I didn't go in my chair yesterday, I promised them I would go in today. They put me in the chair to eat my dinner. It wasn't too bad; I don't know what sort of poultry it was is might have been duck it wasn't chicken so who knows what it was. There were some nice vegetables, so I ate them. Tea was some awful pasta cheese thing even the nurse who served it to me pulled a face. I got talking to her and she is going to London next week for a week and last night she told me she was staying in Manchester. I was thinking all night, so I had to ask her when she came back to work this afternoon. I said are you really staying in Manchester? Because that's a long way from London and there are no tube trains in Manchester. She must have phoned her husband and asked him to check. She came back and said no, no we are staying in Arsenal which is much nearer to London.

As we were chatting, they put me back in bed. They put me back in the hoist, but they got me the wrong way round and I couldn't get my legs on the bed and I tried and they tried and pushed me past the cradle thing and made me scream in pain they didn't mean to do it.

I have not been on the under the tongue morphine today but I am on two small morphines each day and I haven't been on any paracetamol at all today that's quite good but that didn't help the pain after I had strained it moving onto the bed. I am going to give my knee a little bit of a massage because it's stiff, it's about 10:30pm now.

I have just been reading a book called "A shepherd's Life A Tale Of The Lake District" by James Rebanks. I am reading it and it's all about this farmer in the Lake District. It's well written it's not like in chapters he jumps from this to that to this and it works quite well he is just telling you, his story. So, at one part he is at school, next he is a nine-year-old with his granddad. I am thinking well if this recording ever gets put to print it could work if you just say it as it is.

James Rebanks' book won the book of the year and described by the Daily Mail as "A surprising hit of the year" I can't put it down I have nearly finished it. I must go to sleep, so I am giving myself a honey sweet and after that's finished, I have got to stop reading or I am never going to get any sleep. As you can hear I am on a much more positive day today and I have to just keep that way because yesterday was quite a bad one. I think just seeing the family doesn't help well it does help but at first it doesn't because you want to be with them. Anyway, all is good, I think? We will see I hope the doctor takes out my barbecue skewers tomorrow because they are hurting, and I want to get it over and done with. The doctor said it was only four seconds of pain but there's pain and there's pain! Four seconds, how does he know? Anyway, the sooner that's done with the better, I have a feeling he will do it on Tuesday. Bye.

7 Minutes

It's probably the early hours of Tuesday morning, I thought it was a good idea each day to talk to this as my days end in Nantes hospital. Tuesday today should be my last day and night and hopefully if all goes well, Wednesday is when I leave for Niort. The man came Monday to tell me that I would be leaving I am quite hopeful although it has been said before, dates have been given before and it's never happened. But I think this time I need to move so I am sure it will happen on Wednesday, tomorrow.

Prison Or The Paralympics

Today I hope Dr. Pietu is going to take my barbecue skewers out, I am really not looking forward to it. He says it's only four seconds of pain, I am just going to grin and bear it, it can't be like the amount of pain I have been through over these last six and a half weeks, that can't compare to someone just taking out pins from my toes. I'll just pray that I don't have any or too much pain.

Yesterday was a very quiet day but by the time they have washed you changed your bed and put you in the chair it's dinnertime. I am not overenthusiastic about the food but I know I have to eat something I am not hungry or look forward to it. I eat probably more for something to do, a phase in the day, where you have a bit of "What's for dinner?" You look and then think: "Oh right!"

As far as time goes, I have not got a clue. The radio now has no battery so I can't even switch it on to see the time. The physio didn't come yesterday which I was quite pleased about because the day before my leg got hurt putting me back into bed. I think it got pushed the wrong way, so it's been a bit stiff. I do loads of movements I keep moving it, it just won't bend how it should do? I don't know why it's not bending. It's essential that I am back on my feet. I won't be able to do much if I can't at least have some mobility in my legs. The next challenge is probably physio and legs.

Yesterday I just read my book, finished it, stayed here really, I didn't do much. I have been thinking about these recordings and I was trying to get into my head how you would start such a book. I would thank people, my friends and family especially the Golden Girls even though we seem to spend an hour of their visit time talking about poo and farting. I would also want to give all my thanks to every person who has helped me, who's washed me, who's cleaned me, who have assisted me. I would like to give special thanks to the doctor in intensive, he was on nights Louis who spoke to me and gave me some reassurance. There were many good people that I have seen who cared and really wanted to help me, a big thank you to all of those. I cannot thank the surgeons and all the doctors enough. I now know what a mess I was in when I first arrived, and they didn't really know where to start. But somehow, they just started and fixed me up.

I would like to give thanks to my right hand that has now gone it may sound strange but thanks for all that it has done. The degrees, the exams, the decorating and renovating, the gardening, the knitting, the training, the holding of my babies, in fact everything! Everything it has ever done I thank it. I would also like to thank my new replacement Stubby and hope we have a long and active life together.

I think the doctors were amazing, are amazing. The whole hospital in Nantes is of an extremely high standard, I thank you all for giving me my chance. It's important to be aware of what the system is and what the daily routine is. Protect what's in pain because others don't feel your pain. If you are jolly, happy and upbeat they think there's probably nothing wrong and you have no pain.

Always have your politeness always be thankful, grateful and even speak to the cleaners they are so important. Say thank you say hello have a bit of a chat. I know it's difficult and I know at times it's hard, I have been there. Try and keep upbeat it's not their fault that you are in so much discomfort or pain.

Tomorrow I will probably waffle on again and then hopefully it will be a new adventure. I can't say I am sad to leave I just need to move and progress and get nearer home. I don't really know where I am going or what I am going to, but time will tell. So, bye for now.

14 Minutes

Its still Tuesday morning things are going around in my head so I thought I would put them down in this recording.

The date will never be forgotten it was the 2nd of April 2016, it's amazing how one small event, a five minute encounter can change the whole of one's life and one's family's life. It has been a difficult few years just to adapting to change, having in 2008 moved to France. I arrived first with the boys to get them into school, Rob arriving in the November, having to stay in the UK to finish off working.

The French house was in need of much repair even though we had had it since 2004 holidaying there. The doors needed replacing, also the windows and the roof and many internal work to do. I arrived with our old dog Suzie, Harvey was 8 and Elliott 5. I managed to find someone to do the doors, I found a company that did good solid wood and double glazed. I was determined to get the three doors changed so the gusty wind and rain couldn't come through all the broken glass and big gaps and enter the house in winter. It also meant I could surprise Rob when he got here.

We worked hard in 2009 to get things done because we were going to make another move at the end of 2009.

We had applied prior to move to Australia and because of the crash in the economy and the big panic over what I would say was man's greed, banks' greed. To me it was quite simple, people just got greedy that's what happened. The money wasn't there they (banks) were using money that didn't exist and it all caught up with them, especially the banks. I would blame the banks for their greed and not being responsible.

In my opinion the crash was caused by greed, and I don't think you can ignore 911. All those tragic lives lost! The hub of world finance, now gone, caused many opportunities to allow more corruption, as all the documents had gone. I think this must have contributed to the crash somehow.

We were given a date in which we had to be in Australia by. That meant we really needed to get main jobs finished like the roof and windows. I did actually go and start apple picking with my friend Marie who actually fell and broke her finger, so she had to have some time off. At that point I said I had to leave because Rob was getting so stressed at trying to get everything done before we had to leave in October to go to Australia. I could see I was needed more at home so that's what I did. It was crazy and hectic, but we got there and went to Australia.

The boys and I returned to France in a very, very wet February 2014, dog and cat in tow. I think it had rained for months and months and even when we were landing in Nantes (surprise, surprise, little did I know I would spend so much time in Nantes at a later date!) I could see the fields were flooded. We arrived and my dear friends Sheila and Marc came to pick us up, the dog, cat, me and the boys, after a long journey and I was so grateful.

Actually, getting the animals here was a stress in itself. We had little Peggy a cross between a Jack Russell and a Maltese. She doesn't think she is a dog she thinks she is a human and definitely part of the family. Then we had Skitty which we got from a rescue place in Australia, a beautiful black and white fluffy cat who is named well, she is quite skitty at times, but a very clever cat and bigger than the dog, she is a good cat.

Just getting them here was a major feat. I was advised to go via Kuala Lumpur because that was the only route that would take the animals. But a week before we were due to fly the guy at the company said we can't get them on that flight because they don't take your dog because she's got Terrier in her. I am thinking how can you not know that months ago, it's your company's job to fly animals around the world? I wasn't in a position to argue because I was due to fly! So, at the last minute they weren't on the flight which really stressed me out. They had to go with Emirates via Dubai, stay overnight and then fly on to Paris. The boys and I were going on a route which I wouldn't have chosen to fly, Kuala Lumpur and then to Paris. It's a longer flight and I had never flown with them before.

When we got to Kuala Lumpur, we had quite a long delay waiting in the airport. Elliott absolutely hated the place, I was very uneasy I just thought it was tiredness, but I promised myself I would never go to that airport again it just felt eerie! Nothing physically wrong but there was something not right, I felt some real bad vibes and even though we got delayed quite a while I was so pleased when we finally set off for Paris.

Strange enough only a week or so later a plane that flew from Kuala Lumpur, the exact same company we were with, one of their planes disappeared flight 370 also known as MH370 or MAS370, there were 239 people on board. Those poor people, where are they? What's happened to them? There is no closure for their families and friends so very mysterious, tragic and bizarre! Maybe I sensed it before it happened because I really didn't feel comfortable in that airport. There is no closure whatsoever for the people involved their losses and pain incomprehensible.

We got to Paris fine, I try to get the animals not fine! Major drama, I have to go out through the airport, which is massive, it's the International Paris airport, Charles de Gaulle, onto a bus out to the cargo which is not close by and get the animals. Bear in mind I am booked on a flight from Paris to Nantes in a few hours.

I had to leave all the cases and the children tucked away in seats next to Emirates and told them not to speak to anyone. I left them with a pain au chocolat, hot chocolate and told them I had to go and get Peggy and Skitty and it was easier for me to just go, leave all the suitcases there and for them to stay. Any problems I told them, and you go to the Emirates desk and they will look after you. That was a huge stress in itself even though they were five years older and grown up they were no longer young children. Harvey had grown up significantly and was very reliable as was Elliott. Both wonderful boys.

So off I went, I get to the place eventually, it's shut for its dinnertime. Normally in France they have at least a two hour lunch break. I was now even more stressed; I had my knitting so I was knitting away trying not to panic tears rolling down my face. When the time came, I went to see the guy again, he saw my stress and sort of understood. I explained I had the children waiting in the main airport and I was really stressed about leaving them and we also had another flight to catch.

Then I get my animals (there is no need for quarantine because they were coming from Oz) Peggy is so fussy I have got her lead so I can take her out of the box and let her have a wee as we waited for the bus, I am struggling with two big boxes. Skitty I daren't open her box door and she is most mortified and looks at me as if I was evil and why I won't let her out. But at least she knew she was with us again. God only knows what they both were thinking as they travelled the long, long hours in the cargo section of an airplane!

I clambered up onto the bus with great difficulty and get onto the bus, people looking at me strangely. But I didn't care I had got my animals back and was back on route to the boys. So, I clambered back off the bus, I think somebody did help me. The boxes are big, and I am tired and stressed, but I managed to walk all the way through the terminals and get back to the boys. Now it was a matter of racing to the next place because we had another plane to catch.

When we first got to the desk, we were there early but the lady said "You are not on this flight." I think it was because you have to book yourself online or something, I don't know. She continued "You are not on this flight, but the next flight is in a few hours." I said "You can't, please you can't do this to me, I have got two children we have been flying for nearly a day and I have two animals, please, please don't do this to me. Is there any way you can get me on this flight? I have friends waiting for me at Nantes can you please get us on this flight!" As luck had it Sheila just phoned me as this discussion was going on. I told Sheila to hold on I have just been told I am not on this flight, and I will ring you back.

The kind, kind lady did get us on the flight what a massive relief. I don't think I could have done another two hours sitting around, it had been such a hard time getting there. There was a problem with the weight of the luggage. You are allowed more on the international flights than you are on the domestic. So, I juggled everything around and had to pay a big amount of money. We had to let the animals go again, Peggy to her distress had to be put back into her box so they could be taken on the plane. They must have thought no not this again it must have been confusing and stressful for them I bet they thought "What are you doing to us again!"

The boys, animals and I landed absolutely worn out, late at night laden down with suitcases and two big animal boxes. I opened up the sofa bed found some damp sheets and all 5 of us including the cat and dog climbed in, we slept exhausted. (I must admit the house hadn't been lived in for five years we had only visited it once in the summer with our dear friends Sharon and Richard from Australia. But we didn't spend that much time cleaning up and tidying up except in the kitchen, bedrooms and bathroom).

The next morning, we woke up and we had slept in a very mouldy place. The floor was mouldy because the cave (cellar) was under that room, but I set to, got it cleaned up, the fire lit although the wood we had left was really damp. The bit of good wood that was dry only lasted a week. I did get some more but it was poor quality.

It was so damp and cold, and we had all just come from a very hot Australia. I think the cat and dog thought I had brought them to a place with no light because none of us left the room for at least three weeks and the shutters never got opened. We all just slept and then we slowly came back to life.

A few months on here I am in sunny France I had slowly got some animals. I started off with chickens progressed to rabbits, pigs, goats, pintades (guinea fowl) turkeys and geese. Lots of work lots of organising but we were heading towards self-sufficiency. I had come to the conclusion that we lived in a world that was quite crazy really. If you worked hard, you paid taxes but didn't get much for it. Pensions, what's them? They have disappeared I doubt very much if I will get a state pension! My idea was and has always been from a young age, to live off the land. At least if you have got a roof over your head and you can source your food you can live. You can't eat money! I know you have to have money to pay some bills but if you can keep the bills down to a minimum, I think life can be simpler and better.

We were becoming self-sufficient in meat; the vegetables were a bit more sporadic due to me having time but they were getting there. There is no comparison in the difference in quality and freshness, and for me the big thing was the life the animals had been given. This intensiveness of keeping animals is just not right it's not correct! The advertising and supermarkets tell us we need to eat meat or have the supply of meat every day we are told we need this and that. For people to then waste so much of it that the animals have sacrificed their lives for. In my eyes it was way out of balance and wrong. People have often commented but how can you kill them and eat them my response is how can you support such a cruel system just to get your Sunday roast or fast-food fix.

So, there I am in a life of luxury, I am living a dream, hard work though it be, but getting things organised. Rob had arrived back about a year and a few months later at the end of May 2015 having only been over for a visit in the summer of 2014 the previous year.

So here I was with the animals often caked in mud or poo, but it was good. Spring had just started, winter although not awful was cold but everything had managed to survive. We were warm in our one room and jobs had slowly started to begin to get some attention.

20 Minutes

Sorry I can't remember where I was the night nurse came in, so I had to stop recording. I think I had got to the point where I had explained everything about getting here (France) and coming back from Australia.

I was saying we lived in Yorkshire, Yorkshire folk are strange in a way, because they are very proud people. If you look at the history, we are mining villages, lots of history with quite a wild environment. We are grafters (workers) well most of us and we say it as it is we call a spade a spade. We don't really put up with too much crap and we don't like lies or falsehood. We are just really 'right folk' to be honest, well the majority are. So that's a Yorkshire character in my humble opinion.

So why move to France? A number of reasons. To be self-sufficient and to be able to afford somewhere that offers that possibility for it is too expensive to do in the UK.

Prison Or The Paralympics

It's now the 2nd of April 2016, I can't remember much which at first frustrated me. But I thought thank goodness I can't remember anything. Everything I am saying now is what I have been told.

Claire had texted to say they were having pizzas, she had the boys, they had been to the beach for the day with Lewis their son. Rob and I stayed at home to get some jobs done because we had Pat and Robin to stay the next day. I had done cleaning and various jobs and getting all the animals sorted out so I could spend time with them when they arrived.

I think Rob had baked quite a few biscuits; we had got the wood burning oven on. They were in the oven, and I was to put, when I came back from getting the boys a chocolate cake and some caramel slice in, finish tidying the downstairs and then prepare the room for Pat and Robin on Sunday morning, so Rob told me. Also get the meat out for the next day and make a Sunday dinner.

The text came and they said they would meet me. Rob had said he would go but I said no it's not a problem you are tired you just stay here and rest for an hour. So off I went on a normal route that I had travelled many times to go to the supermarket and that was the end of that.

The next thing I knew is that I have got these bright lights shining down on me everything is white with people around me. Rob came to see me I said, "Hi what's happened?" his reply "You have been in a car accident." "A car accident?" I questioned. That was the biggest shock because I drive respectfully, carefully and I have been driving since I was 17 years old. I had a brilliant instructor who taught me you always give at least two car length distance in front so you can see the car in front and also the car in front of that if the car isn't big or a lorry. So, you are always aware of what the cars in front are doing. I also have the policy that I would rather arrive five minutes late than not at all. Risks weren't taken on my part, no accidents, the odd bump in a car park but in my whole years of driving no accidents. No claims on the insurance except when I drove my car through some flood water, and I damaged the engine.

I was in shock when Rob told me, if he had said I had got knocked down by a bus crossing the road I would have been less shocked. I said "They were pissed they were all over the road. Where's the boys?" His reply "Oh they are fine." I looked at him and thought that's what they say on the movies they are fine! Not to upset you, the person who has survived the crash. I looked at him accepted his answer but really didn't believe him. So here I was in a bed wired up, I was in immense pain, I couldn't move, I didn't know what was happening, I was not good at all!

Room number 19, I can remember it being on the door, 19. Rob came the next day with Pat, Robin and Claire. They were all really relieved to hear and see me and my usual craziness. I think they were all worried that I was going to be different, which is quite normal after such a major car accident. But I was myself be it in pain, but I was still myself. It was good to see them and chat.

I don't know when I got to see the boys, I think the following week when they were on holiday from college. Rob had warned them that mum might be different, I think I must have been black and blue not that anyone told me. When Elliott came into ICU he went "Wow!" I thought does he mean 'wow' to me or does he mean 'wow' because of all my wires and tubes. It was good at least I could relax that the boys were alright.

Then things just carried on I had to stay put, I had to be fed, watered, cleaned turned and tortured. Oh God it felt like torture sometimes. I had this extremely painful hand and the rumours and stories went that they were looking for my hand but couldn't find it. It was reattached but it went gangrenous I had this painful smelly hand for nearly a week. I remember these three doctors coming to look at my hand, I said take it off! I could smell it I could see the black fingers I couldn't see the reason why I would spend all my energy compensating, combatting and putting up with a gangrenous hand when I had so many other injuries. I needed to heal, the gangrene was never going to heal it was too bad and dead! I had to say my goodbyes to my hand, and it went six days later. The wait was difficult, the pain got that bad that I couldn't cope. I was on morphine, but I was crying out for more, the pain was crazy and intense.

There was a period of time when they said you are having the operation, you can't eat or drink and then the operation did not happen. This went on for about three days. In the end I said I need this hand off, please, please, please take this hand off!

I think it was a Saturday and I thought to myself they are not going to do an operation on a Sunday so if it doesn't happen today then it is another day and another week I have to put up with the smell and the pain, I don't think I can do it, I know I can't continue with the pain.

Then it happened I went down about 10:30am to the block. Three doctors were there I said to them if you hadn't taken this hand off today, I was going to the butchers. They said "Oh no, no we don't butcher" I said "I know you don't, I just want someone to chop it off." This is all in French and my French isn't the best and my accent doesn't help.

Then I met this really wonderful woman. I am sure she is an angel. I remember her having these really nice blue eyes, she was all gowned up and she said "Oh I remember you, you coming in, I much rather see you like this then when I saw you when you came in." I said, "Oh God thank you for giving me my life back." She could speak English and said "You are welcome" I talked to her, and I said I can't remember anything. She said, "Oh well we gave you something to take it all away." I thought that's good, bit KGB but I thought that's a good idea.

So, whether they did or didn't put me in a coma I am not sure. It was nice to see her and bizarrely I saw her again, she was my anaesthetist for the next operation. Then I saw her again when I had my final operation. She wasn't around at first but then she came after I was waiting in recovery. She had brought another patient in, and she said hi, so it was a sign to me that everything was going to be alright. I will stop now.

18 Minutes

It's Tuesday evening 8-8:30pm I think this is my last day here it's booked for me to go in the ambulance tomorrow at 12, 12:30 or around 12:45. It's been a strange day, a good day. A really good day the staff I get on with really well have been here, the ones I can have a chat with and are really lovely.

This morning it was the usual breakfast. Then the toilet, then it was just waiting for the doctor to come and take the barbecue skewers out. They washed me as normal, they do it so efficiently and I think my hair too.

Then something really bizarre happened, these two guys, one a doctor one a junior doctor, I always read their name badges. They came in and said they were from x-ray I asked if I was going to x-ray? He pointed to my leg. He took the sheets off and started unwrapping the bandages. I asked, "Are you doing it here?" They then left but didn't cover me up or say anything. They then came back starting unwrapping the rest of it and taking my cast off. I am saying no, no I want the doctor my surgeon Dr. Pietu. Then his phone rang, and he suddenly stopped walked out of the door and left me as I was and didn't say anything.

I spoke with the nurse to ask what was happening. I was very stressed about it. Then just as my food had arrived Dr. Pietu came, he said "Eat I will come back." I said, "I will stop eating it's no big drama, it's not as if I really enjoy it." He said, "No I will come back" my reply being "When you come back bring the wine with you" (not that I like wine) he laughed and said, "No wine". Then the nurse came in with the morphine the one you put under your tongue saying you will need it he's taking your pins out. I said I am happy not to take it. The doctor came back and took my pins out, they were so long.

Isn't it amazing, I am reading the book 'The Power Of Positive Thinking' that Mel gave me because after the two guys had been I was worried who was going to take them out. I said to God and the powers that be please give me guidance. I randomly opened on the chapter on how to not stress yourself, believe it or not that's where it opened, the chapter on how to not stress yourself. So, while I was stressing myself I read through a few pages and then I felt much better and then Dr. Pietu arrived. He is a big strong guy, and it took all his strength to pull them out. The fact that he held down the underside of my foot with quite a lot of pressure with his other hand while he pulled them out made it a quick, efficient movement. I was shocked at the size and length of them, but it was good. I was amazed at how little pain there was, in fact the nurse (well some of them) give me more pain taking my blood. Dr. Pietu is a very clever and extremely experienced doctor, and I was grateful he was the one who took out my barbecue skewers. Hopefully I will see him tomorrow, I have to go for an x-ray tomorrow so hopefully he will visit me, and I can say my thanks and goodbyes.

My other doctor came this morning to check me out. He said "Bonjour, bon weekend?" I said, "Yes I went all around the magasins (shops) and then went to the disco this weekend." He is just looking at me laughing his head off in front of me. Because where have I been? I have been in here! How can you have a good weekend in here? We just talked about everything, everything is fine, and he is happy with Stubby. I have to come back in about six weeks, he wants to see me and check everything again so that's good. I might see both the doctors tomorrow before I leave.

Then I got in the chair but before that the physio came, she was good and we had a good chat. She is here for 20-30 minutes but she works me hard. I made her laugh a few times and she was fine and happy.

After they put me in my chair someone said do you know you can have the radio on, on the television free! Hello last day here and I have only just found that out. So, I have had the radio on, finished my other book then I asked them if I could go back into bed (noise of an airplane). See another airplane, it's mental here, there's another going to Nantes airport probably, I think that one's Jet2. Sometimes I can tell what the planes are I can read their logo that's how close they are.

I said to the girls because I had been thinking that surely, I could just get up on the bed and not have to use the harness. There were actually three of them, so we managed to lift me up onto the bed without the harness which is a bit of a contraption at the best of times and quite scary. They said their goodbyes, I thanked them so, so much. What can you say thank you doesn't seem enough. The girl who knew about arnica and we chatted quite a bit went and got me some water and filled my water bottles up. I said thank you, you are so special, it was a bit emotional. But it's got to be onwards and upwards now, you have got to move on! They said to come and see them when I come back, so I will, Rob will know where it is because I haven't got a clue. I was pushed around by porters everywhere, so I don't know where the heck I am going. I hope to be walking in six weeks, I want and need to be a bit more mobile.

She also brought me a phone so I could speak to Rob and tell them I was leaving because I still didn't have a phone. She wrote the address out so I spelt it out to him they can look up the directions and they may visit me tomorrow. It was so good of her and that's why I sound so upbeat.

I am happy because my pins are out, because I am moving and because I got to speak to Elliott on the phone and he was really excited. It's really strange listening to your children on the phone, they sound really grown up it's strange hearing them. He is so excited because Salt and Pepper which are his show birds hatched some chicks, but one was cold. I don't think the mum would have rejected it, but it must have got out of the nest. So, Elliott picked it up with Harvey's help and put it under the heat lamp and asked God to help, for it to stay alive and it did stay alive. He put it back with its mum and she accepted it and it's running around now. She has got three Pekins, potentially show birds, then the black one has hatched some and little Clare the bantam is due to hatch some in a few days. The Combatant is sat in a really awkward place I suggested that they need to try make her a nice place. You risk her coming off the eggs but if she comes off just put the eggs in the incubator. If they cover her up and its dark feed and water her she will go back on them. She is in a dangerous spot in a hole in the wall. If she has sat this long (usually it's 21 days). She will probably sit again even if they move her.

Elliott sounded quite excited that's good maybe I'll see the family tomorrow. I hope so and I hope I do get to move because it's much closer to home.

I have got to work really hard and hope this knee doesn't give me too much grief. The toes might because they have got to heal but if I can bend the knee, I will be fine. I don't know what the ankle will do, I am not allowed to weightbear on the right leg yet, I have two more months from now. I will see what they say at my next place another adventure (airplane noise) looks another airplane, can you hear it? That's not as low as the others I can't see it, it's not a big one that's why you can't hear it as much as the others. Yep, I am on an airplane run but it keeps me occupied, for I keep looking up when I hear them. I am a bit emotional, optimistic and upbeat. Bye.

13 Minutes

I don't know if you can hear this, but this is the helicopter arriving (noise of helicopter). It's probably 9 or 10 o'clock so I am tucked up ready for sleep. The helicopter isn't far from my room, well it is far, but I can see it very well from my room and as you can hear I think that's one just arriving on the helicopter pad. But sometimes they are all night long which I always fear and sometimes they park in a certain position, and I can actually watch them bring people in. I can't see that much but I can see them bringing in a trolley (big sigh) it's always a bit sad for me. I always send them strength and love because that's how I arrived and look at the condition I was in. You hope the people who arrive like that in the helicopter are going to pull through. I often wonder if the same doctors and anaesthetist I had sees to them as well.

1 Minute

It's Wednesday night I think it's the 18th of May. Today I moved. This morning after another good sleep I had a shower. The girls are really nice the one who is a student and is going back to the island just off Madagascar and the other girl who is going to London for a week in July. They are good, and good fun they get me straight into the shower after breakfast and washed my hair. They managed to do that and then the nurse started to redress my legs but the guy came for me to go down for x-rays, so they only dressed one, the other still needs looking at in the place where they pulled the pins out. So hopefully here today they will change that.

I went for my x-rays came back missed the physio, but she came back, she did a little on my shoulder and then I said my thanks and goodbyes. Doctor came said my goodbyes and thanked him. The psychologist came for five minutes gave my thanks and said goodbye. Then it was just waiting for the ambulance. Two guys arrived and we set off. I was lying on the ambulance bed, so I had to go backwards, one of the guys sat next to me.

It rained, rained and then rained some more. It was bizarre to be outside, to see green, to see buildings and cars. It was as if I had just entered another world, it was as if I had been cocooned, I don't know a strange feeling. It must be a similar feeling for people when they are released from prison, very weird feeling. You suddenly see all these trees, buildings, sky and this space after you have been looking at four walls for weeks, months or whatever length of time it's really a bit surreal and weird.

I decided to have a sleep because the guy was reading something on his phone. How could he read in a car, well an ambulance I would only have to send a text and I would be feeling sick and headachey. I admired him to be able to do it and the size of the writing was small, they are all going to end up with bad eyes this generation of spy phones!

I got here (Grand Feu) checked in, but the bizarre thing is they asked if I wanted a single room or will I share. If I have a single room and the insurance company don't cover it, it will be 45 euros a night/day. I said I will share, thinking I don't really want to share. I had to leave 50 euros; well Rob did when he visited for the telephone. I won't

Prison Or The Paralympics

use the TV or the telephone because it's so expensive to use and seeing I wouldn't be working anytime soon I didn't want more stress of unnecessary bills.

I got taken to my room by the ambulance man it's quite a big place and guess what I am in a single room. The ambulance guy said it's all for insurance, they probably haven't got any double rooms, if you choose to be in a single room then it's an excuse for them to charge you more on your complimentary insurance. I said God that's a right mean bloody scam! I am hoping that it is documented that I choose to go in a shared room so they shouldn't ask for any money off my insurance just for the privilege of a single room, when we came to the conclusion that they probably didn't have any shared rooms anyway. It's a bit naughty but probably not bordering on illegal but very ruthless none the same, because how would anybody know there were no shared rooms. It's also funny because there was a piece of paper with my name on it in this single room, so I was never going to go into a shared room if there are any.

It's so very naughty that's one thing that's really depressed me, but I won't let it, it's annoyance, everything is about how much money they can get out of people. But hey let's hope they haven't got that out of me. We can't afford to pay 45 euros a day I might be here months, hopefully not!

I met everybody, the doctor, Dr. Belkacemi, I am having physio twice a day 11:30 and 4:30 lots of talking some I couldn't understand but possibly I will be able to go home at weekends. Now I am in a different bed just waiting to see what happens.

Fortunately, they gave me my evening meal in the room and my breakfast will be given in my room but I have to go to the restaurant for my lunch and evening meals but I have no clothes I have only got this Nantes hospital gown.

Rob and the boys came tonight, he will have to come back because he didn't bring me any clothes he will have to come back tomorrow. So, the reason for not allowing me a phone is starting to backfire, I could have let him know if I had been given this invisible phone of Eric's. The only reason he is not given me a phone is so I can't make contact which is extremely strange and not normal. At least it's only 40 minutes to an hour away for them now. So now that can't be an excuse, it will be much easier for them. Let's see what happens.

Quite sad today. Not because I was leaving the place Nantes hospital, but because some really good people have looked after me. Sad to say goodbye to the doctors though I will see them again. I have got here let the next phase begin!

7 Minutes

This chapter documented my last recordings while in Nantes hospital. I did many, some repeating and some going on a bit, but it was real and raw in a situation I had never envisioned myself to be in. Also included in this chapter was my first recording at my new home the Grand Feu.

I continued to record as my journey unfolded and in doing so, I captured and preserved a moment in time, unedited, not rehearsed and from a deep place within me. It not only allowed me an insight to myself five years later but also how not just a physical and mental part of a human can be changed, but their spirit, their soul and energies that have yet to be named. It allowed me to be opened up and accepting to a much bigger environment than the one I lived in. It gave me a sight I had never seen with and a hearing that I had never heard with. I was now better equipped to understand that which couldn't be seen or heard in the normal human realm that we limit ourselves to. I was given a blessing to strengthen and guide me to a place free for anyone who reaches for it. A place of peace, love and harmony within. But first you have to complete the journey that you have been challenged to undertake and grow from.

Chapter 20: Dubai 7s And New Year In Perth

"Beautiful people are not always good but good people are always beautiful."

-Buddha

It was now time to start heading back to the UK, from my world trip and remember I had that small task of finishing my 20,000 word research paper for my Master's degree. Oh, shit I forgot about that!! But there was one more stop to make and that was Dubai.

When I was doing my degree in the 1980's one of my friends was Kathy Wringley, her degree was also physical education but also computer studies. Kathy ended up working in Dubai for a few years and then went to live in South Africa. She was married to Michael Burke and had a lovely son called Nick. They were involved in the Dubai 7's rugby union tournament providing the shirts via their company called the Ultimate Clothing Company. It just made sense to have a stopover in Dubai to break up the long difficult flight from Oz to the UK. Kathy had the contacts and friends still living there. Like I said before it all comes down to who you know and who they know. I told Rob if he wanted to stop off and watch the 7's I would be able to get him into the tournament. Being a crazy sports fan, it was a no brainer for him. Rob sat for three days watching the tournament whereas I ended up volunteering. I told Kathy that if there were any team in need of help, I was happy to help them. That offer was snapped up by a team called the Warblers. This team consisted of up-and-coming young New Zealand players the team being different every year.

On the 1st of December 1998 I headed for Dubai. In 1998 Dubai was not the place it is today the airport was extremely basic and small.

By the 3rd of December the teams were training in preparation for the tournament. England was there (I managed to get on their team photo, why? Because I just happened to be there), Scotland, Tonga, New Zealand, America, yes America and of course no 7's would be complete without Fiji. And don't forget my team the Warblers, the young New Zealanders.

The Warbler's first game was against America which they won. We then went back to their hotel, in 1998 the best and biggest (probably the smallest now). My humble hotel which Kathy organised for me was the Golden Sands. I was very grateful there was a bed. It was also on a very busy working street for the local ladies of the night and day, making going for a bottle of milk or food to the nearby shop a challenge. Unlike my accommodation the Warbler's hotel we went to was draped in gold, had 25 floors and God knows how many swimming pools. We went for the lads to swim and relax, have treatment and mentally prepare for their next game which just so happened to be England with the likes of Underwood being part of the English team.

Preparations were going well; they were nervous about playing England. They were all so young but where they lacked experience they made up for with fitness and passion. We all got back into the minibus to go back to the tournament. We had to go on a motorway kind of road which had a few lanes and was fast. There were men waiting to cross this road with the constant fast traffic and I thought gosh that's crazy it's like trying to cross the M1 or M62. Then there was a bang and a swerve, and we came to a standstill. I did see something white fly past, but I was in the middle of the bus not the front. What had happened is that some vehicle in front of us had hit a person trying to cross which threw them in front of us and we hit them too. The whole bus was in shock especially the bus driver. I just went into automatic pilot. I told them all to stay on the bus, not to look and I would go and see if I could help. I was the first and only person there and it became like a slow-motion movie.

The man looked straight at me he was wearing a long white robe and he was trying to pull his robe down over his legs. No screaming just silence and looking straight into my eyes. The obvious injury was that his foot was in another lane, yet I don't think he knew he had lost part of his leg. I spoke to him and touched his arm and told him help was coming and he will be alright. He probably didn't understand a word. I looked up behind him there was absolute madness going on. Other cars bumped into other cars, people arguing but still only me by this man's side. Something told me there wasn't anything I could do for this man, and I needed to get the young players away. I ran back to the bus checked that the driver was okay and if he was able to drive, if not I would drive, he was able to drive. We got back to the ground, but the event had affected everyone we did get some extra time by the organisers for the players to have some recovery! It was a bad accident a very bloody scene and all the guys saw it. Forty minutes after this they were on the field playing England. In the changing rooms before the game the atmosphere was very sombre and quiet, they needed more time they were still in shock. They lost to England and their next match was against Fiji. Even without the accident the Fijians are hard to beat, they are so powerful.

They played Fiji the next day and lost so now my team was out of the tournament. One of the young Warblers played for the English team in the England v Australia game. England lost but the young warbler did us proud.

The Fijian team beat the Samoan team and were in the final against New Zealand. Before the final the Warblers performed the Haka behind the sticks (goal posts) and what a good performance they gave. I think it must be in New Zealanders blood for they all seemed to know how to do it. It didn't put the Fijians off though because they beat the All-Blacks and won the 1998 Dubai 7's. I think that was morally uplifting for the Warblers the team that beat them also won the tournament. I personally think it was my rub downs and treating the Fijians granite thighs that gave them the advantage! (Remember I helped them out by treating one of their players with a dead leg)

If our Michael Thomas had the same atmosphere and experience of an extremely fast and amazing sporting event, then like me when he played there, he will never forget it. Playing for your country of Botswana against such other great athletes must have been exciting and rewarding. So pleased you got to live the experience too Micky!

Regarding the accident Kathy said that the law in Dubai was that the last one to see someone alive can be made responsible for the death, it goes back to something to do with camels! I suffered for a few nights after the accident every time I tried to close my eyes; I saw the poor man's face even though it was calm his eyes haunted me. Through the day as well as during the night and whenever I saw a man with a turban on I saw his face.

The mind is amazing, a person can go through an extremely traumatic experience, see, hear and smell the trauma yet the mind will selectively push that image deep, deep away in a compartment. But does the process of hiding those scars change that person for the rest of their life?

We all left Dubai at different times. Kathy, Mike and Nick were visiting the UK to see family and friends before heading back to South Africa. They managed to come and visit me in Yorkshire and my mum gave Kathy for the second time after fifteen years Yorkshire puddings with gravy. Mike and Nicholas got some too!

I hadn't quite finished with 1998 there was still a couple of weeks to go before Christmas which I spent sleeping due to jet lag and looking at my work for my master's degree and also catching up with my patients. But there was one last thing to fit in, another adventure.

The next adventure was with Andy, Lisa, Bobby, Rob and Rob's girlfriend Vicky in Perth. Yes, it could well have been Perth Australia when Andy was involved for you never knew where you would end up whilst in his company. With Andy a different country not a problem, the card would come out and the next thing you know you were at the other end of the country or in another country. Fortunately, that didn't happen to me and Perth Scotland was all my fault.

At some point it came up in conversation that Andy had always wanted to spend a New Year's Eve in Scotland. Me too was my reaction, okay let's do it. That's how we ended up in a lovely hotel for three nights in Perth Scotland. I booked the hotel well in advance and I asked Bobby if he would like to go. Being the easy-going adventurous person, he was he said yes. We arrived in cold Perth, it felt particularly cold to me having just been in the other Perth Australia and the hot dry climate of Dubai. The hotel was a big Victorian house a nice welcoming place. On the first night we ate our evening meal, Rob was not impressed he said it was like an old folk's home, but in the bar later he got into the mood of things and even sung a song on the karaoke.

Bobby was adopted by my friends, and he went on to impress them with his tall stories of being a high diving champion at the Rome Olympics, but he slipped because someone had put soap on the diving board. He slipped and lost his gold medal. He also had a story about how he had to move an F1 car on one of his long-distance lorry driving jobs, think he said it was in Germany. Obviously that story was for Rob's benefit. Bobby's stories were always enchanting he gave a lengthy introduction, dropped names and places and let his imagination loose if I hadn't of known him all the years I had, I would have probably believed them too.

I don't know if anyone remembers Eddie The Eagle, Eddie Edwards. Bobby looked just like him, the same milk bottom glasses a small built man down to earth. A contagious real and honest personality with a bit of his own added fantasy and stories, loved by all.

For those who don't know who Eddie The Eagle is, he was a construction worker from the UK who decided to compete in the Winter Olympic Games in the ski jump. This event involves skiing off a high 90 metre ramp. He competed at the 1988 Calgary Olympic Winter Games and got 58th position out of 58 competitors. Though he did beat the previous British record which he had held. The show of determination going against all odds never giving up made the world notice this down to earth, courageous and brave character. He became famous and a movie was made of his life and his journey to the Olympics. A lesson of perseverance never giving up on one's dreams and being humble and grateful can be the lesson taught by his courage to us all.

New Year's Eve arrived everyone made an effort and looked very smart. Bobby liked expensive quality clothes and looked very dashing in his colourful bowtie. The place was packed, and Rob was warming up to the old folks home! We were all sat at our tables ready for our New Year's Eve meal. It is traditional in Scotland to pipe the meat in and two bagpipe players in full traditional Scottish attire piped the meat in. They stayed for a drink, and I was chatting to them about this tradition and playing bagpipes. Just an interesting fact about Jimmy Barnes, remember him from Bathurst in Australia, he is also Scottish and also can play the bagpipes.

I decided that I would go on the pub crawl with these two guys and actually be a part of this tradition. We were in a small village near Perth but there were plenty of pubs. The guys would play in the pubs which the people there loved. They would get a drink and then on to the next. It was freezing trying to snow and I wondered if the kilt was practical on such a cold night and then I realised I was in a dress with the same problem too.

When we got back the party was in full swing. Bobby was covered in sweat doing his crazy dancing. My new friends the pipers piped the New Year in it's now 1999. We danced the night away and eventually went to bed. Vicky and Rob were going to get a surprise as big brother Andy had turned their room upside down. You can take the rugby out of a player, but you can't take away their mischievousness. We definitely had a great evening and welcomed 1999 in with style.

We had one more night left and when we got up we went for a walk around Perth. That evening was karaoke and lots of dancing. I am so pleased we had this time it was amazing, good company, good atmosphere, good food and most of all good and loving friends.

Bobby died of cancer a number of years ago but his spirit and love for life is still with me. He showed me that happiness with oneself, being different, kind and caring makes life so much more purposeful and real. He taught me to deal with problems head on and not to be afraid of walking away and letting go of people, places and things that stifle who you really are. Live a life of peace and love and be around people who also vibrate on the same wavelength. Life comes and goes and it's up to us to embrace it, learn from it and grow into a better person because of it. Life will be cruel, will be harsh and will let you down but with self-love and good loving friends it can be an amazing journey filled with love, happiness and inner peace.

Chapter 21: The Grand Feu, No One Understands Me And Neither Do I

"Even if you are on the right track, you will get run over if you just sit there."

-Will Rogers

The journey to my new home was long, about two hours. I was pushed into the back of the ambulance, strapped in my bed travelling backwards which always made me feel sick and why I tried to avoid this position if ever I travel by train. I was always better being the driver on long journeys or at least sat in the front or I would get travel sickness.

One ambulance man drove the other sat on the side of me also travelling backwards. I was amazed he sat reading his phone for most of the journey a thing that would have definitely guaranteed me vomiting. I kept talking to myself close your eyes go to sleep then you won't be sick.

The weather was very heavy rainfall and we travelled on the faster roads similar to motorways in the UK. There were two windows in the doors of the back of the ambulance and I could see the weather and the traffic behind us. It was so scary for me, the traffic behind travelled so close to the back of the ambulance even in the bad and wet road conditions that the torrential downpour was causing. I was so scared that we were going to be hit and have an accident.

I have never understood why people drive so close behind other vehicles what do they gain from doing that? I was taught by Betty my advanced driving instructor to leave at least one and a half to two car spaces between the car in front and yourself, and I always have done. It makes logical sense you have left yourself enough braking space even in wet or bad conditions. Also, you not only see the car in front of you, and what it's doing but the car in front of that car and what it's doing too. If the car in front of you isn't paying attention and the car in front of them, for whatever reason has to break suddenly you are able to see that even if the car in front of you doesn't. What is the point of being so close to the car in front, it's not only dangerous but not nice for the driver in front to have that pressure put on them by an impatient idiot that's up their arse!!

That's exactly what the cars and trucks were doing on this fast motorway in very wet, heavy rainy conditions. I had no option but to see them because of the position I was put in within the ambulance. My whole being was tense with fear, I closed my eyes and prayed we would arrive safely.

We were heading for a place called the Grand Feu in Niort. Niort was about 40 minutes away from the place I lived so I was pleased it made it easier for visitors. I was lucky that the rehabilitation place was closer to home, it could easily have been further away.

When we arrived, I was pushed into the reception area while the ambulance men handed in the paperwork. I was sort of in a bit of a daze, there were people around most being in wheelchairs, but I was exhausted and not paying much attention. I was asked a few questions; did I want to request a single room or share with someone? I would share. Did I want a TV or a phone? I said I wasn't bothered about the TV, or the phone and I later found out they all cost extra money anyway.

My ambulance men took me down some corridors looking for my room. When found he pushed me in and transferred me into a different bed world which would soon have an extension to it in the form of a wheelchair, fauteuil roulant as they are called in France. I said goodbye and gave my thanks for getting me here safely, they had no idea how petrified I had been throughout that long journey.

It was the 18th of May 2016 and according to the paperwork I was admitted to the Grand Feu at 14:00 hours so I had been in Nantes hospital about six and a half weeks.

Once in my new bed world this lovely lady came to see me with an equally lovely man. They took some details explained things and said I didn't need to go down to the restaurant area that evening to eat, they would bring my food to my room. They also informed me that the physio and doctor would come and see me.

The room was designed for wheelchair access, including the bathroom within the room I was on my own not sharing. I think I had always been allocated a single room because of my length of stay, my extensive disabilities and probably because my French wasn't fluent. Whatever the reason the question at my administration of do you want a single room being pointless. Maybe if I had requested one, they could have charged me more, just saying!

Having listened to my recordings at Nantes hospital and put them in chapters, I will now just write my experience at the Grand Feu from my recordings, adding anything that I remember as I write the chapter. This I believe will bring a more accurate writing about my actual feelings and psychological health as I try and get some sort of normal life back.

In Nantes I was sort of cocooned and protected from the outside world. My bed world being tiny but safe, a place I could have easily decided to stay in because the other journey that I was about to embark on was one hell of a journey in a physically, mentally, psychological and spiritual way. A journey that revealed hidden truths, cruelty of my fellow man, blatant lies, cowardism, narcissism, bullying, mental and physical torture, pain, desperation, loneliness, heartbreak which all took me to depths of darkness that are impossible to describe.

I would also be taken down a path of sheer injustice, corruption, lies, cover ups, non-lawful behaviour, ill treatment, prejudice, omission of information, manipulation of information, loss of evidence, mysterious loss of 'vital' evidence, violation of my basic human rights all from the people and establishments we are brought up to trust and believe in. The ones given power and resources to get away with it!

But the pen is more powerful than the sword, a thing I didn't know at the time. The clue being in my unknown reason for wanting to record my experiences within the first few weeks of my accident. Now an obvious divinely guided action, that would allow the truth to eventually be exposed years later.

On this journey as I stumbled over boulders placed in my path and with all my might moved them to one side, I would find the tiniest particle of goodness shining up at me showing me hope, love, encouragement, support and understanding, all wrapped in kindness. Amongst the many boulders, dirt and obstacles these particles were very few in number, but their shine and sparkle never wavered as I reached out towards them, they were shining some light along this treacherous dark lonely path. These hidden treasures, giving hope and guidance as my whole being was about to fall off the path over the sheer drop that the darkness was beckoning me to. I will always be grateful and never forget these people of kindness.

My recordings were difficult for me to listen to but by listening, putting it down on paper, not sugar coating it, I will set myself free from these cruel tetherings. My heart's desire is to set others free too, some may read this and also have situations and experiences that continue to bind them. We have a right to be free of cruelty, injustice and fear for all our soul craves is a peaceful and a loving existence.

Some of my first recordings at the Grand Feu were very emotional, I was very upset, I sound as if I have a cold, but I was so upset and crying throughout the following six minute recording.

My first day at the Grand Feu:

It's the first day of the new place, it's fine everyone is really nice. It's totally different here, they had to lend me some clothes because I had none and I had to go down to the restaurant at midday, there were a lot of people with a lot of problems and disabilities.

They sat me next to this English lady Vivian, I was in a wheelchair which the staff pushed. Vivian had been here on and off for a year. My God everyone has been here so long. She had various problems with her leg, she had an infection and I think at the end of this month she is having most of her leg off. She is quite an elderly woman who has had stokes so she says she can't remember French words and was glad to speak English which was fine.

I really don't want to be here too long, if I can work really hard and get out quick but I do think you go home at weekends. It seems hard to get in here but once you are in you can't get out! But that might just be me reading it wrong.

Today, yep fine I had a shower, really good they have a table they put you on and then shower you in the bathroom that is part of your room. They were really nice girls who showered me and then I was pushed in my new wheelchair world for my lunch and then brought back. I had a sleep. All this time they have been moving me into this wheelchair. This guy arrived, Christopher I think he is called, to take me down for physio. They have this plastic thing to slip you onto the wheelchair from the bed and vice versa. This plastic thing is put in place (I don't know if it's any good or not, but you have to do what you are told). They make you put your hand on the arm of your wheelchair. That means I am out of control of my leg. He pulled me across, a biggish guy, just pulled me across and forgot about my legs. Oh, what a frigging nightmare! It sent me into loads of pain (at this point in the recording I break down in tears, very, very upset).

Then I wasn't happy going to physio all upset in physio. The physio only really measured me and did little bits she didn't really do much with me at all. But the thing is now where my scar is, I am so soft (still very upset while talking), where my scar is I have got loads of pain. I think it's ripped some of my muscle and my stomach. Because I screamed, I couldn't get hold of my bloody legs because he had hold of me. Nightmare, nightmare, nightmare! He was so boom, boom so he might have set me back about a week oh! (a long pause very upset) I have him all the time apparently. Then he came back for me and put me in bed but at least I have got a thing above my bed that I can grab hold of, so with all my strength I take as much of my body weight as I can. We got me back into bed reasonably well with no problem. But if I am going to have him every day I am now scared but I am sure he will be a lot slower next time (my words are broken because I am so upset and crying heavily), anyway it's stupid.

Not a bad sleep last night, the boys and Rob came yesterday, didn't bring me any books, no clothes I had to still borrow clothes. It's really hard I have no way of talking to them. He has brought me Eric's phone, but I still can't talk to them because it's not got any credit on it and it's complicated, well it is for me but at least Rob can phone me. I did manage to phone him, well the nurse phoned him for me this morning to say can you bring some shoes and socks as well and some towels.

That's all good, I might have already said this the boys came, and Harvey had made me a Sudoku and it really passed the time away last night. I am sure now it's not far off the evening meal (teatime). I don't really want to go to the restaurant I might ask if I can stay in here because I am waiting for Rob, we will see if they will let me or not. Probably won't let me, I have got a bit of fruit and stuff I can always eat that, all is good I suppose? The only problem was I was still upset when the doctor came in. I don't like them seeing me upset because potentially they can put you on bloody antidepressants which I don't want, I don't want any more tablets she has already brought me two for my pain. Anyway, onwards and upwards I am sure it will be a better day tomorrow.

6 Minutes

In the above recording at the Grand Feu, I was very upset possibly because I had hurt myself and the reality of the extent of my disabilities slapping me in the face. In Nantes hospital I didn't have to physically participate in life, but now I had to, and the future didn't look good. My subconscious was afraid of the what ifs. What if I never walk again, what if I stay in a wheelchair for the rest of my life, what if I can never do anything again. Never go for a walk, never garden, never dance, never train, never be independent and never be me again?!

Fear being very powerful and if allowed, a destructive force. But it can also give you strength when you face it head on. There is a Japanese proverb which says, 'Fear is only as deep as the mind allows.' I believe that my emotionally upset mind seen on this recording was the beginning of a very long battle with my mind that had just witnessed my accident, a very traumatic event, with more trauma ultimately being added to it in the following months and years by various sources. My mind and soul craving healing and peace, but it's environment not permitting it.

It must be noted that I went on to have a good relationship with Christopher he was a very caring and kind person. It was just unfortunate that on our first meeting he didn't realise my injuries especially the fact that my groin was all stitched up.

I also think on this first recording the beginnings of how I was going to be treated by those around me was starting to occur. It took me a very long time to realise it but the person I was before, doing everything for everyone, often while they watched, being extremely reliable, hardworking and spinning loads of plates all at the same time no longer existed. I was now a burden, a strain on their energy, something that didn't sit well and down the line his true colours were shown.

This next recording was after a few days of being at the Grand Feu:

Hi, it's the early hours of Sunday morning I have just been massaging my knee because it's quite stiff and painful. I am not on morphine anymore and I am taking doliprane (paracetamol) but not all the time. I get two red capsule things which are for Stubby, I think they are to do with the nerves and to just look after him.

How long have I been here now? Got here Wednesday, so had Thursday and the first physio, the day the guy hurt me, and I was really upset. Boys and Rob came on Wednesday, then Rob came back on the Thursday with some clothes. At least they can now phone me because they left me Eric's phone, which hasn't any credit on it, but it doesn't matter. At least Rob can give me a quick ring and then he doesn't have to come, because he has got so much to do at the house. He is here on Monday afternoon because we have to have a meeting about what their aims are and what to do with me, the outcome and time scales. Physio is good you have to go (some don't want to). So twice a day I have to go. Yesterday I actually wheeled myself around, the only thing is I am going to have to watch the left hand because it's all I have to wheel myself; it's broken with a plate in I must remember that I don't want to put that back. My fingers, especially on a morning, my little finger and the one next to it are stiff and they don't sit right when you fold them, but I can't massage it. So, I stretch it and try and move it, but I am just going to have to be careful. I must not be too eager pushing myself, but it gives me independence. I am trying to do as much stuff so I can get some weekends at home.

I thought I was going to have a fairly boring weekend stuck in my room. A lot of people go home at weekends, so the restaurant, I call it restaurant but it's more like a canteen, the restaurant is half empty because so many go home. But I was fortunate to have visitors. I had three, the Golden Girls, with Sheila's friend who had come over to look at some houses and she had actually put in an offer, and it was accepted. I am so pleased for Sheila because she will have a good friend around. I am going to stop, I think they are going to come in, the light has just gone on in the corridor. If I stop, I stop. (The recording then stopped).

4 Minutes

I am back they did come in I always pretend to be asleep because then at least they can report back that I am sleeping well. I am trying to do everything so that I look like I am independent, I dress myself though the bra is very difficult, I don't even know why I am wearing one. I have lost that much weight. Only yesterday I was taken into the bathroom, stripped down to the waist to be left to wash myself. It's the first time I have looked in a mirror since my accident, God that was scary! I have no muscle tone; I just look like a wrinkled up old lady. It just shows if you don't use muscle, it just disappears and is so weakened.

That's my aim to build myself up again and is one of the reasons I want to push myself not just for independence but because it's building up my arm, the muscles, tendons and ligaments. I suppose at least I have the knowledge and the desire.

Now what I am doing because I can move around in my room in the wheelchair (the wheelchair is a bit uncomfortable to be honest), I can exercise in the mirror and Stubby is quite stiff. I am sure I have got a frozen shoulder; tennis elbow and God knows what. It will improve, shame I can't get more massage on the shoulder. The physios here are all about (like in the UK) degrees of movement. They move you and move you, but they don't think of massaging you beforehand. If your muscles are all in spasm, there is no way you are going to be able to move. If they spent an hour massaging everybody, which they won't then you would get far more movement.

That's what I have just done, I do it twice a day, massage as much as I can. I have just found, I think it was from the machine in Nantes hospital, that my right leg, abductor muscle right into the groin is in spasm compared to the other side. I am massaging that because that leads right down to my knee. It will affect the movement of the knee and the bending of the leg. That's my new obsession to try and get that out of spasm. If I can reduce it, it might give me more flexibility even though everything else is so stiff, I have to keep going.

Yesterday, Saturday a physio did come into the room, and she moved me quite a bit. My toes have been a bit inflamed since, but I suppose they have got to move you. I am massaging them as well both my feet and ankles are swollen. Before I always had skinny ankles and you could see my tendons and the veins, so I know that there is swelling there.

The Golden Girls were brilliant they were here for quite a while, we just talk about everything and anything.

Prison Or The Paralympics

My pig Myrtle May is going on Friday which I feel sad that I am not there at the end. I always said that my job was, if we decided that we were going to be self-sufficient and eat meat, my job was to be there at the end, no matter how upsetting it could be, I think I owe it to the animals. I wasn't there at the end for Christopher the male pig, I wasn't there at the end for Marcus our goat and I don't think I will be there at the end for Myrtle May.

I have got a problem with Myrtle May going because Dolly is pregnant, and I really don't want her to stay with Buster the male on her own in the field. I probably would get Dolly into the barn as she gets nearer to her due date but that means keeping Myrtle May a bit longer to keep Buster company and as a distraction. If Myrtle May goes that leaves Dolly in danger if Buster mates her. She is pregnant and it's not a good idea, I am a bit worried about that. I can't even see Dolly to see what stage of pregnancy she is. They need separating, you can't leave her in the field, Buster will just bust through the fence to get to the female. I don't know I am here; I am not worrying about it, I am just putting it into the hands of God, please God and just hope everything goes well with everybody. I am hoping that when Dolly's three months, three weeks and three-day pregnancy time arrives, I will possibly be at home. I am not saying I will be home for the birth but at least I can talk to her when I go home at weekends. The animals I have brought up from babies, so they are so use to me.

Animals are not stupid, I really think if the world doesn't get its act together with this intensive farming, there is going to be an 'Animal Farm' episode. There is definitely going to be a revolution from the pigs and other animals. I don't know what, but something has to change. I so hate the intensive farming I hate the cruelty. People say well you kill your own animals, but they have had a good life and there is no stress involved throughout their lives, just a little at the end but it's so quick.

My aim now is to get out of here, back with the boys and Rob, back with the life I have chosen to live. I think I had a bad moment a few days ago, because I am in physio surrounded by handicapped people some badly handicapped and I just didn't want to be handicapped. I just didn't want to admit that I was handicapped and here I am in a wheelchair. But amazing things happen, like yesterday for example, I am slow pushing my wheelchair, it's a bit complicated because I only have one hand. You have to get used to what you do and what you don't do to get the chair moving. So, I am slow but then if someone comes behind and let's say they have a shoulder problem they will help push you into the restaurant, so I am being pushed in by another handicapped person how wonderful no judgement just genuine kindness. I am thinking in my head, I'm not handicapped but I am!!

I have to accept that and that was the hardest thing. To be honest the film 'The

One Who Flew Over The Cuckoo's Nest' has entered my mind many a time and all I need now is to see Jack Nicholson walking around and that will be it. That's how I feel really. I don't belong here I am sure everybody else must feel the same. But it is the place I need to be I have enough intelligence to work that out. I don't really want to be here so all I can do is work really hard to do what they say and get the hell out of here!

Everyone I talk to seems to have been here for a minimum of six months, but I don't know, that seems a long time. I am feeling more optimistic if that's the right word. I am sure I will continue to have my moments of ups and downs. I am surrounded by magazines and books so that's all I can do and put the radio on. I have got the charger back, so I put the radio on and read and that's it.

What else have I got to say? I don't know, I do think the care you receive here is amazing. I can't complain about the amount of care you are given and what I have had (I would hope that I would have got the same if I had been in England or Australia, but I am not sure). I think I was lucky that I got taken to Nantes hospital. A very, very good hospital, I suppose you wish you never have to experience hospitals at all but I was blessed to be taken to an excellent place.

I said to the Golden Girls yesterday, that I have had a pre-run on what getting old is like. Having your bum cleaned for you sometimes by a man, having someone turning you and everyone having to help you. I told them it's not good old age, you have to keep fit and healthy and hope no problems comes your way. Sheila is brilliant, she's 65 and she has probably got less aches and pains than any of us. You have just got to keep active. I would love to set up a rehabilitation place just for me, a gym. I have got some of the equipment, the know-how, the desire, I have just got to find a little place I can set it up. I would offer some people help, not a money-making thing, just if anybody after an operation or just wants to get some fitness. There isn't much around where we live at all. We will see what the future brings, I have just got to keep working, keep positive and accept my downtimes, deal with them and move forwards.

15 Minutes

It's still Sunday it's probably 11ish, we haven't been down to dinner yet, but I just wanted to say (knock on the door) Orr?

12 Seconds

Sorry I got disturbed, the guy came to take me for dinner, so it was 12:30. But I just wanted to report that probably 11:30 I went to the toilet!! In the sense that I sat on a toilet. The girl was really good, it depends on who you get, if they have got experience and know what they are doing. She said do you want the bassin or the toilet? I said can I go to the toilet (nobody had offered me this choice before). So, I did the toilet, a bit hard in the sense that I was wobbly, but she was really good and then I was even able to flush it afterwards, there you go progress yesss!! I have been to the toilet, the first time in seven and a half weeks! People take so much for granted, as I did, just being able to go to the toilet is just amazing!! Bye.

1 Minute

    It's now Tuesday early hours of the morning it is probably towards the end of May. I am not sure of the date quite a few things have happened. My first weekend was okay although I did overdo it trying to wheel myself in my wheelchair, I am stopping that because my left wrist is just inflamed a little bit. I now just let them push me down to the restaurant but push myself back to my room myself.

    As you know I did the toilet a few days ago and I did it again yesterday. I also managed to sit in a shower chair rather than the shower bed. I am trying hard to be independent.

    I have been lucky with visitors; you might know that on Saturday the Golden Girls arrived which I told you about. On Sunday Phil and Sharon arrived. The weekend passed fairly quickly. Yesterday Monday I had them all, the nurse, doctor and everyone came to see me. I told the doctor I am only on two tablets now for the phantom pain in my arm. I told him every time I took a tablet it just went buzzy and quite painful. He therefore has reduced the medication dose from 100 to 75 which I think will be better. I suppose I won't know for a couple of days.

    I also have my new physio Frederick who I feel is very good, very gentle, very methodical, very hands on. He had me sitting on the end of a bench with both legs bent amazing. The only thing is there is pain, I have given them a good massage. I don't seem to be able to bend it, only a certain amount, I need patience to keep going. I have only had two sessions with him.

    Also, yesterday Rob came over and Martine came with him to have a meeting with everybody, to ask what we aim to do and it was a good meeting. It's always difficult because it's all in French, but I understand most of it. Basically, everyone was there, the girl that helps me rehabilitate, the physio, the nurse, the student nurse, the lady that helps you in your room and the doctor obviously.

    They want to know what your aims are. I wanted to be walking, I said running, thinking if I get running that means I am good at walking. I don't particularly want to run but I thought if I aim a bit higher, I might come somewhere in the middle. Gardening, cooking and weight training. I told them that no way will I ever be able to do the ironing again, so the doctor said that's your job then Rob. It was more of a joke I could probably try to iron if I have to but if I can get out of that job I will.

The good news was that I thought I was just having a plastic hand that you stuck on and frighten people with when you are out in the public. But it is going to be connected to muscle a robotic hand which is going to well and truly please Elliott. I am like, I don't know the level of advancements they have made in this area, so I just said thank you, it's a cadeau (gift). It's a pleasant gift because I was told in Nantes hospital that it would be a plastic thing stuck on the end of my arm, that's what a women told me. She said, "Oh no it's not functional it won't move, you just put it on when you go to the restaurant or out in public." To have a robotic, have it connected up to your muscles is going to be good. It will be an interesting challenge.

I did ask them if they would put a Swiss army knife in there just for the convenience of it or even a torch in my hand. I don't know if that's possible it was a joke anyway, but maybe not a bad idea!

What else? Monday, yesterday was busy. Kathy and Dave called, I only got to see them for ten minutes because I had to go for my physio. Kathy has got loads going on with her veins and all sorts of stuff. She has got more appointments than me!

Then in the evening Jenny came so that was really nice, and we had a good chat. She must have got out because she didn't come back to my room. You are supposed to leave at 8:30, but she got out alright. While she was here, I got a phone call from Kay and Dennis. They were back home from a few days at Scarborough. So good to hear their voices.

Yesterday Claire rang but there were people there with me, so she is going to ring today at 3 to have a good chat with her. They are here on Friday Jenny is picking them up and she will prepare their house for them. That was a busy Monday in fact.

Another big thing was a girl came to the room who is an organizer, and it was arranged at the meeting because I want to get home at weekends, that she could come and see the facilities at home. In a fortnight on a Monday, we are going to my home and look at what the facilities are. Rob might have to do a little bit of preparation for that. It's got to be good news.

Fortunately, we have a shower and toilet downstairs, but you have to be able to get a wheelchair in the house. If Rob measures the wheelchair, he can move stuff around before she arrives. So, all is good I hope. I am going to try and get some more sleep now and see how life goes.

10 Minutes

It's Wednesday morning early hours I just can't sleep which is normal so what I do is exercise my shoulder and Stubby, try and massage my legs and then hopefully I go back to sleep. Yesterday was okay I went out to do some work in the garden with three other people. Twenty to thirty minutes in the sun which was quite hot it was the first time that Stubby has seen the outdoor world. We weeded some areas and some big containers, high for wheelchairs and tomorrow, Thursday weather permitting we are planting some things, I can't remember what we are planting. It was good to get outside.

Also, while I was in physio a guy came in and introduced himself and next week he is looking at the muscles for the robotic hand. Today 10ish I have a meeting with the social worker. I have everything written down so that should hopefully be fairly straight forward.

Rob told me the insurance company is coming to see me, I don't know what that will be about. Claire rang we had a good long chat and that's it really.

I need to get a bit of food in here because I am starving now. I have got my dry rice cakes and I know Rob can't get to the shops but as soon as he can he can get me some things. I don't go to breakfast; I have fruit in the room. Dinner is not too bad but then I never like teatime (evening meal) that much. I just feel I need something to nibble at certain times to take the edge off.

What else is there? I went to the toilet again was it yesterday, I can't remember. It might have been yesterday or the day before when I actually after the toilet dressed myself and put myself into the wheelchair. One girl came in and went "Hooray" the other girl tutted and said, "We haven't got your x-rays back yet, we don't know whether you should be doing that!" But I know this foot is alright, just a bit wobbly. The good foot the left that had the barbecue skewers in I think it can take standing. I stand more on my heel than my toes at the moment. So, there you have it.

3 Minutes

As can be seen my life and daily routine rapidly changed once at the Grand Feu, a shock to my system and disabled and weak body. The mental challenge was also there but I felt progress would be and could be made if I participated and worked hard with the expert guidance that was being offered to me.

Chapter 22: Study Must Come First And A Trip To China

"The most wonderful motivational speeches that I've ever heard came from people who told me I couldn't do something. I was bound and determined to show them that I could."

- C.T. Fletcher

It's 1999 I had to put all of my energy into finishing my master's degree. I had a meeting with my tutor, and he told me it wasn't probably going to pass, and I needed to make some adjustments. Re-do my paper of twenty thousand words in the style that the University wanted. He was a lovely tutor, and I was lucky to have him he gave me some guidance and said he needed it done in a month so he could check it again. He also suggested that it may be a good idea to defer the master paper part of my degree and do it next year. No way was I going to do that. If I did like some of my fellow students had done that would be another year of stressing over it. No as T. Fletcher says, "I was bound and determined to show them that I could." I had a couple of days of self-pity and crying and saying how could I get this done. Then I kicked my own arse and got on with it. Getting on with it was locking myself away until 4 in the morning re-writing my dissertation. I still had my clinic to run but by now I was not working with any rugby teams. In four weeks, it was done I had my meeting with my tutor, and he was pleased, he couldn't believe I had re-written my paper. So, it was sent to Banga University. We then had our last weekend at the York college in April 1999 after four years and a lot of hard work. We had a great group of students who helped each other through the demanding course, we had got to the finish line!

On the 29th of May 1999 with our cap and gown proudly worn we graduated. My mum and dad always giving their support and my grandma Walker at another of my graduations. Granddad Sam Walker had died but I am sure he was beside my grandma watching on. I did get my master's and it was thanks to help and support from my fellow students and my tutor who gave me the opportunity to prove I could do it. Out of the eight students who did their master's only five passed, I was one of those five.

My studies didn't end there, I was still studying Chinese medicine with Shulan Tang at her college in Manchester, the Shizen college. I had a couple of years left there, finishing in 2001. Being so interested in the herbal side, I also in 1999-2000 did the Northern's diploma in Chinese patent herbal medicine. Patents were traditional herbal formulas 1000's of years old that were put into 'Wan', pill form so the person didn't have to boil up a bag of Chinese herbs and then drink it. Then in 2001 I continued at York and the Northern College of Acupuncture and started the three-year diploma in Chinese herbal medicine which would finish in 2004. Also, between 2002-2003 I went back to Dabtac in Dewsbury, the college I had done my 'A' levels way back in 1984, to do the 7407 teaching diploma.

If all this studying wasn't enough plus running my busy clinic which now offered traditional Chinese acupuncture (which meant I could offer patients so much more than rehabilitation and treatment of injuries) I was still hitting the weights at the gym, I still did manage another adventure at the end of 1999.

The reason I wanted to add acupuncture to my treatments was because I wanted to treat the whole person. Yes, I could identify an injury and give treatment which helped to fix it but I always knew that I was only part of this process. A person's whole being had to recover too. If they weren't eating right, sleeping rights, thinking right or moving right the recovery would be slow or never happen. Traditional Chinese acupuncture treats the mind, body, and spirit of an individual. Being injured affects the whole person, for example an injury or any disability can create stress and depression. The injury giving stress of pain, discomfort, and if not able to work, stress about money, about losing a job, losing a place in the team of the sport that one loves. The therapist has a huge responsibility and an effect on so much more than the actual physical problem that is presented to them. With adding traditional acupuncture to my treatments, I felt I could treat the whole person.

My Master's research was about the menopause and hot flushes and being Shulan's student with her vast knowledge and expertise of treating gynaecological problems, I became interested in infertility both for men and women. If I had continued studying and maybe done a doctorate this would have been the area I would have researched into. It fascinated me, giving a couple a precious gift, they thought they could never have was also a gift given to the practitioner who helped them. I am so pleased and grateful to say that there are a few bundles of joy in the Yorkshire area that I helped to be born into this world.

Chinese medicine is powerful and logical when administered by well trained and knowledgeable people. It is such a shame that the West diluted it to fit into their politically and profit driven boxes, taking away the core purpose of traditional Chinese medicine which is to treat the whole person as an individual not as a symptom, to heal that individual's mind, body, and spirit at the same time. Any symptom just being a small part of a much bigger picture which often Western treatment and medicine don't put into the equation.

My adventure at the end of 1999 was a trip to China. Shulan was going back to her hometown, to sort out some business and visit some hospitals and her old university. It was a once in a lifetime chance to see China in a real way not as a tourist. Shulan was a well-respected and famous Chinese practitioner, and we were even invited for a meal at the British consul in Nangjing. We flew to Shanghai, did some sightseeing, and had a New Year's party in the hotel before going to Nangjing. China was very Chinese in the late 90's but you could see the influence of the West creeping in. McDonalds had arrived but soon would be followed by the other fast-food giants.

We went to places not normally visited by Westerners, visiting Shulan's village, parents, temples and Shulan's herb factory. We brought in the Millennium in Shanghai, the entertainment being quite different than the year before, no bagpipes but a good evening. China is full of tradition and history the temples being so colourful with giant ancient Buddhas that you can pray to, a very peaceful and atmospheric place.

We then went to Nangjing University a place Shulan had studied and lectured at. We had a tour of the classrooms and Nangjing hospital including its herbal department. Imagine that in a Western hospital a choice between nature's cure or chemical filled medicine. Don't get me wrong if it wasn't for drugs after my accident, I probably would have died from maybe an infection and having to have operation after operation was made possible due to Western medicine. But the big pharmacy doctrine has so much power that it slowly and quietly gets rid of any competition even that provided by Mother Nature!

My visit to China was for two weeks but it was cut short because I was extremely ill. So, I returned to the UK after ten days with Maria who worked for Shulan in Manchester. Maria was English and had worked for Shulan for a number of years, a lovely fun person to be around.

The day before I left to go to Shulan's house in Manchester, I was working, and a number of people were recovering from the bug that had affected them over Christmas. I think I got the virus then. By the time I was at Shulan's I had a fever, she boiled me up some spring onions and ginger to help disperse the fever. We got our long flight to China from Manchester airport and boy did I feel weak. The plane wasn't full and there was one advantage to how I looked, nobody wanted to come near me, the coughing had started, and people kept their distance. The advantage of that was I had a row of seats to myself and so spent most of the flight laid out trying to sleep when my cough allowed me to.

I took the patent herbs that Shulan gave me, but I was so ill and weak. For the first day I just stayed in bed it took me an hour to get the strength to walk to the toilet an extremely difficult task. When the others returned Shulan suggested the hospital, but I didn't want to go into a place I didn't understand the language (that would turn out to be ironic nearly 20 years later). I felt a little better a day later and joined the group I was still weak, but Maria took care of me, and everyone helped me. I didn't miss out on much but knew if there was the chance to return home, I should take it. Maria was flying back home earlier than us so I came home with her.

We nearly missed our connecting flight in Amsterdam. The security checked our bags saw all my Chinese herbs, took one look at me and let us through, I don't think he wanted to get what I had. The trip had been very informative and a fantastic experience even though I wasn't feeling my best. I think I got a glimpse of China before it dramatically changed to be more Western. I probably wouldn't recognise the places that I visited if I visited them now. Change is inevitable but sometimes it comes with a price, like in many countries, China's sacrifice for progress was the more simple, more real and soul filled ways that a long tradition had offered. I know that traditional ways offer many challenges but at least these traditional challenges are visible and not hidden under bureaucracy, power games and profit agendas. I think a little more balance between the two would bring about a more real and happier existence.

I was still quite ill when I got back home the cough was constant and I felt quite weak. A lot of people in Yorkshire and the UK had got this bug. I had to smile because there was all this media stuff warning everyone about the Millennium bug that would affect the computers. When 2000 arrived it wasn't the computers that suffered the virus but a whole load of humans.

Chapter 23: A Friend For Stubby, Life At The Grand Feu And Visits Home

"Better to be slapped with a truth
than kissed with a lie."

- Buddha

It's about 1am on Thursday morning. I have had my first week at the rehabilitation place. Over the last couple of days to get you up to speed I had a meeting with the social worker who basically didn't know if I should stay with her or the other social worker. Now I have been put with the other social worker because they can find you employment. We will have to just see what happens with that I don't have a meeting with her for another ten days probably.

Next week I have got a meeting with the guy for the robotic, just to test my muscles, I think on Stubby's arm. What other things have I got, oh yes, tomorrow 10ish the insurance company are coming, whoever is coming to visit me. Marc is coming as well so I don't know if it's just a general procedure or what's happening, but we will see won't we?

What do I think about my first week? After my initial shock of admitting that I am in an institution, really, be it a relaxed one, and that I have got a handicap. Admitting I was actually one of the inmates, I have sort of got used to my surroundings I accept, I have always accepted that I am probably one of the lucky ones.

People here have all got their stories, horror stories for most of them. Some people look to be in a very bad way. There are quite a few young twenty-year-olds here in wheelchairs. I am just glad that I have got what I have got to a certain extent.

I still ask my friends up there to help me every day, to just give me the strength to look forwards. With the physio I am lucky that I have Frederick. I always look at their badges and he is the oldest, but he is the chef (boss), the boss of the department. He doesn't act like a boss, they are all so relaxed in there (physio department) which is good. If they were all uptight the people would be uptight, it's quite a good, relaxed atmosphere.

In the last few days Fred has got me at the end of the bench with both legs down. Fred has moved the wheelchair's footrest a bit more so instead of my leg being stuck out he moved it first, then I moved it a little bit more so the angle, I think the degree where the right leg bends is now much more comfortable. If you had it stuck out straight it's always going to stay out straight, the natural position is to have it bent when you are sat down. I think we are getting there, definitely getting there.

I believe the pain, in the right knee is coming from the metal because it is always in one place. It may be the bolt I don't know, I have just spent 40 minutes massaging my legs. I have now only got the right leg in the like a plastic padded cast which you put your foot in while you sleep. It's good they have taken the left one away because they are hard, uncomfortable and makes it difficult to sleep. The purpose of them is so your foot doesn't drop to keep the foot up.

I am going to massage my scar around my groin because I think it's pulling. I massage a lot, I massage as soon as I get into bed. The inside ankle is quite numb plus under the foot and heel.

They did give me some stockings while I was at the physio treatment. Then the physio put them on because as I hang my foot over the edge of the plinth it is buzzy, and the colour is quite purple. Today and yesterday, it wasn't as bad so that's improvement. Stubby is still giving me a little bit of awareness and tightness but what I try and do is visualise the hand, because it seems to be all screwed up and in spasm, I just slowly visualise it relaxing. It seems to work very slowly opening my phantom fingers and let the hand relax. I don't know if I will have this forever, but it's got to get weaker over time.

I had a visit from the boys Harvey came first because he had been in Niort with school doing his presentation, so he got dropped off by the teacher. It was nice I got some time with him. He was showing me the photos of the chickens, I said where's the photos of the new geese? The three baby geese that had hatched for he still hadn't taken any photos of them. Harvey being such a wonderful soul, a pretty, pretty soul that doesn't give any hassle and is a really kind and good kid as is Elliott who has a bit of mischief about him which is lovely.

I said Harvey tell me the truth, I would rather know. So, I got to know everything yesterday when Harvey and I were talking. I managed to ask him how he was, he is working really hard because he is doing the animals and helping Rob. Harvey is getting up early to help and he is also out till 9 o'clock just trying to keep everything going so he is just a real star. Elliott who is only 13, a young 13 is a great kid and helps too, I do want them to enjoy their childhoods.

The three beautiful goslings which I was imagining growing up and looking forwards to seeing, died. Harvey went in one day and all three of them were dead. I don't know what's happened there, it's really weird.

Another thing that's happened is one of my favourite original chickens Snowy got a prolapse and so she has died, but we have got some offspring from her, we have to keep them going. What other stories, they still haven't found my mama rabbit, so she's gone! I don't know what's happened to her she was beautiful as well!

Also, which is upsetting and annoying, Dave who is a bit like a bat out of hell, I told Rob I didn't want him to touch my rabbits. Apparently (long pause) which is quite upsetting Rob and Harvey had to go to the Lion d'Or which is the place where Harvey is going to start doing his apprenticeship. They left Dave (big sigh) not a good idea!! They did show him which rabbits, but he then chose to take, I don't know why? He took them out of the cages (there were some in a run to take). He then chooses to take Petra my first rabbit from mama and papa rabbit, who was a beauty God!! He took Petra out of the cage when she had just given birth! How he didn't see the nest is beyond me because he is supposed to have all this experience with rabbits, and he has had hundreds and thousands of rabbits (so he said) and killed her. He not only did that, but he took my breeding male that I paid 10 euros for who was beautiful and killed that one Orr!!

Rob said he went ballistic with him but I would never have left him on his own, well I would have never had him near my rabbits to be honest (a big sigh of disappointment and frustration) so that was another thing.

People don't understand I spent so much time with taking care of the animals. I am not saying that they are not working hard they are, but I had a routine. There are now five motherless babies left, they managed to rear two, three got out I think they were outside near the bench and there was a gap in the cage. I think it could have been a rat or some other creature.

It wouldn't have happened if I had been around because they would still have their mother. He wouldn't have killed my rabbits (Orr big sigh!) because I wouldn't have had him anywhere near them!! I did say to Rob just take them down to Marina (the small local abattoir) for three euros you will have the rabbits done!! Oh God (deep sighs)

So, they were planning this Friday to take Myrtle-May the big Gloucestershire Old Spot who is infertile. This always bothered me, same as it bothered me to have Dave near the rabbits! I have told them about things that have bothered me before, but they don't listen.

I was talking to Harvey, I didn't get upset, I had spent two years stocking up, it's difficult to explain to someone, I had a plan. I said to Harvey "Why are so many people lying to me?" He said, "Because we don't want to upset you." I understand that but lying to me makes me think what else are they hiding. That's why Harvey told me everything. There were a couple of other things. Harvey, bless him said "Is there a problem?" I said "No, there isn't a problem I am not going to get on to Rob!" I am just glad I know because it's not fair to me being in here imagining my rabbits and that all is well, it's better to know the truth. Anyway, that's how it is isn't it?

The pig Myrtle-May they had planned this Friday to take her. The other pig Dolly is pregnant. My logic is we are then left with a strong boar with pregnant Dolly. She must come into the barn to have her young. Buster can't be trusted, and you can't keep her with him I wouldn't want her outside anyway to give birth. She did alright before with her first litter. I know I looked after her really well and she only had three, but she did alright and was a great mum. If they take Myrtle-May away and bring Dolly in the barn, you are left with a boar outside without a female not a good position to be in. We manged to persuade Rob to cancel taking Myrtle-May this Friday, tomorrow. It's probably better to leave it until November depending on if Buster gets sold, he is a pure breed and an endangered breed a Berkshire so it would be better if he goes as breeding stock. I am glad I have made the decision because when he said he was taking her, and she was going I was just really uncomfortable with it.

At least Buster is going to have a girl, if he doesn't have a girl he will be out. I found out that he got out anyway when Robin and Phil were there doing some work. They had trouble putting him back in. He will get out and run the electric fence if there is no female. If he has a female, he is more likely to stay in and be happier and content! My suggestion to them is to get some more picket fencing they are not expensive, move them down to the bottom of the field and let them turn everything over they have got to be occupied.

It's the same with some of the chickens they have nothing to occupy them so their run needs extending so they have somewhere to scratch around in. So, a bit of drama, what can you do? People are trying so hard, and I am really appreciative but if you have not got the interest and the passion, they have got some interest but not the passion. Rob just sees the animals as an inconvenience to a certain extent. Anyway, that was my life before the accident, I am hoping it will be my life after. I will try and keep my two years breeding programme, I don't want to lose it all. I have done well to get to the stage that I have. We will see at least I don't think there are any more lies going to be told, it wasn't intentionally done. People try and protect others by not telling them everything and eventually you get to know. Though I tend to say it as it is, honesty being the best policy.

After a week here all is good. I have got used to the place. I would rather be at home but I know I can't be yet. Not fit enough I can't function enough so that's it.

20 Minutes

It's now Friday 5 o'clock and another week has gone. Today has sort of been busy, I went for x-rays this morning. God it was so painful not compared to the pain I have had but painful to just have to lie on the x-ray table. They had to lift me onto the platform, in the hospital they just wheeled your bed to x-ray, and you stayed on your bed and they x-ray you while you are still in bed. But here I was obviously in a wheelchair, so Christopher lifted me up, the lady who happens to be Christian's wife who is a really nice guy and he helped me so much on the first day, also helped she lifted my legs up onto the cold metal table. I was there for quite a while on this really solid metal x-ray table. It hurt my back more than anything it got really stressful. She was really nice and said it won't be for too much longer.

They x-rayed the legs, the hips, my ankle, my left hand, my left foot so that was good. I then was taken to physio by Christopher. Immediately after that I was taken to the restaurant and then I just got myself back to my room went to the toilet and Corrine came for me to take me to gardening. I didn't know I was going today but she took me. I didn't do much because I am not pushing myself for it really hurts my left broken wrist, but I managed to sow a few seeds. Then she said she wanted to keep me, so she kept me and now I have got an electric chair. This will be really good once I can work it out, it's very sensitive so you only put a little bit of movement on it now I can be independent!

If I can get the hang of it, I still kept my other chair because I said I am worried about getting an electric one in the car when the time comes for me to go home at weekends. She said you will keep your other one and have two chairs so that is fine. They had to do quite a lot of messing about with it but as they were messing about with my chair this woman started waving at me. At first, I didn't know who it was then I realised it's Marc's friend Delow then she came down to see me. She said she had brought me some stuff, fruit and some drinks but they wouldn't let her put them in my room, she did give me some fruit which I hid in my pocket (three sneezes) I hope to God I am not getting a cold because everyone around me is bloody sneezing, I don't want a cold as well as everything else.

After that about 3:30 I had to go for my physio, I didn't do much, but he had my x-rays. I said I had my x-rays done this morning he said the x-rays came from Nantes hospital today, I said that's bizarre but good, so he showed me them. Basically, the left foot, the one that had the barbecue skewers in the four metatarsals not the big toe which I was pleased about, were all broken all look to have healed, so they just need re-educating. I am hoping we are going to start standing on it. As you all know (our little secret) I am already standing on it. Fred is happy with them. The ankle that has got metal in it looks fairly straight forwards, it's got two pieces of metal in it, the only problem with that is that it's still numb so I don't know how the nerve is. The x-rays didn't show the hips so we will have to look at the x-rays I had this morning. The right knee, how can I explain, at the bottom of the femur the big bone it's broken like a T shape at the bottom, and it's got some breaks further up as well it was shattered so the reason for the pole. At the bottom there are four plates or four screws, I don't know what you call them, bolts? Four bolts. There is one that looks to be sticking out a bit and I think that's what's causing me all the problems in the knee. I am hoping it's not rubbing against my medial ligament. You can't really tell from the x-ray if the knee is fine, but I suppose the patella is okay. I don't know how far up the dancing pole goes but we will get to know that from their (Grand Feu) x-rays. The leg had a significant break, quite complex, to me it looks quite a complicated break.

The hand looked to have healed, which is good, I hope I haven't unhealed it last Saturday wheeling myself in my wheelchair.

All looks good but complicated, the knee is going to be complicated mainly because of that bit of the bolt sticking out that's going to stop me bending it. If I can build the muscles up and get my left leg moving that will be a start. I have got to build these muscles up and get some strength. I don't think I will get full range of movement in that knee until that bolt is removed. But they probably won't remove it until the bone is healed which will take a long time. I can't see it being before a year. So, I am hopefully going to have a bit of a rest now the weekend is here. The weekends difficult and lonely.

Corrine has booked me in for two hours every afternoon. You just start to rest and then you have to be somewhere. So, in the afternoon from 1:30 to my evening meal I am not free.

I am glad I saw the x-rays because I now have a picture in my mind what is going to happen and what I am working with. I am still standing up on my left leg because I think it's just a matter of getting the toes working. Bye.

9 Minutes

It's now Sunday about 10:30, I am in my new electronic chair which is better in the sense that I can be independent. It's slightly more difficult to get in and out of because I can only get in one way, the electrical control is only on my left side, obviously because I only have my left hand. It means I have to be transferred from the right side but it's not too bad I am sort of getting better at the bottom shuffle.

It's interesting, or maybe not but you have to be quite canny, I now cross my right leg onto my left leg because the support in the chair isn't there as you transfer from your bed or from your chair to your bed. It's a big chair the electric wheelchair and it takes a bit of getting in and out of as long as I get sat on the piece of plastic thing, the transfer thing it's okay. At the bed you can at least get hold of the triangle above your head. You just get used to doing it a certain way.

I would love to challenge you all to the toilet it's quite an amazing thing to say the least. You have got to imagine, (I will let you have both hands to make it easier for you). Imagine having one leg straight out and you can't really bend it. Keep that leg straight out, get off your chair, get your clothes down so you can have a wee and then get back up, get your clothes back on and back into your wheelchair or chair. It is quite difficult, especially one handed you can't support yourself on both sides. It is most difficult getting your clothes back on because of the straight leg.

I am managing to put weight on my left foot and leg I think it's the right time. I think the physio is probably going to start me doing that in the next week or so.

It isn't easy it would be interesting for all of you to go and have a try make sure you have a small stool to put your leg on because you can't let it drop because of the groin and the scar.

The problem I have got with my left leg is it hasn't been stood on for a long time, over eight weeks so the muscle is weak, balance has gone and there is no strength, plus it's had broken toes and a fibula. But you have to just do it and start somewhere. I can manage to get off my chair and get on the toilet without the girls coming in. But I always have them here when I get onto the chair, I don't think I am quite ready to do it on my own. My goal is to get out of the chair and have a stick but the results from the x-rays will dictate that and the specialist in Nantes. Bye.

5 Minutes

Hi, it's Monday night 11 o'clock, I am in bed just finished watching another DVD, Claire and Steven got me a small DVD player and Jenny has lent me some Doris Day and all sorts of good movies.

The weekends passed quick I had Claire, Steven and Lewis. I had Marie and Chris and Jenny as well.

Today Monday I had the shower and the girl Christine who I think just doesn't want to be here. She is always huffing and puffing, I try and be nice to her, but she never seems happy. I showered, I want to be independent but there are things I need help with like my toes. She doesn't pull out all the stops like the others. She does what she has to do but no more, she can be a bit overpowering to say the least.

I had to wait for the doctor. The doctor arrived and had got the x-rays from here (Grand Feu). So, we had got the full leg and it was broken in two places. Then the wrist looks okay, the foot on the right and the left looks okay too. The ankle on the right leg seems to be doing okay but the amount of damage in the right leg (the dancing pole is all the way up the femur) is a lot it is well and truly broken. I am just going to have to hope it heals and then give it loads of muscles and hope that I can bend the knee. On the 28th of June I go back to the specialist at Nantes hospital so that's good.

Then I had to go to the physio 11:30 then straight to lunch 12:30 I came back to my room, went to the toilet on my own. Someone came to say I was going to see Corrine, I thought it was 14:00 but it was 1:30.

I went and they did loads of tests, trying to tie my shoelace, trying to cut paper, all sorts of tests. Then Corrine made me a plastic cast for my wrist which I use some of the time. I stayed with her until 4:00 then back to physio till 17:30.

I got back to my room just before 6 o'clock. I thought I will just lie on my bed because the wheelchair is uncomfortable, and it was starting to get on my nerves. I had been in it all day and my leg bent it needed a change of position. So I buzzed for assistance this woman I didn't know I had never had her before. She came in the room and first of all she said she didn't understand me (all the others do!). So I said exactly the same again but slower. I just wanted to be put on the bed. Then she asked "Why? When you are going down to the restaurant" I said, "Because I have been in this chair all day and I just want a change of position." She asked, "Have you got pain?" "No just stiffness" was my answer. Her attitude was really bad, then she said, "But you usually do it yourself." I said, "No I have never done it myself." I have tried to help people and I try to be independent with the toilet, but I had never transferred myself to my bed it's too difficult. I asked her "Who has told you I do it myself?" Christine no doubt it would have to be her. I said, "I have never done it on my own!"

She went on and on and I said "Wow" Then she stripped my bed down and I said, "I don't want to get into bed I just want to lay on the bed." Her attitude was so bad I said, "Forget it!" I then said, "Have you got a problem with me?" Her reply "No, no, no." "Right, I am staying in the chair, forget it!" I concluded.

So, I had another hour in the chair, why couldn't she just put me on the bed it's not that hard it would have taken five minutes! It would have made such a difference to my legs. I could have massaged them, and I could have relaxed.

Anyway, I went down to the restaurant I wasn't very happy. I asked the ladies on my table, "If someone is not very kind what do you do or who do you speak to?" the answer "The nurses" so I said, "Right then, thanks."

The woman did upset me quite a bit and then I thought no, don't get upset, don't let one person get you upset, just get on with it, deal with it. She sort of ignored me I don't know what her problem was, I had never met the woman before. Most just nod and smile but she ignored me, I thought fine. She said hello to the other person behind me, I thought what is your problem! So, I thought forget it, then Rob came which was great because I had finished eating.

We went back to the room, she saw us in the corridor and started saying something I responded "Oui oui" and then I thought I don't know what the hell you've said, and we went into the room. Rob had to go so I said I will get ready for bed and then you can help me get into bed if you will. The woman came in as I was cleaning my teeth. She said something I said no problem, Rob's here then she went off on one saying something about that he couldn't do it, but I thought frig off, I am not asking you to do it.

Rob transferred me into my bed, but he left the bumbag, but I couldn't phone him I hope he isn't searching for it everywhere!

So that's the end of today, a good day, a tiring day and an upsetting day created by one person that I had never met before in my life. Trying to bully me, trying to be nasty to me and just not doing her job. I don't know we will see what happens tomorrow, but I won't ask her ever again to help me! Bye?

8 Minutes

It's Friday morning the 2nd or 3rd of June, so another month has passed since the accident. I have just had my breakfast fruit which they let me have in my room. I am still not dressed yet, but the weekend is soon which is good.

Monday we will visit the house so I don't know what will become of that, hopefully she will recommend weekend visits, and all will be good.

I have been practising with the Robocop (Stubby's new friend) on the computer. You have to learn which way to flex your muscles or extend and flex your muscles for different movements, but you have got to know which muscle to move.

Tuesday, I stood up for the first time. I had had a full day with Corrine and her room is really hot. I stood up a couple of times in physio and then I just felt really warm and a bit sick, so I had to sit down. It could have been the standing up for the first time. I only put weight on the left leg. It may have been just tiredness because I felt quite tired as well. But I stood up! I think Frederick is going to make sure I go slow and don't rush things. The next thing will be actually to walk on one leg. Right, that's it, bye.

2 Minutes

I forgot to say I had quite a few visits, Gigi from the boulangerie came with Jan, then Jenny came, and she gave me a head massage unfortunately we had to cut it short because I had to go to physio. Then Mel came with Deirdre who is back from Australia, she gave me a little angel Raphael.

Tonight, hopefully Rob and the boys are coming. Claire and Steven have been again so that was good, so I am very lucky with my visitors.

44 Seconds

It's about 11ish on a Monday night I am quite restless, I don't seem to be able to get comfortable tonight. I have just been watching 'The Sound Of Music' and trying to rest.

Last weekend, Friday Rob and the boys came Claire, Steven and Lewis were here. Then Mel and Della came which was lovely, lots of people, they all went around teatime when I had to go to the restaurant.

Saturday, nobody came, and Sunday Claire, Steven and Lewis came again, they have now gone back to the UK.

Today (Monday) I was so very lucky. This morning I went with Corrine to visit the house so she can assess the house and see if I can get weekend visits. They have all worked really hard. It was lovely to see things, I am still in a wheelchair but all the little chicks, that I had hatched are all big now. We had to get the wheelchair in which was fine. Corrine seemed to think that everything was good it's just a matter of speaking to the doctor and getting paperwork. I am not sure if it will be this weekend.

At least I got to go home, I didn't feel bad about leaving, I knew I had to leave again. What was weird was the smell it smelt of something, maybe damp I had never noticed it before. I know we have had a lot of rain, that may have been it. Everywhere looked tidy but cluttered, but I have been in a hospital situation for so long. I have not seen leaves and the grass had grown. The last time I saw it there were no leaves on the trees and the grass was short, it was good to see.

Little Mars the baby goat, which was only a week old when I last saw him, he is growing well. Dani from next door came to see me to say hello and as we drove past, we said hello to Eric and Michelle and Angelique. Marc was at the house to help. It was good, a good meeting, I think.

I know I am not ready to work outside but if I can just have weekends, just to be there. A very big surprise was I said to my parents I would save up to get a Kitchen Aid (food mixer) which I have been trying to save up for. There was one there on the table. My mum and dad had bought one while they were here so kind of them, they need a telling off. I will pay them back they can't afford to buy it.

I am trying to get comfy it's going to be one of those nights where I just can't get comfy. I suppose I have been in and out of a car and doing more things, so the legs are having to do a bit more. I still can't do much until I know that it's healed.

A good day, tired but I can't sleep (yawning). Tomorrow at 10:00 I have a meeting with the social worker and Marie is coming after dinner so I am hoping I can get an hour out of being with Corrine. I am going to try and settle Stubby down because he is buzzing a bit and try to get comfy and some sleep, bye.

5 Minutes

It is the 9th of June at about 5 o'clock it's a Friday I am just waiting in the room for Rob to arrive for a weekend at home. This week on Monday I went with Corrine to visit the house so she could see if it was possible for me to go home, I suppose to see if it was safe. She said it was okay and we just needed a bed which I managed to get a prescription off the doctor for a bed which I gave to Rob on Tuesday or Wednesday and he put it into the chemist shop, and they then delivered me a hospital bed. The visit at home was good, I don't know if I have already recorded this so I may repeat myself.

It was bizarre being wheeled into the house because I hadn't been in for so long it just seemed different. Peggy our small dog seemed different, and she was really fussy, and it was good. I had been so cocooned in a clinic situation that I found it a bit of a shock to go back to the house seeing things and all the jobs and the organising that stared back at me. They have done so well for two months to look after all the animals and the house as well. It was good.

I have just got to wait another hour now for Rob. I do need to get away from here it's so hard not to be at home. It may be hard coming back but at least I get two days at home. We work hard here I am tired. At 10:30 I go practising my Robocop on the computer then straight to physio at 11:30 and although it seems as if you don't do much but you do and feel it later. It's progress, I am able to stand up now and tonight's physio was standing up and moving the right leg. I can't stand on the right leg yet.

I am then back with Corrine in the afternoon doing things and then I am back at physio so it's hard, but if ever I get a chance to rest, I do.

I have been here three weeks; I am toileting myself and I am transferring myself onto the bed. On a night I need them to move the electric chair to charge it.

I have finished my injections this morning for the anticoagulant which I am glad about because I have had them for that long I think it's about time they stopped. But I still have the two tablets for the phantom pain. I hope I can reduce the medication for Stubby then I won't be on medication.

Hopefully I can have some nice home-made food, it's good that I am getting out.

4 Minutes

It is Monday morning the 20th of June I think I haven't recorded for a while because I left my recorder at the house. On the 7th no the 10th of June I had my first home visit. Rob picked me up at 6:30 on Friday we get home and I returned at 6:30 on the Sunday.

It was strange, good but strange. As we were going home Sharon and Phil rang to see if they could call in not knowing that I was going home. I said yes, no problem which was nice, so they came to see us. It was so weird it all seemed so strange, I have been so used to looking at four walls it just felt weird.

I asked Rob if he could light the fire, I was cold, the weather had been cold, and I wasn't moving that much just sitting in my wheelchair. I was a bit ill on the Monday and Tuesday, I think it's the changes in temperatures and the air conditioning and all the windows open at the Grand Feu. I felt cold and weak I must have caught a virus.

The weekend went alright though I had a few moments of upset. I think it was for two reasons really, one because the last time I was at the house I could do things. I could walk, I could do things and for my mind this was quite hard. The other thing is it is frustrating not to be able to do the things you think you can do the small taken for granted things like making a cup of tea. Also, on the Monday before I had stopped the medication for Stubby, Marie looked it up it was for epilepsy, this that and the other, all sorts of things. I think there was an element of me just being a bit cold turkey from stopping strong medicine.

I have been medication free for a week from today, I am going to persevere with it so my up and down moods may have something to do with that? There is also a realisation that I can't do things at home like I used to do. I found the first weekend at home very good but quite hard. Hard for Rob and the boys too though you try not to you tend to take your frustrations out on the people around you to a certain extent and it's how they deal and respond to it that dictates the atmosphere. So that was the first weekend at home.

Then I am back at the Grand Feu with lots of work to do. Tuesday was the busiest that's when I felt the worst from the virus. I had to see the social worker she is saying I have just got to wait for my carte vital and I am saying I have already been waiting so long for it over a year and she needs to follow it up.

Next, I had to go to get my prosthesis fitted. I couldn't get it to work, I think it was a matter of being stressed, a bit weak and there were so many people there, I couldn't get it to work. I was just tired and out of sorts and then I have to go the physio.

Fred got me to stand up and then on the radio the song from the film 'Rocky' came on 'Eye Of The Tiger'. I said Fred that's a sign I have to walk. So, we walked on the walking railings for a couple of times, there and back so four times. That made my day much better, and I think the paracetamol I had taken half an hour ago because I felt so off colour helped too!

On Tuesday, Wednesday, Thursday, and Friday I did my normal activities. Wednesday, I did a cake, a chocolate cake which turned out fine and I continued to try walking. Then I had another weekend at home.

It was better, I was still a bit stressed, but I tried to do little things. If I can just do that I think I will be fine. I did say to the boys that if they didn't want me to stay weekends then I was okay with that and understood it was difficult. Rob's working three or four days, looking after the boys and the animals. Harvey is doing his brevet the final year exams, getting up early to do the animals, he is constantly thinking that he needs to be doing a job. Harvey was stressed about the chickens, but I looked at them and said Harvey there are no dramas. Those there will be gone in a month because they are cockerels, and they are big. So, when they have gone, we can put the ones that are running loose into that bit and organise it all it's not a big drama. So, he calmed down I said we need another month and then get organised.

On Saturday, Rob said we have got to move the pig, Dolly who is pregnant. I can't go down to the field to see her, so I have wondered and wondered how pregnant she actually is. When Rob said we had to move her I knew she was really near to giving birth. I said "We have to ring Sharon and Phil "Oh no, no, no." was Rob's reply. I said, "But you can't move Dolly with just you and Harvey." Later on, he did contact Phil and they came on Sunday morning. I had to stay in the house, but it was done with no real stress Dolly just went into the barn when I saw her, she was very near to giving birth. I think she has about a week to go but she looked relieved to be in the barn. When I spoke to her, she barked at me, so I think she remembers me. I asked her to just wait for the weekend and I can be here I won't be able to get in the barn to help her, but I can talk to her and de-stress her. At least this is her second time, so she has some knowledge what's going to happen. I doubted that she would have lasted another week before giving birth, now she can be fed and have some peace.

What else is there? Now I am back at the Grand Feu the weekend was good and the boys suggested I still come at weekends. I said to Rob if it's too much stress for you have a weekend off and I will just stay at the Grand Feu. But we do have to have a serious think about the four days of work he does the boys and I need too much help, because I can't really do anything. We will have to see I can't even help with the boys I can't take them anywhere. Rob is off for three weeks in a fortnight so we will have to see but only he can make that decision.

Now I am just waiting for my shower and to get through another five days. I feel a bit tired and low, but I have got to get on with it and try and get another month gone, bye.

10 Minutes

This was the first few weeks in my new home the Grand Feu, a massive change to my system but a place of great opportunity and know how to getting my life back into some sort of normality. I would stay there for quite a bit longer and continue to go home at weekends. I was now starting to wake up to the reality of my situations some of these realities not looking so pretty!

Chapter 24: The Disability Is Seen But Not The Person And Further Recordings At The Grand Feu

"My goal is to change disability into positivity"

-Penny Walker

In previous chapters I have already documented my first few recordings of when I arrived at the rehabilitation institute the Grand Feu between May 2016 and June 2016. I am now going to reflect on my feelings of this first half of my stay there, five years later with the knowledge and understanding I was to discover and be exposed to, including the hidden truths of my situation, revealed within those five years. I will then continue the recordings I made while still at the Grand Feu from July to August 2016, when I was starting to wake up to my reality.

I don't know if we have the ability to know things subconsciously which dictates our behaviour and reactions even though we are not aware of them consciously. For me it is a feeling in my gut, a knowing but not knowing why or how you know. Often this goes hand in hand with an internal mental battle with self not wanting to believe some of the things your gut is shouting be it from fear, ego or just plain non-understanding of how and why you should have this feeling.

When I was taken out of the protective accepting environment of my institute the Grand Feu to experience a less accepting and judging world, my gut was trying to highlight all the red flags to me. But I blocked it, it wasn't true this was my world the one I used to be accepted in loved and cared in, the one that would protect me, guide me and be nice to me after all it was just my hand that had been chopped off not my head.

At the time you are living it you ignore the signs, the red flags and the judgements until you have convinced yourself that it's not happening or it's your fault that these things are happening anyway. People's reactions and treatment of you is down to you, you deserve to be treated like this. The result is misery and anger, a deep depth of depression and a desire to battle and fight against the judgements and actions you receive from others. You trust no one and you don't even like or trust yourself!

After two weekends at home the red flags were screaming but I ignored them.

Now I see that most of the adults around me were not equipped to really accept, understand and help me. It was as if I had a contagious disease and one they may catch.

I see now how it is difficult for people to adapt and accept changes that they have no control over. The ultimate reaction is to not accept it, fight it, judge it, distance yourself from it while justifying these actions. Interestingly enough the young and teenagers don't seem to take this stance. They are accepting, have honesty, openness and loving to people who are different.

I am not saying that the people around me didn't care or try with all their power to understand me and my needs, but if I didn't understand, how was it possible for them to. How was it possible for them to even begin to comprehend the needs and tortures a person was going through after such a big mental and physical adaptation.

The simple fact was I was the same old Penny, just trapped in pain, fear and a disability that I had to learn to grow and develop with. I wanted understanding, normal conversations, not the look, the judgement of my actions which were screams for help. I didn't want the condescending voices or none eye contact. I was now alien to the people and world I once knew.

Many slowly disappeared from my world but the ones I could trust and the ones that never gave up on me stayed. Now they benefit from the wisdom and strength I have been given on this journey.

They stood beside me, trod the path with me, at times having to get out of the way to let me pass unaided but always within watching distance, while praying and caring for me. I believe they too have grown in wisdom and strength, for what they had to witness was not pretty. But slowly something magical and beautiful was beginning to happen, be it very slow and unconsciously.

These are the rest of the recordings which I did while at the Grand Feu:

It is Tuesday the 21st of June, today I had to practise as usual, doing the robocop. I had physio and we are still doing the exercises and then I had to go and get a robocop fitted. The man from the company came and I had a prosthesis put on my arm and then they fitted the robotic arm. It's quite amazing, you have to programme it from and iphone. What you do (recording finished)

1 Minute

Right, I am back I don't know what happened with the phone? I have got this phone (Eric's) I so need to get my own phone!! I don't know how to work Eric's I think it's switched off and now it's buzzing.

I don't know how to receive messages it's all very complicated and I am getting a robotic hand! So, if I can't even work a simple Samsung phone how am I going to work a robotic hand that is controlled by an iPhone? No doubt it will be one of my next adventures in life to try and figure out how to work it.

I did amuse myself because I thought well you could get away with all sorts. You could actually strangle someone and claim it wasn't you, it was your robotic hand, someone else programmed it. I also thought you could probably, if someone got hold of your iPhone, they could programme your hand and control you. It's all a bit futuristic for me but all will be revealed. I have got four weeks practise on it and then I have to make a decision and then my own personal one will be made or cast or I don't know what. I have one now that they gave me just to practise. It all looks good I am very pleased, although it's a bit daunting.

In the afternoon physio I am still walking but only sometimes putting a tiny bit of weight through my right leg, it's hard for me not to but so far so good let's just keep the progression.

I have just spoken to a girl who had just arrived she sat next to me in the restaurant. She is French but speaks very good English, she looked quite sad, in fact on the first night I thought she looked how I felt when I first came here. I have just had a chat with her, her problem is tiredness and back problems. While talking to her I said I think I know what's wrong. I think you need to be kinder to yourself, I think you need to stop helping everyone else. Everybody you have helped, your family and friends have all drained you and you have no energy left. You need to get your energy back. You need to block them energetically, you need to protect yourself, cut cords and get your energy back. Once you do that you will find your energy because now you are so exhausted from giving, giving and giving all the time throughout your life, that you can't give anymore, and you have to now give to yourself.

She is a really nice girl and I hoped it helped we will see. I think I have made her think of something and to look within because she is getting stressed because no one can tell her what the matter is. I think if she can just take the pressure off herself and her mind then her body will relax, and she will make progress.

That's my opinion or is it the angels' opinion? Someone obviously put her next to me on the table for a reason and Vivian too. Vivian who I sat with the first week I arrived has come back, she has had her leg amputated, which gave her so much pain for a year! I think she took my advice, I did suggest that she name it and reconnect with it. She has named it Polly, she has no pain, is very positive and seems really happy.

She came back a few days ago.

Also, back at the ranch they have managed to move the pig which I probably told you about. I am hoping Dolly is alright. I am not sure if this phone is working, but if someone is meant to ring me, they will. Bye.

4 Minutes

It's now Friday teatime I am waiting for Rob to come back and pick me up to take me home for the weekend. This week has been busy I got my hand on Tuesday, the one I am practising with, I got an iPhone which you can programme to whatever movement you want on the hand. The only problem I am having is it is really quite heavy and a long arm. I am finding the balance quite hard. But I have been practising and I am taking it home this weekend to practise with it more I have only four weeks to figure it out and decide what I want to do, I must therefore practise really hard.

I have probably said this before, but last weekend was better, and I am hoping this weekend will be better as well. I will be getting used to it and won't be getting as frustrated about not doing jobs. I spoke to Jenny on the phone and was explaining to her about the post woman, who is alright, but she is nosey and does gossip quite a bit. She had brought a parcel on Saturday, I was in the room just getting dressed and Rob said are you decent which I said no! So, with my knickers around my ankles and in my wheelchair, I had to have a conversation with the post woman. I don't know why Rob didn't understand "No!! I am not decent." Jenny thinks it's hilarious, which it probably was.

Also, last weekend we moved Dolly the pig we had to get help, Rob didn't want to, but we got Phil and Sharon to come and help on Sunday morning and Dolly went into the barn. She looked quite far gone and she seemed to be relieved that she was back in the barn.

Rob came over to visit me on Wednesday and left the boys with Dolly who had three babies when Rob left. He rang me later, Harvey and Elliott had been left in charge to help deliver the pigs and he rang to say she had got 12! He rang me again yesterday so I could find out how they were and explained she had 13 one was a still born and two were runty and one did die. Hopefully in the next hour I will get to see all 11 and I hope Dolly is well! She is a good mum. I have kept my apples for her a little treat which I will give her when I get there so that is good.

This week progress, though the Robocop is quite difficult, it is going to tax my brain. Bye.

3 Minutes

In this recording I was very upset.

It's Sunday night probably 1:00 in the morning. I have had my third weekend at home. I was really looking forward to it and we went to some friends for my son Harvey to help them fill some forms in on the Friday, so we didn't get to bed until late.

Saturday Rob had to go to get some animal food and he had arranged to meet somebody to look at a job. It seems every time I am at home Rob is never there, he has always got things to do probably because he is working three or four days through the week (big sighs, trying not to cry). Saturday was fine James and Jenny came round. James measured up the bathroom. We have to try and change it so it's easier for me to get in there (long pause).

Saturday night I felt really ill and cold then hot, it was about 10:30 that I went to bed, I just felt awful. I don't know if it was too much sun, just too much tiredness or just my body trying to repair from everything (I am getting upset) it's so hard being at home.

I was happy and got to see Dolly and her babies, I don't know how she gives birth to 13, one of the runts died and one was still born. They are all doing well, I hope. The boys have been amazing at looking after everything.

I feel I am just not coping very well (break down crying). I am trying to work it out I think it's because you are there, then you are not there, and you can't get into it so you disturb their routine and their lives. They say they want me there, but I don't know if they do really want me there. I think Rob is doing too much and he is tired and then I am frustrated and probably tired and it's not good. The more I think about it, this is just an extra strain on our relationship. I don't know how you make it any better. I look around at all my friends and I think you shouldn't compare because Rob's not like them but it just I still haven't got a phone (getting more upset), I am still borrowing someone's phone and I can't even make a phone call. I was left in Nantes hospital without any phone, and it just doesn't seem to be right. I don't talk to Rob every day he doesn't phone me, I know he is busy, but it does not seem the correct way to have a relationship. I have told him he doesn't have to stick around and be with someone who is disabled. I just get that daft laugh that he gives, but no answer. I honestly think he doesn't want to be around for a number of reasons (long pause).

Being with someone who doesn't love you is quite hard especially when you love them so much. So, I have prayed hard for answers. I get all the blame because Rob won't talk about things that happened before the accident usually when a person is trying to get away with something they blame the innocent person not discussing the issue but ignoring its existence. He had really shattered my heart from doing certain things and I was just starting to repair it.

Now I feel so vulnerable because I can't help myself as much as I want to. I know he is sometimes tired, and he is probably doing a lot and fed up with it all. I think he doesn't even want to help me anyway. He just says I complain a lot, but he doesn't understand I am not complaining about things, I just want my life back (getting really upset now). I know now I am never going to have it back!!

I worry about Harvey and Elliott because they are teenagers, they are so good, and I don't want them to change. I don't know the only thing I have got left is to pray really hard (breaking down upset). I don't think it's going to be enough, I don't want to be here (Grand Feu) but I know I have to be.

I had a fall out today and I don't even know what it was about. Just something little and Rob has got a short temper and I felt so much in the way, and I said I wish I had died (difficult to hear, I am so upset), but I didn't really mean it, I am so grateful that I didn't die because I have been given a chance to see the kids grow up and I don't want to die. But I feel pretty dead at the moment, I just hope things improve.

Everybody around me is telling me you have got to do this, you've got to get rid of your animals, you have got to get Harvey a motorbike so he can get to work on his own without Rob taking him. Just telling me what to do all the time.

I couldn't possibly let Harvey get a motorbike he just isn't a motorbike sort of person. It's also on the route where I had my accident more or less so I would never rest. (Pause deep sigh upset). So, I am trying to be strong I am trying not to think that I'm in everybody's way, but I feel as if I am. I suppose I was thinking what if it had been over, they would have been upset but at least they would have a life without having to push me around in a wheelchair and put up with me (more sighs).

Maybe I am just feeling sorry for myself I hope I am not. It's just the heart has gone out of me (long pause upset) and I don't really know what to do. I suppose the best option is to try and talk to Rob but you don't get anything out of him (really, really upset). All I want is for him to show me that he wants me to be around and if he doesn't, then he has to say so (long pause) I am so tired now I can't sleep but I will try and get some sleep now. It feels as if it's only just the beginning of this pain!!

10 Minutes

The last recording, the 10 minute one was so difficult for me to listen to. I could not see the paper and my writing because my eyes were clouded with tears. Today February 2021 is the first time I have listened to the recording since June 2016. I am listening to a voice, a person in so much pain and despair, it was quite heart-breaking and harrowing to listen to. I felt so much compassion and love for this person, I just wanted to give them a big hug and say it's all going to be okay. I then realised this was me this was the desperate painful journey I was experiencing, and it was a deep emotional shock to me nearly five years on.

Why did I not feel loved, why did I feel abandoned all these whys came flooding into my mind as I tried to listen and write down the words of a very upset individual. The ironic thing was that it was like a premonition, a message given, a knowing, a look into the future of what was about to unfold. I had it spot on, everything I felt was true and with time this would be confirmed. I then choose the path that so many of us do and listened to the false information, taking the blame, convincing myself that every problem was created by me and was because of me.

The surrounding people and environment happy to feed this illusion and strengthen it within my mind because then they did not have to take responsibility. None of the actions of this crazy woman was anything to do with them and their reactions and actions, their behaviour or even their words. There were very few who did not jump on this bandwagon. Those that didn't get on still remain dear, loyal and loving friends today.

I could carry on down this area of discovery, but I feel it is better to finish the recordings first, so the reader gets the true feelings that I had at the time I had them. But listening back to it makes me realise I was like a vulnerable little creature injured and lost, being pecked at by the bigger, stronger and devious other creatures. They would be waiting for the right time to peck at me some more, secretly when it couldn't be seen. Not choosing to pick up this injured, weak, scared creature, offering them warmth, protection or love to help them with their pain and to watch over them until they were strong enough to stand on their own feet. No, it was easier and quicker to stomp on them, leave them to struggle in their pain and misfortune because there are other creatures, uninjured, not in need of help, who don't look battered and ugly, to replace the disregarded one. There is then no choice but for the injured creature to crawl away and suffer on their own.

But eventually they emerge stronger, happier, healed and wiser. Even with their disabilities and their judged ugliness they become transformed into a beautiful loving soul because they choose to love themselves and their disabilities and not to be pecked anymore!!

Now back to the recordings while in the Grand Feu Niort:

Hi, it is Tuesday night the 28th of June, today we have been to Nantes hospital for an appointment at 9 o'clock in the morning with the plastic surgeon doctor. I managed to arrange to stay at home last night and go first thing in the morning. We get there in good time found where we should be and had about a ten-minute meeting which was fine. The doctor just wanted to check the scar on Stubby and the groin and took a photograph of the groin. He said everything was alright. We showed him the robocop and that was it. He signed me off which was good, I am now an outpatient, he has done his job and I have moved on which was really good.

I had managed to get a 24 hours pass from the Grand Feu so I said to Rob I will stay with you guys and go back at 6:30. It was good and compared to my last recording, I have thought about it and giving it up for divine intervention. I decided that we have got to move on and it was probably a combination of everything that's happened to me which is just trying to escape. I have just got to think more positive, take pressure off Rob and just chill a bit more. Today was good no arguments no stress, a little bit of stress because I had to go on the emails, and they have not been looked at so there were loads to reply to.

I suppose you have got to have your downers to get back up. I would much rather feel how I feel today than how I felt the last time I spoke to you. Bye.

2 Minutes

It is Monday the 4th of July it's 5:30 I have just got back to my room after a day back at the Grand Feu. Today was okay I showered and washed my own hair and the only thing I asked the assistant to do was plat my hair and put the bond on my right leg I haven't bothered with one on my left leg.

The doctor came and I asked if I could see the psychologist because I think being too tough isn't always the answer. I think it's fair to the family and to me to talk to someone else because I realise that it is going to be much more difficult than I thought and there are a lot more things that I will probably never be able to do again. Like climbing the tree to get that last apple or just chopping up wood all the things I did before are not going to be able to be done again, at least I don't think so.

The weekend I arrived on Friday at home. All was good, on Saturday two pintades (Guinea Fowl) hatched one with splayed legs Harvey tied it up and then we took it off because I always think they are too tight. I hope it will be alright, when I left on Sunday it was eating and standing up, but he is still a bit wobbly. I think the paper we put in the bottom of the box was slippery, so we put a bit of straw in, so it was less slippery for him.

All was good and then I had a bit of a breakdown because Harvey was shutting the chickens up and my little baby Snowy chick had been attacked similar to what happened with my little baby rabbit. I felt so frustrated, and I wanted to protect the other chicks that needed to be put away and they were just standing there no one was rushing out to see if the creature was still around. So, we had a massive shouting match, and I had an emotional breakdown. Rob shouted back which upset the kids and spoilt the weekend.

I know it's not Rob he doesn't really want to shout at me, and I don't want to shout back at him. It wasn't just the chick, yes, I was very upset about the chick it was my Snowy's chick it was one that I had reared. The mum has gone she died, and I just hate losing anything, it's my job to protect these animals and I can't do it because I am stuck in a wheelchair (big sigh).

I cried and all was good we didn't fall out we have got to sort it out, but they have to accept that it is not going to be easy. That's what I am going to have to accept too.

We went to Mel and Rob's for a drink and Rob the electrician and his wife Kim and his mum and dad were there, so it was really nice. His dad is a show dahlia grower and I love my dahlias, so it was brilliant to chat to him and get all his ideas. It was really nice, I didn't want to go because I felt awful on Sunday, tired and so awful. I have got to accept that days are going to be good and bad.

Norman and Helen arrived (they have a holiday house in the village), they came around Saturday and couldn't believe how well I looked (I thought I didn't look that well) and how well I was doing for the time that it's been. But they then saw me on Sunday as we were leaving and saw how upset I was. Helen was in hospital for 6 months after a car accident when she was younger, she shattered her hip and leg. Norman has been in the army, so he has seen things. They talk a lot of sense they said you have got to expect ups and downs.

Today (Monday) the physio spoke to the doctor this morning, we have decided that the robotic arm is too long and too heavy so we are going to take the 360° movement off it and just do manual turning and hopefully it will be lighter, and I can use it better. So practised with that and then had physio. Just now I have just come back from physio we are walking and putting some weight through the right leg. I know I don't go to the specialist until Wednesday, but I am putting a tiny bit of weight through my foot. I hope it's okay from the x-rays on Wednesday and then we can get going. I did ask Frederick why I can't go in the gymnasium. I want to build the whole of my muscles up, it used to be my sport, so I miss it and know I need it. If I don't, I am going to have problems with my back, with my shoulders, I am going to have problems with everything, I need to get strong and balanced.

There was a student in physio who seems really nice and keen, and Fred went off and found something which we could maybe have made so I can actually hold the dumbbell in Stubby, that should be good. Hopefully another month and I should be walking if I am slow and careful. I feel better but I have to accept things are going to be up and down and my life will never be the same again.

7 Minutes

It's now Friday morning, probably the 8th of July I will get back to today because it's been interesting to say the least but before that I will go back to Wednesday. We went to Nantes to see the surgeon Dr. Pietu. He looked at the x-rays and he is pleased and said I can now start to walk. He has a little concern about the lower ankle the talus he says it could die, I don't know. It could die if the nerve or the blood supply isn't good, he is worried about the nerve in the foot. I am not as worried I will just work it and adapt the muscle. I have got full movement, a little restricted in certain movements and the sensation is different like you have pins and needles. I think with work and exercise and God's intervention we will be good. It was a long day but good. The doctor is a bit concerned about the length of the prosthesis. We didn't take it with us, so we need to take it with us next time. We see him again on the 7th of September in two months. I will have the same x-rays, but we are going to have other x-rays as well and maybe in different positions, but at least now I can try and walk. I can weight-bear on it now I have got permission because it has healed how he wants it to heal.

The pin or bolt in my knee that is sticking out he said categorically that he wouldn't be doing anything with that. So, I will just have to accept that and work around that one and that was it meeting over.

On the way home we just called in to say hi to the kids and poor Harvey and Elliott had been chasing Myrtle-May and Buster (the pigs) for three hours because they had got out, they had come up to the barn to see Dolly and her babies. The boys were not happy, and it was a really hot day. So, Rob got them back in, I think the pigs were just tired and hot. He repaired the fence and then we had to go back to the Grand Feu.

When we came back the woman, (the short skirt high heeled woman) didn't say "Bonsoir" turned her wrist looked at her watch and pointed at it. I am saying we had to stop for petrol, and I had to use a cheque the tearing out of which is difficult enough with two hands and it's slow and impossible with one hand (but I still want to try and do it). She said, "It takes you that long to go for petrol?" and went on and on. I am thinking oh whatever! What is it to her, it's my business what I have been doing? Every time we come back if we are 10 or 15 minutes late, she gives us a problem.

That night Wednesday there was a barbecue, but I didn't eat any and there was a band, so Rob stayed for a while. Mel came and it was nice to have people there.

They stayed about twenty minutes it was really warm. I didn't eat because Harvey had made me some pasta.

Graham who is leaving today had got a couple of beers and had got Vivian a Guinness. We sat in the corner and listened to the band they were good, and I had a bit of a buggy in my wheelchair.

Thursday physio and other stuff, exercising with my Stubby and on Thursday afternoon I had a meeting with the doctor, Corrine and Fred. It was good, all is fine no problems, we have a date which is the 17th. I am just pausing because the social worker, I will tell you about her in a minute, but she was supposed to be there at the meeting, but she never turned up. She's bloody useless, I tell you she wasn't there.

Then we discussed that it is great I can get walking and we are aiming to leave the rehabilitation place for the 17th of August because Rob's birthday is on the 18th, I would like to be home for that. So, I can get out of here in roughly five weeks. I need to just work hard to get moving with the hand, Corrine needs to video it because people who are paying for it need to see that I am going to use it before they shell out any money. I did have a question about work why are they trying to get me a job, what work can I do? I don't know it was the social worker and she wasn't even there to answer the question! So, they just said later, later, so later, later whatever that means!

That was yesterday, I did feel a bit sick and a bit off, but I did go back to physio at 4:30 and we walked with one stick. It's hard getting the rhythm (and the muscles in my legs are obviously not used to walking) but I can do it if I concentrate, I am not too wobbly and I only need one stick, I can't hold two you need two hands for that! I have just got to build it up the strength so I am hopeful that all will be fine. That was it not a bad day.

Then last week I filled out a form for Bastille Day and it says on the form three nights. The doctor signed it not a problem he said I could go. Leave on Thursday the 11th and come back on the Sunday at whatever time. I took the form to the receptionist last week and went to collect it she said it's not possible and it's been crossed out I now can't have a three-day pass. So, I thought about it, it's daft because in the village Marc asked me if we were going to the Bastille celebrations. Rob said no because I will have to be back at the Grand Feu for 6:30. The reason given is stupid and the reason is because I have to have physio on the Friday (there was none on Thursday because of Bastille Day).

The fact that I worked as a physio for years in my own clinic doesn't seem to make any difference. I was talking to the nasty receptionist with all her high and mighty attitude she said, "No you can't have three days!" So, I picked my paper up which had a cross through it and the doctor's signature on it.

Prison Or The Paralympics

On the Tuesday before I left to go home to go to Nantes the next day, I asked can I have a meeting with the director. She said, "It's not possible, it's not possible." I said "Okay" I then went into another area which is administration the one we went to on my arrival, and I asked them. He phoned the director's secretary and she said she would get back to me. No one ever did! It's now Friday and still no one has got back to me.

So, this morning on a mission I went down to speak to the director the office didn't open until 9:00. The woman who looked at her watch when we came back last week the receptionist, said "What do you want?" I hadn't even gone to her and had no intention of doing so. I said, "I will just wait." She said, "What's your question?" I replied, "It's my business not yours." Why should I speak to the receptionist (especially that one) it's a private question, what I wanted to ask the director so what's the problem with that, I have a right to ask the director a question. It's only him who can sign the paper. So, I said "It's not your business, it's my business." She went off on one I said, "It's not a problem madame I will sit over here and wait until 9 o'clock."

Then suddenly another woman appears and gives me it in the neck, blah, blah, blah! I said, "I just want to speak to the director it's not a big problem I just want to speak to the director." She said, "You can't it's impossible he is not here today." I said, "I am not stupid I know he's not here today I will speak to him on Monday then, but I asked to speak to him on Wednesday and now it's Friday and nobody's even told me anything." Her reaction "Oh right" then she went off on one and she was getting quite angry, so I said, "Madame calm." I was fairly calm because you have to be in these situations. They were pissing me off a bit, but I was calm. I said, "I will just wait here there is no problem."

Then she went around into the back of the office which had blinds down, but I could hear her talking. She had only gone and phoned my social worker who's pretty crap anyway. The social worker turns up and starts talking to the high and mighty receptionist. She is stood there talking about me obviously! I asked Claire the social worker "Have you got a problem, why are you talking about me?" Then Claire the social worker came over and gave me loads of bloody yab, yab, yab, yabber. I replied, "I am not stupid I have a right to see the director, I have a right if I want to see the director." Her reply more yab, yab, yab. I said, "I'm leaving, what are you doing here, why are you discussing me with her (receptionist), what are you doing here?" I went off in my wheelchair Claire is running after me I am saying "I am not talking to you I have no reason to I want to talk to the director." (Big sigh) "I will come back."

I have just been back; they have all been told so they know about me. The woman left me there for ten minutes not attending to me. Then she came and I said, "I want to see the director." Her reply "It's not possible he is not here today." I said, "I know that I will see him on Monday." Her annoyed voice said, "You can't see him on Monday I will get back to you." I said, "No ring the secretary of the director now while I am here and book me in for Monday or Tuesday, I need to see him before Thursday." She rang the answer "He is not available he is busy all week he can see you next week." I said, "That's not right I have to see him before Thursday." She said, "It's not possible" I said "I have to see him before Thursday." Her reply "It's not possible". "Okay ring back and ask for next week" was my request. "No, we can't she is busy she is in a meeting" was her cocky answer.

I am not stupid she's in a meeting? I said, "Oh she is in a meeting that's funny you've just put the phone down on her". "Okay you have to go and see your doctor" was her next bullshit. I said, "I have seen the doctor he hasn't got a problem, it isn't the doctor I need to see, I need to see the director not the doctor." I then asked, "Is it a prison here?" "No" she replied I asked again "Why can't I see the director?" "Well, he is busy." She answered. My response "I'm busy I only have two hours he is the only person who can answer my question!!" Again, in parrot fashion "You have to go and see the doctor."

So, I went to the doctor's receptionist and explained the situation, "I will phone them" she kindly offered. I said, "They won't let me see him." She phoned them and said she only wants to see him for 10 minutes. Now I am waiting to hear from him they are going to email her, and I am waiting to see if I get to see him. It's not right what are they scared of I have a right to see the director.

The doctor's receptionist was really good she actually just forced it a bit and she kept saying on the phone "But she only wants to see him for 10 minutes, she wants to ask him a question, it's ten minutes."

What is wrong with everybody I only want to know the answer to a question. There is no point me having a pass for Bastille celebrations if I am coming back at 6:30 what do I do? Stop mid bloody celebration and come back? It's absolutely stupid. The other alternative is for me to sit here at cell block Grand Feu all day on my own, no physio, nothing open for work or rehabilitation. It's stupid and the form says three nights on it what's the big drama? If the drama is physio that's crap because I am a rehabilitator and have rehabilitated hundreds of athletes. I am really not happy with the social worker, I am not seeing her again she can shite! What is wrong with them all. All I am asking or trying to do is ask one bloody question he (the director) is not God!! What is wrong with people? End of moan bye.

13 Minutes

Prison Or The Paralympics

It's me again it's still Friday about 3 o'clock I am in my room. I went to the re-education place at 1:30 to do my hand with Corrine, while there, there was a phone call to say the doctor is coming to see me. He arrived and brought a nurse who could apparently speak good English to explain the situation?

So, this is the situation, I can't stay out on Bastille night because MSA or whoever pays for me to be here won't allow it which (big sigh), which is bizarre so it's not this place (Grand Feu). They are saying it's MSA that won't allow it and the contract will be broken. So, it was a load of blah, blah, blah and the nurse said "It's the same in England" I said "It isn't the same, if you have Christmas 'day' off the festival is that day you don't have the day before off! You have Christmas day off." Her response "Oh no it's not possible, blah, blah, blah." I sat there for a while, there was a woman Sophie sat next to me who is a really nice woman she had a virus, or an infection lost some of her sight and was in hospital for ages she is a lovely woman. I am sat next to her and thought to myself I'm not staying here. I said goodbye to her and Corrine and wished them a good weekend and came back to my room.

I then went to the doctor's secretary who is lovely and very good and asked her if she would please tell the doctor that I want to leave next week. She said I will phone him I thanked her and said okay. Then I thought oh God she said he will come and find you. I was just about to escape outside, and he found me before I could escape. I couldn't be bothered talking to him because I was upset.

He came into my room and spoke to me and said if you leave now it's too early, I said I know it's too early. I needed a few more weeks but I can't stand this prison. I said to the doctor "When you come back, she is looking at her watch, ten minutes late and she is looking at her watch." The French are never bloody on time!! Then if you try and leave five minutes early, she is like "No you can't leave you have to wait till half past six!" Bollocks!! What a load of bollocks it is (big sigh). So, I spoke to the doctor who is a really nice guy Dr. Belkacemi I have a lot of respect for him. The decision was that I will wait for two weeks and when he comes back (he's on holiday) I'll make the decision, so I am going to stick it for two weeks more (getting upset) I am not going anywhere on Bastille Day I will stay here because it's too complicated to get out and it's not fair to the family. We can't even have a celebration; Rob won't be able to drink, and we would have to stop halfway through the celebrations to bring me back it's absolutely stupid.

What's the point, the form said three nights it actually said three nights! I have noticed they have taken the forms away. So, it continues I don't know what I feel like (big sigh). I can't see it's because I just feel down, the doctor said it's my morale. My morale is fine it's the stupidity that's frustrating me. People who talk to you, it's not the medicine I am not really on any, it's not the professional people it's these surrounding me who do it. The receptionist, the social worker, carer who thinks she's God! Even in the restaurant they give you a dish that's not even appetising, throw it at you and then wonder why you can't eat it. So, I am over it, I am over it all!

But out of respect for the doctor, the physio and Corrine I am going to stay here another two weeks until the doctor comes back off holiday. If things haven't improved, which they won't have and if I am walking and not in my electric chair I am frigging out of here!! I don't care if I haven't got the robotic hand, I will just get it from Nantes, the doctor at Nantes has already said he prefers me to be getting it there than here. It's too early anyway, if I am allowed one, I'll get one. We will see another wonderful day in paradise!

5 Minutes

It's the 11th of July Monday morning just reporting in. At the weekend I went home on Friday, I had Saturday and came back here Sunday night all is good. I have managed to persuade Fred the physio to let me have a stick, a cane, to take home I said I would only use it in the house, and I did more or less, with the only other thing I used it for was walking from the car to the house, but we didn't take the wheelchair into the house.

Slowly I am getting my balance it's still very difficult and I must be careful not to rush things. I am keeping my electric chair for now at the Grand Feu, I am not giving that up for at least two weeks, unless they ask me to. So, another week in paradise (Humm!) but I will just see how things go. I will do my work and ignore all the other people that upset me and get through it. Generally feeling okay.

1 Minute

It's Sunday night, it is the 17th of July. This week I went out Wednesday night slept at home Wednesday and then went to the Bastille celebrations, in the village. I had to get back at 6:30 but Helen said she would take me back and I felt better about things because then Rob could have a drink and stay longer. I was in my wheelchair and people from the village were there it was good. I danced a little in my wheelchair, just my upper body. I got a few people staring who knew me before the accident, people do tend to stare at Stubby rather than looking at me but that's what's going to happen from now on.

Prison Or The Paralympics

Everything was good and then this woman who I didn't know just grabbed my wheelchair and started moving it trying to dance with me. But she caught my bad leg and trapped it on the table and started moving me around which really upset my leg. Everyone thought it was funny, but it wasn't. After she finished, I just had to get outside my leg was really hurting. Then it was time for me to go back.

A few days before Helen and her friend Rosemary came to visit me. They had a laugh because unthinking I went to see them off and say goodbye and went outside. It was one minute past 8:30 and I couldn't get back in. They were a bit concerned but I managed to get my electric wheelchair up this ramp, it wasn't even a ramp it was a step and asked this guy if he would let me use his room to get back in. I did ring the night door someone answered but nobody came. It was a bit of a joke to them they thought it funny that I couldn't get back in and it was, but they did look quite concerned.

About the 7th or 8th of July I started walking with the physio, I walked a little last weekend. This weekend has been quite hard, I think partly because I had Wednesday at home and then was busy here at the Grand Feu. After you have finished all your rehabilitation at least in the evening you are quiet in your room, not like at home when all the jobs you can't do are staring at you, it's difficult. I often get a little bit upset, be it tiredness, I don't know be it my new life! Emotions are difficult generally frustrations with it all.

This weekend I got home Friday it was nice though it always seems to be late when I get to bed. Then on Saturday morning we had to get up to go to Parthenay Rob dropped something off at the insurance then we were looking for something in a shop. I went in, I really shouldn't have done, it was too hard, so I came back to the car and stayed in the car. We didn't stay out long and called at Sharon and Phil's which was nice. I then tried to rest the remaining of Saturday.

On Sunday we went to see Jenny and James on the way to take me back. It was hot so the boys went in their swimming pool. I saw the three chickens that I had given them which I was trying to cross breed. Marans with Leghorns. They looked beautiful; they are really big birds, so I am pleased with them. If the accident hadn't of happened, I was going to start up a new breed, for the eggs and the meat. They will let me have some fertile eggs if I want some. I was impressed with the birds they were really good-looking birds.

The piglets are doing well but loads of work for Harvey and sometimes Elliott will help. Rob is now not working because they are on holiday for a while. I think he will feel better when he is not running around as much. I am still having moments of upset and tears, anger, not anger about the accident, it's not really anger but frustration of not being able to get on and help and do things and general life. But I am only here at the

Grand Feu, for another four weeks so I have to make the most of it. Bye.

8 Minutes

It's now Friday evening the 21st of July, I have not gone home tonight because Rob is picking me up Saturday morning and we are going to try and go into Niort to get a frame for the Velux window in case it's the frame that is causing the leak. Rob has also gone out tonight with Martine and work colleagues for pancakes, so it's probably worked out well that he comes for me tomorrow.

This week, Monday usual physio with Colline the student physio, who has worked me really hard, we are still walking and walking better. All week she has got me exercising and walking and started going up steps and down but not many.

With Corrine in the agro place which is the re-education place I continued to weave my basket which is all I seem to do now but that's okay.

The guys for the hand came with my new prosthesis but it didn't fit. He cut it and cut it but I just couldn't get Stubby in all the way and it was uncomfortable. So they told me to come back in the afternoon and I went down again and did my basket waiting for them but they didn't turn up, it got to 4:30 I said I am not missing physio I missed it this morning. Corrine went to see them, but they were busy with someone else. I said that I had already made the decision that morning, we need to put this on hold. This hand the robocop has got to go back in a week they have got to video me using it to justify paying for it. I am only here for another two weeks it's all too rushed. My arm, Stubby is not ready, I need to get him moving better and muscled up and I have enough to deal with at the moment.

That was my decision and Corrine told them my decision then they admitted that one of them was actually going on holiday anyway. I am not going to rush into it, it's for life I don't want it uncomfortable and not functioning correctly, I will just wait.

On Wednesday Rob and Harvey turned up they had been to sort out some paperwork in Niort and they arrived at dinner time. I was making vegetables with Corrine I have just got to show them that I can function. I have managed to get out of the restaurant tonight nobody has come and pestered me which is good.

Thursday the social worker Claire came I was alright with her, but I am not so keen. She was saying we have got to organise this and that, apply for this and apply for that and I have to phone the insurance company. I can't be bothered with whatever she is doing, she seems to be panicking and probably this stuff should have been dealt with way before now! She goes on holiday on the 5th of August Corrine on the 15th and I leave on the 17th of August. It seems to me that everyone is trying to do things that should have been done ages ago. But I am not bothered I am just trying to keep my mouth shut and get through the next few weeks without any hassle and work really hard with the physio.

Corrine has been really good she's tried to get me a disabled driving license. The form arrived so I have to bring some stuff in on Monday. She has booked me a lesson for the driving which is on the day before I leave the 16th. It's all rush, rush, rush but anyway I am just going with the flow.

Also, this week a guy came into my room to tell me that I couldn't have breakfast in my room. Which I wasn't bothered about. They brought me a piece of fruit, so I didn't have to go to the restaurant I hate going in, it just depresses me. I didn't need the piece of fruit they brought because I always had a banana and rice cakes in my drawer. I said to him no problem, but I won't be going down to the restaurant. The next day the girl who was really nice said I had to go to the restaurant, I didn't want to get her in trouble so I said I would go and talk to the restaurant.

I went down in my nighty in my wheelchair and said I won't be coming down here on a morning and I will never be coming down here on a morning. She didn't have a problem with it, so I don't know who has complained about giving me a piece of fruit. I actually don't care if they don't bring me fruit or not it was often bloody sour especially the peaches it's not a big drama. Not at all, I am not worried about that!

What else has happened, not much more. Sadly, Colline my student left today so I am a bit sad because she has worked me really hard. She seems to get it she is an ex-gymnast and swimmer, and she seems to get that you have to be built up with muscle and that I used to be sportive! The only thing is I never brought in my photo to show her when I used to compete so she will never know what I used to look like or train like. If I find it this weekend, I'll bring it to show Fred.

Yesterday I went and they measured me up to make me something so I can hold a weight in Stubby. The way she moulded it I am not quite sure what she is going to do and how it will work. No doubt I will find out next week they don't really rush things here. I need to get Stubby working I need to get some muscle on him. I need to get the shoulder right and I need to get my body balanced.

My doctor doesn't come back until the 1st of August so that's another week. Fred's changed my physio to 9 o'clock on the mornings which isn't a problem. So, another week in paradise I suppose. That's it really and hopefully I will get home tomorrow.

9 Minutes

It's now Wednesday four o'clock, I am just waiting to go to physio at 4:30. I haven't spoken since last week so what's happened. Went home Saturday morning, Rob picked me up and we went into Niort to look for a frame. They have changed in the last ten years so we couldn't get a replacement we got home at dinner time.

All is good, Harvey is doing a brilliant job of looking after the animals and the garden. Elliott is helping clean the house, so it looks fine and cleaner. We rested and watched a DVD. On Sunday we went to Alex and Kelly's. She had invited us for dinner so she came to pick us up so Rob could have a drink, we went at 1:00 and left at 5:00, I was really tired. It was a lovely day the meal was really nice, and all was good we came back, and I just checked and watched the new-born chicks who were fine.

One of the rabbits had died (attacked by a rat) and Harvey was trying to hide it from me (big sigh), so I went to look in the barn. The barn is really stressing me out. I understand there are a lot of things going on. I don't want anyone doing any of my jobs which frustrates me and before I did things to try and avoid rats.

For example, on Saturday in the barn I was cleaning and sorting stuff out and I had a bit of a go at them because there were loads of bags and rope and rubbish just on the floor, having had rats before I didn't want to encourage rats again. So, I started tidying up and doing stuff which is really frustrating because I am not well or fit enough to do it. I know they are doing their best, Rob is not particularly tidy, and Harvey is a young teenager who is doing much more than he should be doing anyway (big sigh). Rob just argues and says, "It was always like this anyway." It was never that bad, things wanted organising, but it was never mucky, my water buckets were never mucky!! (Big sigh) After tidying I came inside there wasn't a problem. Got ready for bed because I was really tired and just wanted to go to bed.

Then I saw this letter that should have been answered to do with MSA (my health insurance) a very important letter in fact. I am thinking it's just another thing (big sigh) the passports should have been sent off weeks ago and now this important letter that no one showed me. Loads of things that are frustrating me.

So, I got into my hospital bed set up downstairs then a big argument started remember Rob had been drinking and probably looking for a fight. It's always my fault every weekend it's always my fault according to Rob. I understand that it's difficult and maybe I could be more grateful, but they don't understand what I am having to deal with they don't understand what I am going through.

Rob had had plenty to drink at Kelly and Alex's so he was cocky and said something that I thought he would never say. He has said some brutal things to me over the last few weekends but this one was really not nice. He said, "I have got more pressing things to think about than your hand!" (Big sigh). He couldn't have said a worse thing (I get upset now) especially when you are trying to deal with it (long pause upset) then he always goes off on one saying how I bully and this and that and the other. To be honest it's getting boring now because he says the same thing all the time. So I said "Well you get on with what's more pressing and I will get on with my hand!"

Then a huge argument, it's not good, it's really not good for me, my health and Harvey, bless him, is trying to sort it out and he is just stressed with it all too (big sigh). So I sort of got over that and just went to sleep.

On Saturday morning in the car, I had told Rob that I needed to get a photo for my driving license. I only now say things once. Every time I am nattering if I ask them more than once, or if I raise my voice which is the only time, they seem to actually hear what I am saying. Rob claims I never asked and when I asked again the response was "What a time to tell me you didn't tell me before!" (I bloody know I did it was very important) So whatever I didn't get my photos done.

You get tired of it all, now I have actually been thinking about it for the last few days. So, he brought me back Monday morning and it wasn't a good Monday morning because I needed this stuff for Corrine, a bill, he couldn't find a bill. He has been going on and others too about my filing system not working. I looked in the wonderful system that had been developed and I still didn't find my bill. All those messing about with my system hasn't worked, has it? I know people are trying to help but there's helping and taking over and quite a few things have been taken over!

So, Rob dropped me at the Grand Feu, we didn't speak in the car. I really didn't want to be near him. As we left the house, I always drop the metal on the gate down into the gravel, the reason I do that are a few. If it's windy (okay, it wasn't windy) and the wind blows it open then the chickens can get out. Also if it's not down next-door's dog has been known to come and jump on it and get in and chases the chickens or lets the chickens out, then Peggy our little dog can also get out, get attacked by the very nasty crazy dog down the road that is allowed to roam free she would get out if there was a little gap, so I put it down for security. I had put it down like I always have done and then Rob comes and picks it up saying "We have it like this!" I thought right that's it!

I don't know where I am really for two days, I haven't had a phone call or any contact, which is quite normal, but we didn't part on good terms. The thing that's getting to me is that I haven't had a phone for months now. Jenny gave me a phone, brilliant I am grateful, but I can't use it because I can't go and get any credit. It's as if the phone and my ability to actually contact my friends has been delayed and delayed all the time. I can't drive, I can't do anything, I am just stuck at the beck and call of Rob, who doesn't even want to help!

To me it's simple he is in control of me, he is just controlling the situation. It's as if I don't matter or have an opinion anymore. It's a preview of old age, it must be what elderly people feel like when their children take over and start telling them what to do and controlling them.

Anyway, it's Wednesday night I feel better I have got on with my work. I have now got an adaptation so I can go into the sports gym. I can do a little bit of exercise and I will progress with that more and more.

At the end of the day, I don't know what the answer is really. I suppose I will work it out, but I think it might be best if I don't go home this weekend and let them have a rest. Bye

10 Minutes

It's now Monday the 8th of August, I didn't record anything last week so I will start there. Two weekends ago I went home fine no problems no stresses no upsets. Some of the baby Guinea Fowl were hatching, I left on Sunday with Elliott helping the others. On the Saturday we went for my photo which I needed for my driving license. On the way back I said to Rob we must really go and see Bernard and his family. We called for an hour, he wasn't there but we saw his mum and dad. Then on Sunday morning we got a visit from John-Paul Bernard's brother and Chris and Marie so nice to see them. Bernard called late afternoon Sunday, but we had to leave so it was sad we didn't get much time with him.

The week here Fred my physio was on holiday, and I got another guy (I think he was Spanish). It started off okay but towards the end he wasn't. On Friday morning he made me step up and down on a step with my right leg that doesn't bend. But he left me for nearly an hour it wasn't good for my leg. I made excuses for the afternoon, and I didn't go back.

I have been going to the gym, I can't do many exercises but it's better than nothing at least Stubby is doing something. I also had to go out into Niort to see the doctor for an examination to fill the form in to apply for my disabled driving license. That was fine my appointment was at three o'clock. I waited at 2:30 in the foyer for someone from the Grand Feu to take me. The guy arrived very late 2:50 and then drove like a mad man (big sigh). Then at one point he had to put his arm across my chest to stop me going forwards because he nearly ran into the back of a car.

That really upset me and put me into a shock for the rest of the journey, I was petrified! When I got to where we were going, I was crying, shaking and very upset. I got into the surgery and there were people there before me. I couldn't speak to the driver I was so upset and panicking. The guy didn't know what was wrong so he phoned the doctor at the Grand Feu who said I can't go in for my examination like that. He spoke to the other doctor, and he said we will give her 10 minutes to calm down. I tried to calm myself down, I didn't want to have to return on a different day because I needed the form for my driving. I calmed myself I was really all shook up, but the doctor let me in, he was a nice doctor. He asked, "What was the problem?" My answer "He drove like a nutter, and we nearly crashed. Seeing as I have just had a car crash, a big car crash, obviously there is something in the depth of my mind that is not happy. I just couldn't help the reaction; I was scared because of the way he was driving." Which is crazy because I have not got a problem with Rob or Corrine driving me and I have even been driven past where the accident was, I didn't have a problem with that. So, there is obviously something in my mind still.

Besides all that in the week I had lots to do with the social worker who was going on holiday. Loads of paperwork and then a meeting with the insurance guy, then a meeting with Corrine and the social worker about things and more forms to fill in. I suppose it helped the week go quickly.

I have only just started finishing my basket off this week, that I was weaving and if I don't get cracking this week it's not going to get finished. I will be concentrating on that and hopefully exercising.

What else? The weekend passed fine no dramas it was hot and when cooler I did spend some time outside. The boys came to see me on Wednesday night with a sandwich that was good. But Elliott had a drama, a sparrowhawk had come down and taken the head off his male Rosecomb chicken. Oh, it was a beauty as well, who he was going to show. He was an absolute beauty he was really looking good! I wasn't there he was really upset, so now they will have to be more vigilant.

It frustrates me because when I have been there at weekends, they get sat watching a DVD and they wait till it gets too dark in my humble opinion. I would always be putting the chickens away as soon as it starts dropping dark. I couldn't sleep on the Friday something was nattering (worrying) me. I was up doing things and Harvey heard me and he got up. I went out and said, "I have to go and check Snowy's chicks because I don't think they have been put away." They hadn't been put in, so they had got forgotten! When I do get back at least I will be able to check things.

Another thing that happened was that Harvey started his apprenticeship at the Lion d'Or restaurant. Rob is running him around but it's not that far away. Rob has taken to moaning a bit (well a lot!). Mainly because he is doing everything, but I did it for years and years that's probably why I moaned, but I think it's not a big thing to take him to work. I will definitely not let him go on a motorbike and he would have to have lessons and pass a test first anyway.

He is enjoying it, it's hard work and he sometimes does double shifts he is doing okay, it's good for him. He has been very missed at home because he did so much of the work.

I came back to the Grand Feu on the Sunday, and I brought myself some dahlias out of the garden. They are so beautiful a lovely orange and yellow. I just keep staring at them, I thought I will have to bring some with me. So far nobody has seen them so I don't know if I will get told off for bringing them, surely not!

So now the last full week at the Grand Feu! The good news was as we came back the nice receptionist was on, and she told me that it was a three night stay (oh no not that drama again!!) this next weekend there must be a bank holiday or something. Bye for now.

8 Minutes

It's 10:00 Tuesday night the 16th of August 2016, the day before I leave the Grand Feu.

Here's my summary of the Grand Feu:

I spoke earlier about my reflections on the first part of living at the Grand Feu, I think it's probably good for me to just talk about my journey while here.

It's been a bit sad today to say goodbye to the doctor and to certain staff. I haven't really said goodbye properly to Fred the physio, but I will try and catch him again tomorrow. We have had such humour and we have worked hard but he has tried to make it relaxed. He loves his music so he would put music on and talk about music. He asked what song do you want for your last song. He got his computer out and I said, "It's got to be 'My Way' or 'No Regrets' (Edith Piaf)." Fred put on various versions of 'My Way' the original one came from a French guy from the 1960's and the Sex Pistols version. But the one I love the best is Elvis', so he put that on Youtube, bless Elvis. The song does summarise my journey to a certain extent.

Looking back when I arrived here, I had to be pushed in a bed out of the hospital into an ambulance. On the bed out of the ambulance into here and transferred onto another bed. So, I arrived by bed and I am leaving on foot. That says quite a lot really!

You forget where you have come from, just the journey to the Grand Feu from the hospital was a major challenge for my whole being. First in ICU not being able to move, not being able to do anything. Then to slowly being able to sit up when in plastics. The next phase I was put into a wheelchair, transferred from my bed world into a new world.

Prison Or The Paralympics

I remember the guy, who I have become quite good friends with called Christopher, who on my first day transferred me and I got pain and went into my first physio in tears. You forget how bad you were, he felt so bad, and I was upset crying and speaking to the physio who was really a nice girl and understanding. I only had her for the first week and then I had Fred. On my last week she said, in fact she said it today "We will miss you here" that was nice because I am one of many.

You forget that you couldn't go to the toilet without assistance, I had to have a bedpan at first, I couldn't shower, I couldn't move without asking for help.

I remember that day when that woman, who I speak to now and say hello to but she still wasn't very kind to me that day. I asked if I could be transferred onto my bed and she said, you are going down to the restaurant soon (yes in an hour!). In the end I said forget it I'll sit in my chair. From that moment on I swore to myself I would never ask anyone to transfer me again. I slowly transferred myself and got better and better and more courageous and I just figured out a way to do it.

Then you get to a point where you think I will go to the toilet myself, once I could get from the wheelchair to the bed and from the bed to the wheelchair, I thought I can get on the toilet myself. Though my leg was stuck out and I was very slow, and it was very difficult but I managed it. As you do that you start doing more and more. Sometimes I got told off, but it just had to happen, I wanted freedom. The thing I couldn't master was to plat my hair but that's only for now I am sure I will find a way.

The memories of this place on my first day, oh how I hated it. The first time I went in that restaurant it was so depressing. It was full of disabled people in wheelchairs with serious disabilities like the film 'The One Who Flew Over The Cockoo's Nest'.

I have sat and watched over the last three months while being here. I can tell when new people have just arrived, they have got that scared look in their eyes. That mad look, it's weird how to describe it, it's just like an unbelievable look of bewilderment, a pain, a confusion, a deep sadness.

There is this particular guy, I noticed him because he had a plat in his long hair. I have spoken to him because I have seen him with Corrine outside. He has been in a motorbike accident, and he has lost his leg and one of his arms is quite bad it needs rehabilitating. I remember him watching his surroundings in the restaurant (you know when there is someone new). I thought that guy is just in the same place I was, and I watched him again today, I thought no he is accepting it and his situation I have talked to him a little, but he is okay. He is working hard he is a young guy possibly in his 30's he will work hard it's good to see people who work hard it's the only way forwards.

Another man I observed while at the Grand Feu I named Monsieur Accepta. He was the only other person I saw who had a hand problem, two of his fingers were gone. I spoke with him, and it had occurred in a fight, I think. The thing I noticed was the way he was holding his arm away from him not looking or connecting with his disabled hand. I told him I had named my amputation Stubby and chatted and included him in as much as I could. I said if we don't accept our disabilities, it makes it impossible for others to and the pain never heals because you are angry with it and don't send it love and acceptance. Every time I saw him I said, "Bonjour Monsieur Accepta". He always laughed I hope he went on to give his amputation full acceptance and the love it deserves.

You become institutionalised, I am now part of this institution, so you say hello to people you ask how they are. You see people come back for a day treatment and you talk to them.

There is a real nice girl Janet on our table she has been in a fire, a horrendous experience she was badly burnt. I said I would go to see her before I leave tomorrow. Then there is the English lady Vivian who has been here a long time. I had a good chat with her today. She has decided that it's too hard for her to walk because of her back so she is going to stay in her wheelchair. I suggested she sees Corrine and becomes busy with something she needs to be occupied; she could work with Corrine to get her driving license which will help her to get back home for she lives alone. So scary in a way but it's amazing how one adapts.

I have had a few moments here, mainly with the silly receptionist woman, jobs worth bullying woman. Then just a couple of carers who have been a bit annoying to me and upset me but there were only a couple the others were so kind, but it really is time to go.

I hope I can be calm at home and not let things get to me and upset me. Just slowly accept that I am not going to be able to do thing straight away that I have to take my time. I have to work on Stubby and my physio get some muscle back, that's my job now to get strong again! Here's hoping that the next phase in this crazy, crazy experience is as smooth as it can be.

I have got to keep an eye on Rob because he has done it all, he is tired, one of the reasons I want to get back driving is so I can help. I also love driving, I have always enjoyed driving I need to get driving again and it's not good to have just one person driving, it's not fair to Rob.

That's it I hope when my time comes to leave this planet (I was obviously meant to stay a bit longer) I just do what John the English man on our table mum did (John has just had a knee replacement). John goes home next week he is in his 80's but does look good for his age, he was telling us about his mum today who was 92. She was found with a cup of tea in her hand and a piece of toast sat watching telly. Now that's the way to go!!

11 Minutes

In conclusion to this chapter and my time at the Grand Feu it is with absolute gratitude and thanks that I got this opportunity and guidance from a place that brought me much pain, frustration and sometimes unhappiness. Yet it gave me strength, hope, the confidence to carry on, and the professional expertise and guidance I needed in so many aspects of my life. It laid down the solid foundation that I so desperately needed to replace the broken, shattered and wobbly foundations I was trying to build upon. It was a gift given to me that so many in similar situations are not offered. It gave me the drive, the force and sometimes the anger I needed to bulldoze myself forwards but it did so in a professional, caring and mostly a very friendly way.

How can words express the gratitude I have? They gave me the guidance that would point me in the right direction. They picked me up dusted me off and set me on my way. At the time I never fully realised how important and lucky I was to be given this. But my gift to all those at the Grand Feu and all the medical professionals throughout this journey from the 2nd of April 2016 onwards is to embrace life!! The one that you all allowed me to have. I write my story because of you! I will endeavour to guide and help others all I can in the future, as you helped me, because the journey is long, lonely and difficult but not impossible.

All journeys have to start with one step, be it small, be it wobbly, be it weak, or be it aided. That is the hardest step to take, it's your decision, no one else can do it for you. But if you don't look back your next step naturally happens and with each step comes strength, vision, hope and courage. You will stumble and fall but by getting back up you indicate to yourself and the universe that there is no going backwards only forwards!!

Chapter 25: The Beginning Of The Next Generation

"The privilege of a lifetime is to become who you truly are."

- Carl Jung

The first few months of the year 2000 involved working, studying and the general routine of life. Then in the first week of April I was given three days of hard labour. It began on the 4th of April; I was giving a treatment at my clinic on Huddersfield Road my colleague from York College Lorraine Harwood was also working there. I finished my treatment which was the last for the evening and the stomach pains I had been getting became stronger. That's when the three days of hard labour began. Having requested no hospital, the nurse arrived but it was stop and start. It continued all night and eventually the midwife left and said she would return the next day. The next day was the same all I wanted to do was eat, but the family around me said I shouldn't in case I needed to go into the theatre. In the afternoon the midwife returned and was concerned about the slowness, I was still only 5cm dilated. We went to the hospital, and they suggested I stay. I just didn't want to and then the very first midwife I ever saw, saw me and came to chat. I explained I didn't want to stay in hospital so she said okay I will come and by 10pm I will be having a gin and tonic and you will have given birth. I thought great what a relief.

Jill arrived late afternoon but by 4am she decided I was getting too exhausted and called the ambulance. I had only had gas as my pain relief and wouldn't take any drugs. I had gotten used to the gas it was my one and only friend, so leaving it to get into the ambulance was stressful and painful and then they forgot to set it up for me in the ambulance. I was not impressed the pain was only bearable with the gas. They connected me again to the gas and we set off.

It must have been the slowest, most bumpy journey that I had ever experienced, I was convinced that the driver was going over every bump he could, but at that time the roads in our area were known to be bad. If it wasn't the water board or the gas board or electric board or cable TV. Whatever happened to that? They dug the whole country up and for what? Does anyone know why they spent billions on laying down the cable TV taking up perfectly good Yorkshire stone paving to replace it with slippery tarmac? Just another waste of taxpayer's money.

When we finally got to the hospital I had again to leave my best friend behind my gas bottle. I was put in a wheelchair and doubled over in pain, pushed to the lift. The ambulance man took us to the wrong floor which didn't impress me I wanted my gas! He said you are only in labour, my response was "You should try being in labour for three fucking days!" When we finally got to the right floor, I was allowed my best friend the gas and air. Then they arranged for an epidural not pleasant but at least the lower half of my body was now totally numb. The pain was still real, but the edge had been taken off it. It is now day three, after two days I had ended up in the place I was trying to avoid, the hospital.

At the beginning of this book, I mentioned my competition for the under 21's championship that occurred on the 7th of April 1985 and meeting my guru Denbo whose birthday was on the 7th of April. When I was given my due date of the 1st of April, I decided I must not give birth to my child on April Fool's Day. Then Denbo added the request that I put a cork in and give birth on his birthday the 7th. The way things were going if I didn't get on with it, I would miss the 7th. It went on and on I was getting fed up and exhausted. My dilation was so slow, and my waters never broke. I thought it was going to be like all those scenes on the TV dramas where they huff and puff and then suddenly a baby appears. The fact that I had never attended any prenatal classes, preferring to go to the gym instead may have put me at a disadvantage. I remember this giant of a doctor who came to examine me he was a lovely gentle black doctor with hands like shovels. I remember thinking surely, he could just pull my baby out. My baby never once being stressed the head was engaged but wasn't bothering to make an entrance.

Throughout my pregnancy I had studied, worked, trained at the gym, been to China (now you know why I didn't want to be sent to hospital in China, being five months pregnant), had acupuncture, Chinese herbs and reiki from my beautiful friend Sally. This child was way too comfortable and relaxed to want to enter this noisy, crazy world.

I had that many internal examinations that when a lady entered my room, I said okay another. "No love" she said, "I am the cleaner."

It was now the afternoon of the 7th of April and at last I was 10cm dilated and things would start to happen. Even though the head had been in position for over two days, it wasn't until now that movement began and more pain. I remember one of the midwives delivering my baby said, "Great just one big push now to get over the ridge." "Fucking ridge!!" I screamed "Who the hell put that there?"

When you are in this situation sometimes the professionals forget that you are there. I heard them say that they would have to use forceps. I sat up and shouted, "No you're fucking not!" I didn't want forceps pulling my baby's head out, no way. "We will have to cut you then" they said. "Cut me but no bloody forceps!" I replied.

I was so lucky to have such wonderful staff who all worked hard and around 3:20 I gave birth to a 7lbs perfect big headed, long bodied baby boy. Just as he arrived Jill the midwife who had spent a long, long night with me the day before, came in to see if anything had progressed (I think the midwife team were taking bets on when my baby would arrive!). I swear the newly born recognised her voice because he looked straight at her when she spoke. I was then taken to the ward for a rest and my tea and toast.

Rest! It was so noisy my new son didn't make one noise, but all the others did, and their mothers didn't seem to hear them. I eventually went to the nursing station when I could get my legs to move the epidural was still in my system. When I got there, I said I just can't get any rest and it's not even my baby, it would be quieter on the M62 motorway, I want to go home. Because my baby had a little jaundice, they wanted to put him under a special lamp for a few days and because they realised how long my labour had been they found me a bed away from the noise.

The name hadn't yet been decided but on the Saturday in my quiet room, baby under the lamp, quiet also, the Grand National Race from Liverpool came on the TV. No, I didn't call him Red Rum or Papillon the 2000 winner but they interviewed someone and I thought that is a good strong Yorkshireman who is a direct person with no messing about, he was named Harvey Smith the Olympic show jumper, so Harvey it was.

Harvey was a good baby and with a lot of support from my parents especially my mum I was able to continue my work and finish my studies. My life now changed in a good way the responsibility of another human being must always be priority and so my future years were mapped out for me.

Just to experience all that pain again on the 6th of January 2003 I gave birth to my second son Elliott. This time I beat my record of three days labour and got it down to one day. There were no real dramas, he was a heavier baby, unfortunately one of the midwives who just came on duty as I was getting close to giving birth was a bit of a cow. All the others had been nice and caring but this one. One of the midwives suggested they cut me to make the delivery easier, she said to make me work! Bitch! So, me being me thought right I'll show her. For some reason in these early hours of the morning the TV was on and the lasting memory I have as I was just about to give birth was an image straight in front of me on the TV of some tribe using a machete to cut off the head of the village goat and its headless body shaking. I requested that they turn the telly off!!

Elliott arrived, I tore myself badly in the process and had to have a lot of stitches but Elliott was a beautiful healthy boy. My next few years now sorted out for me. I just had a couple of years left studying by the time Elliott arrived in 2003. I did have to take him to Dabtac a couple of times whilst finishing my teaching diploma because I was feeding him.

As you know the next decade or so brought a number of changes one of the biggest changes being the family moving in 2008 to live in France. Then in 2009 the family went to live in Adelaide, Australia and then back to France in 2014. But probably the biggest and most dramatic event that would occur and change everything happened on the 2nd of April 2016 in France, the accident. The rest of my story documents the consequences of this and the nearly five year battle I had to endure in a very cruel environment.

Dubai My Team The Warblers

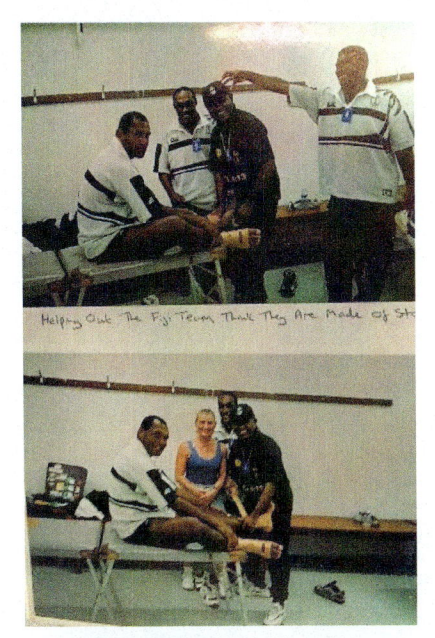

Helping The Fiji Team

The Warblers Doing The Haka

The English Team Plus Me

Yorkshire Puddings, Kathy, Nick, Michael, Mum & Dad

267

Prison Or The Paralympics

Bobby & Andy

Me & Bobby

Rob, Vicky, Bobby & Me

Lisa, Andy & Me

Bobby & Rob Dancing

Dancing The Night Away

The Gang Posing

The Pipers

Bobby

Me In My Clinic

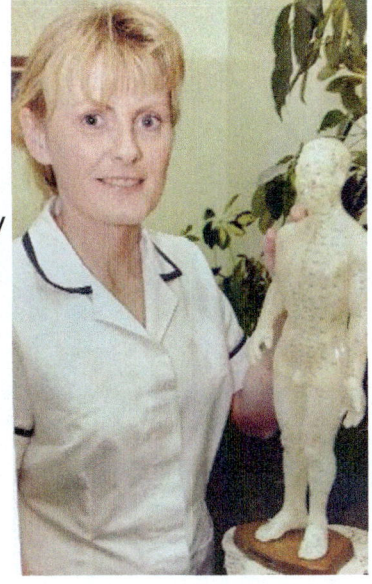

Acupuncture Degree Graduation York

Me & Grandma Walker At My York Graduation

Me & Marie In China

At Nanjing Hospital, China

The First Of The Next Generation (With His Mum, Grandma & Grandad)

Harvey & Jill His Midwife

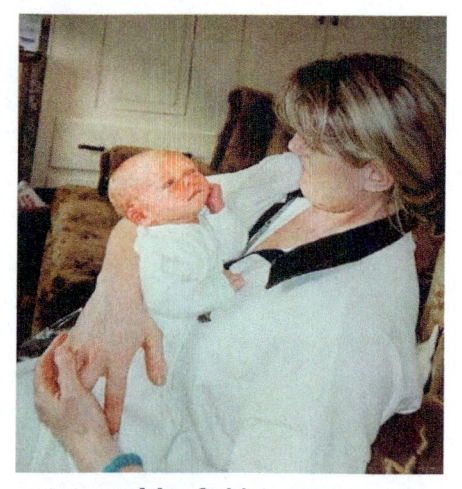

Me & Harvey

Mum & Harvey

Grandad & Grandma With Harvey At Huddersfield Road Clinic

Harvey Working It All Out

Harvey & Denbo

Kay, Denbo, Mum & Harvey On Bonfire Night

Penny Walker

Elliott, A New Friend For Harvey

Brothers In Arms

Bubble bath

Harvey & Suzie

Legoland

Prison Or The Paralympics

'The Tank' With All His Grandchildren

At French School

Off To School

Elliott In The School Play As A Witch

The Boys Grow Up

Chapter 26: My Small World Just Got Bigger And The Strength Of The Young

"There are none so enslaved as those who falsely believe they are free."

- Johann Wolfgang Von Goethe

It had been arranged that I would leave my home of around three months the Grand Feu on the 17th of August 2016. As mentioned earlier I chose this date so I could be back home with the boys and Rob for Rob's birthday on the 18th of August the following day. Claire had prepared some food, a welcome home sign, and balloons for me when we got home which was very unexpected, a lovely thing to do. Rob would never have thought or be bothered with any of that. It was nice to have a feeling you were welcome back into your own home.

I remember for Rob's 50th birthday seven years prior I arranged for a secret party for him. I went off with a couple of friends in three cars to Nantes airport to bring his family and friends back to surprise him. I managed to get a live local band and arranged food with a lot of help from others. We even had a Marquee that someone loaned us in case it rained. But the French weather was good to us, and it was a great success and fun.

When my 50th birthday arrived in 2014 the boys and I were in France, Rob was in Australia. I got maybe a text message and he had got Claire to leave a small gift. But no real thought or effort by Rob to make me feel special on this milestone of a birthday, it was disappointing.

We just accept these things, don't we? We make excuses up for the people that let us down, time and time again. We love them more than we respect and love ourselves and that gives them a certain permission to treat us how they feel fit. Maybe my expectations of how I should be treated were wrong, I just accepted this sort of treatment anyway.

Now things were different, and I knew this re-adaptation would be difficult. Just coming home at the weekends as already stated was stressful but I naively thought it was the back and forth, one minute at home one minute at the Grand Feu which was causing the unsettlement and stress. I needed a new start, to feel a purpose and a belonging again, while still accepting that the mental as well as the physical trauma of the event I had just been through was still real and raw.

Trapped in your car with extensive injuries awake throughout it all, looking at the end of my right arm that had had its hand ripped off. Then trying to find it in the car and trying to stop the bleeding coming from the end of my right arm, seeing all the blood and the blood coming through my clothes my legs being compound broken bones. Trying to get your breath with a collapsed lung and the sheer pain and fear of it all does mess up your mental state, how can it not? It has to be healed, processed and that takes a very long time.

Being back home was difficult Rob had no patience with me. I had gone from doing everything and taking care of everyone's needs to not even being able to stand and put clothes on the clothes horse or separate two tea bags. I was so weak and useless! Frustration for me was an understatement, the hardest thing was seeing all the jobs, the small jobs not being done, the jobs I used to do and be able to do with ease and efficiency.

I tried to put myself in Rob's shoes, could I have had patience with someone I loved if they were hurting so much and disabled? Would I react like Rob? Would I not hold that person in my arms when I could see all the fear and pain in their eyes? Would I not be able to look at them and show them how much I cared, giving them reassurance even though everything I did seemed to be wrong. Would I not get up early to get all the jobs done so they would not feel frustrated, would I not be able to really, really try to take all their pain away and be their rock the solid thing that would never let them down, the thing they could rely on. Could I not only take care of them but the rest of the family too. Could I not give them the feeling that I loved them and their disabilities and tell them that everything was going to be okay.

I hoped I could and would have been there for Rob if the positions had been reversed, but Rob just couldn't or wouldn't for me. So slowly, slowly events would occur that made my transition back into my world much more challenging than I was expecting. He was clever though, he never bullied me or treated me bad in front of anyone, just behind closed doors and in front of the children. My reaction was to protect myself and give back as much as I was given even though my whole being was screaming out for help. For someone to take away my fear and pain not drive me further into the abyss of darkness, loneliness, pain and a feeling of worthlessness. I understood it wasn't easy for Rob but all he needed to do was hold me tight and make me feel safe!

Rob may have a totally different view of the situation, but the fact was that once the friends and offers of help started to die down he had to figure out a way to get organised and make the jobs easier not harder. Looking back the pattern was emerging, instead of doing things to help the situation he just ignored the obvious. Like male pigs and rabbits left with female pigs or rabbits resulting in baby pigs or rabbits. The place I had before my accident was now out of control and it was all my fault even though I wasn't there!!

It was my fault that there were rabbits running everywhere my fault that Buster the 300kg boar and his wife Myrtle-May would get out of the field and take themselves for a walk around the village. It was my fault the fencing was not finished, or the gates Rob promised to make never got made. It was my fault that the care of the animals was only half-heartedly done and it was my fault when we ran out of animal food. All these things could have been avoided with hard work, logic and a desire to fix them. By the time I was back living at the farm in August everything had truly got out of control. The house, the garden and the animals.

As I stated in my note from the author, I do not write this with anger, judgement but the brutal truth. The truth being that Rob didn't cope well with responsibility!

I am to blame really; I had been the one that had got things done even when I didn't want to do them. Maybe it comes from my early years of hard work, studying, training and never giving in. But now I needed someone else to take the reins and sort things out. I do think at times Rob tried but it was too hard, and he just stopped trying. That's when his frustration and my frustration of his frustration resulted in one big mighty battle.

I didn't know in 2016 and 2017 that my frustration from not having my rock to turn to and rely on would give me the strength I needed to get through what was about to be thrown at me. Therefore, thanks and gratitude must be given to Rob for strengthening me be it in a somewhat unconventional and cruel way.

Obviously, this resulted in a difficult return to a normal life, whatever normal may be! In my head it was working on the farm, taking care of the family and the animals, growing my veg and dahlias. Finishing the jobs to fix up the house so winter could be cosy and the family and animals all safe, protected from the wet, cold, bitter winter ahead. The only element that I was able to obtain in my environment was the feeling of coldness with no protection, no cosiness and eventually bitterness.

My physical abilities were very limited, but I couldn't just sit around and watch the situation get worse. So, I began to fix things by organising people to come and pay them to move things on, make the workload easier and take the pressure off Rob.

By the end of the summer, after Rob's long holiday from work he was told that the guy he had been covering for was coming back so he wasn't working. I saw this as a positive thing because the boys needed to be taken places and it would mean jobs could get done to make life easier.

One of the first jobs was to get the bathroom fixed so I could safely and easily use it. We got workmen in to do the bulk of the work, but Rob would do the tiling. I had realised many years ago that it was essential to get materials on site if any jobs were going to be started. I say started because Rob was good at jobs, but he never finished anything without a lot of encouragement which would be met with a lot of resistance. Nothing got finished and that included the tiling in the newly adapted bathroom. I was getting to the point of not even seeing the uncompleted jobs, the house needed a lot of organising, but no room was finished. This would be made more difficult in the next six months.

Being a natural observer of people, an essential part of my professional job, observing people as they walked, sat and talked to you in your clinic was the key to gathering information on their injury and general well-being. Now being stuck in a body with limited abilities my observation skills were very much needed to gain information and feedback about my surrounding environment. One of the biggest observations was the reaction of others towards me, a disabled person and how they dealt with it practically.

My interactions with people were limited only really going out of my small environment to occasionally meet friends, doctor appointments and sometimes shopping, all in my wheelchair.

Being in a wheelchair creates a very interesting state of being, it's like you are disconnected from the environment you are in. The person pushing you, in my case usually Rob takes you where they want to go, if you protest loud enough you will be taken where you want to go. But it would always be a quick visit and then off to where they want to go in my case usually heading back to the car so Rob could get the whole episode over with. In the end I just stopped going out so much, especially shopping.

People also talk to the person pushing you not you. They will have a chat about you as if you are deaf and dumb, it's funny in a very sad sort of way.

The best summary I have heard about being in a wheelchair came off a UK TV series called 'Bread' set in Liverpool around a Liverpool family in the 1980's. It is a comedy highlighting the difficulties of being unemployed in Liverpool in the 80's. In series 5 episode 3 granddad who lives next door to the family sums it up perfectly when they suggest they get him a wheelchair:

"Wheelchair, wheelchair!! Them things that take you where everyone but you wants to go." What a brilliant observation and sadly very true.

My observations also showed me the strength of the young. They are less judgemental, they will actually look at you with interest and curiosity, wanting to find out more until they are pulled away and encouraged to move on.

The two young people in my life my sons Harvey and Elliott were 15 and 13 when I had my accident. I wasn't able to see how they coped, they weren't allowed to see me for about a week maybe because of the state I was in but I, as a child would have found that hard because my mind would not have had the physical confirmation that mum was alright. Kids are much more resilient than us adults think, and it is often cruel to leave them in the dark. They see, hear and are aware of so much more than we give them credit for, even if you think they are absorbed in playing with their Lego.

The reactions of my sons were different, they are both deep thinkers but dealt with their fear, uncertainty and upset in different ways. Elliott was a young 13 year old and he withdrew into games on his computer, keeping a low profile to the crazy atmosphere that had just rocked his world. Harvey suddenly jumped from carefree teenager to trying to fix everything. Once Robin and Pat went back to the UK, after three weeks of madness, Harvey picked up Robin's reins and took over the animals and garden. He continued to work hard even when he left school in June. His preparation the night before his final school exam the Brevet (which he got an amazing result in achieving 18 out of 20) was delivering Dolly's babies all 13 along with Elliott's help. That's how amazing they are and how lucky and blessed I have been to have these two very different, loving and caring sons in my life.

I did continue to do recordings once I left the Grand Feu but not as regularly. I will therefore finish this chapter with the recordings I made from September 2016 to November 2016. I was then back living at home. I hadn't re-listened to these recordings before writing this chapter from memory nearly five years later. My first recording once I was back home being on the 6th of September 2016.

It's the 6th of September I have left the Grand Feu, leaving on the 17th of August. I have been home about three weeks. It was tiring at first and it is still tiring. When I came home, I got some balloons, cards and some flowers, it was nice to come home. Claire, Steven and Lewis were there, and we had lunch prepared by Claire and a chat. Then that afternoon I suggested that we go to Point P and organise the tiles for Steven and Claire's roof and the tiles needed for the bathroom. If we ordered them there and then we had a chance of getting them before the big French three week holidays began, and also while Steven and Claire were still in France. So, we went and sorted that out.

Harvey was busy with his new apprenticeship, so he was in and out a bit and things started happening with the bathroom. James came and did the frame, which was brilliant, the plumber came so things were starting to come together.

I struggled really but I started hobbling around, hobbling more outside because the weather was good. I started slow and then slowly increased my hobbling. I sometimes get a bit short tempered in the sense of tiredness, I don't think I am getting enough rest and sometimes the boys get it in the neck. I am doing too much and not resting my recovering body. I am not lying down with my legs up I need; I really need to realise that I have to rest.

Tomorrow we go to Nantes to have more x-rays again and see the surgeon. Then on Thursday the doctor from the insurance is coming to see me. I will be glad when all these appointments are over, then we can get into some sort of routine.

At the moment Harvey is not here because he is at college until Friday, he has to do three weeks work and a week at college, and he sleeps there. He is missed a lot and I do hope everything is going well for him.

Another thing that happened on Sunday this week was Elliott said there is a fire engine in the village. What was there was a fire truck, and they were having a meeting because the girl in the village is a volunteer fire fighter. I said to Harvey, I would like you to go and thank them or their colleagues who were at my accident and who helped me. We went it was really good because three of the people who helped me on the 2nd of April were there. They were really pleased and interested to see me and very interested to see progress. We chatted for a while, there was a girl there who said that I didn't panic, I wasn't panicking. I told her I had lost my hand and it was in the car somewhere. I kept saying to her my hand was off. I remember being in either intensive care or trauma in Nantes hospital telling Rob I was looking for my hand, I was just looking for my hand in the car. She said that the hand when found went in a bag and into the ambulance. She said, you were so calm, there was blood everywhere and you were just calm. They said they had not got a clue what had happened. They said that the two cars didn't touch, and it was just a mystery. They also said you are doing so well; your morale is so good. It probably is but sometimes I have a bit of shouting and down time usually when I am tired and not rested enough. Like now when I should be sleeping but I'm recording.

It was good to talk to them, good to see the people who helped to keep me alive. I said to the guy, that looks a good truck he said I will show you what we used to cut you out of your car. He showed me the back of the truck it was full of cutting out equipment, massive equipment to cut the roofs off cars, which they had to do with me. So yep, good to talk to them!

Harvey said, "God how can you just talk to strangers like that?" I said, "Well I wasn't really, I was just thanking them." I think Harvey will be having to overcome that on his course. So over and out.

9 Minutes

Well, it's been a very long time since I spoke to this it is now probably the 25th of November. I came out of the Grand Feu on the 17th of August. It was good, the boys, Rob, Claire, Steven and Lewis greeted me and there were cards, gifts and food it was a bit overwhelming really. The weather was really good, Harvey had just started his work at the restaurant, so he was backwards and forwards a bit. Elliott was off school so that was good and generally things were progressing, I could only walk a little.

It was good to sit on the bench, the dahlias were amazing, full of colour. They have all died down now it's November, I am just in the process of ordering some more and must get that posted tomorrow. They gave and do give me such joy!

We had plenty of pumpkins, butternut squash and potatoes that people had kindly put in for us. The Guinea Fowl had grown, all the chicks were growing we still had some to hatch but all was generally good. The baby pigs were doing well.

A very, very hard time for me frustrating, tiring, angry, lots of arguments, lots of shouting and lots of frustration. I remember really not wanting to be around people. People annoyed me, people angered me, everything was so difficult! Then I would have a week of being normal. We still had to get on with jobs and finish the bathroom.

The cleaning that was arranged by MSA, took forever, I think we had three meetings and to be honest by the time the girl came I was already organising stuff and friends were helping. When we did finally get a cleaner it was too late really, and it was stressing Rob out. He earmarked her four hours a week and because we are still renovating and organising the house, it isn't ready for a stranger to come in and clean. After a month Rob more than me, said it's too much money, we can't afford the money and we are not ready for a cleaner. So, then we muddle along, between us we are getting there.

At first it was so tiring to do anything, I had no stamina and no energy. But now although my walking is not good and my numbness in my foot is still there and Stubby buzzes and hurts, but even he is getting stronger, I am doing the weights and some strengthening exercises for the muscle to come back.

I haven't really exercised a great deal, partly because the room where the weights are needs juggling about and organising. I am hoping because I have to sort the room out for the Christmas tree, so I am hoping that I can get to do the weights strengthening exercises, the legs, arms and all the body very soon.

Loads of things have happened because I am so late in talking to you. I don't know if I have mentioned this before, but we had a meeting at the Grand Feu a whole day of meetings and we got to meet everyone. But the doctor forgot us, so a disappointment he just wasn't there which really annoyed and upset me. We rearranged for another time and day. At this new meeting there were people already in the meeting at 11:30 and we were still waiting to go in after 12:00. I was just so stressed with it, so I told the receptionist that I was leaving. I was already feeling low, you are already feeling low because people talk to you differently and all you want is to be treated normal, but people can't treat you normal because they see your hand.

When I got into the meeting I wouldn't speak and was very upset and cross. I told the doctor that he forgot me last week and I just feel like a number and not of any consequence. The meeting was okay, and all was good.

I will try and remember anything that I have left out and speak to you more. To summarise a very rocky road, a very steep hill to climb and I don't know which direction I am going in. But you have got to keep going and I just hope that my head keeps strong, and I can get some sort of normality back.

9 Minutes

Though I would return to the Grand Feu in the future, for now my time there had come to a close. I was out in the big wide world I had come from, but I was unaware that it's reaction to me would not be the same. It never registered in my mind that I would be treated and seen differently for I was still me.

The sad consequence of this is that you have to stop being you and become someone you don't recognise in order to survive these strange reactions in your now same but different world. You have to learn fast what to expect, and you quickly get to know and come to accept this treatment. But by accepting it you become it, you settle for it and lose who you really are in it.

That's when the internal battle begins. Now looking back, I really only had two choices, two paths I could go down. The one of accepting this treatment, an emptiness of my soul, taking the drugs to temper me down, keep me quiet and accept that I had to accept how society now saw me. A damaged good, not as useful, a burden, different, crazy and generally to be side stepped and avoided. Or path two which meant I fought for my real identity, the one that I had buried deep inside, the one that loved myself and didn't feel different, but special and the one that was worthy of this life in a fun and unlimited way.

This second path was my choice, and this was the path with all the resistance, obstructions, judgements, avoidance, ridicule, harsh treatment, loneliness and fear!

But I was on this path now, I wasn't going to look backwards, only forwards, I knew I would be given guidance, strength and wisdom to stay on the path. The universe had my back because I was prepared to suffer and fight to be my true soul, the one gifted to me and the one I wouldn't let man destroy.

Chapter 27: Police Interrogation And My January 2017 Recordings

"Condemnation without investigation is the height of ignorance."

- Albert Einstein

As can be seen from the previous chapters things were not easy. I believed that getting out of intensive care was all I needed to do and then everything would be sweet. That was not the case, in trauma I was put through hell with the pain, the diarrhoea, loss of basic human activities and mental stress. I believed getting out of the hospital would be the answer to all my problems, in reality it created a whole bunch of new problems. Problems no one talked about, no one warned you about, problems you never believed could exist.

I then thought getting out of the Grand Feu and going back home would be the answer. The place of safety, love, caring and peace. The place I had been before my world suddenly changed. The place of hope, kindness, warmth and happiness. But as you are about to find out the things I believed, the people and establishments I gave respect and faith to would not provide this for me! Instead driving my smashed-up body and mind into a place of deep, deep darkness, providing cruelty, lies and condemnation of my whole being and existence. The body that worked hard and the mind that studied and achieved so many things was destroyed, and I questioned if it was even possible to return to even a small percentage of what they were before. The body that had got me to the UK bodybuilding finals, the body that had ran on and off rugby and football pitches, the body that had carried the sack of coal over the finishing line to victory, now struggled with every little thing I asked it to do.

The mind and body are connected so the pain and frustration of the body did affect the mind. The mind was also at the accident and was actively present throughout it all, so it's had its own battles to overcome. But as the body slowly started to adapt to its fate and make tiny improvements, the mind became the target of attack.

It would appear that this is a common and often used method of undermining an individual, if your mental stability is put into question, those around you can justify their treatment towards you. Be it friends, partners, family or the establishments.

Eventually you start to act and believe that you are crazy, every problem in the world is because of you! You are cruelly and slowly stripped of your self-worth, your beliefs and dignity. You are left to rot in your disabled body and your confused and manipulated mind.

All these experiences at first ICU and then trauma and plastics at Nantes hospital, also at the Grand Feu, are all essential for you to live. Every one of these places showed me nothing but expertise, care, professionalism, and amazing results that importantly laid down solid foundations that I would have to spend the rest of my life building on. My gratitude is beyond words, but the problem now was this cruel world I was returned to, the one that didn't bother with integrity or honesty.

Some in this world would make up stories so they wouldn't look bad, avoiding truths and replacing them with gossip. This was to enable them to look good, to win, to hide the truths that they knew existed. This may appear to empower them and often society believes their lies but there is one thing that they left out while they were scheming, lying, and getting away with it and that was the power of the universe, the true judge of the action of man, karma!

Christmas 2016 was quickly approaching, with help especially from Mel I had managed to prepare for some sort of Christmas celebration. I loved Christmas even before the kids arrived, I always put up a big tree at Huddersfield Road and enjoyed the anticipation of the arrival of Santa. With the advancing age the Christmas celebrations usually involved going to my parents for a wonderful Christmas dinner which my mum prepared, on her own and if it fell on a weekend often went to work in the evening as well. This was more when we were still living at home and as dad was a taxi driver, he was often busy as well, driving around dressed as Santa all week bringing joy to the excited children and humour to those who wondered if it was 'The Tank' or indeed Santa himself, helping 'The Tank' out in his black London cab.

We always got a wonderful Christmas dinner. Often grandparents would be there and my mum's brother and wife uncle Malcolm and auntie Margaret. After I got my own house, I would often have to leave early to get some work done for my studying, Christmas being a time I closed my clinic for a few days and a chance to catch up on my course work.

Christmas 2016 passed we had to have our dinner the day before because Harvey was at the restaurant working on Christmas day. Harvey helped prepare the dinner and did most of the work, I am still pretty useless, preparing veg with one hand it takes so long and like shoelaces it's not worth the frustration. Just buy frozen or shoes without shoelaces!

We had a nice dinner courtesy of one of my geese which had been prepared by the local small abattoir. On the actual Christmas day, it was Santa, chocolate and watching DVDs but Harvey had to go to work.

It can get cold in winter where we are, but I stayed near the wood burning fire for Stubby didn't do well in the cold, he really didn't like it.

The house was cold, very cold even the olive oil would freeze. I remember one particularly cold and freezing winter when the carrots left out on the table froze so we had to use the ones in the fridge. That's how cold parts of the house were with the cat and dog's water bowls sometimes freezing.

The main reason for this was that part of the upstairs area had not been insulated or plaster boarded which meant just thin tiles between the outside and the inside. This allowed dirt and cold especially when the wind was around. We had all the insulation ready in packets and we had even had the doors made by Bernard and the flooring ready to go down. We just needed about 10-15 sheets of plaster board and then we could have a warm house. But the sheets never got bought and the house stayed freezing.

Robin and Pat, my dear friends who saved the day the day after my accident were coming for the New Year, I was so looking forward to seeing them. I wasn't really in a position to see them when they were last here in April so I was happy that I would get to see them.

The living room where I wanted to get my gym set up had been cleaned and organised. I had to do it in stages, but the tree was up, and the fire was lit. It felt like some progress, and once the Christmas tree was packed away, I would sort out my training area, get on with some rehabilitation and pump some iron again. I did have a number of Christmas trees and lots of decorations so I would try to make the downstairs rooms Christmassy.

My hospital bed was in a room downstairs, there was no way I could use the stairs, it was far too dangerous, but it didn't matter the bathroom was downstairs. The thing that I loved the most out of all the Christmas decorations was what Elliott and Harvey did in the hallway. I had an old Victorian dresser, and the boys would put cotton wool (for snow) on it and make a Christmas village from all their Lego. It was amazing, it was a little village with Santa and his reindeer, shops, people skiing, trees, decorated Christmas trees, you name it. They had created it all in Lego, it looked enchanting, wonderful. The imagination and gifts of the young ones are so often ignored but I was frequently in that snowy village going to the shops, waving to Santa, awesome thanks boy, I loved it!

Robin and Pat arrived between Christmas and New Year laden with goodies, chocolates, biscuits, presents and Robin's delicious Christmas cakes that he religiously makes for his friends every year. Believe it or not I had made some Christmas cakes too, don't know how I managed but I did have the KitchenAid that my parents had so kindly bought me back in May, but it wasn't big enough for all the fruit and stuff that went into this cake. The cake was basically a recipe for a wedding cake from an old 1960's cookbook. I had to use my old Victorian giant bowl, like the one that my grandma would have made her stone of bread in every week, so now I could soak the fruit and mix it. It was a challenge, and it took me a long time and they were good but not as good as Robin's.

When Robin and Pat were there or any visitors for that matter, Rob was kinder to me, he didn't let his halo slip and he was the concerned, loving partner who was in need of his ego polishing. This performance and act pissed me off, I was someone who said it as it was, shouted, cried, laughed, and got angry if that's what was going on. You got the truth and the masks that Rob relied on I never possessed, it wasn't how I was.

Big mistake, my openness confirmed to others what Rob was secretly telling people and it fed into his probably calculated plan, that he had to get the hell out of a situation that no longer served him, provided for him, fed his ego, or took care of him. He had nothing to feed off, his source had been dried up and cut off. But how to move on to find another source without looking like a heartless bastard? Now less than four months after my return home Rob had to show others what he had to put up with and become the victim.

Like I have already said I don't write this with anger, just acceptance that that was how things were and how things would be. This feeling of rejection and hate by the one who I loved sent me into a world of confusion and questions. The result being that I fought back but I did so openly in front of people not behind closed doors, I had nothing to hide I just wanted the pain to go and my life back. If treated in a different way maybe things would have been easier, more calming, more nurturing, more peaceful and more loving. But what was to be delivered to me in January 2017 would mean further damnation, ill treatment and lies.

I wasn't allowed to heal mentally which results in the progress in your physical healing being haltered too. You are not permitted to move forwards, you don't want to go backwards, so you just stand still while the environment you are in just keeps throwing things at you aiming for the core of the target, hoping to knock you down and break you.

I often got knocked down and very nearly got broken but there was some deep force within me that kept me standing up, picking me up, feeding me strength and a knowing that I wasn't mad, and this treatment was not what I had to accept.

But besides this force I was destined to stand alone. Finally, and slowly over the years things thrown at me would reduce in aggressiveness, vigour, and frequency. They had knocked me down many times, but I had always got back up. The efforts of them all hadn't broken me but strengthened me and proved to me that the truth is your best form of armour and protection. Eventually you will obtain the peace and harmony your entire being craves and then the healing can begin.

The following events shocked me, angered me, and made me lose faith in mankind which I renamed mancruel. I will present them in the order they were on my recordings. Remembering and stating how I was feeling in these moments. By doing this the reader will see that there can eventually be a fulfilling, harmonious, loving, and happy life after such trauma and though it may take a very long time, it will with your forgiveness of others be given to you.

So, the important key is acknowledgement that it's happened, giving forgiveness to those involved and most importantly becoming a person you like and love again. Not allowing the labels and tonnes of shit that's thrown at you to stick. Go within and the true person that you are will be shown to you. You may have to work on some of the things that have become you but aren't you, but they have served a purpose of protection. You can let go of the anger, the disappointment and the lies told to you. Release it all to the universe and replace it with forgiveness, inner peace, and love.

I was hobbling about with my stick in the barn, with Harvey's help just saying hi to the animals (what else was I physically able to do) when they arrived. Three armed police officers, two female one male. Their appearance and manner were intimidating especially with the guns, growing up in the UK I never saw guns and I didn't really have any encounters with the law. That was all about to change plus any respect or trust I had for them. I was brought up to believe (and I still did right up to January 2017) that they were honest, good people, their job was to help you and to protect the 'goodies' from the 'baddies'. They can be trusted, they never lie and will enforce the law, that's their purpose, their job. They will follow the law of the land with fairness, balance, truth, and justice.

I soon woke up from all that shit, but not soon enough because I then put my trust into another law abiding, truthful, non-corrupt, fair, and honest establishment, solicitors!! The ones that make sure that there was justice, and the law was adhered to, fighting for the truth and highlighting anything that may have been missed. Leaving no stone unturned and at around 300 euros an hour and about seven years of training they should be equipped to do this. But my Allianz solicitor Gatien Hugo Riposseau was not or would not!

It was the 16th of January 2017, it must have been about 5ish when they showed up unannounced. Since the accident on the 2nd of April 2016 there had been no contact with me, no visit to the hospital or the Grand Feu, no contact with me at all. How they did their investigation I don't know they never bothered to ask me anything. On the 13th of April 2016 they did interview Rob at the Brigade de gendarmerie de La Chataigneraie without a translator or a solicitor present. I think I may have still been in ICU then, I was definitely having more operations. This was the first manoeuvre of the game, Rob wasn't even there, he wasn't involved in the accident at all. None of the other party's involved family were interviewed or interrogated.

Rob and Steven came looking for me when I didn't show up where I was going but he wasn't involved in any way with the accident. The purpose of this 'friendly chat' was to find out (trick) information out of Rob about me. What I was doing, was I drinking, could I drive, was I on medication, and what did I remember. Rob told me later at Nantes hospital that he very quickly felt uncomfortable and could see what they were trying to do, frame me! The female officer did ask him questions in English then wrote down his answers in French and had Rob sign something he couldn't read and then they wouldn't give him a copy. The game had begun I didn't know that such games existed, and I definitely never got to know the rules of these games.

All I had was my honesty, integrity, and blind faith in the establishments that we paid taxes for to protect us and uphold the law. What a fucking weak position to be in!

So, the game had begun, they had a mission, they were about to serve me with papers. Elliott was in the house in the main room, Rob, Harvey, and I plus the three police went into the kitchen. The male policeman went looking around the house without asking permission. After they left Elliott was upset and scared the male officer had gone into the room where Elliott was, looking around. Elliott was very scared he thought they were taking me away.

I wasn't too happy either, they were not nice and were trying to get me to sign something I didn't understand. This not so nice woman who had interrogated Rob on the 13th of April 2016 was the star of the show, Karen Payeur.

She announced she had a qualification, so she was recognised (by who I don't know) to be able to be an 'official' translator on the form that she was forcing me to sign. It stated 'le truchement de Karen Payeur, mdi/chef, titulaire d'un CMLEGI en langue anglaise.' It can't have been such a great course because she didn't understand the correct translation of key words.

My gut and a voice in my head said, 'don't sign it, don't sign it.' I was now sat in a chair shaking from head to foot, she had just casually announced that I was charged with double murder. She then handed me a sheet in English that she said was a direct translation of the paper she wanted me to sign. It wasn't! It was a general form of notification of my rights. The first line said, 'It is mandatory that the information we provide to you is in a language which you understand.'

Looking at this sheet now it is so clear how this game works, pretend that people have rights, even tell them that they have rights and then don't give them their rights. Bully, pressurise them, mislead and frighten them into playing the game their way and their way only!

On this sheet it stated that: 'you are furthermore informed that you have the right:

To make a statement (never got that choice) answer questions (which I did but they never answered any of mine and later would actually leave out of the statement what they didn't want in) or remain silent (which I should have done!!)

The form went on to say that you have the right to be assisted by a lawyer (Allianz provided me with one but I would have been better off with the local park keeper)

To be assisted by an interpreter (Karen Payeur was no interpreter, just a nasty bully in a uniform)

To view material relating to your case (now this is an interesting one as you will see).

To benefit from legal counsel, the address, and details of which will be indicated to you in a separate document (that never happened).

So, I am looking at this general form in English that Karen Payeur had said was a direct translation of the paper she was forcing me to sign and I said, "This is not the same as that one, I can't sign something I don't understand." That's when all three especially the male who had returned to the kitchen after going around the house without permission, got mad and started raising their voices saying, "Just sign it, stop wasting time!"

I then asked Harvey to go and get Marc in the village to help. It wasn't Marc but Martine who came and she said, "Just sign it it's routine it's not a big problem." Even in my shaking body of stress my gut was still not wanting me to sign it, being charged with double murder didn't seem like a little problem to me!!

I was now shaking more, and I was feeling really unwell but they still pushed and pushed for me to sign it. In the end I just did to get them out of the house.

This was my recording on the 17th of January 2017 the day after the unannounced police visit. The previous pages about this were written from memory and I hadn't listened to this recording before writing those pages. It is 15 minutes long and I will let you read it before I make any comments on it.

Hi, it is the 17th of January 2017, again I have been bad at communicating with you but I will go through from November 2016. November was fine the weather had changed we had got the cold now. Rob had to visit England for three or four days but he brought my mum and dad back with him, it was really good to see my mum and dad and my mum and I only had one argument but we were good when they left.

I find having people around quite difficult it always seems a good idea at the time to have people coming to stay because you want to see them, but it tires me out and it's probably not the best idea.

Then we had Christmas which was good but Harvey because of the industry he is in had to work Christmas day and Boxing Day so we had our Christmas dinner the day before, we had a good dinner and ate lots of chocolate. It was good to be putting the Christmas tree up again, it's always a pain to put them back down but I suppose at least you remember things when you put your tree up and especially when you have had them for so long. What I found amusing is that I asked Harvey for help and for him to put the angel on top of the really big tree. I have had that tree since before he was born, so it amazed me to think that he is now so tall that he can put the angel on top of the tree.

On New Year's Eve Pat and Robin came to stay, it was good I just had a few frustrating moments. I think they are the two people that absolutely kept Rob (they arrived the day after the accident) going and helped so much. I don't think Pat means to do it but she keeps having a little dig at me. Rob says I am imagining it, but she doesn't do it to him just does it to me sometimes. Pat just, I don't know is judging me, I feel judged for whatever reason. And so, it stresses me out. We didn't have any arguments, I haven't got the energy or want to. I would rather, if she doesn't like me or whatever just to say, I haven't got the energy to deal with it. I know what Pat is doing she is just sticking up for Rob. But I don't know I don't even know if she knows that she is picking on me when she is picking on me. But hey, I just don't know about that one really.

When they were here the weather was really, really cold but they got a few jobs done. They cleared some of the brambles and with the help of Phil and Sharon they cut a pathway through the hedge. I need to get the animals in a better system so they are not near the house so we could sort them out. It's coming together only slowly because of the weather and because I can't do anything to move it on.

That was into January 2017, Robin and Pat leaving on the 7th of January. Elliott went back to school and Harvey had his week at college. Also, that week we had a meeting on the Tuesday at the Grand Feu an all-day meeting.

At the meeting there were the same people but all so different towards me, whether it's since the last meeting when they saw what state I was in or whether they now realised that I did need to be recognised and that I am not just a number I don't know. I was in a good place, I was positive, we were still having battles with paperwork, and we arranged to see them again at the end of May. I don't feel ready to do anything with the hand or driving yet.

Then on the Friday we went to see Dr. Pietu the surgeon who had x-rays taken and basically said I have got to get the metal in my left wrist out as soon as possible. So, he has booked me an appointment for the 9th of March, only a month before, in February, we have to go for a pre-op consultation.

It was said at the Grand Feu by the doctor that maybe the cruciate and the ligaments of my right knee have gone. I am 50/50 with that it does give way a bit. I need to build the muscle up but I can't do anything with it for a long time anyway, so I'll try and build my muscle up and see.

The doctor at Nantes said I will have to have my metal out of my leg eventually in another year so my dancing pole will have to go. I will have to mentally prepare myself for that operation. It's not so much the operation it's the anaesthetic, it stays in my system, it makes me angry, it affects me. But they can't do these things without anaesthetic so I will just have to deal with it like everything else. But it's fine I am thinking good let's get on with it and then Rob just happened to mention to me, "That will really put you out of action." I hadn't realised if they operate on my left hand, I really won't be able to do anything.

The scaring will be quite sore in my wrist, so I am trying to do simple things now. Get the paperwork organised and get some other stuff organised things I can do while sitting down (big sigh). I don't know what will happen there is always a risk with operations. As the doctor said they might find it stuck to the bone, it might break my bone, there's loads of things that could happen. It might not be successful, but it needs to come out, so I have to have the metal out.

That was last week, lots of running around. Harvey is back at home this week, he had the weekend off which is good he worked yesterday, and he is off today and tomorrow. I don't think he is 100% happy there but he must stick at it.

The other thing that happened yesterday was about teatime, Harvey got me into the barn I was just sat watching animals. It's hard staying in the house all the time especially when I want to be doing things. Then he said the police are here, I am thinking they are just driving past but they weren't, they were here to come and visit me.

Rob had just arrived from picking Elliott up from the school bus. He helped me back into the house and the three police followed. One was the one that interviewed Rob after the accident, she could speak English. They served me a paper which was in French she said I had to sign it. I said can you read it out to me because I don't understand it. That was the purpose of her being there as it said on the bottom of the paper, her name and the reason why she was there. She read a bit out and then she skipped a bit and I asked her to go back to it. The other guy and woman were getting agitated because I wouldn't sign it.

Then they gave me another sheet saying that this says exactly the same in English. But I wasn't signing that one, so I didn't think it was unreasonable for me to ask her to, especially when she was there for that reason, to translate it properly. The other two officers carried on raising their voices and bullying me. I was getting more upset.

It is basically a letter they are serving me saying I caused the accident, homicide and murder and there is a chance of imprisonment. It was all bizarre really because we got a message the week before from Marc saying that we have to go on the 23rd or 24th of January to La Chataigneraie to see the police. That was no problem I wanted to help, and I asked if we needed to take anybody (solicitor) Marc said no you are not allowed to take anybody then suddenly they are serving me these papers on charges of murder, unannounced which was one hell of a shock.

So, I had quite a bad day, well evening yesterday, but what can I do? I just give it to the lap of the Gods! I can't remember anything, I wish I could remember everything because then I would be certain what happened. I don't know if I have become a suspect, I am the only survivor, so they are pointing the finger at me because they want to finish the case, get it all 'solved' get a result!

I do know that on that road someone else had died on a motorbike not that long ago. I don't know which is the most frustrating part there are so many. If they can categorically give me evidence to say that it was my fault, then I have to take the consequences. But knowing how I drive, knowing how I respect other drivers, knowing that I wasn't in any rush or emergency and being on a road I know I am struggling with their charges.

Was I in front or behind? Was the other vehicle in trouble? I certainly would have stopped to help if I had seen anything and they were having problems, I don't just want to be made the scapegoat. If it's me, they have got to categorically with undeniable evidence prove it was me. Because it's me who must live with the death of two people.

If it's not me I still won't be happy that two people have died. If it was their fault, I will have a different thought process because I was miraculously saved from death by a situation that was out of my control and caused by risks taken by others.

I don't want to be blamed just to close the case, I accept the facts as long as they are cast iron facts. I have basically (now getting really upset) got to put it into the lap of God, gods, angels, Jesus, or any other energy of truth. They got me through the accident and the horrendous time in hospital. There is nowhere else I could turn to, I was bedridden, and this is just causing (very emotional now) as much pain and stress as the physical pain, but I have to do it. It's just hard because the kids were here, it's hard for everybody and I am sort of angry and trying to accept what's happening. It will be over soon I will keep in touch after the event (police meeting). Bye.

15 Minutes

Listening to this recording for the first time since I recorded it in January 2017 only goes to confirm to me that I didn't cause the accident, my recording is honest and open. I wanted the truth and if someone had solid information and facts that were unquestionably pointed to it being my fault, I was more than willing to accept that and the penalty given. It is also clear to me that there was something inside of me or a guidance outside of me that was trying to tell me the real things that were being hidden and being cunningly carried out to set a trap to which I would fall straight into headfirst.

I am not being dramatic, by now the reader will have a picture of who I am, how I treat people and how I just need honesty no matter what the situation or subject.

At the time of the recording, I had not been interrogated (there is no other way of describing the three-hour persecution I was put through by the police) or knew any information at all as to how they had come to the conclusion that it was all my fault.

In the following years as I tried to find information that would find out what did happen, searching for what I had done to cause this, in order to allow closure, all I discovered were photos and facts that without any doubt showed I was not to blame. It is often the things that people won't talk about the information that they ignore, sidestep, and steer you away from that holds the truth.

The things, actions and none actions of these so called just and honourable establishments was beyond belief, but then again, they held all the power. I was just a foreign woman of insignificance, a murder and it was my fault that I was now disabled.

To the reader I warn you that it may be a good idea to get buckled in, this is one hell of a ride, a roller-coaster that I didn't wish to be on, and it just kept going.

My recordings on the 24th of January 2017 after my second police encounter:

Hi today is the 24th of January 2017 I think I spoke to you about the police arriving last week. Today I had to go to the police station in La Chataigneraie to be questioned (big sigh). A good two and a half to three hours later the result isn't very good. I had a translator and a solicitor from the insurance there which everyone said it doesn't matter, it doesn't matter, it's just a formality, just a formality. Not the case!! Also, they (police) wouldn't let Rob go in, so I was on my own. They have basically served me with more papers. So, I haven't a clue what that means really but everybody keeps telling me things, like it's not a problem you don't have to take a solicitor, you don't need to take one. They are not living the nightmare that I'm living right now! It's too late when it's too late, the solicitor had to leave early so I wasn't even represented just left.

I had to sign this paper and I really struggled with it because this is what it says roughly. 'You have (my name, name of the place of the accident and car details) I did cause a criminal offence and caused involuntary the death of Maurice Dupont and Paulette Dupont and they also said I was speeding, and I think it says in a dangerous manner (big sigh).

I am talking to you today because I feel really framed! This is where I stand, I want to know the truth, I have to live with this. But the thing that I don't understand it's as if they are making it up. They had an expert I looked at some of the expert's computer-generated photos that the police showed me. The expert had the other car wrapped in the tree. When Rob was there that car was quite a few meters away from the tree. When I questioned why it was in the wrong place they said (the police) "Oh no it wasn't!"

So, there are two things happened there. 1. Which I find very unlikely that they have had to move the car and then push it into the hedges for that's the position Rob saw it in. If they had to move the car for the victims, I am saying victims because the police are making me say it for the people that died. They are not victims because I don't believe I caused their deaths. I think there was something else that happened. I think they are assuming because I am alive, that I am someone that they can blame. That's what's happening, I think. 2. They have pulled the car out of the tree but why push it into the hedge I thought that the final position of the vehicles after an accident was vital evidence, Rob saw it in a totally different position. Why has the expert got it in the tree? My car is at the other side of the road where it ended up and where it was when Rob saw it. But their car is put in the tree by the expert but that isn't where Rob saw it!

Also, the police questioned why I overtook when there were broken lines on the road only allowing overtaking of slow vehicles. I know I would not have overtaken I am on the wrong side of the car it's an English car. I would not have voluntarily overtaken the only reason I would have done so is if I thought there was a problem or a danger. If they were swaying and there was a problem, then I would have distanced myself or if I couldn't I would have tried to get out of the way.

I would not have tried to overtake, and I have never, never in my life ever cut in front of a car. It's stupid, it's not how I drive. It's how a lot of other people drive but it is not how I drive!

The other thing that I asked, it wasn't clear on these digitally formed pictures is how do they know if I was overtaking. If that's what the expert said I was doing. How do they not know that I felt endangered? I don't know I can't remember anything and if they have come into me. On the back of my car, there are no marks! It's all smashed up at the front where I had the impact with the tree and other places but the place where the digital photo shows, or where the expert said I touched the other car has not got any mark on it. That's confusion, big confusion number one!!

I have lots and lots of questions. I asked did they (police) test us for alcohol? 'No' was the answer. I know I wasn't drinking; I don't know that they weren't drinking nobody tested them. So, we will never know if they were drunk or not! We will never know.

I asked the question 'What about medication?' He (the police) took time looking through the papers, he said he didn't have any (information) yet he was really annoyed with me for not talking my medical papers. If they had told me when they turned up at my house that night and frightened the children. If they had told me to take all my medical records, they would have had them, but they didn't tell me. They expected Rob to go back, and I said you won't know where they are because they are all in different places. Yet they do not have one piece of information about the other people's medication. I asked if they were on medication, no answer.

There are so many questions. These are some of the questions I didn't ask because I didn't want to ask too many questions. Have they been in accidents before? Have they got a problem with their eyesight? Loads and loads of questions.

8 Minutes

Hi I am back again, I am still on the 24th so what happened is I still have lots of questions. They didn't do any blood test for alcohol or drugs. I know I had not taken any alcohol, I am really against drink driving, I think it should be zero tolerance, not one pint or one and a half pints. I think it should be no pints when you drive. The reason the police gave me, was there was not enough blood. In my case maybe there wasn't enough blood due to my extensive injuries. But in the other two people's cases, Rob says they were working on one person and the other was already in a body bag there was no blood that he could see. Rob probably got there about half an hour after the accident I think, we will never know if they were drinking!!

I think it's the police that are taking me to court and also, they said that the family started to sue me for damages.

I have been waiting and waiting but no one contact us except on that time that they just arrived in a gang at my house unannounced. How can the family have started procedures to sue me if the investigation hadn't started, where did the family get the story from? We kept asking and asking for it this report nothing was ever given to me. I feel as if I have been left well and truly in the dark. It seems to me as if the family had seen an opportunity to sue somebody. If money is so important to them that's fine. The big problem for me is that I need the truth.

I have asked myself this question, I would prefer to know it was me categorically and then I can deal with that. If I feel as I do at the moment, I am sort of an easy target to blame because no one really knows, that's not justice or right!

The expert basically looked at the only thing he can look at the cars and the actual skid marks, but even the skid marks to me don't say the true story. If you look at my car and where the expert said I touched them while 'illegally overtaking at high speed' allegedly, I have no damage to the part that he said I had touched them with. Obviously, I don't know the damage that their car had at that part. There are many scenarios, maybe the elderly people had a problem in the car, and I saw it and I thought I have to get to a safe place and I had to speed up to get to a safe place, then they came into me! The tyre marks can only have been after contact or after the cars weren't going in the right direction, after the alleged collision.

If at the speed they claim I was doing I would think that that position on the car, the position the expert and police concluded was the point of contact, surely it would have been scraped, hit, marked, damaged you name it. From what you can see from the photo there was a dint on my car which was there before the accident caused by a shopping trolley when parked at the shops. Marks also would have been caused while they were taking my roof off and moving the car to the garage.

Another big question which I asked was why does the expert show their car smashed into a tree when both Rob and Steven who went to look for me, saw it wasn't in the tree. Steven happens to be a mechanic who used to retrieve cars off the motorways after breakdown or accident in the UK, so he is an experienced guy looking at cars. How come on the expert's report, remember this is all they are going on to point the finger at me, he has it still wrapped up in a tree that's not where it was at the scene of the accident. Also, how can two cars be wrapped up in a tree at the same time it's all so suspicious.

I am praying that I remember, the only thing I did remember, the first words that came out of my mouth in ICU, firstly I didn't believe I had been in a car accident, I have never been in a car accident. Secondly, I said "They were all over the road, they were pissed, drunk" I said that and then just continued my conversation with Rob and asked about the boys. This never got mentioned to the police by Rob I don't know why maybe because it was the first thing I said and I had just come out of a coma and was drugged up, I don't know.

I know I wasn't in a rush to get anywhere, it didn't matter it wasn't a big problem. I don't know why I would have tried to overtake (if I even did?) as they claim I did unless there was a danger, and I was trying to get myself to a safe place. I don't know if the other car suddenly stopped, I don't know if it was having difficulties and neither does the expert know these things. They cannot say you caused the accident if they don't know why I would overtake I am not that person who drives like that. I am not in a powerful car, people do that sort of thing to me all the time I just say goodbye to them, if they want to take risks okay it's their lives that's their choice. So, this is really confusing me.

If they knew me, I know how I drive they would understand how I am having difficulty in the fact that they claim I dangerously overtook at speed because that's not what I do, I don't do that!! But that's what's been said.

I know there is another reason why this situation and accident happened. We cannot test them for alcohol, they may have been roaring alcoholics. When I asked the question about medication they have no information about it, yet they got annoyed with me for not taking my medical information and the only reason I have any medical information is because of this accident, I have never taken any medication throughout my life.

The police asked me if I was familiar with the road. Yes, I went on it often it was the way I went to the supermarket I asked the question back, were they familiar with the roads? Did they live in the area? They didn't tell me. I think this may have come from the papers or someone else but they lived in Cognac, so miles away not used to the road.

More questions I wanted answering, had they had accidents before, even small ones? Did they have any sight problems or just recently had an operation or time in hospital? Were they on any medication or under a psychologist? Did they have any conditions such as diabetes or heart conditions? I feel I am being put on because I am the one that 'survived' in inverted commas because believe me it's not the life I had and I am well and truly imprisoned and my family and friends (getting upset now), it's like a living dead! I am alive but I am dead, so this is why I am in need, a big need to make sure (very upset now) that in that court there is the truth.

We don't know who this expert is, is he well experienced, is this his first case? Is he a friend of the family's? It's difficult to ask these questions, they wouldn't get answered anyway but it's all relevant to the outcome. I need the truth to be given the sentence of having the blame for two deaths will have consequences for me knowing the person I am (upset). I have spent my life caring for people it matters to me. But I don't want to be made the scapegoat because that's easy and it ticks a box and I get the blame. So, the insurance pays the family out, wonderfully, I don't care about the money I care about having a full active life.

So, to me I feel robbed, I feel really robbed, I feel robbed of my life (very upset), I am getting the blame and it's not fair. So, I have to fight this as hard as I possibly can (break down crying) because I know even though I have no memory, I know that I would not put anybody's life in danger. I know that so I need answers. I hope the solicitor understands this (still very upset). It's difficult with the language barrier because things get interpreted in a different way. But for my sanity which is on a very thin wire at the moment I need to do it and fight for the truth.

I question myself am I just doing this because I don't want the blame, it's not the blame that I am worried about, it's how I am being blamed. I am blamed by an 'expert' who has done some digital photos. On the photos they don't even show you the skid marks before and the fact that he has left their car in the tree, for visual impact. As far as I can see, 'Look where those poor people ended up' and the truth is their car was nowhere near the tree never mind in it! It's all wrong and very misleading. Also, the big thing is that our car doesn't look touched or damaged on that point this 'expert' says it touched. If they cannot prove with actual evidence and cannot prove that we did actually touch and make contact, how can they conclude that I touched that car! There could have been two simple separate accidents that happened. Why is that not a possibility?

If there are photos of the skid marks, I need to see all the photos, where the skid marks were on the road and which side of the road. How do they not know that a deer or wild boar didn't jump out? We have had that happen on the very same road only a year before when all the family were in the car, when a deer did exactly that it bounced out and then ran off. How do we not know that it wasn't an animal the police response to this question was that animals don't talk, no but they can cause accidents and kill people! It was April, spring, how do we not know that animals weren't involved! We don't know anything it cannot be said that it was me without investigating other possible factors, because I don't just cut people up on the roads it's not me it's not how I drive or have ever driven. I can't see why I would have wanted to pass and then suddenly wanted to cut someone up there's no logic to me.

I have spent my life training in medical stuff and had people who have come to me with injuries from various things. I know, I am not stupid, I have got two degrees, I am not a stupid person I know the consequences of cars that's why I have not had a car accident before. If I drove as they assume I was driving, why haven't I had accidents before now? (Big sigh)

It's probably good for me to talk I sound angry, I am angry, I sound upset, I am upset. But I have got to get these questions answered (break down upset) I have so got to get these questions answered because they will be with me for the rest of my life. I will try and write things, get someone to write, I can't write with my left hand. I will try to get questions written down as I think of them. Because if the police as they were today sat there and said, "We don't know what medication they were on, we don't know where they were coming from and doing." They know what I was doing and where I was coming from. Rob was interrogated and told them what we were doing, we were preparing for some visitors, they know I wasn't on medication, I haven't visited a doctor in years since the kids were born. They knew I was not ill, but we don't know what their circumstances were. You have got to assume, just as they are assuming it was all my fault, that at their ages (85, 83) that they must have been on some sort of medication, what did they die of? Did they die of a heart attack? Did they have a heart attack before the accident which caused the accident? The 'expert' says I was behind but what if I was in front?

An animal could jump out and not touch the car, I know because we have been in the car when exactly that has happened. If a deer or wild boar jumps out running towards you or across the front of you both the driver and the passenger jumps with the shock, panics, and reacts. How could that affect an 85-year-old, especially if they had alcohol in their system and had health problems or on medication. There doesn't have to be marks on their car from an animal, it doesn't say that there were no animals involved.

So, my questions are many, do they categorically know I was overtaking, how do they know I was overtaking? Could I not have been in front and something else came out and hit them and startled them? An 85-year-old has not got good reactions or quick reactions even without medication or alcohol in their system it's called the ageing process.

I would say it was my fault if I remembered it was my fault, but I know how I drive and it's not how they are assuming I am driving! I do not drive like that, and I have lots and lots of questions. I have got my life to live as best I can with my family. You can't take away the accident you can't give me the hand back (getting upset) you can't give me my unsmashed body back you probably can't give me my sanity back. But at least I can live my life knowing I did not cause the death of two people if the games are stopped, and the truth is told. I need the truth I don't think this 'expert' is doing his job. It's a lot of guess work he cannot categorically say hand on heart that he knows a hundred percent that I caused it that means there is reasonable doubt.

I don't know (big sigh trying to compose myself). I can't help it, I have always needed the truth (upset crying). I can't abide lies and dishonesty I need the truth (really upset now) and if the family are just trying to sue me to get money because they see it as an opportunity to retire, that says a lot about them. I can't retire, I can't have a simple life and live the way I want to live in old age because that's all been taken away from me (break down crying very upset long pause crying). But I have got to fight because from what I have seen today the pictures are not correct, it been staged the way they presented it especially the skid marks you couldn't see where they started so many unanswered questions and so much left out.

I need some answers, please God give me the answers (breakdown upset). I only wish I could remember. If I could remember I would have said if it was my fault, but I can't remember. I did say and remember my first conversation after opening my eyes that they were pissed and all over the road and that I was looking for my hand. I said in ICU that I was looking for my hand and everyone was looking for my hand in the car and that is exactly what the pompier said I was doing when I spoke to them later in the village.

Were they drunk? Or just having problems? Did the driver have a heart attack? (Big sigh) Now I have got a big fat headache.

I just hope I have the strength to carry on. I feel as if everybody is just wanting to get this done and over with as am I, but it's an easy route to just point at me. Who would they point at if I wasn't here, if I was dead, they would still have pointed the blame at me? Maybe that's why I survived to fight for the truth.

The last thing I will say while I remember. I did ask how the family can have started procedures to sue me when nobody knows what happened. I didn't get an answer to that. I asked if I can start proceedings to sue them, no reply.

Have I just been lucky by sheer God's will and my physical fitness and my quick thinking and driving that saved me? I feel that I have been turned into a victim in a different way, not seen as a victim of a car accident, I feel I am a victim of harassment, unfounded information, information that could be argued in any simple case that it was not concrete and very much not provable. Okay bye.

28 Minutes

Hi, it's the 28th of January 2017, I will continue to make comments as I think of them on this recording because it is so difficult for me to write anything down. After Tuesday this week when I was served the papers for homicide of two people and driving at speed and was supposed to have overtaken! I have spent most of the days following doing research and detective work. I would like to put on record that there are a couple, well more than a couple but these are the things so far as I have not got the file yet, which is concerning. Concern number one is that there was no blood test taken. Why was there no blood test taken, the excuse of not carrying out a legal requirement at the scene of an accident, being there was not enough blood. How did they know if they didn't even try to take the blood test (there is no documented information that states who tried to take blood or what time? Did they even try to take any blood? And if they didn't, how do they know there was insufficient blood?). I have got to find out if I got tested for alcohol and drugs.

How can they not have got blood from them? Steven says he saw no blood on the elderly person they were working on when he was at the scene and neither did Rob. The other person was already in a body bag. The lack of evidence here is a big concern of mine especially when it is the number one cause of deaths on French roads, that is alcohol and drug related problems. The French government having put lots of money and resources, plus campaigns into reducing this statistic, yet here we are two deaths actually at the scene and a person gravely injured and a high chance of death too and there is no test taken. Someone explain that one to me for I am struggling with the excuse given. They conveniently got a blood test out of princess Diana's driver who was dead at the scene in France same laws maybe he was being framed too! In a reversed sort of way. They could test me all day long I don't drink and drive, I don't really drink, I have zero tolerance.

Why? That's the big question, why?! Because all the research shows even a small amount of alcohol in a person's system never mind if they are elderly changes all your reaction times. It changes everything and it's a very dangerous state to be in.

Big question two when I asked if they were on medication again no investigation. Think about it if they had been on medication and had even a small amount of alcohol that would have made a massive difference and they were in their mid-80's. Why have these question not been answered?

5 Minutes

Hi, it's the 29th of January 2017 Sunday morning, I am just documenting a few things that I have been thinking about.

The person that telephoned for help we need to know who telephoned, when they telephoned and did the police get a statement from them. Can they confirm what positions the cars were in as my concerns for the 'expert's' report's information is high. We need to look at the damage on their car as well as mine.

Also was there a motorbike involved who fled the scene. It was warm the boys had been to the beach, and they had suntan cream. How do we not know there wasn't a motorbike involved especially on that long stretch of road with a long clear view of oncoming traffic. A road that would allow a biker to open up his motorbike.

They allege I was travelling at 112km/h and the other car 83km/h so if I had actually taken over how come I didn't easily pass them with that difference in speed. It's all very confusing and the thing I need to get over to the solicitor is that I am not trying to get out of something, but I am trying to get the truth. If they can categorically prove I did something wrong and caused the accident, then I will accept that. But from what I have seen and the questions that they won't answer there is too many doubts. I don't want that crime on my hands, well hand, if it's not my fault. At this point in time, I feel it's not my fault. I feel there are so many unanswered questions and I smell a rat!

4 Minutes

Listening and reading these recordings of January 2017 was not easy, the pain, upset, fear, hopelessness being real and raw in my voice. A person desperately alone with no one listening or believing she could even be the victim in all of this. If this state of being had lasted a few months that would have been bad enough for a person's mental and physical health especially as they were already in a very poor state from the trauma they had recently been through. But this state of being would last years, with more bullying, lies and corruption being thrown into this situation.

I write this now knowing the facts that I was not allowed to see. Now aware of the games that were being played out. But back in January 2017 I was trusting, naive and searching for answers that my logical brain was asking. The games methods even after just two encounters with the game players (the police) though not clear, were already starting to work. I was believing that maybe I had overtaken but couldn't understand why I would do that, it wasn't how I drove. It was and is a case that if lies, gossip or a story is told loud enough, long enough and often enough people will believe it.

The mind game had begun I was in their spider's web of lies, blame and condemnation and the 'evidence' they used to keep me there wasn't even that good! Any fool could see straight through it but yet in the recordings I am trying to find balance, justification and answers to get to the truth. It was as if I was the only one concerned about getting the truth. The police, the French family and even my Allianz solicitor accepting the inconsistencies without questioning the conclusions.

So now they had put doubt in my mind all they had to do was keep pushing it down my throat. Easy I couldn't understand most of it anyway and they never gave me anything in English so I could try and understand it. Even my Allianz insurance company a massive multi-million international insurance company could not even give me a solicitor who could communicate with me, he didn't speak English. Not that it mattered for he never listened and was dismissive and even rude and disrespectful at times. In the time frame of about three years that he was supposed to represent me I saw him about 5 maybe 6 times, he always kept me waiting and always rushed the meeting which needed more time because of the language barrier. He was my nemesis not my guiding force. For such a serious situation I got very little time with him, and his attitude was he didn't believe me anyway. If I had been him, I would have made some excuse to find out the personality of who I was supposed to be representing, their integrity, their character and how they drove. But then he couldn't speak English and he seemed to not be bothered about getting to the truth anyway even though I gave him every bit of information I had found. I even took two toy cars of Elliott's with me on my first meeting to show him how the cars would have reacted if they had been hit as the first expert Maurice Pascal said they did. He just dismissed me as if I was a stupid person with disabilities, in a wheelchair.

As time passed, I got the feeling that the two insurance companies had done a deal and it was my insurance's turn to take the hit. This would be further confirmed by the actions I saw when the two 'opposing' solicitors were together. The Dupont solicitor being from a big famous solicitor in Bordeaux Coubris and Courtis (more on them later).

As it will be revealed in this book, I would go on to find police photographs that would be shocking and prove I did not overtake them and indeed they may well have been overtaking me. Evidence was sabotaged and lost; you will never believe what was lost. Basic routine investigations not even being investigated or carried out.

But my gut, guides or the Universe told me to demand a second expert's report and that is exactly what I did. Now they panicked, this was not part of the game, the trap they had set for me didn't involve me fighting back and even with the proof that was given by the second expert, they openly and blatantly ignored it!!

Chapter 28: Re-living The Nightmare, Boxes, Another Operation And Court

"The elementary principles of all deception is to attract the enemy's attention to what you wish him to see, and to distract his attention from what you do not wish him to see."

-General Sir Archibald Wavell

I will now cover the events that occurred after the end of January up until receiving the second expert's report. The first thing that happened in the beginning of February 2017 was me having a vivid nightmare about my accident. Here is the recording of it:

Hello (extremely upset scared) it's early morning I have just had (can hardly talk so upset) a nightmare about my car accident. I am trying to talk to you because I know that soon you forget what you have dreamt. All I can remember is that there are many people, so many people all around, I was looking down I wasn't sitting. I seemed to be out of my body, I was looking down (really upset, crying and difficult to talk). It was really, really, really scary I am trying hard to remember because I want to remember what happened. It's the first time I've remembered I have had lots and lots of dreams and nightmares, but I didn't want to bother the family because they were so confusing, they were just strange, not clear like it has been tonight. Oh God I don't know where I am going and it's just, it's just I want to know what's happened. I was there it was so real there were so many people it was like a busy street that I saw. I kept going back I kept watching myself from above and I was sort of lifted into fresh air. I don't know.

It's been the first time I have actually felt to be in the car, I ask the powers that be to just show me the time before the accident. If I am starting to remember I need to know everything, please someone show me everything. I don't know what day it is 17th - 18th of February (2017).

3 Minutes

Prison Or The Paralympics

This short recording was extremely difficult to listen to, I was so upset just as you are as a child when you wake up from a nightmare, lost, confused and petrified. It's so real and vivid and you are living the nightmare and can't escape until your mind and body brings you back to your existence on the earth plane. I know I was present and conscious during the accident and somewhere in my mind that information is stored. But whether I am allowed to access it I do not know.

Once I calmed down, I did two more recordings.

I have tried to calm myself now. I am sat in darkness in the kitchen, everybody is asleep. I am trying to remember. All I see are lights, flashing lights everywhere and voices. Voices lots of voices that are just everywhere. I can't really, I can only feel the top half, I can't feel or move the bottom half. I can't feel or move the bottom half I am struggling, I am squashed, I can smell earth, like an earthy smell, like I suppose an engine smell when you lift the bonnet up after you have been driving. I can also just hear people, very, very noisy, the lights are just flashing.

I don't know I seem to be next to a tree, not a tree, hedge, grass I don't know where. I also, oh no I am trying to stop the bleeding I have got my arm pressed against something. I am not sure if I can move, I think I can move my arm to try and stop it bleeding, oh no I can see blood! What's happened, please tell me, I want to remember, I need to remember all of it. What happened?

Right, I don't know there is a silvery blue car, silvery blue car. Could that be mine? Mine is grey silver it's not my car, it's not my car (pause crying). What's happened? (Struggling to talk through my upset) They are not driving very well, I can't see what happens to them. If I have got memory, please show me everything. I don't know whether I am going to remember.

I am travelling, I hear singing, I can hear singing on the radio. It's warm it's a nice evening. I don't know if I am singing or the radio, I can't remember, I can hear singing (break down crying). There's a car in front not driving very well. I can't remember I can just see a car but it's spinning, or is it? I can't see it very well, it's not driving correct. I don't know what's happening, what's happening? Is it stopped there's no brake lights, I don't know why they were weaving? Oh no it's too difficult. (Long pause upset)

Now I can hear voices again and flashing lights and people talking to me really nice voices I am talking back, I'm talking back. I think I can hear my own voice, I am talking to them, and I can't seem to get any oxygen I feel as if I am floating away, I am floating out of my body, I am looking down, I am looking down. So much noise, noise I can't see my hand, I don't know what's happened to my hand. I am worried about the eggs, I am worried about the eggs. What's happening? I don't know I can't remember anymore it's all so vague. If I am meant to remember it, it will slowly come back, maybe the brain thinks my body isn't strong enough to take it. But I can't remember much before, what was I doing? I will continue to talk to you and see. I need to try and go back to sleep now.

9 Minutes

I think it's still the 18th of February I am still sat in the kitchen, I am having a drink of water. I feel calmer now I am just sat in darkness closing my eyes because I am sat in darkness everyone is still asleep. Things are flooding back to me and I remember it being a warm evening I was coming to the junction near the church and the restaurant, Lion d'Or and turning onto the road that I was taking.

Then not far from coming through the village I can see a really dark car, quite a biggish car coming and it's behind me. He is behind me it's really up close but that never bothered me I just continue at the speed, if they want to overtake, they can overtake. He, I am saying he the car's quite dark, I don't know if he's got windows that are dark, darkened windows. It's quite close but I am pottering along if they want to overtake let them take over.

Now I am coming nearer to another car in front this car is going slower than me (sigh talking to myself thinking to myself "now think what happened"). It's a bit weavey, they seem to be just going from one side to the other side. They just seem to be (big sigh). I have got my awareness that I am backing further off which is irritating the dark car behind me. But this car in front is weaving a bit and I am thinking oh pissed! They have been for a meal and drank too much.

Then the dark car I don't know oh gosh! (Getting upset) Oh no Orr, he has gone really fast he, I don't know I couldn't really see it looked like a he. He's gone really fast to overtake both of us (upset crying) why do people drive so bad? (upset) It's all gone now I can just hear noises and I don't know what to do (very upset). It's all gone, all I can see is a car turning and the other car (crying heavily). Please tell me what's happening and now I hear voices and I can't find my hand, I am looking for my hand (long pause). A voice is it my own voice? He's talking on a phone very panicky, oh God I hope I remember more.

7 Minutes

I thought at times in my recordings at Nantes hospital and the Grand Feu that they were difficult to listen to, but these last three recordings devastated me. To hear someone is so much pain and I was that someone!

The pain I was in was so heart-breaking, I was re-living the nightmare of my accident. Though not wanting to go through it at the same time needed to remember. It is significant to me that I had this nightmare in February 2017 before I had any information given to me. Only a couple of weeks before I had very briefly been shown (by the police) some information from the report by the expert Maurice Pascal when I was being interrogated in a room full of police working at their desks, talking, and using their computers, I was under immense pressure and being bullied in a very unfriendly atmosphere. So, the fact that I remembered can have only come from my memory of the actual events not from looking at reports or other material connected to it because I hadn't seen any.

These three recordings were done in February 2017 before I was feed constantly that I was overtaking. Like I have said before if something is repeated long enough and often enough it gets planted in the brain it's a method of mind control and causing confusion, which is used by certain 'authorities', people in shall we say certain situations. Humans naturally soak it up it's how advertising works. I won't go deep into the subject here, but you get the picture.

In some of my later recordings I am questioning why I would have overtaken. Offering and giving different scenarios that could have forced this action such as animals, getting to a safe place to avoid a dangerous situation. Very quickly once repeatedly told I was overtaking by the police, my solicitor, gossip, friends, even Rob I was starting to believe it myself, even though my whole being was confused to why I would have done something I would not normally do!

The mind game was implemented and its power starting to affect my thought process. Yet here in my nightmare of re-living the accident I don't mention overtaking once. I mention concerns about a car behind me that overtakes, and I have concerns about the way the car in front is driving and I back off, my alarm bells ringing loud and clear. No thought or attempt to overtake. Then I go into vivid detail of being trapped in my car. Remember I was awake throughout this horrific ordeal! I was aware of my hand and was even trying to treat it by trying to stop the bleeding. If the reader could hear the recordings, they would immediately hear the genuine stress, upset, fear and honesty in the recordings.

Maybe as my angel anaesthetist said they did give me something to make me forget but I believe those three recordings in February 2017 says what did happen.

I had never re-listened to them until February 2021, four years later. Should I have used them in my case? I believe they would not have been accepted, excuses given, they were in English or other excuses. I had some sort of subconscious feeling these recordings were for my private benefit and it was dangerous to let them out of my sight. They would have been mysteriously lost or damaged as so much of the other vital information was. I was guided to not trust them or anyone for that matter.

This same feeling applied to me finding one of my plastic wheel covers in the hedge at the scene of the accident a year later. This wheel cover was intact, it wasn't damaged, broken or marked and it was later proof to me that there were no lengths these people would not go to, in order to frame me. It also proved to me that this investigation was crap, or non-existent, surely the area would have been searched, looked at and investigated, isn't that what they are trained to do? Isn't that their job description or am I missing something here? I have still got a bag of bits, including the intact plastic wheel cover and car parts I found at the scene.

I am so glad I didn't tell anyone involved in the case about it, every time I thought I would a voice in my head said, "No this is for you to allow you to see you are not going mad to show you that something is not right, a gift, a sign from the universe that you must not give up!"

What happened in the following years just proved to me that if they had got their hands on any of this it would have been lost on purpose. This perfect plastic wheel cover, off my car was my confirmation that I did not kill two people. My confirmation they could not destroy with their games and words. My confirmation and guidance from a honest and loving energy that was beside me in my car, in ICU, trauma, plastics and the Grand Feu. My team who would guide me and never leave my side. Guiding me as I put pen to paper with my non-writing left hand, guiding me to give hope to others that eventually the truth is exposed and with every exposure the powers of cruelty and dishonest energies are weakened and one day they will be powerless.

As I write this in March 2021 another sign was given to me. My eldest son Harvey went to pick his brother Elliott up from the school bus on the 9th of March. On Tuesdays Elliott's lessons finish late so he doesn't get off the bus until after 6pm. At this time in France, you are not allowed to be out after 6pm and need a piece of paper. Harvey was stopped by the police his car searched, fined 135 euros, and tested for drugs and alcohol!! Hold on a minute my son gets tested for alcohol and drugs for being out after 6pm, no driving offence, just being out after 6pm. Yet they do not test for anything at a scene of an accident where there are fatalities and grave injuries. It sounds about right! What bullshit!!!!

February 2017 also involved me going back to Nantes hospital to have a pre-operation appointment before returning in March to have the metal in my left wrist taken out. You have to meet with the anaesthetist, they weigh you, ask you questions and you can ask them questions. My only question which was more a request was to have the tablet under my tongue before the operation. It probably wouldn't be necessary because I would only need a local anaesthetic, I was a day patient and would be going home on the same day as the operation. Great you know my fear of general anaesthetics so this was good news to me. I would return on the 2nd of March for my operation.

Also in February 2017 our belongings from Australia were due to arrive. Though I was going through it with the police, the charges and my general battered body and mind I managed along with Sharon and Richard two native South Australians, to get our furniture and things shipped to France. The company was Chess Moving, who I was impressed with, they even expertly wrapped the wheelbarrow up.

Sharon and Richard are the salt of the earth a very special couple with a beautiful family, so kind, genuine, considerate, helpful and loving. I often talk with Sharon, and I tell her the only reason I was meant to spend some time in Oz was to meet them. They and their family are extremely important to me proving distance does not mean that support, love, and an amazing friendship cannot be given. I love you guys so much.

Because of my next operation being a day appointment and not a general anaesthetic it was arranged that Jenny would take me, wait, and bring me back. It would be an early start because of the two hours it took to get there but Jenny was happy to take me. It allowed Rob to feed the many pigs we now had and to pick Elliott up from school. I have a feeling that it may have also been a week when Harvey was residential at his college so he wasn't at home to help not sure but anyhow it was arranged that Jenny would take me not Rob.

The container of belongings from Oz were due the Friday or Saturday before my operation which was on the Monday. The big container couldn't get close to the house so the four French guys who had the job of unloading it had to go and get a van the container parked on the outskirts of the village, and they would fill the van up drive it to our gate and then place our belongings in the house. It was a long job but at least it didn't rain or snow even though we were still in February.

I tried to direct the things into the right rooms every box or piece being well labelled by the removal company, essential for there were probably nearly a hundred boxes plus the furniture. The huge container was full, and it took all day to empty it. We now had corridors of boxes and rooms filled with items covered in white protective bubble wrap. Just another little job for me to deal with!

I talked to myself not to panic with the task that faced me and that I couldn't open anything because I was about to lose the use of my hand in a few days. Seeing as it was my only hand if I wanted any sort of independence and function from my left hand I hadn't to push it post operation, that's if it was a successful operation. I Prayed hard to my team that it would be, and they would watch over me and guide me.

I think this team of mine has a very wicked sense of humour because the odds of what happened next was very high and very unlikely, but I took it with an element of disbelief, a sign, guidance, humour, and love to encourage me.

So now the house is packed with boxes and wrapped up furniture, you couldn't move. There were pathways left to squeeze past but that was all. I said we can't start unpacking any boxes until I can get upstairs and organise some place to put the contents. I still wasn't going upstairs, it was too dangerous. I was looking on the hallway at the writing on some of the boxes. One said toys and games so I thought I will open this one and then Elliott or Harvey might have some of their things that had been left behind. This box was on top of another so I couldn't see into it, but once opened I reached up and put my hand in and pulled out the first thing I touched.

What I pulled out was something that Elliott had got for his trick or treating when it had been Halloween. I pulled out a plastic arm with the image of blood and bone painted on one end of it. I looked up and said, "Nice one, very funny but it's the wrong one I need a right one not a left!" Out of about a hundred boxes that was the only one I opened and that was the first thing I touched and took out. Mad right?

A few days later I was up early to be ready for the operation. You need to shower make sure you were clean, the guidance paperwork emphasising your feet. I wasn't allowed anything to eat or drink so I just waited for Jenny.

I had spoken a little to Jenny how things were after I returned home but not in much detail, I thought it was either my imagination or my fault. Rob's constant words of "You are needy, it wasn't all just about you." and that I was "Paranoid" starting to be believed by me. When Rob didn't even get out of bed to wish me luck, hug me (which he hadn't done at all anyway) and say goodbye, I could see that Jenny was a little shocked. I just said he is still in bed. Jenny didn't say much but her face told me what she was thinking. We set off, arrived in good time and I waited to have my operation.

I recorded this so that's what I will write now my recordings in March and April 2017.

I think it's the 14th or 15th of March 2017, it's a while since I spoke to you and quite a few things have happened. I suppose the main thing really is that I have been back into Nantes hospital for an operation on my left hand. I thought after going the month before for a pre-operation consultation that I was just going to have a local anaesthetic. But as I was down on the trolley waiting in what I call the bus station because you have just got loads of different places where different people are lined up, the anaesthetist said I would be having a general (big sigh). I didn't really want a general because I think I have had that many anaesthetics and I don't think I react so well later on with them, I think it takes a while for it to come out of my system and I was just starting to get a bit of normality back inside of me! There was a problem putting a line in. Three people tried to put a line in my arm, and it didn't work. Then I got wheeled into the theatre and this guy put it in my right leg.

I was a bit stressed at this point because it's not good when things are not going to plan. Then doctor Pietu arrived and that calmed me a bit because at least I knew he was doing the operation which he said he was. I just thought let me get this gas stuff in so I just took as much in as I could. I thought if I am going to be knocked out, I will just have to be knocked out.

I don't know, I think I went down about 12:30 and came back about 3:30. Jenny took me, I think it was easier with the animals and the boys then Rob taking me. To be honest it was good to have a chat, she kept me calm so that was really good. She brought me back the same day. We did have to stop for me to be sick, I wasn't feeling very well and as soon as I got back, about 8 o'clock I just fell into bed and fell asleep.

So now I have still got the stitches in, they are due out on Thursday, and I am due back to see the specialist on Friday. Probably I have not rested it as much as I should have but it's so difficult, so difficult here, I can't ignore some jobs. I just (big sigh) find the whole thing quite frustrating really. But hopefully I haven't damaged anything, and it will knit together. I had a good first week after the operation but having a bad week this week.

I don't know things are too difficult, mainly people, people irritate me. I do a lot of shouting which isn't really my personality. I suppose I was getting frustrated with life and certain things because I used to try and do too much before. But now it's just multiplied and multiplied. If I think about it everything has been concentrated on the physical healing, the physical treatment. I know that I have been so lucky with the people who have looked after me, the surgery and everything else. I am very grateful for that, but surely the mind has been part of it all, how do you deal with that? Because I am someone determined (some would say stubborn) I think my mind seems to be coping but I think it needs some sort of treatment (love and acceptance by a certain other would help).

I am not sure, I have seen a psychologist at the Grand Feu, and I am going to see one tomorrow. I don't know what I need, I definitely need some peace and calm and I just don't seem to be getting that!!

It's annoying that we have not heard anything from the solicitor. I have worked it out, if you take away the weekends, we have only 18 days to go before court. Am I expected to be prepared to be cross-examined in 18 days? I have emailed him (the solicitor) a couple of times, but I think it's just annoying him. So now I am not going to contact him anymore and if I don't feel confident, I will ask for a postponement. I will be in touch with you again maybe sooner than I have been this time, bye.

7 Minutes

It is now the 20th of March early Monday morning, I don't know when I last spoke to you but I will start from my operation. I probably mentioned that on the 2nd I went in for another operation and that it was a general when I thought it was going to be a local. The operation went okay, I feel the scar is okay. I feel physically things have been okay even though it was another big operation, I think it was three hours long. I have pottered along with help from family and friends because in effect it meant I was handless.

I have had some extremely bad days. Part of me thinks it's just the process of recovering from such a horrendous accident. Part of me thinks it may have been the chemicals coming out of my body after the anaesthetic. But I have been as low as you could be and it obviously makes it difficult for everybody around you. It's bizarre really because when I was at my lowest point and really thinking it was all not worth it, any of it and it was time I put an end to it. It was the simple things that encouraged me that it was worth carrying on. I saw a little wooden letter E that Elliott had made in school. It's just a letter E for his name, that's as daft as it sounds, when I got a hold of it I felt it and touched it, it brought me round (I found this little wooden E in my smashed up car when I went to look at my car before the court date).

What is more bizarre last week because the court case is on the 10th of April and we had still not got any information (information came through on the 16th or 17th of March, only last weekend). But last week because Harvey wasn't working, we went on Wednesday morning to the garage where my car was taken after the accident to see the damage. Basically, what's been said is that I caused the accident and I hit this other car of the elderly couple at a certain place on the car. While I was in the Grand Feu Harvey and Rob went to the garage to take some photos randomly, mainly because at a later date they could show me the car. This was done before any information was given to us and not knowing that I was getting the blame. So, it was a 16-year-old lad taking photos of his mum's car for his mum. Not taking photos for a specific reason other than for his mum not for a defence or anything like that. On these photos on the exact spot where they say the contact was made it's not touched. Last week when we went, and this is a big frustration for me the car had been violated and contaminated. They had moved the car, there were big red scratches in the exact spot where the supposed contact had been. The plastic wheel covers had been removed don't know how they vanished or where they are, and my car was being used as a storage place for other car parts and bits.

The guy who was there was really good he told us that the police or whoever said it was done with! But it's the only evidence they're using (the cars) in the accident where two people died and another almost dead and was left with grave injuries and 80% disabled. The guy was really informative by sheer chance he was a volunteer fireman and attended to me first at the accident. We got some information, it's difficult in French because he spoke quite quick. He told me my hand was in the tree that he was the first there and he thought I was the passenger because he didn't realise it was an English car and the steering wheel had gone. I just kept saying my hand, my hand. This guy didn't speak any English, but I am sure he will remember that word until the day he dies. He also said that there was a 15-year-old kid just stood staring at me who had probably come across the accident just going on the same road. So he had to attend to this young guy because he was in shock and then he attended to me, he came back to me after the young guy was attended to. So that was some information.

Then I had some really bad days Thursday and Friday were horrendous just so horrendous for me. I don't know thinking about it maybe it could have been flashbacks. Maybe it could have been just again my body trying to process the whole thing that's happened to it. I didn't check my emails or do anything because I couldn't be bothered. But then I just checked them for some reason and I came around quite a bit. Mainly because Elliott came home on Friday and was really upset because someone had been nasty to him on the bus and shouted at him and swore at him and he was in tears. So that brought me round and back to planet earth, I started to function again.

Now the situation is I have spent the weekend looking at the file. I think it is absolutely important that I get another experts report done even though the car and evidence has been violated. I have a right because it's the police who have asked for this first report and there are loads and loads of things that are shocking in this file.

One of the biggest shocks is that the son of the family within 72 hours after the accident on the 5th of April was in a police station in Cognac starting procedures to sue me for damages. He had to make a statement of how I hit the car. They hadn't even instructed an expert at that point, so where has this information come from. How can he even say that I even hit the car when there is no evidence, no witness, there was nobody there. So that's annoying to say the least. What sort of a person is he? What sort of character is that person who can do that?! He can't have even buried his parents and he is in the Police station making a story up. A normal person with any normal feelings would be in so much shock and upset. They would be surrounded by their family, they would generally not be able to function, they will be just in a daze and shocked for days. But no this guy can go and make a statement, totally made up and start to sue me.

There are lots of things, I am going to spend a lot of time going through things. The expert report, it seems as if there are lots of things missing. For example he circles a bit on the road where he says it is the place of the accident. But on that circle which is quite large it is on equal sides of the road.

As I have and maintained from day one I did not cause that accident. I do not drive how they say, well guess I was driving! I have never had an accident and I would not drive that way and I would not have overtaken unless there was some serious problems with the car in front if in fact they were in front!!

There are lots of things and I will probably keep talking to you about it. The police took a photo of my speedometer saying it was stuck at 112 and then the expert says I was doing 106. They have said they were doing 83 but do not tell us how they know. They haven't included their speedometer photo. There are 13 photos of their car and 14 photos of mine one of which is the speedometer. They were in a Peugeot Partner year of make 2004, our car was a Seat and 2003 only a year's difference. Ours had a hundred thousand on the clock theirs had twenty one thousand on the clock and our car was parked up for a year when we went back to Oz. If the couple bought that car in 2004 as new and it's only got twenty one thousand on the clock then they do not drive much, for what reason do they not drive? If it's their second car and they use another car more than that car then they can't have been used to driving it, but I feel that it is more likely that they just don't drive that much. And yet they have taken on this long journey from Cognac. We don't know because there is no information of what they did before the accident. The only thing noted was they visited some friends or family in Saint Pompain and that's it. In the file there has been nobody interviewed, nobody asked questions like Rob had to do on the 13th of April. There is no information, we don't know what the couple were doing before the accident. They know exactly what I was doing.

If they had driven from Cognac which is about two hours driving for them. If they had gone to their friends or family did they have a big meal, were they drinking, were they drinking contraband which in that age group, he was 85 years old, in that age group they traditional drink it. It's a thing I know happens, that generation have made it for generations especially the farmers and I believe their friends and family were farmers.

The French would not sit and not have a drink with family or old friends, it's what they do. When I went on the 23rd or 25th of January, I can't remember the date to be 'interviewed' by the police I was told off for not bringing my medical records but they didn't have any medical information on the 85 year old or any blood tests for alcohol which I thought was a legal requirement. Then there was no autopsy done, why? So they just guessed the cause of death and pointed the blame at me!

I have a strong feeling that this character the son, knows something, it is probably general knowledge within the family and friends that this 85 year old did not belong on the roads and shouldn't have been driving. Did this son who was a retired accountant see an opportunity and had to sue me before the truth about his father's ability to drive came out? It's just not normal or right to do it in 72 hours and I believe he didn't even get to know about the accident until the Sunday. It's all strange these things are very suspicious.

So to me it's a big fight, a difficult fight, a dirty fight, a fight that I hope I have strength to go through. At times I think I am just not physically fit to go through this court case but then what would have happened if I had not survived? It was questionable if I would at the time, I think it's only the will of God that I am still alive and the experts at Nantes hospital plus all the people who attended to me on the 2nd of April. I am here because Rob couldn't or wouldn't fight against all this he would have just accepted what the police were saying.

There were no photos from what I have been allowed to see that really investigated the scene I have yet to see any of the tyre marks. The policeman in charge didn't go back until 4:00pm the next day to take photos by then all the evidence would have been contaminated the road was not closed off. It's disgusting there are two people dead and possibly a third one and they didn't seem to carry out basic normal procedures. Why is this investigation not being an investigation? Why was the expert's report so basic, poor and putting in wrong information to do his DVD he didn't even go to measure the scene until August 2016 the accident happened on the 2nd of April 2016! (big sigh) I will continue to read, read and read even though it's in French. Bye for now.

19 Minutes

It's the 10th of April 2017 the day of the criminal court hearing, the day I go before the judges and be tried for double murder and for causing an accident.

The expert, the police report and now a solicitor from Bordeaux (Courbis, Courtois and Associates) for the family are against me. They are all saying I over took this vehicle, cut them up pulled in and caused the death of these people. And I did this 'aggressively' and at speed!

The last two months have been difficult. First on the 2nd of March it was the operation, the surgeon is excellent but I fear the stresses of the anaesthetic which stays in the system. It's difficult it makes me have mood swings and makes me very down.

Then we had to go to the solicitors, I had worked really hard and studied the 'experts' report and found out a number of things. Mainly that it is alleged that my back right tyre and their front bumper, come wheel arch, come tyre is the point of collision and black rubber marks were found.

But if you really think about it it's impossible to turn the back wheels while in motion so the only way any black rubber marks can be made would indeed be the Peugeot turning it's front wheels which do turn in motion so turning and touching me. I have tried and tried to get this through to the solicitor and there are loads of other problems too.

The fact that this so called expert can't count, twice he documented on his report that there were three dead. Red flag there! How 'expert' is this 'expert'? The simple things that Maurice Pascal got wrong like the number of dead makes me question his capability and quality of work and I am being charged with double murder on his work!! This is a really serious situation and the fact he can't get the number of people dead right twice is very concerning. So I asked the insurance Mr. Herve who is really kind and the only one who seems interested in getting to the truth, for a second expert report. He commissioned another expert, who didn't have a lot of time around three weeks (Maurice Pascal took nine months to produce 19 pages of very basic information the second expert a national expert had less than a month and he produced 156 pages of high quality scientific findings). The second expert report came late Friday before the court date but the difference is amazing. The quality, professionally, scientifically, the physics it was in a totally different league.

I tried (it's all in French) to work it out and it basically concludes that there is no possibility that through analysing the tyre marks on the road, there is no possibility that the Seat my car could have come into the Peugeot. The only possibility is that the Peugeot has turned his wheel left then rapidly corrected himself and then turned right, that was the national expert's conclusion.

So now we will have to see what happens. The thing I want to be able to do is express how bad this devastation is that the family have lost their parents but also to ask why nobody can answer my questions. Why can I not find out what medication they were on, why can't I find out if they had a drink that day. Why can't I even find out what time they had set off from their home in Cognac. I ask all the powers that be that have helped me so far to just give me the right words, in the right manner today.

Prison Or The Paralympics

It was only last week that it was the anniversary, Sunday. I was pottering about I just sat on the bench at the time it would have happened. I said goodbye to my hand again and I asked the Lord that the two people were okay and they didn't suffer. It was a very strange time and every year for the rest of my life, on the 2nd of April around 8:30pm I will have a minute of silence for my hand and for the elderly couple.

So now I am going to get ready. Claire is coming, Marc, Harvey, Jean Louis and Rob. I think Kelly and her mum and Phil and Sharon are coming. I am not too scared here maybe when I enter the building but at least someone other than me (the second expert) believes I didn't do this accident. The only thing I want is the truth!!

8 Minutes

It's Friday the 17th of April it's been some week. On Monday the 10th it was the court hearing. I was quite relaxed I wasn't really nervous, it was just I knew I had to go. I knew I had to be questioned and just hoped I could get things out that had been on my mind.

I was still in my wheelchair when I went to court so I had to go into the lift and as I came up (it was a glass lift) I saw the other party, probably about 10 maybe more. They looked to be family and an elderly lady, they wouldn't look at us or me they were in big conversation with this female solicitor who was crazily trying to re-enact the accident with her hands.

We were waiting outside the court waiting to go in. I stayed sat in my wheelchair and we all sat at the front, the family at the back. There were quite a few people there and I didn't realise that it had other cases going on. This young kid got called in front of the judges (there are three) and was sentenced for drug abuse. I think he was given rehabilitation and community service.

Then it was my turn but there was a ten minute break so we had to wait and I was turned around looking at my friends but I could see the family. The elderly sister looked really shocked and lost as if she didn't want to be there. There was a guy there who had curly hair and sat next to him was a guy who looked more official. It would be interesting to know which one started procedures, probably the one in the checked shirt, but they wouldn't look at me only if they thought I wasn't looking at them.

I had to go up and be given my sentence or accusation. I had an interpreter I didn't say much I just listened, I didn't agree with what he was saying anyway. I just listened and acknowledged with a slight nod. Then he went on to explain that there is an expert report that said blah, blah, blah that I at speed of 106km/h the others at 83km/h, that I overtook, blah, blah, blah and caused the accident. But then he said we have another report which is by a national expert and it can not be ignored and this says that basically I could not have possibly caused the accident and it wasn't overtaking that caused the accident but them drifting into me and then rapidly going right. So the judge said that he cannot possibly start to make a judgement and he was considering a third expert at the top level to come and look at this. They went away for ten minutes.

They came back and the decision was that he would get a third expert and we had to return on the 18th of December.

The solicitors got a chance to speak before this decision was made I was still in my wheelchair facing the judges. Their solicitor was directly behind me I turned because she was absolutely going on slagging me off. I am thinking I am sat here with my hand chopped off in a wheelchair and where is her respect you know I am still alive and you know your clients caused the accident.

From the bit I could understand she was saying I brutally did this and did that and she cannot comprehend how it's possible that they had touched my car when I would have gone to the left and not to the right if they had knocked my right back wheel. At that point the judge said that's ridiculous which it is because if you touch the back end on the right it's going to flick you into the right not to the left. So she couldn't even get the basic logic of that. She was really agitated and spoke really rapidly and she showed the worst photography of all and didn't do them any favours. I could tell the judge wasn't happy with her.

Then the prosecutor (acting for France) spoke and she was quite annoyed at the fact they had got the report so late, she gave my solicitor a bit of a telling off. My solicitor did briefly talk as well to agree that a third investigation was in agreement.

So that was it about an hour in court still unpleasant and uncomfortable especially when they are arguing with each other the prosecutor being particularly nasty. I am just sat there in my wheelchair thinking to myself, it's not about people. It's about an insurance company versus another insurance company and it's about a solicitor versus another solicitor and I am sat in the middle of them and do I count anymore? They don't even know the journey of hell I have been through and continue to travel, an innocent person in the wrong place at the wrong time! That gave me sadness and I looked and I thought I am not going to cry, I am not going to cry!!

Apparently the female judge looked at me constantly with empathy so Claire and Sharon said. There were two male judges, the one on the end towards the end started looking at me and the middle one I found quite fair, he seemed okay. As I left I did look up to them and say thank you, they acknowledged me, waved and said no problem I think they realised I was a human being and that was it.

Prison Or The Paralympics

How did I feel, disappointment in a way that we have to wait until the 18th of December. I won't go in my wheelchair I want to aim to just have a stick because I will probably still be very unstable. I have a long way to go to be back walking properly.

I will now just go and get in the garden get jobs done move forwards. I can't sit around until December. I will do a little bit of research on things but I have got to leave it alone and rest my mind.

Everyone was relieved, they thought it was a good result. The other expert report coming through only on Friday night brought good news. Very, very technical in comparison to the first report. There is no comparison to the level of technology of the mathematics, of science, it's quality and content cannot be ignored. I feel there can be two results here. One that they will say everyone has suffered enough forget it. I will be slightly disappointed in that or it will be that it was definitely them and it's not my fault. I feel that would be more closure for me.

Even with a third expert report the second expert surely cannot be ignored just because of the quality of the report that Marc Puech produced he is a national expert. I smelt a rat with the first expert's report but I am in the middle of it and have to deal with it. So onwards and upwards (big, big sigh). I have no doubt I will have more meetings with everyone, the psychologist, the doctor at the Grand Feu. Everything is going to still continue but my main thing is to get driving again. So a year on and it's still going on.

12 Minutes

So now my first court appearance was finished and at last I had a professional person with integrity and honesty batting on my side, Marc Puech. Although the future was still uncertain and difficult. But the difficulties that would slap me in the face in the coming months would take my life's challenges to a whole new level. This new level required strength, determination, self-worth, self-love and going it alone. Once again picking myself up after being knocked down.

Chapter 29: Dahlias, The Return To The Grand Feu, Driving Lessons And The Spitting

"First they ignore you, then they laugh at you,
then they fight you, then you win."

-Mahatma Ghandi

We are now heading towards May 2017, the weather is getting warmer, and I am trying to get some sort of normal life back. My plants from Halls of Heddon, a nursery in Heddon England (not far from the famous Hadrian's wall) were potted up when they arrived and now it was time to plant them out. My dahlias, why dahlias? I don't know I just love them, they are very giving and once in the ground and supported they last until the first frost. In the Victorian era they were grown for the tubers which were eaten, but I am sure they will have used the beautiful flowers too, how could they not!

My granddad Sam always grew dahlias and I remember seeing them growing, but he only had the purple and white ones. Funnily enough out of about 50 plants that I have, I don't have that, I think it's called Mystery Day. I remember my granddad carefully wrapping them in newspaper in late autumn and placing them in boxes under the spare room's bed. It was a ritual he did every year and each year he would separate some tubers so he would have new plants for the spring. He would only plant them when all the chance of frost in spring had gone.

I have the same ritual now, around the end of October, depending on the weather I start to dig my tubers up. Often I have objections from the bees who have spent the summer visiting the beautiful flowers. (This last year 2020 I had to buy bigger plastic boxes because the tubers had doubled in size). Then I take any surplus soil off, place them in the box and cover them with empty paper feed sacks and find a frost-free place for them. Once or twice I check them during the winter and spray them with water if the tubers look to be drying out.

Around April to May I start putting them back in the garden. Once in they need no attention except watering in dry spells, give them support (some can grow tall) dead heading and cutting the beautiful flowers for the house and to give to friends. At first I got this ritual wrong but now I have learnt from my mistakes and manage to over winter them just as my granddad used to.

One of my biggest helps however came from the Halls of Heddon nursery in the UK. They have been growing and showing for over a 100 years, the history and story of their journey is in a wonderful book called 'The Highs And Lows Of A Nurseryman'. The story of Halls of Heddon's Morton Stanley Hall.

I was told about this company by Rob the electrician's dad who showed dahlias and always got his new plants from them. They are a company not only of knowledge and expertise, especially in dahlias and chrysanthemums, but also with their kindness and genuine interest in the needs of their customers. (I can no longer get orders from them because of government regulations on EU shipping but at least up until January 2020 I was able to stock up and now have a wonderful display of very good quality plants. I did however lose some of my plants after my accident and then again in 2017 due to certain events that occurred in the middle to the end of 2017, but I managed to re-stock some in 2018 and 2019).

Just like music, these plants were my medication, my therapy, my healing, my need to make my body work to get them planted and the need to see their beauty. To care for and love an honest real thing in my life when all around me I was being given ugliness, dishonesty, cruelty and false realities. I was forced to look at these things and have them shoved in my face. But my dahlias were not just beautiful plants they were my friends, my sanity and my guidance to hope, a hope of better days ahead. Allowing me to see that not all of this beautiful planet which we live on, is filled with ugliness and deception but that there are things provided free to us with an unconditional love. All mother nature asks for in return for these gifts, is kindness, appreciation, acceptance and a love of these gifts. These gifts allowing the soul to breathe and sing from the energy they offer. Awesome!!

Harvey was still working at Lion d'Or restaurant at this time, doing his course work and his exams for his first year were coming up. Harvey was very busy worked hard and never complained. He still pulled his weight a lot at home because I was still so unsteady and weak. Attempting to take care of the pigs was not a sensible option. Harvey often worked late not getting home till after midnight, not that at his age of 16 it was correct or legal. But he did it and the more he did the more that they expected him to do.

Rob constantly moaned about having to pick Harvey up and even took money off him for petrol, a thing I wouldn't have done seeing as he was only getting around two euros an hour. But I was already struggling with some of Rob's actions and attitudes so I kept quiet. What could I do I couldn't drive I was only just hobbling about and Rob wasn't even working much, but that didn't stop the complaining.

Then late one Friday night Harvey came to see me in the hospital bed that was set up downstairs. He was obviously very stressed, trying not to show his anguish and I said, "What's up Harvey?" His reply "What if I don't want to go back mum?" So, we had a chat about how he was being treated I said, "Don't go back if you are so unhappy, I will support your decision."

Basically, he never finished when he was supposed to, didn't get any extra payment for it, he was being abused really. I said, "If you go tomorrow or don't I understand and support you." He did go back the next day but rang to say he would be finishing late which annoyed Rob. I said, "Just go get him he isn't even legally meant to be doing all these hours at the age of 16." But drama, drama, drama from Rob. When Harvey finally got back Rob was not happy, Harvey was trying to please everyone. I was useless and couldn't fix it. I said "Harvey you have your exam on Monday, you shouldn't even be working again on Sunday. I will come as well to pick you up and I will come into the restaurant and get you." For some reason Rob never went in but sat in the car so they often didn't tell Harvey he was even there when the staff saw Rob sat there.

So, on Sunday I went with Rob at the correct time that Harvey should have finished and hobbled with my stick into the restaurant. Harvey looked uncomfortable and stressed. He came out and said, "I just need to finish some desserts, but I don't know how long I will be." "No problem" I said, "I will sit and wait." There was a party of 80 people in as well as a full restaurant, Harvey should have finished nearly 40 minutes ago.

I sat and waited, Rob went back to do the animals it was a very hot day and they needed feeding and watering and also Elliott was still at home. The woman in charge wasn't happy to see me sat there but she couldn't avoid passing me because of where I was sat. She had to acknowledge me and came to give me some bullshit.

I said, "He should have finished at least 30 minutes ago, and he has got his final exams tomorrow, when is he going to rest and prepare for that?" She didn't even know he had his exam, that's how much training and supervision he was getting. She didn't like it so decided to call a meeting with myself and Harvey.

She spoke perfect English until she didn't want to answer my questions and then she ignored me and started talking or picking on Harvey (by the expression on his face) in French. I won't go into all the details but basically, they didn't give a shit about his apprenticeship and were abusing his kind nature and hard work ethic. She then disappeared and went into hiding but I just continued to sit waiting.

She did at one point come back and in perfect English came out to say, "I like you, but I don't agree with you." My reply "Hey I don't need you to like me, I don't care, it's my son's welfare I care about!" I thought to myself you have sat there told me he should get a motorbike to ride late at night in winter on dangerous roads not far from the place of my accident and then insinuate that there are other issues going on with Harvey's unhappiness and you think I need you to like me! Go multiply, I thought, you have managed along with your husband to knock all the passion Harvey had for his cooking just because you hate your job. Eventually Harvey finished and Rob came back, and we left. Harvey knackered but still had to do his exam on Monday.

Harvey was at his college all week did his exam and decided to leave the college. One of his tutors tried to make him stay because he said he had so much potential, but Harvey's heart was no longer in it and so he decided to leave. He phoned the restaurant to ask if he could call on Friday on his way back home to see his boss, but he said he didn't have time to see him. Harvey wanted to explain face to face what he had decided. A young person with the right frame of mind of how things should be done in such a situation, the adult however, his so-called boss wouldn't even give him ten minutes of his time!

Harvey therefore had to tell them on Monday when he went back, and they said he had to work another two weeks before he could leave. He hated the atmosphere and how they treated him, but he went. I personally would have had a long bout of sickness and not given them another minute of my time.

Harvey got himself a place at the lycée in Bressuire to start a three-year BAC general, I suppose the equivalent to 'A' levels in my day and then he could decide what he wanted to do after that. Elliott was glad that his big brother would at least be at home for some of the summer holidays, they were both due back around the 2nd of September. Meanwhile I had a little holiday of my own back at the Grand Feu.

I recorded this, so that is what I will document now.

Hi well it's probably the 9th of July 2017 I haven't spoken to you in quite a while in fact I don't even know the last time I spoke to you but there has been quite a few things going on. I may have spoken to you after the court case which was in April and the operation on my left wrist.

I have visited the doctor again and basically; I have got until October to decide what to do with my right leg which is full of metal. Doctor Pietu sort of put me off saying yes there are lots of risks of infection, you could break the bone in the operation, there is a risk in any operation, and it won't give you any more mobility. I don't really agree with that because I was convinced from day one that one of the bolts in my knee was too long and that it was definitely restricting movement. I can't squat and I cannot get full range of movement.

I know I haven't really started training my legs again, but I am doing quite a bit of moving and walking about and general activities. So, the muscles have come back in that sense but there is no depth of muscle in my quads because I haven't physically trained them. I may not be able to squat because of the ankle. The metal in the ankle cannot be removed because the bone has laid down on it.

With the leg it's the areas that the doctor would have to go in on my leg that I fear. What if he did damage anything in my knee joint, my ligament or cruciate which I actually think are alright at the moment, or a nerve gets damaged there are always risks.

Now at the moment I am at the Grand Feu, I have been here since Monday. I am here in the house which is great because I don't have to go in the restaurant. Believe me you can survive here if you don't have to go in the restaurant! I can choose what I eat and people don't come in three times a night to see if you are still alive. Although it's an adapted place, wheelchair friendly and you have got a buzzer and a phone to call if you need help, but generally you are left alone.

I am here because I am going to learn how to drive. Unfortunately, I found out yesterday which is quite annoying because they must have known before, or someone didn't bother to find out. The thing is I can't continue next week and take my examination because I haven't got a French driving license, I only have my English driving license. If they had let me know I could have got it changed before I came here. So now I have cancelled next week's lessons I don't see the point in paying 42 euros an hour when I might not even get my exam until September or October.

I had my lesson today, the instructor is good the lessons are hard. On the first lesson I was literally three minutes away from getting back here (Grand Feu) and burst his front tyre on a curb. He didn't give me a lot of notice when to turn so I over steered and it was a fairly big curb, and it just went down, and he had to change the tyre. No damage to the car but a Formula 1 pit stop it was not, but the tyre was changed, and we continued.

That was a bit difficult on my first time. The adaptation is also difficult because I don't know it's like a joust stick with some buttons at the top for indicating, but when you are going round a roundabout it's quite difficult because it drops due to gravity. Then trying to hold onto the steering wheel with this handle with three or four fingers and indicate at the same time. It is extremely frustrating and annoying. I need to invent something better. I don't know why it's so complicated I am sure it could be easier.

I went out this morning and I went out Tuesday, Wednesday, Thursday and

Prison Or The Paralympics

Friday. Today was fine, he seems pleased with me, and he takes me on some difficult routes. There are lots of problems to overcome. One I have never driven a left-handed car, never driven on the left in a left-handed car. I don't know the car, don't know the roads and I don't know where he is taking me. I don't even know where I have to go because I have to wait for him to give me instructions and then it's in French!

You try and concentrate on the road, try and listen to French try and translate it into English and then you have to drive with one hand with a thing that keeps falling down (big sigh). Talk about a challenge!! I have only made that embarrassing mistake on my first lesson with the tyre, but I have managed to get through the rest of the other lessons with no dramas.

I am booked in the Grand Feu for two weeks, I am just going to stay here to get some paperwork done. I don't know if I am recording this right (recording stops).

7 Minutes

Hello, I'm back everything is okay, it's just that this screen isn't working very well I hope I am not recording over recording. I have decided to come back next week even though I have cancelled my driving lessons. I need to get all the paperwork correct and I am booked in here, I need space away from everything and everybody because I realise that since the accident as I described to Corrine "Penelope has not been with Penelope." I have not had a chance to just be.

It's a nice place, it is a house, and I am having to deal with things on my own. I am having quietness I don't ever have. I don't have to tidy up after anybody and I don't have to talk to anybody if I don't want to. I just think it's really, really important to have that time because since the accident I have never been on my own.

When you can drive, even nipping out to the shops you go out for ten minutes on your own without anybody around you and seeing that I am such and independent person I missed it. I always have thrived on my own and don't mind my own company. I think it's the key to progress, I just needed a break. I also seriously think Rob and Elliott need to go away for a few days for a little holiday, but we will see.

At times it's been really difficult at home and at times I have just wanted to be left alone and on my own. But coming here you have a lot of time to think. I have realised that I have to accept that it's early days, my mind is still up and down. My mind is still healing, recovering or whatever it's doing. My body is getting stronger although it's still not what it was. I now need to find a way of dealing with my mind. There are lots of issues really. The accident, the court case, my age, my injuries, my hand or non-hand Stubby, my memories that I can't remember but are locked away in my head. I suppose post dramatic stress syndrome, I would get diagnosed with that.

3 Minutes

The recording just stopped, and I didn't record again until October so it was either someone arrived or the batteries died. But I will continue from memory up until October 2017.

In the second week of being back at the Grand Feu with a lot of help from Corrine we got the paperwork sorted out and even Elliott came to stay with me for a few nights. We also went to sort out my driving license because the place was actually in Niort (the same place as the Grand Feu) it made sense to do it while I was in Niort.

It was the middle of July and often a lot of things close for three weeks in August for the holidays in France. If I wanted to be driving (I had some more lessons booked for September), then the paperwork had to be done before August. I also had a meeting with the doctor and a few others in the second week at the Grand Feu and that's when I announced my new goal.

In the meeting at the Grand Feu, we talked about progress and my goals. In the house I was staying in, it had a TV, at first, I was happy for this novelty, remember we didn't have a connection to TV, we just watched DVDs, but after a few days of watching it I was over it. It's so stop and start whatever you are watching interrupted by advertisements. You have no choice but to constantly flick the channels. There were some positive things that I got from it though, two of them being programmes I hadn't watched for years, which Santa then kindly got me one Christmas. The two programmes being 'Little House On The Prairie' which Elliott loved and 'Desperate Housewives' which I absorbed and enjoyed over the winter months.

A third thing that came out of it was the announcement that it was between Los Angeles and Paris who would get the 2024 Olympics which would also mean whoever got it would also get the Paralympics. The decision was instant it was like a message directly given to me I knew it would be in Paris even though it hadn't been decided, so I would train and get there no problem, mental challenge set, game on but what sport?

In the Grand Feu a few times a week there is a small bureau run by Handisport to help and advise people with handicaps to find a sport. I headed there during the week to see what the Paralympics had to offer. My logic was aim high and you may get there, aim low and you are limiting your own potential. Corrine helped me to look on the internet, I (still!!) didn't have a phone and I had no desire for one of those spy phones, smart phones to you.

When the doctor, in the meeting asked me my goals I told him and the others in the meetings my goal. The doctor laughed a reaction that would be repeated time and time again. I told the doctor it was not a joke and that was my goal. I said it's probably going to be in France anyway so it makes more sense to aim for it, and you can all be my team and go with me too.

The doctor said he would prefer Los Angeles I said that's only because of all the boob jobs they have over there. But now it seems the UK and Europe is following the trend. I had my own plastic surgeon in Nantes hospital who did all that stuff but after all the operations, cutting open and chopping off I had had and would still have to have done in the future, I struggled to see how anyone would voluntarily ask for such an invasive intervention when it was not a life-threatening situation.

"What sport?" the doctor asked. "Haltérophilie" I replied. "Oh okay" was the doctor's response. "I know it will be difficult with one hand, but I used to compete in bodybuilding, and I love training with weights and my body needs to be built up again, weights will do that." was my answer.

Haltérophilie is French for powerlifting and in the Paralympics, they only do the one movement which is the bench press. So, all I have to do now is make the thing that they made for me at the Grand Feu more solid and practical so I could place the barbell in it to bench. It was very early days, not something that had really been attempted before but my theory was that sprinters use their prosthetic leg to race in the Paralympics, I just need to design something for Stubby.

There are two sayings that come to mind "Impossible is not a fact it is an opinion, things are impossible until someone does it" and "How do you eat an elephant? One bite at a time".

If I listen to the naysayers or took on board the facial expressions of those I told, even the professionals, I would fill my mind with doubt and questions. I knew this would be a lonely road to travel, but I knew what it meant 'to walk along the lonely street of dreams', as the song by Whitesnake says. This song describing my position perfectly 'Here I Go Again On My Own'!!

At this point in time my understanding of 'On My Own' was more that I alone could get my arse training, I alone would have to find the way, the drive and desire to train hard and I alone needed to focus on my dreams. I knew or thought I wouldn't be literally alone or on my own, I had my friends and Rob but my above interpretation of the word alone would be changed in the coming weeks and months.

I left the Grand Feu grateful and happy that I could now rebuild my shattered life. Yes I knew I had the ongoing court case but the quality and depth of the second national expert Marc Puech categorically concluded that I could not have caused the accident and even challenged the legal aspect of using such unprotected and contaminated evidence (that was the cars). The cars that were not even protected from the elements, which gave me hope that the truth would come out.

Also, I had been back driving and it felt good, liberating me and giving me my independence back, hopefully when I passed my driving test in September. My future was looking up!!

As I write this and got to this part of my journey, I questioned how detailed should it be? Should I just skim over it, not say how it felt and how it affected me? But I had to include the facts the actions and the consequences that resulted from these facts and actions so I couldn't leave details out!

It is my take on things, what I experienced, watched, heard and felt. Those involved may have a different take on things but that's their story and experience and not how I felt and experienced it.

While writing this book there are questions, I continue to ask myself. Why are you writing this? From where are you writing this? Is it anger, bitterness, revenge? If so that is a total waste of time, it's not healthy and it also means I wish to continue to carry these heavy burdens. Which I don't! So, all events had to be included to allow closure and healing.

Forgiveness is so powerful and healing it's the only way anyone can move on from pain, disappointment, and cruelty. Forgiveness is for your own soul not for the ones you are forgiving. It sets you free to live your life with peace and harmony but giving forgiveness doesn't mean hiding the truth. If the truth is hidden, then forgiveness is powerless, and healing cannot take place.

Up until this point things had been a strain, there were many arguments, and it would take me years later to realise that all the red flags had been there, but I just wanted a quiet, peaceful life with no sneaky behaviour, lies or shouting. But somehow that's all there was.

My accident should have made it so much better after all I very nearly died! But my accident seemed to piss Rob off and the fact that he now needed to take care of the family and a disabled person was not part of his plan.

Looking back, I was despised by the man I had given up my world to build a new one with. One ignores and ignores the signs because we just want to fix it and it's probably all my fault anyway. Well, that's what I kept getting told. But then one day one act occurs which changes everything, it gives you a whole new view of your situation and it happens instantly. No questions, no doubt, no self-blame and not even a second thought. You are done. The universe shows you your reality which it has been trying to show you for years. But this time you take notice!!

The thing that brought me to my senses happened at the end of July 2017. We had been invited to Audrey's birthday party in the village and although I was still weak and tired, I agreed to go. Talking to people was tiring for me I was still struggling with getting comfortable sitting and still had a lot of pain so a couple of hours would have been more than enough for me. But Rob was knocking the drinks back like they were going out of fashion.

Eventually I had had enough it was starting to drop dark and the chickens needed putting away. I was struggling to get them in their house and asked for help. Elliott was moaning and complaining, I was tired and in pain and lost my patience I said don't bother I'll do it myself. Then an argument started. Rob being well and truly cocky with booze ignited the situation.

I limped off swearing and cursing to myself, telling myself to just leave them, go to bed and not to get into yet another argument, especially with the amount of alcohol Rob had drunk, I had not drunk any.

I went inside and was sorting out the tropical fish before I went to bed. Rob came in and carried it on, then another argument. We are in the hallway in front of the fish tank. There are outside doors at both ends with glass so you can see in. Harvey was at one door and Elliott at the other, on their way into the house.

The argument continued and then Rob came close up to my face and spat at my face with such a look of contempt and hatred which then started a physical fight and I ended up at the other end of the hall. Though I was being pushed in a violent and forceful way I fought back but couldn't do too much because of my unstable legs and my one arm, but I bloody tried. The bastard had just spat in my face! I wasn't going to put up with that!!

When I saw my two boys and the fear on their faces, I thought that's it I am done. But then I don't know who this statement from Rob was aimed at but he said, "Don't ever hit a woman boys!"

No but you can spit at, hit and push your disabled mother from one side of the hallway to the other that's okay! I never got an apology for him spitting in my face but in a way, it was the kindest thing he could have done for me. Now I realised who he really was and if I was prepared to stay with a person who could spit in my face what sort of person does that make me?

I had to get me and the boys away from this toxic atmosphere how I didn't know. But from that moment on I never once argued again with him in front of the boys. I had no respect, no love and not even any anger for this man, he had just given me the best gift ever, my freedom to become me again.

I took myself off to bed and that was the end of another day in paradise. So now we were not talking but I needed things to move on for all our sakes. Rob carried on pretending it never happened, I think it was easier for his ego to let himself believe that he hadn't stooped that low to spit into someone's face. I had no doubt in the months to come and even years this 'little' factor of our breakup would not be mentioned. His ego and how others saw him being his main concern, not the welfare of others, like his partner or family.

He had to spread the word that I was crazy, violent, unreasonable and God knows what else. I quickly found out who my friends were and so I kept silent and to myself. The only two people that mattered, Harvey and Elliott, knew the truth lived with the ugliness, saw their mum at her worst and saw the reaction and actions given to her.

I believe everyone involved has a contribution to these situations and it is never just down to one person. Where I was open and public with my feelings, anger and my sheer frustrations of not being able to do the simplest things, Rob was quiet, laughing, eyes rolling and charming in public and wore many masks. I was authentic and raw and it made Rob's task of being the victim so much easier and people around us were starting to make judgements and feel sorry for poor Rob.

The next day I tried to talk to him and said, "You need to move out." His reply "How can I? I have nowhere to go and no money." My reply "Get a job then, you have had the form for apples since May hand it in they start thinning out in August." I then said, "We need to sell this place" his reply "You wouldn't get anything for it look at the state of the place." We were outside in front of the barn, I looked around at the untidiness and the unkempt wilderness surrounding us and thought yer and who's the untidy one!! I then suggested I would leave he could have the house, I didn't want any money just Harvey and Elliott's name on the deeds when my name came off. The reply "I am never going to fucking do that!" my response "Well if you are saying it isn't worth anything the boys can have my share rather than sell it for peanuts, they need somewhere to live." With that suggestion he stormed into the house.

This conversation being continued in the kitchen where suddenly Rob's view of the value of the house tripled! There was no possibility of discussing any practical solution. Rob's conclusion was things were good I wasn't talking to him, so he was happy. My concluding statement was "Okay I will move out I can't work, handicapped, waiting for more operations, on charge for double murder, can't drive, but I will move out!!"

A few days later I had already arranged to go out with Sheila to get a phone, I still hadn't been given one that I could actually phone people with, and I had given Eric's his back as soon as I left the Grand Feu. As Sheila drove us to the phone shop, I told her about my situation and did she know of anywhere that was available for me to move into. She said she would ask around and let me know.

The following weeks were not pleasant I kept out of Rob's way but did try and talk about getting it sorted out. He was adamant he was never going to leave the house. I think it was his weapon to use against me for he knew I loved the house, the animals and had worked hard trying to make it a home even with all the boxes and the hundreds of unfinished jobs. But something had happened inside of me the moment he had spat in my face. It was an instant feeling of death, loss, ending and pain which had broken my spirit.

All I wanted now was peace and quiet and to try to learn to live with my disabilities and work through all the challenges that were being hurled at me. I was physically, mentally and spiritually drained, exhausted, I needed to start to think about my health, my welfare and my future. If I didn't remove myself from a difficult loveless relationship, I would be alive but dead inside. The faces of Harvey and Elliott as they watched us arguing and fighting, which would turn out to be the catalyst for their future, told me this was not how children should spend their teenage or any years, they deserved better than that. They didn't have any choices or could move away they were more stuck than me. It was my responsibility and desire to make this situation better for them. If Rob wouldn't leave, I must find a way to leave. Harvey and Elliott deserved better!!

Chapter 30: Peace Pad, My Daily Walk, A Driving Test, A Trip To The UK And The Announcement

"Pain is temporary, quitting is permanent."

-Unknown

Sheila had found me somewhere to move to and she took me to see it and I accepted with gratitude. I moved in on the 9th of August 2017.

I couldn't take much with me just some clothes and toiletries, I couldn't exactly ask Rob to help! This place was like the barn part of the house that Sheila's friend Debbie had bought. You walk into a space that had a sink, an electric hob and then you walked through an area with a bath, sink and a toilet, into another small area which had two single beds in it, this room having a connecting door to the main house where Debbie lived.

It was very compact and no windows, but it was my place of peace and quiet a sanctuary from the hell I had been trying to survive in, heal in and become strong again in. Here I was given the space to begin my healing without judgement, resistance, conflict or mental manipulation. My shattered body and mind were allowed to be without input and demands from the environment which it now found itself in. I called the place my Peace Pad.

I had this little white DVD player that Claire and Steven had gifted me while I was in the Grand Feu. I had got myself a 'spy' phone (smartphone) so I could get access to my emails which may include information on the court case. I could for the first time since my accident, contact and talk to my friends, chatting to them was therapy in itself. I didn't know where I was going and how I would get there but I had made the first step. I was on my own but in reality, I always had been.

In August about a week after I left, it had been arranged prior that Phil, Sharon, Claire, Steven, and Lewis would come round for some food for Rob's birthday, the 18th. Rob was joking, laughing, and drinking like nothing had happened. It was a show but that's not how I am I couldn't put a mask on.

I was still raw from the incident and unbelieving about the spitting and the lack of shame shown by Rob. Claire, Sharon, and I went to sit on the bench outside. The dahlias looked beautiful, and I needed to get away from the act that Rob was performing in the kitchen.

They all knew of the incident, but it didn't seem to bother them that much, but I just couldn't accept the spitting. The conversation was what had become a regular topic, the animals. Why have you got so many? Why don't you get rid of them all? On and on it went. My response being do you ask Rob why he hasn't even started making the gates? Why the pigs still get out? Why there are three times as many animals now than before my accident? All running around where the hell they want to! Have you asked Rob any of this?

Claire's response well if it was me Steven would say I would have to get on with it myself. Sharon also giving her opinion. What about the spitting in my face then? Is that okay? In the end I got up and said, "If you think Rob's so fucking wonderful you live with him." I then left to walk back to Peace Pad.

I have no doubt I served Rob's little plan of making everybody think I was angry, unreasonable, and crazy and no doubt it was discussed around my kitchen table in my absence. I had just helped Rob's cause, plan, and escape route.

I knew Claire and Steven talked about me, how bad I was and how poor Rob was having to put up with so much. They saw Rob as the victim in all of this. The place he needed to be to be able to fulfil his ultimate plan. Elliott confirmed this a few years later when he said he didn't like going to see Lewis because they would slag me off and talk about me and if dad was there, they would all talk about his mum, which upset him. He said, "One day I was pretending to be asleep on the grass at Sharon and Phil's, Claire and Sharon were talking about you not dad and it upset me, I don't think they knew I could hear."

Not long after my chat on the bench with Sharon and Claire, Sharon and Phil called at the house (though I had left I walked there to help Harvey with the animals and wash their clothes). Rob was outside and I was in the kitchen. Sharon had come to chat to me. She still didn't get how upset I was at being spat at, then she said something that really hurt. She said, "Well you have got your wish, what you had wanted, what you said at the Grand Feu, that you needed to be on your own, well now you are!" It was the way she said it cold and judging. I said "What mother wants to voluntarily leave her children? That is not the peace I wanted, I had no choice but to leave!" I then said, "I am off I don't have to listen to this!" Sharon then went outside and said, "We are going Phil, come on." I was on my way out of the farm and said, "No I am the one going, you stay and chat to Rob!!"

Again, I was helping Rob's cause of appearing the poor victim, from being this mental person, who shouted and got angry and who you couldn't reason or talk to. I was all those things but only because of how I was being treated and the mental and physical pain I had with me constantly due to my accident and near-death experience.

It was a very clever game to discredit a person so those doing the discrediting looked like butter wouldn't melt in their mouths. I was unaware until years later that such games existed and who possessed the rulebook. But I was doing exactly what the game player wanted me to do, discredit myself but more importantly it needed to be done in public in front of an audience for all to see.

The location of Peace Pad meant about a thirty-minute walk, well hobble to the farm which I had to do twice (there and back). I would go to help feed the animals, wash, and iron the boys and my clothes (I refused to do Rob's). I was mad but mainly disappointed in being so badly let down.

I was also disappointed in who I had become, I was in a place I didn't recognise, everything around me getting to me because even the simple little tasks were often impossible for me to achieve. I finally gave up on shoelaces and zips they just took far too much time and frustration. However, I had to find a way to get on with a lot of jobs, especially the animals.

Harvey and Elliott were still on holiday and wouldn't go back to college until September. Harvey was already doing all the animals and the situation with them was not easy, there were rabbits everywhere and chickens, although I had pushed and employed James to help put the fencing up to try and get some sort of control back. James had worked really hard and put loads of posts in physically a very demanding job. Rob and Phil then attached the fencing which I had had to push Rob to take me to buy. It was the summer, if we didn't get it done now the winter would be a nightmare. I already had chickens sleeping in trees in my garden, well what used to be a garden, it was now a jungle.

There were broody hens sat on eggs all over the place, some very inventive places, some very dangerous places. Buster and Myrtle-May were still out in the field but parts of it were just not good and would just be mud when the wet weather arrived. They got out on a regular basis even though Harvey worked so hard to keep an eye on the electric fencing. Before I left and before the spitting I was communicating with Rob, and I had tried hard to get materials on site so we could have one big push before the winter to bring back some sort of organisation and sanity back to the farm. I was met with much resistance from Rob but there were people around us who could see the chaos and wanted to help that meant Rob was sort of shamed into getting things done.

Not all the materials I managed to get to the farm got used. We got metal for

Rob to fabricate three gates to put in the spaces that had been left between the newly erected fencing. That was left to rust in the barn and never got made along with the expensive and ornate metal that we had bought for Rob to put on the stairs, so it was safe for me to use them. The only delay for this job was having to get about ten sheets of plasterboard upstairs first to be able to finish the upstairs bedroom off. I was excited to eventually have the stairs finished I knew it would look amazing with the metal pieces we had chosen. But the plasterboards never got bought and the ornate metal pieces were left to rust too.

Another idea I had to solve the problem of escaping pigs and the dangerous terrain for me to attempt to walk on and to get to them, was to bring them inside. The barn was sort of divided into like three areas one of these areas was dangerous due to the roof. It was about to fall down, wet and couldn't really be used for even storing wood. As we had already done the house roof this area was small in comparison. Harvey and Elliott were up for helping so a good week or 10 days would have seen it done. Then with some breeze blocks and a gate we had a pig pen.

This would make it easier for taking care of the pigs and better for the pigs, they would be out of the heat in summer and the wet, cold, frost and wind of the winter. It had to be done before September before the boys were back at college.

He delayed and delayed taking me or going himself to order the tiles, so it never got done but Rob did manage to give a former work colleague a full day doing his roof out of the kindness of his heart and obviously getting his ego polished at the same time. You may have guessed our roof never got done.

So, things were challenging for an able-bodied person never mind one who had been classed as 80% disabled but what could I do?

Dolly had had her babies that were now over a year old I think we had managed to get two in the freezer, and I think some others had gone to someone else. That left 6 plus Dolly and her daughter Titch. We did have the space but at the back of the barn was a lot of rubbish that needed sorting out, lots of it needed to go to the tip. Because of the warm weather we had to wait for the weather to cool down hopefully about September or October before we could reduce the number of pigs as there were still some male pigs. I was concerned.

The summer continued into October but at last we had arranged for the boys to go they were starting to fight and feeding time was a mad and dangerous occupation for me plus the amount of cleaning out that was required.

I was still living at Peace Pad, walking down to the farm every day and not communicating or speaking at all to Rob. Or was it that his pride wouldn't allow him to acknowledge me? By now September 2017 Rob had left working at the apples (he went for about two weeks in August) and had returned to the part time job where he had previously been a caretaker working with Martine from our village so they car shared.

The boys were back at college, Harvey in his first year at Lycée having left his apprenticeship and Elliott in his final year of college before hopefully going to the same Lycée as Harvey to do woodwork.

Rob would drop them off at the school bus early so he could get to work, he worked three or four days with all school holidays off.

I was left with the animals so I would set off each morning to slowly hobble to the farm. It was difficult at first and I definitely needed my stick, but my attitude was it was rehab, it was making me stronger.

For the first month I didn't attempt to clean the pigs, Harvey did that at weekends. It was too dangerous for I needed to climb over things to get into the pigs. It wasn't an option but at least I could feed and water the animals and try and slowly, little by little clean the chickens and rabbits out. I knew I had to be sensible. I was still very unstable and weak, but my situation would strengthen me, I had to get on with it somehow in some sort of fashion. I didn't go down at weekends, I needed to rest, and I didn't particularly want to see Rob.

However, I did have to go down one weekend, because Harvey had phoned me with a problem with the animals and he needed help. Harvey and Rob's relationship at this point was not good, though Harvey would not argue, he was extremely intelligent, and he was now waking up to the truth of the situation. He was only seventeen and the responsibilities he was taking on to fix and help the situation were both physically and mentally draining. I had already observed this and was keeping a close eye on him, though he never complained and made light of it, this was a heavy burden to bear.

Harvey would not have asked for help from Rob, so I went down. Rob was doing something outside and I went straight into the house. For a very long time Rob had been obsessed with his phone never letting it out of his sight and definitely not wanting me to see it. This obsession made me suspicious of it and if I had had a phone (remember for some reason I wasn't allowed one for months and months), he could have looked at my phone anytime, surely that's normal in a relationship!

My suspicions of things he was hiding and lying about, probably for years, was confirmed on the day Rob didn't expect me to be there.

I went straight into the kitchen to find Harvey and there for the first time in years I saw Rob's phone sat on the kitchen work surface. I thought what's so secretive on this phone. But I didn't have time to find out, Rob came rushing in within minutes agitated and picked up his phone giving me his usual greeting of aggression and hatred, then stormed back outside. That's when I knew I wasn't going mad, and my gut had been right all along.

Harvey and I sorted out the problem he had phoned me about. The atmosphere in the house was not good, I felt sorry for Harvey and Elliott. They had been dragged into the shit that was going on around them, innocent bystanders battered and emotionally bruised by the two adults that were supposed to protect them from such things.

Being at Peace Pad alone was difficult but peaceful and safe. It gave me the time to have the deep sadness, heartache, difficulties, and frustrations but it also gave a deep healing.

I believe even though extremely difficult and at times mentally, emotionally, and physically challenging, you have to go through this hell to recover and grow from the process. It is not something I would wish to experience again for it was cruel, dark, and lonely. But eventually you see things and feel things from a more enlightened place, and it gives you many insights and strengths which would not have been given if the journey had been a simple and unchallenging one.

I received messages and signs from so many different sources indicating I was not alone, I was being watched over, guided, and protected. It would take me five years to embrace this and to trust it. I was in such a low and dark place, the light though visible was only a flicker in the far distance and on many occasions, it was pure darkness.

One source of guidance and enlightenment came from the DVDs I would watch. I remember staying up into the early hours watching 'Happy Valley', the scene after Sarah Lancashire leaves her hospital bed to return home was painful for me to watch. Her wonderful portrayal of loneliness, no one understanding and deep anguish was as if the writer was watching my life, looking into my mind, and searching my soul. It was scary and so painful to watch yet allowed me to recognise that I was not the only person who had challenges. However, these challenges can only be faced when that individual is ready and has a certain amount of self-love and peace within.

It didn't take Elliott long before he moved in with me. I didn't ask what was happening at the farm, I just set up the bed for him and welcomed him. He would stay with me through the week, going to the farm at weekends. Each school day he would walk to the school bus that was only 10 minutes away. Harvey stayed at the farm, there wasn't any more beds, but I would have put one in the living area if he wanted me to. I had my concerns he looked stressed but said nothing. I didn't know what was going on with Harvey and Rob and I didn't ask, but they weren't talking.

Once a month I needed to see my own GP mainly for forms to confirm I was still unable to work. I could walk there so that wasn't a problem, but I also needed to go to the shops. I employed Jenny about every three weeks to take me shopping so that was taken care of.

While at the Grand Feu in June I had booked some more driving lessons and my driving test. This being more important than ever now, not just for my independence but to help Harvey and Elliott too. Harvey had passed his theory for driving but he still needed to have his lessons which he began at a local driving school in the December of 2017.

My driving lessons were in the first week of September, again at the Grand Feu and then two more lessons in the third week of September, my driving test being on the 21st of September. I had not told a soul. I was having a very strong intuitive feeling that there were spies in the camp who were feeding information back to Rob. I withdrew from everyone.

Rob had become threatening and angry saying I couldn't have anything out of the house even though most of it I had bought before meeting him. He constantly stated he wasn't going to leave the house, wouldn't sort it out legally and wouldn't get a new bank account. In effect my small amount of sick pay was paying for all the bills at the farm. He had his part time job and complained that his money went so quick, but he didn't seem to register in his head that things like water and electric didn't come free. I took care of anything for the boys and school fees I did constantly tell him I wasn't going to carry on paying the bills at the farm. All I got back was I will just get into a load of debt then. I think the fact that I had walked away from the farm both puzzled him and angered him he thought that was how he could control the situation. I was that tired of it all and wanted a fresh start and the boys to be happy, I didn't care about the farm, I knew deep inside I would be okay.

I would later realise that Rob probably stayed around waiting for my insurance settlement to arrive, but it never did. As far as I was concerned, he could have the house but the boys, Harvey and Elliott's names needed to replace mine on the deeds.

Because of my concerns of gossip and people talking to Rob I booked a local taxi to take me for my driving lessons. I would walk down early to get the animals done then the taxi would come and pick me up. It was about forty minutes away at the Grand Feu, an hour-long driving lesson and then the taxi would come back for me.

The taxi driver I got was also a fireman and who had cut me out of my car at the accident. It was wonderful to chat with him and he was so pleased to see my courage and progress (he didn't know my situation at home), he was encouraging and kind. This guy had seen me at a time that it was looking very slim if I would survive and it was this man's will, expertise and desire as it was with all those around me that day, that gave me any chance that I had to survive and to live. It pleased him to be taking that same person to her driving lessons and on the 21st of September wait thirty minutes while she took her driving test.

My driving test was at 9:00 am and by 9:45 I was back at the Grand Feu, the examiner announcing I had passed my driving test and could now drive an adapted car. I was over the moon, it was one of the bigger pieces of the jigsaw that I needed to put my life back together. With the help from Corrine and Thierry Rimbault, the expert driving instructor from école de conduite Du Port, I had been given my independence back!! I was so grateful this was a huge step for me. I still didn't tell Harvey and Elliott, I wanted to surprise them once I could get a car.

Trying to find a car was a task in itself, the budget I had would only buy me trouble and then I would have to invest 3000 euros in it to adapt it. With winter around the corner, I needed a reliable car. I decided the best option was to rent and then try and claim it back from the insurance.

I searched and found the company Handynamic who have all sorts of adapted cars that people would rent usually for a weekend or a week. My driving license for a disabled person arrived in the third week of October so I couldn't do anything until after that.

Also, in October I had booked Elliott and I some cheap flights to the UK to see friends and family. I needed their love, for I was surrounded by untrustworthy people and my soul was crying out for good down to earth honest people and to be surrounded by the ones who truly did care. To have honest conversations and a feeling of being loved.

Elliott was on holiday from school and very pleased. Harvey was glad to help and do the animals and I promised him that after Christmas I would send them both for a break in the UK to get away from all the negative atmosphere and to see grandma and granddad.

I wanted them to see that there was a future life that wasn't weighed down by dark thunderous clouds, that people did love them and had their best interests at heart. They had been through a lot at a young age, their foundation shook and crumbled. They needed to start to rebuild their foundations again with confidence, external love, self-worth and fun.

Jenny and Jude were going to the UK as well, so we shared the cost of getting to the airport and then travelled back together after our week in the UK.

Elliott and I stayed with Kay and Denbo for part of the week and then at my amazing friend Susan's. The time was special, loving, peaceful and healing. Elliott got to see his grandma and granddad who he adored, and he also got fish and chips, a carvery at a wonderful place in Wakefield with huge Yorkshire puddings which he managed three of. He never stopped talking about how delicious they were. He also fell in love with Gregg's chicken pasties, which later on a school trip to London he would introduce his French classmates to.

Our trip was a tonic a moment of normality away from all the added stresses. I had physical and often mental stress too. It is never free from your mind! I worried about Harvey but decided as soon as it was possible, he needed the same tonic.

We got back on the 3rd of November Harvey had had some dramas, Elliott's kitten that someone had given him, a pure black one that he named Whitney was not well and Sheila had helped Harvey take her to the vets. The vet keeping the kitten for a few days. Elliott loved that kitten so much; he was extremely sad when he heard the news that she was at the vets.

Whitney had been ill before and Rob had taken her to the local vets, and she had to have drops in her ear. One day when I got to the farm, I saw she was not good. I threw some food to the animals put Whitney in a carrier bag and set off hobbling to the vets a good 40 minutes away. By the time I got there they were just shutting and wouldn't help. I was so upset. I sat for a while with this dying kitten and cried. It was just one more thing! I wanted this gift of love given to Elliott to live, it would hurt him so much to lose the thing he loved so dearly.

I called Debbie and she kindly agreed to pick me up and take me to another vets. When we got there, they were shut for lunch, so we had an hours wait. When they did open there wasn't a vet there. This tiny kitten needed help now! We phoned Sheila to see if she had any ideas. She rang her vets and arranged for us to have an appointment there. The lovely vet said the kitten hadn't been given the right treatment, so she treated her differently.

With Elliott's and Debbie's consent I said I would take Whitney with me and take care of her at Peace Pad. Elliott was relieved he was mad with Rob for not taking her to the vets sooner (Elliott said, "He was too busy on the X-box!!"). I felt so sorry for Elliott he felt so let down.

When we went to the UK Whitney went back to the farm and Harvey religiously did what he needed to do for Whitney. But she wasn't looking good, so he contacted Sheila. When we get back from the UK Whitney was still at the vets, but she did come back to live with me. She pulled around but she seemed to have a brain problem and struggled to balance. She lasted a few weeks but died during the night. I found her curled up in her bed and part of me was relieved that her suffering had ended. But now I had to tell Elliott who was living with me only going back to the farm to see Harvey at the weekends. (Elliott did get another kitten a few years later who was given to me one day when I went for the animal food at Cavac. Wilson is a beautiful white and ginger cat loved by all of us, especially Elliott).

On Monday the 6th of November, Handyamic brought me my rental car a VW Polo, funnily enough the same make of car I had my lessons and took my test in. I needed to take the two people who had drove it to me all the way from the north of France to the nearest train station which was Parthenay. I had to drive, a bit scary but I took a deep breath and got on with it. These two people did not appreciate what they had just brought me. My independence and a means of moving my life in a new direction, a direction of hope, a renewal of faith and peace.

I did do two recordings in October 2017. Things may be repeated that I have already written but the recordings state how I felt while I was in the middle of my challenges and in that moment of time.

Hi sorry about the last recording (at the Grand Feu) but the batteries went so I had to stop mid-sentence. There has been many things happened since the last recording. One of the reasons I didn't record before is because I kept forgetting to get batteries and then when I did get them there never seemed to be a time to put them in and record but hey this is it now.

It's the 4th of October 2017, it's a Wednesday evening 10 o'clock it's three days off my 53rd birthday and life has changed dramatically.

Since the last recording I did go back to the Grand Feu for the second week. I spent a busy week sorting out paperwork and I made a decision there that I would try and do something positive, and, on the television, it was saying that Paris was going to try and be the next Olympics which meant it would be the place of the next Paralympics too. So, I went to a place in the Grand Feu that helps people who want to look for a sport, Handisport. I am going to seriously try to get into the Paralympics for the bench press. It's very early days not even started but that's my aim.

After another argument, like it always is, over stupid things! We had been to Audrey's birthday party, and I realised that Rob had been drinking quite a lot and it was something really daft between me and Elliott because we were trying to put the chickens away for it was dark. Anyway, there was an argument and it got violent though Rob denies that it got violent and that he spat in my face. I just thought to myself I can't do it anymore. I know most of the tension is the stress, but he won't talk about things, about what's happened before, he won't talk to anybody about his stress levels.

I looked at the two gorgeous boys Elliott and Harvey and I thought I can't do this to them anymore and so I asked Rob if he would leave, he categorically said he fucking wouldn't leave, blar, blar, blar, not leaving, not leaving!! Even though he won't do the animals, is not interested in the garden, not interested in anything (big sigh) there's not one job finished. Over a year now since he started the bathroom and it's still not finished.

I don't know, but without going into all the little details, it was over. What's the point in carrying on, you need to go forwards not round in circles! Like Harvey said, "It's not sad, it's progress." How wise of him.

So, on the 9th of August I was guided to move on, and I would find somewhere to move to. I found somewhere a one-bedroom little place at Deb's, a friend of Sheila's. I can walk (well hobble) down to the house/farm which I do every day so that I can look after the animals. Harvey is at Lycée and Elliott back at school. It's difficult but sometimes you are forced into situations, so you find a way and by having to walk, it's about a 20–30-minute walk there and then the same back, I have got stronger, my legs have got stronger they have had to get stronger.

So, the situation now is that I am actually sat in Josie's gite because Debbie had already booked her friends to stay at her place when I moved in in August so I always knew I would have to go to Josie's. It's been nice to have a change it's really nice the garden is beautiful. Elliott stayed with me this weekend it was a change for him and peaceful. It's clean, it's tidy and it's finished a rare experience for Elliott.

I have still been going to the animals. I did walk it once from here, but it took an hour and a half, and my knees knew about it. I think I pushed myself too much that day.

Since I have left, I have had to do a lot, I have had to sort things out. Jenny has been brilliant; she has helped me, and I employ her to help me. I have also had to use taxis and pay them to get to the Grand Feu I went there 3 times in one week for driving lessons then after another week went twice for lessons and then my exam in September. I have just got to sort out some paperwork now.

I have decided to rent a car be it an expensive way to go because I need an adapted car and I can't afford much of a budget for a car.

Rob started to do the apples for a few weeks and then he got his old job back being a maintenance man. I don't know what's going to happen with the house, it's been totally ruined for me now, I have to move forward I have to find somewhere. I have put it out to the universe to find me somewhere!

Whatever Rob wants to do he can do, if I was to summarise, I know it's been difficult, but Christ I have had a lot in my head, I have had a lot to deal with and Rob just can't deal with it. It's the way he attempts to deal with it and how he treats me. When I am having a bad moment, he just makes it worse by his shouting, I can't remember him ever holding me or saying nice things to me after the accident. I know it's difficult when someone is struggling and in a bad mood and I have been. But Elliott knows how to deal with it and Harvey knows how to deal with it. You just have to let someone know that it's alright and that you care. Rob didn't know how to do that or wouldn't.

I honestly think he doesn't want to be with me anyway, but he doesn't want to look bad leaving a one-handed woman with two kids. So, I have probably done him a massive favour, but it feels as if I had to do this, I have to go forwards. I know in the Grand Feu I appreciated the time, but I have realised there are only two people really important in this world and that's Elliott and Harvey. They know what's gone on, they know everything.

I do not need to justify anything to anybody, I just need to find a way to move forwards to have a peaceful life to have a full life. To focus on the Paralympics, to focus on getting strong and with the will of God and everybody else who is helping me it will happen.

I have been very strongly led or spiritually guided that some people have to go those who have judged me not understanding the situation between me and Rob, I have got to back right off them I have lost my trust in them. They are weakening me in the sense that they are draining me.

Some people have said I have never looked after myself even after the accident. I have always been worried about the kids, Rob and the animals. Even when I spoke to my mum (it was weird three different people said it to me, you have got to look after yourself now) you are not looking after yourself was my mum's observation.

I have faith that it will be okay it's not going to be easy, it's not going to be easy at all, as in any separation, it's going to be nasty (big sigh) I just think I can't go back, I have got to keep moving on.

The first DVD series I watched when I got to my little one room Peace Pad, was 'Moving On'. You have to sometimes just move on. I am worried about Harvey and especially Elliott. I think he understands. At first, I think he thought it was his fault and then he realises that mum is not going to leave him. That's the thing, I have not left them, I just couldn't bear them being in that unhealthy environment any longer. Rob said he was quite happy for it to stay like it was, but how can you live like that? He might be able to deal with things by ignoring it, I just can't it's too tiring, it's too unsettling, I need peace and tranquillity. I need honesty!

The crazy thing was everyone was saying to me, making judgement, you have got to get rid of the animals. I know there are too many animals but it's not down to me. The two teenage pregnant pigs was because they were with males. The number of rabbits is because they were with males too. Harvey and I have tried so hard to just get it organised, it's gone mad! So now I am left with living things that need looking after. I go each day it's my job and I go no matter how much pain I am in. I don't do anything in the house, I wash and iron the boys and my clothes the best I can. I used to clean the house and I thought what am I doing, I don't live here!

I have just got to find somewhere and make a place where the boys feel comfortable and happy. I think Harvey is just feeling really lost, it's really difficult. I am trying to be upbeat and happy for them, but Harvey is stuck at the farm. I hope the lycée will distract him, he only has to put the animals away on a night and then spend some time cleaning the pigs out at the weekends. The only thing Rob did was get the food for the animals from Cavac because he is the only one driving. I have even taken that job back and pay Debbie to go once a week for the food because Rob would wait until we ran out not a good idea with winter round the corner and hungry pigs.

By November I will hopefully be driving which will make a massive difference to my life. Then Rob doesn't have to worry himself about the farm. It's bizarre he won't leave it but he doesn't want it, so I don't know what game he is playing. God talk about a year and a half (big sigh). You have got to just stay strong. People have worse things happen. I saw someone in the Grand Feu who had not got his arms or legs, I have only lost my hand and broken bones some people have way more to deal with.

I will go forwards I am just asking for guidance with the boys, if I thought there could be some resolve between Rob and I then I would do it. But he won't go to speak to anyone professionally I think he just doesn't want to be with me and maybe that's what he wanted before the accident, and it just snookered his plans. One thing that does really upset me is that on a number of occasions he has mentioned when I have asked what are we doing about selling the house, what do you want me to do. Rob said, "Well I don't know what you're worried about you are going to have some money." My response "That doesn't even enter my head to me that's blood money, my blood!!" That money (getting upset) that can never replace my right hand or give me my mobility back it can never change me being in intensive care with a gangrene hand, it can never compensate me for all that stress or sadness it could never compensate for anything, the whole family has had to suffer. I don't think about any money, but he obviously does!

We haven't even got any answer to the court case yet and we are now in October 2017. But you know I am going to conclude this by saying if everybody wants to think and that Rob wants to let them think that I have gone mad, I'm unreasonable, I have gone crazy it's down to the accident and I have changed so much let them all think what they want. I know I am not mad; I know I have suffered and I know I have had to overcome a lot of things. But you know what I won't put up with any lies and crap or anything else and if that's what's changed since the accident then that's a good thing! Because you don't have to put up with that. I definitely don't want to live with it through old age, I want peace and quiet not wondering if anybody is lying to me or I am blamed for something I didn't do. It's peace that's what I want!! Here's me saying goodnight.

20 Minutes

Hello today's my birthday the 7th of October 2017 I have been okay most of the day. But I just feel really bad at the moment (crying) and I feel you are my only friend because no one understands what I am going through. I don't want to pester people I don't want to phone people with my down times. I was doing alright I didn't really expect my sons Harvey and Elliott to remember my birthday.

Then about an hour ago Harvey came up with a card and some tomatoes that I keep forgetting to pick up that he has grown and a plant I can't carry. I really got upset when he left because as soon as he walked in the door, I asked if he had walked up and he said no and Rob brought him up and was waiting. After he left after about five minutes, I thought to myself (crying a lot) I walk everyday back and forth with this gammy leg to sort out the animals and do things for them. My own sons couldn't even walk up here to say happy birthday or spend an hour with their mother, so that how bad I must be and how they feel about me.

It's not right and what has Rob done today gone to play in a fucking petanque game, he is not even there when he is there, taking care of them, what a selfish individual. He has taken the kids, he's taken the house, he's taken the car my right hand paid for!! And he's the one who was playing around, ohh God!! (Very upset)

I am recording this because I hope it will make me feel better once, I have finished because at least I am talking to someone even if it's to myself. I really feel I should just vanish somewhere.

Harvey is doing so well he is doing all the work down there at the farm. I am trying to help him so much but if I go down at weekends it's just arguments. I will never forget what Robert fucking Mitchell has done to me, never! But he won't beat me even if the boys have to stay wherever, they can and if they don't want to stay with me that's okay.

It's now frigging awkward even with my own sons because they listen to Rob. I have spent all their lives bringing them up to be decent people and they are lovely boys but now they are turning to what Rob thinks. I have just got to let them go and get on with it there's nothing I can do about it.

I am on my own now and there are two choices I have, I either move forward or I don't go anywhere. What a birthday!!

5 Minutes

Now just two months left of 2017, like 2016 I was looking forward to it going. But as if I hadn't had enough to get through the end of 2017 had just a couple more surprises up its sleeve.

I was encouraged that things were going to get better, I had my rental car which allowed me to become more independent, be more involved in the boys' day to day lives and seeing as the weather was turning to winter it was a blessing to not to be walking everywhere.

In December Harvey began to take driving lessons at a local driving school Thime S.R. Although expensive I told him I would find a way to afford. I saw it essential for Harvey to gain some independence, to build up his self-confidence and just like my situation feel more self-reliant not depending on others. For me it was a valuable investment to his future. I had wanted him to go to my instructor in Niort, he was good, really tested you and very consistent and reliable. But the arrangements had been made for Harvey to go to Thimes S.R.

In the first week of December, I was doing the animals. Harvey was off ill for the day so was asleep in his bedroom, Rob at work and Elliott at school. I was just watering the pigs and trying to clean them when one knocked my legs from behind which made them buckle and I fell onto the concrete floor. Falling to the right due to the weakness and instability of that side which meant I could not break my fall; I hadn't got a hand. I lie for a while to get over the shock but then couldn't move without immense pain, I couldn't get up.

The pigs were getting interested in me, they probably smelt the pig food traces on my clothes. I thought I either get up and move or I get eaten by pigs!! I managed to drag myself through the straw covered floor, it was where they slept so it was clean which was a blessing and got myself up somehow onto the old feeding trough. The pigs were still interested in my wellies and trousers I knew I could not fight them off, there were too many and strong, seeing me as interesting and possibly tasty and edible. I had to get out the pain was not good, but neither was being eaten alive.

I got to the gate which I had to climb over difficult at the best of times. I was desperately shouting Harvey, but he couldn't hear me. In sheer agony I got over the metal gate, believing this would be less painful than being eaten by pigs!! I couldn't put any weight on my right at all but at least I was out of the pigs. I continued to shout now I was outside the barn Harvey eventually heard me. He helped me inside to my hospital bed downstairs and I knew I had to lie down. Lifting my right leg onto the bed was a matter of screaming out loud and doing it. Nurse Peggy out little dog jumped up to protect me and lie with me she knew there was something wrong, I was in so much pain and felt very unwell.

I asked Harvey if he could phone Mel to get me back to Peace Pad and maybe then he could go with her to get the animal food because I didn't think I would be driving for a while.

Mel and her husband Robert came and got me back to Peace Pad in my car Mel driving and then in their car went to Cavac for the animal food with Harvey. I took some paracetamol and just sat I couldn't really put weight on my right leg.

Elliott arrived back from school and was like a mother hen. The next morning, I got up and used my stick to get Elliott and myself a cup of tea and breakfast before he went for the school bus. As Elliott was having his cup of tea in bed, I was talking to him and then suddenly I fainted onto my bed. It really scared Elliott and the next thing I knew was him shaking me and shouting "Mum, mum wake up!" He wouldn't go to school that day because he didn't want me to be left alone. I think I fainted due to the level of pain I was in.

I thought to myself I am in court in two weeks and here I am in all this pain. Mel and Robert wanted me to go to the hospital, I didn't want to, I had an appointment with my main man Dr. Pietu at the end of January and also an appointment with my MSA doctor the following week I would ask him to check it out.

I was back driving after a couple of days I needed to get Elliott from school as they finished at 12:00 on Wednesdays, once I was in the car, I was alright.

The following week Jenny took me to my MSA doctor in Bressuire who examined me and said I had damaged my groin. I thought I had either totally ripped some tendons or ligaments in my groin or broken my hip. I knew how painful a bad groin strain could be from working with the rugby players but all I needed to get through now was court on Monday and then have a total rest from the animals for the two weeks over Christmas when Harvey would do them in the school holidays.

I hadn't had any contact from my solicitor at all, that's how good he was! My gut was telling me there was something wrong, so I contacted the solicitor's office where the receptionist, yes, the receptionist informed me that it had been cancelled!! So, when were they going to let me know?

I think the reason was the third expert Christopher Ledon hadn't completed the report, he had only had 8 months to do it in! The national second expert Marc Puech did his very high-quality report in a month. Remember the one that categorically stated I did not cause the accident. Christopher Ledon took so long, and you will never believe the amount of mistakes Christopher Ledon made.

Christmas was on its way I put a little tree up and had managed to get some things organised with Santa, so he left some gifts for Harvey and Elliott at Peace Pad. Elliott was spending more and more time with me even though he was off school as was Harvey. Harvey too would stay with us watching DVDs till quite late, it was as if he didn't want to go back. Now I was driving I would take him back or pick him up no problem. I think he was confused and lost, and Elliott hinted that Rob wasn't so nice to him. What could I do but keep an eye on him and give him hope, with his driving lessons and his future independence.

Also, in December Rob announced that he didn't want the house and wanted some money. I think someone had told him I was starting to look at other properties. I couldn't stay at Debbie's forever and she had told me she wanted to rent it out in the Summer.

Rob was getting scared that he would be left with the farm and all the work, and I think he had already got other plans back in the UK (remember his secretive phone). I didn't want the farm either it was physically too much for me. I didn't want this shit to carry on like it was, just going round and round in circles for years and years to come. He wanted money!

The housing market was slow, and our place needed so much doing to it to prepare it for market. Remember those boxes from Oz, well they were all still stood there. I had to take the bull by the horns, pay him off take on the work and see where things were in a year or two. By then the boys may have gone down their own life path and I could sell it then.

I wasn't happy but I knew it was the only way to move this stalemate relationship forwards and begin a new life. I could have insisted on putting it on the market but that would have meant more stress more arguments and no doubt me doing all the work.

So that was the end of 2017, dare I say it bring 2018 on it can't surely be any worse than the last couple of years! Or could it?

Chapter 31: Confirmation, Boys Get A Holiday, The Runner, A New Hospital And Back To Nantes

"There is a stubbornness about me that never can bear to be frightened at the will of others. My courage always rises at every attempt to intimidate me."

- Jane Austen

I was due to see Dr Pietu in Nantes hospital on the 31st of January 2018 my last appointment and x-rays had been in October 2017. He had indicated that at my next appointment he would check everything and if I had decided to have my dancing pole removed that would be arranged.

Mel offered to take me which was wonderful because we could have a good chat on the way there and back. As we were both from West Yorkshire talking is part of our DNA and character.

I got my x-rays done and then went to see Dr Pietu who had them on his computer. He examined my legs and hips and asked me various questions one being had I had any problems or pain? I informed him that I had after a fall, and I wasn't sure if I had damaged or totally torn my ligaments or even broken my hip.

He went back to his desk to look at the x-rays and there it was I had broken the head of my femur at the neck part, but it was healing. When I looked, I thought shit that's all I need a broken hip! It could clearly be seen that my neck of femur on my right leg was shorter than on the left femur. Now I really am going to walk like Quasimodo!

My doctor was a bit shocked and concerned I didn't dare tell him that I had been lifting 25kg bags of animal food and pushing wheelbarrows of pig poo for the last month. But he said it looked to be healing well. The only problem now was he couldn't possibly take my metal out because it was an aggressive procedure and he needed to know that the broken hip was fully repaired, so a delay was inevitable.

I had made the decision to have my metal out even though it carried no guarantees with many risks because at our last meeting in October Dr Pietu did say in years to come if I did need a hip or knee replacement then they would have to remove the metal before they could do it anyway. I thought get it done now with the surgeon I trusted and while I was relatively young and active all which aids recovery.

The date was set the 12th of September 2018 if the nerve to my femur didn't die due to my broken hip in the meantime. Great not a problem just another walk or limp in the park. Here I go again back on the block!! I told the doctor I will have my own personal block at this rate. I did have strong suspicions that I had done something bad when the pigs had knocked me down and now it was confirmed.

The pain was very bad, but I do think like muscle tissue, which I believe has some sort of memory, your pain threshold must have too. The higher the pain you have experienced before, the more you can take at a higher degree the next time. It's as if you have a memory bank in your system already prepared for the pain and in the case of muscle the demands and resistance that comes when you push yourself training.

Patience now having to be installed in me again not only for a new court date but for my operation to have the metal removed out of my right leg.

January 2018 would prove challenging; I was getting in the mindset that as soon as one thing was dealt with or moved to a different time and things were starting to seem 'normal' the universe would throw me just one more challenge. The challenge thrown to me at the end of December of Rob suddenly doing a u-turn on his need to have the house caused quite a number of challenges.

Once Rob knew I could and did walk away from his threats and attempt to control things he panicked, the only thing he really wanted was money!! To be able to walk away from the whole thing as a victim a person who had been treated so bad, left homeless without any banker's card (I had the card he had the cheque book for obvious reasons I couldn't use a cheque book with one hand). He also wanted people to believe that the boys were being manipulated to not want to see him. On and on went the things he told people that he had to endure. He needed to look good and for people to feel sorry for him it was part of his bigger plan.

One resulting challenge was getting this all sorted out legally going to a solicitor and him basically selling his share of the house to me. I asked him to make an appointment with who he wanted, and I would use the same one. He never did so I had to do all the running around and hoped he would show up. It would take until March to get it sorted and me having to pick up the solicitors fees.

I just wanted the mess over with and I knew it was money that he was interested in. Not me, not the nearly 20 years, not even the boys a thing I never thought he would do. None of our separation was their fault, why punish them? In future years his halo would slip and his true colours exposed.

I may have been imprisoned by the accident and the disabilities it gave me. But Rob had just given himself a life imprisonment and disability in his head and karma would eventually knock on his door. I did not and do not wish him ill or anybody else in my life's story what happened, happened. How I was treated only served to make me stronger.

It taught me the power of forgiveness. It is the foundation of a person's health and inner peace. It allows you to love and like yourself to be a better person and also having the tools and ability to not allow others the power to take away your inner peace and love. It's the protection you are given when the universe sees your worth and has your back.

January wasn't all bad, I was given the chance to be connected to APF, Association des Paralysés de France and an appointment was made to have a meeting on the 9th of March in Niort not far from the Grand Feu. That was great but I had to get through February first.

Part of the agreement for Rob to get his money was that he had to be out of the farm by the 9th of February 2018. I knew Debbie wanted me gone by February so she could get prepared for Easter and the summer. I would be on manoeuvres again but at least I had my car which made it easier.

I was so grateful for Peace Pad and Debbie's kindness; I always knew it was only a short term stay. But I never thought I would be heading back to the farm!

Rob didn't put any effort into moving on he just went a few minutes' walk away to stay at Helen and Norman's in the village. I was a little disappointed in them they knew the difficulties of the relationship but a few weeks later I would get a message from Helen asking what was Rob doing in her house. She had only just found out he was in her house. I didn't know, I had guessed about a year ago he had a plan, but he wasn't going to enlighten me was he? I wasn't interested in that drama, and I was too busy trying to get the house clean again.

Before Christmas I had booked Harvey and Elliott flights to go to the UK for a week in February not knowing that I would be back at the farm. I just wanted them to get away from it all, especially Harvey who had never moved away from the farm. I had managed to get them into a hotel near Kay and Denbo and they were well and truly taken care of including going to the Carvery to challenge Harvey with the Yorkshire pudding eating record that Elliott had set a few months before.

When the boys returned my dear friend Susan Deakin came back with them. She is such a wonderful friend a solid and loving person who was always at the end of a phone with support, wise words and understanding. Her friendship meant so much to me and when I had sent Kay and Dennis their roses, 'Nostalgia' and 'Simply The Best', I also sent Susan one called 'Friendship', it's a beautiful red rose. Susan only had a quick visit, just four days but boy was her timing right!

This first week back at the farm I was on my own, the boys in the UK. Rob was only a few minutes' walk away and I knew he was spying, what a weird game he was playing. I just worked hard trying to clean the house. It obviously, like his relationship with his family hadn't had much attention. His close proximity was a bit of a concern, but I thought a few days to a week and then he will move on to a new place, where I did not care. Over six weeks later he was still there! But at least in the second week Susan was there it was so comforting I had someone I could talk to and someone who really listened. When Susan left, I just threw myself into jobs and taking care of Harvey and Elliott. Slowly the animals were being brought back under control, but it was still out of hand.

At this time, I was as low as a person could get. I still had the court case, operations, pain, disability, frustration and the gossip from my so-called friends and neighbours. People love a drama and my drama got juicier with every event.

People were nosey, disguising it as concern but in reality, they were talking behind my back. I withdrew my connections with them which helped the mental game that Rob was playing. He now had to make it appear that he was the one that walked away. If he could achieve this illusion, it makes it so much easier for him to cry his sob stories and play a victim.

He needed to get their sympathy which would then make it easier for him to create a more successful smear campaign against me and to discredit my character. He encouraged and allowed people to think I had and was still doing this, that and all these things so he had to leave.

I wasn't in a good place I shouted a lot, cried a lot, was frustrated most of the day and Rob just kept feeding the fire making me defend myself more. I wasn't just coping with my mental and physical anguish, but I was being bullied by Rob and the police. I also wasn't believed by a non-English speaking solicitor and being accused of double murder!!

At times I sat in very dark places but were the boys and my true friends would try and give me a light and a strong helping hand to hold onto, Rob made my world darker, more frustrating and he did it with this strange smirk on his face. I ask you who really had the mental problem in this failed relationship. The runner was planning his course of escape, but as Bob Marley's song 'Running Away' says "Ya running and ya running and ya running away but you can't run away from yourself".

In Niort my meeting with APF arrived and I was curious to know what it was all about. At this meeting I met people who would help me get my life back to some sort of function if I choose to allow them to assist me. They were all so caring and supportive, a wonderful company of people that helped so many disabled individuals,

I was lucky to be offered and be given this support.

The main people I would be involved with included Emeline Mallereau the Ergotherapeute who would help me with the practical everyday things. Anne Leroy assistant de service social, she patiently helped me with paperwork which was constant and Nadege Cholet the best psychologist ever.

I had seen three psychologists before who were little help. The last one I saw Sebastien-Marie Nicolas a psychologist in Niort supplied be my Allianz insurance company, and like the solicitor they gave me he would ignore me and didn't listen. I was just a source of good money from the insurance company not a person in need of help, to be listened to and be given his actual attention.

On my last appointment we got disturbed twice by phone calls, he left me waiting 10 minutes into my appointment time and he was working on his computer that he was sat in front of. I was on a chair opposite him and his computer. He asked what I would like to talk about with his eyes fixated on the computer screen. I began to talk (he could speak English). Without looking at me he kept saying "Mumme mumme". I just stopped talking but he kept saying mumme. Then he realised, eventually that I wasn't talking. "Oh you have nothing to say?" My reply "What's the point when you are not even listening and playing on your computer." His excuse was that he was looking at my file and taking notes which obviously affects his hearing because he kept saying mumme even after I stopped talking. I told him "I would not be coming back it takes me 40 minutes to get here and 40 minutes to get back home. When I set off, I am in a good place and after 15 minutes with you I feel ignored, worthless, insignificant, a meal ticket and fucking depressed!"

When your shrink can't be bothered to listen to you, that really fucks you up and makes your already low self-esteem non-existent! And they are supposed to be the professionally trained ones. A good hour and a cup of tea with the remaining true friends I had served my mental health far better than he did, he made me feel worse.

Not Nadege, she was fantastic, she was so caring and actually knew about my situation. She sat at my kitchen table with a cuppa and listened! She even spent time with the boys, making sure they were okay too. They not only had lost the life they had once known and the mother replaced with a struggling, hurting, emotionally battered disabled person but also the fact that the person who should have been there for them had just pissed off! In the six and a half weeks he lived a few minutes away, he never took them anywhere or spent any time with them. No sorry maybe ten minutes. He was too busy going round to people's houses having alcohol and meals so he could get his ego polished and perform his play of being the victim.

Also, from APF I was helped by Claudia Caillard animatrice sociale in charge of my social well-being and social activities. At the first meeting they were all introduced to me and their aims and the assistances that they could offer me. At this meeting in March 2018, I said to Claudia "Well I have got a challenge for you I want you to help me get to the Paris Paralympics in 2024, are you up for it?" A shocked expression but sure she was up for it.

On that day some beautiful and caring relationships were begun. I no longer felt alone, abandoned by society, cast aside and judged because I had been in the wrong place at the wrong time two years before, I felt supported and that I mattered! They now without judgement took my hand and guided me forwards in a slow, gentle and loving way.

It was now June 2018 and Harvey was still having his driving lessons, but he didn't seem confident, the lessons being sporadic and often changed or cancelled. I was throwing good money after bad, and I asked if he would change and go to my instructor Thierry Rimbault. He said he preferred to stay where he was, I said okay but you need to find out when your test is, remember you need to be driving before September because I have my operation then.

Rob had left the village towards the end of March 2018 once he had his money. The only thing he asked for was his welder, his dart board and his petanque boules.

There were a number of incidents in the village before Rob left and I just thought you can all go to hell; you can hang out with Saint Rob! By treating me how you are, you are not only judging me, but you are turning your backs on two young men that probably could have done with some outside support. No one came near us while Rob was around and then expected to say hi and worm their way back into our lives once he left. Go forth and multiply was my motto you will realise one day that you backed the wrong horse. I was half expecting the village to club together and erect a statue of Saint Rob to place in the middle of the village, he was seen as such a hero!

Harvey's driving exam was booked for the 14th of June. I had been in the car with him a couple of times and I had already decided to book him a few lessons with my man in Niort even if he did pass, he just didn't have the confidence, he should have had after all the lessons he had taken. Thierry Rimbault was on par with my excellent driving instructor Betty who had taught me all those years ago. I wanted Harvey to be taught well, for there are so many bad drivers around and some that shouldn't even be behind a wheel, as I know only too well to my cost!!

He failed his test and informed me that the other girl who went with him from the same school was taking it for the third time and still failed. I said Harvey you have got crap instructors let's get you booked in at Niort we need you driving before my operation which is only a few months away.

Prison Or The Paralympics

This next event just went to show me that this company was more concerned about the money they made than producing good safe and well instructed drivers. We had to go to the school to get Harvey's paperwork. She had not given him any feedback about why he had failed and didn't seem that particularly bothered. She was annoyed that we were going elsewhere, and she refused to give him his documents until I paid her 250 euros. She was a bit of a bitch. So, I asked her why the lessons hadn't been consistent and various other questions. She tried to say, "Well it's different in France" (a normal bullshit statement when you challenge anyone). I said, "No it isn't, I have just had driving lessons and I knew exactly how many and when my lessons were." Anyway, she got a cheque and we left.

We managed to get Harvey an assessment lesson in Niort on the 23rd of June and booked some lessons in July before everyone had their three weeks August holidays. Thierry knew the importance of getting Harvey passed before September and he manages to get Harvey an exam date for the 25th of August, a thing the other school had said was impossible to do.

After his assessment drive Harvey said he had learnt more in that hour than he had in all the months with the other school, that summed them up really.

A few days later from Harvey's assessment lesson on the 25$^{th\,of}$ June it was my court date, but it had been cancelled again! I think because the third expert Ledon still hadn't finished his report. It was now moved to the 16th of November 2018.

We are now in July; the weather was hot, and I was feeling quite tired with the heat. I asked Harvey if he could do all the animals for a few days so I could rest. Elliott said I should go to the doctors, but I spent so much time with doctors I didn't want to bother my lovely doctor Dineu. I just rested more, out of the heat.

Harvey had a lesson on the 12th of July, I would take him wait in the car and then drive back so a good three and a half hours in Niort. As I waited in the car in Niort that morning, I felt really unwell and thought maybe I should make an appointment to see the doctor. I rang and the receptionist said I could go that morning. I explained I was in Niort, and it wasn't possible was there anything this evening?

That evening I set off to the doctors she took my blood pressure and temperature. Dr. Dineu said I needed to go home and wait for the ambulance, I needed to go straight to casualty! "No, no" I said bursting into tears "Not the hospital, please don't send me to hospital." She said, "If you don't go you have to promise me you will call the ambulance if you get worse and I want to see you tomorrow."

A voice in my head said just go to the hospital! So, I agreed, went home and started to pack a bag and sort out things giving instructions to the boys. When the ambulance men arrived, I shouted just a minute I will be with you soon. I really didn't have time for this.

One of the guys was the driver who had taken me to the Grand Feu for my driving lessons and exam and the one who had cut me out of my car. He said, "What have you done now?" I said, "I don't know."

As we drove the 40 minutes journey to Niort hospital, I started to feel bad and sick, he had the monitor on me and said something to the driver who then put the blue flashing lights on.

They got me to casualty, and he was telling me that England was playing in the football world cup semi-final tonight. I didn't have a clue. As they left me with the staff in casualty he said to the person "Take great care of her for me please!" which touched my heart.

I was then wired up to machines and left for hours not knowing anything. I wanted to know what was wrong I didn't feel well but I thought it was the stresses of the previous couple of years that was catching up with my body, I just needing a rest and peace.

Eventually I was taken to a room and told I would be staying the night. I was put in a shared room that already had an elderly French lady in the other bed. She was not impressed that I was in the room and made it quite clear she wasn't happy. I daren't breathe or move all night.

The next morning, I was given hot chocolate and a croissant. Having spent that long in hospital before I knew this was a good sign. They don't feed you if they are going to operate on you, I was relieved. I was then sent for a scan and sent through a big tunnel thing, the first time for me.

Around dinnertime a female doctor called Dr. Jouan came to see me. She announced that she wanted me to get into the shower with this special washing stuff, the nurse would come and shave me, and I would be operated on. My reaction was "Wow, wow, no, no, look I am booked in on the 12th of September to have an operation for my metal to be taken out of my leg, I'll come back after that." I pleaded I wanted to get the metal out of my leg I didn't have time for this operation whatever it was for. The doctor said, "If you don't have the operation today you will be dead and won't need the other operation." Well, that was straight to the point!

So, I got into the shower much to the horror and objection from my roommate and off I went again on the journey of unknown outcomes. Different hospital, different staff but the same fear and the same feeling of shitting myself.

I don't know how long I was on the operating table, the block but what they did was cut me open from the top to the bottom of my stomach, take out my large intestines put them to one side to get to 10cm of my small intestines that were black and green.

Then put it all back and that was that. Easy right? I also got my appendix removed while they were digging around, there was nothing wrong with them, but it was normal procedure to take it out anyway (maybe there was a market for healthy appendixes somewhere, just saying!).

I was now stuck in bed again. Your stomach muscles are used in most basic movements. My abdominals, the ones I had got ripped and defined for my UK bodybuilding final, were now cut wide open and had God knows how many stitches. It was painful, uncomfortable, and very restricting.

I remember thinking the previous night as I lay being monitored in casualty yet again, that this was not right, how many bloody challenges do they want me to pass? I was starting to get fed up with all this shit! Hadn't I proved myself enough to these powers that be? Could they not give me a break, a time out, a bloody bit of good luck and hope in my life?

The words had stuck in my mind what my ambulance mate had said "Take care of her." Then I remembered him telling me that England was playing in the semi-final that night and if they beat Croatia they would be in the final with France. This pissed me off because I was alone again in casualty, where was my fucking partner of nearly 20 years? In the pub playing the victim, splashing the money around that he had taken from the family, watching his beloved football in the World Cup semi-final. I wouldn't be surprised if he hadn't planned his arrival in the UK with that in mind. I prayed that England would lose! Somehow it did not feel fair.

I spent ten days in hospital, the doctor not prepared to let me go until my drip and drain was out. I had had a poo (remember they are obsessed with that in hospital!!) but at least this time I could carefully get to the toilet in my room and didn't have to go through the drama of bedpans again.

I realised I couldn't do a thing and if I bust these stitches open that would really set me back. I needed to be good enough for my operation in September to take place in Nantes in about a couple of months from now.

On the 15th of July at 2:35 I paid four euros to watch the football final in my hospital bed on my hospital TV. France v Croatia, result France 4 Croatia 2.

Harvey and Elliott had held the fort while I was in hospital a show of their characters and strength. My wonderful earth angel Marie helped them out a lot because Harvey was still not driving, and I think Mel had even taken him to Niort for some of his driving lessons.

Once I returned home, I had no choice but to be back driving and with the corset I had bought while in hospital I could manage but I didn't lift or do a thing. I wanted to get the okay for my operation in September.

I had nurses coming to dress my scar and to check on me. I also had an appointment with Dr. Jouan on the 24th of August and I was hoping she would give me permission for my operation at Nantes hospital to go ahead.

A few days before on the 22nd of August I had had my pre-operation visit at Nantes with the anaesthetist, one I hadn't had before but I requested my little pink tablet under my tongue. I had already seen Dr Pietu who said he was happy to do the operation after my intestine operation if the anaesthetist was okay with going ahead. I think Dr Pietu must have thought what's with this patient, last time I saw her in January she came with a broken hip and now she's had a major operation on her small intestines. I asked him if he thought I had that disease of needing to have operations the Munchausen syndrome, he just laughed. But I was starting to think I was heading for the Guinness book of records for surgical procedures!

The anaesthetist was okay to go ahead so all I needed now was Dr. Jouan's approval and then I could look forward to yet another risky operation. My theory if I could get this operation over and done with, I could then rest both areas and just get to the end of another interesting and challenging year.

My training again put on hold and now my core was totally buggered as well as the rest of me. On the 24th Dr. Jouan said she was happy for me to have the operation is September, okay bring it on.

What a busy week and on the 25th I took Harvey to the place he would take his driving test. I waited for his return. My ace instructor was with him, on their return he announced he had passed with flying colours. Great, wonderful I was so pleased for him and the family, a bit of good news at last.

I was booked in the Nantes hospital from the 12th to the 16th of September. I arranged the taxi to take me and to pick me back up. Harvey and Elliott were back at lycée, Elliott starting his first year of woodwork at the same lycée as Harvey which made things easier for them. Harvey was driving so he would take them to the school bus, park his car up and return later in the day. Again, they would have to hold the fort while I went for my operation. We all just had to get on with it. At some point, at some time in the future our lives had to get easier, but I had thought that before.

I arrived at Nantes hospital by ambulance-taxi, not the helicopter this time, which was a good thing, it was the 12th of September 2018 over two years after my first visit.

I was in a shared room, I think the lady had had a hip operation, she was nice we chatted a bit. I was prepared the next day and off I went on that scary trip that I had grown to know so well but I had my best friend with me, my little under the tongue pink tablet. I knew this was a big operation, but I had Dr Pietu and that filled me up with confidence and a certain amount of calmness.

Prison Or The Paralympics

The effect of what seems a never-ending journey, staring up at the lights flashing past up above in the high hospital ceilings as you were pushed on your bed to the block, was always petrifying. My only distraction was trying to make conversation with the person pushing me.

At the bus station (the waiting area) the usual happened, questions asked, and the line put in. As I waited, having a word with my team who had watched over me in the car and had never left my side over the last couple of years, a young boy was pushed into the area. He was about nine or ten years old, his parents by his side. Seeing him gave me strength, at least I was an adult, how must all this feel at his age? I sent him strength and love and asked my team if they could keep an eye on him too.

I was back in recovery and the usual fears and feelings of being disconnected were there. I just had to wait for the reconnection of my soul and spirit back into my earthly vehicle, my body and mind. I was eventually taken back to the room the other lady was still there. I slept for the rest of the day, I had no clue how long I had been operated on or what time it was I believed it was still the 13th of September.

The next day was like going back in time, same routine, same looking room, same colour of paint on the walls, same noises and smells and even some of the same nurses who were so lovely, and it was great to see them again. The one big difference was that I didn't need a bedpan, I could actually get out of bed, be it painful and needing a stick.

Beforehand Dr Pietu came to see me and wanted to know what I was doing about a prosthesis for Stubby. He had arranged for someone to come and talk to me. I had given up on the idea of the robotic hand I wasn't ready for it and in some ways, it wasn't so practical for me, it couldn't get wet or really go outside, no good for mucking out the pigs then!

Two people came, one guy who had been one of the group who came to see my hand way back in ICU in April 2016 before the decision was made to remove my gangrenous, dying hand. Dr. Pietu had explained that to get a prosthesis, just a normal one not even robotic, those flesh looking ones. (If I was going to have one of them it would have to be bright orange or tattooed so I wouldn't get those looks off people 'Is it or isn't it?' we all, do it.) Dr. Pietu had said I would have to have another operation and some of Stubby chopped off because it was too long for a prosthesis to work properly.

No way was I going to put Stubby through that, not because I didn't trust the doctor or the need to do it but because I had become attached to Stubby. He had become my friend; we had been through a lot together I didn't want to lose him. He was doing good, working hard, still a bit skinny and his skin baggy but he was less painful and could now carry a half full watering can. No, I would not put him through an operation.

I explained this to the two visitors, the woman watching me closely as I was talking away. Stubby was joining in, a thing he did naturally, he wasn't going to hang lifeless by my side. He had been accepted from day one and now he was finding his feet and expressing himself after all he was Yorkshire.

The lady made a comment "Look how much you use your arm when you talk." My response "He's called Stubby, that's his name." Then me, Stubby and I went on to explain the importance of acceptance and love to anyone's amputation. It's vital that there is a strong connection to the person and the rest of the body if pain is going to subside, function regained, or a bond made.

They were happy and impressed with our attitude and said if I ever changed my mind about the prosthesis I knew where they were. Thank you I am so grateful for that.

My aim was for Stubby to be able to pump iron, lift weights not to be hidden behind a plastic hand and arm. We had things to do and places to go didn't we Stubby?

My roommate left on Saturday morning and so I was left with my thoughts, lying in a position I knew all too well, in an environment that had been my world for over six weeks. In a world of pain, anguish, confusion, acceptance, healing and caring. I was in trauma/orthopaedics again, different room not number 56 but the same noises, smells, colour of paint on the walls with my bed even facing the same way, I could hear the helicopter but not see it as I could when I was in plastics, it was Saturday afternoon the weekends always being quieter than through the week.

I was feeling tired and lay there in the deafening silence my mind drifting back in time. I was transported back to April 2016 as I lay in the very same hospital, I had laid in unable to move, paralysed and helpless. I could hear the helicopter in the distance, it had been a busy day for the pilots, but I am sure there are many not just one helicopter.

Then I heard a familiar sound, a sound of a motorbike that I had heard every morning and afternoon in April 2016. In 2016 it got to the point where I waited for it so I could get an approximate time of day. Here it was again that very distinctive motorbike noise, it freaked me out a bit.

I closed my eyes and tried to rest, then I heard the helicopter noise and it seemed louder than ever but this time I was in it. My eyes closed my breathing not good and then I saw it all a person in front slumped over the driving wheel, the car weaving an arm reaching over to hold the wheel by the other person in the car. I had to get out of this dangerous situation, I had to get to a safe place. By now I had tears rolling down my cheeks, couldn't get my breath and was really panicky and scared.

From my hospital bed I buzzed for help. I was not feeling well I had just had a very vivid flashback to an event that was still buried deep inside my psyche, mind, brain and memory.

I was not good, I was sweating, crying, hyperventilating and shaking uncontrollably. My logic mind trying to intervene "Calm yourself you are safe, you are in hospital, it's not happening to you again, you are safe now!" I say logic mind but looking back now it was more a voice, a guidance that became stronger and stronger as the months and years after the accident continued to deliver a whole load of cruelty and lies.

The nurses came in one of them being the one who had helped me so much in 2016 when I was so ill with diarrhoea. She was one of my guardian angels, the one who gave me my first kiwi fruit and pineapple juice which allowed me to slowly recover from all the cruel medication I had been given to make me poo. Then she understood and could see the situation, she fed me back to health. Now with the other nurse she was so concerned and caring.

The two nurses looked concerned when they saw the anguish and stress, I was in. I managed to express the need for a pen and paper, I had just remembered what had happened and what I saw at the accident, and I needed to try and see if I could somehow write it down with my left hand. Writing was not easy for me as I had never done it with my left hand before, but I needed to get it down I hadn't got my dicta-phone, so this was the only way.

When I finished, I was exhausted. It felt to be in the evening but the nurses who came back to check on me said it was late afternoon. One nurse asked if I needed some medication to help me calm down, I said no thanks I will try and sleep, I feel a sort of relief that I have remembered what happened.

It was planned that I would go home on the Saturday but there was some question because of the drain on my leg so I had to stay another night. I just wanted to get home, I didn't like the memories this place brought me. It was a place that saved my life but also the place that brought all my nightmares back. I felt suffocated, fearful and trapped. I needed to leave and go home.

I now had two things to deal with the small intestines operation, which was very limiting, plus a painful, swollen, stitched up leg that complicated matters! Me and the boys had to get through it I knew it was essential that I did nothing for the first two weeks, risking an infection or bursting open my wounds was really not an option. That would make me out of action for longer and not help the boys. I really had to be good and not do a single thing that could slow my recovery.

I was due back at Nantes hospital on the 28th of September to let Dr. Pietu see how I was healing; I would try and be good at least till after then.

By the middle of October, I could do so much more but avoiding any heavy stuff. I had told myself that I needed to get to the end of 2018 to allow my strength to come back and lay low in the winter so I could get on with my plan to start training in 2019. But before that I had that 'little' thing the court case on the 16th of November.

I found out that it was cancelled again because it was noticed that the whole report by Ledon had been done using the wrong car! Yes, you heard me correctly, he had calculated everything using two left hand drive cars, I was in an English right hand drive car. How could such a major mistake be made?

I now had alarm bells ringing where are they getting these 'experts' from? I am being charged with double murder here! Eventually when I started to do my own investigating the things, I revealed on the first report by Maurice Pascal and the third report by Christophe Ledon, left me in no doubt that there was some cover up, corruption, you name it what you will, but it certainly was manipulated to try and fit the story that had been told. But karma will sneak up and bite their arses, I am sure of that! Now the new court date was the 15th of April 2019.

I did a recording on the 31st of December 2018, here it is:

It is the 31st of December 2018, I have just listened to my last recording which was my birthday the 7th of October 2017. It's been a long time since I have recorded anything for a number of reasons. The last recording was stressful, it was after a very difficult time I had only just left the farm in August. I was living in a one-bedroom place, I wasn't driving, I was just alone. Life was difficult.

As the last recording said Harvey came up for 10 minutes for my birthday. It put me in a bad place because I just felt all alone but looking back I had to go through that. I had to go through that pain and that stress, I had to! Look how wonderful the boys are now, we were all in a very difficult situation.

I will go through the situation as it is now as quickly as possible and stage by stage. At Christmas 2017 Rob was playing the game of not doing anything and saying blarr, blarr, blarr, threatening to not pay bills, threatening to do this and to do that, whatever! Elliott basically moved in with me and just went down to the farm on Saturdays. I was driving by November so I could help the boys more, so they didn't have to ask Rob who wasn't a willing helper anyway. Also, at the end of October into November Elliott and I went to the UK.

In December 2017 I fell and broke my right hip fortunately it was the Christmas holidays, so Harvey took up the work with the animals. I didn't go to the hospital because I had an appointment with my specialist at the end of January. The x-rays confirmed my hip was broken and the operation to have my dancing pole out had to be delayed.

Before the new year I had managed to get Rob to talk with the help of Helen and Norman where Rob announced that he no longer wanted the farmhouse even though I had offered him the house without taking any money as long as he put the boys' names on the deeds. His response to that offer given in August 2017 was he wouldn't fucking do that!

I didn't want the house, I wanted to move and get a smaller house to adapt it for my disabilities. But at this 'meeting', which wasn't very pleasant, he asked for money, and he said he didn't want the house. I said I didn't want the house either. To be honest I just needed it to be over.

I ended up doing all the running around because Rob wouldn't. I organised the solicitor hoping he would show up. I was still paying the bills at the house even though I hadn't been there since August. I told him he had to get a new bank account it made sense for me to keep the old one where the house bills were paid from, and that he no longer could have the chequebook because he was no longer putting anything into the account. This sent him into craziness, and he got very angry. If he wanted money, he had to get a job not live of his disabled partner that he had rejected and spat at six months before!

To cut a long story short it was arranged that on February the 9th 2018 he would leave the house. He did leave and I moved in on the Sunday, I had arranged for the boys to go to England to stay near Kay and Denbo and to also see Peter and Susan. I had booked them into a small hotel in Ossett.

I could see Harvey was really, really stressed he wasn't talking to Rob, he had lived with him and done all the work, he needed the hell out of there. I booked this long before I knew I was moving back into the house.

When Rob left on the 9th, he walked a few minutes to Norman and Helen's and stayed there. Apparently, he told them he would stay there for three days but stayed for six and a half weeks, which was not good for me.

He got the money that he demanded and the car, the only thing he asked for out of the house was his petanque boules, his dartboard, and his welding machine. That says a lot, no photos or anything to do with the boys that was it. In the six and a half weeks he had spent probably 10, maybe 20 minutes with the boys, well Elliott really. He never picked them up from school, never took them out, never had them round at Norman and Helen's but spent most of his time with his ego polishers, people in the village also with ex-friends of mine, well so called friends, Claire, Steven, Dave, Kathy, Sharon, and Phil. He also went for a meal at Alex and Kelly's, but Kelly always kept in touch with me, not really taking in and believing the stories he was telling. So, all these people he went to have meals with, went out with, drank with but didn't have time for the boys.

The night before he left the village a Saturday he went out, (he left the Sunday or Monday), he was out in the new pub with Sharon and Phil not with the boys or had even seen them that day. Before during these six and a half weeks he asked Elliott if he wanted to go to Claire and Steven's, but he didn't want to be with anybody else he wanted a one to one with Rob. He didn't want to be babysitting while he watched him drink, talking about his mum with people.

It was hell, it was hell to think that everybody was talking and gossiping I withdrew and didn't speak to anybody except Mel and my good friends in England. I kept a low profile and cut myself off from these people.

After he had got his money about a few days before he left, I took his welder round and tried the house, but he wasn't there. The car was open, so I put the welder in there. I told Harvey who had carried it round for me that Rob would probably be at Marc's so I will let him know that it's in the car so he can lock the car later. "You go back I won't be long." I said to Harvey.

When I got to Marc's Rob is sat there having an apero (the French tradition of drinking and talking with friends and family). Also, there was Eric and Michele who I no longer spoke to because of their treatment of me and the boys and their gossiping. I knocked at the door Martine answered. I didn't go in I just gave the message to Martine and asked her to pass it on to Rob, she was especially friendly with Rob they had drove to work together. As I turned to leave, it wasn't yet dark, Martine shut the electric shutters. Now you might say I was a bit stupid in how I reacted but bear in mind where I am at this point in my life. There was so much gossip and lying going on I was very defensive and protective of the boys. This action felt so dismissive, like swatting an annoying fly it felt so "Just go away we are with Saint Rob." So, I turned and re-knocked on the door and said, "Martine I am not interested in what you are doing I don't want to listen or be part of your cosy group." She said, "I didn't shut them because of you" I said, "Well you haven't shut the other ones." and then she dismissed me with her hand like she was shooing a dog away. So that was it I went into the house and told them all to basically fuck off I told Eric and Michele to go to hell and never to speak to me again. Rob then joined in, and his halo slipped and he 'F'ed and blinded at me he was very aggressive. I said "Why are you still here? You have got your money why don't you fuck off?" I also said, "Why aren't the boys speaking to you?" he said, "Well someone's influenced that" I said "Really I want you to have a good relationship with them." Michelle and Eric had things to say I responded to their bullshit and left.

Prison Or The Paralympics

So that was that. I don't speak to any of the previous people who I used to speak to in the village. It's the only way I can survive and get away from their gossip and false friendships. They have really shown their true colours who needs people like them in your life?

So that gets us to March, Rob buggered off. We still have no contact with him, we don't know where he is or if he is still in France. I don't know why he is taking it out on the boys.

On the Sunday before he left, he requested by text that they go round to see him. Elliott was ten minutes Harvey wanted to talk to him. When Harvey returned after some time he was as white as a ghost I was concerned about him. I said, "Harvey I am really sorry you feel like this, you don't have to tell me anything, I just want you to know I am here to support you."

He said "I now know how not to treat people, don't I? I have been shown how not to be, it was just a load of bullshit and lies, he has just lied to me!" I said "Well" Harvey interrupted me and said, "I will never speak to him again!" I said, "Never is a long time Harvey".

So, I picked the pieces up or tried to and just hope I can take the pressure off Harvey and get organised more at the farm. Harvey and Elliott will be at the same college in September and Elliott will finish at school a place he doesn't like going to by June and then the summer holidays so they can be more relaxed and rest.

So, we were slowly starting to get more organised and then boom! In June we had some baby pigs because nothing was organised to prevent it so that had to be dealt with but slowly, we are dealing with that be it hard work. Then in July I was rushed into hospital for another operation to have 10cm of my small intestines cut away because it was twisted and black and green, they also took my appendix out. That was a shock to my system, a big operation it took me a long time to recover because they basically cut my stomach open.

I was in hospital about ten days but couldn't do anything when I came out. Nobody knew except Mel and Robert and Chris and Marie. None of the village knew, I didn't need them I wasn't going to have anything to do with them, they let me and the boys down badly. I won't rely on them ever again.

It was really bad I didn't want to bust these stitches open. I asked Harvey if he could just cover until he goes back in September. Elliott would be at the same Lycée doing his joinery course (which he loves). Harvey passed his driving test with a different driving school in August.

I went back to my specialist in Nantes, and he said there was no problem to do the operation if the anaesthetist said it was okay so soon after a major operation. It was agreed I would go in on September the 12th. I went back to Nantes hospital and had my metal taken out of my right leg all went fine.

Then on the Saturday I had a really bad time because everything came back. The room looked the same, the colour on the walls, the smells, the helicopter again and I could even hear a motorbike that used to come when I was bedridden in the hospital for over six weeks. It was horrendous I had flash backs, so I was in a real state. I asked the nurse if she would bring me a pen and paper. I sat there and wrote what I remembered.

My memory was I came upon this car (getting upset) and it was slowing down but I had no indication it was slowing down because there were no brake lights on. It was weaving and not driving correctly. I had to make a quick decision to get to safety. I saw a person slumped at the wheel and another person's hand holding the steering wheel. There was a big problem in that car. Then all I remembered after that was a big bang spinning, white light and saying I am not going, I am not going because I have got my boys to look after. I heard lots and lots of noise, shouting noises and looking for my hand, looking, looking for my hand.

I had just remembered the horror of the accident I was in such a state. After I tried with my left hand to write it all down.

I came home late Sunday afternoon. I was so relieved to have remembered I wanted to know what had happened. The court case has been cancelled again! It's not now until 2019 but I am relieved that I know what happened. They can pass their judgement that it's all my fault, I've been blamed from day one anyway. In my heart and my soul, in my being I know I didn't cause that accident. So that is judgement enough for me.

So now in September I am laid up again with the knee and leg after the operation. Because of my circumstances I had to get on with things as carefully as I could. The stomach was still healing, and I had to be aware of getting an infection, so I had to be slow and careful.

Into October it's funny the boys forgot my birthday again, but it didn't bother me, not like the last year did, I feel as a trio we are happier. I know they have gone through hell and back and things were difficult, I was not easy company with all that has been thrown at me. They had to watch a very unhealthy relationship. Rob continued to lie, be secretive and bullying. He never once embraced me or sat with me, and he never once reassured me that things were going to be okay.

When I was in the hospital in September, I laid there thinking and realisations came to me. I thought wait a minute I was rushed here in a helicopter; with really grave injuries it was 50/50 if I would even make it. Rob didn't even know if I would survive, and he didn't even come. He sent Claire and Steven because he said he had to stay with the boys in case he had to tell them the bad news.

I thought to myself no one would have stopped me being at Rob's side. Nobody would have stopped me being with my partner and at their side on their deathbed. My partner of many years just left me to die on my own. I don't know any other couples where one of them would not have been at their partner's bedside.

I accept that some people can't deal with things, but I believe 99% of people would have been at their dying partner's hospital bedside. Rob couldn't or wouldn't. Claiming to be there for the boys was just an excuse as time would confirm.

Rob did cheer up when he got his money, you will all be pleased to hear. I wish he had been more honest for the boy's sake more than anything. I didn't expect him to stay with me for I was now 80% handicapped, not if he didn't want to.

I am glad for him whatever he is doing or wherever he is. I am free from all his baggage and crap. I know it will be difficult for the boys and me, but we won't be manipulated, judged or harassed by others. It's just us now and that's a good thing. We had a good Christmas, and I can't kid you I am over this year, it's been a rough, rough year.

I think mankind shouldn't be called mankind, it's mancruel, it really is mancruel! I need to move forward and just be quiet and I accept that people are that way because of the way the world has gone. The main thing is Elliott and Harvey's smiling face and enjoyment.

I know I am going through the mill, and I have had trauma after trauma. It's funny the pompiers came just before the New Year to sell me a calendar a thing they do every year. The girl who came was at my accident and she said her team had the job to go and look for my hand and they couldn't find it. I was, she said screaming about my hand and that it was gone, there was blood everywhere, you were aware, you were looking for your hand. They couldn't find my hand. A guy went to have a pee and found my hand (laughing) you have to laugh, so my hand got peed on basically.

I don't know, the future has got to be good. We are here, we are on this planet no matter what anybody says we are on this planet for a reason. We have just got to let that reason be revealed to us. I hope to go forwards, I hope to be busy. I am withdrawing myself from main society, because I don't like how mankind, mancruel, has gone.

I have had fifty dahlias delivered, I am going to concentrate on simple things, grow things, have minimum animals that are organised not running everywhere. I want to just prepare for the Paralympics. That's something I have still to do, my body is battered it needs repairing, it needs strength, it needs training!

Compared to the last conversation on this dicta-phone I feel it's been a year of horrendousness but a year without the lies, without the demoralisation, without the bullying, without the gossip, (well sort of) without the nastiness, without the unknown and without the dishonesty from a partner.

It enables you to cope better when you know someone isn't going to kick you in your head just because you are down. That's how it was for the first few years, and I really believe Rob has built himself a massive prison, he has imprisoned his mind. He may be jolly and sat drinking with his 'friends'. He may have watched the world football cup in England or wherever he is. He may be the man around town, he may have money in his pocket and may not even have any stress. But deep, deep in his soul he knows that he has not been good or honest. The consequences of his actions may not come towards him until later in life. But I am not wishing that for him or making a judgement that's the universe's job, for the universe will always deliver what it feels is right, what it feels is just for any individual's actions.

It is a shame Rob didn't have the balls to do more. I know I would never have let him down. I would have argued back with him, and he may have been a nicer patient. Or he may not have had the will to have done what I had done. He may have stayed in his bed and stayed in his wheelchair because I feel he is quite a weak person. They say if you still have hate or anger with someone you still love them. I have no feelings for him, as long as the boys are alright. If they ever want to visit him, if he ever contacts them! If the boys want to, I will support whatever they want to do. But me personally I have no anger I've moved on. I was just fed up of being trampled on and probably Rob didn't even think he was doing it! If he doesn't contact Elliott next week on his birthday we will know, won't we? We will see.

So, here's saying a Happy New Year to you all. May the gods, the angels and the forces that be, guide my life and the boy's life and all the people around me I care about, please take care of us. Love them guide them and protect them. Bring on the New Year in a wonderful way. Give us opportunities, give us choices, give us health, give us peace and energy. I am looking forward to a New Year. Bye for now.

26 Minutes

It seems I always have so much optimism for a new year. After getting through the trials and tribulations of the one I was leaving behind. As the previous couple of years had not failed in sending me one or two challenges 2019 would not fail to disappoint. The universe continued to throw me some curve balls, some I could catch and run forwards with, others I couldn't, and I knocked on and got trampled by my team who had a different victory in sight, the one I wasn't told about in the brief 'team' talk! Now I would have to play the game on my own, just me and Stubby.

Chapter 32: The Gifts From APF And Thrown To The Lions

"Unthinking respect for authority is the greatest enemy of the truth."

- Albert Einstein

January and February 2019 passed quick with not too many things going on. I still needed to get stronger both in my core and my legs. I was still careful how I moved and what I did and lifted.

The operation that cut open my abdomen being a challenge to recover from a cough or a sneeze could be a dangerous thing. The winter always brought a respite from the many outside jobs and I was grateful for that, and that Harvey was driving.

March was a busy month I had so many appointments. All my wonderful team from APF Association des Paralysés de France, contributed immensely to me moving forwards. They were pointing me in the right direction putting me on the right path. Even going with me to start my dream of being back hitting the weights, helping me to get that up and running.

Also, in March I had the usual, rushed non-English speaking meeting with my solicitor on the 23rd of March with Riposseau in Bressuire, where I found out that he had not sent my memory of the accident. I had this memory in Nantes hospital back in September 2018. He hadn't sent it to the court even though he had it in October 2018. I didn't really get a reason why it hadn't been sent. I was not happy the alarm bells were going off again! What was his game?

The court date was less than a month away on the 15th of April, that's if it didn't get cancelled for a fourth time. The 'little' problem of Christophe Ledon, the third expert putting the wrong car in for his calculations didn't seem to matter according to Ledon. He didn't even change the photos showing a righthand car and just left two lefthand cars in his 'expert' report's calculations!!

Now I am no expert but to me if you are driving a righthanded car oppose to a lefthanded car doesn't your whole field of vision and how it is presented differ isn't it different? Or I'm not getting something here?

The so called 'expert' Ledon did however suddenly add a paragraph saying that there must have been a third car involved. Why not make it up as you go along! Others seem to use that method of investigation. What about a UFO? Or Star ship Enterprise (Star Trek) beaming me up with Scotty?

Now I was really pissed off. I spent every minute I could analysing these three expert reports even though they were all in French. My basic human rights clearly stating it was my right to have the information in my native tongue which was English (well Yorkshire really). I got nothing in English, a violation of the basic human right to a fair and just trial which is the law set down by the European convention of human rights.

In a case of Foucher v France 18th of March 1997 it was concluded that each party must be afforded a reasonable opportunity to present his/her case in conditions that do not place him/her at a disadvantage vis his/her opponent.

The convention also maintains that everyone charged with a criminal offence has the following minimum rights:

a) To be informed promptly in a language which he understands
b) To have adequate times and facilities for the preparation of his defence.
c) To defend himself in person.

So you get the picture, the rat I smelt on the 24th of January 2017 while being interrogated by the police, had many brothers and sisters. All with the same odour and the same agenda, to not reveal the truth and to not give a person their basic human rights! The stench was overpowering!!

The rest of March gave me some positive vibes. My team from APF visited me on different days and I felt their concerns and desire to help my situation. I was disabled, left abandoned to take care of two teenagers, run a smallholding, have doctors' appointments, have major surgery and deal with a double murder charge plus rely on a very poor legal assistant in a foreign language. I needed the APF's professional and amazing help that was unquestionable. I was very lucky and grateful that I was given it.

I had done some research on powerlifting gyms in my area, and I had a choice of two. One in La Rochelle the other in Poitiers. They were both and hour and thirty minutes' drive away. I decided on Poitiers. I visited the gym and arranged a visit in April.

Claudia from APF would take me and we could get the ball rolling and start on my road to the Power Paralympics. I had the drive and the passion but no muscle or strength the two elements that I needed to religiously work on. It would not be fast, but my main aim was to grow the muscle and progress without getting injured. The date was arranged for the end of April to visit the gym. I had just got that matter of the court now on the 15th of April.

Little did I know that I was about to be thrown to the lions, and they were hungry!

I had little confidence in Mr. Riposseau he just didn't have the desire or even the thought that he could present a very strong case. He dismissed everything I had found and how he would represent me and what he said in court was damming to my case. I concluded (allegedly) that he was either instructed to lose the case or he was shit scared of this big famous solicitor the family had gone to.

The company the Dupont family turned to was Coubris, Courtois and Associés their main cabinet in Bordeaux and a second one in Paris. Though Philippe Courtois appeared to be involved in the case, he signed the paperwork, he didn't bother to show up sending one of his henchmen instead, a woman who would stand and deliver her vicious attacks on me. I wouldn't say she was really that good in my opinion, resorting to personal attacks. Trying to hide the hard facts that an 85-year-old, probably on medication and more than likely with alcohol in his system was driving or trying to!

The reason I believe he was on medication and was a drinker, is the fact that it wasn't investigated or was never mentioned. Also, the crap she came up with on the 15th of April 2019 was further confirmation that there was one hell of a cover up going on and I was the scapegoat.

It's what happened in the Hillsborough investigation, with Schumacher in 1997 (mentioned in chapter twelve), Epstein, the royal Andrew. If you have power, money, fame, and lack of integrity you believe you can lie and trample your way through life, the weak and innocent being the steppingstones to getting more power, fame and money. But sometimes those trampled, used, crippled individuals won't be silent, won't be bullied and fight back. Against all odds, without power, fame, or money but with a power that alludes the tramplers, that is the power of the truth.

It's a bit ironic that the reason for Philippe Courtois becoming a solicitor was after his brother was killed in a car crash and how he wanted to get justice for the victims. Really? Then was that at any cost and by any means of manipulation? The following is Mr Courtois' profile on Google, very interesting reading.

'Lawyers specialising in the defence and compensation of victims of bodily accidents.

The loss of his older brother in a traffic accident explains his great motivation to advise and assist victims of road accidents and their families in all the efforts to obtain the sanction of those responsible and compensation for the victims.

Coming from a medical family Maître Philippe Courtois was sensitised very early on to the problem of medical errors and wished to fully invest in the cause of the victims.

Thus, Maître Philippe Courtois has decided to put his skills at the service of victims of road accidents and medical errors.

Maître Philippe Courtois skills in the defence of victims of bodily injury and his humane qualities are recognised and Maître Philippe Courtois very often intervenes in various media in order to testify or give advice to victims.

He published a book to allow all victims of bodily accidents to be able to have their victim's status recognised, defend themselves and obtain the best compensation for their various damages.'

Maybe I need to read that book! Okay to quote Maître Philippe Courtois 'To invest in the cause of the victims.' and 'At the service of victims of road accidents and medical errors.' Would that include cause of death by any chance? So why is there no autopsy? The only legal way to define the cause of death, no medical records provided from you, you came from a medical family you know the consequences of prescribed drugs. Or maybe that's why there is not one bit of information about the health, medication, or medical condition of an 85-year-old driver. Also, alcohol, why was that not investigated? Just asking!!

Do I fear you using your power and influences to go after me? No! I would embrace it, it would give me material, motivation, and confirmation that I have hit a nerve and getting to the truth and the chance to write about it. Remember the bigger they are the harder they fall! I may be a tiny ant in your world but the strength of such a tiny creature is immense and there is always an army of little ants behind waiting to give assistance.

The morning of the 15th of April arrived. I had decided to go on my own. I thought that Maurice Pascal's report was so poor and the fact that Christophe Ledon had ballsed up the third report not even putting the right car into achieving his report, meant to me, the national expert Marc Puech's report would and could only be the accepted report within the legal courts. It was the only report without any mistakes, it was a very professional high standard report from a national expert with immense experience in his field of expertise. The judges are educated, intelligent people they would see through the unacceptable mistakes of Pascal and Ledon and go with the report that concluded that I couldn't have caused the accident.

Then there was my memory in the hospital the poor driver could easily at the age of 85 have had a health problem and collapsed at the wheel it happens every day with much younger people! Most 85-year-olds and their families, usually decide it's best for them not to drive even short distances for obvious reasons. My dad ('The Tank') stopped driving in his late 70s and he had been a taxi driver for most of his life.

It may be hard to believe that in France you don't need a medical examination by your GP to drive when you get to a certain age. You can be 101, have many health issues and be as blind as a bat and the French law says you can still drive, no questions asked and no medical needed, how crazy is that!!

Yet be in the wrong place at the wrong time, become 80% disabled by an 85-year-old driver, possibly with alcohol and prescribed drugs in their system and you have to see doctors and be examined and be declared physically and probably mentally fit to be given permission to even take a test and have driving lessons. Then every so many years get a medical to have permission to continue to drive!

The Tribunal Correctional was at La Roche Sur Yon, over an hour's drive away. I got ready, I was sat in my adapted car and thought I need a cd the radio is so stop start with advertisements. I went back into the house to get a Guns and Roses cd. I couldn't find it, so I picked up the next one I saw.

I wasn't looking forward to today the music would help. Songs in the last year had started giving me messages, guidance, and peace, which I would eventually get put onto a USB so I could train to them and listen to them in the car. This USB would become part of my healing and therapy, my medication.

It wasn't a particularly good day; the skies were grey, and it threatened rain. I got there in good time and waited for my solicitor Riposseau. I also had an interpreter Caroline, a nice lady but a timid person she had been in the police station back in January 2017, but my gut was saying trust no one!

The time came for us to enter the court, the family were there, I don't think the whole 24-26 of the people who began to sue me three days after the accident were there but there were at least ten or twelve!

As I sat (I was not in my wheelchair) I saw the main female judge, who was dealing with a young man on a different charge. I thought this bitch is going to have me. It's as if I could see right into her soul and it wasn't pleasant. She appeared to be cold and had no empathy, totally different to the three judges I had before back in 2017. I just knew I was about to be thrown into the Colosseum with many lions, Mr. Riposseau being one of them.

I had to stand in the middle of the court my interpreter to my right the three judges, Isabelle De Coux, Elodie Marti-Testeliu and Mr. Pascal Miche directly in front of me. The public prosecutor to my left Emilie Rayneau, Mr. Riposseau also on my left and the Dupont solicitor Géraldine Dauphin to my right further back behind me and Caroline.

Judge Isabelle De Coux stated the charges that the police had come up with which was I aggressively at speed overtook at a place I was only allowed to overtake slow moving vehicles and caused the death of two people.

As I am writing this (2020/2021) I feel so disappointed in the sheer allowance and permission that our society gives to a system that can pick and choose what facts or information it wants to use to get the outcome it is seeking and determined to reach. It picks out the 'laws' that are convenient to allow it to achieve that and brushes aside or ignores other laws that are there that will not take them to the already decided outcome!

Lawfully defining the cause of death being one 'little' thing they chose to avoid. Let's guess the cause of death, better still let's instead blame the other allegedly 'aggressive' driver who has never had an accident or been given any speeding offence in France before and was 52 not 85. Wasn't on any medication, never really drank alcohol, more into fitness and had been driving since the age of 17 and had driven all over the world.

Let's ignore the physical and medical health of an 85-year-old who had travelled many kilometres that day, had been to their friends or family at apero time. Probably on prescribed medication and also probably had alcohol in their system. Let's not investigate any of that, it's her fault (mine) because Hervé Dupont the son, who wasn't even at the accident, said so on the 5th of April 2016 in a police station in Cognac. That will do, she's not French anyway.

This was the justice system I was being thrown into. The first thing that they must do is discredit the person's character and the truth. In my case these people must be clever, they must have all been stood in the field watching. Using the word aggressive. Throwing that descriptive word in aggressive for impact and drama, why not the word carefully?

This is the justice that we are brainwashed to believe and accept. How many other innocent people have been framed?

Judge Isabelle De Coux got very agitated with me. Though I didn't understand much I knew that I was the target, the one to blame and attack no matter what, let's just ignore any truths or uninvestigated information. A strong message came into my head 'this is your only chance he (Riposseau) won't ask your questions; you ask them.'

My recordings may be more accurate to what I asked but this is my memory now in 2021. The only way they could get me to cause the accident was for me to have 'aggressively' been overtaking at speed. Not me trying to get to safety because the car in front was driving wrong and all over the road.

The topic of my memory came up in a sarcastic way "You don't remember the Christmas before how can you remember the accident!" was the judge De Coux's attitude. Has she not heard of Freud and his theory of things stimulating the memory?

I was in the same hospital, same surroundings, same noises, smells and some of the same staff. I was never unconscious throughout my accident it was in my memory somewhere!

Also, if I was going to conveniently remember it as judge Isabelle De Coux was implying, I should have remembered it before the 15th of April 2019. I should have remembered it before December 18th, 2017, the date we should have been in court. The court date cancelled three times because of the incompetence of Christophe Ledon the third 'expert'.

I couldn't believe what judge De Coux said next "If he was slumped at the wheel the car would have slowed down and stopped!" My response "Well his foot could have stayed on the acceleration pedal as he slumped forwards". I am thinking to myself she's a judge? So, when you faint, have a heart attack or fall asleep at the wheel while driving you first put your car out of gear, handbrake on, hazard lights on, stop the car and then you can slump at the wheel!! The very fact that your foot was on the gas before the problem occurs, means it probably stays there and the force of the forward motion of the body may even accelerate the gas more.

Now I had to think on my feet she was going for my jugular. So, I said, knowing that there hadn't been one carried out "The autopsy will give us the time and cause of death". She didn't like that! Judge De Coux turned to the judge to the right and demanded they look up the time of death. With her importance and aggressive manner (here's that word again, but she was aggressive!) she looked straight at me, well through me and said, "It was 10pm!!!" I said "That's the time he was pronounced dead. The first person on the scene who phoned for help in her statement she said there was no sign of life and in at least four pompiers statements, they said there was no life, one even thinking (and stating in his police statement) it had been a heart attack, and that was before 9pm!"

That was it I was now about to get hung, drawn, and quartered by everyone, the pack of hungry lions advancing.

I also asked why we do not have the medical records of an 85-year-old. They asked for mine and I am in my early 50s (52 at the time of the accident). Next up Géraldine Dauphin the Dupont's solicitor.

This is what Géraldine Dauphin said in court on the 15th of April 2019.

She speaks for the family a painful case. Today we have a complete vision of the accident (minus an autopsy, medical records, or an alcohol test!!) I am appalled by the fact that you do not feel (she means me) responsible for their deaths. The family does not like the idea the couple could have drunk (does this mean they did?). They were married for 59 years with a huge family who all wrote a certificate to show the human qualities of the Dupont couple (I believe they probably were a very nice couple but one that should not have been driving and the family knew that!)

They were an aged couple but in perfect health (then prove it, give us the medical records). They were going to have dinner with Mrs Dupont's sister (yes after having been in Saint Pompain with friends or family leaving just after apero time, did the driver have a drink or not? Some bugger ask the question, they asked me!!).

The family want to understand they do not want you (me) to go to prison (stop lying then and tell the truth. Oh, by the way losing your right hand is quite imprisoning!). The family lost two parents (that could have been avoided, driving at 85 years old is not a good idea).

They need explanations and logic (acknowledge the existence of Marc Puech's, a national expert, report the only one who didn't make any fundamental mistakes like the other two 'experts').

Overtaking is not reproached but was dangerous (guessing the facts). She (me) overtook the vehicle that was not disturbing the traffic (she must have been there!). The car is English to overtake a big car (my car was bigger than theirs) she had no visibility (but Christophe Ledon says that doesn't make any difference, he didn't even use a righthanded car in his calculations).

They need to understand why she went back into the right lane (gossip, assuming). Maybe an obstacle arrived in the opposite direction (oh yes, Ledon said that when challenged for putting the wrong car in, let's make it up as we go along shall we?).

Overtaking was inconsiderate (if I ever did overtake). Ms Walker says Mr. Dupont was unconscious, but no expert mentioned that the car moved from one side to the other (yes they did Ledon and Puech stated exactly that!).

The movement on the left mentioned by Mr. Ledon (thought they didn't mention moving from side to side?) was just part of the normal way of driving (it's not how I was taught to drive, weaving from side to side has never been a normal way for me to drive!). We don't know why Ms Walker overtook (she didn't! But how else can you frame me?).

I am appalled (so you should be, with the things you have been hiding) that Ms Walker does not get the logic (I don't get the logic?!! Then she says this next bit).

If Mr Dupont's car went to the left you should have gone to the left too (no my logic would have been to get the hell out of the way, as far away from a car coming left towards me).

If Mr Dupont was unconscious the car should have slowed down (not that one again). If he was not driving correctly, she should have slowed down (I probably did). What she says is not consistent (tell me what's not consistent). If Mr Dupont's car went to the right (it did two experts say so) it means he had seen Ms Walker's car coming onto the right (so, why did he then go left?). If Mrs Dupont was holding the wheel the car could not have turned to the right (why not it could go right or left, it's a steering wheel).

The family would like to understand they need the truth (they already know the truth, their father was not fit to drive that day and they are filled with guilt and remorse because they not only lost their father, but he then caused the loss of their mother, that's why they need to blame someone else, it's easier to accept. That's not an easy thing for the family to admit).

The comments I make are what I would say if I was to ever get the chance, but that was never going to happen. I was silenced but the following years as I started to investigate more deeply, wanting to find real evidence that I caused this accident and that I did actually overtake, would only show me things that confirmed I didn't overtake. There was so much hidden, not mentioned and manipulated it just confirmed what my intuition, guides and the universal justice system was shouting to me and was trying to tell me. Which was I did not kill two people or cause the accident.

It wasn't my ego or my fear of being blamed I would take the blame if they showed the full story not leaving vital evidence out. But the more I tried to find hard evidence that it was me, the more I found hard evidence that it wasn't me!

My solicitor Maitre Riposseau was up next. I say my solicitor but throughout the time in court he didn't speak once or acknowledge me, choosing instead to lean on Géraldine Dauphin's desk and talking to her. Maybe the two of them thought they had accomplished their mission. But they didn't factor into their cosy relationship that I was a Libran from Yorkshire and hated injustice! This scapegoat was not going down without a fight.

I will write Riposseau's summary without any comment please try to believe he was supposed to be on my side.

My nemesis' summary in court 15th April 2019

It's a tragedy, three years after the accident, broken lives for the family and for Ms Walker who is devastated. Ms Walker was a good driver and liked driving. Ms Walker bought a house in 2004 and settled in 2009 and drove a lot. There were no witnesses and a loss of memory.

The first report was by an independent expert, second report by the insurance

Allianz different findings so a third report was requested in order to gather enough elements about the case.

Ms Walker finds it difficult to admit certain things. She has always tried to find the truth and defend herself to continue with her life.

We have the essential elements more objective than before. There was overtaking at a speed higher than authorized. The Peugeot Partner also moved to the left it remained in it's lane. The vehicles touched one another. Both cars hit the tree because the steering wheel was turned abruptly to the right by both vehicles.

I attached the memory of the facts that Ms Walker had in September. I am aware that this memory came back in the same hospital in similar conditions. This memory may contain some truth. I think you can collapse and have your foot on the accelerator. The abrupt turning of the steering wheel to the right could have been done by the passenger. It's impossible to prove it. Medical and legal investigations were not done correctly, no autopsy maybe it would not have been interesting, but it could have revealed a health incident. I cannot prove that this vehicle would have gone slower and that she had to take a quick decision, so she overtook. Maybe the legal truth will not be the source of the actual truth.

There is no penalty that will give peace to the family. She cannot understand her behaviour on the road may have been dangerous. She has to live with the death of two people and that it is difficult to admit, moral pain plus physical pain Ms Walker will go out with a penalty that will not correspond to what she has lived.

We cannot cancel an English driving license. To limit her right to drive on the French territory, for some years it's possible. Three years suspended imprisonment is a lot taking into account Ms Walker's profile.

I only became aware of the civil financial questions on Thursday.

This was the solicitor in my corner. His attitude being no mention of alcohol, no mention of the driver being 85. He stated that things like no autopsy or medical records and the legal investigation was not being done correct and then goes on to state it could have revealed a health incident! He never mentioned the fact that the second national expert Marc Puech was the only one to not make a fundamental mistake, took only a month to produce a very high-quality piece of work oppose to the other two Pascal and Ledon. They took nine months and Ledon over a year with many mistakes, and Puech had concluded a number of things. 1) The way the evidence the cars had been unpreserved and contaminated meant they could not be legally used as evidence and 2) I did not cause the accident.

Mr Riposseau didn't bother with any of that for a student lawyer this case was a gift. All they needed to do was highlight the unlawfulness of the whole cruel, bullying situation. Instead, this so-called solicitor pussy footed around and even states "She has to live with the death of two people and that it is difficult to admit, moral pain plus physical pain." What! I was the only moral honest person in this circus of lies, cover ups and manipulation. So, you can imagine I was not in a good place but the prosecutor, Ms Rayneau hadn't had her pound of flesh yet. Here's what the prosecutor for France stated in court on the 15th of April 2019.

It's a difficult case with two deaths, involuntary homicide, difficult to find the right words (I usually just tell the truth) and penalties. Loss of Mr and Mrs Dupont will bear on you and the family, no peace for them or for you. The judge must say if Mrs Walker committed the involuntary homicide. I reproach Ms Walker with two faults, driving too fast, two reports prove it (these reports made huge mistakes how can that be ignored?), overtaking in dangerous conditions (if I even did overtake!).

Two years because the parties wanted more expert reports but not necessary (What! The first report by Pascal couldn't even get the number of people deceased right).

First expert was appointed by Cassation Court. The first report didn't see any fault from Mr Dupont.

The second report was produced by an expert commissioned by your insurance (she didn't bother to say he was a national expert and concluded that I didn't cause the accident).

The third report was similar to the first (she forgot to mention he put the wrong car in and left it in when challenged). He said that you were driving at least at 105km/h instead of 90km/h you overtook where there was a line intended for overtaking slow vehicles. Second fault Ms Walker went back too quickly onto the right (though my car had no damage at the back at the place of the alleged contact). Maybe disturbed by Mr Dupont's movement to the left (I would instinctively get away from a car coming towards me).

It was dark (again she must have been there, I didn't have my lights on it was not dark), driving quickly, was not allowed to overtake guilty!!

Ms Walker should be sentenced to three years imprisonment, cancellation of her driving license, forbidden to take another test to drive any vehicle (I had been driving since September 2017 with one hand and not had one incident at all, just as I had for all those years before, until I was on the same road at the same time as Mr Dupont!) in France we cannot make the decision respecting abroad but we can sue Ms Walker if she does not comply with the decision if she takes a driving test she may be sued.

Remember back in the 1980's when I was threatened, bullied, and attacked at the age of 12 by Mrs Sanderson the P.E teacher on the first week of high school. I promised myself then I would never allow anyone to bully me again! I would speak my truth and live with my integrity and honesty; I can't do anything other than that.

I would not accept these bullying, fear evoking tactics by people who have the power to cover up, dismiss the truth and corrupt a situation. It's not how I choose to live. I was not having any difficulty in accepting anything except lies and bullying. I would not run away from this cruel and dishonest situation; I wanted the truth that the family and the friends of Mr and Mrs Dupont already had but were keeping it well and truly hidden!

I was destined to expose the way this system operates. To be able to help and show others that they must fight for their rights and not fear the bullies and their false power. I felt that was the reason I miraculously survived.

I tried to plead with judge Isabelle de Coux, that I did not cause the accident, she just got up and walked away shouting back over her right shoulder "You can appeal if you think you are innocent."

Now for the first time Mr Riposseau was actually at my side trying to calm me and move me away, obviously an embarrassment to him. I then went to leave the family still there with their victory. I turned to one of the sons he had a nice face, kind looking and curly hair. I said, "I am sorry for your loss, but I did not kill your parents." He took my left hand and said, "Take care and look after those boys." he appeared a decent sort of bloke I wondered if it was Hervé, the one who started the whole story and gossip off! I then spoke to the daughter, a doctor (so she had the knowledge of medical conditions and how prescribed drugs affect an 85-year-old). She was okay to speak to until Ms Géraldine Dauphin, their solicitor grabbed hold of my right shoulder and pulled me back. I turned she was giving me some shit in French, and I said, "Go away I am talking to a person who has lost their parents, you have your so-called justice!" The daughter said, "It's okay" (she spoke English) and accepted my conversation. But there was something not right, she had a strange look in her eyes, a sadness yes, but it was more than that, like a plea for forgiveness, a look of guilt of shame. In those brief seconds my heart went out to this woman, she wanted to speak but couldn't. I wanted to embrace her and say I would not judge, but offer forgiveness, I wouldn't be angry, I just wanted honesty!! I also tried to speak to another son who dismissed me said something harsh and turned his back.

I was dragged to one side by Riposseau there was the interpreter there also. I was on the verge of having a mental breakdown. I was just sentenced for double murder that I knew I wasn't guilty of. I was upset, angry with the system and wanted to die!!

Once I had calmed myself, I announced to my solicitor that I wanted to appeal. I had already been guided by the universe to research it and knew I had ten days in which to appeal. Mr Riposseau's response "No, no!! Madame Walker you can't do that, you will be given a worse sentence!" my reply "What will they chop off my left hand as well?"

He shit himself, I then said I will make an appointment with him in the next couple of days and make a decision then. His response "I have no appointments free; I can't possibly see you." I said, "It has to be done in the next ten days." "No, I can't see you before ten days." was his cowardly response. Fucking what!!! I had just got charged with murdering two people on very dodgy 'evidence' and he couldn't find me ten minutes to help me appeal? What the hell was this guy being paid around 300 euros an hour for?

While we were talking their solicitor Ms Dauphin came to nosy to see what was going on. I waved to her and invited her to join us, but she scurried off like sneaky rats usually do.

I was in a bad way, words don't really describe the orchestra of emotions that are playing out, not only in my head but in every cell in my body, I had just been sentenced for double murder!

As we parted company, he, Riposseau asked if I was okay to drive "Oh yes." I said "I will no doubt go and kill some more people because I am such an aggressive and dangerous driver. If I do happen to be in the same place as an accident, I will probably get the blame for that too!"

I personally would not have let me drive away without at least taking me for a drink of tea or coffee or even driving behind me to keep an eye on me he was after all going to the same area. But that's me my humanity and care of others, why do I keep thinking that these people have any humanity or care for another human being. They work in a cold, calculated and selfish environment, holding out a helping hand to someone suffering and in pain is not in their DNA, possibly instead being used to the suffering of others and maybe give them a slight kick as they are pushed down by the wonderful, 'just' system they are proud to be a part of.

They both just walked off and didn't even contact me later to see if I had actually got home safely and if I was alright. But I had a much bigger, loving, divine team watching over me and they talked to me through song.

It was raining quite hard now and as I sat in my car distraught and in a very bad place, I needed to hear some friendly voices. I phoned Kay and Denbo and they listened and calmed me. "What are you going to do?" Kay asked. "I don't know" was my reply. "You have been treated really bad Penny; can you live the rest of your life with the judgement that you have just been given?" Kay questioned. I didn't think I could, it would be like a cancer growing inside of me, the lies, the hidden information, the lack of any truth or clarity, would slowly consume me because I knew I was not guilty.

I then spoke to my amazing friend and wise person of words Susan. She also helped me calm myself enough to drive back home. I was so grateful for their support, I was so close to just driving into a wall and fucking giving them something to talk about, all those people who were pecking at me just as vultures do, all taking their pound of flesh.

But as I started the car a song came on from the cd I had hastily picked up before I left the house. It was 'Running Away' by Bob Marley. In that moment I realised I could not run away from this injustice I had to be able to live with myself and if I did not try and get the truth out in the open, I would have done myself so much harm and never be free from the mental torture all these injustices were giving me.

Then as I drove the song 'Get Up Stand Up' by Bob Marley sang a very clear message to me "Half the story has never been told, so now you see the light, stand up for your rights, get up stand up, stand up for your rights. Get up stand up don't give up the fight."

What other sign did I need? I was not alone in this wicked world, someone, some sort of energy was guiding me. I may not have the earthly justice, but a much more pure and truthful justice was being shown to me. I had to get up, stand up and never give up the fight!!

This was not just about me, little disabled one-handed Penny, but about humanity itself. If I was courageous, listened and allowed myself to be guided I would not only heal my own damaged soul, but allow many others to heal theirs as well.

I may be criminalised, laughed at, ridiculed, abandoned, lied to and be on a lonely path but every step would be guided, and I would be protected by a power and righteousness that is often not seen or dismissed because of the fear that has been planted in one's soul. From that moment onwards I felt a calmness and warmth and a beginning of healing of my soul. I was not alone.

It would not be a quick healing and I would stumble and fall and be pushed or tripped many times. But I was now connected to the power of a deep spiritual love that would teach me many things that society could not.

When I had got home on the 15th of April I could not sleep. I was thinking how unsupportive my solicitor was and how he desperately didn't want me to appeal. At 3:56 am on April the 16th 2019 I sent him an email which I tried to translate into French. It said I wish to appeal. The email said:

> The family said they wanted the truth and today they did not get that. I want an appeal!
> I accept things but have a difficulty accepting injustice! All my life I have needed the truth it's who I am thank you
> Penny Walker.

I needed a change, a change of scenery and asked the boys if they could cope if I went to the UK for a week when they next had a holiday from Lycée. No problem, so I booked a cheap flight in May.

Throughout April, APF had visited me and helped me in so many different ways. Nadège Chalet the psychologist having to listen to my feelings and disappointments about the court case.

Mr Riposseau had given me an appointment after the 10 days cut off time so for the next ten days, I constantly chased him up to make sure he had put my appeal in. I also contacted Mr. Ravet from the Allianz insurance to make sure my appeal was lodged. I didn't actually trust that it would be, but it was my human right to appeal.

I also sent Mr Riposseau an email translated to the areas that was needed to be investigated and mentioned at my appeal. I doubt he even bothered to read it.

I eventually got a meeting with the solicitor after the ten days and all he kept saying was I could get a different solicitor if I wanted. He must have said it four times!

I had Harvey with me as a translator and a witness, I was really not trusting that this guy had my best interest at heart, especially after what he had said in court.

I was sort of ignored and told to be quiet a number of times, he didn't want to answer my questions. Twice I got up to leave but was persuaded to sit back down. I finally got to ask a question "What was the time of death of Mr Dupont?" "10 pm" was Riposseau's answer. My response "So you haven't looked at the police witness reports that clearly state from at least five people that no one saw Mr Dupont alive, all saying he did not appear to be breathing and even one of the witnesses a pompier stated they thought he may have had a heart attack. That's in the police witness statements! And you sit there and tell me 10pm!!"

I got up and said, "We are off Harvey". As I stood to leave Mr Riposseau had a big pile of my files, probably as tall as a two-litre bottle if not taller on his desk and he raised his hand and slammed it down on the top file on the pile stating "Madame Walker there is nothing in there that will show you are innocent!" My reply was "You know who Bob Marley is?" Riposseau nodded his head. "Well listen to his song 'Get Up Stand Up' because half the story has never been told!!!" and as I hobbled out of his office, I thought to myself you can fool some of the people sometimes but you can't fool all the people all of the time.

On the 4th of May I had another meeting in Niort at APF at their offices. The meeting was good and positive, and it was arranged for Claudia (we had already bonded at the first meeting) and myself to go to the powerlifting gym in Poitiers, so I could begin my training.

I had a bench and some weights at home and the adaptation that they made for me in the Grand Feu, but I needed to be coached in powerlifting and get my license to compete. I needed to be affiliated to a powerlifting gym.

Claudia and I set off to the gym in Poitiers. The coach Patrick wasn't there he was on holiday a bit of a mix up in the arrangement, but a really kind lady phoned Augustin and said if we came back in about an hour, he would be able to see us.

Claudia made a phone call to her office to explain our delay and we went for a drink of hot chocolate and cake until it was the right time. It was great to have this time with Claudia, for we had bonded on our first meeting. She was full of enthusiasm and had a belief in me.

We went to meet Augustin a really great guy who sorted out some paperwork and arranged for me to go back to train with Patrick the following Wednesday.

With the distance there and back and my training, it took up all the afternoon but the boys weren't at Lycée on Wednesday afternoons so they would feed the animals and sort them out for me. Now my road to regaining strength had begun.

I also did some research in the UK and contacted Taylor's gym in Liverpool and spoke with Danny Taylor the owner. He was willing to help me and take me on, so I arranged to call and see him for a quick visit when I went to the UK in a couple of weeks.

Danny had a sudden emergency on the date we had arranged, he offered me a different time, but I couldn't make it I was up north and didn't have much time in the UK, maybe only four days. There wasn't a problem I would visit Liverpool on my next visit to the UK.

My visit to the UK was very short. I stayed with Kay and Denbo and also Susan I was well looked after, and it was so wonderful to be amongst friends.

Susan took me to see my parents. My mum looked ill she had lost a lot of weight and had spent a lot of time in bed. We chatted and I told them I would try and see them again before I left the UK.

Denbo took me on the second visit to my parents, they loved Denbo and were pleased to see him. As we left, I said "Denbo my mum is dying, I can see it in her eyes, she is really sick." It was a difficult thing to accept but now I had a different take on life after my accident, I didn't fear death or loss I just prayed that people didn't suffer and my mum would leave earthly sufferings behind, to allow herself a peaceful energy within her soul and embrace the beautiful energies and love she would receive as she left the earthly plane. I would later, gratefully be able to return to say my goodbyes.

Chapter 33: A Massive Pile Of Nothing And My Last Recording In July 2019

"What is that which stands higher than word? Action. What is it that stands higher than action? Silence."

- Francis of Assisi

Back in France I had got into the routine of going to the gym on Wednesday afternoons. On Wednesday the 5th of June 2019 Patrick had to video me lifting to send to Handisport so they would allow me a license. I had already sent them a medical certificate from my doctor Dr. Dinu in March, so they just needed this to complete the application.

I continued to train with Patrick each week and then on the 15th of July I began my training online with Danny Taylor four times a week. I was now getting stronger, but it's not just your physical body that benefits from the training, you also benefit you mind and mine still had loads to deal with.

I was also looking forward to having a meeting with Pasquay in the Grand Feu to try and fabricate a new sturdier adaptation for Stubby to be able to bench press. At last, I was back in the gym!

Around this time, I had signed a letter from Allianz to say I wanted a different solicitor, one that could speak English, for my appeal. But I heard nothing back from them, this big all singing, all caring and all doing international insurance company, Allianz just ignored my signed document they did nothing! It was as if I was swept under the carpet, their duty of care to their paying customer non-existent.

The fact that Mr Riposseau had gossiped how bad I was at court in April 2019 and how I was 'aggressive' here's that word again! (It must be a textbook word you have to use to try and discredit a person and hide the truth) His client confidentiality not being honoured or carried out because I got to hear this from Sandra the office worker at the Allianz office in Parthenay, nice very professional Mr Riposseau, but his need to gossip about his clients' private information would not stop there. I thought these 'professionals' had a code of conduct to uphold. Don't they?

So, I never got contacted and was never offered another solicitor, though I had signed a document to say I requested and needed one. Be careful which insurance company you choose to have your back. Allianz in my case did not live up to all it's wonderful PR and sales pitches. They totally abandoned me and their duty of care that they were legally bound to.

Now I had to represent myself, so I needed that big pile of files that Riposseau had aggressively (I may as well use the word too!) slammed his hand on at our last meeting. The information he said that wouldn't prove my innocence. Okay let's see what's in this massive pile of nothing!

In the years I had now been exposed to this French 'justice' system, I realised that it was far from just and they had the cheek to have an insignia in the courtrooms and on the police, uniform showing a balanced set of scales for the justice they so efficiently provide. Really! Is that what it symbolises? Who are they trying to kid? How very bizarre and ironic! I now took heed from Albert Einstein's wise words "Unthinking respect for authority is the greatest enemy of the truth.". Every encounter I had with authority was only proving Einstein's quote time after time, after time and it wouldn't even stop at the appeal court!

Seeing as Allianz had abandoned me though I was still paying them monthly for the privilege. I needed to get the documents to prepare for the appeal. I had very little given to me throughout the years, though requested and the little I had was all in French.

On the 11th of July 2019 I sent a signed for, registered letter to Cabinet AVC in Bressuire addressed to M. Maitre Hugo Riposseau. On the 12th of July 2019 I got the AR form back from La Poste confirming the letter was received and signed for.

This letter requested my documents and the time I would be there and if not convenient to let me know and I would gladly come at a different day or time to fit in with his availability. I didn't really need or want to see him just my files. No letter, no contact, no reply. So, Harvey and I went to collect my case files, I even had a big shopping bag to put them in because there were that many. Remember the pile he had indicated, that held nothing to help my case, sat on his desk.

The game was now about to start. I had realised in January 2017 in my police interrogation that some sort of dishonest game was being played. Now in 2019 I had more understanding of the way these games were played. With their arrogance and their egos plus the stolen power, they never thought anyone would actually challenge or question the rules of their games. So, they panicked and were desperate.

The lies got bigger, and they exposed themselves with more clarity, the smoke and mirrors becoming clear and transparent, the hole they had dug and pushed me into, they were now being forced to jump in. By now I had painfully, determinedly crawled and dragged myself out of that dark evil abyss and was behind a wall of safety, the wall built out of integrity and truths, a wall unavailable for them because they just couldn't stop lying so they would never be able to get out of the hole, trapped by their own lies and cover ups.

Due to staffing shortages, they had not had time to prepare the file. Prepare? The file? All that was needed was for them to carry the pile of files to reception and I put them in my shopping bag and that's it. Why did they need to be copied he was no longer involved in the case? This information coming from the receptionist (we all know how they can be!) I requested that I speak to Riposseau. He arrived and said a load of bull and that if we returned on the Friday the 26th it would all be ready for me. Okay thank you, we will return on Friday, "Is that a good time for you Mr Riposseau?" I politely asked. "Yes" was the reply. Round one, game on, mess them about, piss them off and tell lies, they will eventually go away and give up. Don't underestimate me Mr Riposseau I am a Libran and from Yorkshire!!

Round two, 26th of July 2019, we arrived. This dismissive, self-important receptionist presented me with this thin file and a paper to sign all in French which I believe stated that I accepted what they gave me.

Harvey explained that we needed all the files, she said that's it. I looked through the thin file which she was trying to hide below the counter (I reached down and got it) and I looked through it. There wasn't one photo! I asked, "Where's the photos from the police?" Then she got really nasty and said something like "We can't afford to print all that out!" I said, "You don't, just give me the originals, this case is no longer Riposseau's."

Well, she went off on one "Then you should have brought a USB." My response "Why didn't you tell me that?". She continued with her cocky tone "We have sent you the files via your email." "No, you sent me blank pages" was my reply.

She then started pointing her finger at me. I thought why am I talking to a receptionist? I said "I am not talking to you; you aren't even a solicitor! I would like to see Mr Riposseau please." Her answer "You can't he is at the Niort office." That summed him up, make an appointment when you are not here so you can hide! My small female dog Peggy had more balls than him!

"Okay" I said, "I am going to sit in the waiting area until you get me ALL my files!" I went to sit down, she followed me into the waiting area shouting some bloody abuse pointing her finger at me again. I said, "I am not talking to you go away!"

Then she got Riposseau on the phone who requested to speak to Harvey not me. I was quite pissed off by now. I said "Harvey don't speak to him he wants to trap you! He can speak to me." but he wouldn't speak to me. I wonder why coward!

Then this woman appeared a solicitor I think and started throwing her weight around. I said, "It's quite simple just give me my files and I will leave." her superior sounding voice said, "You can't have it, you have to be a solicitor" (I thought, and these people have studied the law for years?). My informed reply "No I don't! Okay you sign and date a statement saying you are refusing to give me MY files, which I am lawfully entitled to, and I will leave without the files." But for some reason she wouldn't do that, why not?

Then she got angry and aggressive (that word again but she did I was at the other end of it) and said that she would call the police! I said "Do you think that scares me! Call them and I will tell them that you are refusing to give me what I have a legal right to have. Call them I will sit here and wait for them."

Yes, you guessed it, funnily enough she never called them. You see weak bullies can only bully and usually lie, when you stand up to them you expose how weak and pathetic, they really are!

I requested a piece of paper and pen and started writing. She was now ignoring my existence and asked Harvey what I was doing and why I was taking so long. I said, "Because I have only one hand and I can't write so good with it."

She then wrote some address down if I had a complaint, I could contact them. Batonnier des Deux Sèvres, order des Avocats Espace Thenis Rue Noncel Paul, 7900 Niort. Guess who sails that ship, another load of solicitors. They set up these complaint procedures by the very same establishments and people you are complaining about it's part of the game. The average person doesn't really have any human rights if you dare to question the rules of these powerful, controlling establishments, you are given the run around and usually have to stand alone.

This is what I wrote on the sheet of paper:

Penelope Walker DOB 7/10/64

I arrived to collect my files on the 26/7/19 the information was at AVOdes office Bressuire 79308 Bressuire. The file offered was not complete, no DVDs, photos or other information which I asked for and needed. I asked them to sign a piece of paper saying that they would not give me the full number of files which I have a right to under the equality of arms act. This is the second time I have been to collect my files. It must be noted that I am representing myself and not using a solicitor. They acted unlawfully, unkindly, and threateningly.

I then signed and dated it.

This was for my records because I was in a game that could be, shall I say untruthful. But the bully had given me an idea, I will go to the police, they are breaking the law not giving me what is lawfully mine. Let's see what these enforcers of the balanced scales of justice do, it's what the badge that's sewn on their uniform displays. Surely, they must believe and honour what it stands for, equality, fairness, and a person's rights. Or are all these rights a smokescreen to keep the masses quiet, in their place, unchallenging and swimming in an ocean of injustice.

Yep, you guessed it, not interested. The young man on the desk said he would take details and got hold of a small post it pad. Where do you think that would go as soon as my back is turned and out of the door? "No" I said "I want to make an official complaint" I wasn't allowed, it wasn't what they dealt with was his response. My next question, pointing at his uniform "So why the badge then? I have been treated unjustly and it's not your department?!" I think their training programme must have a high percentage of training to teach them how to avoid a person who is being unjustly treated and has the courage to ask for help. There must be a hell of a lot of insomniacs in these sorts of jobs how do they sleep at night with the cover ups, untruths, and the manipulations of situations they turn a blind eye to. But it's slowly changing, the universe has had enough, and the people's justice is getting stronger by the day because this justice comes from the love of their fellow man, woman, and child.

Round 3 now began. Mr Riposseau on the 29th of July 2019 sent me an email with the third expert Christopher Ledon's report and three videos showing the Seat, my car overtaking the Peugeot with the Seat being a left-hand car not a righthand car to simulate this alleged 'aggressive' high speed overtaking and pulling in too early. Unbelievably he didn't even bother to put the correct car in even when told he had made that mistake. Is that because it would have resulted in a different conclusion then that which was asked for? This major mistake surely was not a lawfully submittable piece of evidence! Yet that's the one they all quoted and used in their kangaroo court.

Mr Riposseau also stated that the full file had been sent via LRAR a registered and signed for postal method.

My email back on the 29th of July 2019 translated into French was:

Hello Mr Riposseau, I am going to request through a different channel my FULL files including all correspondences, all DVDs, USBs and photos, from all parties involved including the three experts and the information, including all photos from the police and madame Simon cabinet Erget's USB.

I am shocked that you withheld this information from me on both the 22nd of July and Friday the 26th of July 2019. In your email dated the 29th of July 2019 you state my FULL files have been sent by LRAR. Let's hope this is true. However, my lack of trust and confidence that ALL my files will be sent gives me no choice but to continue down my other options to obtain my FULL files which I am lawfully entitled to!

Yours sincerely, Penelope Walker.

I had refused the envelope when it arrived, it was so thin, it had open edges so the USBs could have easily fallen out, it had no security, I wasn't going to accept it, what happened to the big pile in his office? What was he hiding in those files?

On the 31st of July 2019 I got this email from Mr Riposseau:

Dear madame,

The registered mail containing a copy of your file, as well as a USB key containing the video reconstruction of the accident has been refused by you.

This letter was returned to me today with the following message "letter refused by recipients". I take note of this and deplore your questionable and paradoxical attitude, of which I admit to not understanding the reason.

Please be advised dear madame the expression of my distinguished feelings.

My response was to send the following email on the 31st of July 2019 at around 10:30 – 10:45 am.

Dear Mr Riposseau I received your email on the 31st of July 2019 at 09:38. I refused the letter because I requested my FULL files, the weight and size of the envelope clearly indicating that this was not my FULL files. Security was a problem there were gaps on both sides of the envelope the contents in transit could have easily fallen out i.e the USBs.

If you were to send my FULL files as requested already with a list of the contents prior to its arrival then I would gladly sign for the FULL files, if I believe it's complete.

The fact you confess not to identify the purpose of my request for my FULL files only goes to strengthen that my decision to no longer want you to represent me is indeed the correct decision!

My next email to Mr Riposseau was sent on the 3rd of August 2019.

Dear Mr Riposseau, today Saturday the 3rd of August 2019 I again refused to sign for an envelope sent by you. Although the envelope was more secure, with no gaps for any items to fall out, the size and thickness was the same as that sent and refused on the 31st of July 2019.

I will repeat myself again, I have no problem signing for my FULL files and if you refer to the email sent to you on the 31st of July 2019 a list of the contents prior to you sending it would be a logical thing to do so I know what I am signing for. I am sure you will agree that it is FULL files that I need to be able to prepare for the appeal. I look forward to receiving my FULL files.

Yours sincerely.

I then received a reply on the 5th of August 2019 at 10:30am from Mr Riposseau:

Dear madame,
My registered mail included in accordance with your request, a summary slip of the part of the complete file.

As indicated in my last registered letter, I will no longer send your file back by registered mail, because I am tired of incurring unnecessary costs.

You can bring a trusted relative to my Bressuire office and collect the documents from your file when it has been returned to me by post. I refuse to let you disturb my staff and the other clients of the firm again with your indignant attitude.

Your new lawyer, if you appoint one can also, if necessary, write to me so that I can send him the documents in your file, which I will do upon receiving his request. Please be advised.

Please accept dear madame, the expression of my distinguished feelings.

Signed by Mr Riposseau.

My reply on the 5th of August 2019.

Dear Mr Riposseau,
I thank you for your email which arrived on at 10:30am on August the 5th 2019. You are well aware that you are not sending my FULL files which is essential for my appeal. The reasons for your withholding some of its contents is disturbing and unlawful.

In the email you also state you refuse to give me my FULL files. You have yet to provide a list of what you are prepared to give me.

I will no longer be contacting you on this matter for it is obvious that you will not give me my FULL files. I therefore have to try and get the information from a different source. Your refusal to hand over my FULL files fills me with suspicion, but it also fills me with strength to get the truth and to fight for my rights.

I pray that you and your family are never served an injustice! Thank you for your email. Have a great day.

Penelope Walker

After so many years of being blinded and not given the rules of the games that these people were playing, I started to see some basic tactics of the game. Never give them the information you don't want them to see or talk about, ignore a person's basic human rights to a fair and just trial and give them the run around to wear them down. If that person is at a disadvantage because their native tongue is not that of those playing the game, just use that to your advantage. Don't provide anything in their native tongue and bully them to sign legal documents they don't understand. They will be such an easy target; they won't fight back!

When you do fight back, they play the game even dirtier with more bullying and more ignoring of your basic human rights, I am a human being, am I not? But that's okay, I have got an appeal, they will play fair without things going missing and being sabotaged, it's the whole point of an appeal!

They will see that Christophe Ledon didn't put a righthand car into his calculations to obtain his report. They would also see that nobody actually did a legally required medical procedure, that is an autopsy to legally define the cause of death of an 85-year-old and what was actually in the system of an "Aged person of perfect health", (a quote from Géraldine Dauphin in court on the 15th of April 2019). What was really in his system? Prescribed drugs maybe? Or dare I mention the word alcohol? Also remember Geraldine Dauphin their solicitor stated in court that "The family does not like the idea the couple could have drunk". See the game, she didn't even say alcohol.

As I have said before it's not what people say it's what they don't say, what they go to great lengths to avoid saying, hiding and camouflage, if forced to go anywhere near the truth they are desperately trying to hide.

So why is it that no autopsy was done? Why aren't this big family jumping up and down demanding why madame Walker wasn't tested for alcohol. Who knows, maybe I was tested but I don't drink and drive. It is one of the biggest causes of fatalities on French roads. Plus, aged drivers on prescribed drugs!

This is my last recording (my dictaphone is now full). It was on the 27th of July

Prison Or The Paralympics

2019:

Hello it's the 27th of July 2019. It is quite a while since I actually recorded anything, there are so many reasons for that. I will quickly go through the time in December 2018 when I reached an extreme low with a feeling of sheer disappointment in everything and everybody, by the way I was being treated, just a real, real downtime. But I realised that you have to get so, so low to have a choice. You either climb back up or you give up!

I chose to climb back up. The struggle has been really difficult, there has been many, many knockbacks and knockdowns! Today I decided it was time to record and get things up to date.

So, the main thing that happened this year (2019) was on April the 15th. It was the court date. I told no one about the date and went on my own. The solicitor saw me maybe a week before. The communication with the solicitor has been extremely poor and I mean extremely poor!! At this last meeting he discussed my memory that I had in September 2018 while in Nantes hospital having an operation to remove the metal out of my leg. I gave this information to the insurance in September 2018 we are now at the end of March 2019 and the solicitor has yet to send this information to the court. His excuse was he needed to discuss it with me. He could have done that in September or October. From the information I thought there is something very, very odd going on here. He has no compassion, has got nothing about him to even desire to defend or believe me.

The meeting was very short and a great disappointment and this would continue throughout the court day of April the 15th 2019.

I realised as I saw the judge that she was going to have me. The day was beyond words, it's difficult to describe. I was thrown to the lions, and everyone had a piece of me, even my own solicitor!

In Riposseau's summary he said I had difficulty accepting things (yes lies and injustice!!). I was distraught I had to defend myself. On questioning I brought up questions that nobody would bring up or answer. I brought up the point of all these people suing me. I got dismissed with that. I brought up the point of alcohol, got dismissed with that. I brought up the point of not knowing anything about medication and the health of an 85-year-old and there being no autopsy. That was dismissed! I actually said when she (judge) asked me about, which was very sort of uninterested and vague questioning, she never listened to me. I asked, "You know about my memory you have seen it?" she more or less said it was convenient stating "You didn't even remember the Christmas before." I said "Yes but the situation was in an environment that I was put in directly after the accident, after being helicoptered there. All this brought my memory back."

I had written my memory down and it consisted of me remembering that there was a problem with the car, the driver was slumped at the wheel, they had either fallen asleep or having difficulties, the car was moving from side to side and the passenger had hold of the wheel. She, judge De Coux dismissed it, just dismissed my memory!

Then I said, "We can find out from the autopsy, (I knew they didn't have an autopsy) what the time of death was." she got quite annoyed about this and she stated, "That it was 10pm." I said, "That's when the doctor pronounced him dead."

Judge Isabelle De Coux also stated to me "If he was slumped at the wheel the car would have slowed down!" I said, "Not if his foot was still on the acceleration pedal." I am just stood there thinking they are just going to absolutely slaughter me and for what reason? Because I asked important questions that to this day have never been answered! The only possible source of legal evidence to determine the cause of death was swiftly removed from the equation, what do they do then? They guess, pull possible causes of death out of a hat? Make it up or just blame someone else surely, they can't and won't question this illegal manoeuvre, they will probably not survive anyway!

The driver was 85 years old, and that information had never been mentioned in court (I only found out recently they (the other party) were allowing people to believe he was younger, but he wasn't, his date of birth 12/12/31, that makes him 85). Think of all the people in their 80s that you know, would you be comfortable allowing them to drive such a long way on a hot day. My dad was a professional rugby player, didn't really drink from around the age of 60 and had been a taxi driver for years. Before he even reached 80, he gave up driving.

In the summary from Geraldine Dauphin, the solicitor acting for the big famous solicitor Phillipe Courtois made this statement in court. She said, "That they were concerned that they could have been drinking." The family were concerned that they could have been drinking, which means that they could have been drinking. She didn't outrightly say they didn't drink!! Never daring to mention the actual word alcohol. She also stated, "They were an aged couple but in perfect health." At 85 you can't be in perfect health!

She continued to say, "That the weaving been documented by the experts was a normal way to drive!" Hello!! Not in my life, I don't weave about on the roads. All this absolutely reeks of bullshit!!

I was so distraught, my solicitor did not help in fact he never communicated with me at all, not once while in court.

Prison Or The Paralympics

After the hearing or should I say the kangaroo court I got sentenced for three years, a suspended prison sentence. I got charged with double involuntary homicide, which means murder. I got banned from driving, I got banned from taking a test I got everything they could throw at me. I could not believe it the judge dismissed me.

Nobody was on my side at all and that included my insurance Allianz and my solicitor employed by Allianz. After this, me being the person I am, (that's the problem nobody knows who I am and my personality), I was distraught I went to the family members and said to them I am really sorry for your loss, but I did not do it. I did not kill your parents. One of the sons shook my hand and said, "Just look after those boys." I spoke to the daughter their solicitor grabbed hold of my shoulder and dragged me away. I said to her "Just you leave off it's over now you have got your 'justice' I am talking to someone who has lost their parents." The daughter spoke English she is actually a doctor and I said, "I didn't do this, I didn't kill your parents." She was a decent lady, but her eyes were trying to tell me something, she knew the truth.

I know, I bloody know that they know something, why will they not release the medical information?

I am now absolutely distraught, they interpreted that as aggression. They want to try having the amount of treatment I have had. Losing your right hand, being accused, accused and accused some more! Year after year for something that has never been investigated. Yes, if you want to call it aggression, I call it absolute desperation!!

Desperation to be heard, desperation to just get the truth out there. I asked the solicitor Riposseau "I can appeal" "No, no, no!! Madame Walker, Madame Walker do not appeal you cannot appeal! You will get a bigger sentence and you will not win; you will not win!!" I said "What sentence will I get? Will they chop my left hand off as well?". I said to him "The only reason you don't want to appeal is because you don't believe me."

So that was his response for his client who had just been given a sentence of double murder and they didn't even know the causes of death. Only an autopsy can give you that!

I knew I only had 10 days in which to appeal, I said I will not make the decision now I will come and visit you before the 10 days expires. "Oh no madam Walker I can't possibly see you in ten days." was Riposseau's reply. Ridiculous!

I was so distraught, if I had a gun I would have shot myself (getting upset). To be attacked and to be accused like that, it is so destroying. The crazy thing is if for one second, I had thought I had caused any accident because of my actions I would have said it the moment my eyes opened in intensive care.

I get home I don't sleep I read some of the notes the interpreter had made, and I realised that he said, Riposseau "That Madame Walker finds it hard to accept things."

At around 4:00 am on the 16th of April 2019 I sent Mr Riposseau an email requesting that I have my appeal, it's my right to have an appeal and I want an appeal.

I think, shall I say allegedly that this has been prearranged by the professional companies and they are all in it together. I know people say that's being paranoid but what other reason is there for such an injustice?

On a better note I picked myself up and said "Right that's it! I will turn to training." I train once a week in Poitiers in a powerlifting gym, and I now have correspondence training from a gym in Liverpool by Danny. I am focusing as hard as I can and I will continue to make that more of a priority, to try and compete in the Paralympics. It's the only thing I have got at the moment to stop me being mentally and physically destroyed by a corrupt, manipulative, dishonest, governmentally created system.

I am continuing with the case, I requested to Allianz that I wanted a new solicitor, one that could speak English so I could at least communicate with them and them with me.

Not one piece of information or any documents have been translated into English or any correspondence. It is outrageous this is an international company surely Allianz can access and has access to English speaking employees.

Nothing has come back about a new solicitor. I continued to look at the pages of the few documents I had though difficult because it was all in French. The things I found in these few documents was horrendous and very revealing. I cannot believe what has been going on.

I decided that there is only one person on this planet who is going to look after me and that's me. I have no choice but to represent myself as Allianz is ignoring my request for an English-speaking solicitor. This brings us to yesterday.

I have an interpreter, a translator who is going through the paperwork with me. I am getting a file together to present to the appeal court in Poitiers. It's amazing what is going on and being hidden.

Val, from Val Assist composed a letter for me which I sent by registered post to the solicitor Riposseau and told them that on the 22nd of July I would be coming in for my file, I also notified them that if there was a problem with this date to send me an email so a new date could be made. No reply or response.

Harvey and I turned up on the 22nd, we got nothing. They had acknowledged acceptance of the letter; it was on their computer. The solicitor Mr Riposseau came to see me, I was not happy he said, "The staff have been on holiday, it's not ready." I said "Okay when do you want us to come back?" "Friday" was his answer.

We went back Friday he happens to not be there, the coward that he is. The receptionist gives me three articles. I flipped through them; one was the expert's report the other to do with the money the family was claiming. The third was another report that had been sent that morning by email, the email was blank! I said to her that's blank showing her the email that doesn't work, I can't see it. Her cocky response being "We can't photocopy, it's too expensive to photocopy!" I am thinking at 300 euros maybe more an hour and you can't afford photocopying! Also why are they photocopying it? Why isn't it just being given to me, they are no longer acting for me. They are no longer part of my life! Why would I want them to work for me? They have done a very poor job so far! Why have I got to get photocopies? Why are they keeping my file? All these questions swimming around in my head.

This is what happened yesterday, Friday when we went back. I took a shopping bag with me knowing that when we last had a meeting with Riposseau there were a lot of files. The tall pile of files that he slammed his fist on, and said, "Madame Walker there is nothing in there that can get you an appeal." and three times in that meeting I got up to leave. I was disgusted with him. This is me who is getting done for double murder! It's not a parking fine.

The receptionist was giving me a load of bull "You haven't a right to have these files" she obviously didn't know the law. This was a receptionist not a solicitor, not anybody with any legal ability whatsoever, I said "Look no problem, I am going to sit in that waiting room and you get someone who has got some authority, you get your boss to tell me what's happening with my files because this is not my full file! There are no DVDs, where's the DVDs?"

Her response "If you wanted DVDs you should have brought a USB." My answer "Nobody mentioned bringing a USB and the fact is why should I bring a USB when it's my files!"

This solicitor came and started throwing her weight. Before when I was sitting in the waiting room the receptionist came into the waiting room shouting at me and pointing her finger blar, blar. I didn't understand a word she was saying it was all in French. I said "Look I have got a right to them files, I am talking to a professional. You are a receptionist; you shouldn't even know what's in my file!"

The professionalism of this group is ridiculous. This different woman the solicitor starts going on at me she said, "Are you going to sign that?" I said, "No I am not!"

You can't have a civil conversation with these people they are just treating you like an imbecile; they treat you like you are stupid.

There are two people in the waiting room, obviously two of her clients waiting. So, my next vision is that they will have signed witness statements from them saying I was aggressive (they like to use that word). Remember even two days after the accident the police have stated I aggressively overtook not she carefully overtook, if they were making assumptions, why not assume carefully and respectfully? The word aggressive seems to be used in the French language when they are wrong, when they are trying to lie and trying to cover something up and dishonour a person's character.

So, what if they want to use the word aggressive, that's their problem. They want to try having their hand chopped off twice!! They want to try being bloody accused of double murder. They want to try not having their questions answered and be interrogated let's see what they feel like. This is not aggression this is sheer desperation and sheer disappointment on the way I have been treated in this so called 'justice' system.

So, she then threatened that she would phone the police, I replied "Phone them! I want to see your manager." She the solicitor then gave me a name of a place, a place I think you can complain, a place you write with your complaint if you have a complaint about a solicitor. Four times I said to her I need the name; I can't just contact nobody. Her reply "You can't have that."

At some point the solicitor Riposseau is on the phone, requesting to speak to my son. I said "Harvey you don't speak to him, it's a game they are playing, you don't speak to him. Let him speak to me."

He should have been there he arranged it for Friday. The amount of paperwork they were offering me, what the hells the delay? I bet there wasn't even 50 sheets, there was way less and no DVDs, no photographs. Why did we have to wait? This is the second time I am trying to get my information, which I have a right to under the 'equality of arms'.

Then I asked this female solicitor "Will you write on a piece of paper (she could understand English, but she chose not to) that you are refusing to give me my full documents and date and sign it?" She said, "No I won't, no I won't." I said, "Right then phone the police."

Now I am writing down what's going on, the way she threatened me, the way she refused to give me my files, etc. The solicitor then disappeared with these clients. Why didn't she call the police? And what was she calling the police for anyway? To tell them they were not going to give me my files that I had a right to!

I thought right I'll go to the police. After we left, we phoned the police prior and went to the police and we spoke to the police. At first, they weren't much help it was a young guy. Then this more mature police officer walked past, and I said "Can you help me? I am trying to get my file; I have been given a prison sentence and being done for double murder. There's been no autopsy, no blood taken, and no medical records and this person was 85 years old. No one has listened to me, and they expect me to take the sentence!"

The investigation has been crap!! He doesn't know the half of it I was keeping that well and truly under wraps. I don't trust a soul in the 'investigation'!

He did help, he gave me the same address the solicitor had given but with a name for the place you complain about solicitors. He also suggested we go to Poitiers to the appeal court and request a full copy of our file. He said that's all you can do. The police officer said the solicitor should have asked for the medical records, you can represent yourself because of the sort of sentence you have been given. You are entitled to represent yourself and they should be giving you all that information.

So, there we are! Remember that information form in English, that the police gave me in January 2017 stating, 'you are furthermore informed that you have the right to view material relating to your case.'

So, what happened to that right?

I am giving everything up to the universe and the powers of divine justice. If this goes all the way to the European court so, be it. I feel this is not just for me and my injustice, this is for a lot of people.

I have turned to the universe; I have turned to the powers that be because they have guided me every day. I have books that Mel has given me and books that I have got, and I randomly open them, and they give me a message. Last night the message was have faith in God and have confidence. I think that's all I have left. This society is really, really corrupt!

I am trying to give love to this situation, and I am just trying to see the situation for what it is. But people keep battering me so what I have to do is keep picking myself back up.

I will never have any communication with that solicitor Riposseau and his company again. If people like me in these situations do not make a case of it there is no comparison for other people in the same situation. If I can get this out there, then other people in similar situations can benefit.

I am distraught that this is going on in my life when I have been classed as 80% disabled, I have one hand and I am trying my best to get strong again. This has got to come to an end, and it will, when I don't know. I have just got to be patient and give all the confidence to the powers that are much more powerful than our society. That's it bye.

27 Minutes

I am only about halfway through 2019 and it's been major battles, deceit and lies. What were these people so scared of? Why the cover ups and secrecy? Is this what the human race was about? If so, I wanted no part of it.

What's happened to honesty, integrity, love, and the concern for the well-being of your fellow man? Kindness, the truth, upholding the law, applying the law in a fair and just way? Do I even belong on this planet that allows this dishonesty to be the norm? The way that society is structured and allowed to behave isn't my normality and I never want it to be!

In the following months I would be allowed to see that not all of society functions like this and there are amazing, kind, and honest humans that don't buy into those cruel parts of society. Instead, they care for other humans on this planet of lunacy! That is where the true strength and power of our society resides.

Chapter 34: The Gentle Goodbye, An Appeal, The Gym Gods And My First Competition

"Wisdom is knowing how little we know."

- Socrates

We are now in August 2019, and I had booked a quick visit for Elliott and me to go to the UK, Harvey was holding the fort and taking care of the animals.

We stayed with Kay and Denbo and also with Susan. The time went so quick and we were very well looked after, I even got to train at my old gym in Horbury.

The main reason for the visit was to go and see my mum and dad, and Elliott to go and see his grandma and granddad. They had always been around for him in his early years along with Harvey and their cousins Darby and Georgina. When we moved to live in France, they could not see them as much. Both Harvey and Elliott loved them dearly and got so much love and guidance from them. 'The Tank' often having them both on his knees reading 'Thomas The Tank Engine' or whichever other enchanting book he would have them spellbound with as they received their bedtime story.

Grand parenthood came so naturally to my mum and dad and all four grandchildren were blessed with the love of two amazing grandparents.

I warned Elliott that grandma was not well and dying, but Elliott had just been through a major trauma in his life, as had Harvey. Seeing their mum become handicapped and going through a very dark and painful time which they had to witness. Then his father leaving in March 2018 with no knowledge of his whereabouts. This kid was much stronger than I thought. He made his grandma laugh even as she lay there dying!

My mum had cancer. Back in the 1980s she had battled through breast cancer. I remember coming to see her from Liverpool university. She had taken herself away in her bedroom with a portable TV, just getting up to go to work. My brother, sister and dad were at home then and I asked if they knew what was wrong with mum. They didn't know, I said "Has anyone bothered to ask her?" "No" was the reply. I went to talk to mum and found out she had a lump in her breast. She was terrified to go to the doctors, probably worried about having to have time off work!

I managed to persuade her to go and get it sorted out she would be alright but ignoring it wouldn't be! I had to go back to Liverpool I had exams. My mum did go and get the operation but didn't tell me when until after my exams. She was a brave, strong woman but I wish she and dad had thought more about themselves as we became adults, but mum couldn't let go of caring for us, it's all she knew.

In the care home mum and I had a very loving and deep chat, we had not been speaking at Christmas because of some lies she had told to protect others. Lies at that time were all I got from the court case, Rob before he left, and I was raw and defensive and now my mum was bareface lying to me. But she was sick even though she hadn't been diagnosed and I was in a dark place trying to accept all that had just happened to me. She was nasty when she last came with dad to visit me and the boys in France and I was nasty back.

On the 23rd of August 2019 in my mum's small room in the care home, a place she was taken to after being in hospital for a period of time, we were reconnected in the same loving way we had been for the majority of our lives. Mum had let go of so much pain that she carried around with her and I had found some light in the darkness I was in.

I knew I would not see her again but the love and peace we gave each other that day was a genuine healing and true love that couldn't and wouldn't be broken, even in death. Neither of us blaming each other but embracing the special moment we had and she promised me that she would let go of all the anger and pain she was burdened with and peacefully go to the place she had been shown. Going there willingly and not looking back, accepting the loving arms that she could see open and inviting her. Allowing herself to go to all the people who were waiting for her. She said there was even her cat Tish and my dog Skippy with some of the other pets waiting with her mum and dad and some of her friends. My mum's face full of peace, no pain, and a look in her eyes of brightness and joy, an acceptance it was time and that it was okay to go. My visit had helped to heal the worries and regrets and helped the acceptance that her time had come to move on.

I knew exactly what she was seeing and feeling, I had experienced it in my accident and in my ICU room. But for me I was supposed to stay for a bit longer, for mum it was time and now she would not fight it but embrace it.

Since my accident I have no fear of death and I have no doubt our soul continues in a place of peace and harmony. I wanted my mum to embrace it and not take with her the fear, anger, and burdens that this human life had given her or the generational pain she also carried for others. By what she said and the look on her face I believe she did that.

When Elliott and I arrived back home, Harvey had done well, and I think enjoyed some time to himself. They were now due back at Lycée it was September.

In September I got the good news that my Handisport licence for the 2019-2020 season had arrived. Now I could compete in my first powerlifting competition in December. Awesome now I needed to focus on my training with just over three months to go.

Still in September I arranged for Val Assist to help me with my appeal preparation. I would do the research; with the little information I had and prepare my case and then Val would translate it into French.

The very first thing we did was send an email to the court on the 19th of September via Val's email so she could respond in French, asking for my files. It was short and to the point:

Dear sir, Madame Walker Penelope Ann (then my case number) is representing herself and requests all documents related to her case to be made available. Thank you.

For the rest of the year, I would go every few weeks to work with Val to get my appeal papers ready, she was brilliant!

During this time Val also went with me to the police station in Coulonges to do a preliminaire procès-verbal d'audition victime.

Before we went, I prepared what I wanted to say because it is normal for the police officer to write down your claim and create a plaintiff against X. I wanted to do two plaintiffs, one against the story told by X (Hervé Dupont) back on the 5th of April 2016 at Cognac police station and a complaint or plaintiff against how X (the police) had treated me, not recognised my human rights and the lack of a proper investigation to the cause of the accident. This is what I proposed to say:

I am present here to depose a plainte contre X and all named persons (26 in total). X gave information which was not true and based on assumptions not facts. On the 5th of April 2016 at 15:05, X entered the police station in Cognac and told a story that X and the other people named had not witnessed. The story concerned a car accident that happened on the 2nd of April 2016 involving X's parents and myself madame Walker who became the victim of this accident, resulting in multiple injuries, loss of my right hand and becoming 80% handicapped.

X's father aged 85 the driver Mr Dupont Maurice and X's mother Madame

Dupont Paulette also in her 80s died at the scene.

No autopsy was carried out, so to this day the cause of death has not been lawfully established and there were no blood samples taken so there is no investigation to alcohol consumed or drugs in the drivers' systems. I madame Walker do not drink alcohol and do not take drugs. There was no investigation of the elderly couple's medication or health though this was investigated for me madame Walker who was 52 years old not in her 80's.

I would then describe what was said at the Cognac police station and the sentence that Lucas Philippoteau gave. I also stated that it was based on assumption not facts and how I had been unjustly treated and my stress and anxiety plus the defamation of my character etc, etc.

The second plaintiff against X (police) highlighting the gross misconduct of X, resulting in a biased, assuming unjust, unlawful, and criminal act. X did not act within the law, and this resulted in violation of a person's right to a fair and just criminal procedure. It greatly violated the human rights act Art. 6 (1-3).

So, you get the picture, I had looked up my rights and I could do a plaintiff (complaint) even though time had passed because I was bringing new discovered information.

Bet you can all guess what happened as Val, and I stood in the police station in Coulonge. The not so friendly police office said I had no right to make a complaint. I tried to say through Val that I did in fact have a lawful right. Then I got the superiority act off him, "I have been a police officer for 20 years and I am telling you, you have no right." This was all said at the counter at the reception area he didn't even take us into a room for privacy or to get the form to start the plaintiff I had a lawful right to make. His twenty years policing obviously just gave him understanding how to not be a nice person and throw his weight around while ignoring the actual laws that he was supposed to enforce. We left this was just another massive kick in the guts, yet again administered by the upholders of the scales of justice.

I was training once a week in Poitiers, Patrick guiding my benching and then I would go off and use the other machines and train the rest of my body. I still had the attachment that the Grand Feu had made me, but it wasn't strong or safe enough as I would hopefully increase the weight load.

I had some meetings with Pasquay, the company I met at the Grand Feu and the one that worked with me to try and get the robotic hand to work, but it was way too early for that. Stubby was weak and skinny and when Dr. Piteu explained that I would need to chop some of Stubby off to help get just a normal prosthesis, my mind was made up, Stubby and I would find another way to get on with life.

Pasquay listened to my goals (probably thought I was crazy) but worked with me to develop a more sturdy attachment for my benching. They knew that I had a competition on the 8th of December so hopefully it would be ready for then.

My hidden gem in Liverpool, Danny from Taylors gym was also sending me training four times a week. I had to video it and send it to him. I didn't like being on video but just got on with it. Now looking at them I can see how weak my poor battered body was and how much work it needed, it would be a slow process.

Both Danny and Patrick helped me understand the strict movement that had to be done to get a good lift. It wasn't a matter of forcing the bar up with all your might, if you didn't do it according to the rules, it was a no lift! Just a hesitation or a small wobble would give you a no lift. It had to be done correctly.

As the time grew closer to my competition date, I discussed the weight I should do for the three lifts. The weight decided was 37kg, 40kg and 45kg. Not any amazing weight there but the competition was more about living it, learning from it and just experiencing it. For me it was my best teaching experience.

I had, way back in the 1980's entered a bench press competition and got second but that wasn't a strict powerlifting competition but more connected to bodybuilding and was organised by Ken Latham at one of his bodybuilding competitions.

The discipline I was entering into now was so different and I had to learn how to lift that way. The tiny matter of only having my left hand to hold the Olympic bar, just adding to the challenge and my desire to find a way for Stubby and his attachment to assist!

Just to test my commitment and perseverance, the universe decided to test my desire to get to this competition, which was way up in the north of France, at Villeneuve d'Ascq. With Patrick's help I had booked my place in the competition and a two night stay in a recommended hotel. I didn't know what to expect but I would arrive on the Friday and all the competitors would have a meal together. The Saturday would be competition day and the Saturday evening another meal with the competitors and all those involved and leaving the hotel on the Sunday.

I booked my train and asked if I could take up the offer of someone meeting me at the train station. Then the train drivers or workers went on strike, so all trains were cancelled. But that wasn't going to stop me! I would drive there but would have to break the journey up it was too far to do it in one go.

I did some research and booked myself into this budget hotel in Rouen Petit Quevilly on the Thursday the 6th and again on the Sunday the 9th on my way back home.

Rouen was more than halfway to Villeneuve d'Ascq, so that left me about 257km for tomorrow's journey. The total distance from my house was about 640 km but I wanted to avoid Paris, so I probably took a longer route. Driving in the middle of Paris was not something I desired to do. I would stay the night in the Ibis hotel, rested and ready for the next part of the drive.

The journey was tiring and difficult, lots of rain so I was very pleased to get to Rouen about four and a half hours after setting off. Having lived in Australia, long distance was the norm, but I could have done with less rain. Passing trucks on the auto-route was a heart in the mouth experience for the water spray blinded your vision, no matter how fast the wipers were going. I prayed every time I had to overtake one. I concluded the hardest challenge this next few days was not lifting the bar but getting there in one piece with the weather conditions.

I gratefully got there in one piece and searched for the hotel. We had received notification that the hotel in Villeneuve d'Ascq was next to Lille football stadium and that weekend there was a home game so parking may be difficult.

I arrived early and found a disabled parking spot close by. I decided I would stay parked there for the two days and nights so as not to lose my spot. I had really had enough driving in the last few days, so I wasn't in a rush to drive if I could avoid it.

I went to my hotel but got told my room wasn't ready and I needed to wait. No problem, I was early but at least I was at my destination.

Another person arrived and he had to wait also. We got chatting, he was there for the competition too. We waited a long time with no information, and I said this isn't right it's past check in time. I wanted a rest, and I was cold the hotel lobby seemed quite cold.

Eventually I had had enough and said I wanted to get to my room, that's when they told me that the heating had broken, and they were trying to get it fixed. To cut a long story short we were moved to a hotel within walking or wheelchair distance (a lot of the competitors were in wheelchairs), so at last I could rest.

We had a meal organised for us and my new friend who spoke some English said I could go in his car. I gratefully accepted for I was hoping that I wouldn't have to use my own car over the weekend.

As with most French meals it was four courses, none of your quick couple of hours, it was the opportunity for people to catch up with friends they hadn't seen for a while, this competition being an annual event.

I sat and watched, I was tired from the journey, didn't feel hungry and was a bit lost, they were all talking so fast. I soaked up the atmosphere. Many there were curious to know who I was, I didn't know anything about them. There were many in wheelchairs and a wide range of ages. There were carers or helpers, coaches, and the judges there too.

Halfway through the meal another person arrived, he was friendly and popular, and I remember thinking he looks like a bodybuilder. He had good biceps.

I had then for some unknown reason thought the English sports car that I had parked behind when I arrived (I noticed the righthand drive) was his. I don't know why I thought that, but sure enough after the meal he drove away in that sports car.

The next day my new friend, who was a judge offered me a lift to the venue and I jumped (well I can't jump!) at the chance.

There was a lot of setting up it was a Coupe de France, and many good lifters were there. I watched, listened, and intently observed. There was a buzz, a happiness, friendliness, non-judgemental atmosphere, and I felt so at home.

All these athletes and all the people involved had their stories to tell. My chauffeur had been hit by a truck as a child and all his family in the car had been injured. It was an English company, and the driver didn't stay around, so it was a long hard battle for his family to get any closure. He had written a book about it and I was touched and encouraged by his story.

There are so many people learning to live a life they thought they would never have had to live and in that room on Saturday the 8th of December 2019 I got the biggest lesson that I had had so far. It was okay to be disabled, it made you special, not different. It made you stronger, and much more accepting of the gifts that you had and how far you could work with them.

That day I felt I belonged, I wasn't different, except I spoke poor French. I was welcomed and I was accepted and encouraged. Being disabled mattered!

We did and do have a place in the none disabled world. By accepting our disabilities personally, what other's opinions were did not matter. We were able to achieve whatever we set our mind to and were prepared to work for within the bodily limits we were given.

I was now shown that this, in the future was my task, my mission, to help other see their self-worth, no matter what the disability! We are beacons of light, that others could learn so much from, including able-bodied people.

The competition started. All competitors had been weighed in and their competition clothes checked. Stubby's adaptation had to be looked at, I still had the old one, there had been delays in getting the new one but I had trained with the old one so I was good with it.

Because it was my first competition, I wasn't put into a weight class. I weighed in about 54kg, so would have been in the women's under 55kg class. I also had to go and tell them what height I needed the bench, so I went and tested it.

The bench they use is not the same as the bench used in normal powerlifting, it's wider and there are two places to put the bar on for people who have short limbs. In fact, Barbara Meyer the organiser and director of sport development and musculation of Handisport, asked me if I needed to use it because of my short limb. Then I didn't really know what she meant; I always trained the normal way so said I will lift normal.

Stubby is about 20cm shorter than my left arm and the guys at Pasquay were making the new attachment so Stubby would be the same length as my left arm.

Being a novice and in the novice, class meant my class would be up first. There was a warmup area and most athletes had coaches except me and I didn't see the guy with the English sports car with one either.

I went and did some warmups and just followed the crowd. I hadn't got a clue what I was supposed to be doing.

There were three males and two females (including me) in the novice class. Two of the boys were just fourteen years old the other seventeen. Their lifts were 30kg, 32kg and 34kg for Soukouna, 47kg, 49kg and 50kg for Ben Hadj and first place to Lamdaouar who lifted 65kg, 69kg and 73kg at fourteen years of age, that was amazing.

In my class I was with Coulibaly aged twenty who lifted an impressive 53kg, 57kg and 60kg. Me at fifty-five years old lifted 37kg, 40kg and 45kg which I was over the moon with.

With my emergency intestine operation back in July 2018, then my big operation to have my dancing pole out in the September, I had only really got training just over six months ago. So, the purpose of this competition was research and to get started on the competition journey.

I was so unsure what to do that in my first lift I get the command to start by the judge sat behind the bar, who happened to be my wonderful new friend the chauffeur. So, I lift the bar and just held it there, he then had to get up and tell me to press. For some reason I was waiting for another command. When you have raised the bar, the judge then instructs you to rack. This means put the bar back on the rack. Bit embarrassing, everyone was watching this one-handed woman make a daft mistake.

Now I just had to concentrate on my next lift of 40kg. There was this friendly looking lady in a wheelchair, I hadn't seen her last night at the restaurant, she was watching me, and I exchanged a smile and an expression of I haven't a clue what I am doing! She gave me an encouraging smile back.

I did my next lift okay with no daft mistakes this time and then I was going to go for 45kg. Would I be able to get it? I did my third lift and thought Stubby was a little wobbly and I did not think I had managed to get a successful third lift, but I had. That was it over, my first competition with Handisport. Now the real competition would start with the experienced athletes.

I did get to chat to the female in the wheelchair who had smiled. I said, "I hadn't got a clue what to do." Her reply was "I was so shocked you were only lifting with one hand." I found out that the kind smiling face belonged to Souhad Ghazouani a well experienced lifter who had been to many Paralympic Games. That day she lifted 120kg, now that's amazing! Souhad was in the under 79kg class. If I had not been a novice my class would have been the under 55kg class.

That day there was an under 50kg class and three ladies were competing. The ladies in the under 50kg class lifts were 38kg and 42kg by a young girl called Whitney (one of her lifts was a no lift). Then Martine who was in her 60s, so I wasn't the oldest competitor. She lifted an impressive 58kg, 61kg her 63kg attempt being a no lift. The third competitor Mimozette, another Paralympian lifted 82kg with a no lift for her first lift of 80kg and a no lift for her third lift of 87kg impressive I was truly impressed with that! Now the bar had been set, that would be my goal over the coming years, to get stronger and lift better.

The men's competition included three different weight classes, up to 65kg, up to 72kg and the plus 72kg class. There were also some Paralympians competing in the men's competition.

The winning lift in the up to 65kg class was a lift of 165kg by Axel Bourlan. The up to 72kg class a 130kg lift by David Copien. The over 72kg class was a 179kg lift by Julien Avonembum.

I have already made the comment that many songs talk to me. Remember Bob Marley after my time in the Colosseum (the court) and the songs he gave me. This day it was Queen giving me a message. Just before I went to the warmup area a song shouted out a message at me. Queen's 'Don't Stop Me Now'. I said to the lady who was in charge of drinks and snacks "This song is for me, don't stop me now!" She laughed and I went to warm up.

I did actually get presented with a medal, but I had left with a lovely girl who was also a judge, to go back to the hotel to change for the evening meal. We chatted, her English was good, she was a trained speech therapist and a lovely person. I will probably get my medal one day, it would be more for nostalgia for me, a little sign that I had made some progress.

Once everything was packed away, we all headed for the restaurant not the same one as the night before, but my loyal chauffeur Johann Biree took me there.

I was sat opposite another judge Jean Bernard Gebert and his wife and the guy with the sports car Julian to my right, who spoke good English. I had briefly spoken to Julian after the competition but now I was sat next to him I wanted to know if he was a bodybuilder. He was and he had just won a competition. He had his leg amputated when he was eighteen years old and started training then.

I told him I used to compete with the EFBB, and I think he was impressed. He said he hoped his next competition would be with that federation. The evening was very pleasant, everybody enjoying the friendly atmosphere and tomorrow we would all be back to our different lives.

The next morning after breakfast, everyone said their goodbyes. I wished the bodybuilder sports car guy Julian all the best for he was about to open a gym in the new year. I was encouraging and happy that he was following a deep passion and dream that he had. I was pleased to see a person follow not only his dream but their passion, the two I think go hand in hand with each other. Julian asked if I planned to compete in May 2020 in Drôme in the south of France, yes, I would like to, why not!

I now had my shorter drive to Rouen and then Monday the longer trip home but I was happy with the weekend, the people I had met and the lessons I had learnt. All credit must go to all the organisers and especially Barbara Meyer who worked so efficiently and endlessly to make the event happen.

I was grateful to them all they did not appreciate what gift they had all just given me. The gift of self-love, no matter what challenges may have been thrown at you!

By the end of 2019 I had my appeal ready. I never got any files even though in November I had physically gone to the court who told me all my files were now at the appeal court in Poitiers. Again, my request for something I had a legal right to being ignored, this time by the court! I concluded they all piss in the same pot.

Val Patard was such a wonderful professional and a supportive person. We both thought it would be best to send my appeal file by secure, signed for post after Christmas, in January 2020. The court date being the 23rd of March 2020. I would also send a copy to the Dupont solicitor. I had previously requested my file from the appeal court in Poitiers to no avail. No response and no files why does that not surprise me?!

In the November I had realised that there was a powerlifting competition in Manchester in February 2020 which I would like to go to so I could further my knowledge which I had learnt at the competition in December. Also, some of the people from that competition were going to represent France in Manchester at the World Para-Powerlifting competition. I told them that I was hoping to go and watch.

I made arrangements, I would at last get to see my coach Danny in Liverpool, then go on to Manchester, then up to Yorkshire. I booked a flight from Nantes to

Manchester from the 16th of February until the 26th of February 2020.

Before the trip I had asked Santa for an Olympic powerlifting set, I needed to get used to the bar that was used in competitions and I was sort of running out of options with the weights I had already. I loved going to the gym but that was just once a week. My main office of weight work was at home, and I needed to upgrade things. It was a bit like going back to my small gym in the hut when I was at Liverpool University. If you have the will and desire, you can just get on with it no matter what facilities were available to you.

I felt at last nearly four years after my accident a year was ending on a positive and encouraging note. But why do I keep thinking this? I always end up disappointed and battling my way through another difficult year!

Suzie In France

Peggy

Skitty

Wilson

Prison Or The Paralympics

Waiting To Be Planted

Dahlias In The Garden

Penny Walker

Gifts From Mother Nature

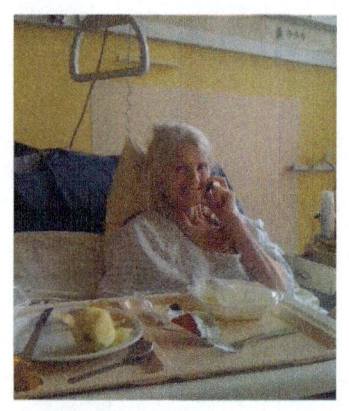

Prison Or The Paralympics

April 2016 Nantes Hospital Trauma Ward

View From Plastics Nantes Hospital (Helicopter Landing Pad)

The Fire That Kept Stubby Warm

The Basket I Made At The Grand Feu

Elliott Enjoying The Snow

February 2018 Harvey & Elliott Having A Snowball Fight Over The Adapted Car Outside Peace Pad

Stubby's Gym

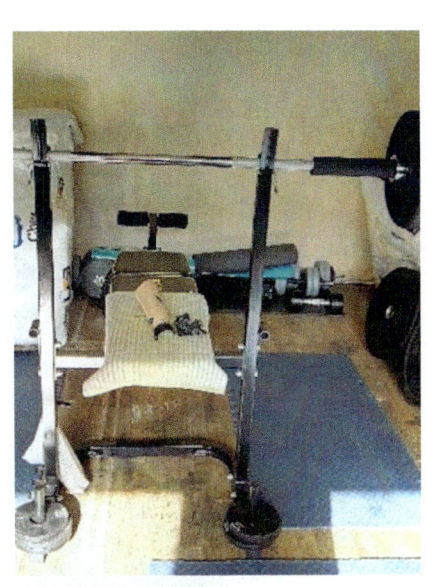

My New Eleiko Gym Equipment

Susan's Rose Friendship

Prison Or The Paralympics

Kay's Rose Nostalgia

Saying Goodbye To Mum

Denbo's Rose Simply The Best

Chapter 35: Appeal Papers, The Volunteer, Fear Of The Truth And My Pen Is Mightier Than The Courts

"When you tear out a man's tongue you are not proving him a liar, you're only telling the world that you fear what he might say."

- George R.R Martin

I like the number two so I was hoping 2020 would bring a good twelve months, but my track record didn't really show that. My appeal pieces were translated even though I had not received anything from the courts after a number of requests. The game obviously still being played out.

My translated pieces or file included the following:

On the front of my red plastic file was my name Madame Walker Penelope, the title 'Pieces Procedure en Appel' and the reference number 19/710. The first page had the Cour d'Appel de Poitiers address 86000 Poitiers and a list of the pieces (documents) included, there were 35 pieces.

Pieces 1-6 were attestations (character references) from people who had been in my life at some point and knew my character and integrity.

The first one was from Philip a retired UK senior police officer who had been seconded by the UK Foreign and Commonwealth Office and had held the post of Head of Police development department, OSCE spill over monitor mission to Skopje. He had supervised a staff of 80 people and negotiated policing policy at government level. He stated that he could recommend her (me) "As an honest, dedicated and talented professional who is an asset to her many patients."

The second was from Steven a company owner of Sandams who I had known for many years. His conclusion "I truly believe wherever Penny goes it will be their gain and our loss."

The third was from Michael the owner of Townsend Planning he stated "I must state that I have always been impressed by her professionalism. Perhaps more importantly, I have been impressed by her care, understanding and empathy with her clients."

The fourth from Andrew the director of Modis, "Penny is a very professional, ethical and reliable physio. She is very skilful and dedicated!"

The fifth from Christine from Kirklees council the Southwest Yorkshire mental health NHS Trust. "An important part of my job is to research and procure the services of a variety of holistic complementary therapists to provide such skills as:

Sound knowledge of their profession.

Good communication and facilitation skills.

To be able to convey enthusiasm and enjoyment in the session.

Valuing people and treating them with respect.

Penny has consistently provided all the above skills and attributes and is always a sought after and popular therapist."

The sixth being from Brenda, head teacher of food technology. "My life is richer for having the support and now friendship of Penny. I cannot recommend her highly enough, Penny is incredibly conscientious, hardworking, and caring with a great sense of humour, a credit to her profession."

I included these to show I was not that person they were portraying me to be, these 'professionals' who had never bothered to find out who I really was.

Pieces 7-16 included my medical records from Nantes hospital and the Grand Feu.

Pieces 17-21, 17 included police photographs, with Piece 18 being photographs from the first expert Maurice Pascal. Piece 19 are photographs of the Seat's (my car) wheels, Piece 20 are photographs of the non-preservation of any evidence on the Seat and Piece 21 a report by the second expert Marc Puech. (Some of the pieces I will put in the appendix but give a brief explanation here why I had included them).

The whole evidence according to Maurice Pascal, the first expert report lay at the black rubber marks on the Seat's back right plastic wheel hub and the Peugeot the Dupont's car front bumper which he also claimed had black rubber marks on it's left. Piece 17 are five police photos. Photo IMG 1567.JPG being taken at the scene of the accident. I was still in the car the emergency team preparing to cut me out. The other four photos were taken the following day on the 3rd of April 2016 by the police at the garage where the cars were stored for evidence, but not undercover or with any protection.

These five photos are of the Seat's back right wheel and it is shown on all five photos that there is no wheel hub on this right back wheel. Piece 18 shows the same five police photos alongside two photos taken by Maurice Pascal (first expert) either on the 28th of April 2016 or the 23rd of August 2016 the two dates he states he visited the garage (so the photos could have only been taken on either of these dates). These two photos taken by Pascal now show the Seat's back right wheel has a wheel hub on it, this being where he concluded the contact took place on the Seat due to the alleged overtaking and the alleged pulling in and touching the Peugeot's front bumper on the left side. I would like to add I did point out this very fact and the five police photographs plus the contradicting Maurice Pascal's photographs to Riposseau who dismissed it! But my simple question is how does a plastic wheel hub or cover take itself off and move itself from the left back wheel and then fixes itself onto the right back wheel on the Seat car, how interesting and miraculous is that?

If someone had found a wheel cover in the road (there obviously was not a search made, remember I found a perfect wheel cover in the hedge off my car a year later) they can't just guess which of the four tyres to put it on and remember the police photos show only one in place less than 24 hours later on the left back wheel. The other three tyres didn't have anything on them. I found one undamaged which was left in the hedge for a year at the scene of the accident. So, this cover must have had magical powers that allowed it to move onto the right back tyre on Maurice Pascal's photographs. Oh and don't forget that this wheel cover from the Seat and a front bumper off the Peugeot vanished when I requested a second expert's report. The only two pieces of the cars that Maurice Pascal claimed made contact.

Piece 19 showing all this with seven police photographs showing all the four wheels of the Seat and only the back left wheel has got a wheel cover on. The front two wheels in IMG 6767 and 6741 clearly showing the damage to the front wheels with no wheel covers and IMG 6768 showing the back right wheel of the Seat without a wheel cover. There is a mud mark on the back right tyre, and I know it's the right because the petrol cover can be seen on IMG 6745 and that was on the right side of the car. It's image IMG 6769 that shows the left back wheel and that is the one with the cover.

As I stated earlier I also over a year later, in the hedge at the scene of the accident, found one of my plastic wheel hubs, without damage or any mark, which was off the Seat's back right wheel because a plastic wheel hub/cover would not have been undamaged if it had come off the Seat's front wheels. If the impact could take my right hand clean off and my steering wheel, I don't think a plastic wheel hub could have survived undamaged!

So, what does all this mean? Well firstly you don't have to take years training as a police officer to work it out! I was not overtaking! It's more probable that the Peugeot had lost control and caught my back left wheel as it was out of control which then sent me into a tree (the only one on that stretch or road the rest being hedging). It also means that somebody moved the wheel hub from the back left to the back right, so it looked as if the Seat overtook. The police photos all say the same and if the wonderful 'technology' used by the expert Pascal could explain the accident I would like them to show me how a wheel hub can, all by itself, move from one wheel to another weeks later and by March 2017 when a second expert is there to exam the non-preserved evidence the magic moving wheel hub vanishes along with the Peugeot's front bumper! The only two areas according to Maurice Pascal that proved the cause of the accident. How do you misplace a full-size bumper in a double murder case? When it is allegedly vital evidence! Just asking.

I thought these photos needed to be seen. At least the appeal court could clearly see from the pieces I provided that there was something extremely dodgy happening with the only 'evidence' that I was being sentenced for double murder with. The fact that my solicitor didn't bother to mention this 'little' inconsistency or mystery, captured on police photos spoke volumes to me.

Piece 20 are photos to show how contaminated the Seat car was before the second and third expert got to examine it, minus the mysteriously vanished Seat wheel hub and Peugeot's front bumper. In fact, in piece 21 I included a response to the report by Christophe Ledon (the third expert) by Marc Puech (the second expert), in which this national expert Marc Puech states on page four of the response in bold print that there is no preservation of the vehicles and basically it can't be used as evidence.

Also, at the top of page five of this response, Christophe Ledon has a photo of the tree hitting the Peugeot in the roof and then suddenly Christophe Ledon changes his mind. Now at the bottom of page five and on page six, he shows the tree hitting the Peugeot in the windscreen. Come on Ledon make your mind up!

You have already done all your calculations with two left-hand drive cars instead of my righthand car and now you can't make your mind up if the impact on the Peugeot was in the roof or in its windscreen come on, after all you are supposed to be the 'expert'!

The court in April 2019 on the 15th did not even mention Marc Puech's faultless report instead relying on Christophe Ledon and Maurice Pascal, the expert with the self-moving plastic wheel hub and Ledon the one who used the wrong cars and couldn't decide which part of the Peugeot the tree hit, if indeed it ever hit the tree. Remember Pascal had it stuck in the tree when at the scene of the accident the Peugeot was in a totally different position and direction. I have to accept my sentence of double murder on that quality of information?! A five-year-old could see these mistakes but police, judges, prosecutors and solicitors couldn't or wouldn't!

Piece 22 is the police statements from the first person who found the accident and phoned for help. Pieces 23, 24, 25 and 26 are all police statements from pompiers who attended the accident. The statements 22-26 all stating that Mr Dupont had no signs of life. He was not worked on to try and revive him, but Mrs Dupont was. This was way before 10pm, the first witness statement stating she arrived at 8:40pm. One of the pompier's statements even mentioning their belief that Mr Dupont had had a heart attack. 'Le conducteur en arrêt cardiaque et sa passagère inconsciente mais qui respire.' (The driver had a heart attack, and the passenger was unconscious but still breathing).

I included these because it clearly showed that there was no question that the driver of the Peugeot was ever seen alive from at least 8:40pm and he did not die at 10pm as judge Isabelle De Coux aggressively (I have got to use the word, everyone else does!) claimed he did, that time 10pm was the time of a pronounced death. But an autopsy, the legal way to define time and cause of death (and consumption of alcohol and prescribed drugs) was never carried out so we will never know, will we? However, he was 85 years old and 'in perfect health' according to Geraldine Dauphin. In a court of law, a solicitor committing perjury, isn't that breaking the law? Isn't that misleading and most definitely stretching the truth if it was in fact true!

Piece 28 was some of my interrogation by the police which conveniently left my questions out and the non-informative answer or unanswered response by the police. My two main questions being "Had they consumed alcohol?" and "Were they on medication or had any medical problems?". The questions, dodged not given a straight answer to or no answer at all, swiftly moving on from having to give one.

Piece 29 was the paper I was served with and bullied to sign on the 16th of January 2017, plus the notification of rights in English. The one that police officer Karen Payeur told me was a copy of the served papers which it wasn't. I didn't understand what I was forced to sign.

Piece 30 was the charge I was presented with after I was interrogated for nearly three hours, and I refused to sign it I didn't agree with it. Eventually I did reluctantly sign it because I was feeling very ill and faint and just wanted to get out of the toxic, bullying and hostile environment. I was still in my wheelchair and was still very unwell from the accident.

Piece 31-34 were papers referring to a visit made by Hervé Dupont one of the sons on the 5th of April 2016 in a police station in Cognac. At this time, I was still in a coma or maybe had just come out and still in ICU and not certain if I would live or die.

The son went to tell a story about the accident even though he wasn't there. You would have thought he would have had the funeral first. There was no delay for the funeral for they didn't bother with that 'small' matter of finding out the cause of death or alcohol or drugs in the driver's system with an autopsy. But for some reason this story needed to be told in just over 48 hours (There is a much bigger window of opportunity than that to start the claim for compensation, maybe he was desperate for money or trying to hide the truth).

It is interesting that the same charges that the police officer Lucas Philippoteau charged me with on the story told by Hervé Dupont, who wasn't even at the accident, were the same that were given to me on the 15th of April 2019 in court. So, the sentence was decided before any so-called investigation to the cause of the accident had even begun. Purely based on a story and assumptions and no doubt gossip told and delivered by Hervé Dupont in a Cognac police station on the 5th of April 2016 at 15:05. Also interesting was there was no mention of alcohol, the age of 85 years or any medical conditions, procedures, or medication for his 85-year-old father. But then that was the whole point, lead them down a path away from the truth, that foreign other driver won't probably survive anyway.

Piece 35 was a document requesting an investigation sent to the magician Maurice Pascal, (remember he can make things move and vanish), what a clever man. It was sent on the 6th of April 2016 at 11:45, the request made for the 'expert' to investigate the cause of the accident. The instructions being to open an inquiry for the homicide (murder) by a road accident that caused, yes it stated caused, the death of two people. I thought the whole point of appointing an expert was to conclude and investigate the cause of the accident. So how at this stage can police officer Eric Gatard put in print that the accident caused the death of two people, how did he know? Oh yeah, he read Hervé Dupont's story, or he told him the story, but let's not worry here there will be an autopsy and then we will get to know the truth and the true cause of death. After all an autopsy is the only legal way of defining the cause of death, isn't it? Or can someone walking by or not even be at the scene where there is a fatality decide the cause of death? Apparently so!

Making assumptions that it was murder before any investigation can't be lawful. What's the point of having thousands of laws if no one follows them? I get it now, you pick out the ones that will fit into the story and gossip, don't bother to look for real evidence, that's not the police's job, is it?

Boy, do I wish I had Columbo on this case he would have not missed the obvious or listened to the gossip, made up stories or the bullshit and lies.

On the 23rd of January 2020 I sent the file to the appeal court in Poitiers, all translated into French, secure, signed for, return notification of arrival post. It cost a bit but I wanted to know that the appeal court had got it. In March 2020 I sent another file again registered post with the exact material in it also translated to Dupont's solicitor.

I received the pieces from Phillipe Courtois on the 18th or 19th of March, less than a week before the court date. It was all in French (remember it's how the game is played, leave a person in the dark don't give them their human rights). You would think that this world-famous solicitor would know that one of the basic human rights was the equality of arms, and I should have equal opportunities as the other party. Not given anything in my native language which I am sure such a big and famous cabinet of solicitors was quite capable of doing meant they weren't giving me an equal opportunity.

This was not living up to the profile he portrayed. The portrayal being Phillipe Courtois' desire for fighting for justice and the truth. Not his desire in my case, instead let's camouflage and ignore the truth and get a victory at any cost. We must not let our famous reputation get dirty now, should we?

I tried to understand the document that they had sent me but with less than a week to go before the 25th of March I couldn't get it translated. As I was endeavouring to do this myself a voice came into my head, don't bother, it's a game, they are only going or trying to direct you away from what they are hiding.

Funny enough there was no mention of alcohol, medication, medical records, health status, ages, or the lack of an autopsy. No reference to the national expert Marc Puech, I wonder why that was?

But just as the undamaged plastic wheel hub in the hedge that I was gifted a year after the accident was a sign from the universe indicating to me that the wheels needed looking at more closely, for it was a sign that I was on point and that the evidence was sabotaged to look as if I had overtaken.

Another gift sent and presented to me in the papers sent by Phillipe Courtois was in piece 30. In piece 30 there was a photo of Maurice Dupont with a glass of alcohol at his right hand in the Summer of 2015 so less than a year before the accident. This showed a number of things. Firstly, he not only 'could drink' as the Dupont solicitor said in court but he did! And they had just proved it with a photo less than a year old. This photo wasn't taken years before the 2nd of April 2016 but only months before.

Now I knew why alcohol is never mentioned and why a test for alcohol is never taken! The police saying there wasn't sufficient blood. Rob and Steven walked the scene of the accident as the emergency teams were trying to get me out of my car. They saw no blood near the Dupont's so no huge amounts of physical loss of blood, more than can be said for my situation.

Also how did this French system manage to test Henri Paul, Princess Diana's driver. Henri, Diana's driver was killed at the scene, same country, same laws. How did they manage to test him for alcohol and do an autopsy? The situation was the same.

Many times, I had asked my team of guardians to give me signs that what I knew deep in my being was true, and there was a reason why everybody is hiding and avoiding discussing the subject or the word alcohol! Like the wheel hub this photo was the sign I needed. I now knew this 85-year-old was not a tea totaller but consumed alcohol.

The only bit of information that the police managed to find out about the Dupont's was that they drove two and a half hours from Cognac to visit with family and friends in Saint Pompain and they left just after the tradition apero time.

Apero time is a very serious time for the French and usually is in the early evening where they have drinks with friends or family between 6pm and 9pm. This tradition of France very much active today especially with the older generations.

The most disappointing thing is that the Dupont couple sat with family or friends who knew what they drank and ate, yet they allowed them behind a car wheel.

Why didn't any of these people or anyone connected to the Dupont's, ever get questioned officially and provide a sworn witness statement? Rob, my partner had to! There are so many people involved in this cover up "Facts do not cease to exist because they are ignored." Aldous Huxley.

I wonder how they all sleep at night. If my two boys had been in the car, they probably have sentenced me for killing my own sons too!

But justice does exist outside any human justice system and my boys were never meant to be in the car just me. I have immense gratitude for that.

I would raise a glass to all those that did and are hiding the truth. Hiding behind their unspoken words allowing the untruths to grow into a jungle of cover ups and deceit. But I can't, I don't drink, and I haven't got my right hand!!

In January 2020 I was also blessed to still be getting support from my team at APF, and I had got my new attachment for Stubby from Pasquay nearly ready. Though I didn't have it for my competition in December 2019, I was pleased to have it nearly finished. It was so much more robust so would work well when I was benching. I just had to go back on the 5th of February to get it slightly altered which they gladly did. I knew that there was room for improvement, but I had something that worked well and by using it I would learn how to improve and develop it further if needed. I was so grateful.

The next week on the 16th of February I would be heading to the UK and see my hidden gem Danny at Taylor's gym in Liverpool. I decided to take my old attachment and leave my new one at home. I didn't want to lose it; I had only just got it.

Penny Walker

I landed in Manchester airport on the Sunday the 16th of April, late afternoon and had a train booked for 17:53 to Liverpool arriving in Lime Street station around 7pm. I knew this station well I had used it many times in the mid-1980s when I was at Liverpool University. I couldn't believe how much it had changed but things tend to in thirty years.

Two friends met me at Lime Street station, and we went to their house to eat and catch up having not seen them for years. After catching up I went to my hotel in Liverpool, the Tune Hotel. They were friendly and the place was just right for what I needed a three night stay in Liverpool. It had the added thing which made Elliott so jealous when I spoke to him, a Greggs next door, his favourite food outlet, he adored their chicken pasties. I got my tea, coffee, and porridge there each day and an occasional cookie. I was now trying to eat for my training what you eat being important to progress in your training. Your car wouldn't function so well if you put water instead of fuel in it and you wouldn't get very far. I saw the food I consumed was a vital part of my training and a thing that was easy to do, the hardest part for me was having the time to eat enough.

I was booked to be coached by Danny at his gym, Taylor's gym a five-minute walk away from my hotel. On the Monday and Tuesday, I had booked my coaching session for 3 o'clock until about 4:30. I had also booked a treatment with another Danny who had a treatment room there, D.S sports massage. Daniel Staples was an excellent therapist, and I am very picky. It's got to be hands on, deep and get to the root of the tightness, injury, or restriction. My poor body having all three. Since my accident I hadn't really had treatment but rehabilitation at the Grand Feu which I was so lucky and grateful to have. I hadn't bothered with treatment I knew what my body needed, machines and ten minutes of light massage was a waste of time, my battered body needed far more than that which Danny Staples expertly gave it. He gave hands on treatment, asking the right questions and listening to the patient. I would definitely seek more treatment from him each time I was in Liverpool.

I had gone out earlier to find the address of Taylor's gym and also found a great sandwich shop. All the workmen in their work-boots and dirt were queuing outside, a good sign. So that was my source of food for the next couple of days. I didn't get the bacon sandwich the workmen were getting, having pigs back in France meant pork was all I seemed to eat so I didn't bother with bacon, though it smelt good. I chose tuna instead.

That afternoon I set off with plenty of time to spare to walk to Danny's gym. It would be great to meet him at last. The guy willing to take on my challenges with belief and an amazing depth of knowledge.

As I walked, I wondered if he knew what he was letting himself in for. A disabled bodied ex-bodybuilder who saw no reason why her dreams could not materialise with the right guidance, a lot of hard work, faith, and perseverance. With an inbuilt stubbornness to do something that not many had done. The path was not well trodden and maybe a new path had to be created, but my belief was that impossibility is only impossible until it is done!

As I got nearer to the gym, I saw a tall bearded man walking in my direction, I thought "I bet that's Danny", he later told me "I saw you and thought I bet that's Penny."

After seven months of energetically connecting via distant training, in a city I had a deep soulful connection to, I would at last meet Danny in the flesh on the streets of Liverpool. I instantly knew, just like my connection with Denbo all those years ago, that this connection would be strong. Danny also getting the crazy, driven, determined me just as Denbo had and I would not be let down.

Danny was on his way for his coffee, I had a feeling this was a daily routine for him and I hobbled along at the side of him, chatting away. Folk from Liverpool love to talk as much as folk from Yorkshire.

I loved his gym, it was a hardcore place, no frills, just a raw fantastic space, oozing with atmosphere and spirit even though there weren't many there at this late afternoon time slot.

I believe gyms breathe, they give off energy and they have a soul all of their own. I always felt it at Muscle World it was at the Poitiers gym in France and most definitely in Taylor's gym in Liverpool. It looked a bit like the Cavern that the Beatles made famous worldwide, that now being a tourist attraction. At Taylor's gym I felt welcomed and at home.

I struggle with what I call the posh marketed gyms. They may be colourful and well equipped, but they lack the soul and the characters of these well-worn grass root sort of gyms. I was there to kick arse, I didn't need the posh sparkling equipment, I needed the grunt and the banter of a down to earth real gym. That's what I got at Taylor's.

Danny wanted to assess my abilities when you are classed as 80% disabled people don't know what to expect. I was nothing like before my accident physically, I had been well and truly smashed up.

People obviously see the missing right hand but that's only the beginning of the story. But you must own your disabilities not let its own you or even define you. I had broken my back in four places in the lumbar region and all the other stuff, but I just about held on to my spirit and soul.

I had two coaching sessions booked with Danny and he spent a good time going through stretches, assessing my mobility, flexibility and balance, all of which required lots of work.

We also went through the benching techniques required and competition rules. The smallest things can make a big difference. The amount of weight not of any importance if you pick up bad techniques, habits, and wrong competition style on the light weight. That's only going to get worse as the resistance increases. Patience being a major element and something that is difficult to have, but you must have it.

My few days in Liverpool were so inspiring. I got brilliant coaching, the technical stuff, position on the bench, hand and Stubby plus attachment position, breathing and an added bonus to meet Danny's powerlifting team. He coaches them twice a week, they were kind, encouraging and inspiring to watch. I was invited to go back to the gym on Tuesday evening to watch, a privilege I was blessed to have been given. They all worked really hard and with humour and enthusiasm.

I got a very good treatment from Danny Stables and I also managed to meet up again with my friends and got more treatment and great hospitality, plus lots of encouragement to achieve my goals. Now it was back on a train heading for Manchester.

I was heading for Wythenshawe south Manchester. I knew Wythenshawe it was at Wythenshawe hospital that I had trained for a year for physiotherapy, living in the tall block of flats close to the hospital with crazy full of life nurses. (I left to continue my training at the Northern College of Massage).

I had been in contact with Eddie Halstead who was involved with the British powerlifting and involved in organising the Para-Powerlifting World Cup. The Manchester 2020 road to Tokyo Para-powerlifting was at the Wythenshawe Forum.

I had booked to go on the Thursday the 20th of February till the finish on the Sunday the 23rd of February. I was booked into Normanhurst hotel about a 15-minute taxi drive away. I had applied to be a volunteer but wasn't sure if I had applied too late for that.

I got there on the Thursday and yes it was okay to be a volunteer, so I get the tee-shirt and was put on the sponsors area (I don't know what else to call it). Food and drinks being on offer for those with the right pass.

I took any chance I could to talk to anyone it was so much easier and even strange to hear all the English accents. I watched the competition with total admiration for all the competitors they were lifting some heavy weights.

I was so happy to have been given the chance by Eddie to soak up this very well organised event. It had organisation, atmosphere, brilliant athletes and for me a humbling experience. I saw it as a blessing that was given to me to see that there are people who work endlessly and tirelessly to assist people with disabilities.

Prison Or The Paralympics

It just confirmed to me that there was a purpose to the horrendous and challenging card I had been dealt. My journey wasn't just for my own benefit, but that one day I would be shown how to give and help others on their rough sea. How and when I didn't know. I did know however it was one of my missions, sent by the universe and I was more than willing to oblige.

Barbara Meyer who I first met at my competition in Villeneuve d'Ascq was there in an official capacity as one of the judges. Also, there was the French lifting team, and they did well. Souhat Ghazouani winning gold in her weight class. It was wonderful to see them again and see them do so well. Hopefully I would see them again in May at the next competition in the south of France.

I was hungry for knowledge and watched and took on board everything I could. I met a lot of very knowledgeable people who were very kind with their time and answering my questions. If you don't ask you never get to know anything the key, I have found is to ask those daft questions, they often provide very informative answers. You soon sense those that don't want to be bothered and that's okay. Find someone who does want to talk, they are often filled with information you had never thought of.

My main questions were about how to get to be part of Para-Powerlifting. I was part of it in France with my license from Handisport and I could enter as many competitions as I liked there but I could not aim for Paris 2024 representing France you had to be a citizen of the country you are representing.

I had already done some research and one of the first things to do was to become a member of the British weightlifting organisation which turned out to be the hub of information. To take part in any competition you had to have an eligible physical impairment. Believe it or not it has been known for some to enter teams into the Paralympics with athletes that have not got impairments and have lied to get to the Paralympics.

What's that all about? I love that sign in a disabled parking spot that states 'If you take my parking spot take my disability too.' That goes for any people out there who try and cheat. We did not request our disabilities. We are just trying to find a positive and enriching way to live with them. Sport being a massive way and part of getting somewhere close to achieving that. Be grateful that you are able bodied, don't insult us any more than some of you do by taking this away from us.

To participate nationally your eligible physical impairments must be named in the World Para-Powerlifting classification, rules and regulations which is acknowledged and evidence by your GP or consultant by completing a World Para-Powerlifting medical diagnostics form and then sending it to your organisation.

In the UK it would be the British weightlifting and in France it is Handisport. Then it will be determined if the minimum impairment criteria is met for your specific physical impairment. In Para-Powerlifting athletes with hearing, visual or intellectual impairments only are not eligible to compete. This is maybe a safety issue after all benching is a dangerous occupation as I learnt in my training hut at Liverpool University 30 years ago.

To go down the international path the world Para-Powerlifting minimum must be met. A world Para-Powerlifting license is essential and can be purchased once all the documentation has been submitted.

I managed to chat briefly with Eddie Halstead and some of the judges who were very encouraging and informative. I also got to pick the brains of a very kind and knowledgeable man who was watching the competition. He was Glyn, a coach based in Salford and was involved with the Para-Powerlifting sport. I learnt a lot and said I would love to visit his gym the next time I was in the UK. He said he would be happy to introduce me to people at his gym and I would be most welcomed. So now full of inspiration, I signed up for my membership at the British Weightlifting organisation that was there.

I also went to get Stubby his own tee-shirt with his name on the back. I felt alive, uplifted, and knew this was the path I was meant to be treading. Where I was going, I hadn't got a clue, but someone, somewhere would guide me, of that, I was sure.

I spoke to the man and woman from the tee-shirt company Uneek who were selling and printing logos on the merchandise for Manchester 2020 and discovered they were from my neck of the woods. I spoke a lot to them they were really nice, and we had quite a lot in common coming from the same area.

I was due to leave and get a train to Dewsbury on Sunday and I found out that the tee-shirt man was going back to Huddersfield on Sunday afternoon, so I asked if I could have a lift because the trains on Sundays were not as frequent as throughout the week. He was happy to take me, and we chatted away as we drove over the Pennies on the M62.

I was so grateful, he dropped me off at Huddersfield train station and Susan came to get me. I was so lucky to have had such a friendly, enlightening few days in Manchester. Now I could have a quick catch up with Susan, some of my friends and see my dad.

I managed two training sessions at my old gym and a catch up with Darren. I got to see Pat and Robin and Robin trained with me. I even got Denbo to come and spot for me, it meant the world to me to have him back by my side in the gym, the gym we had worked so hard together in, the gym that allowed us to make an unbreakable bond of an amazing friendship, trust, and unconditional love.

Denbo hasn't stepped foot in the gym for years and I asked if he would just come to the gym for 15-20 minutes to spot for me. At first, he was reluctant but then he didn't let me down and said he would.

It was like going back in time my mind, body, and soul back in the place I had worked so hard and more importantly back with the person who had allowed me to achieve so much. I wanted and needed him to be part of my new dream, challenges, and direction. We had both been thrown some dark places that we had to visit. But now there was a glimmer of light and I wanted us both to benefit from it, embrace it and heal within it.

Mine and Denbo's souls were intertwined, and we felt each other's challenges and pain, so it was important to feel each other's joys too! I was not going to leave my mate behind even if that meant me dragging him along behind me. That's how powerful a bond we had created over the years and together we would be Cedi Nulius.

I also managed a quick visit with another important and influential man in my life, my dad. He looked a bit lost and confused, he was missing my mum but putting a brave face on.

It saddened me to see this but what I took from it, like so many other things shown to me on my challenging journey, was that we have got a choice to how we want to live. We can be angry, disappointed, and non-forgiving of life's cruelties and the things that happen to us, and the things people do and say to us. Or we can choose to live in peace and harmony, yes facing and battle through our troubles, but not allowing them to own us, define us and dictate to us our sense of well-being and happiness. My dad was strong, accepting of his situation and loving.

No, you don't lay down and be trodden upon but you are grateful of the lessons and stay in your own lane. Being your authentic true self, connecting to your heart and soul and walking away from anything or anyone who attempts to alter that. We have only a short phase of time in which to be truly happy because we are often too busy fighting it.

The visit to see dad was so good in a sad sort of way we talked a lot about his rugby, but he did seem to avoid talking about my mum, he did seem organised and content with his life. I was proud to be his daughter, I missed him and enjoyed our time together, he is a very special soul. I didn't know that world events would mean that that would be my last visit.

Another visit I managed to fit in was seeing my dear friend Debbie and her amazing husband Lee, I got a few hours with them. A lovely couple who work hard and are very genuine and caring.

I was booked on the train from Dewsbury station to Manchester airport and

Susan, another caring and amazing friend coming on the train too because she liked to have outings on a train. The only problem was the previous train hadn't turned up so this one was way too full and for most of the journey we couldn't sit together. We said our goodbyes at the airport an emotional time for me. This beautiful person stood in front of me, had been and was a solid foundation for me, a big slab of granite, always on the end of a phone always there to pick me up, listen and guide me. Susan did this even though she was taking care of her ageing mum another wonderful person who I always went to visit and have a cuppa with when at Susan's. I loved her mum's company she was also a special lady.

As I waited for my flight to Nantes in Manchester Airport, again my team of guardians would show and highlight another reality to me, one that I had guessed to be in existence but now it was confirmed.

I was learning and accepting that information I was meant to know would be given in divine timing. Just as the information on the wheel hub I found in the hedge and the photo of Mr Dupont drinking only months before the accident, today would reveal another truth.

On this occasion it involved two friends, now ex-friends, who had believed Rob's stories and chose to back that horse. I knew they discussed me because Elliott had heard them, so their friendship wasn't the kind I respected.

It was around three years since any contact although I had heard that they had moved to France permanently. I spotted Claire and Lewis going to the shops in Manchester airport and the actions I saw when we landed in Nantes airport confirmed to me, they had spotted me too.

The plane was small, it wasn't full and Nantes airport is small too. But they must have been in a bit of a rush because Claire and Lewis were already there in the airport waiting outside the male toilets, no doubt for Steven, before I even got into the airport (we had been on the same small plane).

They had their backs turned and didn't see me as I went to get my bag. I then placed myself against a wall so I could sort out my bags. They had to walk past me it wasn't a large area and there weren't that many passengers.

Steven looked straight at me and marched past, throwing me an unpleasant stare. Lewis passed too but had a look of fear and uncertainty when he saw me (The stories Rob had woven about me must have been good). Then Claire had to pass me I looked straight at her and said "Hello." She pretended to not have seen me but that was impossible and there was no surprise on her face just a look of 'Oh bloody hell'. They were probably getting away as fast as they could and knew I was on the flight.

Lewis came back and I spoke to him, asked if he now spoke French and commented how tall he had grown. He left quickly to get to his dad who was way ahead and didn't move but stayed there. With the look on Lewis' face stories had obviously been told. Claire had to make small talk, asked if I had been on the same flight. I said "What flight were you on?" "Manchester" was Claire's reply, which I had guessed "Have you been to see family?" Claire uncomfortably asked, she looked so nervous and guilty. My reply "I have been doing this and that." She then asked about Harvey and Elliott and then made her excuses of needing to get to the car.

I actually felt sorry for them, they had been my friends a lot of years, but they had made their choice. I had nothing to hide or bow my head about but obviously they did. I was offering an olive branch, but it wasn't taken, they believed the gossip and lies that Rob had spun and that's their prerogative. I wish them well especially Lewis, a very special young person.

We had had Hugo a Danish student stay with us and on the 1st of March Harvey left for a week's exchange in Denmark through Lycée. He loved it and I am sure he will revisit there one day. Harvey got back on the 15th of March he had had an amazing time; I was so pleased for him. The timing was good for Harvey he gained a lot from the experience.

Life carried on and I posted a copy of my appeal papers to the Dupont's solicitors. Though I had not received a thing from anybody. I was obviously seen as a mushroom that needed to be kept in the dark.

Then at noon in France on the 17th of March a change occurred which would affect the world. We also had a further issue to face which would clearly show the truth of the situation and the true colours of those involved.

On my return from getting the animal food on the morning of the 17th of March 2020, Harvey was waiting at the gate and told me that from noon we were on lockdown and weren't allowed to go anywhere without an official paper. Remember I didn't watch TV or listen to the radio preferring to be oblivious to the world's madness. From the time that I had been on planet earth I was inclined to have the same opinion as Voltaire "Planet Earth is the asylum to which the rest of the universe sends it's lunatics." I preferring to avoid the constant misery the media seemed to be obsessed with and ultimately some of that energy I would pick up. It would weigh heavy on my heart. To recover from my own personal, burdensome energies, I could not take on others.

"Okay Harvey let's get the food I have just got into the back of your car, and I will go and get some more because the pigs will not understand lockdown and they will not understand not being fed!" I observed, I just had time before Cavac would shut for dinner at 12:00 and who knows when it would re-open.

When I returned, it had been busy and a lot of panic at Cavac. No one had a clue what was going to happen. I got what pig food I could in my car and left the madness behind.

I arrived back home and as I was getting out of my car a white Seat with an English number plate came down our small lane, stopped, reversed back, stopped again and then came towards me. I stopped and watched at first for some reason I thought "Oh no someone I have stopped talking to is coming and I really can't be bothered with their excuses." But then because it reversed back, I thought maybe it was someone lost and they need directions, then the driver decided not to go backwards but forwards towards mine and Harvey's cars (which were now filled with animal food). It pulled up behind our cars and stopped. The driver getting out of the car, the passenger staying where they were and without shutting the driver's door, started to swagger in a bit of a cocky, John Wayne style, a confident way with a smirk on his face and said "Bonjour", it was Rob.

The last time I had had any contact with him was in the same spot in March 2018, (it's now March 2020) when he asked for some papers which I handed to him before he left, his parting words being "Bonne chance" (good luck) my reply "I think I will need more than good luck with the shit I have to deal with." An apology for spitting in my face, I think would have been more of an appropriate parting expression but of course that never happened or would ever happen. In Rob's head it never took place. So why the fuck was he here now after two years of no contact?

I could see straight through him; he was so transparent. I asked, "Who's that in the car?" his reply "None of your fucking business" I thought you have brought them to my door, it's all my fucking business!!

The driver's door was still wide open, so I went over to put my head into the car to say hello. Rob had come for a fight so he could show his new friend that all the stories he had been vomiting out to all that would polish his ego, have pity for the poor victim (by the way this victim still had his right hand) and who had been so battered by his partner which meant he just had to leave were true.

It's funny but for a number of months I had dreams, messages that he would show up. However, I didn't think he would be so insensitive to the boys to show up with another woman. I was their mum after all, and they were very protective of me naturally. They had also lived the hell and knew the truth.

Rob then said he had come to see the boys, lie number one, the way he had reversed in his car showed me that he had had no intention of seeing them but putting the single piece of paper with his details on in the letter box and not facing them, just scouring off like a crafty, sly fox.

By doing this he could convince himself that he had tried, and it wasn't his fault there was no contact. Hello! You have been gone over two years that's called abandonment! And now you can choose to show up with your girlfriend. You also left them with someone you were telling people was crazy and violent. So, if I had ill-treated them in those two years that was something you didn't give a shit about or was it you really knew they were safe. Don't worry as long as you were having your needs met. I actually felt sorry for him. I said it was not my decision if they wanted to see him or not, but I will go and tell them, it's their choice.

Rob was not happy that he couldn't sneak away, and he actually had to face them (bit of karma there then). I told him he could not come through the gate, the same gate he had bullied me about once on our return to the Grand Feu. I told him he could not come through the gate we were on lockdown and he and she had just arrived from another country looking at their car's number plate. How they were allowed into France I didn't know but I believed they hadn't just arrived and that he had to see the boys desperately, insistently as he was trying to make out, lie number two.

The boys were slow in appearing Elliott was first and he sat on the stone wall a little distance from the gates, Rob on the outside of the gates. All I heard of the conversation was that Elliott said, "You look old!".

I then went to talk to the person in the car that was none of my fucking business even though she had been brought to my house. I wanted to know who she was. We chatted and I think she said her name was Vicky but not sure. She had known Rob before (interesting) but they had only just met a few months before at Christmas (now she was lying my gut telling me a different story remember the obsession with his phone and not letting it out of his sight). She had been married twice and divorced twice. Had some children one also called Elliott and that Rob needed to make amends with all his family (Rob having three children from his marriage before I met him).

I didn't judge this woman, but I sensed she knew how to play the game, with two marriages behind her looking to be in her late forties or early fifties she was not wet behind the ears or even green at all. Her opening statement to me had been "I know you will have bitterness towards Rob." My reply "I am not wasting my energy being bitter towards him, I have more important things that I need my energy to go to. But Rob does have issues he doesn't know how to love someone. I think there is so much he has never dealt with from his childhood and his marriage, he just keeps running and never deals with anything". As we continued to talk, I didn't dislike her, I suppose I was indifferent to her. A big part of me grateful that I no longer had Rob to deal with and take care of and that I was set free! Well, I hoped he would set me free but he was still full of anger buried under that smirk of his. He really wanted a reaction from me, a fight and I just wasn't giving him one. This meant he may have had a bit of explaining to do to his friend sat in the car. I wasn't the person he had lied about but how much she would be misled would depend how far she was under his spell.

I had had over two years of not being put down, backed into a corner, or shouted at and I was starting to get rid of all those bad habits that you have to defend yourself and that become stuck to you in any false or toxic environment. Yes, I still had a lot of toxicity around me from other things, but now the home environment was slowly being cleansed. Slowly the stress, shouting and fears were no longer the norm but dancing in the kitchen, singing, playing music and laughter being allowed and it was slowly, very slowly, beginning to be a place that me and the boys felt happy in.

Our conversation continued as Elliott continued to have his with Rob. I said to Rob's partner "You will have been given some stories." Her reply "There is always two who cause problems in relationships, it's never just one." I said nothing but thought well you must know with two divorces behind you or is that what people lying choose to believe. If one is cheating it's not the other's fault but the person cheating often projects that onto the other person, to justify their actions of cheating on a decent innocent person so their ego driven cheating can continue.

I believe that often there is a person oblivious to the lies and sneaky behaviour (at first and often for years) who is hard working at the relationship but then gets picked on and blamed and this could be either a woman or a man. Then the slow process of discrediting the non-cheating person begins. Instead of the sneaky person moving on from the relationship they don't want and being honest they carry on with their side hustle!

My next statement or observation was "What kind of partner leaves their partner to die on their own? Not even being at their side, at their deathbed or possible deathbed."

If that doesn't tell someone how they are thought of, I don't know what will! Yet I still was trying to fix it all with a person who couldn't even be at my bedside in what looked like my dying hours or embrace me and ensure me that it was all going to be alright.

I then continued to say to Rob's friend "I am happy for you both but don't expect true love, he doesn't know what it is."

Harvey was out now so I went to the gate, their last meeting had not been good I didn't want it to turn into anything nasty. I should have known better; Harvey wasn't going to stoop to Rob's way of dealing with things and he calmly handed Rob a piece of paper with his number on and said, "You can contact me if you want" and returned inside.

Elliott was given the one piece of paper with Rob's details on and then Elliott went inside. I was already back talking to Rob's friend when he came back and got into the car. He said to me "Thank you for letting me see them" I said, "It wasn't my decision it was theirs." I also said, "I wish you both well but Rob you have got to let go of your anger from your marriage and probably your childhood, if you want a good, loving relationship you need to change." His reply was "I like who I am." I replied, "Well you keep being and acting as you have done then but it's nobody's fault but yours, the situation with the boys, you just abandoned them." His response "I had to look after me." I thought, yer it's always been all about you. When the time came when I desperately needed you and you wasn't able to take from me anymore you ran to the hills as fast as you could. But not before trying to destroy three other people's lives, which by the way you didn't manage to do!

Then I said, "You don't need to thank me for you speaking to the boys, but I sincerely wish to thank you because for all the things you did to me you have made me ten time stronger than I ever was, so I thank you for that." I waved to them as they drove off.

I suppose his unannounced appearance with his girlfriend upset the apple cart a little, but I was actually relieved. He didn't trigger me a thing he thought he could still do and that told me I was moving forwards. When someone can still make you angry, they still have some energetic connection to you. But when you are not bothered or triggered by a word or an action you know they have no power over you anymore and you are set free.

At times you may have to cut cords as they try to reconnect that power again, but generally you are free. I felt I could be myself again, the one I liked and the one that could move forwards to a better, kinder, and more fulfilling existence.

Harvey was contacted by Rob, but Elliott didn't want to phone him he was still angry, he needed time to heal and think. I told Harvey I didn't want to know when he spoke and what they said, just talk to me if something bothers you. He was bothered that Rob had requested him to put Elliott on the phone. My advice was "Don't do that Harvey we have to let Elliott decide when he is ready, he has the number. Rob should be trying to build bridges with you, not using you to get to speak to Elliott. Don't be used."

I didn't say anything until around May when I asked, "Do you still keep in contact and chat?" Harvey's answer "Well he said he would phone me on my birthday, but he never did, and he hasn't contacted me since." I felt so sorry for Harvey but didn't say anything. I thought what a cruel game this person is playing but it will all return and bite his butt one day.

Also, in March just before the runner's return I had to go to Andouard-Flisseau huissieres de Justice in Niort to sign something. I naively thought at last, be it a little late I was about to get my files, you know the ones I was lawfully entitled to! So, I set off to Niort, again with a shopping bag to Andouard-Flisseau huissieres de Justice in Niort to collect my documents or that's what I thought they had summoned me for.

The universe again would give me a very big sign regarding the games that these 'enforcers' of justice and the law were playing. Plus, their lack of integrity and client confidentiality, isn't that another code of conduct they are supposed to uphold in this facade of justice?

I arrived and entered the Andouard-Flisseau huissieres de Justice building, to be greeted by a very stern-faced typical jobs worth receptionist (must have been the sister to the one in the Grand Feu). I had the letter with me which had summoned me and handed it to her. She then handed me some sheets of paper and told me to sign them.

I read them slowly, they were in French (why bother given this accused person anything that would be complying with their rights of having it in a language they could understand, we don't bother with the law unless it suits us!!). I then read the second copy of the same information, didn't really understand but I wasn't not going to carefully look at anything this unjust system was involved with. It's not as if I trusted their integrity. This really annoyed the woman and she tried to hurry me. I took my time and ignored her.

I then tried to ask if I was getting my files, I had my shopping bag ready. She did that usual thing of not understanding but when I had to go back on another occasion this time taking a witness, Mel with me who had been by my side throughout this whole charade, this woman actually spoke some English.

I was trying to communicate with this non-cooperative woman when the universe brought someone to see me the wonderful, brilliant, empathic and professional upholder of justice Mr Riposseau. Boy was he not happy to see me stood there. Thanks universe a little bit of karma maybe? He didn't look pleased to see me, but I said "Bonjour" and asked if he was okay in French. He was not comfortable; you could see the steam coming out of his ears as he tried to stay composed.

I tried to finish my conversation be it a one-way conversation, with the jobsworth and he decided to get involved. I told him I didn't need his sort of help and that it was no longer any of his business. He then went off on one about my files. This woman then got even cockier and more obstructive. In the end I said to Riposseau whose agitation was becoming more visible, that it was okay I didn't need the files I had the power of the truth and karma. I then left.

I did a quick u-turn back into the room looking for my glasses, which were on my head. But as I re-entered the room again Mr Riposseau was in a full-blown conversation about me and my case with this woman. I tutted and shook my head and said, "That's not very professional, talking about a client's case, gossiping, how very professional!" What is it with these people? They come across or pretend to, in their fancy clothes and posh language, ego and self-importance and in reality, many of them are just so shallow and weak.

We are now in lockdown, it's May 2020, my appeal date on the 25th of March cancelled. The lockdown didn't really bother me I had put myself on lockdown about three years ago when all the gossip and backstabbing started. We were okay and my life, except not being able to go once a week to train at the gym in Poitiers, hadn't really changed.

I had already decided I needed to invest in some competition weights and a bar so I would start to look into that. I still could distance train with Danny but no actual visits to a gym. But no problem I was used to training on my own with limited equipment and space I had done it at Liverpool University.

I tried to find the weights on Amazon but most of the world was now training at home, so most things had been sold out. It was sad but also my competition in the south of France in May had been cancelled the whole world in fear and on lockdown.

This fear continued into June and July and then the usually French holidays in August would be upon us. One of the best things I saw during this time was something sent to me showing how the wild animals of the world had claimed their planet back. Walking with their families in the cities of the world. We selfishly claim this planet and ignore the rights that other creatures have to belong to it. I bet all these animals were not full of panic stockpiling totally inflated priced toilet paper!

After searching with no luck for some weights on Amazon I turn to Eleiko why not go for quality that the Power Paralympics use, I did.

The quality amazing the shipping cost very good and the service and attention to detail of packaging so high I couldn't fault the company at all I highly recommend them.

Eleiko, a Swedish company provided the Para-Powerlifting World and Olympic competitions with their high quality sexy looking equipment (well it looked like that to me). I would now get to know the feel and weight of the same equipment that was used in competitions.

I got on their website, and they had the stuff I wanted in stock and the delivery charge from Sweden was a good price. I made the investment. I had promised myself that I would not stop training, it's only society that ages training. As long as you are sensible training can continue all your life no matter your age!!

My order in June 2020 was an Eleiko XF set, an 88kg men's set. This included a 20kg Olympic barbell, 2 x 15kg, 2 x 10kg, 2 x 5kg plates with some 2.5kg and 1.25kg plates. I also ordered some wrist wraps (I had to get a pair though I only needed one, Stubby doesn't have a wrist). Then in July I put another order in for 2 x 7kg, 2 x 20kg and 2 x 32kg dumbbells. Plus, a pro-resistance band and some fitness tube with PVC handles. I was now able to have good equipment at my disposal.

September brought the return to Lycée for Elliott and the start of a degree in philosophy for Harvey at Poitiers University. On the 2nd of September, I took Harvey to the halls of residence he would be staying at to take his bedding and other stuff. We also called to see if my gym was re-opened, and it was. Great I will be back to train next week.

Either every week or fortnight I would call to briefly see Harvey and to give him some food and clean washing, bringing any washing back before heading off to the gym. That routine continued throughout September. Harvey was settled and enjoyed his degree, Elliott still at Lycée doing his woodwork. There was always lots to do in the house and outside, but I still got my weekly session at the gym in Poitiers and did my four sessions of distance training from Danny in mine and Stubby's gym.

The people at the Poitiers gym were very supportive, friendly and there was a good atmosphere. The competition I did last year in Villeneuve d'Ascq would more than likely be cancelled but I hoped it wouldn't. I sent my deposit off, the meals at the restaurant not allowed but at least the competition may go ahead.

I had trained in Poitiers on the Wednesday before and with the programme Danny had sent me. But as we got to October the 1st I didn't feel well. The worrying thing was my new court date for the appeal court in Poitiers was in a week on the 7th of October, my birthday!! I couldn't decide if that was a good or a bad omen, but they now had my appeal file.

The appeal court could now see with the file the police photos showing the mysteriously moving and then vanishing vital evidence the plastic wheel hub and front bumper. There was also that little matter of cause of death, alcohol, and medication plus medical records of an 85-year-old. Any judge would see that this was essential information, a lawful and necessary procedure of investigation to go through in any case never mind one in which someone is charged with double murder.

My appeal file also showing the grave mistakes of Maurice Pascal and Christophe Ledon in their reports plus the unlawful, non-preservation of evidence. The vehicles being contaminated, damaged, and not preserved.

On the 2nd of October 2020 in the afternoon, I received an email from Elisa Pelisser court clerk at the appeal court in Poitiers. It stated that from the information they received on the 23rd of January. Let me repeat that again on the 23rd of January 2020 (and they contact me now with just over four days before my court date! Game still being played but they had something up their sleeve to get around this one). Have I received a copy of procedures? They wait till now to ask me? And no doubt they won't bother to send it in my native language of English which I have a legal right to. My answer was "No". This legal document arrived by normal post on the 9th of October, two days after the court date. How many laws are they allowed to break or ignore? It appears as many as they like and repeatedly that's their scales of 'justice'!

I had felt ill on the 1st of October but carried on. However, by the next day I was extremely ill. It was like going back to Nantes hospital when I had the excruciating pain and diarrhoea. I spent the next four days on the toilet with a bowl on my knee both ends challenging my desire to live.

I was not eating, barely drinking, and trying to throw the animals food in and water them before I had an accident in my pants, thinking I wish I had some of those nappies that they had put me in at Nantes hospital. I was so ill, sat on the toilet, I daren't leave it. Both the vomiting as well as the diarrhoea being extreme pain. A couple of times I fainted in the process. Woke up on the bathroom floor and then had to start cleaning up after myself.

I really thought if I die before being able to say my piece in the appeal court that would not be fair. But what part of the last nearly five years had been fair?

I didn't care if I died but if I was still alive on the 7th of October on my 56th birthday I would be in that appeal court. I would just have to wear a pad and if I had an accident while stood there in the courtroom, so be it. It summed up the whole situation anyway, full of shit! But I would be there, it's time the truth got told (how bloody naive of me).

Elliott never got it so it can't have been contagious, not that I allowed him anywhere near me and Harvey was away at university. Maybe my intestines were blocked again? Maybe a gallstone or kidney stone? Or maybe my body was just totally exhausted with all the shite and lies it had had to deal with in the last four and a half years.

I never called the doctor because then I wouldn't be able to go to my appeal and she probably would have sent me to hospital. By the 6th of October I only needed the toilet once and I managed to eat some plain rice and a slice of toast.

Mel and Davina were coming with me, and Harvey was going to meet us there. I drove I knew the route I used it every week to get to my gym and to see Harvey at university.

The girls brought me some beautiful cards and birthday gifts a message from Davina and Warren saying, 'Age doesn't matter but friends do!' They had got that one right. It really made me feel happy even as I prepared to go to the appeal court. I had a peace within, it surely couldn't be like the 15th of April 2019, this was the appeal courts. They were used to seeing injustices and correcting them by realising the mistakes and the unlawfulness that had been served in the other court.

As I drove, I spoke and told Davina some of the stuff that this so called just system had done. Davina knew some of the story but there were very few who did instead they relied on gossip to get their information.

Mel and Davina were not gossipers and very trustworthy which is more than I could say about a lot of the people who I now have nothing to do with.

Before lockdown or prisondown I had started to train Mel and Davina in Davina's small gym and we had all bonded well. Warren, Davina's husband, and Robert Mel's husband were great people also. I got a lot of help from them; they were my sort of people.

Slowly the universe was guiding me to the right vibrating souls and allowing me to see that not all people are out to gossip, judge or put you down and that some do care about their fellow man. I was lucky to have them on my team, especially on this day.

We got there in good time and got parked. The appeal court was massive and looked like Versailles on a smaller scale. Harvey was there, he had a lecture around four o'clock so he would have to be leaving to get to that.

We had to wait a while outside but eventually we could go in with our masks on. We then had to wait outside the court room, there were many different ones.

Riposseau was there for Allianz insurance company, not me, he looked uncomfortable, but I had this calmness within me I didn't need to hang my head I knew that I had been in a very wicked, cruel game and the players knew deep in their beings that I had been made a scapegoat. They also knew that things had and were still hidden, both Riposseau and Geraldine Dauphin, the Dupont's solicitor could not look at me and appeared very nervous.

Something had happened to me in my accident and throughout my traumatic journey I just knew things. I suppose I always had from being really young but now it was clearer and went so much deeper, it's as if I could see a person's soul, their heart, guilt, lies and personal sadness so clearly. They both looked hot under the collar.

I watched them and I mentally sent them forgiveness and peace and a prayer that they would not continue down the same path in the future. But it was their decision if they wanted to continue searching for power, importance, ego and money. Their souls just couldn't or weren't allowed to see how destructive and debilitating these things are to their soul's journey. It would not be good for their souls.

Prison Or The Paralympics

On this day there was only one family member Dominique Dupont but another son I think arrived later. There were other appeals going on in the same court and we were in and out a bit and delayed so Harvey had to leave before it was my slot.

As we waited a woman approached me and said she was called at the last minute to replace the other translator that I had been notified of when I got the new court date, and she would be my translator. My immediate thought was here we go, games again. They know I had to have a translator my gut telling me this one did not look up to the job, way too nervous, as if she wasn't used to being there.

I had to stand in front of three judges. The president Mrs Isabelle Lauque and the two counsellors Mrs Delphine Roudiere and Mrs Delphine Portal. To the left was the public prosecutor Mrs de la Landelle to debate Mr Hervé Drevard's delivery, Geraldine Dauphin to the left also. Hugo Riposseau there for Allianz to the right.

My interpreter wasn't even registered with the court so had to take an oath before the court. So, my gut was on point again and she didn't fail to prove why she was not registered. It's just part of the game, silence the person but do it so it appears to be within the law.

This was further demonstrated to me when one for the three judges sat in front of me asked if I had seen and received all the information and was I happy to continue and ready to continue. I received nothing but I said I was happy to continue because I knew my appeal file had been received because I got it confirmed by AR signed for and received notification back in January 2020.

I was well prepared in what I wanted to say. But this woman I had been given to translate for me didn't install much confidence in me, after hearing her as she said her oath before the court. I was now going to be thrown to the lions again.

I was asked lots of questions by these three judges. Both the French and the English giving my translator problems and the three judges had to repeat themselves to her a number of times. What chance did I have?

It was as if I would not be allowed to say what had never been said but on paper they had looked to have followed all the rules. Having someone by your side who couldn't do the job, and she started getting mad at me! I would have been better trying to tell them in French myself at least I understood the English part of it.

Then it was madame Landelle the prosecutors turn to interrogate me, and she was not nice. It was so hard with the translator I had been given to even understand what she wanted she was pushing and pushing the overtaking the obviously important thing they had to find me guilty of in order to scapegoat me for the deaths.

I was under the impression that they have all seen and taken the time to look at my file. I was trying to tell her that police photos clearly showed the wheel hub on the left back wheel not right back wheel and then by the 28th of April 2016 the wheel hub was then on the right back wheel according to Maurice Pascal. Then that and the front bumper vanished by March 2017 so no one else was able to analyse them.

In the end I had to walk over and show her the photos. I will never ever forget the look on the woman's face. This vicious, clever, probably well experienced prosecutor had a look of horror, a disbelief in what was there in front of her eyes. There was no denying the fact, and these were police photos, one of the photos still had me trapped in the car. But she still dismissed it and carried on with her vicious interrogation and attack.

At one point she said, so are you saying that someone took the wheel hub from the left and put it on the right? I said yes!! I thought well it couldn't have bloody moved itself, and you are thinking that too, but you are still going to have me! I was standing having to look at this black insignia in front of me of the scales of justice in perfect balance. That's funny here I am presenting police evidence and they just ignore it. How balanced is that? They seem to all piss in the same pot, even in the appeal court.

I was then told to sit back down and now the frustrated Geraldine Dauphin (just like Scarlet in Gone with the Wind she was about to put on a performance). She began to give her performance of personally attacking me and my character, not that I could understand much the woman sat next to me supposedly translating shushed me when I asked her what she was saying in her dramatic performance.

Then Riposseau spoke for the Allianz insurance company saying how the company couldn't keep paying money out, agreeing with me being guilty. So please don't believe all the expensive advertising and PR stunts they give (they have money for that but not a client wrongly charged with double murder). They couldn't even find me an English-speaking solicitor! Ironically enough you will find Allianz' logo on the sponsor board at the Paralympics, wonder how much that cost in sponsorship. You would do more good looking after your clients that have become disabled through no fault of their own. Exposing the truth instead of pretending that you actually care about a disabled person. I would welcome and invite you to explain, it would be nice to hear the reason your duty of care was so, shall I say bad for one of your policy holders. Now a disabled one!

Then I was invited to speak which lasted all of ten minutes before the whole charade was brought to a close. I got to say nothing. I then asked if they had seen my file, they didn't know what I was referring to when I tried to explain the pieces I had sent. I walked over to the judges to show them my file, the one I knew they had received in January 2020. The judges had never seen it!!

See how the game continues and is played out they had that file since January

2020. It was now October 2020. Who signed for it? Who had hidden it? Maybe it had been conveniently lost in the expensive bureaucracy of bullshit!

The judge concluded that they would make their decision at a later date, and we were to return on the 23rd of November 2020.

I never got the pleasure of being back in front of the insignia of the balanced scales of justice which they have all over the place in these so-called establishments of justice. Maybe their scales are balanced with lies, cover ups, loss of vital evidence, targeting the vulnerable and not seeking the truth.

It's been the same throughout history but now they add insult to injury by pretending every person has the same rights in this system.

In my experience nothing could be further from the truth. In fact, the 'little' factor of truth is often extinct, whitewashed, ignored, avoided, camouflaged, hidden, and purposely sabotaged to allow their justice system to function the way they dictate it should. Honesty, integrity, and humanity not being part of their somewhat corrupt 'elitist' bullshit circus.

The second bout of lockdowns resulted in my sentence being posted (with no security or signed for, how do they know I even received it?) the information again violating my right to understand because it was in French with no copy in English. There were a few lines saying a translated copy would follow.

By this time, I had begun this book and was writing about my life and what I had achieved. This gave me the courage and confirmation that I wasn't the person that all these people and establishments had tried to portray me as even though they didn't bother to find out anything about who I really was.

I had never before in my life ever thought or wanted to write a book, who wanted or would be interested in what I had to say. But even when in the ICU guidance was given to me to get a dicta-phone. I then believing it was more to say goodbye as I left this world. Slowly it's true purpose would be revealed but as I spoke into it I did not realise what lay ahead. Now I see the true need to document my journey and print it. Maybe I can help others in their struggles with disabilities and not being believed.

I had to be me again and not give anyone the power to turn me into someone I wasn't. I now needed to work and turn to my heart, soul, and spirit to heal myself and take out all the swords that had been stabbed in my back, left there, often twisted by the placer to give constant pain, fester, and become infected. I was to carry these swords with me for the rest of my life because others had decided to stab them there without just cause or reason. I now needed to get physically, mentally, and spiritually strong in order to remove them.

I now had a small insight to my purpose of having to go through this and getting to this point, enduring this dark, difficult, lonely, and cruel path. I had to dedicate the rest of my time in this human existence to making things better. Showing others that they can overcome the injustice and pain that has been forced onto them. Now being disabled, I would encourage and help others to see their worth and to be proud of who they were. Not to become what circumstances and people have made them think they were. We are all worthy of honesty, love, and inner peace. It's what our soul needs to continue to breathe.

Chapter 36: The Sentence

"Although I am a typical loner in daily life, my consciousness of belonging to the invisible community of those who strive for truth, beauty and justice has preserved me from feeling isolated."

- Albert Einstein

Today is the 29th of November 2020. I am writing this to document how I feel regarding the sentence from the appeal court in Poitiers France.

On the 26th of November 2020 by regular post, no security or sign for posting, I received a large brown envelope I knew it was from the court because it had the address on the envelope.

I felt it was thick and I guessed it was my plastic file which I sent by secure, sign for post on the 23rd of January 2020. The file was evidence and information, vital information, to the truth of the circumstances of the accident. It included information that had never been brought forward, not even by my Allianz insurance solicitor Riposseau who I had given the information to. He dismissed it.

Having this file returned to me I found a bit odd for at my appeal on the 7th of October 2020 judges Isabelle Lauque, Delphine Roudiere and Delphine Portal said they had never seen my file when I stood in front of them and showed it to them.

This mysterious loss of my file goes hand in hand with the mysterious loss of my wheel hub and the other car's front bumper. Yes, a real size front bumper lost from a place the cars were supposed to be stored for safety, security and an uncontaminated environment in order to preserve the evidence. How do you get that in your pocket and leave the garage without anyone seeing it? Don't forget that these were the two vital car parts that were the only evidence used to sentence me for double murder, and they vanished? How very convenient!

I opened the envelope, yes it was my file, they did have it yet the judges said they had never seen it before. For some reason this vital information never got to be seen in my case in which I was being charged for killing two people. Is this big, powerful, expensive system so incompetent that they can't manage to get a file to the correct place? Or did they fear the truth being exposed? I will let the reader decide that one.

Also in the envelope was the judges' decision all in French, no translated copy in English (even the appeal court ignores my human rights). There was a badly written sentence in English from the clerk stating that the sentence in English will be sent soon. It has still not arrived. If they send it by normal post, how will they know it's arrived and that I have actually got it, not that they care about that or my rights!

So, I think that the French document says I am found guilty of causing the accident and causing the death of two people. The sentence was reduced from an 18-month driving ban, cancellation of my driving license and having to do a driving test again to a 12-month suspension of my driving license. Remember I had been driving since November 2017 when I passed my driving test in an adapted car with one hand and have not had one issue. But now three years later I was such a risk to society and don't forget that word aggressive that I was now banned from driving. Yet be 85 years old and you are not even tested to see if you are even capable of driving due to the natural reduction in ability to do so, due to the ageing process and the usually prescribed medication that that brings.

They also gave me a three-year suspended prison sentence. Wonder why they didn't send me to prison? Was that because I was being framed and they acted unlawfully? Blaming me for the deaths of two people when they never bothered to investigate what they died from! Surely an autopsy vital and the only lawful way to conclude the cause of death. If I am guilty of killing two people as your 'justice' system says I am, then I deserve to go to prison surely? Send me, I don't fear your man-made prison and I will not fall prey to the mental and spiritual prison you desperately tried to force me into. I am not mental, not aggressive, and not crazy. I am honest and you never destroyed my soul! But quoting William Ernest Henley from Invictus 'It matters not how straight the gate, how charged with punishment the scroll, I am the master of my fate, I am the captain of my soul.'

My feelings, disappointment in the lack of honesty of the whole system. They basically used gossip and very questionable information to come to their conclusion. This questionable 'powerful' system may be able to stop some of my freedoms, but they can't stop me writing. My true judgement or sentence will be given by a much more powerful, honest, and real environment, the universe.

I write with integrity, truth, and love. That's all this world needs to put an end to the corruption, lies, cruelty and greed that we are all forced to be surrounded by. The power of the universe has our backs, and our new decade will see the 'mighty' fall. Then allowing the return of balance and love for our souls.

Prison Or The Paralympics

I am not angry with those in my case who choose to walk down the path of dishonesty and manipulation for the sake of their egos. Their own private sentence will be served to them at some time by the universe.

There is a cleansing happening to our planet which will result in a loving, kind, peaceful, honest, and real life for all of us to be part of on this beautiful planet once we let go of fear and replace it with love.

I send love to all those involved, and I continue the journey of my soul, stronger and wiser for my challenges. It has also enabled me to continue my journey with love, peace, and my integrity intact.

Chapter 37: Closure, Handing It Over To The People's Justice And The Universe

"The truth is like a lion, you don't have to defend it. Let it loose, it will defend itself."

- Saint Augustine

I continued to write hours and hours a day, it was a time of cold, dark nights and no demands from the garden. I had lots of jobs in the house, big cleaning and sorting jobs but that I could catch up with once I got this book finished.

I gave myself until the end of February then the end of March and then it continued into April. But in April 2021 I had finished. There still remained the editing, the organising, and the massive task of typing it up and hopefully I would get help with that.

The only thing that happened from January to April 2021 regarding the court case was three police officers arriving unannounced to take my driving license, but I said I needed the paper they wanted me to sign translated before I would sign it. The date of their arrival being the 20th of February 2021. I spoke with them and said if they would let Harvey translate it then I would know what I was signing. I had been forced to sign papers I didn't understand twice before I wasn't going to do it a third time. By the way these officers were from the Coulonge station the same one that refused me my right to make a complaint.

I tried to see the sheet, but the police officer wouldn't let me see it he also had the bottom corner bent over which I thought odd. We went out to the police car where his boss and a female officer were sat waiting, the officer who came to the door saying he would have to speak to his boss.

The boss said, "We will just go back and say she has refused to sign it." I said "You can't say that I have a witness" pointing at Harvey "And I am not refusing to sign it, I want to be able to understand it before I sign it. It's one of my basic human rights." The boss then said, "You have no rights you are in France." I thought to myself, you've got that fucking right!! I went on to say, "I only need ten minutes for Harvey to translate it." His response "No we have an emergency we can't wait" (I thought yer doughnuts)

"Well come back then" I suggested. "No, you will have to come down to the police station in Coulonge and we will get a translator" he concluded.

Right, I thought, but I will have my own translator Harvey with me. The boss went on to say, "We will phone you to let you know when." It's now the middle of April and there has been no contact. What games were they trying to pull again!

As I put the last few pages to this book I hope and pray for closure. It is not my intention to forget all that was done to me but for my own health and healing I forgive those involved.

I also hope those involved find closure but in order to, they need to admit the truth, if not to others, then at least to themselves. They can choose to continue to blame me, after all this 'very just' French system says it was me. But they know the hidden truths!

I may only have my integrity and honesty but by having that the universe guided me to the truth that was being hidden. I have no anger or judgement of what was done to me, but I have disappointment in how people in certain positions can misuse their position. I do not know what they intend to gain but I do know they eventually gain a deep illness of their souls.

My choice a long time ago was not to hold on to the injustice of my journey, instead handing it over to a much more just and honest energy that will always deliver the last and final verdict. That is the power of the people's justice and the power of the universe. One of my biggest lessons was that you need to give yourself protection so that others can't attach their negative energy to you, for many will try.

This has been my truth; I invite you to make what you will out of my words. On this journey I have been given a gift to not be affected by what others think of me. Reactions cannot affect truth; a truth can never be a lie. I send you all love, peace, and the will to carry on your amazing soul's journey, with love and integrity. Do not sacrifice your own soul to please others, be your authentic self. Our soul is a gift given to us and we must love and nurture it. Forgiveness of others is one way to keep your soul loving. When your soul is loved it protects you from harm and soulless people. I, my soul and Stubby thank you for taking the time to read about our journey a soulful love is sent to you all. Love is all there is, and all there needs to be.

In this closing chapter I would like to share with you writings that I did throughout this period of my life, plus some poems, quotes, books, and a list of my songs on my USB. All of these offering me guidance, direction, realisation, and hope. I was strengthened and they really made me think about the challenges I had to face. They allowed me to pause, breathe and have faith when I believed there wasn't any. I was awoken in the early hours, compelled to put pen to paper. I would like to share these messages with you. Thank you all for reading mine and Stubby's story.

Me & Stubby

Messages

I can't remember the date for this message, but it was in the first half of 2020.

If you don't fear death, you give yourself permission to live. The key is getting to a place of inner peace within your soul which allows you to be the best version of yourself. This may not come until you have experienced darkness, pain and many fears but it is necessary for these to strengthen you and prepare you for the peace and love that is waiting for you. All you have to do is see the beauty within which exists in every single human soul.
Penny Walker

This one I wrote on the 29/4/20.

One force has the power to 'control' the whole world which means that the force in 'control' is able to manipulate all actions that go on in the world. Famine, poverty, wars, money, disease, hatred, killings, cruelty, and greed. What it can't 'control' is unconditional love that each and every spirit and soul has the capability and possibility of giving when they escape the force's power. Love is all there is and all that is needed for planet earth.
Penny Walker

The Soul's Journey 7/5/2020

When a human arrives on this planet it's being is filled with two elements, a soul, and a spirit. The soul is pure love, the spirit is the knowing.
Within hours these tiny elements crave human stimulants to survive. Food, water, warmth, protection, contact and love.
The human time scale passes and the spirit and it's knowing becomes confused and doubting. The soul becomes lost and unloving but keeps trying to shine its love into the world around it only to be rejected, judged, laughed at, and abused.
In time the soul becomes buried under the human life experience, struggling to breathe, not being shown, and never being listened to or heard. The knowledge the spirit once had is replaced by a doctrine from its external influences which slowly suffocates it so it finds it hard to breathe and very slowly it dies. The beautiful light and

love the soul once beamed out is put into darkness and love is replaced by fear.

Now the human being can conform and be accepted on the planet where it exists. It's existence now is for growing, achieving, and accumulating all that its planet says it is due, the only charge is to sacrifice its spirit and soul.

As the spirit and soul slowly, slowly dies they leave behind a tiny seed of hope and purity which some beings discover after the planet they live on just knocks them down once too often. Then their spirit starts to open they get guidance and support from a pure and loving energy and their spiritual knowledge starts to be awakened once again.

The soul still very much dead and lifeless, starts to receive healing from its spirit and recovery begins. It is very slow and outside energies constantly sabotage its progress. Then the spirit realises that the only thing the soul needs to grow and become stronger is love. That is because that's all there really is, and all there really was the moment the soul entered the human body. The spirit and soul now reunited grow together and love pours out of them into the environment around them, bringing peace to the human. Fear no longer exists for the human and the human's soul journey can begin.

    Penny Walker

    A message from spirit about letting go 4/6/2020

You need to move to bring in brighter days,
look up to the sky for you are soon about to fly,
The love you deserve is about to explode, if you stop thinking and looking at the old,
Be strong, move on and bring joy and peace into your world,
We have a lot of love to let your soul unfold.
    Penny Walker

    To See 19/8/2020

To allow yourself to see there are a number of things that must no longer be
Telly vision, radio, and magazines too, cloud your mind and visions blocking the divine truth
Open your being with the things that are true, the light and the dark and believing in you.
Do not imprison your thoughts and your mind in a world that is cruel and so very unkind.
The world has been tortured in cruelty and pain just for a few to make their gain
But all is not lost and soon it will be free because the universe can rely on you and me

With love, honesty, and happiness from you this world will blossom and become divinely true.
   Penny Walker

June or July 2020

Fill your soul with love, feed it with hope and faith, believe in its strength and love will never fade.
Know that anger, disappointment, and fear cripples the soul's atmosphere leaving it empty and all alone never able to thrive and to be known.
So, give your soul the love it desires then your heart will expand and be inspired
Then with hope, peace, and love within the true meaning of your life will begin.
   Penny Walker

Poems and quotes that kept me sane

'Invictus' – William Ernest Henley

Out of the night that covers me,
Black as the pit from pole to pole,
I thank whatever gods may be
For my unconquerable soul.

In the fell clutch of circumstance
I have not winced nor cried aloud.
Under the bludgeonings of chance
My head is bloody, but unbowed.

Beyond this place of wrath and tears
Looms but the Horror of the shade,
And yet the menace of the years
Finds and shall find me unafraid.

It matters not how strait the gate,
How charged with punishments the scroll,

Penny Walker

I am the master of my fate,
I am the captain of my soul.

'The Proof Of Worth' – Edgar Albert Guest

Though victory's proof of the skill you possess, defeat is the proof of your grit. A weakling can smile in his day of success, but at trouble's first sign he will quit.
So, the test of the heart and the test of your pluck isn't skies that are sunny and fair, but how do you stand to the blow that is struck and how do you battle despair?
A fool can seem wise when the pathway is clear and it's easy to see the way out. But the test of a man's judgement is something to fear, and what does he do when in doubt?
And the proof of his faith is the courage he shows when sorrows lie deep in his breast; It's the way that he suffers the grief that he will bear for a cause which he knows to be right, how long will he suffer and fight?
There are many to serve when the victory's near and few are the hurts to be borne. But it calls for a leader of courage to cheer the man in a battle forlorn.
It's the way you hold out against odds that are great that proves what your courage is worth. It's the way that you stand to the bruises of fate that shows up your stature and girth.
And victory's nothing but proof of your skill, veneered with a glory that's thin unless it is proof of unfaltering will and unless you have suffered to win.

'The Victor' – C.W. Longenecker

If you think you are beaten, you are.
If you think you dare not, you don't.
If you like to win but think you can't,
It's almost a cinch you won't.
If you think you'll lose, you're lost.
For out in the world we find
Success begins with a fellow's will.
It's all in the state of the mind.
If you are outclassed, you are.
You've got to think high to rise.
You've got to be sure of yourself before
You can ever win the prize.

Life's battles don't always go
To the stronger or faster man.
But sooner or later, the man who wins
Is the man who thinks he can.

'The Man In The Glass' – Peter Dale Wimbrow Sr.

When you get what you want in your struggle for self
And the world makes you king for a day
Just go to the mirror and look at yourself
And see what that man has to say.
For it isn't your father, or mother, or wife
Whose judgement upon you must pass
The fellow whose verdict counts most in your life
Is the one staring back from the glass.
He's the fellow to please never mind all the rest
For he's with you, clear to the end
And you have passed your most difficult, dangerous test
If the man in the glass is your friend.
You may fool the whole world down the pathway of years
And get pats on the back as you pass
But your final reward will be heartache and tears
If you've cheated the man in the glass.

Quotes

There is no perfect time. No perfect opportunity. No perfect situation. No perfect moment. You either make it happen, or you don't.

Mattie Rogers

When I train, I erase all the limits and expectations of what I can do. I am powerful and anything is possible.

Camille Leblanc-Bazinet

It's not the will to win that matters everyone has that. It's the will to prepare to win that matters.

Bear Bryant

Penny Walker

Impossible is not a fact, it's an opinion things are impossible until someone does it.
Carl Jung

If you don't know where you are going you don't know what it takes to get there.
Carl Jung

Thinking is difficult, that's why most people judge.
Carl Jung

That which does not kill me makes me stronger.
Friedrich Nietzsche

To live is to suffer, to survive is to find some meaning in the suffering.
Friedrich Nietzsche

Anything that costs you your peace is too expensive learn to let it go
Ralph Marston

Love is the absence of fear, evil is the absence of love.
Ralph Marston

Happiness is a choice not a result. Nothing will make you happy until you choose to be happy. No person will make you happy unless you decide to be happy. Your happiness will not come to you. It can only come from you.
Ralph Marston

When we are no longer able to change a situation, we are challenged to change ourselves.
Viktor Frankl

The biggest coward is a man who awakes a woman's love with no intention of loving her.
Bob Marley

You can't do in a lift what you haven't prepared for.
Penny Walker

Prison Or The Paralympics

My attitude is that if you push me towards something that you think is a weakness then I will turn that perceived weakness into a strength.

Michael Jordan

Every session I try and improve to set myself up better in the long run.

Unknown

I hated every minute of training, but I said don't quit, suffer now and then live the rest of your life as a champion.

Muhammed Ali

There is an old saying a champion is someone who is willing to be uncomfortable.

Unknown

The key to immortality is first living a life worth remembering

Bruce Lee

Hard work and training. There's no secret formula I lift heavy work hard and aim to be the best.

Ronnie Coleman

I like to see people doubt me.

Sheryl Swoopes

You have to do something in your life that is honourable and not cowardly if you are to live in peace with yourself.

Larry Brown

Buddha Quotes

If people don't make an effort to be in your life don't try so hard to be in theirs, it's not worth it.

When someone leaves it's because someone else is about to arrive.

Penny Walker

Better to be slapped with a truth than kissed with a lie.

Always be in love with a soul not a face.

Beautiful people are not always good but good people are always beautiful.

Love is not what you say but what you do.

Success isn't the key to happiness, happiness is the key to success.

Freedom comes when you stop caring about what others think of you.

Stop expecting loyalty from people who can't even give you honesty.

The best revenge is to improve yourself.

You don't need someone to complete you, you only need someone to accept you completely.

A beautiful face means nothing when the heart is ugly.

Everyone is trying to find the right person, but nobody is trying to be the right person.

Don't choose to love the most beautiful person in the world. Choose to love the one who makes your world beautiful.

A real man doesn't love a million girls, he loves one girl in a million ways.

Books

The Power of Positive Thinking	Norman Vincent Peale
Stay Alive All Your Life	Norman Vincent Peale
How I Became The Fittest Woman On Earth	Tia-Clair Toomey

Prison Or The Paralympics

Start Your Engines My Unstoppable-CrossFit Journey	Sam Briggs
Dottir My Journey To Becoming A Two-Time Cross Fit Games Champion	Katrin Davidsdottir
Meat Rack Boy	Michael Tarraga
A Hard Road To Travel	Michael Tarraga
The Prophet	Kahill Gibran
Flip It	Michael Heppell
Just A Boy	Richard McCann
The Boy Grows Up	Richard McCann
The Hospital	Barbara O'Hare
Silent Sisters	Joanne Lee with Ann and Joe Cusack
Shine On	David Ditchfield and J.S. Jones
The Convent	Marie Hargreaves with Anne and Joe Cusack
Chariots of The Gods?	Erich Von Daniken

My USB songs

Imagine – John Lennon
Creep – Radiohead
Soul Love - David Bowie
Rock & Roll Suicide – David Bowie
Oh! You Pretty Things - David Bowie
Get Up, Stand Up – Bob Marley

Mustang Sally – The Commitments
November Rain - Guns N Roses
One More Try – George Michael
Paradise City – Guns N Roses
Because The Night - Patti Smith
One of my posing songs for my bodybuilding competitions
Photograph – Nickelback

Penny Walker

The song given to me just after being charged with double murder
It's My Life – Talk Talk
A Change Is Gonna Come – Sam Cooke
A Girl Like You – Edwyn Collins
Reminds me of Silverstone F1
Under – Alex Hepburn
All Cried Out - Alison Moyet
I changed this to all caught out and dedicated it to my ex-partner
Invisible - Alison Moyet
Love Resurrection - Alison Moyet
All I Wanna Do Is Make Love To You - Heart
Amazing Grace – Elvis Presley
I love this and later realised Mark Burgess had the hymn version at his funeral
Angie – The Rolling Stones
Another Day in Paradise – Phil Collins
Another One Bites The Dust - Queen
Always Remember Us This Way – Lady Gaga
Babe – Take That
Woman In Love – Barbara Streisand
Wind Beneath My Wings - Bette Midler
Bitter Sweet Symphony – The Verve
Blasphemy – Robbie Williams
Blaze Of Glory – Bon Jovi
Bed Of Roses – Bon Jovi
Wanted Dead Or Alive – Bon Jovi
When I Was Your Man – Bruno Mars
Believe – Cher
Johnny B Goode - Chuck Berry
I remember Damon Hill's version at Silverstone.
Civil War – Guns N Roses
Don't Cry – Guns And Roses
Personal Jesus – Depeche Mode
Don't Give Up – Peter Gabriel, Kate Bush
Brain Damage, Eclipse – Pink Floyd
Wish You Were Here – Pink Floyd
Proud Mary – Tina Turner
Purple Rain – Prince
Don't Let The Sun Go Down On Me - George Michael, Elton John
SOS D'un Terrien En Détresse – Grégory Lamarchal
Living On My Own – Queen
Under Pressure – Queen, David Bowie
Rebel Yell – Billy Idol
Never Gonna Give You Up – Rick Astley
Angels - Robbie Williams
Rockstar - Nickelback
Romeo And Juliet – Dire Straits
Ruby Don't Take Your Love to Town – Kenny Rogers
Running Away – Bob Marley & The Wailers
Shape Of My Heart – Sting
Unstoppable – Sia
Stubby's training song
Shine On You Crazy Diamond – Pink Floyd
Simple Man – Lynryd Skynyrd
Gold – Spandau Ballet
Gonna Fly Now – Bill Conti
Eye Of The Tiger – Survivor
Song on the radio when I took my first steps
Sweet Child O' Mine – Guns N Roses
The Exodus Song – Pat Boone
The House of the Rising Sun – The Animals

Prison Or The Paralympics

A song from 'The Tank'
Comfortably Numb – Pink Floyd
Don't Stop Me Now – Queen
The song for my first Para Powerlifting competition
Hotel California – The Eagles
If I Can Dream – Elvis Presley
In The Ghetto – Elvis Presley
Bridge Over Troubled Water – Elvis Presley
If I Am A Fool For Loving You – Elvis Presley
My Way – Elvis Presley
I did throughout my journey keep true to who I am. It also reminds me of F1 Suzuka Japan
Suspicious Minds – Elvis Presley
Unchained Melody – Elvis Presley
A song for 'The Tank'
Can't Help Falling In Love – Elvis Presley
Always On My Mind – Elvis Presley
A song for 'The Tank'
A Little Respect – Erasure
Piece Of My Heart – Erma Franklin
Everybody Hurts – R.E.M.
Princess Diana's song
Feel – Robbie Williams
Parisienne Walkways – Gary Moore
Here I Go Again – Whitesnake
Sums up my journey
I Hear You Knocking – Dave Edmunds
I Am Your Man - Seal
I Want To Break Free – Queen
I Want To Know What Love Is - Foreigner
In The Air Tonight – Phil Collins
It's My Life - Talk Talk
It's A Man's, Man's, Man's World – James Brown
Cry To Me – Jimmy Barnes

The Power Of Love – Frankie Goes To Hollywood
It describes what a true soulful love is
The Show Must Go On – Queen
My ICU song
The Wonder of You – Elvis Presley
Three Little Birds - Bob Marley & The Wailers
Love Walked In – Thunder
The Best – Tina Turner
Denbo's song
Unchain My Heart – Joe Cocker
Wake Me Up Before You Go-Go – Wham!
We Are The Champions – Queen
Dedicated to all the disabled people in the world
What About Love - Heart
When I Fall In Love – Nat King Cole
White Wedding Pt.1 – Billy Idol
Who Wants To Live Forever - Queen
Why Does My Heart Feel So Bad - Moby
Wicked Game – Chris Isaak
Wonderful Tonight – Eric Clapton
Reminds me of Liverpool University
Would I Lie To You – Charles & Eddie
You Can Leave Your Hat On – Joe Cocker
You Gave Me A Mountain - Elvis Presley
This song helped me to climb them
Young Lust – Pink Floyd
You're Beautiful – James Blunt
You're So Vain – Carly Simon
You're In My Heart – Rod Stewart
Where No One Stand Alone – Elvis Presley
Private Investigations – Dire Straits

Penny Walker

Stone Cold – Jimmy Barnes
Sunshine On My Shoulders - John Denver
Take Me Home, Country Roads - John Denver
Just Pretend – Elvis Presley
Piece By Piece – Kelly Clarkson
Dedicated to my sons
Knockin' On Heaven's Door – Guns N Roses
Let It Be – The Beatles
Listen To Your Heart - Roxette
What A Wonderful World – Louis Armstrong
Love's Divine - Seal
Thunderclouds – LSD
Lucille – Kenny Rogers
Money – Pink Floyd
Mother – Pink Floyd
Nothing Compares 2 U – Sinead O' Connor
Non Je Ne Regrette Rien – Edith Piaf
This reminds me of leaving the Grand Feu
Hurt – Elvis Presley
Nessum Dorma – Luciano Pavarotti
For the strength of character of my dad
Working Class Man – Jimmy Barnes
Driving Wheels – Jimmy Barnes
Where Do I Begin – Shirley Bassey
Song for mum and dad
All You Need Is Love – The Beatles
You Took The Words Right Out of My Mouth – Meat Loaf
You'll Always Find Me In The Kitchen At Parties – Man Like Me
Jar Of Hearts – Christina Perri
Smile – André Rieu & Jermaine Jackson

'The Tank'

It's the 29th of June 2021 11:08am English time the day of my dad's funeral. Due to restrictions, I could not go to St Michael's and All Angels Church Thornhill at 10:30am English time to say my goodbyes. But I was blessed to have others go in my place. Johnny Harpin a fellow rugby player and 'Tank's' friend and Kay and Denbo who knew my dad and went to represent me as well.

I asked Kay if they could take a rose from their garden that I had sent them as a plant a couple of years before called Nostalgia, to give to my dad and mum. Mum had been patiently waiting for the love of her life so they could be united again in a place of peace and unity at Thornhill Church.

As the time approached 10:30 English time 11:30 for me here in France I took my photo of my mum and dad which was on my phone outside into the garden so I could be with them. Dad having worked in the garden for me and my mum loving it too.

I closed my eyes and watched the funeral through my imagination/third eye. I could see the people arriving and enter the church. I then played on my phone 'Smile' the version by André Rieu and Jermaine Jackson seeing in my mind my dad's coffin going down the church aisle, a church I had spent a lot of time in in my younger years, the image clear and real in my mind.

Though being overcome by emotion and tears I spoke with my mum and dad and told them I would smile and knew they would be by my side guiding me, healing me and watching over me. Then the heavens opened for ten minutes a torrential downpour, I stood in the doorway, the rain pouring into the entrance, but I had to be connected to the outside, the universe.

I then played a Shirley Bassey song 'Where Do I Begin' as I imagined the coffin being taken out of the church to its final resting place. This song being for the both of them and how I would remember them.

The rain suddenly stopped, and the sun came out. I let all my emotion out and said my goodbyes and played Pavarotti singing 'Nessun Dorma'. This strong voice and figure of a man Pavarotti reminding me of my dad's strengths and personality.

I know through the journey I went through that all is good, they have no pain, upset, disease or anger. Just pure love and forgiveness for themselves and for all. Their loving energy always there for me and anyone else to access.

Dad confirmed this the moment he left his overcoat behind in the early hours of the 15th of June 2021. I had phoned Croft house in Cleckheaton, and a beautiful kind lady answered with a soul of an angel and allowed me to say goodbye to my dad and also for him to hear his grandsons Harvey and Elliott's voices say goodbye too.

As I spoke to my dad, I told him it's okay to go now he would be alright, and he can visit me anytime and help me in my garden. I told him just as he had phoned me in hospital in May 2016 and said how proud he was of me for being so strong. I told him I was so proud of him for being so strong now, but could he make me even more proud by letting go for he has done all he was meant to do and now he could leave his overcoat behind and go to a peaceful place with mum, all his friends like Bobby and his family who will be there for him.

The lovely lady said he is raising his eyebrows, he hears you! I will be forever grateful to that beautiful soul who gave me a chance to say goodbye.

Unable to sleep that night I played some of my dad's favourite songs one being 'Smile'. At 2:12am French time I made a cup of tea and went outside it was warm and the sky a mass of stars. I looked up and asked if my dad would let me know when he had gone "Give me a sign dad, how about a shooting star?" I had never seen one.

I came back inside and tried to sleep. At about 3am French time 2ish English time my phone rang it was my sister Caroline who had been by his side. My dad had left the building, his overcoat left behind.

The connection on the phone wasn't good and we got cut off. I moved to the side of the house I was outside and phoned back. Peter, my sister's boyfriend who had been amazing at keeping me informed throughout my mum and dad's last few years answered. As I emotionally talked to him the most clear and defined shooting star went flying past. I said to Peter "He has gone I have just seen him going flying across the sky, he is probably looking for the rugby pitch!"

Thanks dad! I know you visit me as a robin, sitting on the garden fence and you bring mum with you as you are two dancing butterflies. Love to you both, I know you both have peace and love and the energies of the universe at your disposal now.

Until we meet again, I will be grateful, content and blessed to tap into your soul's energy for guidance and love. I already feel and see you thank you. A soulful love is sent to you every day, your loving daughter Penny.

P.S You sent me five shooting stars the other day, now that's just showing off! Thank you for showing Elliott one too though I am not sure he believes it's you. But I do!!

I wish to thank all the kind messages that were given and for all who went to say goodbye to 'Tank'. I am so pleased that my mum is reunited with my dad, she was left alone for a while waiting but she is now in the place she should be, with dad.

Kay was able to put the rose 'Nostalgia' into the coffin for my mum and dad, so I felt my love and energy was with them.

The following days were a roller-coaster of emotions my dad's photo by my side. Again, the universe sent me messages and signs. The robin, dad and I talked about weeks before he left his overcoat behind, visits and stares through my kitchen window. I don't normally see the robins in summer, but I do now.

I was also given messages from songs Guns N Roses' 'Don't Cry' I feel that was from dad to all his children and grandchildren. And two Elvis songs 'Always On My Mind', I think we would both sing that to each other and 'Unchained Melody' a song expressing a deep emotional loss and a deep love, but a love that wouldn't and couldn't ever die. As the days passed, I allowed myself to smile and tapped into dad's energy. I feel him everywhere, by my side guiding me, strengthening me, and protecting me just as he had always done.

He is now back in the gym with me a thing we did back in the late 1980s and 90s. Inspiring me, encouraging me, and assisting me with each rep I do.

Our loved ones are very much still alive, but we can only reach them if we accept that they have moved on to the next phase of their soul's journey. We should be happy and excited for them to reach that point in their journey and with divine timing we all will get there as one beautiful, harmonious, peaceful, and loving soulful energy.

Love You Dad

Appendix

Martyn's gym equipment can be found here: www.nytramgymequipment.co.uk

Qualifications

University Of Liverpool	B.A General	1982-1986	Psychology, Physical
Northern College Of Massage	Diploma	1986-1987	Remedial Massage
Northern College Of Massage	Diploma	1988-1990	Sports Therapy
Northern College Of Massage	Diploma	1991-1993	Advanced Remedial
Football Association Management Centre Of Excellence	Diploma	1992-1994	Treatment of Injuries
Northern College Of Acupuncture	Diploma	1995-1997	Acupressure Massage
Northern College Of Acupuncture (Univ. Of Wales)	Master's Degree	1995-1999	Acupuncture
Shizen College	Diploma	1998-2001	Chinese Medicine
Northern College Of Acupuncture	Diploma	1999-2000	Chinese Patent Herbal Medicine
Northern College Of Acupuncture	Diploma	2001-2004	Chinese Herbal Medicine
Dabtac College Of Further Education	Diploma	2002-2003	Teaching, 7407

Penny Walker
PHYSIO & PHILOSOPHY

Penny Walker of Muscleworld in West Yorkshire, has been quietly training away over the past six years in order to build her physique of matured petite quality. As a junior she showed enormous potential and fully expected to explode onto the senior ranks of competition, but instead she disappeared into obscurity. At last, Penny returned to competition in 1988, to become the winner of the 0/52kg section of Lathams Winter Classic. Her physique, still of petite proportion, but improved rapidly over her two competitively dormant years. Penny explains to Muscle & Co. her unique bodybuilding philosophies. I've found that if you study the muscles it makes training much more effective. I know exactly which muscles are being worked with a particular exercise, because I know what direction they need to be worked in".

It has to be pointed out at this point that Penny has a B.A. in Physical Education and psychology and she is qualified as a sports therapist. At the moment she is in full study for advanced level physiotherapy which is taking up most of her time, but such study has led to her individual approach to bodybuilding.

"People think bodybuilding is very complex", explains Penny, "they make it complicated themselves. It is really very simple but they get too bogged down with all fancy exercises and diets that they lose track of what they are doing. They would be much better off getting a basic physiology book and just read what muscles are comprised of. A big problem with a lot of bodybuilders is rest and recouperation. They just don't rest enough. They overtrain all the time. The muscle grows during the rest period. Also, people make competition preparation very complicated when it doesn't need to be. All this sodium loading and carbohydrate loading, your body wants to be balanced, if it's not balanced it tries desperately to balance itself. If you don't have water, your body will retain the water that you have got. It automatically thinks there is a drought on so it holds water even more. People make the sport too complicated".

Well how would you advise them to go about bodybuilding Penny?

"The main thing in bodybuilding is getting the years of hard training in. A lot of people, especially women, don't train hard enough. You have to train especially hard if you're a woman. People start talking in between sets when they should get on with their training. I train with men because a lot of men seem to train much harder. Bodybuilding should be fun, and hard training is good fun. I get a terrific thrill out of knowing I have done my best. Life's too short to have bodybuilding as a labour. What people do get enjoyment out of is results I think. There should be more awareness out there of what people are doing. Every bodybuilder should have a Gray's Anatomy".

Where do you think bodybuilding will lead you?

"I realised a long time ago that you can't make a lot of money out of bodybuilding unless you are prepared to do a lot of things that I'm not prepared to do".

What's that?

"Drugs!"

"I speak my mind and feel very strongly about certain things, but I don't know if it will reflect on my performance. For in-

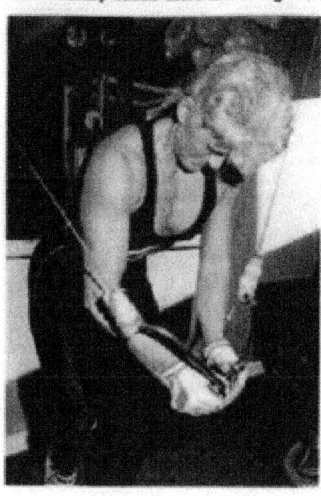

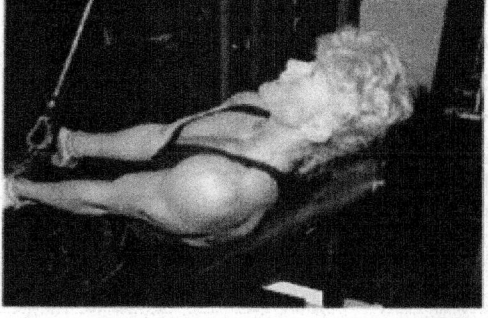

> PEOPLE MAKE THE SPORT TOO COMPLICATED. THEY JUST DON'T REST ENOUGH. THEY OVER TRAIN ALL THE TIME, WHEN REALLY, THE MUSCLE GROWS DURING THE REST PERIOD!

Prison Or The Paralympics

> PEOPLE ON DRUGS TAKE TWO STEPS FORWARD AND ONE STEP BACK. A NATURAL BODYBUILDER WILL ONLY TAKE ONE STEP FORWARD, BUT *WON'T* STEP BACK UNLESS HE OR SHE STOPS TRAINING!

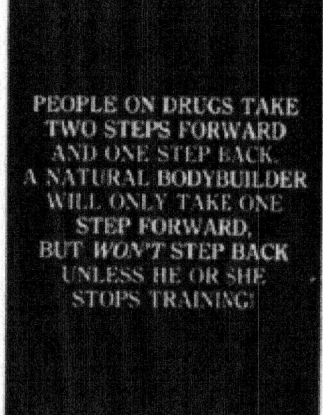

stance, the judges - I feel there are a lot of judges who have never competed before, and I just don't think that's right. Also the drugs situation. I don't want to criticize anyone at all in bodybuilding, but the people I don't agree at all with are those who won't put their time into their sport. They don't read their bodies, and then take drugs, which is the lazy way out. What is it worth to your health. If someone was to offer you a lot of money then it could be contemplated, but there isn't any reward in bodybuilding at this level. What I like to prove is that you can look good and be healthy through bodybuilding. Some people only think bodybuilding is going onstage and competing for a plastic trophy. People on drugs take two steps forward and one step backwards. They're forever increasing and decreasing their bodies composition. A natural bodybuilder will only take one step forward, but won't step back, he/she stops training altogether".

Does anything else annoy you Penny?

"Yeh!"

"When you go into a gym and see some of the characters, and a lot of them don't seem to use their brains. We need to project a more intellectual image to the public, not the brawny one of the past".

Obviously Penny has very personal feelings upon the subject of drugs in sport. Which is a good strong message to the younger athletes involved in bodybuilding. To the older ones - you should know better anyway. The question was brought up - what do you have as a release from physio and bodybuilding Penny, how has your personal life developed?

"I feel I have too much going on around me at the moment to have much social life. I go out with my friends now and again but not very often. I'm studying, training, which doesn't leave too much time for anybody else. Maybe I'm too selfish to settle down just yet. I want to do what I want to do, and follow my own path. I want to get my own life into some kind of direction. There's a big world out there, there's loads of travelling, loads of things to do and I want to live a little, for now.

I'm hoping to open my own clinic which will cater for all athletes and help to promote the sport. On the competitive scene I would like to compete to the standard of EFBB but I don't know if I can really. I'll just keep training and enjoy my bodybuilding, and be on the stage when I feel the time is right".

Appeal Papers

This is what I would have said if I had been given the opportunity at the 2020 appeal court.

INTRODUCTION

Madame Walker suffered a massive injustice on the 15th of April 2019.

The sentence, which included being charged with killing 2 people, was based on assumption - not fact.

Evidence confirming this has been presented.

Mme Walker is now representing herself as only half of the story has been told and vital information has been withheld.

Madame Walker is a person of integrity and truth, who is horrified by the way that she and her family and have been treated.

At the appeal, Madame Walker prays that just one person will listen to the injustice that has so far been served and sees in the eyes of the law a great mistake has happened.

FACTS:

1. During the legal process, the only evidence presented to the court that claimed Mme Walker had caused the accident, was contaminated, and left unpreserved, lost and thus not available for examination by 2 of the 3 experts.

    This fact alone makes the sentence given to Mme Walker on the 15th of April 2019 unlawful and thus not enforceable.

2. The cause of death of the elderly couple has never been lawfully established as no autopsy was carried out, nor medical records investigated.

    This therefore leads to the unlawful sentence given to Mme Walker for double manslaughter

3. Involuntary manslaughter can only be given as a sentence if an unintentional killing results from criminal negligence, recklessness or from committing an offence.

    This has not been lawfully proven to have occurred in the sentencing of Mme Walker.

4. There is no lawful evidence that has been provided to prove that Mme Walker committed any of the above.

    Thus, Mme Walker is not guilty of involuntary manslaughter.

5. Mme Walker argues that her actions did not rise to the level of negligence necessary to constitute criminal negligence.
6. Mme Walker argues that the deaths were truly an accident and did not result from the careless actions of her driving. Indeed, it is more evident that the deaths resulted from the careless, reckless actions and possible criminal negligence of Mr. Dupont's driving.

Mme Walker objects to her sentence:

- Prévu par Art.221-6-1 - not true as there is no evidence
- Prévu par Art.221-6 - not true as there is no evidence
- Prévu par Art.221-8 - this cannot be enforced as Mme Walker is not guilty of Art.221-6-1 and Art.221-6

There are overwhelmingly reasonable doubts in this case. Therefore, a new investigation to establish the health of the 3 people involved in the crash and the ability, experience and driving history of the 2 drivers is essential and necessary to bring truth out as to the cause of the accident.

Mme Walker Penelope would also wish to enforce her right to lodge the following articles:

- Art 121-3
- Object under Art 414 of CCP
- Art 420 (1-2) of CCP
- Art 424(1) of CC

Question:

Were the experts looking for the truth, or leading us down a path which had already been decided?

On the 5th of April 2016 15h05, Mr Hervé Dupont and Mr Lucas Philippoteau in Cognac (16100) decided Mme Walker's sentence.

PLEASE NOTE:

1. This was before the expert, Mr Maurice, had been contacted, before any witnesses had been interviewed or statements taken, and therefore relied on an account from Hervé Dupont who was not involved in the accident and who is a retired accountant, not a person qualified to decide Mme Walker's sentence.

2. Mr Philippoteau is a police officer – however, he had not visited the scene of the accident, had not seen the cars involved, nor had he read any documents related to the investigation, as the investigation had not gathered any information by the 5th of April 2016.

3. The sentence suggested and documented on the 5th of April 2016 at 16h55 was decided on gossip - not fact - and served to Mme Walker on the 15th of April 2019.

4. This violates all Mme Walkers human right for a fair and just trial.

5. It must also be noted that on the 6th of April 2016 at 11.45, Eric Gatard an Officier de Police Judiciaire de Pouzauges stated the following: " une investigation d'homicide involontaire faisant suite à un accident de la circulation routière ayant causé le décès de deux personnes."

6. This statement is misleading, implying, assuming and grossly unlawful. The words "homicide involuntaire" cannot justly be used as the investigation by an expert had not taken place at this point; no witness statements (for example Annie Girard) had been taken; and the Pompiers had not given their evidence.

7. The fact that it was assumed that the accident had caused the death of the elderly couple is somewhat concerning and a gross misconduct of justice.

8. Even today, over 3 and half years after the accident, the cause of death has not been investigated, no autopsies have been carried out and no medical records or history have been made available for the two deceased people. Mr Dupont was 85 years old, and Mme Dupont was 83 years old.

9. Any possible evidence available to the experts was contaminated as it was not protected, and in the case of the second and third expert, was not even available for examination (Example: The Seat wheel hub and the Peugeot front bumper).

Therefore, the sentence given to Madame Walker relied on contaminated, unpreserved, unavailable, manipulated, unexaminable, unreliable and assuming information.
This is not lawful and therefore not able to be submitted in a court of law.

The conviction is based purely on the following disputed evidence:

1. That Mme Walker was overtaking the car of Mr. Dupont

2. The black rubber marks on the Seat wheel hub and the Peugeot front bumper which also had black rubber marks.

If, **as the police photographic evidence shows**, the wheel hub was on the left rear wheel of the Seat, and not the right, then the Seat was not overtaking Mr Dupont's car.

Madame Walker has constantly questioned why she would drive in such a manner as she would never normally drive, and believes that it was the Peugeot that was either having a problem in front of the Seat and lost control, or it was indeed overtaking the Seat and lost control

IT SHOULD BE NOTED:

1. The Seat wheel hub, as the photographic evidence shows, was not in place on the RIGHT rear tyre at the scene of the accident, nor for the following few weeks after the accident.

2. The photograph from the Police on the 3rd of April 2016 clearly shows the wheel hub on the rear LEFT tyre of the Seat!

3. After August 2016, these 2 car parts (wheel hub and bumper) had disappeared, meaning that only the first expert was able to see and examine these parts.

How is this possible?

The photos from the first expert were taken on either the 23rd of April 2016 or the 28th of August 2016 (the 2 times he visited - according to his report) and these clearly show the wheel hub now on the RIGHT rear tyre.

As can now clearly be shown, any evidence used with regards to the Seat was contaminated due to non-preservation of said evidence.

Photographic evidence confirms this.

Other avenues of investigations to the possible cause of the accident were not carried out, fully or not carried out at all. This includes:

1. Consumption of alcohol or drugs (no blood test carried out)

2. The ability of the drivers to drive in a safe and correct manner.

3. No investigation was carried out looking at activity on the day of the accident (2nd of April 2016) by the elderly couple – except noting that they drove from Cognac to St Hilaire de Voust which is about 130kms. This is a 2.5 hours' drive on a hot day.

    Investigations were carried out on Mme Walker's activities for the whole day of the 2nd of April 2016. She was cleaning the house, preparing for friends who were arriving from England on the 3rd of April 2016. She had a 15-minute drive from her home to the place of the accident - on a route she used every week to go shopping.

4. <u>Cause of death not known – NOT KNOWN as no autopsies were carried out.</u>

WITNESS STATEMENTS

1. Witness statements which confirm the driver of the Peugeot Mr Dupont was not alive from 20h40 onwards and that no medical intervention or assistance was given.

2. The 6 witnesses came to the same conclusion that there was no sign of Mr Dupont being alive.

3. That is Mme Walker saw the driver of the Peugeot slumped at the steering wheel, unable to drive and causing the tragic events that followed.

SERVING PAPERS

An exact copy of the paper served to Mme Walker on the 16th of January 2017 at 18.00 was not given to her in a translated form of her native tongue of English "PROCES VERBAL DE CONVOCATION EN VUE D'UNE AUTION LIBRE".

The paper given in English was a general form and not as the police said a direct translation of the paper served "NOTIFICATION OF RIGHTS".

Mme Walker did not understand what she was signing.

On the 24th of January 2017 at 9.30am, at the Brigade de Gendarmerie de La Chataigneraie, Mme Walker was questioned for approximately 3 hours in a room full of people - with no privacy, no concern for her well-being or even an offer for a rest or a drink of water.

This harsh treatment was given to a person who is 80% handicapped, was still having medical procedures and had only a few months previously left the "Grand Feu" centre of rehabilitation in Niort in a wheelchair.

Mme Walker had a solicitor provided by her insurance company and an interpreter supplied by the police.
The solicitor had to leave after about an hour for another meeting, so for more than half of the meeting
Mme Walker was not represented by a solicitor.
At the end of the convocation, Mme Walker did not agree with the charges given, but was forced to sign the documents after about 30 minutes refusing to sign them. The reason that she eventually signed them, was because she felt unwell and wanted to go home.

On the 13th of April 2016, Robert Mitchell, Mme Walker's partner, was also interviewed - without a translator or solicitor being present at the Brigade de gendarmerie de La Chataigneraie.

None of the Dupont family, or the friends that the deceased visited on the day of the accident were interviewed by the police.

OTHER UNLAWFUL ACTIONS OF THE INVESTIGATION

1. Assuming Mme Walker was guilty before the investigation had begun or Mme Walker had been interviewed by the police on the 24th of January 2017.
2. There were numerous statements made with reference to 'homicide involontaire' before the investigation had begun and information of the events involved in the accident had been collected.

This violates Mme Walker's right to a fair and just trial and violates the law that a person is innocent until proven guilty.

The investigation provides no lawful evidence that proves Mme Walker is guilty of the sentence given.

Further information required before a conclusion can be drawn:

The decision and conclusion to this case cannot be made until all information is provided.

This includes:
- Establishing the abilities of the two drivers to drive on Saturday the 2nd of April 2016.
- The information given by the experts was not legally allowed to be submitted in a Court of Law, therefore the cause of the accident cannot be established using this information.
- There is no lawful information available to confirm that Madame Walker was speeding, overtook, caused the accident, or caused the death of the elderly couple.

What did happen?

If evidence of the following had been investigated, then a clearer and more honest investigation could have been achieved.
The information used to sentence Madame Walker is unlawful, biased, assuming, non-preserved, contaminated, manipulated (especially Seat wheel hub), and mysteriously lost.
Evidence that would have made the investigations less unjust has been withheld.

This includes:

1. **Cause of death**
    - No autopsy or medical information provided

2. **Ability and safety of the drivers to drive that day**

    - History of any insurance claims in the last 10 years
    - Any traffic violations (for example speeding)
    - Driving experience and driving test
    - Alcohol consumed
    - Tiredness, what activities were done on that day, kilometers travelled that day, familiarity and regular use of the roads in the area

3. **A fair and just investigation**

    - Facts not assumptions
    - Truths not gossip
    - Integrity and honesty

It is logical to conclude, that with the above information provided, this tragic accident would still have occurred if Mme Walker had never left her home on the 2nd of April 2016.

CONCLUSION

It is often the case that it is the subjects that people avoid talking about or investigating, that hide the truth.

In this case there are three areas which no one will talk to Mme Walker about:

1. What time the couple left their home, exactly what did they do on that day, where, and with whom?
2. What, if any, medications were the elderly couple taking – what was their medical history? (The driver was 85-year-old)
3. Alcohol – was this present in the driver's blood stream?

Mme Walker was asked for all this information about herself, and she willingly provided the answers.

Under the Equality of Arms Law, this amounts to gross inequality and violates Mme Walker's human rights for a just and fair trial.

May it also be noted that not one piece of information - legal documents of information – presented, has been offered to Madame Walker in her native language of English.

Penny Walker

All meetings with the insurance company and solicitor were conducted in French, and no information by either was provided in English.

This is a violation of her human rights.

Madame Walker struggled to understand the information provided in French (written and oral) at a time when she was trying to recover from the loss of her right hand and many other disabilities due to the accident.

This results in an insensitive treatment of another human being whose sentence is based on assumptions, not facts or evidence.

For the sake of others who find themselves in a similar unjust situation, Madame Walker will continue to fight for her rights, for a fair and just treatment which is everyone's human right.

Prison Or The Paralympics

Photographic Evidence from the Police.

The following photos were taken by the police on the 2nd and 3rd April 2016.

The photos taken by the Police clearly show that there is NO wheel hub on the SEAT's rear RIGHT wheel.

The Police photos also show that the SEAT has no damage to the back of the vehicle - which would be present if the SEAT had pulled in too early in the alleged overtaking of the Peugeot.

Police image 6769.jpg clearly shows the rear LEFT wheel has the wheel hub on. The police photos taken on the 3/04/16 also show this.

BACK TYRES

IMG_6768.JPG

IMG_6769.JPG

Photographic Police evidence showing no wheel hub on the SEAT back RIGHT wheel

(Police photos taken of the SEAT on the 2nd and 3rd of April 2016)

IMG_1567.JPG

IMG_6751.JPG

IMG_6744.JPG

IMG_6752.JPG

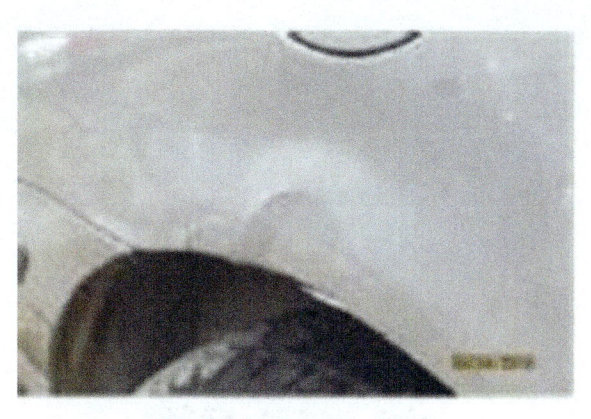

IMG_6745.JPG

FRONT TYRES

IMG_6767.JPG

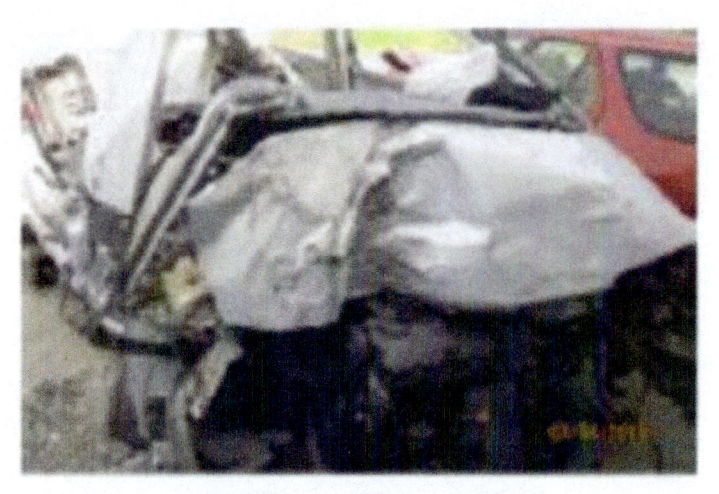

IMG_6741.JPG

03/04/2016
SEAT Rear Left Wheel

03/04/2016
SEAT Rear Right Wheel

Unexplainable Information

The whole investigation and resulting sentence that claims Mme Walker is responsible for the death of two elderly people is based on gossip, and the SEAT wheel hub (Mme Walker's car) and the front bumper of the Peugeot (M Dupont's car).

However, after August 2016 these two car parts had disappeared!

Therefore, only allowing the first expert to see and examine them.

The SEAT wheel hub, **as Police Photographic evidence shows**, was not in place on the RIGHT rear wheel at the scene of the accident or for the following weeks after the accident. The photograph from the Police on the 3rd of April 2016 shows the wheel hub on the rear LEFT wheel of the SEAT

The first expert's photos taken either on the 28th of April 2016 or the 23rd of August 2016 (the two occasions he visited the cars according to his report) clearly shows the wheel hub now on the RIGHT rear wheel.

How is this possible?

Any other possible evidence on the SEAT was contaminated due to non-preservation of evidence, photographic evidence confirms this.

Expert Photos

Photos from the 1st expert Pascal MAURICE taken on April 28th 2016 or August 23th 2016.

Here the wheel hub is on the SEAT's rear RIGHT wheel.

There is no documentation by either the police or Mr. MAURICE as to why this wheel hub would be taken off the LEFT rear wheel of the SEAT and placed onto the RIGHT rear wheel of the SEAT.

Neither is there any documentation of who decided to do this, why and when.

The SEAT's Wheel Hub
First Expert's Photos (28th April or 23rd August 2016)
April 2016) / Police photos (2nd & 3rd April 2016)

3.2 Examen des déformations

La violence du choc par contact direct contre l'arbre a déformé de manière importante la structure AVD du véhicule.

Impact et déformation par collision contre l'arbre et le véhicule PEUGEOT PARTNER (B):
A1: point de collision initiale contre B, faible déformation de l'aile ARD et frottement contre l'enjoliveur de la roue ARD et parechoc.
A2: déformation importante de la structure AVD par collision contre l'arbre à droite de la chaussée

Traces de frottement contre l'aile AVG du Peugeot PARTNER

Traces noires résultant du contact avec le pneumatique AVG et parechoc AV du Peugeot PARTNER

Hauteur des traces de gomme (noire) sur le parechoc AR / sol : de 46cm à 57cm
Hauteur du frottement contre l'aile ARD de 67 à 81cm.

IMG_1567.JPG
IMG_6751.JPG 
IMG_6744.JPG 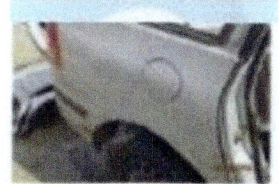
IMG_6752.JPG 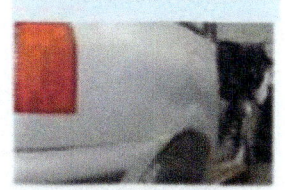
IMG_6745.JPG

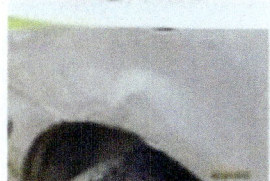

Lack of Preservation of the Evidence

Photographs taken on the 15/03/2017.
These photos show the non-preservation and the contamination of the evidence. It also shows the reason for there being so much more additional damage on the SEAT after the accident (Accident date: 02/04/2016).

As the evidence was not preserved, the Experts only had contaminated evidence upon which to base their reports.

It must also be noted that by March 2017 the two vital vehicle parts showing the alleged contact of the SEAT and the Peugeot, (I.E., the wheel hub from the SEAT, and the front bumper from the Peugeot) have disappeared and were not available for the second or third experts to see and examine.

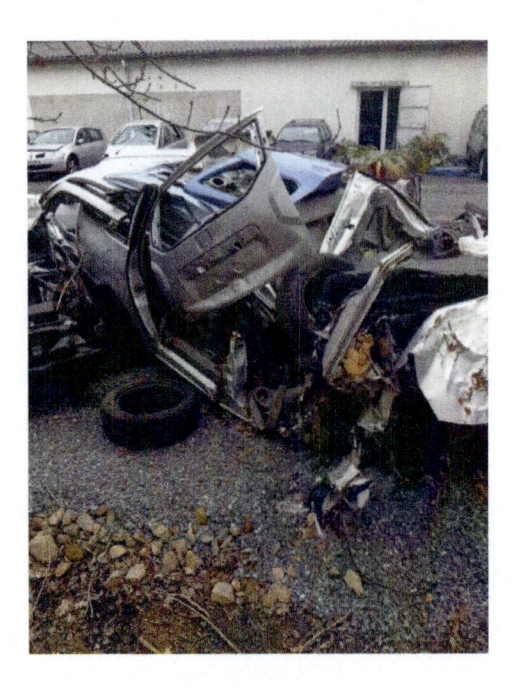

SEAT SPEEDO

The instrument panel has suffered physical damage during the accident. There is colossal damage to the front engine compartment. The electrical system may have suffered gross malfunctions due to cables breaking and short circuits occurring within the engine bay. These in turn corrupt the data supplied to the on-board computer which in turn gives signals and values to the speedometer. The needle may have therefore swung about wildly not giving accurate reading.

In addition to the above it is likely that during the collision one or both front driving wheels were not in contact with the ground. These wheels supply the primary speed data from ABS sensors and override the rear sensors. If the front wheels were able to spin freely in mid-air with the engine power applied, they would accelerate very quickly. The resulting speed registered on the vehicle's speedometer would therefore not be an accurate reflection of the vehicles actual speed

It is not normal for the speedometer needle to stay in any position other than zero once power is cut. This is another indication of damage & malfunction

For the above reasons it is not safe to use the photo of the speedometer as a gauge of speed at the time of the accident.

The expert has been fair and not referred to the speedometer at all. He has correctly used the computer model to establish estimated speeds. The photo should not be used at court as this would be unfair and discriminatory & will prejudice the court against Mme Walker. The courts may often not fully understand all the technical aspects of the case. A photograph however is very powerful and if it infers something that is incorrect it should not be used. It would also give support to the expert's findings as correct when in fact they are not 100 % correct or true but are the best explanations that can be arrived at with the known facts (not all the facts can be known)

HOW DID IT HAPPEN

Expert Pascal Maurice claims and concludes that rear wing of Seat came in contact with Peugeot by the Seat pulling back in onto the Peugeot whilst overtaking. This led to both cars going off course to the right and the subsequent crash.

It would be difficult to prove that the SEAT turned in on the Peugeot rather than the Peugeot swerving to the left and hitting the SEAT as it passed. The resulting initial damage to both vehicles would be the same (rear wing SEAT front wing PEUGEOT) the resulting forces on the two vehicles following the initial contact would be the same and the crash would happen. If this was simulated on the computer software it is likely that there would be much the same outcome. Bear in mind that the expert's model whilst good is not 100% it is the best explanation they could come up with.

Did the expert try it on the software with the PEUGEOT going left into the SEAT to see what the result was?

Why would he veer left?

1	Falling asleep

2	startled by passing car,

3	Had been drinking and not in full control

4	Was unwell and not in full control

5	Driver is 85yrs old driving at night (eyesight etc.)

6	Unfamiliar with road

There could be reasonable doubt about how the primary contact happened. The truth of this can most likely never determined 100 % from the known facts and models.

NOTIFICATION OF RIGHTS
Provided to individuals testifying voluntarily before Court
(General Form)

It is mandatory that the information below be provided to you in a language which you understand.

You are hereby informed that you are being heard because there exist one or more plausible reasons to suspect that you have committed or attempted to commit an offence.

You have the right to be informed of the designation and presumed date and time of the offence of which you are being accused.

You have the right to leave the premises at which you are heard at any time.

YOU ARE FURTHERMORE INFORMED THAT YOU HAVE THE RIGHT:

To make statements, answer questions or remain silent.

Once you have stated your identity, you have the right, during your hearings:
- to make statements,
- to answer the questions asked of you,
- or to remain silent.

To be assisted by a lawyer

If the offence for which you are being heard is a crime or a felony punishable by imprisonment, you have assisted during the course of your hearing or open confrontation.

- **Choice of lawyer**

You may request to be assisted by the lawyer of your choice. If you are not able to designate a lawyer or if the lawyer you have chosen cannot be contacted, you may request that a lawyer be appointed by the President of the Bar Association.

You will be responsible for the related expenses, unless you fulfil the conditions for free legal assistance, as listed in the appendix document provided to you.

- **Legal assistance**

The lawyer may:
- speak with you under conditions that guarantee confidentiality;
- be present at your hearings and open confrontations.

You may agree to continue the hearing without your lawyer's presence.

To be assisted by an interpreter
If you do not speak or do not understand French, you have the right to be assisted free of charge by an interpreter during your hearings, open confrontations and communication with your lawyer.

To view material relating to your case
At your request or that of your lawyer, you may ask to view the proceedings of your hearings and public confrontations.

To benefit from legal counsel
You may benefit, if applicable free of charge, from legal counsel in a legal services structure, the address and details of which will be indicated to you in a separate document.

Observations on the pre-report of the Expert Justice (By Mr. Puech)

II – Observations sur le pré-rapport de l'Expert de Justice

1. <u>Remarques générales :</u>

   a. Absence de mesure de conservation des véhicules et scellés non conformes :

   Les véhicules n'ont pas été conservés dans des conditions normales à ce type de procédure, notamment dans le cadre d'un accident corporel grave :

   - Absence de scellés,
   - Les voitures laissées à tout temps sans aucune couverture,
   - La perte du bouclier avant du PEUGEOT PARTNER.
   - Les véhicules présentent de nombreux dommages complémentaires :
     - Pour le SEAT ALHAMBRA :
       - La roue avant droite a été démontée sans mesure conservatoire.
       - Il y a des dommages supplémentaires sur l'aile avant gauche et le capot moteur.
       - Il y a des dommages supplémentaires sur l'aile arrière droite, endroit du contact litigieux entre les deux voitures.
       - L'enjoliveur de roue arrière droite a disparu (endroit du contact litigieux entre les deux voitures).
       - Etc.
     - Pour le PEUGEOT PARTNER :
       - Absence du bouclier avant, endroit du contact litigieux entre les deux voitures.
       - Dommages supplémentaires sur le bouclier arrière et le panneau latéral arrière droit.
       - Etc.

   <u>Ces manquements inadmissibles sont de nature à avoir privé les parties de défendre correctement leurs droits et intérêts.</u>

b. Analyse générale sur le rapport de l'Expert de Justice :

Les observations ci-dessous ne sont pas exhaustives. Elles sont de nature à montrer que même l'Expert de Justice fait des imprécisions et des erreurs d'analyses.

L'Expert de Justice explique dans son rapport (notamment page 48) que le choc contre l'arbre sur le PEUGEOT PARTNER a lieu au niveau du pavillon, à hauteur des portes avant.

La photographie ci-contre montre les déformations du pavillon.

L'écrasement du pavillon se situe clairement au niveau des portes avant.

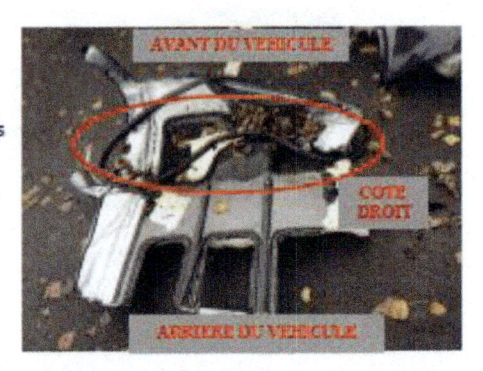

Or, sur la simulation réalisée, le choc contre l'arbre a lieu au niveau du pare-brise, au lieu de la partie avant du pavillon à hauteur des portes avant !!! Cette simulation n'est pas compatible avec la position réelle au choc.

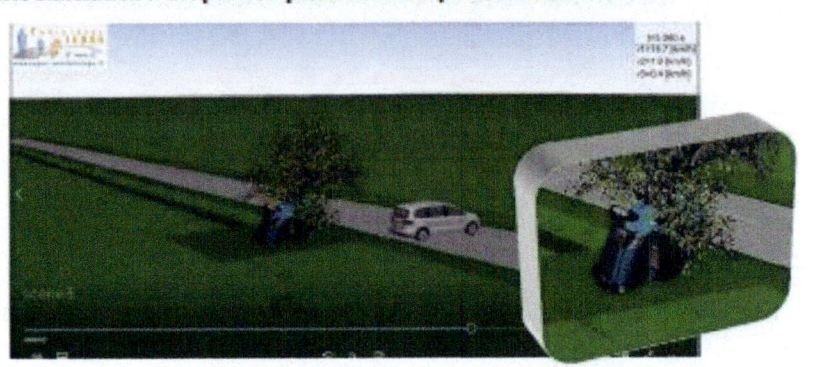

De plus, ce point d'impact ne correspond pas à la vidéo « driver-PEUGEOT.mp4 », dans laquelle l'arbre n'est pas visible.